W9-DDF-992

Microsoft

Microsoft®
Exchange 2000
Server
Administrator's
Companion

Walter J. Glenn
Bill English

PUBLISHED BY
Microsoft Press
A Division of Microsoft Corporation
One Microsoft Way
Redmond, Washington 98052-6399

Copyright © 2000 by Microsoft Corporation

All rights reserved. No part of the contents of this book may be reproduced or
transmitted in any form or by any means without the written permission of the publisher.

Library of Congress Cataloging-in-Publication Data
Glenn, Walter J.
  Microsoft Exchange 2000 Server Administrator's Companion/Walter J. Glenn, Bill English.
    p. cm.
  ISBN 0-7356-0938-1
  1. Microsoft Exchange Server (Computer file) 2. Client/server computing. I. English,
Bill, 1961- II. Title.

QA76.9.C55 G6 2000
005.7'13769--dc21   00-027100

Printed and bound in the United States of America.

1 2 3 4 5 6 7 8 9   WCWC   5 4 3 2 1 0

Distributed in Canada by Penguin Books Canada Limited.

A CIP catalogue record for this book is available from the British Library.

Microsoft Press books are available through booksellers and distributors worldwide. For further
information about international editions, contact your local Microsoft Corporation office, or contact Microsoft Press International directly at fax (425) 936-7329. Visit our Web site at
mspress.microsoft.com. Send comments to *mspinput@microsoft.com*.

Macintosh is a registered trademark of Apple Computer, Inc. Intel is a registered trademark of
Intel Corporation. Active Directory, BackOffice, FrontPage, Microsoft, Microsoft Press, MS-
DOS, NetMeeting, Outlook, PowerPoint, Windows, and Windows NT are either registered trademarks or trademarks of Microsoft Corporation in the United States and/or other countries. Other
product and company names mentioned herein may be the trademarks of their respective owners.

Unless otherwise noted, the example companies, organizations, products, people, and events depicted herein are fictitious. No association with any real company, organization, product, person,
or event is intended or should be inferred.

Acquisitions Editor: David Clark
Project Editor: Barbara Moreland
Technical Editor: Nick Cavalancia
Manuscript Editor: Rebecca Pepper

Dedication

I'd like to dedicate this book to my father, Bill English.
(No, this is not my co-author—just a curious coincidence.)

Walter

To Kathy, David, and Anna, you are the joy of my life.

Bill

Contents at a Glance

Table of Contents

Part II
Planning

Part III
Deployment

Part IV
Clients

Part VI
Maintenance

Acknowledgements

This book represents the culmination of a personal and professional journey for me. Five years ago, I was in private practice in the health care field when I decided to make a career change. Over the last five years, many have helped me along the way and all of them, in one way or another, have played a part in this book.

First I'd like to thank David Clark, acquisitions editor at Microsoft Press, and Walter Glenn, my co-author, for taking a chance on me as a book author. I hope you both feel that you made a good choice. I'd also like to thank Barbara Moreland, the project editor, for her professionalism, calmness, and leadership. She knew when to push me and when not to, and I appreciated both very much. Barbara, I hope we can work together in the future. Rebecca Pepper, the manuscript editor, made my rough manuscripts smooth and pleasant to read while offering key advice on structure and flow. RP, I never knew I could sound so good (is this edit OK? <g>). Nick Cavalencia, the technical editor, was learning this material at the same time I was, and he graciously put up with my many phone calls asking about how to do this or that. Your patience is a virtue and your energy is boundless. Thanks for all your help! Bill Teel helped with producing screen shots. Bill, you're a master with that Paint utility!

The following developers at Microsoft added significant value to this book. Even though they were heads down writing code, they took time to help me understand the finer points of Exchange 2000 Server. I'd like to thank Mark Wistrom for his guidance in developing the clustering chapter, Jeff Bachmeier for his patience and technical support in explaining to me the intricacies of Instant Messaging, David Lemson for his welcome corrections and instruction on routing concepts and the LST, Aaron Szafer for his help with the counters and instances for the Performance Monitoring chapter, Dalen Abraham for his explanations on the finer points of Chat Service, Erik Ashby for his help in explaining mixed mode concepts, and Philip Hupf for providing insight into ESE, store maintenance, and how database restorations work. Any mistakes in these chapters are mine, not theirs.

Back here in Minnesota, I'd like to thank Tina Rankin, who gave me my first break in the training world and believed that I could become a good trainer. I will never forget your kindness. I'd like to thank Jane Holcombe, whom I consider a mentor and friend, and who has given me very good, strategic advice at key points in my professional development. Jane, you're a class act and one of the best trainers in the Twin Cities. I also thank Dave Fletcher and the folks at MindSharp, who worked with my ever-changing schedule to give me the time away from the classroom necessary to do this writing. Thanks for your flexibility and kindness.

To Neil Salkind, David Rogleberg, and the folks at StudioB, I deeply thank you for your efforts in seeing this book through to the end in a rather difficult and accelerated situation. Neil, you are the best agent anyone could have.

Finally, I must thank my family. My wife, Kathy, who endured my long hours at the computer and was very patient and supportive of my efforts. Kathy, I'm so glad I married you. And David and Anna, my two adoring children. Every time you came into my office, you reminded me of what was really important. Books will come and go, but the love of a child is to be cherished for life.

Most importantly, I want to thank Jesus Christ, who gave me the opportunity and talent to co-author this book and without whom I would be lost forever.

Bill English
Maple Grove, Minnesota
June 26, 2000

As usual, a lot of people did a lot of work to put this book into your hands. Foremost, I'd like to thank my co-author, Bill English, for all his work. He signed on to this project at the last moment when another author dropped out. Bill took up the challenge and did a great job. I'd also like to thank Nick Cavalencia for a grueling technical review and for contributing updated chapters to the book as well.

The folks at Microsoft Press also deserve special thanks for guiding this book through its various stages. David Clark, acquisitions editor, and Barbara Moreland, project editor, both helped to make sure that this book is of the best quality and that it was published on schedule.

Walter J. Glenn
Hunstville, Alabama
July 5, 2000

Introduction

Welcome to Microsoft Exchange 2000 Server! Whether you are an experienced Exchange administrator or just learning this product, you are going to be impressed with its new features, increased flexibility, and expanded information management capabilities. The development team at Microsoft has done an outstanding job of continuing the Exchange tradition of offering superior messaging services—Exchange 2000 Server is the best ever!

Microsoft Exchange 2000 Server is designed to meet the messaging and collaboration needs of businesses of all sizes. *Microsoft Exchange 2000 Server Administrator's Companion* is designed not only to bring you up to speed in setting up the various features of Exchange 2000 Server, but also to show you how these features work and why you might want to use them. We also offer advice from first-hand experience in the real world of Exchange networks.

It's impossible to cover every element of Exchange 2000 Server in detail in one book. However, this *Administrator's Companion* is a great place to start as you consider implementing Exchange 2000 Server in your Windows 2000 organization. This book can be used in several different ways. It can be read as a

- guide to planning and deployment,
- ready reference for day-to-day questions,
- source of information needed to make decisions about the network, or a
- thorough introduction to the particulars of Exchange 2000 Server.

We assume that the reader has a fundamental understanding of networking concepts and of Microsoft Windows 2000 Server. We have attempted to provide background at appropriate points as well as references to additional resources.

Overview of Contents

Exchange 2000 Server Administrator's Companion is divided into six parts, roughly corresponding to each stage in the implementation of an Exchange 2000 network.

Part I: Introduction

We begin by outlining the new features of Exchange 2000 Server. Then we dive in for a close look at the program's storage and routing architecture. Chapter 1 is designed to get you up to speed quickly on what Exchange Server is and some of the features it offers. This first chapter also serves as a roadmap for the rest of the book. Chapters 2 and 3 show you how to plan for and implement your routing architecture. They introduce Exchange 2000 Server's new Web store, demonstrate how the databases and transaction logs provide you with a high level of recoverability, and discuss the new link state protocol—all dramatic improvements over the routing architecture of Exchange Server 5.5. Chapter 4 explains the tight integration between Exchange 2000 Server and Windows 2000 Server, particularly the integration between Exchange and the Windows 2000 Active Directory directory service, Internet Information Server 5.0, and Windows 2000 DNS.

Part II: Planning

Every successful implementation of a messaging system requires good planning, and Exchange 2000 Server is no exception. Two chapters are devoted to planning issues. Chapter 5 looks at methods for taking stock of a current network and assessing the needs of users on that network prior to an Exchange 2000 Server deployment. Chapter 6 examines ways to create an actual deployment plan, based on the needs assessment methods outlined in Chapter 5.

Part III: Deployment

After learning about the architecture of Exchange 2000 Server and how to plan for its deployment, you're ready to get your hands dirty. In this section (the longest) we outline how to install Exchange 2000 Server and how to implement its various features in the way that best suits your organization. Chapter 7 details the various methods of installing Exchange 2000 Server, including installing a new organization, installing into an existing organization, and upgrading an Exchange 5.5 installation. This chapter also shows how to make sure a server is ready for Exchange 2000 Server installation. Chapter 8 introduces you to the Microsoft Management Console (MMC)—the new management interface included with Windows 2000—and it provides a tour of the management resources in the Exchange System snap-in for the MMC.

The next group of chapters—Chapters 9 to 13—covers a whole host of other topics: creation and management of recipients (users, contacts, groups, and public folders), storage groups, routing and administrative groups, and routing group connectors, such as the SMTP and X.400 Connectors. Since many of you will be performing migrations, Chapter 14 covers this very important topic. Here we discuss the Active Directory Connector and Site Replication services and explain how Exchange 2000 server can co-exist with Exchange 5.5 servers on the same network.

Part IV: Clients

The best implementation of Exchange 2000 Server won't do your organization much good if there aren't any clients to connect to it and use it; in this section we've provided an overview of the clients for Exchange 2000 Server. The topics presented here could easily be expanded into their own book, so we've covered the more important topics and referenced other materials where appropriate. Chapter 15 gives a general introduction to the various types of clients that can be used to connect to an Exchange 2000 server, Chapter 16 focuses on Microsoft Outlook 2000 and examines the issues surrounding its deployment, and Chapter 17 covers some basic protocols—NNTP, SMTP, IMAP4, and OWA. We go over the basic commands of each and discuss how to use the logging features for troubleshooting purposes.

Part V: Functionality

Exchange 2000 Server ships with several new and interesting features. Among them are two real-time collaboration programs: Chat Service and Instant Messaging. Chapter 18 discusses Chat Service, both the client and the server sides. (Chat Service is most often used in conjunction with video conferencing, a topic not covered in this book.) Chapter 19 covers Instant Messaging, detailing how to setup routing and home servers and outlining how to setup the client for this service.

Exchange 2000 takes advantage of the new Active/Active clustering services of Windows 2000 Server, which is covered in Chapter 20. Chapter 22 looks at the procedures for connecting Exchange 2000 Server organizations to foreign messaging systems, such as Microsoft Mail for PC Networks and X.400 systems.

Security is a primary concern of any network administrator, and Exchange 2000 in collaboration with Windows 2000 offers enhanced options for protecting your organization. While this is another topic that could easily fill a book of its own, in Chapter 21 we offer as comprehensive a look at security as this space permits, including details on Certificate Authority and Key Management Service.

Part VI: Maintenance

Every system—even Exchange 2000 Server—needs maintenance. We've addressed the most important maintenance tasks in this section. In Chapter 24, we cover the critical topic of backup and restoration of your databases. Moreover, we outline how to monitor your Exchange 2000 servers (Chapter 23), how to perform basic troubleshooting for a server (Chapter 25), and how to tune your Exchange 2000 servers for maximum performance (Chapter 26).

Overview of Conventions

Within the chapters we've tried to make the material accessible and readable. You'll find descriptive passages, theoretical explanations, and step-by-step examples. We've also included a generous number of graphics that make it easy to follow the written instructions. The following reader's aids are common to all books in the Administrator's Companion series.

Note Notes generally represent some information that needs to be highlighted or alternate ways to perform a task.

Tip Methods of performing tasks more quickly or in a not-so-obvious manner will show up as tips.

More Info References to other books and sources of information are offered throughout the book.

Caution Don't skip over these boxes because they contain important warnings about the subject at hand—often critical information about the safety of your system.

Planning As we stress throughout the book, proper planning is fundamental to the smooth operation of any network. These boxes contain specific and useful hints to make that process go smoothly.

Real World

Everyone benefits from the experiences of others. Real World boxes contain elaboration on a particular theme or background based on the adventures of IT professionals just like you.

Talk to Us

We've done our best to make this book as accurate and complete as a single-volume reference can be. However, because Exchange 2000 Server is a large and complex product, we're sure that alert readers will find omissions and possibly some errors—though we really hope that there aren't too many of those! If you have suggestions, corrections, or comments, you may write to one of the co-authors, Bill English, at *benglish@networknowledge.com*. We genuinely appreciate hearing from you and sincerely hope you will find the *Exchange 2000 Server Administrator's Companion* to be enjoyable and helpful.

Part I
Introduction

Chapter 1
Introducing Exchange 2000 Server

Microsoft Exchange Server has been a leading collaborative product since its introduction in April 1996. Part of Microsoft's BackOffice product suite, Exchange Server has become the fastest selling server application in Microsoft's history. With each new release, Microsoft has added new functionality to enhance Exchange Server's capabilities. The latest version, Microsoft Exchange 2000 Server, builds on the superior performance and features that Exchange users have come to expect.

This chapter provides an overview of the capabilities and structure of Exchange Server, discussing the components of Exchange Server architecture, how those components are organized, and how they interact to provide a comprehensive messaging system. It also offers a look at the powerful new features of Exchange 2000 Server. Exchange Server is a complex program, but with a little dissection you will see how its complexity can benefit any enterprise.

What Is Exchange Server?

As you know, Exchange Server is one of the most popular components of Microsoft's BackOffice suite. But what is Exchange Server? Ask three different administrators and you're liable to get three different answers. Is it a messaging system? Is it a groupware product? Is it a development platform? The answer is all three.

As a messaging system, Exchange 2000 Server represents the state of the art in reliability, scalability, and performance. Over the past couple of decades, electronic messaging has become one of the dominant methods of business communication, and Exchange Server is one of the most popular messaging systems in the world.

The term *groupware* was coined in the 1980s to describe products that could be used to create collaborative applications in which people share access to a collection of centralized documents and resources. These days, we just call it collaborative software. Exchange 2000 Server breaks new ground in online collaboration through the support of real-time data and video conferencing, instant messaging, and an enhanced chat server. In addition, it lets you store virtually any type of document within the Exchange system, allowing the document to be shared. Exchange Server can also automatically send copies of documents to different physical information stores, making the use of shared documents across an organization much more efficient.

Microsoft Outlook 2000 is the newest version of Microsoft's premier messaging and collaboration client for use with Exchange 2000 Server. It allows users to send and receive messages that include many different types of data, to share scheduling and contact information, to participate in public folder discussions, and even to access both network and local file systems.

Exchange Server is also increasingly being used as a development platform—that is, as a basis for creating applications and systems to address the specific needs of organizations. For example, you can use it to create forms that extend the capabilities of a simple message and even attach application logic to those forms. You might then configure Exchange Server to route the forms to specific users or destinations, where they can undergo further modification. Additional tools allow you to access and manipulate the information stored in Exchange Server or to take advantage of Exchange Server's delivery services.

As you can see, Exchange Server is a multifaceted and complex product. By the time you complete this book, you will have a full understanding of how to use Exchange Server to implement and administer all of these features, and you will be equipped to exploit Exchange Server to its fullest.

Versions of Exchange 2000 Server

Microsoft provides three distinct editions of Exchange 2000 Server. Each is basically identical in function, but includes a different set of features. The three editions are Exchange 2000 Server, Exchange 2000 Enterprise Server, and Exchange 2000 Conferencing Server.

Exchange 2000 Server

This edition is designed to meet the basic messaging needs of small to medium-sized companies. It is built on the new Web Store technology and includes a transacted data store that can reach a maximum of 16 exabytes and fault-tolerant SMTP routing.

Exchange 2000 Enterprise Server

This edition is designed to meet enterprise-level messaging and collaboration needs. Exchange 2000 Enterprise Server includes all of the features in Exchange 2000 Server and also provides a transacted data store that can grow to an unlimited size, that can be partitioned into separate physical databases for increased reliability, and four-way, active/active clustering.

Exchange 2000 Conferencing Server

This edition provides tools that allow users to participate in data, voice, and video conferences. The major distinguishing factor is that the server provides tools for reserving and allocating corporate conferencing resources. It supports load balancing, failover, and control of attendee access to conferences. In addition, by allocating bandwidth for each conference technology provider, you can run any combination of the conferencing services simultaneously. Exchange Conferencing Server is a separate product that will be available soon after Exchange 2000 Enterprise Server is released.

Note   Throughout this book, we refer to Exchange Server in different ways, and each has a different meaning. Typically, we will refer to the software product as "Exchange Server." If you see this term, you can take it to mean Microsoft Exchange 2000 Enterprise Server. When necessary, we will use "Exchange 2000 Server" to draw attention to the fact that we are discussing a feature that is new or has changed in the most recent version of the product. Each of these terms means essentially the same thing. If we refer to a previous version of Exchange Server, we will always do so specifically, such as "Exchange Server 5.5." Finally, we will often use the term "Exchange server" (note the lowercase s in "server") to refer to an actual server computer, as in "There are eight Exchange servers in this routing group."

Basic Concepts

The next few chapters give you an in-depth look at the architecture of Exchange 2000 Server. Before learning the specifics of Exchange Server, however, you need to understand some of the concepts that form its foundation. This section describes the basics of messaging systems, how an Exchange Server environment is organized, how Exchange Server stores information, and the key services that make up Exchange Server.

Messaging Systems

When most people think of electronic messages, they first think of e-mail, but an electronic messaging system can do more than just deliver e-mail. The term *electronic messaging* describes a more generalized process that can be used to deliver many different types of information to many different locations. A messaging system has several specific characteristics. First, it involves the participation of at least two parties: the sender and one or more recipients. Second, when a sender dispatches a message, the sender can count on the message being delivered. If the messaging system cannot deliver a message to a recipient immediately, it keeps trying. If, after repeated tries, the messaging system fails to deliver the message, the least it should do is inform the sender of this failure. Although a standard messaging system can guarantee the reliable delivery of messages, it cannot guarantee exactly how long it will take to deliver a message. This uncertainty is due to the asynchronous nature of a messaging system. In an asynchronous system, two related events are not dependent on each other; in a messaging system, for example, the sending of a message and the receipt of the message are not tied together in any fixed span of time.

There are two basic types of messaging systems: shared-filed systems and client/server systems. Although client/server systems have almost entirely replaced shared-file systems in modern messaging products, administrators need to have a good understanding of both.

Shared-File Systems

Many older messaging products, such as Microsoft Mail, are shared-file systems. A *shared-file* e-mail system, as shown in Figure 1-1, works fairly simply. A messaging server contains a shared folder (a mailbox) for each user of the system. When a user sends a message, that users' e-mail client places a copy of the message into the shared folders of any designated recipients. Clients are generally configured to check their shared folders at set intervals. If the recipient client finds a new message in the folder, it alerts the user. Shared-file systems are generally referred to as *passive* systems, in that it is up to the messaging software running on the client to carry out the operations of the e-mail transaction. The messaging server itself plays no active role (other than housing the e-mail system's shared folders) in passing the message from sender to recipient.

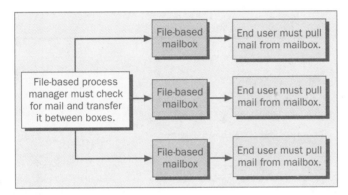

Figure 1-1. *A shared-file e-mail system.*

Client/Server Systems

An Exchange-based system is a form of *client/server* system (Figure 1-2). This type of system is referred to as an *active* system because the server takes a much more active role than the server in a shared-file system. In an Exchange-based messaging system, client software delivers outbound messages to a service on an Exchange server. That service places the messages in the recipient's mailbox or in a queue destined for another Exchange server or for a foreign messaging system. Exchange Server itself is then responsible for alerting users that new messages await them. In addition, Exchange Server takes on many other responsibilities. For example, each Exchange server does the following:

- Manages the messaging database
- Manages the connections to other Exchange servers and messaging systems
- Indexes the messaging database for better performance
- Receives new messages and transfers them to their destinations

To provide these services, Exchange Server is typically installed on more powerful server machines than those used for shared-file messaging systems, which means that a client/server system such as Exchange Server is inherently more scalable than a shared-file system. The server-based agents that implement Exchange Server can also provide a higher level of security, reliability, and scalability than a simple shared-file messaging system can. All of these features allow Exchange Server to support many more users than simple file-based systems.

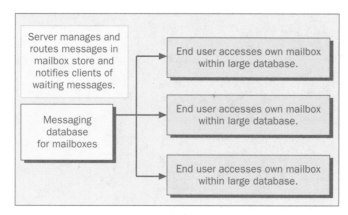

Figure 1-2. *The Exchange client/server system.*

As the name implies, a client/server system has two distinct components: a client and a server. The client and the server use a specific interface to cooperate. The fact that Exchange Server distributes functions between the client and the server means that more processing power is available systemwide for messaging in general. In comparison, a shared-file system depends on the client to constantly check and pull mail, a process that can result in poorer performance as well as increased network traffic on a workstation client.

Note Exchange Server is the server component of an Exchange system, but the server does not exist in a vacuum. You will also learn about the clients that participate in an Exchange system.

Multiple clients can access a server at the same time. As a result, a server must be designed to handle many types of requests from many sources simultaneously. The need to service many clients is one of the primary factors that led to the architecture used to implement Exchange Server, in which several separate processes in the server cooperate to handle client requests. These server processes and the way they interact are described later in this chapter. Each Exchange Server process handles one type of task. This structure means that Exchange Server can execute different functions simultaneously rather than sequentially, as a monolithic, single-process messaging architecture would do. The overall result is that Exchange Server is a robust system that improves upon legacy messaging architectures.

The Organization of an Exchange Environment

In previous versions of Exchange Server, each group of Exchange servers was known as a site, and each site defined the group's boundaries for both administration and routing. Exchange 2000 Server does away with sites and instead allows Exchange servers to be grouped into administrative groups and routing groups. This split allows administrators to deploy their organizations along boundaries that are more closely aligned with the real world than was previously possible. In addition, the integration of Exchange 2000 Server with the Microsoft Windows 2000 Active Directory directory service has brought about changes in the way the various recipients are managed. This section outlines the basic organizational features of Exchange 2000 Server.

Administrative Groups

An *administrative group* is a collection of Exchange servers and administrative objects that are logically grouped together for common administrative purposes. For example, your organization might have two system administrators, one responsible for administering collaborative services and the other responsible for administering servers and connectors. You could use administrative groups as a way of assigning permissions and policies to each administrator. An administrative group can contain policies, routing groups, public folder trees, servers, and more.

Routing Groups

A *routing group* is a collection of Exchange servers that are all physically connected by a permanent, high-speed, reliable network. A server is contained within one—and only one—routing group. The routing group is the closest thing to a site in previous versions of Exchange Server. Messages sent between servers in a routing group are delivered directly from source to destination. Messages sent between servers in different routing groups must be routed through *bridgehead servers,* servers that are specifically designated to route messages from one routing group to another over specialized connectors.

Policies

Policies are another feature new to Exchange 2000 Server. *Policies* are collections of configuration settings that are applied to one or more Exchange configuration objects. For example, an administrator could configure a set of parameters to govern a certain aspect of server behavior and then assign those parameters, as a policy, across tens or even hundreds of servers. Once policies are implemented, changes to the policies affect all objects to which the policies are assigned, making it easy to change the configuration of entire groups of objects at a stroke. Exchange 2000 Server uses two basic types of policies: system policies and recipient policies.

System policies are used to configure servers and the message store databases on those servers. Three classes of system policies are defined: mailbox store policies, public folder store policies, and server policies. A system policy defines configuration settings for a class of objects (such as public folders). Once you have defined a policy, you can apply it to existing objects or create new objects using that policy. You can then change the configuration for all of those objects with one stroke. For example, you might create a system policy that limits the size of messages that can be posted to a group of public folders. Once that policy has been applied to those folders, you could change the limits at any time for all of the folders simply by changing the policy.

Recipient policies are used to configure objects such as users, mailboxes, groups, and contacts—objects typically associated with the user side of the system. Because much of this directory information resides in the Windows 2000 Active Directory, recipient policies actually apply settings to the Windows 2000 domain containers. Recipient policies work in much the same way that system policies do. You can use them to apply and modify configuration settings to groups of recipients all at once. For example, you might configure a recipient policy that defines how an SMTP address is created for certain recipients. Once that policy has been applied, you can change the addressing scheme for all of the recipients by changing the policy.

Servers

Server is the term used in the Microsoft Exchange topology to refer to an individual computer that has the Microsoft Exchange Server messaging application installed and running on it. The name of the server is typically the same as the name of the Windows 2000 computer that hosts the Exchange Server application.

There are no hard and fast rules as to how many servers you should have within a particular routing group. The size of the machine acting as the server will have some bearing on how many users and how large a store the machine can support. In addition, you should put some thought into which servers to place users on. When individual users on the same server communicate through Exchange Server, they do not add to network bandwidth because the message does not need to move across the network between separate physical machines. By grouping users according to how they interact with one another, you can improve the Exchange server's performance and even the performance of the entire messaging system.

Recipients

Although the recipient is the lowest level of the Exchange hierarchy, it is a critical component of the Exchange organization. As the name implies, a *recipient* is an entity that can receive an Exchange message. Most recipients are associated with a single, discrete mailbox, although this mailbox can be represented by several addresses, depending on the addressing types implemented within Exchange.

In previous versions of the Exchange Server, a separate tool—the Exchange Administrator—was used to create recipients and to associate them with Microsoft Windows NT user accounts. With the introduction and integration of Windows 2000 Server and Exchange 2000 Server, all that has changed. When you install Exchange 2000 Server, it adds Exchange-related functionality to the Windows 2000 Active Directory Users and Computers snap-in. This tie to Active Directory means that, in addition to mailboxes, Exchange 2000 Server supports other types of recipients, including groups and contacts.

Mailboxes   A *mailbox* is an area of an Exchange Server's mailbox store database where a particular user's private messages are stored. A Windows 2000 user object that has been given a mailbox is referred to as *mailbox enabled.* Only user objects can be mailbox enabled.

Note You can make other objects participate in Exchange 2000 Server routing simply by giving them an e-mail address. Such objects are referred to as *mail enabled* and are not associated with an actual mailbox.

Groups   A *group* is a collection of users, contacts, and even other groups that is able to receive messages. When a group receives a message, Exchange Server sends a copy of the message to each of the recipients within the group. The term *group* also refers to a Windows 2000 security object that is a collection of users and other groups. An Exchange 2000 Server group is always based upon a Windows 2000 group. A group is the functional equivalent of a distribution list in previous versions of Exchange Server.

Contacts   A *contact* is a Windows 2000 object that is not an actual user and thus cannot log on to the network. Contacts can receive e-mail from Exchange users, just as standard Exchange recipients can, after their addresses are defined in the Exchange system's Global Address List. Through the use of contacts, you can integrate external recipients, such as Internet e-mail addresses, into the address list of your Exchange system. Contacts are the functional equivalent of custom recipients in previous versions of Exchange Server.

Address Lists

An *address list* is simply a list of recipients. The Global Address List is the list of all Exchange Server recipients in the entire Exchange organization. Exchange Server uses address lists to hold and organize the names of the recipients associated with the system.

An Exchange system can have hundreds of thousands of recipients, making it difficult for a user to locate an individual recipient's name. In addition, e-mail addresses can be somewhat cryptic. Various legacy messaging systems have restrictions on the length of the user's mailbox name, and some administrators assign puzzling mailbox names. All in all, it can be difficult to guess a user's e-mail address. The primary purpose of an address list, from a user's point of view, is to provide a way to locate an e-mail address for a recipient. When the administrator of an Exchange environment creates a recipient, the person's name—not a cryptic e-mail address—shows up in the Global Address List, making it easier for Exchange users to locate and send mail to recipients.

In addition to the Global Address List maintained by Exchange Server, individual users can create their own personal address lists, called address books. Personal address books can contain a portion of the Global Address List, as well as other custom addresses added by the user, to make it easier to access the addresses they use most frequently.

Connectors

You should understand one more piece of the Exchange Server topology before moving on: connectors. A *connector* is a piece of software that acts as a gateway between Exchange Server routing groups or from a routing group to a non-Exchange mail system (such as foreign X.400 messaging systems). A connector enables the Exchange system to interact directly with a foreign e-mail system, as though its users were part of your Exchange system. Connectors can integrate foreign address lists into the Global Address List, enable message exchange, provide access to shared messaging folders, and make other functions available. Some connectors simply enable a consistent mail-forwarding and receipt operation. In addition to providing a link between Exchange Server and other messaging systems, a connector can be extremely useful if you are in the process of migrating to Exchange Server or connecting to nonmessaging systems such as fax or voice mail.

Exchange Server Storage

Exchange Server uses several types of *message stores,* or storage databases, to hold the messages that make up its information environment. Within these stores, Exchange Server organizes the messages and other material in folders. A folder has the same relationship to its messages that a directory in a file system has to its files. Because Exchange Server manages the storage of its own data, there is not a strict one-to-one relationship between a folder in an Exchange Server store and a directory in the operating system. Exchange Server uses two types of stores: a mailbox store and a public folder store.

When you install an Exchange server, you have to specify locations for the public folder store and the mailbox store. Each store acts as a database for all the objects that it contains: mailboxes for the mailbox store and public folders for the public folder store.

Note   Exchange 2000 Server makes use of a technology named *Web Store.* The term actually applies to the Exchange Server store technology and does not represent an actual store of data on the Exchange server. You'll learn more about the features of the new Web Store in the section "Web Store," later in this chapter.

Mailbox Store

The mailbox store is a database on an Exchange server that contains all of the mailboxes of every Exchange user associated with that Exchange server. The mailbox store manages the data within the mailboxes, tracking deleted messages and mailbox sizes and assisting in message transfers. A *private folder* is a secured folder component within a mailbox for an Exchange Server recipient. Each private folder holds information that is available only to a single Exchange user and to others to whom that user has granted access permissions.

Exchange maintains private folders and the mailboxes that contain them within the mailbox store of the associated Exchange server. Although the folders are "secured" in the sense that an Exchange user must have an account and a password to access each mailbox, Exchange Server does manage the contents of mailboxes. For example, the mailbox store is included in standard Exchange Server backup and recovery operations.

Exchange users are not limited to using the Outlook or Exchange client to access their mailboxes. They can also access private stores through various Internet mail protocols and even through a standard Web browser, if the Exchange environment is configured to allow those types of access.

> **Note** Many companies using Exchange also make use of *personal stores*, which are databases of messages controlled by a messaging client rather than by Exchange Server. Typically, personal stores reside on a user's local machine or on a shared network volume. After materials are placed in a personal folder, they are the exclusive responsibility of the user. Other users cannot access the materials in a personal folder. If users create or modify any of the documents in the personal folder and want others to access these documents, they have to explicitly place these documents in a private or public folder in order to put them back under the care of an Exchange server.

Public Folder Store

The public folder store is a database that stores public folders, indexes their contents, and assists in the replication of the folders with other Exchange servers. As the name implies, a *public folder* is accessible to more than one user. Administrators can define the specific security restrictions on a public folder to limit the types of users who have access to it. Public folders are the basis of a great deal of Exchange Server's functionality. They are ideal places to keep information that is accessed by large numbers of people. If, for example, your organization has marketing materials or human resources policies that you want to make available to everyone as soon as they are created, you can put them in a public folder.

The reason for the separation between the Public Folder Store and the Mailbox Store lies in the way Exchange Server treats the information in the Public Folder Store. Because everyone in what could be a widely dispersed organization can access public folders, Exchange Server allows you to set up automatic replication of the contents of public folders. Exchange Server handles the replication of documents in a public folder with no intervention on the part of an administrator after the replication is defined. Users who request a document in a public folder retrieve it from the closest copy of the public folder, rather than having all users access the requested document from a single location. In this way, public folders help expand the scalability of Exchange Server by reducing the bandwidth requirements for the access of common documents.

Exchange Server Services

From the outside, Exchange Server looks like a single, monolithic software system. Internally, Exchange Server uses three key services to perform its tasks: the Information Store service, the Routing Engine service, and the System Attendant service. A *service* is a piece of software that runs in the background on Windows 2000, performing its tasks without requiring any specific administrative intervention.

When you install Exchange Server, you must specify a Windows 2000 user account that the various Exchange Server services will use to access the Windows 2000 server system. This account is called the Exchange service account. User accounts can be granted varying levels of system access. When an Exchange 2000 Server service accesses the Windows 2000 server, it must be able to act as part of the operating system. Thus, the user account that you specify as the Exchange service account during the installation of Exchange Server will automatically be granted extended access to the Windows 2000 server in order to act as an intermediary between Exchange users and the operating system. All Exchange Server services normally use the same service account. The following sections describe the three basic Exchange Server services.

Information Store

As you know, Exchange Server information stores are kept as database files that are managed by the Exchange server. The Information Store service is responsible for storing and retrieving information from those stores. It is involved in sending messages and also handles certain automatic functions of Exchange, such as replication.

Routing Engine

The most active part of an Exchange server is the Routing Engine. If this service shuts down, the Exchange server can no longer move mail through the system. The Routing Engine service is responsible for coordinating the transfer of messages between Exchange servers. It acts as a traffic cop and a crossing guard combined, directing messages to their destinations as well as ensuring that the messages arrive safely.

System Attendant

The System Attendant (SA) is the background manager for the Exchange system. The SA maintains the link state tables used for message delivery, monitors the connections between servers, and collects feedback that is used by other monitoring tools. These unseen activities are vital to the continuing successful operation of your Exchange environment.

Some optional features of Exchange Server create their own services, and so additional Exchange Server services may also be running on your system, such as the Key Management Services, which provides an additional level of security for your Exchange organization.

What Is New in Exchange 2000 Server

Some of the features new to Exchange 2000 Server have already been discussed, such as administrative groups, routing groups, and policies. This section takes a look at the other important enhancements to Exchange 2000 Server.

Active Directory Integration

With each new version, Exchange Server has grown more integrated with the Windows operating system. Exchange 2000 Server integrates seamlessly with the Windows 2000 Active Directory and offers the combined and centralized management of messaging, collaboration, and network resources. Active Directory is a scalable directory service built using Internet technologies and fully integrated into Windows 2000. All Exchange Server directory information is now stored in the Active Directory. You will learn much more about the integration of Exchange 2000 Server and the Windows 2000 Active Directory in Chapter 4.

Active Directory Connector

The Active Directory Connector (ADC) is a tool designed to allow Exchange 2000 Server and Exchange Server 5.5 to exist within the same organization. The ADC lets administrators replicate directory information between the Exchange Server 5.5 directory and the Windows 2000 Active Directory. The ADC allows for multiple-master, bidirectional replication.

Multiple Message Databases

Exchange 2000 Server allows message stores to be partitioned into smaller, separately managed databases with no size limit. Previously, a message store could have only one database. A logical database can be split into separate physical databases on a server, and those databases can even be stored on different servers. You can perform administration, and even stop a database altogether, while sibling databases are still running. This is a great advance, in that it allows administrators to further localize the number of users affected by routine maintenance and recovery.

Storage Groups

Exchange Server 5.5 stores data in two main databases, Priv.edb for the mailbox store and Pub.edb for the public folder store. Exchange 2000 Server replaces the single private and public information stores with support for multiple folder stores contained in storage groups. A storage group is a collection of databases that share a single transaction log and a single point of administration, backup, and restore. You can create multiple databases per storage group and can have multiple storage groups, making it possible to have many different databases, even on the same server. You'll learn much more about storage groups in Chapter 2.

Distributed Configuration

Different pieces of the Exchange Server environment, such as protocols, connectors, and storage databases, can be hosted on separate servers in Exchange 2000 Server, making a distributed environment possible. For example, you could dedicate one server to hosting connectors, another to fielding incoming Internet mail protocol requests, and yet another to hosting messaging stores. This allows a great deal of flexibility and scalability in your Exchange deployment.

Simple Mail Transport Protocol Message Routing

With Exchange 2000 Server, Simple Mail Transport Protocol (SMTP) has become the default messaging transport protocol for routing all messages between servers. Further, a fault-tolerant implementation of SMTP has been embraced, allowing for the delivery of messages even when servers or network connections fail.

Administration Through Microsoft Management Console

The Exchange System snap-in for the Microsoft Management Console (MMC) serves as the single seat for Exchange 2000 Server administration. The MMC provides a customizable framework for management utilities. Windows 2000, Exchange Server 2000, and many other Microsoft and third-party applications use MMC snap-ins to provide a common console for multiple-resource network administration.

System Monitoring

Exchange 2000 Server provides a new monitoring interface that is a simple flat view of all of the servers and connectors in an Exchange environment. All servers are monitored for disk space usage, service status, and queue trends.

Windows 2000 Security

Exchange 2000 Server is tightly integrated with the Windows 2000 security model. Administrators can use a single set of security groups to administer both Windows 2000 and Exchange 2000 Server. You'll learn more about this model in Chapter 4.

Field-Level Security

Exchange 2000 Server allows permissions to be set for individual messages and even for fields within those messages, instead of only at the folder level. This capability gives administrators greater control over workflow and message tracking.

Web Store

The Exchange 2000 Web Store is an Installable File System (IFS) that provides local and remote users access to the file systems. Drive M on the computer running Exchange Server provides direct access to all data in the Web Store and is automatically given the share name BackOfficeStorage. Each Web Store exists as a folder under the M drive on the local machine, which means that applications that save directly to disk can now store files in the Web Store from local or remote locations. Users can access all data in the Web Store, including messages, documents, and objects, by entering a URL into a Web browser. For example, a user might access his or her Inbox simply by entering *http://servername/username* into a browser.

The Web Store includes built-in indexing that enables speedy searching of all Web Store content. Users of Microsoft Outlook 2000 can easily search for messages, documents, and users. The Web Store is also tightly integrated with Internet Information Services (IIS) and Active Server Pages (ASP) technology, enabling developers to use known tools and skills to build powerful, high-performance Web-enabled applications that include Web-based forms, business logic, and workflow services.

Web Forms

Web forms are browser-based forms that Exchange 2000 Server transmits directly to a Web browser, using the Hypertext Transfer Protocol (HTTP). For example, a Web Store folder could contain a sales order form that a user accesses by typing a URL into a Web browser. Web forms can be created with Microsoft FrontPage 2000 and are used to create and modify items in a Web Store folder.

Multiple Public Folder Trees

Exchange 2000 Server supports multiple public folder trees, giving administrators a good deal of flexibility in deploying collaborative applications. In previous versions of Exchange Server, an organization could have only one public folder hierarchy that was exposed to all users. This restriction made it difficult to have public folders that were limited to certain sets of users, and it made administration of public folders a bit more complicated as there was no good way to divide up the administrative chores. Having multiple public folder trees allows system administrators to separate databases according to functional, business, geographic, or administrative requirements. For example, you could dedicate an entire public folder tree to each major department in your organization, providing a much more natural organization of resources.

Data and Voice Conferencing

Exchange 2000 Server data and voice conferencing allows dynamic, on-demand sharing of data and information using any T.120-compliant client, such as Microsoft NetMeeting. This enables users to talk and easily share visual information. Exchange 2000 Server also offers complete audio and video conferencing using Internet Protocol (IP) based multicast technology to provide audio and video teleconferencing services. This technology is based on the Telephony API (TAPI) 3.0 standard, which is included as part of Windows 2000; it allows more simultaneous participants in a videoconference than other solutions do.

Instant Messaging

You have probably seen instant messenger software such as the MSN Messenger client and AOL Instant Messenger. Instant messaging lets users send text-based messages to other users on a network. Unlike e-mail, these messages are displayed immediately to the other user's screen, and they can be received only if the other user is logged on. Instant messaging has become very popular for Internet users in recent years and is poised to play a significant role in businesses as well. Exchange 2000 Server includes an instant messaging service built on a secure architecture suited for both internal and Internet deployment. The client software for instant messaging in Exchange 2000 Server is the MSN Messenger client. Presence information is part of instant messaging; it enables one computer user to see whether another user is currently logged on to a network, a corporate LAN, or the Internet.

Summary

This chapter introduced you to Exchange 2000 Server, giving you the background you need to delve into the Exchange Server architecture in detail. It described basic concepts, including how an Exchange environment is organized, how different types of information are stored, and the services that work behind the scenes to accomplish the many tasks that Exchange Server performs. In addition, the chapter gave an overview of the new features in Exchange 2000 Server, including Active Directory integration, the new Exchange System Manager snap-in, and the Exchange 2000 Web Store. The next two chapters take a deeper look into the Exchange Server architecture, beginning with its storage architecture.

Chapter 2
Understanding Exchange 2000 Server Storage Architecture

The explosive growth in the number of e-mail users in the average corporate environment, together with the increasing complexity of the messages being transferred (containing, for instance, video, voice, and large graphics), have led to a dramatic increase in the size of many Microsoft Exchange 5.5 databases. It is not uncommon to find databases exceeding 20 GB. In this environment, a robust storage architecture is an absolute necessity. Exchange 2000 Server meets this need.

This chapter describes the storage architecture in Microsoft Exchange 2000 Server. It covers the database file structure, the Extensible Storage Engine (ESE), the Installable File System (IFS), and changes in the way Exchange 2000 Server handles public folders. It also discusses indexing and how clients access Exchange 2000 Server stores, as well as the front end/back end server architecture.

Storage Design Goals in Exchange 2000 Server

In designing the storage architecture of Exchange 2000 Server, the creators had three goals in mind. The first was to minimize loss of productivity when a database goes off line. Exchange 2000 Server achieves this goal by spreading users across multiple databases that can each be mounted (started) or unmounted (stopped) individually. If one database in a storage group goes off line for some reason, the other databases continue to run, minimizing the number of users who are affected by the downtime.

A second design goal was to allow a single server to host more users than is pragmatically possible in Exchange 5.5. Spreading the users across multiple databases on a single server accomplishes this goal as well. Since the databases are smaller, creating more databases on each server allows each server to host more users. For instance, it is easier to manage six databases with 1000 users per database than it is to manage one database of 6000 users. Not only can backup and restore times be scheduled individually and run faster, but if one database becomes corrupted, only 1000 users are affected instead of 6000 users. In addition, Exchange 2000 Server can group multiple databases into a single storage group and host multiple storage groups on a single server.

The third goal, better recoverability in the event of a disaster, was a major concern of the design team and is also achieved by spreading users across databases, allowing individual databases to be restored while other databases are running. The result is shorter downtimes and greater productivity for users because only a subset of the organization's users are affected when a database goes off line.

Database File Structure

Each Exchange 2000 database consists of two files: the rich text file (ending in .EDB), which holds mail messages and Message Application Programming Interface (MAPI) content, and the native content "streaming" file (ending in .STM), which holds all non-MAPI information. Hence, a mailbox store (formerly known as a private information store) now consists of the files Priv1.edb and Priv1.stm (Figure 2-1). Similarly, a public folder store (formerly known as a public information store) now comprises the files Pub1.edb and Pub1.stm (Figure 2-2). Each database incorporates both files, and Exchange 2000 Server treats the files as one unit. When Exchange reports the size of the store, it gives the combined size of the rich text file, the native content file, and the transaction logs. Both types of data are stored in an Extensible Storage Engine database format. (ESE is discussed later in this chapter.)

Figure 2-1. *The Database tab for a mailbox store property sheet.*

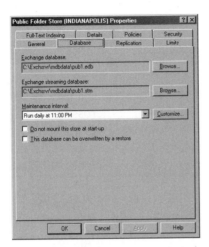

Figure 2-2. *The Database tab for a Public folder store property sheet.*

Rich Text File

The rich text file holds messages from MAPI clients, such as Microsoft Outlook. MAPI clients access these messages without a conversion process running on the server. The rich text file is the same as the Exchange 5.5 information store. It is an .EDB file that uses transaction logging just as it did in Exchange 5.5.

On-Demand Content Conversion

When a MAPI client attempts to read a message from the rich text file, no conversion is necessary, since the message is in the client's native format. However, if another type of client, such as an HTTP client, attempts to read a message from the rich text file, Exchange converts the message to the requested format. This process, in which messages are converted for dissimilar clients, is known as *on-demand conversion*.

Exchange 2000 Server does not automatically convert data when it writes it to the database. Instead, client actions, such as a dissimilar client requesting data from the rich text file, cause the data to be converted. This is known as *deferred content conversion*. For example, suppose that a Web-based client posts a message to an Exchange server. It is stored in the native content file. If another client requests this message over TCP port 80, Exchange streams it out of the native content file without converting it. However, if an Outlook client requests that message, that client is attempting to read information from a database that is not in its native format. In this case, Exchange converts the message in the memory of the server and then passes it to the client. The message is not moved from the native content file to the rich text file before being sent to the Outlook client.

If the Outlook client makes a change to the message and then saves it, the message is copied from the native content file to the rich text file and then deleted from the native content file. During the copy process, the updated message is converted from its native content to rich text before being written to the rich-text file.

Native Content File

In Exchange 5.5, messages are always written to the database in Microsoft Database Encapsulated Format (MDBEF). If a message in non-MDBEF format needs to be written to the database, the Imail process converts it to MDBEF format so that it can be written to the information store.

In Exchange 2000 Server, the native content file holds all non-MAPI messages in their native format, including HTTP and IMAP4. Native content files can include audio, video, voice, and other multimedia formats. This file simply holds the raw data with no overhead, such as compression or B-tree overhead. In addition, the page checksums and space-usage information (information that tells ESE which pages are used and which ones are free) are stored in the .EDB file.

> **More Info** For a discussion of how B-trees work, see Chapter 17 of *Microsoft SQL Server 7.0 Administrator's Companion* (Microsoft Press, 1999).

Messages delivered from the native content file are streamed to the client. The streaming is fast due to the presence of the Win32 kernel mode component ExIFS. (See the next section, "How Streaming Works," for more on this component.)

Any Win32-based client is able to access the data in the native content file over server message block (SMB) architecture. This capability means that any kind of data can be placed in the native content file, and it will be accessible to your LAN-based clients as regular file shares as well as being available over standard Internet protocols such as HTTP.

How Streaming Works

Figure 2-3 illustrates how streaming works in Exchange 2000 Server. Let's assume that a Post Office Protocol 3 (POP3) client requests a message from the native content file. The POP3 client connects to the POP3 server in Internet Information Services (IIS), and the server asks the Store process (Store.exe) to manifest a handle to the message inside the native content file. The Store process negotiates a handle for the message with the kernel mode Exchange Installable File System (ExIFS) driver. The ExIFS driver locks the message, creates the handle, and presents the handle back to the Store process. It is also worth noting that page checksums are not verified during outbound transmission. Once manifested, the handle is handed back to the POP3 virtual server across the epoxy layer in user mode. (The section "Front End/Back End Servers," later in this chapter, discusses the epoxy layer.) The POP3 virtual server then issues a TRANSMITFILE command, which is a high-performance API that uses both the handle and sockets to transmit the file. The TRANSMITFILE command is issued to the Auxiliary Function Driver (AFD), which essentially acts on behalf of Winsock, streaming the file out of the NT Cache Manager by talking to the ExIFS driver. It is important to note that at no time does the streaming data enter user mode, which makes this architecture very fast and very reliable. The handle contains the list of database pages that hold the information being requested. During the locking phase, ESE reserves the pages that hold the information and gives them to ExIFS.

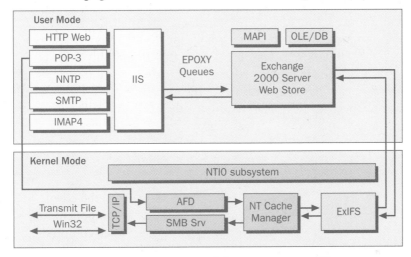

Figure 2-3. *Streaming architecture of the native content file.*

IIS can write to the native content file as well. ExIFS will make the native content file appear to IIS as multiple, yet virtual, files. When IIS wants to write to the native content file—as would be the case, for example, when an inbound message has a graphics attachment—ExIFS creates virtual files to which IIS can write. Then ExIFS streams this data into the native content file and passes the list of pages to the Store process. ESE then commits the pages by logging the information in the transaction logs. Page checksums are stored in the rich text file, so that only data is held in the native content file.

ExIFS requests database space from ESE when necessary and allocates space for new messages from its reserved space. This allocation makes the write operation faster than if the space was not previously allocated.

Single-Instance Message Store

Exchange 2000 databases continue to support the Single-Instance Message Store (SIS) feature, meaning that a message sent to multiple recipients is stored only once as long as all the recipients are located in the same database. SIS is not maintained if a mailbox is moved to a different database, even if it still resides in the same storage group. Moreover, it does not span multiple databases in a single storage group.

Here is an example of how SIS works. John, the Exchange administrator at Oak Tree, Inc., has deployed two storage groups consisting of four databases each. Each group contains two mailbox stores and two public folder stores. Mary, a user in John's network, sends a 1-MB message to a distribution group of 40 recipients, all of them residing in the first storage group, with 30 of them on mailbox store 1 and the other 10 on mailbox store 2.

Without SIS, the message would be copied 41 times (40 copies for 40 users plus 1 copy for the transaction log), requiring a whopping 41 MB of total disk space to store the message. However, as Figure 2-4 shows, with SIS only three copies of the message are held, one in the database of mailbox store 1, one in the database of mailbox store 2, and one temporarily in the transaction log. Hence, sending this message to these 40 recipients requires only 3 MB of total disk space, saving 38 MB.

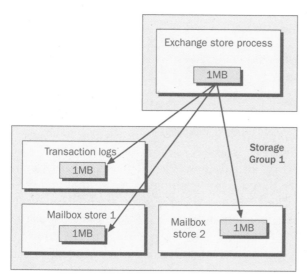

Figure 2-4. *How the Single-Instance Message Store feature works.*

Storage Groups and Multiple Databases

A storage group consists of an instance in memory of the Extensible Storage Engine (ESE) transaction logging system (described later in this chapter), the set of transaction logs, and their corresponding databases in the group. The ESE instance is managed by the Store.exe process, which runs as a single process. Each storage group can hold up to six databases. There can be up to 4 storage groups per server and each group can hold up to 6 databases, so the limit is 24 databases per server. However, as we'll learn later, you'll want to reserve some of these databases for recovery and maintenance functions. Each database can be either mounted (started) or dismounted (stopped). Although a corrupt database cannot be mounted, it also cannot stop the Store.exe process from running or stop other stores in the storage group from being mounted or dismounted.

Having multiple databases in multiple storage groups gives you great flexibility regarding how you manage your users and databases. For instance, you can group your users together by department or location and create their accounts in a common database. You can also control your user-to-database ratio, so as your company grows, you can keep your databases at a predetermined size and simply create another database for new users when necessary.

Also, the databases are very scalable, meaning that a single database can have from one mailbox up to (theoretically) an unlimited number of mailboxes. Neither extreme is recommended, however, and the actual limit to the number of mailboxes in a database will depend on factors such as hardware capacity or the amount of time necessary to back up or restore your databases. In addition, databases can be scheduled individually for backup, and you can perform multiple backups on multiple databases to multiple tape drives simultaneously. This feature helps reduce the window of time necessary to back up your databases.

The process of restoring a database is just as flexible. You can perform multiple restores simultaneously. In the event of a disaster, if you lose four databases that are each 4 GB in size, Exchange 2000 Server gives you the option of restoring all four databases simultaneously, thus reducing the restoration time by 75 percent. Exchange 5.5 doesn't have multiple databases or storage groups, so you would have to restore one 16-GB database. It's easy to see that it's faster to restore four databases simultaneously than it is to restore one 16-GB database.

Data Recovery and Transaction Logs

Three of the top ten questions that Microsoft's technical support receives are related to the ESE and data recovery. This section discusses the role of transaction logs and describes how they are used in the recovery of your databases in the event of a catastrophe. It also covers why databases fail and looks at some of the common error messages that accompany a database failure. See Chapter 24 for a step-by-step description of how to restore a database.

The Extensible Storage Engine

The Extensible Storage Engine is a transaction logging system that ensures data integrity and consistency in the event of a system crash or media failure. The design of the ESE was guided by four criteria. The first was a question: "What happens if there's a crash?" Every development was guided by the notion that it should improve recoverability in the event of a disaster. Second, every effort was made to reduce the number of I/O operations that ESE would perform. Three I/O operations are better (faster) than four, and four are better than five. Even if it means expanding an I/O operation to include additional calculations, eliminating one I/O operation greatly improves performance. The third criterion was for the database engine to be as self-tuning as possible. The ESE team is moving toward having all maintenance activities performed online. Finally, ESE is designed to provide an uptime as close to 24 hours a day 7 days a week as possible. Achieving the online maintenance level will enhance the success of this last goal.

How ESE Works

The main function of ESE is to manage transactions. ESE applies four tests to the databases to ensure their integrity. They are sometimes referred to as the ACID tests:

- **Atomic** Either all of the operations performed in a transaction must be completed or none will be completed.

- **Consistent** A transaction must start with a database in a consistent state and leave the database in a consistent state when finished.

- **Isolated** Changes are not visible until all operations within the transaction are completed. When all of the operations are completed and the database is in a consistent state, the transaction is said to have been *committed*.

- **Durable** Committed transactions are preserved even if the system experiences significant stress, such as a system crash.

Note Durability can be seen when the system crashes during the performance of the operations. If some of the operations were completed before a system crash (for example, if the e-mail was deleted from the Inbox and copied to the Private folder but the item count on each folder was not updated), when the Store.exe process starts on reboot, it will detect that the database is in an inconsistent state and will roll back the operations. This precaution means that the mail message cannot be lost while it is being moved, nor will there be two copies of the message upon reboot. ESE ensures that, when restarted, the database is in the same state it was in immediately before the operations began.

Real World What Happens When a Change Is Made to a Page in the Database?

Let's say that you move an important e-mail message from your Inbox to a private folder named Private. The following operations occur to complete this transaction:

Deleting the mail message from the Inbox folder.

Inserting the mail message into the Private folder.

Updating the information about each folder to correctly display the number of items in each folder.

Committing the transaction in the temporary transaction log file.

Because these operations are performed in a single transaction, Exchange either performs all of them or none of them. This is the Atomic test. The commit operation cannot be carried out until all of the operations have been performed successfully. Once the transaction is committed, the Isolated test is passed. And since the database is left in a consistent state, the Consistent test is passed. Finally, after the transaction is committed to the database, the changes will be preserved even if there is a crash. This meets the Durable test.

How Data Is Stored Inside an ESE database file, data is organized in 4-KB sections called *pages*. When information is read from an ESE database file and loaded into memory, it is done in the form of a page. Each page contains data definitions, data, indexes, checksums, flags, timestamps, and other B-tree information. They are numbered sequentially within the database file to maximize performance. Pages contain either the actual data or pointers to other pages that contain the data. These pointers form a B-tree structure, and rarely is the tree more than three or four levels deep. Hence, the B-tree structure is wide but shallow.

A *transaction* is a series of modifications to a page in a database. Each modification is called an *operation*. When a complete series of operations has been performed on an object in a database, a transaction is said to have occurred.

Note An ESE database can contain up to 2^{32} or 4,292,967,296 pages. At 4 KB per page, an ESE database can hold 16 terabytes (4,292,967,296 × 4096 = 17,583,994,044,416 bytes). Practically speaking, your database size will be limited by hardware space or backup and restore considerations rather than by ESE design.

When a page is first read from disk and stored in memory, it is considered *clean*. Once an operation has modified the page, it is marked as *dirty*. Dirty pages are available for further modifications if necessary, and multiple modifications can be made to a dirty page before it is written back to disk. The number of modifications to a page has no bearing on when the page will be written back to disk. This action is determined by other measures, which we will discuss later in this chapter.

While the operations are being performed, they are being recorded in the version store. The version store keeps a list of all of the changes that have been made to a page but have not yet been committed. If your server loses power before the series of operations can be committed, the version store will be referenced when ESE starts again to roll back, or undo, the unfinished operations. Figure 2-5 illustrates this process.

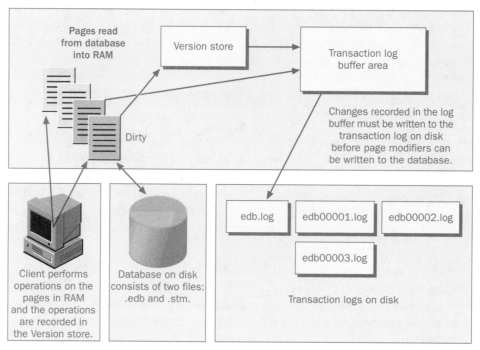

Figure 2-5. *How ESE handles transactions.*

To actually commit a transaction, the operations must be written to the transaction log buffer before being written to the transaction logs on disk. ESE uses "write-ahead" logging, which means that before it makes a change to the database, it notes what it's going to do in the log file. Data is written to a cached version of the log in the log buffer area, the page in memory is modified, and a link is created between these two entries. Before the modifications of the page can be written to disk, the change recorded in the log buffer must first be written to the log file on disk.

> **Tip** It is possible that one operation will hang or be so large that the version store takes up hundreds of megabytes. This situation could occur if your operation is indexing a large table or writing a very large file to the database. Since the version store keeps track of all of the changes that have occurred to the database since the oldest transaction began, you might get a "-1069 error (JET_errVersionStoreOutOfMemory)." If this happens, consider moving your databases and stores to another disk with more free disk space, and also consider increasing the RAM in your system.

Oftentimes, the cached version of the changes to the pages is not written to disk immediately. This does not present a problem, since the information is recorded in the log files. Should the modifications in memory be lost, when ESE starts, the log files will be replayed (a process discussed in more detail in the section "Replaying Log Files During Recovery," later in this chapter), and the transactions will be recorded to the disk. Moreover, not writing cached information to the database right away can improve performance. Consider the situation in which a page is loaded from memory and then modified. If it needs to be modified again soon thereafter, it does not need to be reread from the disk because it is already in memory. Thus, the modifications to the database can be batched to increase performance.

Database Files The database itself is a combination of the .EDB and .STM files stored on the hard disk. Eventually, all transactions are written to one of these files. Before a page is written to disk, however, a checksum is calculated for that page, and the checksum is then written to the database along with the data. When the page is read from disk, the checksum is recalculated and the page number is verified to be sure that it matches the requested page number. If the checksum fails or if there is a mismatch on the page number, a -1018 error is generated. This error means that what was written to disk is not what was read by ESE from the disk into memory.

> **Note** Beginning with Service Pack 2 (SP2) in Exchange Server 5.5 and continuing in Exchange 2000 Server, ESE attempts to read the data 16 times before generating a -1018 error, reducing the chance that a transient event might cause a problem. Hence, if you receive a -1018 error, you know that ESE attempted to read the data repeatedly before warning you.

ESE and Memory Management   Before it can load a page into memory, ESE must reserve an area in memory for its own use. *Dynamic buffer allocation* (DBA) is the process of increasing the size of the database buffer cache before the memory is needed. More than a few Exchange administrators have complained that Exchange eats up all of the memory on their server. This situation is by design, although the design doesn't necessarily call for using all of the memory, nor is the allocated memory unavailable for other system processes.

In Exchange 4.0 and 5.0, the size of the cache was set by the Performance Optimizer. In Exchange 5.5, the process was changed to be dynamic: ESE observes the system and adjusts the size of the database cache as necessary. To observe how much of your RAM is being reserved by the Store process, use the Cache Size performance counter.

At this point, it might be helpful to take a look at the overall design goals of the DBA process. Understanding these will answer any questions you might have about memory management in Exchange 2000 Server. The two design goals of DBA are as follows:

- **Maximize system performance**   The Store process uses the amount of overall paging and I/O activity, among other factors, to determine how much RAM to allocate for the database buffer. Overall system performance really is the focus of this goal. It does no good to have Exchange running quickly if the operating system is constantly paging.

- **Maximize memory utilization**   Unused system memory is wasted dollars. ESE will allocate to itself as much memory as it can without negatively impacting other applications. If a new application starts that needs additional memory, ESE will release memory so the other application can run efficiently.

As you can see, you don't need to be alarmed if you go into Task Manager and see that, for example, out of the 512 MB of RAM on your system, only 50 MB is left and the Store.exe process is using 330 MB of RAM. You're not running out of memory and the Store.exe process does not have a memory leak. All it means is that the DBA feature of ESE has allocated additional RAM to increase your system performance. Figures 2-6 and 2-7 illustrate what this looks like in Task Manager. Note in Figure 2-6 that DBA has allocated a total of 133,688 KB of system memory for the Store.exe and Mad.exe (System Attendant) processes. Figure 2-7 shows that only 49,176 KB is available in physical memory.

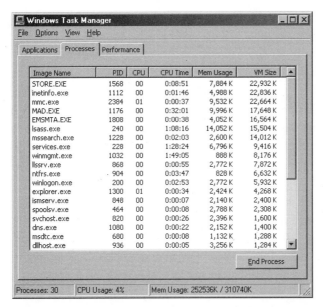

Figure 2-6. *The Processes tab in Windows Task Manager, showing the memory allocated to Store.exe and Mad.exe.*

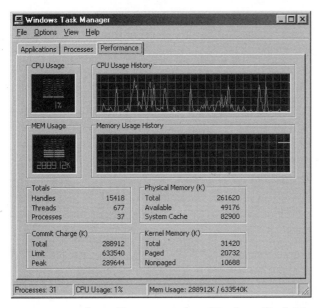

Figure 2-7. *The Performance tab in Windows Task Manager, showing memory usage and availability.*

Transaction Log Files In theory, the transaction log file could be one ever-expanding file. But it would grow so big that it would consume large amounts of disk space, thus becoming unmanageable. Hence, the log is broken down into *generations*—that is, into multiple files, each 5 MB in size and each representing a generation. The generations are named Edb*XXXXX*.log, where the *XXXXX* is incremented sequentially, using hexadecimal numbering.

The Edb.log file is the highest generation. When it becomes full, it is renamed with the next hexadecimal number in sequence. As this happens, a temporary log file, Edbtemp.log, is created to hold transactions until the new Edb.log can be created.

Each log file consists of two sections: the header and the data. The header contains hard-coded paths to the databases that it references. In Exchange 2000 Server, multiple databases can use the same log file, since the log files service the entire storage group. From an administrative perspective, this arrangement simplifies recovery. No matter which database in a storage group you're restoring, you will reference the same log files for that group. The header also contains a signature matched to the database signature. This keeps the log file from being matched to a wrong but identically named database.

You can dump the header information of a log file with the command Eseutil /ml (Figure 2-8). The dump displays the generation number, the hard-coded database paths, and the signatures. The data portion of the log file contains the transactional information, such as BeginTransaction, Commit, or Rollback information. The majority of it contains low-level, physical modifications to the database. In other words, it contains the records that say, "This information was inserted on this page at this location."

When a database is modified, several steps occur. First, the page is read into the database cache, and then the timestamp on the page is updated. This timestamp is incremented on a per-database basis. Next the log record is created, stating what is about to be done to the database. This occurs in the log cache buffer. Then the page is modified and a connection is created between these two entries so that the page cannot be written to disk without the log file entry being written to disk first. This step guarantees that a modification to the database will first be written to the log file on disk before the database on disk is updated.

Hence, there is legitimate concern over the write-back caching that can be enabled on a log file disk controller. Essentially, write-back caching means that the hardware reports back to ESE a successful disk write even though the information is held in the disk buffer of the controller to be written to disk at a later time. Write-back caching, while improving performance, can also ruin the ESE process of writing changes to the log file before they are written to the database. If a controller or disk malfunction of some sort occurs, you could experience a situation in which the page has been written to disk but not recorded in the log file—which will lead to a corrupted database.

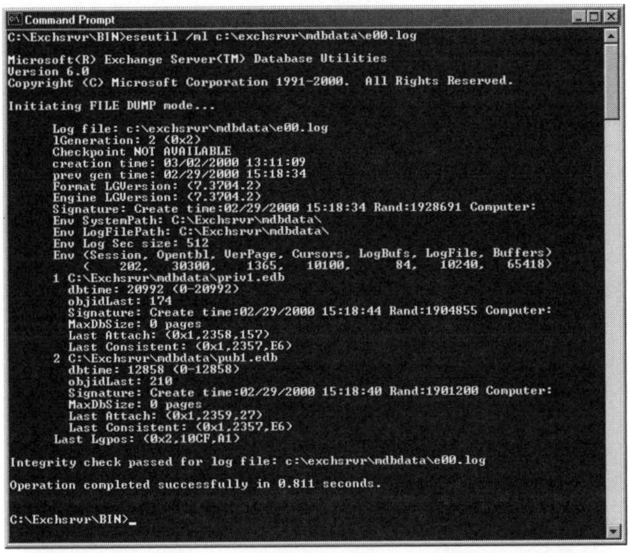

```
Command Prompt
C:\Exchsrvr\BIN>eseutil /ml c:\exchsrvr\mdbdata\e00.log

Microsoft(R) Exchange Server(TM) Database Utilities
Version 6.0
Copyright (C) Microsoft Corporation 1991-2000.  All Rights Reserved.

Initiating FILE DUMP mode...

   Log file: c:\exchsrvr\mdbdata\e00.log
      lGeneration: 2 (0x2)
      Checkpoint NOT AVAILABLE
      creation time: 03/02/2000 13:11:09
      prev gen time: 02/29/2000 15:18:34
      Format LGVersion: (7.3704.2)
      Engine LGVersion: (7.3704.2)
      Signature: Create time:02/29/2000 15:18:34 Rand:1928691 Computer:
      Env SystemPath: C:\Exchsrvr\mdbdata\
      Env LogFilePath: C:\Exchsrvr\mdbdata\
      Env Log Sec size: 512
      Env (Session, Opentbl, VerPage, Cursors, LogBufs, LogFile, Buffers)
          (    202,    30300,    1365,   10100,      84,   10240,   65418)
      1 C:\Exchsrvr\mdbdata\priv1.edb
        dbtime: 20992 (0-20992)
        objidLast: 174
        Signature: Create time:02/29/2000 15:18:44 Rand:1904855 Computer:
        MaxDbSize: 0 pages
        Last Attach: (0x1,2358,157)
        Last Consistent: (0x1,2357,E6)
      2 C:\Exchsrvr\mdbdata\pub1.edb
        dbtime: 12858 (0-12858)
        objidLast: 210
        Signature: Create time:02/29/2000 15:18:40 Rand:1901200 Computer:
        MaxDbSize: 0 pages
        Last Attach: (0x1,2359,27)
        Last Consistent: (0x1,2357,E6)
      Last Lgpos: (0x2,10CF,A1)

Integrity check passed for log file: c:\exchsrvr\mdbdata\e00.log

Operation completed successfully in 0.811 seconds.

C:\Exchsrvr\BIN>_
```

Figure 2-8. *A header dump produced using Eseutil /ml.*

How Log Files Are Replayed During Recovery   After you have restored your database, the logs will be replayed when you start the Store.exe process. Replaying the logs and then rolling back operations that might exist in the version store constitute the "starting" of the Store process; this is often referred to as the recovery process. Replaying the transaction logs is the first part of the recovery process, and it consumes most of the time necessary to start the Store.exe process.

Replaying the transaction log files means that for each log record, the page is read out of the database that the record references, and the timestamp on the page read from the database is compared to the timestamp of the log entry that references that page. If, for example, the log entry has a timestamp of 12 and the page read from the database has a timestamp of 11, ESE knows that the modification in the log file has not been written to disk, and so it writes the log entry to the database. However, if the timestamp on the page on disk is equal to or greater than the timestamp on the log entry, ESE does not write that particular log entry to disk and continues with the next log entry in the log file.

In the second and last phase of the recovery process, the version store plays a very important role. The version store keeps track of any operations that were performed but not finished because the transaction could not be committed. These operations are rolled back: If a piece of mail was transferred, it is untransferred. If a message was deleted, it is restored. This is called *physical redo, logical undo*. Recovery runs every time the Store.exe process is started. If you stop and then start the Store process five times, the recovery process runs five times.

Tip You can also run the recovery process with the Eseutil /m command and the Isinteg command.

Even though the recovery process is run on the log files and not on the databases, if you've moved your databases, recovery won't work because the hard-coded path to the database in the header of the log file will no longer point to the database. At the end of recovery, it will appear to have been successful, but when you attempt to use that database, you'll get an error with an event ID of 9519 from MSExchangeIS in the application log, indicating an error in starting your database (Figure 2-9).

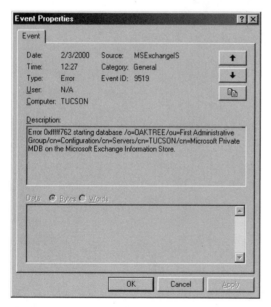

Figure 2-9. *Message indicating that an error occurred when starting the database.*

If you move the database back to the location where the log file is expecting to find it and then start the Store process, you should find that recovery brings your database to a consistent and usable state. If you need to change the location of your databases, use a recovery from tape backup and modify the Restore in Progress key to alias the new location of your databases. Although this doesn't rewrite the headers in the log files, it causes the alias to be referenced during the restore process. For more information on how this works, see Chapter 24.

Checkpoint File   The checkpoint file is an optimization of the recovery process. It records which entries in the log files have already been written to disk. If all of the entries in the log files have been written to disk, the log files don't need to be replayed during recovery. The checkpoint file can speed up recovery time by telling ESE which log file entries need to be replayed and which do not.

Faster recovery of a database is sometimes why circular logging is enabled. Circular logging deletes log files older than the current checkpoint location. The problem with circular logging is that you lose the ability to roll forward from a backup tape. If some of your log files since the last full backup have been deleted by circular logging, you'll be able to recover only to the last full backup. However, if you have all of your old log files, restoring the last full backup of your database from tape will allow for a full restore up to the point of your disaster because all of the log files can be replayed into the restored database. Remember that in order for a full restore to work, the database must be in the same physical condition as it was when the log files were written. A physically corrupt database cannot service a restore process.

Caution   Never, never, never delete your log files. Here's why: Assume that log file 9 contains a command to insert a new page at a particular place in the database. Log file 10 contains a command to delete this page. Now suppose that an administrator deletes log file 9, perhaps thinking that the file's timestamp is too old, and also deletes the checkpoint file. The administrator then needs to reboot the system for unrelated reasons. When the Store.exe process is started, ESE automatically enters recovery mode. Finding no checkpoint file, ESE has no choice but to replay all of the log files. When log file 10 is replayed, the delete command will be carried out on that page, and its contents will be destroyed. ESE won't know that there was an earlier command to insert a new page in that location in the database because log file 9 was deleted. Your database will be corrupted. Whatever you do, *do not delete your log files or the checkpoint file.* Furthermore, be aware that *write-back caching can have the effect of deleting log files.* The best practice is to disable write-back caching and never delete your log files or checkpoint file.

How Log Entries Are Written to the Database As we mentioned earlier, modified pages in memory and committed transactions in the log buffer area are not written immediately to disk. Committed transactions in the transaction log file are copied to the database when one of the following occurs:

- The checkpoint falls too far behind in a previous log file. If the number of committed transactions in the log files reaches a certain threshold, ESE will flush these changes to disk.

- The number of free pages in memory becomes too low, possibly affecting system performance. In this case, committed transactions in memory are flushed to disk to free up pages in memory for system use.

- Another service is requesting additional memory and ESE needs to free up some of the memory it is currently using. ESE flushes pages from memory to the database and then updates the checkpoint file.

- The database service is shutting down. In this case, all updated pages in memory are copied to the database file.

Bear in mind that pages are not copied from memory in any particular order and may not all be copied at the same time. The random order in which the pages are copied back to disk means that if there is a system crash while pages are being written to disk, the database file may have only portions of a committed transaction updated in the actual file. In this event, when the Store.exe process is started, the transaction will be replayed from the transaction log files and the database will be updated completely.

Installable File System

One of the problems with document management for an organization has traditionally been the need to choose a technology for saving users' data. Until now, users have had to choose between saving their documents in a file system, on the Web, or in a public folder. Once they chose the location, they were locked into using a single interface to retrieve and work with their information.

Installable File System changes all of this. With IFS, users can place any kind of document in the native content file (the streaming file) and then access it from almost any client, regardless of whether that client is a browser, a MAPI client, or Microsoft Internet Explorer. This section expands on how ExIFS can be managed and how it will revolutionize the way you think about file and document management.

Data Access Through IFS

IFS treats each item of information in its database as an individual object that is exposed to network clients as a normal file, which means any folder, mailbox, or other information object can be accessed as though it were a normal network share. Clients can map drives to information objects in the database and have the ability to read and write data directly to and from the native content store.

The store is mapped automatically as the M: drive for the Exchange 2000 client. The share name on this store is BackOfficeStorage. Hence, clients can map a drive to *servername*\BackOfficeStorage. The M: drive is called a *portal* into the Store.exe process. If you run the Dir command on your M: drive, it becomes a Win32 call for a list of files. The ExIFS driver moves this call into the database, which determines which files are being requested and returns the results of the call to the user, in the form of a listing of files in the database (Figure 2-10).

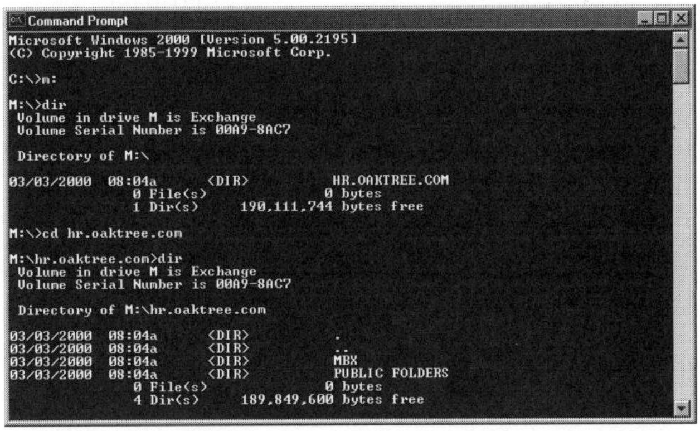

Figure 2-10. *Using the Dir command to list files in the native content file.*

Inside this share will be two folders: Mbx and Public Folders. The Mbx folder is the root folder for all mailboxes on the server. Users with permissions to do so can navigate the hierarchy using explicit folder names that equate to the mailbox alias names.

Information in the IFS can also be subject to full-text indexing and can be accessed by HTTP clients. This means that Internet users can utilize the Exchange Web client to query the information store for document properties as well as for search terms, get the results quickly, and then view the results in their browser with an Outlook-style view. Moreover, with Extensible Markup Language (XML), a user can make changes to a document over the Internet via the browser and save the document in the same way that one would save a document on a file server.

Web Access to IFS

As we mentioned earlier, information that is held in the native content file can be accessed over the Web, using HTTP. This is accomplished by giving each object in the file a unique URL that lets the object be accessed from the browser, allowing a customized application to call directly into the Exchange store to retrieve data from both mailboxes and public folders.

WebDAV, an update to the HTTP protocol, is now available to meld Internet technologies with file and print technologies. WebDAV is an extension of the HTTP protocol and represents a standards-based layer that is built on top of HTTP 1.1. Specifically, it supports a more complex command structure, adding commands such as COPY or MOVE that manipulate individual objects on a Web server. In addition, this new protocol allows read/write access to the information store over HTTP for any client. It supports relational database structures, semistructured databases (such as Exchange databases), and standard file systems. Furthermore, WebDAV clients can be synchronized to server-side stores over the Internet through replication, allowing efficient online access and offline usage of data. This feature enables you to, for example, publish an hourly update of current inventory to a nationwide sales force. Each salesperson would be able to view this information over the Internet, enter orders and comments, and have current information at a client site as long as Internet access was available.

WebDAV can accommodate all types of content, which means users can use WebDAV to work collaboratively on a word processing document, a spreadsheet, or an image file. Potentially, anything you can put in a file can be authored using WebDAV. WebDAV makes the Web, from the point of view of the client, a writable medium. Microsoft Internet Explorer 5 and Microsoft Office 2000 are WebDAV compatible. Some of the features of WebDAV include the following:

- **Overwrite protection (file locking)** Users can write, edit, and save shared documents without overwriting another person's work, regardless of which software program or Internet service they are using. This is a key collaborative support feature.

- **Namespace management** Enables users to conveniently manage Internet files and directories, including the ability to move and copy files. This process is similar to file management in Explorer.

- **Property (metadata) access** Permits metadata information about a document, such as the author's name, copyright, publication date, or keywords, to be indexed and searched to find and retrieve relevant documents. (For more information on this, see the section "Indexing," later in this chapter.)

Web folders are designed to let clients access a Web server in the same way they access a file server. Exchange 2000 Server allows a client to access directories and items in the information store just as it would access them on a file server and to manage the data in the Web folder as if it were a file server. Public folders are also exposed as Web folders in Exchange 2000 Server.

Public Folders

Exchange 2000 Server makes several important changes to public folders. These changes include the following:

- Administration of public folders is accomplished through the Exchange Folders Microsoft Management Console (MMC) snap-in.

- Public folder trees are far more scalable and flexible. No longer are all of the public folders in your organization grouped into one large, mono-lithic hierarchy. You can now create public folder trees by geography, department, or function. The next section, "Multiple Public Folder Trees," discusses this feature in more detail.

- Public folders are integrated with Active Directory, which means that mail entries enable you to send messages to a public folder instead of having to post directly to the public folder.

- Public folders use the users and groups in the Active Directory directory service for security.

- Accessing a public folder over the Web is more direct and much easier. With a standard URL, it's possible in Exchange 2000 to open up the contents of a public folder.

- ExIFS, using SMB, makes public folder contents accessible from the file system for your LAN users.

- Full-text indexing is built in with public folders. Outlook clients auto-matically use this new index when performing a Find or Advanced Find search. In Exchange 5.5, indexing of public folders is supported through Site Server, and that index is available only for Web clients to query.

- Referrals are enabled by default. Public folder referrals enable clients to gain access to any folder in the organization because referrals between routing groups are now enabled by default.

- Public folders can be created with the Exchange Folders snap-in. You are no longer required to use Outlook to create a public folder.

Multiple Public Folder Trees

In Exchange 2000 Server, you can create multiple public folder trees for a variety of purposes. For instance, suppose that you have a project team composed of three internal LAN clients, two users in your company at remote locations, and three consultants outside your organization. You can create a public folder tree for these users that is separate from the default public folder tree (Figure 2-11).

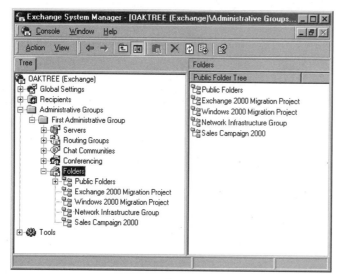

Figure 2-11. *Multiple public folder trees.*

Each public folder tree stores its data in a single public folder store on a per-server basis. You can replicate specific folders in the tree to every server in your company that has a public folder store associated with that public folder tree. The default public folder tree is available via MAPI, IMAP4, Network News Transfer Protocol (NNTP), and HTTP. Additional public folder trees are available only to HTTP and NNTP clients but not to internal LAN clients unless they use HTTP or NNTP to connect to the public folder tree.

Replication and Public Folders

By default, when a public folder is created, only one copy of it exists within the organization. If you like, you can replicate this public folder to other servers for redundancy, accessibility, and fault tolerance. Figure 2-12 shows how to use the Replication tab on the folder's property sheet to specify folders that will receive a replica of your public folder. You can also configure the replication schedule and the priority of the replication messages.

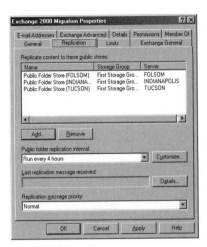

Figure 2-12. *Specifying replication for a public folder.*

Exchange 2000 clients really don't care which replica of a public folder they connect to. However, we administrators do care, for a variety of reasons. It is worth noting that when a client attempts to connect to a replica of a public folder, it looks for the replica in the following sequence of locations:

1. The client's default public store. This default is determined on the mailbox store's property sheet (Figure 2-13).

2. A server to which the client already has an existing connection.

3. Every other server that is in the same routing groups as the client's home public folder server.

4. Any other server in remote routing groups, based on the connector values between the home routing group and the remote routing group.

If two or more remote routing groups have the same connector costs, the servers containing the public folder replica are pooled together and selected at random as if they were in the same routing group. You should consider carefully before configuring a mailbox store to use a server in a remote routing group as its default public folder store. If you have slow or unreliable WAN links between your routing groups, your users may very well saturate your bandwidth if they heavily access public folders across the WAN link. It is best to choose a default public folder server that is in the same Windows 2000 site and Exchange 2000 routing group as the client's home mailbox store. In addition, consider pulling in replicas from remote public folder servers for clients who access these folders heavily.

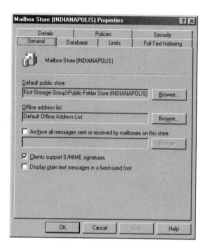

Figure 2-13. *The default public store for a client.*

Security and Public Folders

Whereas previous version of Exchange used the security system embedded in the information store, Exchange 2000 Server uses the Windows 2000 Active Directory to enforce security. Hence, the new security model implements several important principles.

The first is that access control can be applied to any resource, not just the public folder. This capability enables you to apply security settings individually to items in the folder and to properties on the items. Second, Exchange 2000 Server no longer uses roles because the security system no longer emanates from the information store. Instead, permissions to administer Exchange 2000 Server are created in Active Directory. Third, as a further integration with Active Directory, the security identifiers (SIDs) for the user and group objects are used in the object's access control list (ACL). Anonymous access permissions are assigned to the special anonymous logon account, and default access permissions are assigned to the Everyone group. Finally, permissions can be denied on a per-user, per-object, or per-property basis. Deny permissions are processed first and take precedence over granted permissions.

Note You can still use the Outlook client to assign permissions to a public folder. It will show the Exchange 5.5 style of roles and permissions, but Active Directory will not directly map these roles to Active Directory permissions.

Client Access to Exchange 2000 Stores

There are more ways than ever for an Exchange 2000 client to access the Exchange store. Clients can access the information store through POP3, NNTP, IMAP4, HTTP, Simple Mail Transport Protocol (SMTP), property promotion, standard URLs, and WebDAV.

The information store specifically supports NNTP and SMTP so that users can create and view Internet newsgroup discussions in addition to sending and receiving e-mail. The store also provides an automatic Hypertext Markup Language (HTML) 3.2 view of a folder of objects by using property promotion on each object to render this view inside the browser. (Property promotion is discussed more fully in the next section, "Indexing.") For instance, if the documents inside the folders requested are Office documents, the document properties are automatically parsed and promoted to the store. Once promoted, users can create views or queries on these documents that use the promoted properties.

As each message or file is created in the store, Exchange creates a unique URL for that object. For example, a document named Memos.doc that has been saved to the Memos folder in the Administration public folder tree can be viewed with the URL http://*server_name*/administration/memos/memos.doc. A user's Inbox can be accessed via the URL File://./BackOfficeStorage/*server_name.domain_name.com*/mbx/*user_name*/inbox/*document_name*.

Indexing

The information store process creates and manages indexes for common key fields for faster lookups and searches of documents that reside in a store. An index allows Outlook users to search for documents more easily. With full-text indexing, the index is built prior to the client search, thus enabling faster searches. Text attachments can be included in the full-text indexing. As Figure 2-14 shows, each information store can be indexed individually for flexibility.

Property promotion allows for advanced searches on any document property, such as Author, Lines, or Document Subject (Figure 2-15). When Exchange stores a document in a supported file type, the document's properties are automatically parsed and promoted to the information store. Hence, the properties become a part of the document's record in the database. Searches can then be performed on these properties.

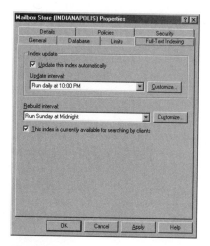

Figure 2-14. *Scheduling indexing for a mailbox store.*

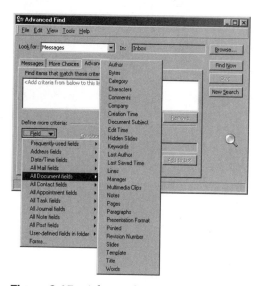

Figure 2-15. *Advanced search for document properties that have been promoted to the information store.*

This feature offers outstanding flexibility. You can build your indexes around those attributes that are most important in your document management structure and expose those attributes for fast searches to your clients.

The index is word-based, not character-based. This characteristic means that if a user performs a search for the word "admin," only those documents that have the word "admin" will be returned. The word "administrator" will not be identified as a match. Both the message and attachments can be indexed. Binary attachments and document properties are not indexed. Not all file types are indexed either; the following documents are the only types that are indexed:

- Word documents (*.doc)
- Excel documents (*.xls)
- PowerPoint documents (*.ppt)
- HTML documents (*.html, *.htm, *.asp)
- Text files (*.txt)
- Embedded MIME messages (*.eml)

Indexing is provided by the Microsoft Search service. Both the information store service and the search service must be running for the index to be created, updated, or deleted. Depending on the size of your store, completing a full index could take hours. Therefore, it's best to have this activity occur at a time when your server will be underutilized. Remember that indexing consumes about 20 percent of the disk space of your database. Also, individual indexes cannot be backed up; they must be backed up at the server level. Finally, even though multiple instances of a message might be held in the database, the message is indexed only once. This single-instance message indexing results in smaller indexes that can be created more quickly.

The Indexing Process

Microsoft Search builds the initial index by processing the entire store one folder at a time. The Search process identifies and logs searchable text. During the indexing process, you will see heavy CPU utilization; depending on the size of the store, this process could take hours.

After the index is created, any change to a folder within the store causes a synchronization event to notify the Microsoft Search service of the change. Depending on how you have configured the Search service to run, either it will wait for the scheduled time to regenerate the index so that the new change is included or it will update the index shortly after the change is made.

Updating the Index

The time delay for an immediate (automatic) update of the index will vary based on the current server load. You can optimize this setting on the Full-Text Indexing tab of the Information Store's property sheet (Figure 2-16).

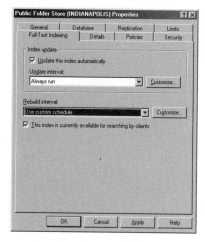

Figure 2-16. *The Full-Text Indexing tab of the property sheet for a public folder store.*

Scheduled updates allow granular control over when the index is updated. The advantage of scheduling the index update is that it can be planned for off-peak hours when the server is not heavily accessed by users. The disadvantage is that the index can become out-of-date over the course of a day. However, this may not be a big problem, since most users search for documents that were received and indexed more than 24 hours before the search. Try to schedule your updates to occur at least once each day.

Automatic updates will keep the index up-to-date. Changes to documents are queued for a short period of time, and then the index is updated. All changes that are made during the wait period are incorporated into the index as a batch job. The disadvantage of automatic updates is that you cannot control when server resources are used to perform the index update. If your store is becoming increasingly busy—meaning that an increasing number of documents are being posted, deleted, or changed—the server will expend more resources to keep the index up-to-date. It's best to configure automatic indexing on stores in which documents change infrequently, or on servers that are not heavily used for purposes other than document management and indexing.

Search Architecture

If you want to implement full-text searching widely in your organization, you'll need to consider which messaging clients to deploy. Only online MAPI and IMAP4 clients are able to perform full-text searches on the server. POP3 and WebDAV clients do not have search capability.

Exchange 2000 Server can perform two types of searches. The first is a full-text query of the index that has been built using Microsoft Search service. The second type is a query based on the properties of the documents that are not available in the full-text index.

When a user performs a search in the Outlook client by choosing Advanced Find from the Tools menu, several options are available (Figure 2-17). Once the user enters the desired variables, the query is sent to the Query Processor, which determines how the search should be conducted. If the search is based on both a string of text characters and a desired property variable, the Query Processor splits the query request into two parts. For instance, suppose that the request is for all documents that are larger than 5 MB *and* that have the phrase "building plan" in the subject line. The Query Processor splits this request and has the Microsoft Search service generate a list of documents that have "building plan" in the subject line. It then evaluates the size of each document that the Search service returned to find all those larger than 5 MB and generates a new list of documents that meet both criteria.

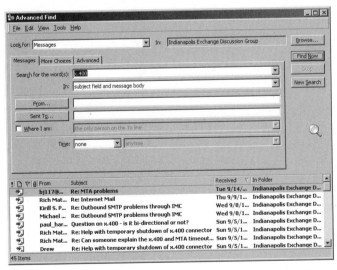

Figure 2-17. *The Advanced Find dialog box in Outlook 2000.*

Finally, Exchange 2000 Server applies security restrictions to the remaining documents to ensure that the client does not receive a document that the client is not supposed to see. After this security enforcement, the matching results are returned to the client.

Gather Files

If a file is attached to a message or is placed in a public folder that cannot be indexed, it will be recorded in a gather file. Gather files are created during each index process; they are located by default in the \Exchsrvr\ExchangeServer\ Gatherlogs directory and end with the extension .GTHR. You can use these text files to identify every document and message that was not successfully indexed. For example, if a document is named with an extension indicating a supported file type, but it is not actually that type, the indexing component halts, fails the index, records the URL of the document in the gather file (Figure 2-18), and then continues with the next message or document.

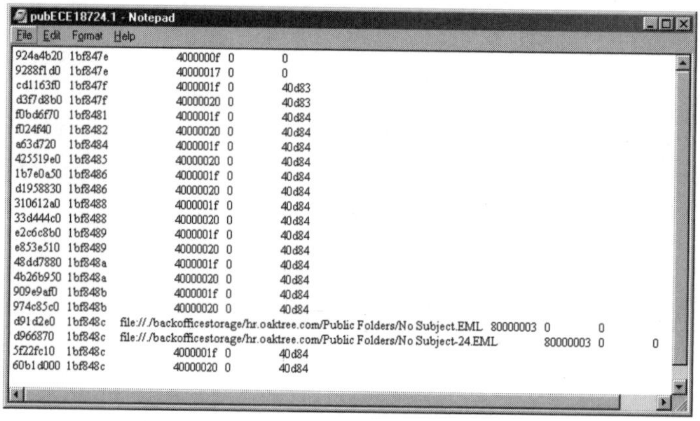

Figure 2-18. *A URL in a gather file.*

In addition to the URL, the subject or filename and the error code are also recorded in the gather file. To decode the error number, use the Gthrlog.vbs utility in the \Program Files\Common Files\System\MsSearch\Bin directory. The syntax for this utility is

```
Gthrlog <filename>
```

where *<filename>* is the name of the gather file. You will be prompted with a series of dialog boxes that contain the data found in each line of the gather file, as shown in Figure 2-19.

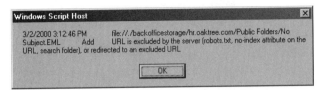

Figure 2-19. *A dialog box containing a line from the gather file.*

Moving the Index When It Gets Too Big

If your catalogs become so large that you're running out of disk space, you may want to move the index to another server. To do this, stop the Search service and use the Catutil.exe utility located in the Program Files\Common Files\System\ MSSearch\Bin directory. For help in using this utility, type *Catutil Movecat /?* at the command prompt.

Front End/Back End Servers

Between the Exchange store architecture and the Internet access protocols lies a layer called the Exchange Interprocess Communication Layer (EXIPC), now known as the *epoxy* layer, which is an efficient, asynchronous shared area in memory to which both the Store.exe process and the IIS protocols can read and write. This queuing layer permits information to be exchanged very quickly between the IIS protocols that run inside the Inetinfo.exe process and the Store.exe process. The epoxy layer uses shared memory to communicate between these processes and is optimized for small packet communication.

To keep track of the binding, connection to, and use of the epoxy layer's queues, Exchange 2000 Server uses the Central Queue Manager. This manager is also responsible for unbinding and queue cleanup in the event of a catastrophic failure in the other process. This revised architecture, known as a front end/back end architecture, makes it possible to run some of the Internet protocols on different servers than the servers on which the store and the databases are running. The major advantage to this feature is the ability to scale Exchange for any installed base that is desired. To enable Exchange 2000 Server to act as a front end server, you simply select a single check box on the General tab of the Exchange server's property sheet in the Exchange System snap-in (Figure 2-20).

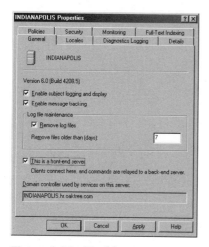

Figure 2-20. *Enabling a server to act as a front end server.*

When this check box is *not* selected, the protocol DLLs, such as Pop3be.dll, Imap4be.dll, and Httpbe.dll, are loaded into memory. When the server is marked as a front end server, these protocols are unloaded and front-end-specific DLLs are loaded into memory, such as Pop3fe.dll, Imap4fe.dll, and Httpfe.dll. To fully balance the load between client requests on front end servers, you will need to use either a DNS round-robin scheme (in which multiple IP addresses are assigned to one host name) or third party software.

The Windows 2000 version of DNS, when implementing a round-robin scheme, does not handle the failure of a front end machine very well. For instance, if you have five front end servers and one of them fails, DNS will still pass out the IP address of the failed machine, resulting in a 20 percent failure rate for client requests. Third-party software overcomes this issue via a concept called convergence. This technology recognizes failures in the front end and will stop advertising that server while it is offline.

Summary

This chapter has brought you up to speed on the storage architecture used in Exchange 2000 Server. You learned, for example, that the Store.exe process can manage many databases on a single server and that databases are divided into stores, each of which can hold up to six databases, either private or public. You have also seen some of the new architecture for public folders, WebDAV, indexing, ExIFS, and front end/back end servers. The next chapter takes a look at the message routing architecture in Exchange 2000 Server and describes how messages are passed between servers.

Chapter 3

Understanding Exchange 2000 Server Routing Architecture

One of the most significant differences between Microsoft Exchange Server 5.5 and Microsoft Exchange 2000 Server lies in the basic architecture of an Exchange system. The message routing topology in Exchange Server 5.5 is based on sites. A *site* is a logical grouping of servers that enjoy permanent, high-bandwidth connectivity. Architecturally, each site defines three distinct boundaries: the boundary for single-hop routing, the administrative unit, and a namespace hierarchy in the directory structure.

In Exchange 2000, these three boundaries have been separated into individual elements. Single-hop routing is defined by a routing group, the unit of administration is defined by the administrative group, and the namespace hierarchy exists in the Active Directory directory service in the form of a domain. This architecture gives administrators much more flexibility in determining how Exchange 2000 Server is administered because administrative assignments can be divided along functions and activities rather than geography.

This chapter focuses on the routing architecture used in Exchange 2000 Server. It describes what routing groups are, how to plan and name them, how they connect, and how link state information works to provide better message routing than Exchange 5.5 Server. We'll also look at the transport architecture and introduce some of the new architectural features.

Routing Groups

Each routing group in an Exchange organization consists of a collection of well-connected Exchange servers for which full-time, full-mesh connectivity is guaranteed. Most often, routing groups will closely map to the physical topology of your network. Connectivity among servers in a routing group is based entirely on Simple Mail Transfer Protocol (SMTP).

Using SMTP as the native protocol provides several advantages over the remote procedure call (RPC) -based communications in Exchange 5.5. First, it allows for a more flexible routing and administrative scheme because SMTP is more tolerant of low-bandwidth and high-latency topologies than RPC-based communications. This tolerance allows you to group servers into a single routing group in Exchange 2000 Server that you could not place into a single site in Exchange 5.5. Second, the use of SMTP allows a division between the routing architecture and the grouping of servers for administrative purposes. In Exchange 5.5, both of these elements were dictated by the site, forcing many companies to map their administrative boundaries to their site boundaries. Finally, SMTP requires less overhead and bandwidth than RPC-based communications.

In addition, Exchange 2000 Server features a new routing calculation engine that eliminates the problems associated with the Gateway Address Routing Table (GWART), replacing it with link state information (discussed in the section "Link State Information" later in this chapter).

Note SMTP doesn't replace the Message Transfer Agent (MTA) in Exchange 2000 Server. Instead, the MTA has been improved and works in both Exchange 5.5 and Exchange 2000 systems. However, it is now used mainly for connectivity to external X.400 systems.

In the object hierarchy of Exchange 2000 Server, routing groups are located beneath administrative groups (Figure 3-1). Within an administrative group (which is a logical collection of Exchange servers that you administer as one group), you can configure the servers so that some of them route messages directly to one another while others forward their messages to a bridgehead server. (Bridgehead servers are discussed more fully under the section "Message Routing to Other Routing Groups" later in this chapter.)

Exchange 2000 Server stores its routing information in the configuration naming partition of Active Directory. Even though this information will be made available through replication to your entire Exchange organization, you still need to define the connectors between servers, because these connectors help form the routing topology in the configuration naming partition. Using connectors, you can create customized routing topologies for maximum flexibility.

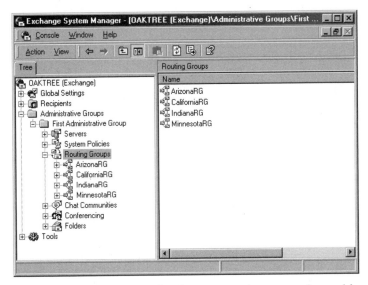

Figure 3-1. *Object hierarchy showing routing groups located beneath administrative groups.*

Routing Groups and Public Folders

An Exchange 2000 client uses the routing information in the configuration naming partition in Active Directory to locate a public folder server. By default, users will attempt to connect to a public folder replica on their home server and then on another server in the local routing group. If a client attempts to connect to a replica of a public folder that resides on a server in a remote routing group, the connector costs determine the order of the routing groups to which the client is directed. You can also set a flag on a messaging connector to prevent public folder referrals across the link (Figure 3-2), which was not possible with site affinities in Exchange Server 5.5.

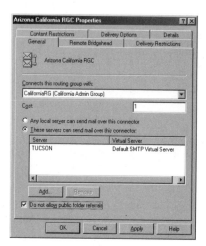

Figure 3-2. *The property sheet for a messaging connector, showing the Do Not Allow Public Folder Referrals option.*

Note Connector costs are arbitrary "costs" that you assign to the routing group connector (RGC) to reflect the bandwidth associated with the connector and the amount of messaging you wish the connector to receive. For instance, if you have an RGC configured over a T1 link and an SMTP connector over a satellite link, you would assign the RGC a cost of 1 and the SMTP connector a cost of 100. Message routing will attempt to use the lower-cost connector first.

Let's look at an example of how this works. Suppose that you have three routing groups, each with two servers named Server1 and Server2. In each routing group, Server1 is the e-mail server and Server2 is the public folder server. Sally is a member of routing group A.

Let's say that Sally attempts to connect to a public folder called Memos in her home routing group. Unfortunately, Server2 in routing group A is down for maintenance. In this instance, Sally is directed across the RGC to the public folders in routing group B and routing group C to access a replica of the Memos folder. If the connector cost on the RGC between routing group A and routing group B is 10 and the connector cost between routing group A and routing group C is 30, Sally will first be sent to routing group B because it has a lower connector cost.

Now let's say that the physical connection between routing group A and routing group B is severed by a construction crew. The administrator in routing group A could select the Do Not Allow Public Folder Referrals check box on the connector to routing group B, thereby taking that connector out of consideration the next time Sally needs to access the Memos folder. When the line is repaired, the administrator could clear the check box, permitting public folder referrals to once again flow across that connector.

Tip   Another situation in which it is a good idea to enable the Do Not Allow Public Folder Referrals option is when you know that a public folder server in a remote site is down and will be for a sustained period of time. Selecting this option will eliminate public folder requests across that connector. You might also want to use this option if all instances of public folders are housed in one routing group and you want to focus client traffic on that routing group. In this scenario, all of the RGCs that connect to the routing group containing the public folders will have this check box cleared, while all other RGCs will have this check box selected.

Overview of the Transport Architecture

Before we discuss how messages are routed within the same group or between groups, it might be useful to have a basic understanding of how messages are transferred internally within an Exhange2000 server. Knowing how messages arrive in an outbound SMTP queue, for example, will help complete the overall routing picture that will be presented in the next several pages.

Messages can flow into an Exchange 2000 server in one of three ways. The first is through the SMTP service. An example of this type of message is Internet e-mail. The second is through a store submission, such as a message created by a Microsoft Outlook (MAPI) client or an Outlook Web Access (OWA) client. The third way is for the message to come in via the Message Transfer Agent (MTA). Messages arrive in this way via an X.400 connector from a foreign e-mail system or via any Exchange Development Kit (EDK) -based connector.

As Figure 3-3 shows, SMTP messages are first sent to the NTFS queue because not all messages coming in from SMTP are destined for the local Exchange store. Thereafter, SMTP messages are sent to the precategorization queue for further processing.

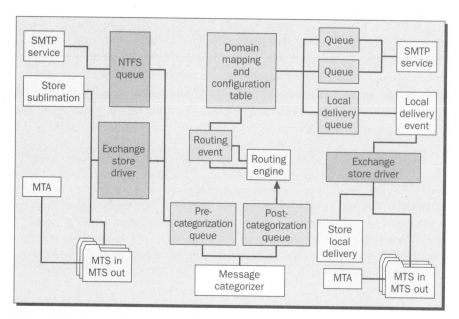

Figure 3-3. *Internal transport architecture for Exchange 2000 Server.*

Messages submitted via either a store submission or the MTA are dropped into the Exchange store driver. The Exchange store driver picks up these messages and passes them to the precategorization queue. The precategorization queue is the first opportunity you have to fire your event sinks. *Event sinks* are scripts that can be run against the message to perform certain functions, such as adding a disclaimer or running an antivirus program.

The message is then passed to the message categorizer, which is essentially a collection of event sinks that perform address resolution on both the originator and recipient of the message. In addition, it retrieves attributes from Active Directory that apply to the message, such as the originator's or recipient's size limits for outgoing and incoming messages, delivery restrictions, forwarding specifications, and other settings that might restrict the message in some way. Any restrictions that do exist are applied to the message. Once these tasks have been accomplished, the message is placed into a postcategorization queue, which allows more event sinks to fire on the message if you choose to set them up.

After the message is processed in the postcategorization queue, it is given to the routing engine, which parses the destination address against its domain mapping and domain configuration table. The routing engine then decides whether the message is destined for the local store, or if a temporary outbound queue (called a destination message queue) should be created to pass the message to another SMTP server.

Destination message queues are created based on the destination domain name. The advanced queuing engine is able to create as many destination message queues as needed. From these queues, the SMTP service reads the message out of the queue and then passes the message to the next SMTP server. If the message is destined for the local store, it is placed in the local delivery queue. The Store.exe process then reads the message out of the queue and writes it to the local database. Thereafter, the message is associated with the destination mailbox, and the recipient is notified that new mail has arrived.

Note   The SMTP service comprises two components: the protocol stack and the advanced queuing engine (AQE). The AQE makes up the majority of the SMTP service and manages the passing of messages through the queues from the time they enter the transport core until the time they are placed in an outbound queue or delivered to the Exchange store driver. Thus, even though the AQE isn't depicted in Figure 3-3, it is the managing component that works behind the scenes to move message through the transport core.

Message Routing Within the Same Server

When Exchange 2000 Server determines that the recipient of a message is on the same server as the sender, it delivers the message to the recipient's Inbox. The steps involved, shown in Figure 3-4, are as follows:

1. The client sends the message.
2. The message is passed to the categorizer, parsed against the domain mapping table, and then placed in the local delivery queue.
3. The information store associates the message with the recipient's mailbox.

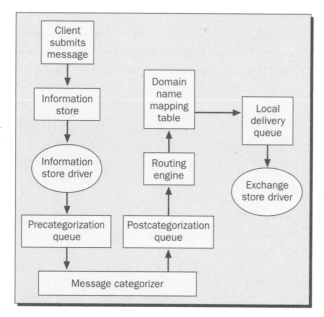

Figure 3-4. *How Exchange 2000 Server routes a message to a recipient from a sender housed on the same server.*

Message Routing Within the Same Routing Group

Messages sent between servers in the same routing group use SMTP as their transport. The steps involved in routing a message between two servers in the same routing group, shown in Figure 3-5, are as follows:

1. The client sends the message.

2. The message is passed to the categorizer, which applies any restrictions found in Active Directory. It is then passed through the postcategorization queue and on to the routing engine.

3. The routing engine parses the message against the domain name mapping table and then places it in the outgoing SMTP queue for the destination server. This queue is dynamically created for the message based on the destination domain name, which becomes the name of the queue—in this case, hr.oaktree.com (Local Delivery).

4. The sending server looks up the recipient's home directory in Active Directory, conducts a DNS lookup for the mail exchanger (MX) record associated with the destination server on which the recipient's mailbox is stored, and then creates a TCP connection to that server over port 25.

5. The message is transmitted to the destination server.

6. The destination server accepts the message from the SMTP service and places it in the NTFS queue. The AQE reads the message out of the queue and takes the message through the transport core.

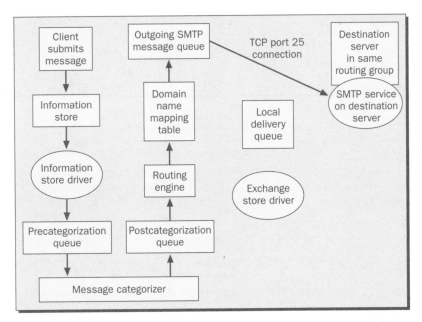

Figure 3-5. *How Exchange 2000 Server routes a message to a recipient on another server.*

Message Routing to Other Routing Groups

Messages routed to servers in other routing groups must pass through a bridgehead server (BHS) at each end of the connector. The steps involved in routing messages to servers in different routing groups, shown in Figure 3-6, are as follows:

1. The client sends the message.

2. The message is passed through the transport core and then placed in an outgoing SMTP message queue.

3. The routing group information is gathered from the configuration naming partition of Active Directory.

4. The link state information is consulted to determine the best routing path. (See the section "Link State Information," later in this chapter, for more information.)

5. The message is passed to the BHS over TCP port 25.

6. The BHS passes the message over TCP port 25 to the BHS in the destination routing group

7. The receiving BHS passes the message to the destination server in its group over TCP port 25.

8. The message is brought into the destination server via the SMTP service and is placed in the NTFS queue.

9. The message is taken out of the queue by the AQE and associated with the recipient's Inbox.

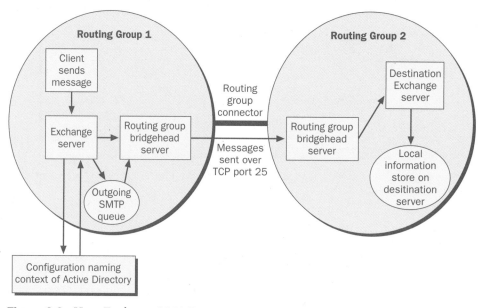

Figure 3-6. *How Exchange 2000 Server routes a message to a recipient in another routing group.*

Message Routing to Foreign E-Mail Systems

Messages are routed to foreign e-mail systems over the X.400 connector if it is a direct, continuous connection. Otherwise, they are routed over the Internet via

SMTP. Here are the steps involved in routing messages to another e-mail system when using SMTP:

1. The client sends the message.

2. The message is placed in the outgoing SMTP message queue.

3. The SMTP service reads the message out of this queue and sends it over TCP port 25 to the destination SMTP server.

If the message is being routed to a foreign e-mail system over an X.400 connector, these steps are essentially the same as routing over SMTP, except that an X.400 connector is used and no port number is involved.

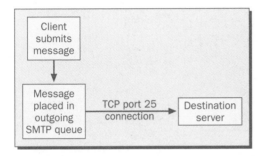

Figure 3-7. *How Exchange 2000 Server routes a message to a recipient in a foreign e-mail system over SMTP.*

Routing Group Topologies

You can connect your routing groups in several ways. The most common topologies are the hub-and-spoke and the modified mesh topology. A hub-and-spoke topology, as the name indicates, will have a central routing group to which all other routing groups are connected (Figure 3-8). Administration is easier in a hub-and-spoke topology because there aren't as many RGCs to create and maintain. The one huge disadvantage of this topology is that there is a single point of failure. If either the Exchange 2000 servers or the physical connections into and out of the hub become unavailable for any reason, messaging between routing groups is effectively terminated until the problem can be resolved.

In a mesh topology, each routing group has an RGC configured to every other routing group in the organization. This topology provides redundancy in the event of a link or server failure at any given point; the link state information will reroute the message via another path. However, administration is more difficult since there are more RGCs to create and maintain. Figure 3-9 illustrates a mesh topology.

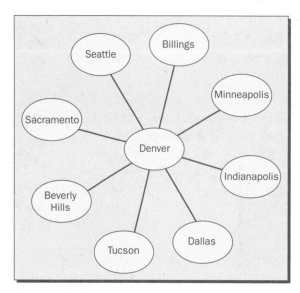

Figure 3-8. *Hub-and-spoke topology.*

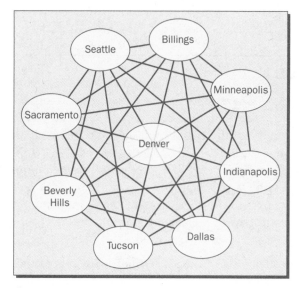

Figure 3-9. *Mesh topology.*

A less common method of connecting routing groups together is the linear topology (Figure 3-10). In this topology, all of the routing groups are connected by placing them in logical order in a straight line. Although this topology might be the easiest to set up due to the limited number of RGCs needed, it is fraught with potential problems. For instance, there is no redundant routing; therefore, the loss of a link between any two routing groups means that messaging will be hindered across the entire organization. Second, messaging from one end to the other may take longer than is pragmatically good for the organization. In the absence of alternate routes, messaging latency could become a real problem. This topology is the least desirable, and best practice would favor either the hub-and-spoke topology or the modified mesh topology described next.

The modified mesh topology (Figure 3-11) has multiple routes to each routing group but does not concern itself with making sure that each routing group is connected to every other routing group in the organization. In most cases, a modified mesh topology will be the best choice.

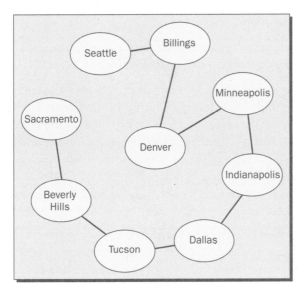

Figure 3-10. *Linear topology.*

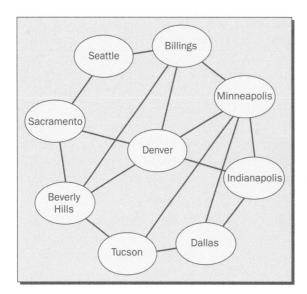

Figure 3-11. *Modified mesh topology.*

Link State Information

The link state protocol is a binary protocol that greatly improves message routing in Exchange 2000 over Exchange 5.5. Message routing in Exchange 5.5 is based on the GWART, which is a table that keeps track of each available connector in the Exchange 5.5 organization, along with the cumulative cost of using those connectors. The GWART is limited in that it contains only next-hop information. It doesn't monitor whether the link is actually up or down. The GWART is located in the Site Addressing object and is referenced by the MTA when determining messaging paths to a destination server.

The link state protocol operates over TCP port 691 within the routing group. In each routing group, one server is configured as the *routing group master* (RGM). The RGM receives link state information and propagates this information to the other servers in the routing group, including the BHS. When one BHS connects to another BHS in a different routing group, the exchange of link state information occurs over TCP port 25, using SMTP. The RGM keeps track of which servers are up and which are down and propagates that information to the RGM in every other routing group.

Link State Algorithm

The *link state algorithm* is new to Exchange 2000 Server, although it has been around for many years. First developed by Edsger Dijkstra in 1959, it forms the foundation of the Open Shortest Path First (OSPF) protocol, used extensively by routers today. Although Exchange 2000 Server incorporates routes and costs, it also relies heavily on link state information to route messages between routing groups.

The link state algorithm propagates the state of the messaging system almost in real time to all servers in the organization. There are several advantages to this:

- Each Exchange server can make the best routing decision before sending a message downstream where a link might be down.

- Message "ping-pong" is eliminated because alternate route information is propagated to each Exchange 2000 server.

- Message looping is eliminated.

Given the extensibility of this protocol, it is possible that future versions will be able to interact with network routers to achieve even greater routing capabilities. Networks that collaborate in this way are known as directory-enabled networks.

Link State Concepts

Link state information is rather important when an organization has multiple routing groups with multiple paths between the groups. The RGM maintains the link state information, sending it to and receiving it from the RGMs in other routing groups. The RGM is not necessarily the same server as the BHS, which is the server that you designate to send and receive messages across a given connector to another BHS. You can, however, manually configure one server to perform both roles.

The RGM ensures that all the servers in its routing group have correct link state information about the availability of the messaging connectors and servers in other groups. In addition, it ensures that other groups have correct information about its servers.

Link state information is propagated among the servers within a group over SMTP. Between groups, however, link state information is replicated from RGM to RGM over TCP port 25. There are only two states for any given link: up or down. The link state information does not include any connection information, such as whether a link is in a retry state. This information is known only to the server involved in the message transfer.

Note Connectors such as the Lotus cc:Mail Connector, the Microsoft Mail Connector, and other EDK-based connectors will always display their link state information in Exchange System as up, even if the link is unavailable.

Link state information is held in memory, not on disk. If the RGM goes down or needs to be rebooted, it will need to replicate in all current link state information from other RGMs in the organization. Since the routing group information is held in the naming partition of Active Directory, the definitions of connectors and costs are also held in Active Directory. The link state protocol references each connector by its globally unique identifier (GUID).

Tip When a BHS determines that a link is unavailable, it marks the link as down. It then sends this information to all the servers in its own routing group (over TCP port 691) and to the bridgehead servers in the other routing groups (over TCP port 25). If you are performing a trace for link state data, look for the X-Link2state command verb, which denotes this type of data. The information is sent in chunks labeled "first chunk," "second chunk," and so on, up to "last chunk."

Figure 3-12 and 3-13 illustrate what you'll see in Network Monitor. Figure 3-12 shows the link between Folsom and Minneapolis as DOWN. After you restore the link, you can see that Figure 3-13 shows the link as being UP. However, the X-Link2state command doesn't appear in the description of the packet. You'll need to read the data in each packet to find the X-Link2state command packets.

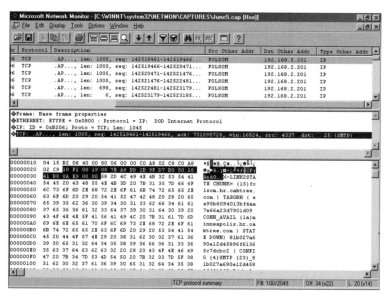

Figure 3-12. *Trace showing link state as DOWN.*

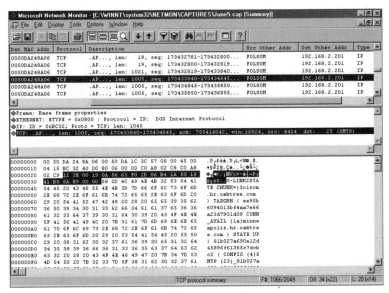

Figure 3-13. *Trace showing link state as UP.*

How Link State Information Works

Let's look at how link state information works and what happens to messages in the event of a failure. Figure 3-14 shows the topology for a network consisting of five routing groups and indicates the connector cost for each connector. We will assume that all connectors are RGCs.

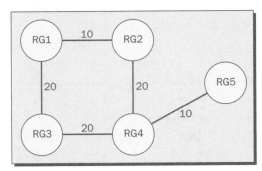

Figure 3-14. *Routing topology for link state example.*

Failure of a Single Link

Normally, a message sent from a server in RG1 to a server in RG5 will pass through RG2 and RG4 because it is the route with the least cost. Let's assume, however, that there is a link failure between RG2 and RG4. In this type of single-line failure, the link state protocol causes the routing processes to carry on as follows:

1. The BHS in RG1 sends the message to the BHS in RG2.

2. The BHS in RG2 attempts to open an SMTP connection to the BHS in RG4. If RG4 contains more than one BHS, the BHS in RG2 attempts to open a connection to each BHS in sequential order.

3. The BHS in RG2 is unable to contact any of the BHSs in RG4 because the physical link is down. Therefore, the BHS in RG2 places the connection into a glitch-retry state. The BHS waits for 60 seconds and then attempts to retransfer the message to the BHS in RG4

4. After three unsuccessful attempts to connect to RG4, the BHS in RG2 marks the link as down, updates the link state information on the RGM in RG2 over TCP port 691, and makes a call to reroute the message that is sitting in the SMTP out queue.

5. The RGM, upon receiving the notification that the link is down, immediately floods this data to all other Exchange 2000 servers in the routing group.

6. The BHS in RG2 recalculates an alternate route to RG5 via RG1, RG3, and RG4.

7. Before rerouting the message back to RG1, the BHS in RG2 sends the information about the down link to the BHS in RG1. This communication occurs on TCP port 25 and consists of an EHLO command and a X-Link2state command. (For more information on these and other SMTP commands, please see Chapter 17.)

8. The BHS in RG1 immediately connects to the RGM in RG1 over TCP port 691 and transfers the information about the down link.

9. The RGM in RG1 immediately floods this data to all other Exchange 2000 servers in the routing group.

10. Using the new link state information, the BHS in RG1 calculates the best route to RG5, through RG3 and RG4.

11. Before routing the message to RG3, the BHS in RG1 propagates the link state information to the BHS in RG3. This process continues until all of the routing groups know of the down link between RG2 and RG4.

It is highly likely that subsequent messages will be sent to RG5 from RG1. When this happens, the messages will be routed through the alternate route (RG1-RG3-RG4-RG5) because each server in the organization knows that the primary route is down.

The BHS in RG2 will continue to try to contact the BHS in RG4 every 60 seconds, even if no messages are awaiting transfer. This value is not configurable. When a link becomes operational again, the new link status is replicated to all of the other Exchange servers in the organization. The BHS transmits the "up" status to the local RGM, which in turn floods the Exchange 2000 servers in the local routing group. Then, similar to the way in which the "down" message was propagated, the "up" message is sent to the rest of the Exchange organization.

Note   As Figure 3-15 shows, by default the SMTP virtual server will check the status of the link after 10 minutes for the first retry interval, after 10 minutes for the second retry interval, after 10 minutes for the third retry interval, and then every 15 minutes for each subsequent check. Reduce these intervals if the link is passing mission-critical information between two routing groups. Each retry interval can be as short as 1 minute.

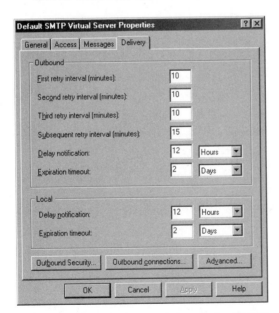

Figure 3-15. *Default retry intervals for SMTP virtual server.*

Caution In both this example and the next example on multiple link failures, it may seem that link state information is transmitted only immediately ahead of a user-initiated message. This is not the case. Link state information is always transmitted immediately, independently of whether other messages need to be transmitted or not. We mention that the link state information is transmitted ahead of a user's message to indicate the importance that Exchange 2000 Server places on replicating link state information to all its servers. There is no necessary connection or correlation between the transfer of a user-initiated message and the sending of a link state message to another routing group master.

Failure of Multiple Links

If more than one link fails at any given time, the link state protocol ensures that the message doesn't bounce back and forth between routing groups in a continual attempt to find an open message path. Let's look again at the example of a server in RG1 attempting to send a message to a server in RG5. This time, however, let's assume that both the link between RG2 and RG4 and the one between RG3 and RG 4 is unavailable. RG1 sends a message to RG2, and RG2 returns the message to RG1, as it did in our single-link-failure scenario. Here are the steps that the link state protocol will then perform:

1. The BHS in RG1 opens a connection to the BHS in RG3. Before sending the message, however, it propagates the down status of the link between RG2 and RG4 to the BHS in RG3. The BHS in RG3 forwards this information to the RGM, which floods the other servers in the routing group with this information.

2. Then the BHS in RG1 sends the message to the BHS in RG3. The BHS in RG3 sees that the message is intended for RG5, attempts to open a connection to the BHS server in RG4, and the attempt fails. The BHS server marks the link as being in the glitch-retry state and retries three more times at 60-second intervals.

3. If it cannot establish a connection, it marks the link as down and notifies the RGM, which in turn floods the other servers in the routing group with this new information.

4. The BHS in RG3 attempts to calculate a new route for the message, given the new information. With both the link between RG2 and RG4 and the link between RG3 and RG4 in the down state, the cost of routing a message to RG5 becomes Infinite.

5. Once the cost has been calculated as Infinite, the message remains in the queue of the BHS in RG3, which makes calls to routing, based on the schedule you have configured on the Delivery tab in the property sheet for the SMTP virtual server, to see whether either link has become available.

6. When a link becomes available, the message is rerouted as appropriate. If the message stays in the queue for more than 48 hours, it is returned to the sender in RG1 as a nondelivery report (NDR).

If additional messages are sent to RG5 from RG1 while both links are down, the messages remain queued at the BHS in RG1 until one of the links becomes available and a fully functioning route can be established. This is the best place for the messages to remain queued.

> **Note**   The 48-hour time period is the default length of time for messages to sit in a queue before a Non-Delivery Report (NDR) is generated and sent back to the user in Exchange 2000 Server. You can configure this value on the Delivery tab of the property sheet for the SMTP virtual server.

Failure of a Routing Group Master

If the RGM goes offline, a new master is not automatically nominated. Therefore, the link state information held by other servers in the routing group could, over time, become increasingly antiquated. If the RGM will be down for a period of time, it is very important that a new RGM be manually configured. This action will ensure that other servers in the routing group have up-to-date link state information.

To manually configure a server to become the RGM, navigate to the routing group in which the server resides, highlight the Members folder for the server, right-click the server in the details pane, and choose Set As Master. Figure 3-16 illustrates this process.

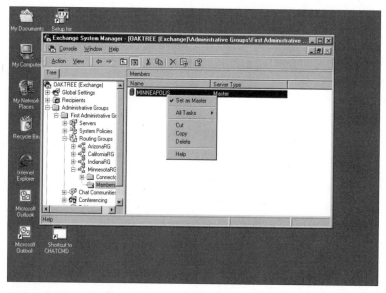

Figure 3-16. *Selecting a routing group master in Exchange System Manager.*

Summary

In this chapter, you have seen that Exchange 2000 Server improves upon the site concept in Exchange Server 5.5 by introducing routing groups and link state information. SMTP, which is now the default protocol for message transfer, is more tolerant of higher latency and lower bandwidths than an RPC connection, and hence has several advantages, which were outlined in this chapter. You also saw how link state information works after certain kinds of failures. The next chapter introduces you to the Active Directory Connector and provides an overview of how Exchange 2000 Server integrates with Windows 2000 and Internet Information Services.

Chapter 4
Understanding Windows 2000 Integration

In the last two chapters, you learned about the storage and routing architectures in Microsoft Exchange 2000 Server. This chapter builds on that knowledge by describing how Exchange 2000 Server integrates with Microsoft Windows 2000 and how it uses the services in Windows 2000 to its advantage. We'll begin with a brief overview of the Windows 2000 Active Directory directory service and then finish the chapter by describing how Exchange 2000 Server uses Active Directory and discussing some of the more important Internet information protocols.

Brief Overview of Active Directory

Even though a full explanation of Active Directory is outside the scope of this book, a brief overview is warranted. Because Exchange 2000 Server is heavily dependent on the underlying network operating system, it is important to have a basic understanding of Windows 2000 Active Directory.

> **More Info** For a more thorough discussion of Active Directory and the other concepts discussed in this chapter, see *Microsoft Windows 2000 Administrator's Companion* by Charlie Russel and Sharon Crawford (Microsoft Press, 2000).

Directory Structure in Active Directory

Before we discuss what Active Directory is, you should first understand what a directory is. As an analogy, think of a generic file system. Perhaps in this file system, you have a C: drive, and on that drive, you have a root folder named Memos. Under C:\Memos, you have a folder for each of the 12 months of the year, so you would find a folder in the structure named July. Under C:\Memos\July, you have a folder named Departments, which means the full pathname to Departments is C:\Memos\July\Departments.

What we have just described is a hierarchy of folders in a file system. A directory is no different, except that the hierarchy consists not of folders but of *objects*. An object is an entity that is described by a distinct, named set of attributes. And instead of using Windows Explorer to search through this hierarchy of objects, we'll be using a protocol designed to search a directory, called the Lightweight Directory Access Protocol (LDAP).

> **Note** The original protocol for accessing a directory was called Directory Access Protocol (DAP), but it had a high overhead and tended to be slow. Lightweight Directory Access Protocol (LDAP) is an improved version that is faster and requires less overhead. For more information about the LDAP protocol, see Chapter 17.

With Active Directory, Microsoft has taken the directory concept and made significant improvements to it, such as dynamic DNS. The "Active" in Active Directory describes the flexibility and extensibility that has been built into Microsoft's directory service.

Logical Structure of Active Directory

The components that form the logical structure of Active Directory include domains, organizational units, trees, and forests.

Domains

A *domain* is the core unit in Active Directory and is made up of a collection of computers that share a common directory database. The computers that share this common directory database are called domain controllers. A *domain controller* is a Windows 2000 server that has Active Directory installed. It is able to authenticate users for its own domain. Each domain controller holds a complete replica of the domain naming partition for the domain to which it belongs and a complete replica of the configuration and schema naming partitions for the forest. Dcpromo.exe is the utility used to promote a Windows 2000 server to a domain controller.

All Active Directory domain names are identified by a DNS name as well as by a NetBIOS name. The following is an example of the two types of names:

DNS-style domain name:	sample.microsoft.com
NetBIOS name:	sample

Generally, the NetBIOS name is the same as the first naming component in the DNS name. However, a NetBIOS name can be only 15 characters in length, whereas each name in the DNS naming convention can have up to 64 characters.

During installation, both names can be configured to meet your needs. In the initial release of Windows 2000, Active Directory names cannot be changed.

The domain is also a security boundary in Active Directory. Administrators in a domain have the permissions and rights to perform administrative functions in that domain. However, since each domain has its own security, administrators must be given explicit permissions to perform administrative tasks in other domains.

A Windows 2000 Active Directory domain can be in either mixed mode or native mode. The default installation is mixed mode. In mixed mode, a Windows 2000 domain controller acts like a Microsoft Windows NT 4 domain controller. Active Directory domains in mixed mode have the same limitations on the security accounts database as Windows NT 4 domain controllers. For example, in mixed mode, the size of the directory is limited to 40,000 objects, the same restriction imposed by Windows NT 4. These limitations allow Windows NT 4 domain controllers to exist on the network and connect to and synchronize with the Windows 2000 domain controllers.

To run Windows 2000 in native mode, you must not have any Windows NT 4 domain controllers on your network. The switch to native mode is a one-time, one-way switch and is irreversible. Native mode allows your Windows 2000 domain controllers to have millions of objects per domain. In addition, native mode allows the nesting of groups, something that is advantageous if you anticipate large distribution groups in Exchange 2000 Server.

A Windows 2000 network running in native mode can accommodate Windows NT 4 stand-alone and member servers. Windows NT 4 workstations must be upgraded to Windows 2000 Professional in order to participate in Active Directory. Microsoft Windows 95/98 clients can install a Windows 2000 Active Directory client that allows them to participate fully in the native mode domain.

Windows 2000 implements Active Directory in a multimaster model because objects in Active Directory can be modified on any domain controller, which accounts for the emphasis on directory replication between domain controllers. However, some roles are either too sensitive to security issues or too impractical to perform in a multimaster model because of potential conflicts that could arise from the replication traffic. An understanding of these roles is important; if a domain controller that is performing a particular role becomes unavailable, the function it performed will not be available in Active Directory. These roles are schema master, domain naming master, relative identifier master, PDC emulator, and infrastructure master.

Schema Master The schema is the set of object classes (such as users and groups) and their attributes (such as full name and phone number) that form Active Directory. The schema master controls all aspects of updates and modifications to the schema. To update the schema, you must have access to the schema master. There can be only one schema master in the forest at any given time.

Domain Naming Master The domain naming master controls the addition and removal of domains in the forest. This is the only domain controller from which you can create or delete a domain. There can only be one domain naming master in the forest at any given time.

Relative Identifier Master The relative identifier (RID) master allocates sequences of RIDs to each of the domain controllers in its domain. Whereas the schema master and domain naming master perform forestwide functions, one RID master is assigned per domain. Since each domain controller can create objects in Active Directory, the RID master allocates to each domain controller a pool of 500 RIDs from which to draw when creating the object. When a domain controller has used more than 400 RIDs, the RID master gives it another batch of 500 RIDs.

Whenever a new user, group, or computer object is created, the object inherits the security identifier (SID) of the domain. Appended to the end of the domain SID is the RID, which makes up the unique SID for the object. In addition, when an object is moved from one domain to another, its SID changes, because it receives a new SID (made up of both the domain SID and the RID) in the destination domain. By allowing only the RID master to move objects between domains, Windows 2000 ensures SID uniqueness, even across domains. Objects maintain a SID history for security access to resources.

PDC Emulator Each domain in the forest must have one domain controller that acts as the PDC emulator. If Active Directory is running in mixed mode with Windows NT 4 domain controllers on the same network, the PDC emulator is responsible for synchronizing password changes and security account updates between the Windows NT 4 servers and the Windows 2000 servers. Moreover, the PDC emulator appears to downlevel clients, such as Windows 95, Windows 98, and Windows NT 4, as the PDC of the domain. It functions as the domain master browser, is responsible for replication services to the BDCs, and performs directory writes to the Windows NT 4 domain security database.

In native mode, the PDC emulator receives the urgent updates to the Active Directory security accounts database, such as password changes and account lockout modifications. These urgent changes to user accounts are immediately replicated to the PDC emulator, no matter where they are changed in the domain. If a logon authentication fails at a domain controller, the credentials are first passed to the PDC emulator for authentication before the logon request is rejected.

Infrastructure Master   The infrastructure master is responsible for tracking group-to-user references whenever the user and the group are not members of the same domain.. The object that resides in the remote domain is referenced by its GUID and its SID. If an object is moved from one domain to another, it receives a new SID and the infrastructure master replicates these changes to other infrastructure masters in other domains.

Organizational Units

An *organizational unit* (OU) is a container object that is used to organize other objects within a domain. An OU can contain user accounts, printers, groups, computers, and other OUs.

OUs are strictly for administrative purposes and convenience. They are transparent to the end user and have no bearing on the user's ability to access network resources. OUs can be used to create departmental or geographical boundaries. They can also be used to delegate administrative authority to users for particular tasks. For instance, you can create an OU for all of your printers and then assign full control over the printers to your printer administrator.

OUs can also be used to limit administrative control. For instance, you can give your help desk support personnel the permission to change the password on all user objects in an OU without giving them permissions to modify any other attributes of the user object, such as group membership or names.

Because an Active Directory domain can hold millions of objects, upgrading to Windows 2000 allows companies to convert from a multiple-domain model to a single-domain model and then use organizational units to delegate administrative control over resources.

Trees and Forests

The first Windows 2000 domain that you create is the root domain, which contains the configuration and schema for the forest. You add additional domains to the root domain to form the tree. As Figure 4-1 illustrates, a *tree* is a hierarchical grouping of Windows 2000 domains that share a contiguous namespace. A contiguous namespace is one that uses the same root name when naming additional domains in the tree.

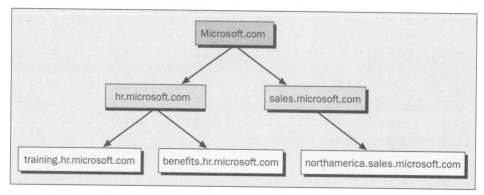

Figure 4-1. *Fictitious tree of Microsoft.com.*

A collection of trees that do not share a contiguous namespace can be placed in the same forest. They then share a common configuration, schema, and Global Catalog. By default, the name of the root domain becomes the name of the forest, even though other trees will not share the same name as the root domain.

Even though they don't share the same name, transitive trust relationships are automatically established between the root domain servers in each tree, as long as they are members of the same forest. Figure 4-2 shows two trees, Microsoft.com and oaktree.com, in the same forest.

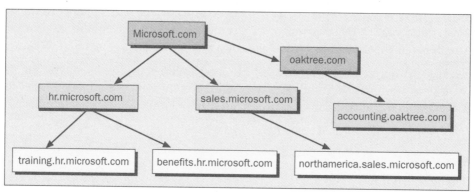

Figure 4-2. *Forest consisting of Microsoft.com and oaktree.com.*

The schema and configuration partitions for Active Directory are replicated to all domain controllers in each domain. While a domain represents a boundary for security and the logical grouping of objects, a forest represents the boundary for Active Directory and the Exchange 2000 organization.

The first domain within an Active Directory forest plays a very important role. It can never be removed. This restriction means that when you install Active Directory on a Windows 2000 server (using Dcpromo.exe), the server can never be demoted back to a stand-alone server if it is the first domain controller in the first domain of the first tree in the forest.

In addition, other domain names cannot be represented above the first domain name. For instance, if your root domain name is hr.oaktree.com, you can never install a domain named oaktree.com in the same forest. You can join other domain names to the forest, such as microsoft.com, as long as they are in a different namespace.

Tip   The design strategy for most companies is to create the first domain as a placeholder for the rest of the company. Initially, this domain doesn't contain any user or group accounts, other than the defaults. However, as departments become ready to migrate to Windows 2000, they will have the option of either joining the current domain or creating a new domain in the tree structure.

Groups

Windows 2000 enhances the group structure of Windows NT 4. Groups are used to reduce administrative effort and to enable the management of many user accounts simultaneously. Windows 2000 uses groups to reduce the number of objects that require direct administration.

There are basically two kinds of groups in Windows 2000. Each has its own advantages and restrictions that you must take into account when using them. Exchange 2000 Server uses both kinds of groups from Windows 2000:

- *Security groups* are security principles within Active Directory. They are used to group users or computers for the purpose of reducing the points of administration and providing permissions to network resources.

- *Distribution groups* are the replacement for distribution lists in Exchange 5.5. You cannot use them to assign permissions to network resources. They exist solely for the purpose of creating distribution lists for e-mail.

Global Groups   Global groups, in mixed mode, can contain users only from the domain in which they are hosted. In native mode, they can contain users and global groups from the local domain in which they were created. However, they can be used to assign permissions to resources in any domain. Global groups can contain users, computers, and global groups from the local domain. They can be members of any other type of group.

Typically, you'll use global groups for administering user membership that has permissions to a network resource. The group itself is replicated as part of the Global Catalog, but its membership is not. This restriction means that adding user accounts to or removing user accounts from a global group will not trigger a new replication of the Global Catalog. Global groups can be converted to universal groups (discussed shortly) as long as the global groups do not contain other global groups and the domain is in native mode.

Domain Local Groups   Domain local groups in native mode can contain other domain local groups, users, global groups, and universal groups from any domain in the forest, but they can be granted permissions only in the domain in which they reside. In mixed mode, they can contain only user and global group accounts.

You'll grant permissions to domain local groups only for objects in the local domain. The existence of the domain local group is replicated to the Global Catalog server, but its membership is not replicated. Domain local groups are flexible in that you can use any other security principle inside the domain local group (when running in native mode) to reduce administrative effort. You can convert a domain local group to a universal group in native mode as long as it does not contain other domain local groups.

Universal Groups   Universal groups can contain users, global groups, and other universal groups from any Windows 2000 domain in the forest. The domain must be operating in native mode to create security groups with universal scope. You can grant permissions to resources anywhere in the forest to a universal group.

Universal group membership must be determined at the time of logon. Because the scope of the universal group is universal, this group is propagated through the Global Catalog. Hence, not only is the group itself propagated in the Global Catalog, but its membership is propagated as well. A universal group with a large membership will generate additional replication overhead if the membership changes. Universal groups as security groups are available only in native mode. Table 4-1 summarizes group membership rules.

Table 4-1.   Comparison of the various types of groups

Group Scope	In Mixed Mode Can Contain	In Native Mode Can Contain	Can Be a Member Of	Can Be Granted Permissions For
Domain local	User accounts and global groups from any domain	User accounts, global groups, and universal groups from any domain in the forest, and domain local groups from the same domain	Domain local groups in the same domain	The domain in which the domain local group exists
Global	User accounts from the same domain	User accounts and global groups from the same domain	Universal and domain local groups in any domain and global groups in the same domain	All domains in the forest
Universal	Not applicable	User accounts, global groups, and other universal groups from any domain in the forest	Domain local and universal groups in any domain	All domains in the forest

Other Active Directory Components

Active Directory is a complex system that includes far more than this basic logical structure. This section highlights several other components that play a critical role within Active Directory.

Naming Partitions

You can think of Active Directory as being divided into three parts: domains, configuration, and schema. Each part is called a *naming partition* because it is a self-contained section of Active Directory that can have its own properties, such as replication configuration and permissions structure. A Windows 2000 domain controller will always hold three naming partitions in its database file (Ntds.dit).

These partitions are:

- Configuration (sample LDAP path: cn=configuration,dc=sales,dc=microsoft,dc=com)
- Schema (sample LDAP path: cn=schema,cn=configuration,dc=sales,dc=microsoft,dc=com)
- Domain (sample LDAP path: dc=sales,dc=microsoft,dc=com)

In a multidomain structure, domain controllers belong to different domains. These servers share a common configuration and schema naming partition but have a unique domain naming partition. Exchange 2000 Server stores most of its information in the configuration naming partition. Because this partition is replicated throughout the forest, global administration is easier than in Exchange 5.5.

Sites

A *site* within Active Directory is a collection of IP subnets that enjoy permanent, high-bandwidth connectivity. Active Directory assumes that all computers in the same site have permanent, high-speed connectivity with one another. Sites tend to map to the physical structure of your network: slow WAN links will be considered outside your sites, and high-speed links will form your sites.

Site and domain topologies are not dependent upon each other; a single domain can span multiple sites, or multiple domains can be located in a single site. Since the bandwidth between sites is assumed to be slow or unreliable, it stands to reason that some type of connector is needed to connect the sites. That connector is call a *site link*.

Site links are built manually by the administrator and form the physical topology of the network. To create replication paths between domain controllers across the site links (as well as between domain controllers within the same site), Windows 2000 employs the knowledge consistency checker (KCC), which runs automatically but can be configured manually, if necessary. The KCC creates *connection objects* on each domain controller in the configuration naming partition that form the overall replication topology over which Active Directory information can be replicated. The KCC is a service that runs on each domain controller to create the connection objects for that domain controller.

Location Service Providers

In Windows NT 4, to find a service such as the server service on a domain controller, the client needs to contact the Windows Internet Name Service (WINS) to obtain the IP address of the server offering that service (WINS offers dynamic mapping of NetBIOS names to IP addresses). In Windows 2000, DNS takes on this role and helps the client find the services it needs on the network. Dynamic DNS is supplied with Windows 2000 and is a standard part of the Active Directory installation. With dynamic DNS, clients query DNS service (SRV) records to locate services on the network.

Global Catalog Servers

In a multidomain environment, it is reasonable to assume that some users will need access to objects outside of their own domain. For instance, a user in domain A may need access to a color printer located in domain B. Since domain controllers maintain only a replica of objects in their own domain, a special service is needed in the forest to gain access to objects located in remote domains. The Global Catalog server performs this function. This server holds a replica of all objects in the forest, with a limited set of attributes for those objects. The schema defines which attributes are listed for each object in the Global Catalog.

Tip   By default, there is only one Global Catalog server in the entire forest, and that is the first domain controller installed in the first domain of the first tree. All other Global Catalog servers need to be configured manually. You can do this by opening the Active Directory Sites and Services snap-in, navigating to the NTDS settings on the server you want to install this service on, right-clicking NTDS Settings, choosing Properties, and selecting the Global Catalog Server check box.

In addition to users needing access to services outside their domain, some applications need access to a forestwide listing of objects. Exchange 2000 Server is one of those applications. For instance, when a user wants to browse the Global Address List, this list is generated by the Global Catalog server, which gathers each mail-enabled object into a list and returns it to the user inside the address book interface.

Even in a single-domain environment, Exchange clients are referred to the Global Catalog server for address book lookups. In this scenario, the default is to refer all those lookups to the root domain controller. The best practice is to create two or more Global Catalog servers for redundancy and scalability.

A Global Catalog server is represented as an SRV record in the DNS database. There are two ways to locate the Global Catalog server: by service and by both service and site name. To find a domain controller without specifying the site name, you would specify a node path of ._tcp._gc._msdcs.*domain*. The entry name would be _LDAP, and the entry data would be [0][100][3268] *server-name.domain*. Figure 4-3 illustrates what this entry looks like in the DNS snap-in. Table 4-2 shows node paths for other DNS resource records in Windows 2000.

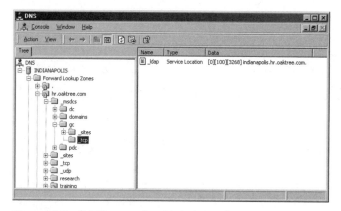

Figure 4-3. *DNS entry for Global Catalog services on indianapolis.hr.oaktree.com.*

It is helpful to note that a Global Catalog server will pass back different attributes depending on the TCP port used for the query. For instance, a query to port 389 (the default LDAP port) allows a client to search for objects only within the home domain, and the full set of attributes for the object is returned, whereas a query over port 3268 allows a client to search for objects in the entire forest, including the home domain of the Global Catalog server. However, a query over this port returns only a subset of the attributes available, even if the object is in the home domain of the Global Catalog server.

Table 4-2.   Resource records registered by Windows 2000 domain controllers

What the Record Does	Node Path
Finds a Windows 2000 domain controller in the domain named *DNSdomainname*. Each domain _ldap._tcp.hr.oaktree.com	_ldap._tcp.<*DNSdomainname*> Example: controller registers this record.
Finds a domain controller in a specified site. Each domain controller registers this record.	_ldap._tcp.<*sitename*>.sites.<*DNSdomainname*> Example: _ldap._tcp.defaultfirstsitename.sites.hr.oaktree.com
Finds a PDC in a mixed mode domain. Only the PDC of the domain registers this record; it is responsible for unregistering any other registrations of this record.	_ldap._tcp.pdc._msdcs.<*DNSdomainname*> *Example:* _ldap._tcp.pdc._msdcs.hr.oaktree.com.
Finds a Global Catalog server. Only Global Catalog servers register this name.	_ldap._tcp.gc._msdcs.<*DNSdomainname*> Example: _ldap._tcp.gc._msdcs.hr.oaktree.com
Finds a Global Catalog server when the site name is specified.	_ldap._tcp.<*sitename*>.sites.gc._msdcs. <*DNSdomainname*> Example: _ldap._tcp.defaultfirstsitename.sites.gc._msdcs.hr. oaktree.com

Finds a domain controller based on its GUID.	_ldap._tcp.<*domainGUID*>.domains._msdcs.
	   <*DNSdomainname*>
	Example:
	_ldap._tcp.
	   4f904480-7c78-11cf-b057-00aa006b4f8f.
	   domains._msdcs.hr.oaktree.com

Finds a domain controller that holds a modifiable copy of the directory in a specified domain. In mixed mode, the PDC always registers this record. In native mode, all domain controllers register this name.	_ldap._tcp.writable._msdcs.<*DNSdomainname*> Example: _ldap._tcp.writable._msdcs.hr.oaktree.com
Finds a domain controller that holds a writable copy of the directory in a specified domain and a specified site.	_ldap._tcp.<*sitename*>.sites.writable._msdcs. <*DNSdomainname*> Example: _ldap._tcp.defaultfirstsitename.sites.writable._msdcs. hr.oaktree.com
Finds a domain controller by a normal A (host) record DNS lookup. This record is registered by the Net Logon service	<*DNSdomainname*> Example: Hr.oaktree.com

Client Authentication

When a client attempts to log on to the domain, it queries DNS SRV records to locate a domain controller. DNS attempts to match the client's IP address to an Active Directory site and then returns a list of domain controllers that can authenticate the client. The client chooses a domain controller at random from the list and then pings it before sending the logon request. In native mode, the authenticating domain controller passes the client's credentials to the local Global Catalog server so that the Global Catalog can enumerate universal security group access.

Active Directory Names

Both users and applications are affected by the naming conventions that a directory uses. To locate a network resource, you'll need to know its name or one of its properties. Active Directory supports many naming schemes for the different formats that can access Active Directory.

Distinguished Name

Each object in the directory has a *distinguished name* (DN) that identifies where the object resides in the overall object hierarchy. For example,

cn=benglish,cn=users,dc=microsoft,dc=com

would indicate that the user object *Benglish* is in the Users container that is located in the microsoft.com domain. If the *Benglish* object is moved to another container, its DN will change to reflect its new position in the hierarchy. Distinguished names are guaranteed to be unique in the forest. You cannot have two objects with the same distinguished name.

Relative Distinguished Name

The *relative distinguished name* of an object is that part of the distinguished name that is an attribute of the object. In the former example, the relative distinguished name of the *Benglish* object is Benglish. The relative distinguished name of the parent organizational unit is Users. Active Directory will not allow two objects with the same relative distinguished name under the same parent container.

User Principal Name

The *user principal name* that is generated for each object is in the form *username@ DNSdomainname*. Users can log on with their user principal name, and an administrator can define suffixes for user principal names if desired. User principal names are required to be unique, but Active Directory does not enforce this requirement. It's best, however, to formulate a naming convention that avoids duplicate user principal names.

Globally Unique Identifier

Some applications require that an object be referred to by an identifier that remains constant. This is achieved by adding an attribute called the *globally unique identifier* (GUID), a 128-bit number that is guaranteed to be unique. A GUID is assigned to an object when it is created, and it will never change, even if the object is moved between containers in the same domain.

Exchange 2000 Server and Active Directory

Previous versions of Exchange employed a dedicated directory that provided a central location for the organization's objects, such as addresses, mailboxes, distribution lists, and public folders. A separate directory service was installed to manage object replication among the Exchange servers.

Exchange 2000 Server no longer uses a dedicated directory. Instead, it integrates with the Windows 2000 Active Directory service. Integration with Windows 2000 provides several benefits, including the following:

- **Centralized object management**   Administration is now unified for Exchange 2000 Server and Windows 2000 Server. Directory objects can be managed from one location, with one management tool, and by one team.

- **Simplified security management**   Exchange 2000 Server uses the security features of Windows 2000, such as the system access control list (SACL). Changes to security principles (such as user or group accounts) apply to data stored in both Exchange 2000 and Windows 2000 file shares.

- **Simplified creation of distribution lists**   Exchange 2000 Server automatically uses Windows 2000 security groups as distribution lists, eliminating the need to create a security group for each department and a corresponding distribution list for the same department.

- **Easier access to directory information** LDAP is now the native access protocol for directory information. In earlier versions of Exchange, look-ups in the directory were conducted over the Named Service Provider Interface (NSPI).

Storing Exchange 2000 Data in Active Directory

Earlier we mentioned that Active Directory is divided into three naming partitions: configuration, schema, and domain. In this section, we'll discuss how Exchange 2000 Server uses each of these partitions and which kind of data is stored in each.

Domain Naming Partition

In the domain naming partition, all of the domain objects for Exchange 2000 are stored and replicated to every domain controller in the domain. Recipient objects, including users, contacts, and groups, are stored in this partition.

Exchange 2000 Server exploits Active Directory by adding attributes to user and group objects for messaging purposes. Because Exchange 2000 Server uses the same database as Windows 2000, some terminology has changed from previous versions of Exchange Server. Table 4-3 lists directory objects in Exchange 5.5 Server and their Active Directory equivalents, and Figure 4-4 shows the dialog box used to mail-enable a user object.

Table 4-3. Comparison of Exchange 5.5 and Exchange 2000 directory terminology

Exchange 5.5 Directory Object	Equivalent Active Directory Object	Comments
Mailbox	Mailbox-enabled user	Mailbox-enabled users are security principles in Active Directory that can send and receive messages.
No direct correlation with a 5.5 object	Mail-enabled user	Mail-enabled users are those who can logon to your domain with a user account in your domain, but whose e-mail is sent to an external address. This type of user is best suited for long-term contractors who need access to resources on your network but who need to send and receive e-mail through their employer's e-mail system.
Custom recipient	Mail-enabled contact	All mail-enabled contacts have an SMTP address. These are always users outside your Exchange organization.
Distribution list	Mail-enabled group	Domain local, global, and universal groups can be mail enabled.
Public folder	Public folder	Mail-enabled public folders can be created only in the Exchange System snap-in or the Active Directory Connector.

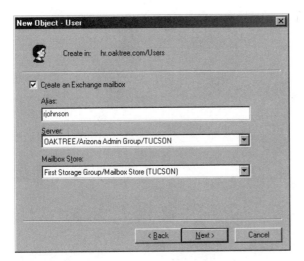

Figure 4-4. *Mail-enabling a user object.*

Designing a Group Implementation Strategy   Previous versions of Exchange use a distribution list to send the same message to a large number of recipients. Exchange 2000 uses groups for this function. Any user accounts that are placed inside the group will receive the message. In Windows 2000 native mode, groups can be nested inside of groups, effectively creating a multitiered distribution list. The two types of groups you will use most often for large distribution of a message are global and universal.

If you want to optimize the universal security groups that have been set up in Active Directory, you can mail-enable the groups (Figure 4-5) and then add an SMTP e-mail alias (Figure 4-6). Once completed, the group will be visible in the Global Address List (Figure 4-7). To mail-enable a group, right-click the group, choose Exchange Tasks, and then follow the prompts in the Exchange Task Wizard.

The largest downside to universal groups is that membership is fully replicated to each Global Catalog server, which means that replication traffic occurs when membership changes. Therefore, it is best to populate a universal group with other global groups, so that when membership changes in the global group, the universal group is not changed and traffic is not replicated.

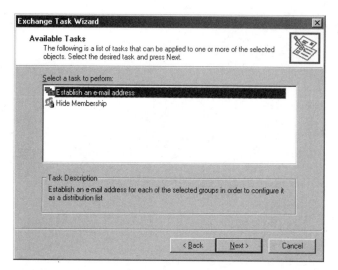

Figure 4-5. *Mail-enabling a group using the Exchange Task Wizard.*

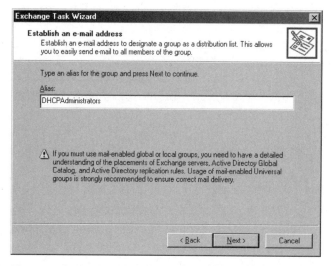

Figure 4-6. *Creating an SMTP alias in the Exchange Task Wizard.*

Global groups can also be mail-enabled for message distribution. If you choose not to use universal groups, you can mail-enable global groups. Membership for a global group is not promoted to the Global Catalog server, which presents some issues to consider when working in a multidomain environment.

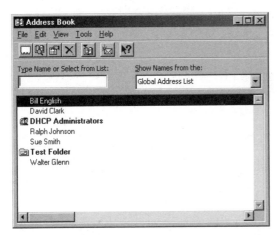

Figure 4-7. *Viewing the mail-enabled group in the Global Address List.*

When a message is sent to a global group in a remote domain, the expansion server must connect to a domain controller in the group's home domain and retrieve the membership list. In addition, the expansion server must have IP connectivity to a domain controller in the group's home domain. Retrieving membership from a remote domain may take time and slow down message delivery, which will affect overall performance. It is best if there is an Exchange 2000 server in the remote domain. Then you can set the expansion server to that server instead of retrieving the membership remotely.

When deciding which group type to select, consider the following implications:

- **Whether you have a single-domain or multiple-domain environment**
  If you have a single domain, you don't need to use universal groups, because all of the domain objects are local. If you have multiple domains, use universal groups if the membership is fairly static (global groups as opposed to individual users), and remember that users may not have access to all object attributes from other domains in universal groups.

- **Whether direct IP connectivity is possible between all domains** If you have IP connectivity, use global groups if membership changes frequently or if you have Exchange servers in each domain that can act as expansion servers. Otherwise, use universal groups, since membership is static and the local expansion server can expand the list.

- **Whether membership changes frequently** If membership changes often, use global groups. If membership changes infrequently, use universal groups.

Outlook users will not be able to view the user memberships of a group that has been created in a remote domain. They can view membership only in global groups and domain local groups that have been created in their home domain.

An Expansion server, which has been mentioned several times, requires some explanation. When a message is sent to a mail-enabled group, the message needs to be expanded and individually addressed to each member of the group. By default, the local SMTP server performs the expansion and uses LDAP to contact the Global Catalog server to deliver the message to each member of the group. If the message is intended for a local group in the domain, the local Global Catalog server is contacted.

By default, an SMTP message can be routed to only 100 recipients. This is a limitation of the SMTP protocol, not of Exchange 2000 Server. You can adjust this limit as required in one of three places:

- On the Message Delivery object properties sheet under Global Settings, where the default for the entire organization is 5000 recipients per message

- On the properties sheet for each SMTP virtual server in the Exchange System snap-in (Figure 4-8)

- On the individual user's account properties sheet in AD Users and Computers (Figure 4-9), where you can input the value needed for that user.

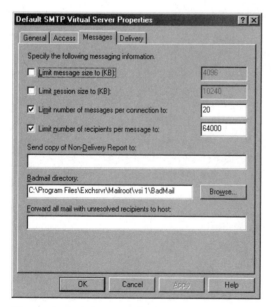

Figure 4-8. *Adjusting the SMTP recipient limit in the Exchange System snap-in.*

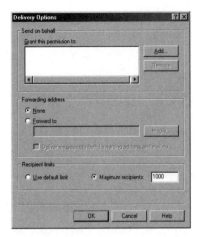

Figure 4-9. *Adjusting the SMTP recipient limit in AD Users and Computers.*

Note   SMTP messages with more than 100 recipients are divided into multiple messages before being expanded, each with 100 recipients or less. And if the number of recipients exceeds the limit specified in the global SMTP settings, the message will not be processed. Limits are imposed by the transport core categorizer, which is discussed more fully in Chapter 3.

Configuration Naming Partition

The configuration partition of Active Directory stores information regarding how your Exchange 2000 system is organized. Because this information is replicated to all domain controllers in the forest, the Exchange 2000 configuration is also replicated throughout the forest. The configuration information includes the Exchange 2000 topology (such as routing group information), connectors, protocols, and service settings.

Schema Naming Partition

The schema partition contains all object types and their attributes that can be created in Active Directory. This information is replicated to all domain controllers in the forest. During the first installation of Exchange 2000 Server in the forest, the Active Directory schema is extended to include new object classes and attributes that are specific to Exchange 2000. These new classes start with "ms-Exch" and are derived from the LDAP Data Interchange Format (LDIF) files on the Exchange 2000 Server CD-ROM.

Given that these extensions represent more than 900 changes to the schema and that these changes will be replicated to all of the domain controllers in your forest, it's best to install Exchange 2000 Server at the beginning of a period of time when you anticipate that network activity will be relatively light—for instance, on a Friday night. This schedule will give the domain controllers time to replicate all of the schema changes into their own databases.

> **Tip** You can install Exchange 2000 Server using the /forestprep switch, which will write the new Exchange object classes and attributes to the schema but will not install Exchange itself. Plan on this activity taking anywhere from 30 to 90 minutes, depending on the speed and capacity of your hardware. For more information on installing Exchange 2000 Server, consult Chapter 7.

Generating E-Mail Addresses

Exchange 2000 Server gives you flexibility regarding how your e-mail addresses are generated. As Figure 4-10 shows, e-mail address generation is controlled by the recipient policies in the organization. The user's e-mail address will likely be different from the user's principal name. Since the e-mail address is just another attribute of the user object, you can set it up so that the user's logon name and e-mail address are simplified, thus hiding the complexity of the underlying domain infrastructure.

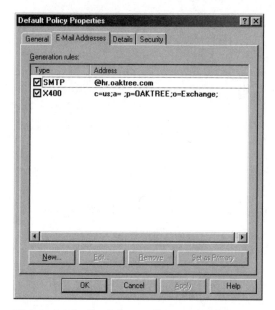

Figure 4-10. *Recipient policy properties.*

Exchange 2000 Server and Forest Boundaries

Since Exchange 2000 Server stores much of its information in the configuration naming partition, an Exchange 2000 organization cannot be extended past the boundaries of the forest. This is one area where your Active Directory structure will directly influence your Exchange topology. Having multiple forests in a company incurs the following limitations:

- You'll have separate Exchange organizations to administer.
- You'll have separate Global Address Lists, with no automatic directory replication between them.
- You'll need to use SMTP and/or X.400 Connectors to connect the multiple organizations.
- No link state data will be transferred because Routing Group Connectors (RGCs) cannot be used.

If you want to synchronize directory information among multiple forests, you can use DirSynch Control. This utility provides the sharing of information between dissimilar directories in a mixed-directory environment, using LDAP calls to both directories. At the time of this writing, it has been submitted to the Internet Engineering Task Force (IETF) as an open standard. In the initial release of Windows 2000, there is no automatic way to synchronize two directories. If this is a requirement for your environment, you'll need to use third-party tools.

Public folders can be synchronized with the Public Folder Inter-organization Replication tool. This tool will also replicate Free/Busy system folders as well. Even with this functionality, users cannot open calendars across forest boundaries. In addition, bear in mind the additional administrative overhead of synchronizing public folders in this manner compared to performing this function in a single organization. If possible, the best practice is to create additional domains rather than forests to eliminate the need for multiple Exchange organizations in your company.

Integration with Global Catalog Server

Exchange 2000 Server needs regular access to the Global Catalog server for activities such as producing a Global Address List for mail-enabled users as well as for use by DSAccess and DSProxy. (These two Exchange services are discussed in the sections that follow.) Unless your network is small, with fewer than 20 light users, consider implementing at least two Global Catalog servers per site for scalability and redundancy. In a multidomain environment, be sure to place a Global Catalog server in each domain as well. Large installations may require more Global Catalog servers.

> **Tip** One test environment recently found that having more than 17 Exchange servers referencing the same Global Catalog server caused a significant decrease in performance, resulting in extended periods of unproductivity for the end users. You'll need to regularly monitor the Global Catalog server to discern the load being placed on it by the Exchange 2000 servers. If you're company is growing, this will be a key area for you to manage. Microsoft doesn't give any hard and fast numbers or benchmarks to work with. The proper ratio of Exchange 2000 servers and Global Catalog servers is left to you to decide because each environment is different and unique.

DSProxy

When determining how many Global Catalog servers you need for your site and domain structure, you'll need to understand how a Microsoft Outlook user and an Exchange 2000 server access Active Directory. In Exchange 5.5, every server has a complete copy of the directory, which enables Outlook clients to refer to the directory on their home server. The Message Transfer Agent (MTA) uses the local directory to route messages. Now that Exchange 2000 Server uses the directory in Windows 2000, directory calls need to be referred to Active Directory.

DSProxy acts as a facilitator to allow Outlook clients to access the data within Active Directory. It performs two important functions. The first is to proxy directory requests on behalf of clients to Active Directory through the Name Service Provider Interface (NSPI). Older Messaging Application Programming Interface (MAPI) clients, such as the older Exchange client or Outlook 97/98, make MAPI Directory Service (MAPI DS) requests to an Exchange server over a remote procedure call (RPC) connection.

When an older MAPI client makes a directory request, the request is made to the Exchange 2000 server, as shown in Figure 4-11. The DSProxy NSPI then blindly forwards the MAPI DS directory call to a Global Catalog server. It does not open and evaluate the RPC packet, because doing so would incur too much system overhead for the Exchange 2000 server as well as complicating the security structure. It also does not change the request into an LDAP call over port 389. Active Directory can be accessed over a number of protocols, including LDAP and MAPI DS, so the forwarding of the packet has no effect on its ability to access Active Directory.

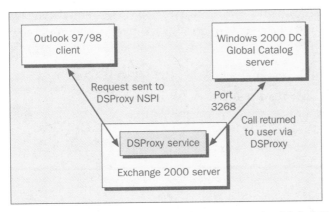

Figure 4-11. *How older MAPI clients access the Global Catalog via DSProxy.*

The Global Catalog server returns the results of the request to the Exchange 2000 DSProxy service, which in turn passes the results to the client. This entire process is transparent to the user.

Tip   If you need to specify the server that DSProxy uses manually, you can do so with the following registry entry:

HKEY_LOCAL_MACHINE\System\CurrentControlSet\Services\MSExchangeSA\Parameters

Value name: NSPI Target Server

Value Type: STRING

Value data: *GC-Server-name*

HKEY_LOCAL_MACHINE\System\CurrentControlSet\Services\MSExchangeSA\Parameters

Value name: RFR Target Server

Value type: STRING

Value data: *GC-Server-name*

The second function that DSProxy performs is to request that more recent versions of Outlook, such as Outlook 2000, send all future directory calls directly to a specified Global Catalog server. Outlook 2000 clients first go through the DSProxy process for the initial directory lookup. DSProxy then passes back to the Outlook 2000 client a referral to send all future directory calls to a specified Global Catalog server, thus reducing the load on the Exchange 2000 server and minimizing any possible latency issues for directory calls. If the Global Catalog server fails, the Outlook 2000 client will need to be restarted to obtain a new referral from DSProxy.

The Outlook 2000 client writes the referral in its registry under the following key:

1. HKEY_CURRENT_USER\Software\Microsoft\WindowsNT\ CurrentVersion\Windows MessagingSubsystem\Profiles\ profilename\cda7392.....2fe19873
2. Value name: 001e6602
3. Value type: STRING
4. Value data: *Directoryserver.domain*
5. Example: \\indianapolis.hr.oaktree.com

If your clients need to access Active Directory through a firewall, you can open up the firewall to allow the Exchange 2000 server to access Active Directory and turn off the DSProxy referral process to your Outlook 2000 clients. You can instruct the Exchange 2000 server not to give out referrals in the following registry key:

1. HKEY_LOCAL_MACHINE\System\CurrentControlSet\ Services\MSExchangeSA\Parameters
2. Value name: No RFR Service
3. Value type: DWORD
4. Value data: 0x1

If the Global Catalog server being used by DSProxy fails, DSProxy issues a callback to the System Attendant service (Mad.exe), which, in turn, issues to DSProxy a new server name to use. This process is known as *retargeting*. The System Attendant will not retarget unless it receives a request for DSProxy to do so. When the Exchange System Attendant service starts, it finds the most appropriate Active Directory server by referencing DNS, and then it passes the server's name to the DSProxy process (Dsproxy.dll).

It is also possible to determine which Active Directory domain controller a given Exchange server is using by viewing the properties of the Exchange computer in the Exchange System snap-in. In Figure 4-12, since Tucson is both an Exchange server and a domain controller, it is referring to itself for Active Directory services.

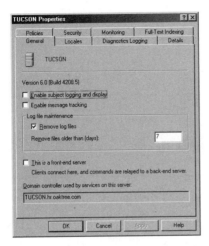

Figure 4-12. *Property sheet for the Tucson server.*

DSAccess

To reduce the number of calls to the Global Catalog server from your Exchange 2000 server, Exchange 2000 implements a directory access cache (DSAccess). This cache holds recent directory lookup information so that if the same information is requested within a specified period of time, the results can be returned to the client from the cache.

Increasing the cache size or the cache time will decrease the number of calls DSProxy and Outlook 2000 clients make to a Global Catalog server. You'll want to first measure the stress on the Global Catalog server and then, if necessary, modify the registry on the Exchange 2000 server.

The default parameters for cache size and cache time are a maximum of 4 MB of directory entries, which can be cached for up to 10 minutes. You can change these parameters in the registry of the Exchange 2000 server as follows:

- To adjust the expiration time for cached entries, use the following registry entry:
  1. HKEY_LOCAL_MACHINE\System\CurrentControlSet\Services\ MSExchangeDSAccess\Instance0
  2. Value Name: CacheTTL
  3. Value Type: Reg_WORD
  4. Value data: 0xXXXX (where XXXX = number of seconds desired)

- To adjust the size of the cache itself, use the following registry entry:
  1. HKEY_LOCAL_MACHINE\System\CurrentControlSet\ Services\ MSExchangeDSAccess\Instance0
  2. Value name: MaxMemory
  3. Value Type: Reg_DWORD
  4. Value data: 0x*XXXX* (where *XXXX* = number of kilobytes desired)

- You can also specify the maximum number of entries in the cache, rather than its overall size, as follows:
  1. HKEY_LOCAL_MACHINE\System\CurrentControlSet\ Services\ MSExchangeDSAccess\Instance0
  2. Value name: Max Entries
  3. Value type: REG_DWORD
  4. Value data: 0x*XXXX* (where *XXXX* = number of entries)

Note Each cached entry requires about 3.6 KB of memory, and the overhead to run DSAccess is approximately 2.5 MB.

Configuration Partition and Directory Data

The two Active Directory services that an Exchange 2000 server uses most often are the Global Catalog server for address book lookups and the configuration naming partition for routing information. It is possible that two different domain controllers will be referenced, depending on the type of request being made by the Exchange 2000 server.

When an Exchange 2000 server boots up, it establishes a number of LDAP connections to domain controllers and Global Catalog servers. If it needs routing information to route a message, it can contact any domain controller to obtain this information, because each domain controller in the forest has a full copy of the configuration naming partition. If the Exchange 2000 server needs to obtain the Global Address List, it will contact the closest Global Catalog server. Best practice is to place a Global Catalog server near the Exchange 2000 servers and make sure that they are in the same site and domain.

Manually Configuring Exchange 2000 Servers for Global Catalog Lookups

You can hard-code which servers Exchange 2000 Server contacts to obtain data. This task involves merely specifying a preference for your Exchange 2000 server. Should the specified server be offline, Exchange fails over to standard DNS lookups.

To specify the domain controller to contact for configuration partition information, use the following registry key:

HKEY_LOCAL_MACHINE\System\CurrentControlSet\Services\
MSExchangeDSAccess\Instance0

Value Name: ConfigDCHostName

Value type: REG_SZ

Value data: *DirectoryServer.domain* (for example, Tucson.hr.oaktree.com)

Value name: ConfigDCPortNumber

Value type: REG_DWORD

Value data: 0x389 (the default LDAP port number is 389)

To specify the domain controller to contact for address book lookups, use this registry key:

HKEY_LOCAL_MACHINE\System\CurrentControlSet\Services\
MSExchangeDSAccess\Profiles\Default

Value Name: UserGC1

Value type: REG_SZ

Value data: *DirectoryServer.domain* (for example, Tucson.hr.oaktree.com)

Value name: PortNumber

Value type: REG_DWORD

Value data: 0x3268 (the default port number for a GC server)

Value name: IsGC

Value type: REG_DWORD

Value data: 0x1 (always set to 1 if the server specified is a GC server)

Address Book Views

In Exchange 5.5, the view consistency checker (VCC) service runs in the background every 5 minutes, creating a new address book view (ABV) for each unique string of characters in the field that is being sorted. This method is not flexible for larger organizations and creates unwanted ABVs when words are misspelled or entered incorrectly.

Exchange 2000 Server eliminates ABVs and replaces them with address lists, which are created with *build rules*. These rules use the LDAP search filter syntax defined in RFC 2254 and are extremely flexible. In fact, as Figure 4-13 shows, the Global Address List is built using a filter rule.

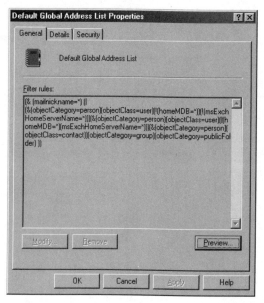

Figure 4-13. *Property sheet for the Global Address List, showing the filter rule.*

Tip When you click the Preview button shown in Figure 4-13, you'll get to test your build rule by having it used to search through the directory and find matching objects. If you get a list that isn't what you expected, you can modify your build rule. By testing your build rule here, you are not forced to close and open the address book properties multiple times to see the effects of a newly written rule.

Address lists are updated when the System Attendant service (Mad.exe) makes a call to Wldap32.dll. You can specify the frequency of this action on the property sheet for the Recipient Update service (Figure 4-14). To perform an update, the System Attendant service contacts a local domain controller, searches Active

Directory for the objects and attributes specified in the build rule, and creates the new address list.

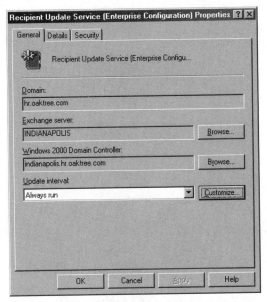

Figure 4-14. *Property sheet for the Recipient Update service.*

Several default address lists are configured in Exchange 2000. Table 4-4 lists the build rules for each of these default lists. Figure 4-15 shows where you can find the default lists in the Exchange System snap-in.

Table 4-4.   Build rules for default address lists in Exchange 2000

Address List	Build Rule
Default Global Address List	(&(|mail=*)(proxyAddress=*)(textEncodedORAddress=*)) (|(objectCategory=person)(objectCategory=group) (objectCategory=publicFolder)))
All users	(&(|mail=*)(proxyAddress=*)(textEncodedORAddress=*)) (|(objectCategory=person)(objectClass=user))))
All groups	(&(|mail=*)(proxyAddress=*)(textEncodedORAddress=*)) (|(objectCategory=group)))
All contacts	(&(|mail=*)(proxyAddress=*)(textEncodedORAddress=*)) (|(objectCategory=person)(objectClass=contact))
Public folders	(&(|mail=*)(proxyAddress=*)(textEncodedORAddress=*)) (|(objectCategory=publicFolder)))
All conference resources	M(msExchResourceGUID=*)

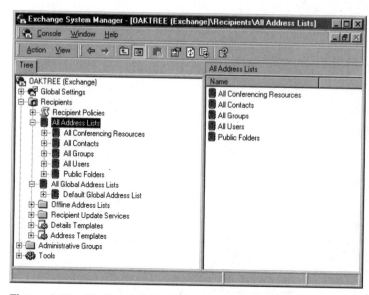

Figure 4-15. *Finding default address lists in the Exchange System snap-in.*

Integration with Internet Information Services 5

When Windows 2000 is installed, the base version of SMTP is installed. Network News Transfer Protocol (NNTP) may also be installed when Windows 2000 is installed, but it must be selected manually. In Windows NT 4 and Internet Information Server (IIS) 4, these services were part of IIS.

Because these protocols are now basically transport stacks for the operating system, Windows 2000 no longer relies on RPCs. For instance, it is possible to have Active Directory information replicated over SMTP rather than RPCs.

Note An RPC allows an application to execute code that resides on a remote machine. RPC-based applications use the network to transport the request. The client computer issues a call to "stub code" that takes the place of a local procedure. The stub code uses both communication and data conversion utilities to execute the request within the memory of the remote computer. Because RPC uses the network for its transport, TCP handshakes must be established for each new RPC between two machines, which results in high overhead on the network. RPC also requires permanent, high-bandwidth connectivity to ensure that the TCP connection can stay active. Compare this to SMTP, under which commands can be passed between servers in the form of messages. SMTP is thus more tolerant of lower-bandwidth environments and as a result is a better protocol over which to conduct server overhead functions, such as directory replication.

Given the ability to exploit Active Directory information via traditional Internet protocols, such as HTTP (and the improved version, WebDAV) and SMTP, as well as via Outlook Web Access (OWA), Web-based applications will become more popular, especially in environments where the work force is distributed but the information is centralized.

In addition, because IIS is now installed as part of the operating system and can run the transport protocols independently, the ability to host the protocols on different servers allows you to design an Exchange 2000 topology that will scale into the millions of users. Using a bank of front end and back end servers, Exchange 2000 can work with any size of installed base. For example, you can design your Exchange 2000 server topology with a bank of front end servers that allow non-MAPI clients, such as HTTP clients, to connect to virtual IP-addressable front end servers while storing messages and collaboration data on separate back end servers.

The protocols shipped with Exchange 2000 Server, such as SMTP and NNTP, lead to services such as OWA, instant messaging, and data conferencing. These protocols and services are discussed in the sections that follow.

Instant Messaging

Instant messaging allows users to see presence information for other users (that is, which people are online, out of the office, or not receiving calls) and lets users communicate instantly when an immediate response is necessary. The interface is lightweight, and it is designed for ad hoc communication. The major difference between instant messaging and e-mail is that instant messages are not stored in the Exchange 2000 store; after a message has disappeared from the screen, it is gone forever.

Instant messaging uses DNS and Active Directory to locate the home server for a user. It also supports front end/back end configurations for scalability into the tens of thousands of users. Instant messaging is hosted via virtual servers and realms. Virtual servers group users by e-mail address, and one physical server can host multiple virtual servers. Realms map an e-mail address (for example, research.microsoft.com) to a virtual server that is designated through a URL, such as http://im.research.microsoft.com.

A user principal name, such as benglish@research.microsoft.com will be translated by Exchange into a URL, such as http://im.research.microsoft.com/aliases/benglish. To learn more about instant messaging, see Chapter 19.

Data Conferencing

When more than two users need to collaborate in real time, they can use data conferencing. This powerful tool enables information to be exchanged through a shared clipboard, file transfer, a shared whiteboard, chat, audio, and video in real time. This service is T.120 compliant, meaning that any T.120 client can interoperate with a data conferencing server. The server is H.323 compliant. Audio and video streaming is accomplished through IP multicast technologies.

Exchange 2000 Server installs two Windows 2000 services to enable conferencing. The first is the Microsoft Exchange Conferencing Management Service. This service manages the virtual resource mailboxes and conference profiles. In addition, it routes clients to the appropriate server when they join the conference.

The second service is the Microsoft Exchange Data Conference Service. This is the hosting service for the conference session. It implements the T.120-compliant conference bridge (known as a multipoint conferencing unit, or MCU). Although a single Conferencing Management Service normally manages the conference facilities for an entire site, scaling can be achieved by deploying multiple MCUs. Each Exchange 2000 server can host exactly one MCU.

Simple Mail Transport Protocol

Exchange 2000 Server relies entirely on the Windows 2000 operating system to provide SMTP services. During the installation of Exchange 2000 Server, the IIS SMTP protocol is extended to include additional command verbs that enable link state routing and other advanced features. In addition, an advanced queuing engine and an enhanced message categorization agent are installed. For more information on the SMTP protocol, see Chapter 17.

Network News Transfer Protocol

NNTP, used by Exchange 2000 Server to access newsgroups, is part of Internet Information Services 5 and Windows 2000. Exchange 2000 does not extend or modify this protocol when it is installed.

DNS Configuration

On the Internet (or on any TCP/IP network, for that matter), every device is represented by an IP address— using a four-part dotted-decimal notation, such as 192.168.0.1. A device with a TCP/IP address is called a host and is assigned a host name, which is a character-based name that is easier for humans to recognize and remember than its numeric IP address. The format of the host name is *hostname.domain.com.* When a host name identifies a resource on a TCP/IP network, computers must translate that host name into an IP address because computers communicate using only IP addresses. This translation is called *name resolution.*

There are two basic methods of resolving host names to IP addresses on a TCP/IP network. The first involves using a file called a Hosts file. The Hosts file is a single, flat file that simply lists hosts on a network and each host's IP address. To use the Internet Mail Service (IMS) with a Hosts file, you must enter into that file the domain name and IP address of the hosts to which the IMS may need to transfer messages. As you might imagine, this process can be time-consuming.

The second method of resolving names is more efficient. It involves the Domain Name System (DNS), a hierarchical, distributed database of host names and IP addresses. In order to run Exchange 2000 Server, you must have already installed Windows 2000 Active Directory and DNS services on your network. Although host files are still available in Windows 2000, given the dynamic nature of the new implementation of DNS, there are few times when you'll want to use them.

You are likely to want outside SMTP hosts to be able to transfer messages to your SMTP service. To enable this capability, you must create two records in the DNS database so that those outside hosts can resolve your server's IP address. The first record you must create is an address record, or A record for your Exchange 2000 server. This can be registered dynamically with DNS in Windows 2000. The second record is a mail exchanger record, or MX record, which is a standard DNS record type used to designate one or more hosts that process mail for an organization or site. This record must be entered manually in your DNS tables.

More Info This chapter provides a simplistic discussion of configuring TCP/IP and DNS, but these topics encompass a monstrous amount of material. If you need more information about using TCP/IP and DNS in the Windows 2000 environment, see *Microsoft Windows 2000 Server Administrator's Companion* by Charlie Russel and Sharon Crawford (Microsoft Press, 2000).

Summary

This chapter described the ways in which Exchange 2000 Server is integrated with Windows 2000. It gave an overview of how Active Directory is structured and described how Exchange 2000 Server works with Active Directory. It also discussed the Internet information protocols installed with Windows 2000 as well as services available in Exchange 2000 Server, such as Outlook Web Access, instant messaging, and data conferencing. In the next chapter, you'll learn how to assess your needs as an organization as you begin the planning process for migrating to Exchange 2000 Server.

Part II
Planning

Chapter 5
Assessing Needs

Proper planning is valuable in any project. In a Microsoft Exchange 2000 Server deployment, planning is critical. Many Exchange Server components are difficult or impossible to change after installation. Poor planning can cause problems that range from inadequate performance to outright failure of components.

We've broken our discussion of planning into two chapters. This chapter helps you gather the information you will need to plan your implementation of Exchange 2000 Server. It looks at the business requirements of the enterprise, examines how to assess the needs of future Exchange users, and describes how to evaluate the resources of the current environment for the new messaging system. Chapter 6 discusses how to plan specific elements of your Exchange organization based on those assessments. Exchange Server is a complex program, but with suitable preparation, implementation of the new Exchange organization becomes a much easier task.

If you are reading this book from start to finish, you might want to skim these two planning chapters and then go on to read the rest of the book. After you have a firm understanding of how the various components in an Exchange organization work, come back and read these two chapters more carefully. In the real world, planning should always come before implementation, but it helps to understand the implementation before working on your plan.

More Info   This chapter and Chapter 6 provide an overview of planning an Exchange 2000 Server deployment that, coupled with the specific component knowledge you'll find throughout this book, should put you well on your way to designing an effective Exchange organization. You can also find many other books that can help you make detailed plans for certain aspects of your Exchange system. One of our favorites is *Deploying Microsoft Exchange Server 5.5 (Notes from the Field)*, also from Microsoft Press.

Defining User Needs

Your first step in designing any system should be to determine what that system needs to accomplish. In an Exchange system, this means asking yourself several questions:

Will the system provide basic messaging services, a way for users to send mail to one another?

Will the system provide access to Internet resources? Can users send and receive Internet mail or participate in Internet newsgroups?

Do you plan to offer public folders as a means of group discussion?

Do you plan to offer conferencing, instant messaging, or chat within your organization?

Are there any custom applications you want to use Exchange Server for? For instance, do you have a database of contact information that you want to make available as a public folder?

Your goals at this stage include gathering business requirements and understanding the corporate culture and technical environment—including the network topology and desktop systems—where you will use Exchange 2000 Server. When designing an Exchange organization, you must also find out what services and functionality your users require. After you've answered the questions presented in the following sections, you can effectively group users according to their needs. You can then use those groups to plan Exchange Server resources to accommodate user needs, as described in Chapter 6.

Messaging

Exchange 2000 Server is typically implemented as a messaging system. The odds are that your Exchange users will want to be able to send e-mail to one another. Ask the following questions to help describe the specific needs of your users:

- **To whom will most users be sending messages?** Messaging on most networks follows a fairly typical pattern. Users tend to send messages primarily to other users in their workgroup. Users also need to send messages to other workgroups or to outside recipients, such as people on the Internet. Developing a picture of these traffic patterns can help you plan user and server placement.

- **How much e-mail do users expect to generate and receive?**   Some users rarely use e-mail; others send and receive dozens of messages per day. Knowing the average volume of messages for your users allows you to plan the capacity of your servers, the limits on your information stores, and the bandwidth requirements of your network.

- **Will users exchange scheduling and contact information?**   Microsoft Outlook 2000 provides the ability to share scheduling and contact information dynamically between users. This generates extra messaging traffic and needs to be accounted for when designing your system.

- **What kind of messages and attachments will you allow users to send?** If your users will transfer large files to one another using e-mail, you must make allowances for this volume. Some organizations put limits on the amount of information that can be transmitted in a single message. Others put limits on the amount of space a single mailbox can consume. You can also apply different limits to different users. Executives, for example, may be given more flexibility than other employees.

- **Will user messages be stored primarily on an Exchange server or in local personal folders?**   If server-based storage is to be the primary repository of user messages, how much space do you intend to allot for your mailbox stores? Your organization might have business policies that require mail to be stored for long periods of time. For example, some government units must store e-mail forever. Such information can help you plan hardware capacity for both servers and clients.

- **What kind of security will users need?**   Do your users need to encrypt or digitally sign messages and attachments? If so, you will need to implement some sort of certificate server on your network, such as Microsoft Certificate Services. Exchange security is covered in Chapter 21.

Public Folders

Public folders are the foundation for collaboration within Exchange 2000 Server. They enable public access to, and collaboration on, centralized messaging information. Public folders require considerable planning. In addition to planning storage capacity for the Exchange servers that will hold public folder replicas, you must plan public folder replication and user access to public folder servers. The following questions will assist you in assessing public folder usage in the new Exchange organization:

- **Which users will need access to which public folders?**   Some workgroups will collaborate on certain documents and messages more than others. This information helps you decide where replicas of certain folders need to be placed and how often replication needs to occur.

- **Which users should be allowed to create public folders?**   By default, top-level public folders in a public folder tree are created on the home server of the user who creates them. Subfolders are created on the same server as the top-level folder in which they are created. By restricting which users can create top-level folders, you can govern the placement of public folders on servers. Such restrictions also help you keep the structure of public folder trees manageable.

- **How much information do users expect to post within those public folders?**   Both the type of information—documents, forms, executable files, or simple messages—and the size of a typical file help you determine the storage capacity required for public folder stores.

- **How long will the average message need to remain in a public folder?** This information helps you determine the storage space that your public folder stores will consume and the load that users will place on your servers when accessing the public folders.

- **How often will users access the public folders?**   This information helps you further determine the load that your public folder servers will have to meet and to schedule public folder replication.

- **Will you use public folders to allow access to Internet newsgroups?**   It's not uncommon to see thousands of messages come through an Internet newsgroup every day, and there are tens of thousands of groups available. You can create public folders that synchronize with Internet newsgroups, but you need to make sure your server can handle the message load.

Connections to Other Systems

Will any of your users need to access the Internet or a preexisting messaging system? Having this information can help you plan the placement of users and foreign messaging connectors. If one group of users tends to use a connector heavily, you might want to place those users on the server on which the connector is installed, to reduce the number of hops that messages have to take from your users to the foreign system. Any Exchange server can host a foreign messaging connector, and that messaging connector can be made available to all users in the organization. You might want to configure more than one connector to a foreign system to help balance the messaging load to that system.

You must decide between connector types when multiple connectors can support the same system. You will need to consider the types of foreign systems and the types of connectors they support, as well as the performance that those connectors will be expected to provide. For example, an X.400 Connector is highly reliable, but its reliability is due to a higher overhead that can affect performance. The X.400 Connector can also send and receive mail at scheduled times, thus reducing the impact e-mail has on other network applications.

Connectors also vary in the additional services they provide. A connector that enables the use of shared storage may be preferable to one that enables only e-mail between users. If a connector is used only to migrate from one version of Exchange Server to another, it will be a temporary addition to the Exchange organization. In such cases, choose the connector that makes the transition easiest for the users. In many cases, you can migrate the users transparently, with little interruption to their daily business, just by selecting the right connector. You'll learn more about connectors in Chapters 13 and 22.

Remote Access

Often, you will want to allow users to access private and public folders from a remote location. In planning an Exchange organization, you need to take the requirements of these remote users into account. This information can help you plan the placement of users, as well as plan a Remote Access Service (RAS) or virtual private network (VPN) server for your network. Various manufacturers offer solutions that can enable remote access to Exchange. This information is also valuable in security planning. Ask these questions to assess the remote access needs of the organization:

- Which users need to be able to access the Exchange organization remotely?
- Will users dial in to a RAS server or access your network over the Internet? Dialing directly into a RAS server usually provides better control and security. Accessing the network over the Internet is often much cheaper and more convenient.
- Where will you locate your RAS server?
- On average, how many users will need simultaneous access to the network? This information helps you determine the number of RAS servers you will need and the number of modems and phone lines.

Custom Applications

Do your users have special needs that can be met only by custom-tailored applications? If so, can the users themselves design these applications, or will you need to hire special personnel? The time to think about custom applications is during the planning stage. The use of custom applications could change many of the answers to the questions in this section.

Training and Support Services

Your users will likely need special training in using the new system. Don't make the mistake of assuming that e-mail is simple to use. Outlook 2000 and other messaging clients are sophisticated programs. Users may need to be taught how to use public folders or how to sign and encrypt messages. Do you plan to have users install the mail clients themselves? If so, they will need training, and you may need to set up a convenient method for them to do so.

Remember that users are often called upon to learn new things, including new versions of operating systems and software. Take the time to make sure that your users understand the system you are putting in place, as well as who they should go to with questions or problems. Public folders are a great place to store training materials so that they are available to all users. You could also use a public folder to list the contact information for support personnel. A public folder can use the same forms and views that are found in a user's mailbox folders. In this case, a public folder that stores contact information and uses the Exchange Contact form is ideal for a list of support personnel contacts.

Assessing Current Resources

Once you have determined the needs of your users, the next step in planning your organization is to assess your current resources. To make this assessment, you must put together three diagrams: a diagram of your company's geographic profile, a diagram of your network topology, and a diagram of your Microsoft Windows 2000 networking model.

Defining Your Geographic Profile

The easiest place to start your assessment is with a geographic profile of your company. Get out a pen and paper, and start drawing maps. If your network is global, start with all of the countries in which your company has offices. Work your way down through states, cities, buildings, and even in-building locations.

Defining Your Software Environment

After you have a firm idea of how your company is laid out geographically, gather information on where users and resources are located within those geographical regions. This information helps you determine where the users are, where the computers are, whether the computers are ready for Exchange 2000 Server or your chosen messaging client, and how many licenses you are going to need. The following are a few considerations to think about along the way:

- Where are existing servers located?
- What are the servers' names and functions?
- What versions of which software are installed on the servers?
- How many workstations are in each location?
- What operating systems and software are used on those workstations?
- How many users are in each location?
- What are the users' needs?

Defining Your Network Topology

After you've created diagrams of your company's geographic profile, you need to diagram your company's network. Unlike the geographic profile, a network topology tells you exactly how your network is physically put together. When reviewing the geographic topology of the network, be sure to mark out the wide area network (WAN) links between the various locations and their bandwidths. This step will help you assess the site boundaries, the connectors required between sites, and the replication schedules. Figure 5-1 shows an example of a network diagram for a companywide WAN.

Real World **Systems Management Server**

Ideally, you will already have a detailed inventory of your existing network assets. A comprehensive inventory includes a list of all of the hardware and software on all of the computers on your network. The inventory should also take into account how your network is constructed and maybe even some of the network's use statistics.

If you don't already have a network inventory, you could actually go to all of the computers on your network with notebook in hand. A better method, however, is to use an automatic inventory system such as that built into Windows 2000 Server or, for larger networks, Microsoft Systems Management Server (SMS). You can use Windows 2000 Server and SMS to gather hardware and software information from computers on your network automatically. You can also use SMS to push installations of software (such as messaging clients) to workstations throughout the network from a central location, to control and support client software remotely, and even to keep track of licensing information on your network. SMS really is must-have software for any up-and-coming Exchange administrator.

Note, however, that SMS is not a simple install-and-run application. Instead, it is a comprehensive, enterprise-capable network management software package. SMS requires SQL Server to provide the underlying database that captures and manages the network's data. To implement SMS and Microsoft SQL Server, you should have defined and executed a project plan and systems design.

For more details on the systems management capabilities built into Windows 2000 Server, see your product documentation. For more information on using Systems Management Server, check out the *Microsoft Systems Management Server 2.0 Administrator's Companion* by Steven D. Kaczmarek (Microsoft Press, 2000).

A clear definition of your network's topology allows you to plan site boundaries, site connections, and server placement and to understand replication issues. Whether your network is a single local area network (LAN) within one office building or a WAN connecting thousands of users around the world, you should design the Exchange organization to optimize its messaging functions over the network topology.

Areas that can be optimized include the following:

- Routing group definition
- Server placement
- Message routing
- Public folder replication

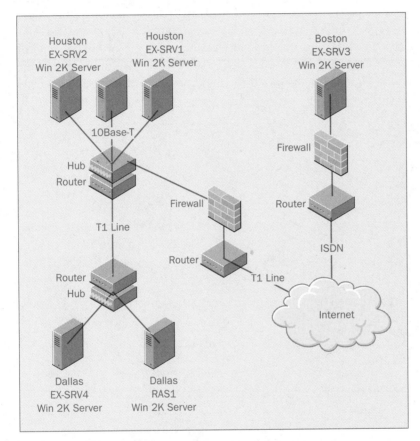

Figure 5-1. *Diagramming your network topology.*

The first step in defining a network topology is to determine the size of your network. The size of your network dictates how you will make many planning decisions and even whether you need to make them at all. On a large WAN, for example, especially one that is geographically dispersed, you might want to consider setting up multiple routing groups. Using multiple routing groups means that you have to consider such things as messaging connectors, directory replication, and public folder replication among sites. If you are setting up a relatively small LAN, you may decide to configure only one routing group in your organization, which makes many of these decisions much easier.

In a small company, all of your computers are likely to be connected on one high-speed LAN. In larger companies, networks usually consist of many small LANs connected in various ways to form larger, interconnected LANs or WANs. In your network topology diagram, you need to include all of the segments that make up your network. Figure 5-2 shows an example of a simple network diagram for a LAN.

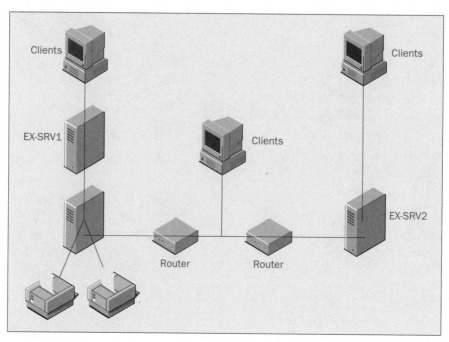

Figure 5-2. *Diagramming a LAN.*

For each segment, ask yourself the following questions:

- How big is the segment? How many computers are there? How large a geographic area does the segment cover?
- How is the segment wired? Does it use thin or thick Ethernet, shared or switched Ethernet, 10 Mbps or 100 Mbps, Fiber Distributed Data Interface (FDDI), token ring, or something else?
- What is the bandwidth of the segment? Determine the optimal bandwidth according to the type of network being used. (See the Real World sidebar "Determining Bandwidth.")
- How is the segment connected to other segments? Is the network segment connected to the rest of the network directly; is it connected through a router, switch, or bridge; or is it connected through a WAN link? Is the connection permanent or switched? What is the bandwidth of the connection?
- What protocols are used on the network?
- What are the traffic patterns on the network segment? At what times of day is network traffic within the segment heaviest? What application and operating system functions account for this traffic?
- What are the traffic patterns between this segment and other segments? At what times of day is network traffic heaviest between segments? What application and operating system functions account for this traffic?

Real World   Determining Bandwidth

Although doing so can be somewhat tricky, you need to determine the available bandwidth of each segment of your network. The available bandwidth is the amount of bandwidth not consumed by average network activity. For example, if the throughput of a WAN link is 1.544 Mbps and the bandwidth consumed on that link can peak at 1.544 Mbps but averages around 512 Kbps (equivalent to 0.5 Mbps), the available bandwidth will be 1.544 Mbps – 0.5 Mbps, or 1.044 Mbps. You subtract the average value, not the peak value, because all network links experience peaks that don't represent the usual network bandwidth consumption.

Defining Your Windows 2000 Networking Model

The final step in assessing your current resources is to document your Windows 2000 networking model. Again, constructing a diagram is helpful. Whereas the topology diagram illustrates the physical layout of your network (cables, routers, etc.), the diagram of the networking model will illustrate the logical layout of your network. This logical layout includes how many domains your network has, how those domains are configured to interact, and the functions of those domains and the servers in them. Figure 5-3 shows a basic example of a Windows 2000 networking model.

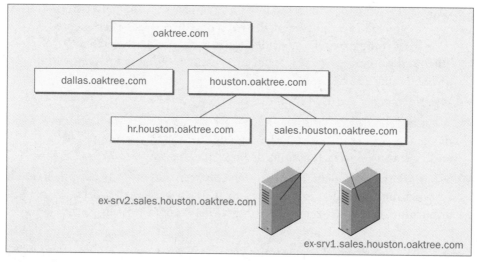

Figure 5-3. *Diagramming a networking model.*

Although Exchange 2000 Server routing and administrative groups differ from sites and domains in Windows 2000, Exchange Server resources rely on domains to perform essential security operations. For example, to access an Exchange 2000 Server mailbox, a user must log on to a domain using a valid user account. Because Exchange 2000 Server services are Windows 2000 services, they too need to be authenticated by a domain controller before they can perform their functions. Each server in an Exchange organization is configured with a special user account called the Site Services account, which is used to validate Exchange services. For a detailed look at the integration of Exchange 2000 Server and Windows 2000 Server, see Chapter 4.

If your network contains only a single domain, the task of diagramming the networking model is easy. If your network consists of multiple domains, for each domain on your network, ask the following questions:

- What is the name of the domain?
- What is the function of the domain?
- What domains does this domain trust?
- What domains trust this domain?
- How many user accounts are configured in this domain?
- What resources are configured in this domain?
- Who are the administrators of this domain?
- In what domain are the user accounts of the administrators configured?

Putting the Diagrams Together

After you've diagrammed your networking model, it's helpful to see how the networking model diagram, the geographic diagram, and the network topology diagram fit together. No real rule defines how Exchange routing or administrative groups should correspond to Windows 2000 domains. It is tempting, and sometimes appropriate, simply to create a routing and administrative group for each domain. However, this approach does not always work. A single domain might cover several geographic regions that a routing group might not be able to span, due to the topology of your network. You may end up with one group spanning several domains, or you may end up with one domain spanning several groups. These decisions are more an art than a science—an art that is the topic of the next chapter.

Defining Administrative Needs

Your last step in the assessment stage of the planning process is to determine how administration will be handled. In previous versions of Exchange Server, Exchange administration was mostly separate from other forms of network management. Now that Exchange 2000 Server makes extensive use of the Windows 2000 Active Directory, Windows and Exchange administrators must learn to get along.

In a small organization, it is likely that one or two administrators will be able to handle administration for both the Windows network and the Exchange organization. Planning the administration of larger networks requires a bit more thought. Here are a few factors to consider:

- **User management** Since Exchange and Windows now share Active Directory, it usually makes sense to let one person or group manage both Windows 2000 users and their Exchange mailboxes. Because the same interface is used to manage both, little extra training is required.

- **Routing** You will likely need one person or group to be responsible for managing routing in your organization. The administrative model in Exchange now separates routing and administrative topologies. Servers can be grouped in administrative groups for permission management and applying system policies, but they can belong to routing groups that span administrative groups for message routing. Responsibilities of this group include defining and maintaining routing and administrative groups, building and maintaining connectors between routing groups and to foreign systems, applying user and system policies, and managing permissions. You can think of this group as your core Exchange administrative unit.

- **Public folders** It is often useful to designate a separate person or group to manage public folders and public folder replication. You may even want to designate a person to manage each distinct public folder tree. Since public folders take on an even greater significance in Exchange 2000 Server than in previous versions, their management can be quite a complex task.

- **Collaboration** If you plan to provide real-time collaboration services, such as chat, conferencing, or instant messaging, in your organization, you may want to designate a separate administrative group to oversee the management of these services.

Summary

Good planning can make or break your deployment of Exchange 2000 Server. This chapter covered the first stage of planning an Exchange organization: assessing your current situation. It described how to assess the needs of your users and how to document your current resources by creating a geographic profile as well as profiles of the physical and logical layout of your current network. It also discussed considerations in planning how your Exchange system will be administered in a Windows 2000 environment. Now that you have collected the information you need, it's time to put that information to work. In Chapter 6, you will learn how to plan the actual Exchange organization.

Chapter 6
Planning for Development

In Chapter 5, you learned how to assess the needs of your users and how to take stock of your current network situation. In this chapter, you'll learn how to put that information to use.

We divide the task of planning a Microsoft Exchange organization into three distinct subtasks: designing the overall Exchange organization, planning the location of Exchange routing groups, and placing individual Exchange servers in those groups to optimize the messaging system. This approach will provide you with a logical placement of resources developed with users' needs in mind.

Beginning at the organizational level, you'll establish organizationwide naming conventions, determine the number of routing groups you'll need and the boundaries of those groups, and plan how to link those groups. Next, at the routing group level, you'll plan the services that the group must provide. You'll also plan public folders and gateways. Finally, at the server level, you'll determine the functions each server will perform and plan the server hardware to accommodate those functions.

Planning the Organization

The best place to start planning an Exchange organization is at the top—with the organization itself. Planning at the organizational level primarily involves determining the number of routing groups and administrative groups that you need in the organization and deciding where the boundaries of those groups should be. You also need to plan any messaging links between those groups. Before you get started on these plans, however, you need to establish a convention for naming the various elements of the organization.

Establishing a Naming Convention

The requirement that names be unique is common to any system with a directory of users, resources, and servers. Because Exchange Server provides various migration tools, duplication can occur when different systems are migrated to an Exchange system. An administrator should review the systems for possible duplication and take appropriate precautions—such as changing a name or deleting old accounts—before migrating multiple systems to Exchange Server.

Exchange systems can grow to include hundreds of thousands of users worldwide and many routing groups and servers. Most names cannot be changed once an object has been created. Certain objects, such as user mailboxes, have different types of names as well. Before you install your first Exchange server, you need to establish a convention for naming the primary types of objects in your Exchange organization: the organization, groups, servers, and recipients.

Establishing a naming convention for distribution groups, as well as for users and contacts that appear in the Active Directory directory service, is a great help to Exchange users. Furthermore, if administration is distributed among multiple administrators in different regions, it can help to apply a naming standard to connectors and other Exchange objects.

Real World   Illegal Characters

Network and messaging systems should avoid using illegal characters in their names. These are characters that some systems do not understand and that other systems misinterpret as special codes (sometimes called escape sequences) that cause them to try to interpret the remainder of the name as a command of some sort. The result, of course, is failure to communicate electronically and, perhaps, errors on the network or messaging systems. Although the list of illegal characters can vary, most systems consider some or all of the following, along with the space character (entered by pressing the Spacebar on the keyboard), illegal characters:

\ / [ ] : | < > + = ~ ! @ ; , " ( ) {}' # $ % ^ & * - _

Avoid using illegal characters in any names, even if you find that Microsoft Windows 2000 or Exchange 2000 Server will allow you to do so.

Organization Names

The organization is the largest element of an Exchange system, and its name should typically reflect the largest organizational element of your company. Usually, an organization is named after the enterprise itself, although it is possible to create multiple organizations in an enterprise and for the organizations to communicate with one another. Organization names can be up to 64 characters long, but to facilitate administration, it is a good practice to limit their length. Keep in mind that users of external messaging systems might need to enter the organization name manually, as part of the Exchange users' e-mail addresses.

> **Caution**   When you install the first production Exchange server, be absolutely sure that the organization name you specify is correct. If this means waiting for management's approval, so be it. Changing the organization name later requires a huge amount of work. Also, be aware that the Simple Mail Transport Protocol (SMTP) address space uses the organization and routing group names to construct e-mail addresses for the Internet. The SMTP address space can be changed, but doing so can be a hassle and a cause of confusion for other Exchange administrators later.

Routing Group Names

The convention for naming routing groups varies, depending on how the boundaries of the groups are established. In a typical Exchange system design, routing groups are named by geographic region or by department because routing group boundaries are determined based on wide area network (WAN) links and workgroup data flow. Like the organization name, routing group names can be 64 characters long, but it's best to keep them as short as possible. Again, users of some external messaging systems may need to enter the name of the routing group as well as the organization name when sending e-mail to users of your Exchange system.

Server Names

The server name for an Exchange server is the same as the NetBIOS name of the Windows 2000 server on which Exchange 2000 Server is installed. Therefore, you should establish naming conventions for servers before installing Windows 2000 Server. You can determine the name of a Windows 2000 server on the Network Identification tab of the System utility in Control Panel. NetBIOS server names cannot be more than 15 characters long. Note that you will not be allowed to change the NetBIOS name of a domain controller.

If you are installing Exchange Server on the first Windows 2000 server in an enterprise network, one recommendation for naming the server is to use its location or the type of function that the server will provide. You can end the name with one or two digits to allow multiple Windows servers in the same location providing the same network function. For example, an Exchange server in a company's London office could be named LON-EX01.

Recipient Names

Recipient names work a bit differently from the names of the other objects. Exchange Server allows four types of recipients: users, contacts, groups, and public folders. Public folders are discussed later in this chapter. Each of the three other types of recipients actually has four key names, which are shown on the General tab of the object's property sheet (Figure 6-1):

- **First Name**   The full first name of the user.
- **Initials**   The middle initial or initials of the user.
- **Last Name**   The full last name of the user.
- **Display Name**   A name that is automatically constructed from the user's first name, middle initial or initials, and last name. The display name appears in address books and in the Exchange System snap-in, so it is the primary way in which Exchange users search for other users. Display names can be up to 256 characters long.

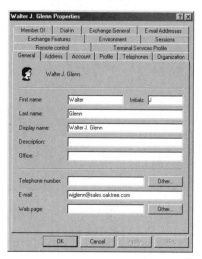

Figure 6-1. *Elements of a recipient's name.*

A naming convention should take into account the outside systems to which Exchange Server may be connecting. Many legacy messaging and scheduling systems restrict the length of recipient names within their address lists. Although Exchange 2000 Server allows longer mailbox names, the legacy system might truncate or reject them, resulting in duplicates or missing recipients. In addition, messages could show up in the wrong mailboxes or might not be transmitted at all. A common length restriction in legacy systems is eight characters. You can avoid many problems if you keep mailbox names to eight characters or fewer.

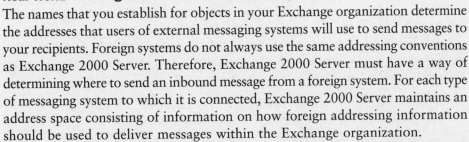

Real World **Naming Conventions and Addressing**

The names that you establish for objects in your Exchange organization determine the addresses that users of external messaging systems will use to send messages to your recipients. Foreign systems do not always use the same addressing conventions as Exchange 2000 Server. Therefore, Exchange 2000 Server must have a way of determining where to send an inbound message from a foreign system. For each type of messaging system to which it is connected, Exchange 2000 Server maintains an address space consisting of information on how foreign addressing information should be used to deliver messages within the Exchange organization.

Suppose that you have set up Exchange 2000 Server so that your users can exchange e-mail with users on the Internet. In this situation, Exchange 2000 Server would support the SMTP address space by maintaining an SMTP address for each recipient object. A user on the Internet would then address messages to your users in the typical SMTP format—something like *user@organization.com*. (You will learn how address spaces work in Chapter 13. For now, just understand that the way you name the objects in your organization has fairly far-reaching effects.)

Defining Routing Groups

In general, you want to keep the number of routing groups in your organization as low as possible. If you can get away with having just one routing group, you should generally do so. Many of the communications between servers in a group, such as message transfers, are configured and happen automatically, greatly reducing administration on your part. However, there are also many good reasons to use multiple routing groups. This section covers some of these considerations.

Geographic Considerations

If your company is spread over two or more geographic regions, you might want to implement a routing group for each region. The primary reason for doing so is to help manage network bandwidth consumption. A single routing group is easy to set up because much of the communication between the servers in a routing group occurs automatically. Unfortunately, this automatic communication consumes a considerable amount of bandwidth, which grows with the size of the routing group. If your network contains WAN links, which typically have a smaller amount of bandwidth available, it is best to divide the organization so that an Exchange routing group does not span a WAN link.

Network Considerations

Several physical factors determine the possible boundaries of a routing group. All Exchange servers within a routing group must be able to communicate with one another over a network that meets certain requirements:

- **Common Active Directory forest** All servers within a routing group must belong to the same Active Directory forest.

- **Persistent connectivity** Because of the constant and automatic communication between Exchange servers within a routing group, these servers must be able to communicate using SMTP over permanent connections—connections that are always on line and available. In addition, all servers within a routing group must be able to contact the routing group master at all times. If you have network segments that are connected by a switched virtual circuit (SVC) or a dial-up connection, you must implement separate routing groups for those segments.

- **Relatively high bandwidth** Servers in a routing group require enough bandwidth on the connections between them to support whatever traffic they generate. Microsoft recommends that the connection between servers support at least 128 Kbps. Keep in mind that if a network link is heavily used, 128 Kbps will not be sufficient for Exchange Server traffic. The network link should have a fair amount of bandwidth available for new traffic generated by Exchange Server, if an Exchange routing group will span that link.

Routing groups in Exchange 2000 Server—like sites in Exchange Server 5.5—are based on available bandwidth. However, Exchange 2000 Server uses SMTP, which is more tolerant of lower bandwidths and higher latency. This capability means that you can group servers into routing groups that you could not have grouped into sites in Exchange 5.5. You might want to divide Exchange servers into multiple routing groups for a number of reasons:

- The minimum requirements outlined previously are not met.
- The messaging path between servers must be altered from a single hop to multiple hops.
- The messages must be queued and sent according to a schedule.
- Bandwidth between servers is less than 16 Kbps, which means that the X.400 Connector is a better choice.
- You want to route client connections to specific public folder replicas since public folder connections are based on routing groups.

The most important factor to consider when planning your routing group boundaries is the stability of the network connection, not the overall bandwidth of the connection. If a connection is prone to failure or is often so saturated that the pragmatic effect is a loss of connectivity, you should place the servers that the connection serves in separate routing groups.

Be sure to have a Global Catalog server in each routing group and preferably in each Windows 2000 site. This arrangement will decrease lookup traffic across your slower WAN links and make the directory information for client lookups more available to your clients.

More Info   Planning an Exchange organization involves more detail than two chapters of this book can cover. For particularly large organizations, planning involves many additional factors, such as whether to use mesh or hub-and-spoke architecture. For more information on advanced planning of Exchange organizations, see *Microsoft Exchange 2000 Server Administrator's Pocket Consultant* (Microsoft Press, 2000).

Planning Routing Group Connectors

After you've determined how many routing groups your organization will have and what the boundaries of those groups will be, you need to plan how those groups will be linked. Routing groups are linked by connectors that allow servers in the different groups to communicate. Exchange 2000 Server provides three connectors that you can use to link two routing groups: the Routing Group

Connector, the SMTP Connector, and the X.400 Connector. These connectors are covered in detail in Chapter 13. This section briefly describes the advantages and disadvantages of each connector.

Routing Group Connector

The Routing Group Connector (RGC) is used only to connect one routing group to another. The RGC is by far the easiest of the connectors to set up and, everything else being equal, is also the fastest. It has some of the strictest use requirements, however, needing a stable, permanent connection that supplies relatively high bandwidth. SMTP is used as the native transport for the RGC.

The RGC works using bridgehead servers. A server in one routing group—a bridgehead server—is designated to send all messages to the other routing group. Other servers within the routing group send messages to the bridgehead server, which then sends the messages to a bridgehead server in the other routing group. That bridgehead server is then responsible for delivering the messages to the correct servers within the group. If you want, you can configure more than one bridgehead server in a routing group, for the purposes of fault tolerance and load balancing. Bridgehead servers let you control which servers transfer messages between routing groups.

SMTP Connector

The SMTP Connector can be used to connect two Exchange routing groups or to connect an Exchange organization to a foreign messaging system. It can also be used to connect two Exchange routing groups over the Internet. The SMTP Connector allows finer control over message transfer than the RGC, including the ability to authenticate remote domains before sending messages, to schedule specific transfer times, and to set multiple permission levels for different users on the connector.

X.400 Connector

The X.400 Connector can be used to connect two routing groups or to connect an Exchange organization to a foreign X.400 messaging system. In connecting two routing groups, the X.400 Connector is generally slower than an RGC because of additional communication overhead. It was a preferable choice in Exchange 5.5 because the standard connector (then called a *Site* Connector) had no ability to schedule communications or establish a maximum message size to traverse the connector. Since the RGC in Exchange 2000 Server allows scheduling and maximum message sizes, you most likely will not use an X.400 Connector to connect two Exchange routing groups.

Multiple Messaging Connectors

Generally speaking, it is simplest to configure only one connector between any two routing groups. You can, however, configure multiple connectors. Multiple connectors can be used to provide fault tolerance in case one connector fails or to balance the messaging load over different network connections. For example, you could create two X.400 Connectors between the same two sites using different pairs of messaging bridgehead servers. If one connector went down (most likely because one of the bridgehead servers in that pair failed), the other connector (and its designated bridgehead servers) would remain up.

A cost value is assigned to each connector you create on a routing group. Cost values range from 0 to 999. (There is no cost value assigned to the SMTP connector itself—only to the address spaces associated with the SMTP Connector.)

A messaging connector with a lower cost is always preferred over one with a higher cost. This approach allows you to designate primary and backup connectors between routing groups. When Exchange determines which connector it should use to send a message, it takes into account the cumulative cost of the entire messaging path. In Figure 6-2, for example, a message could move from group 1 to group 4 by being transmitted either through group 2 or through group 3. The path through group 2 has a cumulative cost of 4, while the path through group 3 has a cumulative cost of 2. Thus, Exchange Server will prefer the path through group 3 because it has the lowest cost.

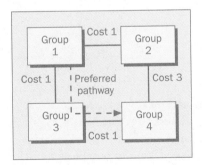

Figure 6-2. *Using costs to determine message routing.*

Use multiple connectors whenever the physical networking between routing groups is unreliable. For a small or medium-sized network with high-bandwidth links between routing groups, having a single connector between groups provides a consistent messaging pathway. This consistency is valuable in developing an accurate picture of network traffic and in troubleshooting message delivery problems. In medium to large networks that have inconsistent traffic patterns or restricted bandwidth availability as well as multiple, redundant links between groups, using two connectors between groups for backup or load balancing can enhance the messaging system's reliability.

Planning Routing Groups

After you've established the number of routing groups your organization will contain and determined how those groups will be linked, you're ready to design the groups themselves. Several elements go into a good routing group design. You need to establish a public folder strategy, and you also need to plan the services, such as foreign gateways, that your users will need. You will base many of these determinations on the assessment of user needs described in Chapter 5.

Designing Your Routing Groups

A good portion of the work of designing an Exchange routing group involves planning the servers that will be members of that group. Planning the Exchange servers themselves is the topic of a later section of this chapter. The following are a few guidelines for deciding how to distribute the services among the servers in a routing group:

- If your goal is to isolate messaging traffic from other network traffic, put users and their home servers on the same network segment in a workgroup configuration. It is important to have high-bandwidth connections between mail clients and servers for the best performance.

- If your goal is to use a hierarchical physical network structure, in order to use its inherent security by grouping servers together, put servers on intermediate network segments that route traffic to the network backbone, and route traffic to the geographically located workgroup segments.

- Put the mailboxes for all users in a workgroup on the same server. Users tend to send the most mail to other users in their own workgroup. Keeping all of the mailboxes on the same server means lighter network traffic and lower consumption of server disk space.
- When possible, create duplicate services on multiple servers to provide fault tolerance. Always place Exchange servers on machines that have fault-tolerant hardware.

Planning Public Folders

Public folders in Exchange 2000 Server can be put to several uses, including as discussion forums, as public collections of documents, and even as the basis for custom applications. Exchange 2000 Server allows you to configure multiple public folder trees, each of which can contain any number of public folders. Folders created in the root level of a public folder tree are referred to as top-level folders. When a user creates a top-level folder, it is placed on that user's home server. When a user creates a lower-level folder, it is placed on the same server as the folder in which it is created. The contents of a public folder can be stored on a single server, or they can be replicated to other servers in the routing group and organization. Chapter 10 discusses the creation, storage, and replication of public folders in detail. A few aspects of public folders are pertinent to routing group planning:

- Decide how many different public folder trees you want to maintain. Each department could manage its own tree, or you could have one companywide tree.
- Decide whether to distribute public folders on multiple servers throughout your routing group or to maintain them all on a single server.
- Decide whether to dedicate certain servers to public folders by having them contain only public folder stores or to have servers that contain both public folders in public folder stores and private folders such as mailboxes in mailbox stores.
- Determine which users will be using public folders for collaborative applications and whether those applications will require other services or special security.

- If users in remote routing groups need to access public folders in a local routing group, decide whether or not to replicate the contents to a server in the remote routing group to keep intergroup network traffic down.

- Consider which users should be allowed to create top-level folders in a public folder tree. Limiting the number of users who can create top-level folders allows you to control both the servers on which public folders are created and the basic organization of the public folder hierarchy.

- When naming public folders, you have a bit more license than with the names of other recipients. Public folder names can be up to 256 characters. However, when you name your folders, keep in mind that only a small portion of the name will actually display in your users' client software, and very long names could become a real hassle. Also, some users may occasionally need to type in the name of a public folder, and smaller names will be greatly appreciated.

Planning Gateways

Any server can be configured with a connector to a foreign system. All other servers in the organization will then be able to route messages over that gateway. When possible, you want to create a foreign messaging connector on the server that maintains the actual physical connection to the foreign system. Also, if one group of users makes primary use of a foreign connection, consider placing those users on the server on which the connector is installed.

Planning Servers

After you've planned the general structure of your organization and routing groups, you can plan your servers. The number of servers you need depends on the number of users in the routing group and the services that you plan to provide to those users. As you've learned throughout this chapter, you accomplish part of server planning while planning your organization and routing groups, after which you should have a fairly good idea of the services that each routing group needs to offer and the number of servers that you need to have to offer those services.

Depending on your needs and resources, you are likely to have decided whether to concentrate your services on just a few powerful servers or instead to distribute the services among a larger number of less powerful servers. There really is no guideline for the number of servers that you need or the power of those servers. What is important is that you make a plan. After you make that plan, you can begin to estimate the hardware requirements for your servers.

When estimating the performance of an Exchange server, you need to consider four distinct categories of hardware: disk, processor, memory, and network. The sections that follow discuss each of these categories in turn.

Disk Considerations

Your server needs to have adequate disk space for Windows 2000 Server, Exchange 2000 Server, directory information, transaction logs, and information stores. The speed at which Exchange 2000 Server can access your disks is another important consideration.

SCSI drives are generally faster than IDE drives. Consider using a caching disk controller with a high-speed bus, such as PCI. Adding more drives allows Exchange 2000 Server to distribute the workload, reading and writing to multiple drives at the same time. Also consider placing your transaction logs on a separate physical disk so that the logs can be written sequentially, increasing performance.

Real World   Calculating Disk Space

When you plan the amount of disk space your server will need, consider these factors:

- Windows 2000 Advanced Server (with IIS, Active Directory, and DNS) takes up about 750 MB, depending on the options you install.

- A standard installation of Exchange 2000 Server will take up an additional 180 MB.

- In addition to these figures, you need to factor in the number of user mailboxes and public folders on your server and the amount of space you plan to allow each type of store to consume.

- Transaction logs are relatively small (5 MB each), but you should use a separate drive for them.

Finally, you need to take into account any additional services you need to run on the server, including other major programs such as Microsoft SQL Server and Exchange extensions such as virus and filtering programs.

If you use multiple drives, you might also want to consider a Windows 2000 software-based redundant array of independent disks (RAID), including disk striping with parity (RAID-5) or disk mirroring (RAID-1) to offer some level of fault tolerance. You can configure Windows 2000 software-based RAID in the Computer Management snap-in. Computer Management allows you to create a *volume set,* which is a group of hard disks that the Windows operating system treats as though they were a single hard disk. Yet another option is to implement a form of hardware-based RAID, which can be costly but offers the best performance and fault tolerance available.

Although it may seem tempting to throw as much storage space at the Exchange server as you can, don't do it. Instead, think about the storage needs over time and the capability of the backup system. If the storage space might exceed the capacity of the backup system, you may need additional servers instead. Many gigabytes of data can accrue on an Exchange server over time. Eventually, the information stores can grow to be too large for the backup system. When defining the storage for a server, ensure that the backup system is adequate to fully back up the information stores, transaction logs, and operating system files. A large information store can take several tapes, and a very long time, to back up on a daily basis. A restore can take several hours. Multiple servers with smaller information stores provide an inherent tolerance to failure: the failure would affect fewer users for a shorter period of time because the restore process is shorter.

As the amount of data on an Exchange server grows, performance can diminish. Exchange Server manages a number of background tasks for the information stores. These tasks take longer to execute when there are more messages in the information store to manage; hence, performance degrades across the server as a whole. One way to keep the mailbox store from growing too large is to configure the server to limit the size of users' mailboxes. Another way is to configure multiple mailbox stores, which you learn how to do in Chapter 11.

Processor Considerations

Using multiple processors significantly increases a server's performance. Adding a second processor to a server, however, does not double its performance. The processors still share a motherboard, adapters, storage, and other components, and data can face a bottleneck in these components. However, Windows 2000 does support symmetric multiprocessing, and Exchange 2000 Server is a multithreaded application. Therefore, multiple pieces of the Exchange system can run simultaneously on different processors within the same system, significantly increasing response time.

Memory Considerations

Memory (RAM) is used to run active processes on a computer. When physical memory is not sufficient, the system supplements it by using a paging file on the computer's hard disk. Ideally, you should have enough physical memory on a server to avoid excessive use of the paging file. Right now, memory is the cheapest way to increase the performance of any computer. We recommend having at least 128 MB of RAM on any Exchange server as the bare minimum; use 256 MB from the start if at all possible.

Network Considerations

The network interface cards on your servers should be fast enough to handle traffic coming from and going to clients and other servers. High-speed network adapters, such as those that use a PCI bus, are best. Fast servers can take advantage of multiple network interface cards, providing the ability to host connections to several other clients or servers at the same time. Furthermore, many server platforms allow you to merge network interface cards into a pool; then, should one of the cards in the pool fail, another card takes over. We recommend using high-speed PCI adapters that are capable of bus mastering whenever you can.

Ways to Add Fault Tolerance

Some standard precautions can be taken to ensure that Exchange servers stay on line, even when there are failures. An uninterruptible power supply (UPS) is a common way to ensure that the server does not go off line if the power in the building fails. A UPS can also prevent power surges from damaging the server components.

As we have already mentioned, a server can have multiple hard disks, multiple processors, and multiple network interface cards. These redundant components provide increased performance, load balancing, and failover options, depending on how they are configured. A server can also have dual power supplies, controller cards, and error-correcting RAM. Whenever a server has redundant internal components, it is better able to tolerate faults in those components. Server-class machines typically come with software that is able to monitor the servers' hardware components from a central management machine.

Besides establishing redundancy for server components, you can also do so for the server itself. Exchange servers can be configured to take advantage of a shared storage system using clustering. This is a system in which multiple servers are configured in a cluster, so that if one server has a problem, the system fails over to the redundant server.

Real World   Load Simulator

The Microsoft BackOffice Resource Kit includes a wonderful utility called Load Simulator (Loadsim.exe), which allows you to simulate the load caused on an Exchange server by a specified number of users sending and receiving messages over a given period. Load Simulator cannot tell you exactly what hardware a server needs to provide a set of services. It can, however, answer one important question for you: What average load will a certain number of users put on your server hardware?

Load Simulator can be set to perform five separate tasks:

- The Inbox task (a user reading new mail)
- The Browse task (a user reading old mail)
- The Send Mail task
- The Schedule+ task
- The Public Folder task

Each individual simulated user performs the selected tasks a specified number of times per simulated day. You can specify the number of simulated days that you want Load Simulator to run. Load Simulator can run many simulated days in a fraction of a real day.

Be sure you use the version of Load Simulator designed for Exchange 2000 Server as earlier versions will not work. For a copy of the latest version of Load Simulator, check Microsoft's Web site at *http://www.microsoft.com/exchange*.

Summary

In this chapter, you learned how to take information about the needs of your users and the current assessment of your network and use it to design an Exchange organization. The design of an organization happens at three distinct levels: the organizational level, the routing group level, and the server level.

Part II of this book has shown you how to collect and use information about your situation in planning your Exchange organization. Chapter 7 begins Part III, which looks at the deployment of Exchange 2000 Server. In Chapter 7, you will learn how to install Exchange 2000 Server.

Part III
Deployment

Chapter 7
Installing Exchange 2000 Server

So far, you've learned a bit about how Microsoft Exchange 2000 Server works and how to plan your Exchange organization. In this chapter, you'll actually get your hands dirty and install Exchange 2000 Server. You'll do this in four basic stages:

1. Make sure that your server is prepared for the installation.

2. Run the Exchange 2000 Server Setup program, click a few buttons, and supply some information about your environment.

3. Verify that the new Exchange services are up and running.

4. Apply other software that may need to be integrated with Exchange Server, such as Exchange service packs, backup software, and virus-detection software.

Regardless of whether you're installing Exchange 2000 Server as the first server or as a subsequent server within the Exchange messaging system, you'll find that if you select the right options, Exchange 2000 Server is not difficult to install. If you choose the wrong options, however, you may end up having to reinstall the software. For anyone involved in installing Exchange 2000 Server, this is a critical chapter.

Preparing for the Installation

Although it's tempting (and easy enough) simply to insert the Exchange Server CD-ROM and run the Setup program, it's best to take care of a few chores first. You should verify that your server is correctly configured, gather some information, and set up special accounts. If you created a good deployment plan, you probably have all the information you need.

Real World Taking Exchange 2000 Server for a Test Drive

If you are considering upgrading your Exchange organization to Exchange 2000 Server from a previous version, we recommend trying the new version on a non-production server first to get a feel for its new features. You may also want to test-drive the software even if you are creating a new system rather than upgrading. Testing Exchange 2000 Server before deployment can help you plan the best ways to implement some of the features offered by the new version as those decisions come up during the "real" installation.

If you do decide to take Exchange 2000 Server for a test drive, we recommend setting up a test network that is physically separate from your actual network. If you do not have the resources for a separate network, you can test Exchange 2000 Server on a server on your existing network.

Gathering Information

The following is a checklist of critical questions that you should ask yourself before starting an Exchange Server installation. The answers to some of them may seem a bit obvious, but taking the time to study them before you begin will prevent problems during or after installation:

- Does the computer running Microsoft Windows 2000 Server meet the hardware requirements for running Exchange 2000 Server? (See the next section, "Verifying Hardware Requirements.")

- Does your server have access to a domain controller with a Global Catalog?

- Do you have access to a user account with administrative rights on the server on which you will install Exchange 2000 Server?

- Does your account have the right to modify the Windows 2000 Active Directory Schema? If not, you can have an administrator who does have rights modify the Schema before you begin installing Exchange 2000 Server. (See the section "Installing Exchange 2000 Server.")

- Is TCP/IP correctly configured on your Windows 2000 server, and do you have access to DNS servers? (See "TCP/IP," later in this chapter.)

- What are the names of the organization and routing group that you will create or join?

- What is the name and password for the Exchange service account you will be using? (See "Creating a Service Account," later in this chapter.)

- If you are joining an existing routing group, what is its name?

- For what connectors will you need to install support during your Exchange Server setup?

- What is the disk configuration of the computer on which you are installing Exchange Server?

- Do you have the 25-digit key number from the back of the Exchange Server CD-ROM jewel case?

- Is Internet Information Services (IIS) 5.0 or later running on the computer?

- If you plan to install Key Management Service (KMS), is Microsoft Certificate Services running on your network? (See Chapter 21.)

- If you plan to use the connector for Microsoft Mail for AppleTalk networks, is Windows 2000 Services for Macintosh correctly configured?

Verifying Hardware Requirements

Before installing Exchange 2000 Server, you must make sure that your machine meets the minimum hardware requirements. Table 7-1 details Microsoft's minimum and recommended configurations for a computer running Exchange 2000 Server. Keep in mind that these requirements indicate the configurations on which Exchange Server will run, not those on which it will run *well*. Many Exchange servers require multiple processors and more memory to execute the desired services.

Table 7-1.   Minimum and recommended hardware configurations

Hardware	Minimum	Recommended
Processor	200 MHz Pentium	400 MHz Pentium II
Memory	128 MB	256 MB
Disk space	2 GB for Exchange, 500 MB available on system drive	Space for e-mail and public folders; multiple physical disks configured as a stripe set or stripe set with parity

Note To allow you to verify that your hardware and software are compatible with a given Microsoft product, Microsoft publishes hardware and software compatibility lists. Because these lists are published for various Microsoft operating systems and applications and are updated often, Microsoft publishes them on line in searchable form at *http://www.microsoft.com/hcl/.*

On this Web page, you can enter the name of any Microsoft product for which you want to view the lists of compatible hardware or software. Of particular interest are the lists for the Microsoft BackOffice suite, of which Exchange 2000 Server is a component. The products on these two lists have successfully passed a series of difficult tests to verify that they take advantage of BackOffice technology and are authorized to display the BackOffice logo on their product materials.

If you plan to add future enhancements, such as a fax service, to the Exchange Server environment, check the BackOffice software compatibility page to help you select a compatible application.

Getting Service Packs

Microsoft provides its service packs on line for free and on CD-ROM for a small charge. A *service pack* is an update to an operating system or application that encompasses the solutions for multiple problems. In contrast, hot fixes, or *patches,* are solutions to single, immediate problems with an operating system or application. A service pack will include all hot fixes up to the point that the service pack is released. Service packs and hot fixes assure you quick access to the latest improvements for your operating system or applications.

To get the latest service pack or set of hot fixes from Microsoft, downloading is the way to go. Be aware, however, that although hot fixes are usually small and quick to download, a service pack is typically several megabytes in size and can take a very long time to download, even with a fast Internet connection. Most— but not all—service packs include the contents of past service packs within them. Check to make sure that the service pack you are downloading does include past service packs if you do not already have them installed on your system. This information will be in the Readme file.

Once you have downloaded a service pack, it is important that you test it on another system before implementing it in your production environment. You should test it on the exact same type of hardware that you have running in your environment.

Defining the Role of Your Server

Unfortunately, Microsoft's minimum configuration—a 200-MHz Pentium with 128 MB of RAM—is not sufficient for anything but a very small organization or test server, and even then, performance will depend on what you're doing with the server. For optimal performance, you should run Exchange 2000 Server on a computer that is not also functioning as a Windows 2000 domain controller for your network. All domain controllers experience some capacity loss due to the overhead required to manage security for the domain. The amount of this overhead is determined by the size and activity of the domain.

Although an Exchange server performs better if it is running on a machine that is dedicated to Exchange messaging, it is not uncommon in small networks to have one machine serve as both a domain controller and an Exchange server because it saves the expense of an extra machine. Saving on a machine, however, may result in meager performance for both Windows 2000 Server and Exchange 2000 Server.

If your computer needs to play the roles of both Exchange server and domain controller, you'll want more powerful hardware than that listed in Table 7-1. Also, running Exchange 2000 Server on the domain controller means that administrators of that machine must be administrators on all domain controllers. Furthermore, there is a security risk in that anyone who uses the Web Connector will need the right to log on locally at the server, which is generally not a privilege allowed for users on a domain controller.

The Exchange 2000 Server architecture was developed to participate in a Windows 2000 network. In fact, you can install Exchange 2000 Server only in a domain with a Windows 2000 server configured as a domain controller with a Global Catalog. You must also have DNS resolution running in your domain. If you do not have a DNS server in your domain, you can configure a Windows 2000 server as a DNS server. For more on this subject, see Chapter 4. The network can have one or more Active Directory forests, each with multiple domain trees in it, and each domain tree can consist of one or more domains. Each Exchange server must be a member server or a domain controller. If it is a member server, the Exchange server must be able to access a domain controller in order to function.

Specifying the role of a server involves more than simply configuring it as a domain controller or as a member server. It also includes indicating the services that the server will provide to the network. One of these services is IIS. Hardware capacity is even more critical if your server is also running IIS or other network applications. IIS, which is required to install Exchange 2000 Server, uses considerable memory and processing power, depending on its configuration. For example, if IIS is configured to provide FTP service as well as the SMTP and NNTP services, it uses many more CPU cycles and much more hard disk space than if it did not provide those services. When determining your hardware requirements, you should list the services that the server will host and the hardware requirements of the various applications. Start with the application with the largest hardware requirements, and then increment the RAM, processor speed, and storage capacity for each additional service by about half of its own recommendation. You will then have a fair idea of your server's hardware needs. For more information on planning your server hardware, see Chapter 6.

Note When you install IIS on a Windows 2000 server (either during setup or afterward), make sure that the NNTP stacks are also installed. NNTP is not included in the default IIS installation, and it is necessary in order to install the messaging components of Exchange 2000 Server.

Optimizing Hardware Through Configuration

Increasing the speed of your processor and the amount of storage and memory on your computer are effective ways of making your Exchange server more powerful. You can also optimize your existing hardware to help boost the performance of an Exchange server if you configure the operating system in the following ways:

- If possible, use one physical disk for your operating system and another for your pagefile. You can also increase the size of your pagefile to 50 MB or 100 MB beyond the size of your physical memory.
- After installing Exchange 2000 Server, designate separate physical disks to house your information stores and transaction log files. This step allows your log files to be written more quickly to disk. The reason for this increase in speed is that logs are written to disk sequentially, while the Exchange database is written randomly. Having the logs and the database on the same physical disk affects hard disk performance because of the extra time required to continually reposition the head. Furthermore, keeping the logs on a separate disk can assist you if the database

disk crashes because the logs are used to recover the database. Because the log files are relatively small (using 5 MB of storage space), you can increase speed even further by placing them on a disk formatted with the file allocation table (FAT) file system. On partitions smaller than 500 MB, the FAT file system is usually quicker than the Windows NTFS. Note that NTFS has other advantages that may outweigh the need for speed, and it also performs well on partitions larger than 500 MB. Choose this optimization only when it is relevant to your situation, and keep in mind that you should never place your information stores on a FAT-formatted drive. Place stores only on drives formatted with NTFS.

- You can also use a stripe set consisting of multiple physical disks to house the Exchange information stores and other main components, allowing the various components to be accessed most efficiently. Using a stripe set with parity has the additional advantage of providing fault tolerance. Because messaging data is considered critical to most businesses, you should avoid striping without parity because using it increases the chances of losing all data at once. Hardware RAID using striping with parity provides better performance than software RAID because the operating system does not have the burden of managing the disk activity.

Verifying System Requirements

In addition to making sure that your computer's hardware can handle Exchange 2000 Server, you need to check certain other settings before proceeding with your setup.

Windows 2000 Server

Exchange 2000 Server can be installed only under Windows 2000 Server. Make sure that the NetBIOS name given to your Windows 2000 server is the name that you want your Exchange server to have. It is simple enough to change the name of a member server before installing Exchange 2000 Server, but it's nearly impossible to do so afterward. You can change the name beforehand by clicking the Properties button on the Network Identification tab of the System Properties dialog box, accessed by clicking the System icon in Control Panel. This displays the Identification Changes dialog box, as shown in Figure 7-1. For more information on Exchange 2000 Server's integration with Windows 2000 Server, see Chapter 4.

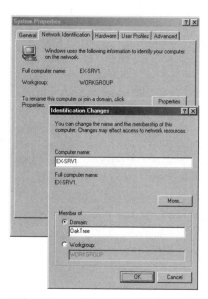

Figure 7-1. *Changing the name of your Windows 2000 server.*

Windows 2000 Domains

When you install the first Exchange server in an organization, you also create a new Exchange organization, routing group, and Administrative group. If you are installing Exchange 2000 Server on a single-domain network or if your new Exchange routing group will not cross any domain boundaries, you should have no problems. However, if your new routing group will cross domain boundaries, you need to make sure that appropriate security has been established before you start Setup.

TCP/IP

Exchange 2000 Server includes support for many Internet protocols, including Simple Mail Transfer Protocol (SMTP), Network News Transfer Protocol (NNTP), and HTTP. All of these protocols rely on the TCP/IP suite to operate. In fact, SMTP is now the default messaging transport mechanism in Exchange Server, meaning that TCP/IP must be configured on your Windows 2000 server before you install Exchange 2000 Server. To do so, open the TCP/IP properties of the network connection you are using, or use the Ipconfig utility, as shown in Figure 7-2. Note that each server's Ipconfig output reflects the actual IP configuration of that server—and varies widely from machine to machine.

```
Command Prompt                                                    _ □ ×
C:\>ipconfig /all

Windows 2000 IP Configuration

        Host Name . . . . . . . . . . . . : EX-SRV1
        Primary DNS Suffix  . . . . . . . : sales.oaktree.com
        Node Type . . . . . . . . . . . . : Broadcast
        IP Routing Enabled. . . . . . . . : No
        WINS Proxy Enabled. . . . . . . . : No
        DNS Suffix Search List. . . . . . : sales.oaktree.com
                                            oaktree.com

Ethernet adapter Local Area Connection:

        Connection-specific DNS Suffix  . :
        Description . . . . . . . . . . . : Winbond W89C940 PCI Ethernet Adapter

        Physical Address. . . . . . . . . : 00-20-78-17-03-B7
        DHCP Enabled. . . . . . . . . . . : No
        IP Address. . . . . . . . . . . . : 10.10.1.1
        Subnet Mask . . . . . . . . . . . : 255.0.0.0
        Default Gateway . . . . . . . . . :
        DNS Servers . . . . . . . . . . . : 127.0.0.1
C:\>
```

Figure 7-2. *Using the Ipconfig /All command to verify TCP/IP configuration.*

More Info For more information on configuring Windows 2000 networking, consult your Windows 2000 product documentation. You might also want to check out the *Microsoft Windows 2000 Server Administrator's Companion* by Charlie Russel and Sharon Crawford (Microsoft Press, 2000).

IIS

IIS 5.0 or later is required on the server on which Exchange 2000 Server will be installed. Fortunately, IIS 5.0 is part of Windows 2000 Server. In fact, a default installation of Windows 2000 Server includes IIS 5.0. The SMTP service is also included as part of the default installation. To install Exchange 2000 Server, however, you will also need to make sure that the NNTP service is installed—something that is not done by default. You can include it during Windows 2000 installation or install it separately at any time thereafter.

Microsoft Key Management Service

In addition to taking advantage of the built-in security of Windows 2000 Server, Exchange 2000 Server provides advanced security in the form of an optional component named the Key Management Service (KMS). The KMS works in conjunction with the Active Directory directory services to manage the encryption keys used to encrypt e-mail messages. It integrates with Microsoft Certificate Services to provide services. For more information on configuring and supporting the KMS, see Chapter 21.

Windows Clustering

Windows 2000 Server provides support for clustering technology, in which two Windows 2000 servers, called *nodes,* can be grouped to act as a single network unit. Clustering is designed to provide reliability through hardware redundancy. If one server in a cluster fails, another server in that cluster can take over, providing near-continuous access to network resources. To install Exchange 2000 Server in a clustered environment, you must ensure that a cluster has a single network name and IP address as well as a shared disk that is part of an external disk array. You can learn more about using Exchange 2000 Server in a clustered environment in Chapter 20.

Note Whenever you add components to or remove components from the clustered Exchange server installation, you run the Setup program on the first node as usual. You must then run Setup again on the second node and choose the Upgrade Node option.

Services for Macintosh

Exchange 2000 Server provides support for a connector that allows Exchange Server and Microsoft Mail for AppleTalk Networks to transfer messages and share directory information. To install this optional component, you must ensure that Windows 2000 Services for Macintosh is installed and configured correctly on the computer on which you plan to install Exchange Server.

Creating Special Accounts

Your last task before starting Exchange Server Setup is creating some special user accounts. The first account, the Site Services account, is required. The second, a special Exchange Administrator's account, is helpful for distributing Exchange administration responsibilities.

Creating a Service Account

Each of the main components of Exchange 2000 Server acts as a Windows 2000 service. For these components to communicate with one another, with services on other Exchange servers, and with the Windows 2000 Active Directory directory service, all of the services within a routing group must have a common security context. This context takes the form of a special Windows 2000 user account called a service account.

When you install Exchange 2000 Server, you are asked to specify this service account. Although you can specify any existing user account, we highly recommend that you create a special account for this purpose instead of using a normal user account.

You can create this new account via Active Directory Users and Computers, assuming that you have administrative privileges in the domain in which you'll be installing Exchange 2000 Server. In the Active Directory Users and Computers console window, select the Users folder, and choose New User from the Action menu. In the New Object - User dialog box (Figure 7-3), enter an appropriate user name and full name. In the next screen of the wizard (Figure 7-4), specify the password. Because the service account has considerable access to the network, select a complex password that cannot be guessed easily. This step further secures your network. (Be sure to write down the user name and password, because you'll need to know them during the installation.) You also need to select both the User Cannot Change Password and Password Never Expires options so that this account does not encounter authentication problems. When you're done, click Finish to create the new account. Setup will assign other rights required by the new service account.

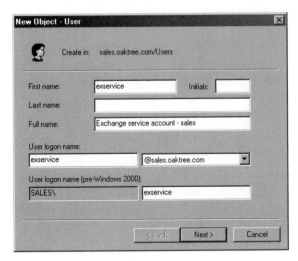

Figure 7-3. *Naming the Site Services account.*

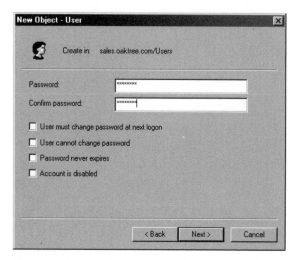

Figure 7-4. *Creating a password for the Site Services account.*

Creating the Exchange Administrator's Account

Exchange administration and Windows 2000 administration are handled separately. Just because an account has administrative privileges in Windows 2000 does not necessarily mean that the account will have administrative privileges in Exchange. When you install Exchange 2000 Server, one user account is given permission to administer Exchange: the account that you are logged on with when you start the installation. If you want to enable other Exchange administrators, you must do so manually, using the Exchange System snap-in.

For this reason, make sure that when you start Exchange Server Setup, you are logged on from the account that you want to use for Exchange administration. This account can be the preconfigured Administrator account, your own account, or a special one that you create just for the task. It should be a member of the following Windows 2000 security groups: Domain Admins, Enterprise Admins, and Schema Admins. Later, you can assign administrative privileges to other accounts or groups.

Playing It Safe

Before creating the accounts, you should perform two tasks to ensure that, if necessary, you can restore the system to the same state in which it started. One of these tasks is to create an emergency repair disk. You use the Windows 2000

Backup utility, available in the System Tools folder on the Programs menu, for creating these disks. In Windows Backup, choose Create An Emergency Repair Disk from the Tools menu, and follow the steps for creating the disk. You will need one formatted 1.44-MB floppy disk.

The second task is to back up your server, for which you can also use Windows Backup. Most administrators select a tape backup system for backing up their servers on an ongoing basis. The best thing to do at this point is to execute a full system backup. Chapter 24 discusses the procedure for backing up an Exchange 2000 server using Windows Backup. Although the procedure for backing up a Windows 2000 server is a bit different from the one described there, you can use that chapter as a tutorial for backing up your system prior to installing Exchange 2000 Server as well.

Installing Exchange 2000 Server

Finally! After all of the reading and planning, you actually get to run Exchange Server Setup. You can run Setup from either the Exchange 2000 Server CD-ROM or a shared network installation point. If you are using the CD-ROM, you have only to insert the disk and watch Setup start automatically. If you're installing over the network, you have to find and run the Setup program yourself. There could be multiple versions of the installation files for different encryption levels and for different languages. Be sure that you find the right files for your situation. If you are performing a typical installation of Exchange 2000 Server on a computer with an Intel processor, for example, you will find Setup.exe in the \Setup\I386 folder on your CD-ROM.

> **Note** Remember that before you begin the installation you must be logged on with the Windows 2000 user account that you want to be given administrative privileges in Exchange Server. This account should be a member of the Domain Admins, Enterprise Admins, and Schema Admins security groups.

If you insert the Exchange 2000 Server CD-ROM and the Autorun feature is enabled on your system, a splash screen appears from which you can run Setup and access other features on the CD. If Autorun is disabled, you will need to run Setup.exe manually from the CD-ROM. In either case, the first thing you will see is the welcome screen of the Microsoft Exchange 2000 Installation Wizard, shown in Figure 7-5.

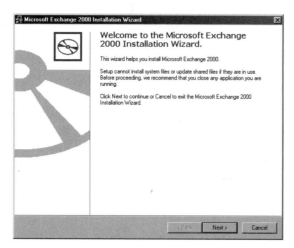

Figure 7-5. *The first screen of the Installation Wizard.*

Note Before Setup starts, it may display a warning to shut down any other applications that are running. The single most common reason that an Exchange Server installation fails is that other MAPI-based applications are running in the background while Setup is running. These applications can include e-mail programs, Web browsers, and even components of Microsoft Office. Use the Processes tab of Windows 2000's Task Manager to find and close any such applications. You also need to shut down all instances of System Monitor that are monitoring the server, whether they are running locally or on a remote machine. Finally, you need to make sure that Event Viewer is not running on the server.

Choosing Components for Installation

After you've made sure that no other programs are running, you will encounter one screen that asks you to read and accept Microsoft's End-User License Agreement and one on which you enter the 25-digit key from the back of your Exchange CD cover. After you've completed these two steps and clicked Next, Setup searches for any components of Exchange Server that might already be installed on the computer. If Setup finds an installation of Exchange Server 5.5, you must choose whether you want to perform an upgrade. Exchange 2000 Server supports upgrading only from Exchange Server 5.5 and not from versions previous to Exchange 5.5. For more information about coexisting with Exchange Server 5.5, see Chapter 14. The upgrade process is described later in this chapter. If no previous installation is found, you are taken to the component selection screen shown in Figure 7-6.

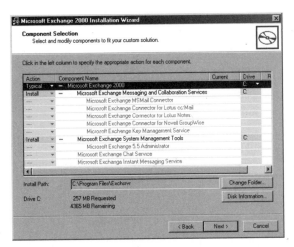

Figure 7-6. *Choosing components for an installation.*

Select one of three installation modes using the drop-down menu to the left of the Microsoft Exchange 2000 Server component. Typical mode (the default) installs all available components. Minimum mode installs the main Exchange component and messaging services but does not install System Manager or the collaboration tools. Custom mode lets you pick the components to install. You can designate the drive on which you would like Exchange 2000 Server installed by selecting the Microsoft Exchange 2000 Server component and clicking the Change Drive button. You can also specify the installation path on that drive by clicking the Change Folder button. All components you select to be installed are installed on the drive you choose; you cannot install individual components to different drives. Clicking on the Disk Information button opens a dialog box that shows you all of the drives on your system and the amount of space they have free.

If you are running Setup on a computer on which Exchange 2000 Server is already installed, you may see additional options as well, including Disaster Recovery, which attempts to reinstall the component, and Remove, which removes the component from an installation.

Note For a basic messaging system, it usually is best to install only Microsoft Exchange Messaging and Collaboration Services and Microsoft Exchange System Management Tools. However, you may want to go ahead and install the other available components if you think you might need them at some point. That way, you won't have to return to your CD-ROM to reinstall it.

Table 7-2 describes each of the components available on the component selection screen. Once you have selected your components, click Next to go on to the next screen of the Installation Wizard.

Table 7-2. Components available in an Exchange 2000 Server installation

Component	Description
Microsoft Exchange 2000	This is the primary node for the Exchange Server installation. To install any Exchange components, you must select Install on this node. To change the default drive on which other components will be installed, change the drive for this component.
Microsoft Exchange Messaging and Collaboration Services	Select Install on this node to install all of the basic messaging components of Exchange, each of which is also described in this table. Once you select this component, all subcomponents are also selected. You must individually deselect any that you don't want installed. You must select this node to install the real-time collaboration components as well. To install this node, your system must be running the NNTP stacks as part of the IIS installation.
Microsoft Exchange MSMail Connector	This item supports message and directory information transfer between Exchange 2000 Server and Microsoft Mail for PC Networks.
Microsoft Exchange cc:Mail Connector	This item supports message and directory information transfer between Exchange 2000 Server and Lotus cc:Mail.
Microsoft Exchange Connector for Lotus Notes	This item supports message and directory information transfer between Exchange 2000 Server and Lotus Notes.
Microsoft Exchange Connector for Novell GroupWise	This item supports message and directory information transfer between Exchange 2000 Server and Novell GroupWise.
Microsoft Exchange Key Management Service	The Key Management Service is an Exchange-specific security enhancement of the Windows 2000 Server Certificate Services. For more information on using the Key Management Service, see Chapter 21.

Table 7-2. *continued*

Component	Description
Microsoft Exchange System Management Tools	This option installs the Exchange System snap-in. You must install this component to manage all Exchange components. You can also install it by itself under Windows 2000 Server or Windows 2000 Professional to manage your Exchange organization remotely. For more information on using this utility, see Chapter 8.
Microsoft Exchange Chat Service	These components allow your users to join and form chat communities. For more information about administering Chat Service, see Chapter 18. If you are installing Chat Service, you must also install Exchange System Management Tools and Exchange Messaging and Collaboration Services.
Microsoft Exchange Instant Messaging Services	This component allows your users to send and receive instant messages. For more information about administering the Instant Messaging Services, see Chapter 19. If you are installing the Instant Messaging Services, you must also install Exchange System Management Tools and Exchange Messaging and Collaboration Services.

Creating an Organization

In the next phase of installation, you create the organization that you've been planning. First you must specify an installation type, as shown in Figure 7-7. You can choose either to create an Exchange 2000 organization or to join an existing Exchange 5.5 organization. If you will be joining an Exchange 5.5 organization, you will want to check out Chapter 14. If you want to create an Exchange 2000 organization, select the default option, Create A New Exchange Organization. After making your choice, click Next.

On the next screen of the Installation Wizard, shown in Figure 7-8, you will name your organization. Do not take this task lightly. After the installation, even during subsequent installations, you will not be able to change the name without tearing down and completely reinstalling Windows 2000 and Exchange 2000 Server. If you have not yet decided on the name, you haven't properly planned your organization. See Chapters 5 and 6 for more information on planning and naming your organization. Click Next when you've entered the name.

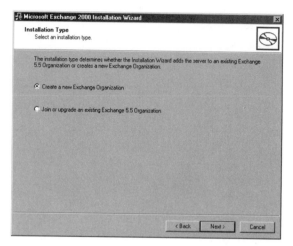

Figure 7-7. *Specifying an installation type.*

Note This section assumes that you're creating a new organization. If you're joining an existing Exchange 2000 organization, see "Installing in an Existing Organization" later in this chapter for a description of the slight differences between the two procedures.

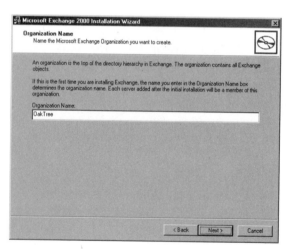

Figure 7-8. *Specifying a name for a new organization.*

Licensing

The next screen of the Installation Wizard, shown in Figure 7-9, shows you the Per Seat licensing agreement. Exchange 2000 Server supports only Per Seat licensing, meaning that any client computer that connects to Exchange 2000 Server requires a Client Access License. For example, a computer that connects to Exchange 2000 Server using Microsoft Outlook 2000, one that connects using Outlook 2000 and Microsoft Internet Explorer, and one that connects using only Internet Explorer would each need a Client Access License. After you've agreed to the licensing agreement, click Next.

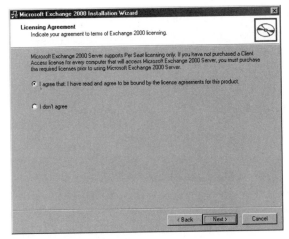

Figure 7-9. *The Per Seat licensing agreement.*

Confirming the Installation Choices

You're just about ready to start the actual installation. After you have designated a service account and clicked Next, you see an installation summary screen that looks just like the component selection screen (refer back to Figure 7-6), except that you cannot change anything. You can, however, back up through the screens in the wizard to change any information you want. When you're satisfied with the summary, click Next. Setup then begins copying files. Depending on the components you selected for installation, this can take several minutes.

During the process, Setup may notify you that it needs to extend your Windows 2000 Active Directory Schema, as shown in Figure 7-10. Assuming that you logged on with a user account that has appropriate permissions to do this, go ahead and click OK. Don't be alarmed if it seems as though Setup is not getting anywhere. The schema updating process can take quite a bit of time (even hours), depending upon your situation. This may be a great chance to go get some lunch. When Setup completes the task, the Installation Wizard will indicate that the installation was successful. Click Finish and the new Exchange services will start.

Real World   What If You're Not Allowed to Update the Schema?

In some large companies, or those with tight administrative policies, only a select few administrators may have permission to mess around with the Windows 2000 Active Directory Schema. How, then, are you, a lowly Exchange administrator, to get your installation job done? Take heart—there is a way. You can run Exchange 2000 Server Setup from the command line, using a switch that causes Setup only to update the Windows 2000 Active Directory Schema without actually installing any of the Exchange 2000 Server components. The command for doing this is Setup /forestprep. This means that you can hand the Exchange CD-ROM to an administrator who has permission to update the schema and let him or her update the schema for you. The administrator could also update the schema by using Exchange files on a shared network installation point. Once the schema has been updated, you can install Exchange 2000 Server yourself. There are two added bonuses to having someone else update the schema. The first is that you don't have to wait around for the update to finish. The second is that if something goes wrong, someone else gets the blame.

Figure 7-10. *Extending the Windows 2000 Active Directory Schema.*

Installing in an Existing Organization

Installing Exchange 2000 Server in an existing Exchange 2000 organization is nearly identical to installing it as the first server in an organization. You need to be aware of only a couple of small differences in the procedure. You start Setup the same way: from either the CD-ROM or a network installation point. The first difference you will notice is that you are not able to change the organization name. The name is displayed (refer back to Figure 7-8), but it is dimmed.

After you've chosen your administrative and routing groups, the rest of the process is no different from the one you used to install the first server in an organization. Make sure you select the Exchange service account used by other servers in the organization. Because Setup will not need to update the Windows 2000 Active Directory Schema again, the installation will take much less time.

Real World **Automating Exchange 2000 Server Setup**

If you plan to deploy a large number of Exchange servers in your enterprise, or if you need to deploy servers remotely, you will be glad to know that there is a way to automate the setup process. Setup places all of the information that controls its file-copying process in a file named Setup.ini. The file is customized for a particular installation when you make choices in the various Installation Wizard screens described previously.

You can create your own Setup.ini files based on samples on your Exchange CD-ROM. Go to the Support folder, and then open the Batsetup folder. You'll find the samples in the Setup folder. You can then create a batch script that runs the Setup program, using the information in your customized file. If you are deploying Exchange 2000 Server on existing Windows 2000 servers in your enterprise, you can also use Microsoft Systems Management Server or a similar application to further automate the process.

More Info To learn more about automating Exchange Server Setup, including all of the parameters for customizing the Setup.ini files, consult the online product documentation.

Upgrading from Exchange Server 5.5

You can upgrade existing servers running Exchange Server 5.5 with Service Pack 3 applied to Exchange 2000 Server. You will have to take the server off line while you perform the upgrade, so it is best to do it during planned downtime. Also, if the existing server is running Microsoft Windows NT 4, you will need to upgrade it to Windows 2000 Server before you can upgrade to Exchange 2000 Server.

Note We suggest that you familiarize yourself with the tools and methods for enabling coexistence between Exchange 2000 Server and Exchange Server 5.5 before deciding to upgrade your Exchange 5.5 servers. Coexistence is discussed in detail in Chapter 14.

When you run Exchange 2000 Server Setup on an existing Exchange 5.5 server, Setup will determine that you are running a previous version of Exchange and give you the option of upgrading the server, as shown in Figure 7-11. Other than this, the upgrade process is nearly identical to the process for installing Exchange 2000 Server outlined previously. The only other difference is that you cannot add any components to the existing server configuration. Once the upgrade is complete, you can rerun Setup to add additional components.

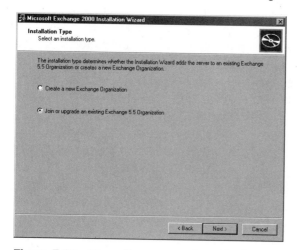

Figure 7-11. *Upgrading a server from Exchange Server 5.5 with Service Pack 3.*

If you are running Exchange 5.5 on a Windows NT primary domain controller (PDC), you will also need to change the LDAP port that the Exchange 5.5 directory service is using to avoid port conflicts. Although you can do this at any time before you upgrade to Exchange 2000, Microsoft recommends that you change the port before you upgrade the operating system to Windows 2000 Server. After you change the LDAP port, you must change the port number on the Active

Directory Connector (ADC) connection agreements that are configured on the computer. To change the port, follow these steps:

1. Open the Exchange 5.5 Administrator program.

2. Expand the Site container, expand the Configuration container, expand the Protocols container, and then double-click LDAP (Directory) Site Defaults.

3. On the General tab, change the value in the Port Number field to something other than 389. Click OK.

4. Open Control Panel, double-click Services, select Microsoft Exchange Directory, and then click Stop.

5. After the service stops, click Start. Verify that service has restarted, and then click Close.

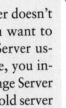

Real World   The Move Mailbox Upgrade

If you find that the hardware on your existing Exchange Server 5.5 server doesn't meet the minimum requirements for Exchange 2000 Server (or if you want to upgrade the hardware anyway), you can upgrade to Exchange 2000 Server using a method called the move mailbox upgrade. In this type of upgrade, you install Exchange 2000 Server on new hardware and join an existing Exchange Server 5.5 site. Once Setup is complete, you can move the information from the old server to the new server and then remove the old server from the network. In addition to mailboxes, you can also move public folders by creating replicas of them on the new server.

Verifying Your Installation

You've installed Exchange Server, but don't pat yourself on the back just yet. You still need to perform some basic postinstallation tasks to make sure that everything is running well. The very first thing you should do is restart your server. After you've done so, check the Windows 2000 event log for any problems. Each of the Exchange components that make up your new server run as standard Windows

2000 services. You can verify that these services are running in the Services snap-in, available from the Windows 2000 Administrative Tools folder on the Programs menu. Figure 7-12 shows the Services console window. You should see the following services listed:

- Microsoft Exchange System Attendant
- Microsoft Exchange Information Store
- Microsoft Exchange Routing Engine

Depending on the optional components you installed with Exchange 2000 Server, you may also see several other Microsoft Exchange services running.

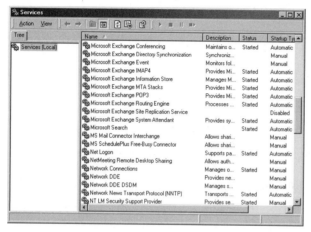

Figure 7-12. *The Services console window.*

Microsoft releases service packs for Exchange 2000 Server, just as it does for Windows 2000. To avoid possible problems later on, it is best to install the latest available Exchange 2000 Server service pack. See "Getting Service Packs" earlier in this chapter for more information. If you are concerned about the latest service pack introducing new problems (and they often do), consider testing the service pack on a nonproduction server first. After you've installed the service pack, you should restart the system again. When the server is back on line, again check the Services console window to ensure that the Exchange Server services are up and running. Your new Exchange server is ready to be configured. *Now* you can pat yourself on the back. And now that you've installed Exchange 2000 Server, you're ready to apply the other software you need to integrate your

Exchange environment, such as third-party backup software, virus-detection utilities, or content filtering applications.

> **Note**   To verify that services are running on a remote Exchange Server, you can use the Connect To Another Computer feature of the Computer Management snap-in. You can also use server monitors to keep watch over services for you in the Exchange System snap-in. You'll learn how to set up these monitors in Chapter 23.

One of the first things you might be tempted to do after successfully installing Exchange 2000 Server is go poking around the system to see what was put where. This is fine, of course, and is a great way to learn more about how Exchange is laid out.

Summary

This chapter described how to install Exchange 2000 Server. It discussed how to prepare your Windows 2000 Server for the installation, including how to verify that the hardware on your Windows 2000 Server meets requirements for installing Exchange 2000 Server in the desired configuration. It then took you step by step through the installation process and described how to check the installation. Now that you have installed Exchange 2000 Server, it is time to learn how to use it. Chapter 8 begins that process with a look at using the Microsoft Management Console and the Exchange System snap-in.

Chapter 8
Managing Exchange 2000 Server

Now that you've installed Microsoft Exchange 2000 Server, you're probably eager to start working with it. You'll want to begin creating users, groups, and other recipients, but first you need to know some basics of managing the Exchange system. For the most part, you will manage Exchange Server with tools called snap-ins, which work within Microsoft Management Console (MMC). The primary tool you will use is the Exchange System snap-in, which provides a graphical environment for configuring the various services and components of an Exchange organization. This chapter takes a look at the general workings of MMC and the Exchange System snap-in. Then, in the next chapter, you will learn how to use the Active Directory Users and Computers snap-in to set up and manage users, contacts, and groups.

Microsoft Management Console

Microsoft Management Console (MMC) provides a common environment for the management of various system and network resources. MMC is actually a framework that hosts modules called snap-ins, which provide the actual tools for managing a resource. For example, you will manage Exchange 2000 Server using a snap-in named Exchange System.

Note The start menu icon that loads the Exchange System snap-in is called *System Manager*. While you can do all of your administration by selecting that icon, this chapter will focus on the Exchange System snap-in itself.

MMC itself does not provide any management functionality. Rather, the MMC environment provides for seamless integration between snap-ins. This allows administrators and other users to create custom management tools from snap-ins created by various vendors. Administrators can save the tools they have created for later use and share them with other administrators and users. This model gives administrators the ability to delegate administrative tasks by creating different tools of varying levels of complexity and giving them to the users who will perform the tasks. For example, you could create a custom console that allowed a user to add users, configure mailboxes, and create public folders in an Exchange organization, but nothing else.

The MMC User Interface

When you first load MMC, you may notice that it looks a lot like Microsoft Windows Explorer. MMC uses a multiple-document interface, meaning that you can load and display multiple console windows in the MMC parent window simultaneously. Figure 8-1 shows the MMC parent window with the Exchange System snap-in loaded. The next few sections discuss the main parts of this window.

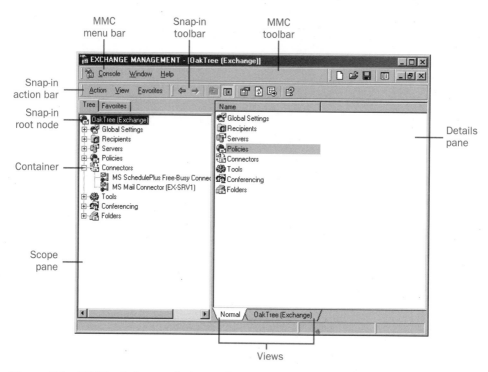

Figure 8-1. *MMC window with the Exchange System snap-in loaded.*

MMC Menu Bar

The main MMC menu bar always holds three menus: Console, Window, and Help. The Window and Help menus are pretty much what you would expect. The Window menu lets you manage console windows if you have more than one window open in MMC. The Help menu lets you access general MMC Help as well as Help for the snap-ins that are currently loaded. The Console menu is where most of the action is. From this menu, you can open and save consoles and even create new ones. You can also add snap-ins to and remove them from open consoles and set general MMC options. Options you can set include the following:

- **Console Title** Specifies the console name as it appears in the MMC title bar.
- **Console Mode** Author mode grants the user full access to all MMC functionality. User mode comes in three flavors: Full Access lets the user access all MMC commands but not add or remove snap-ins or change console properties; Limited Access Multiple Window allows the user to access only the areas of the console tree that were visible when the console was saved and to open new windows; Limited Access Single Window works the same as Limited Access Multiple Window, except that users cannot open new windows.

Other options define whether users can access context menus on taskpads, save changes to the console, and customize views.

MMC Toolbar

The MMC toolbar is a standard Windows toolbar that provides access to commonly used MMC commands. By default, these commands include ones to open and save a console, create a new console, and open a new window.

Snap-In Action Bar

The snap-in action bar is actually a combination menu bar and toolbar; you can separate the two by dragging if you wish. Although the actual menus (Action, View, and Favorites) remain the same no matter what console you have open, the commands on these menus can change a bit according to the open console.

The Action menu typically contains commands that apply to whatever container or object you have selected in your console. These commands duplicate the commands available on the shortcut menu that you see when you right-click an object. The Action menu lets you perform actions such as creating new views and objects in containers, opening an object's property sheet, and accessing tasks.

The View menu lets you control how information is displayed in the details pane of your console. You can, for example, change from icon to list view or customize the columns displayed.

The Favorites menu lets you add items to a list of favorites and organize that list into categories. The Favorites list can include shortcuts to tools, items in the console, or tasks. The Favorites tab in the scope pane lets you view items on your Favorites list.

The toolbar portion of the action bar provides quick access to some of the more commonly used actions associated with selected objects. Many of the icons on the toolbar change depending upon the object selected in the scope pane or details pane of your console.

Scope Pane

The scope pane contains a hierarchy of containers referred to as a console tree. Some containers are displayed as unique icons that graphically represent the type of items they contain. Others are displayed as folders, simply indicating that they hold other objects. Click on the plus sign next to a container to expand it and display the objects inside. Click on the minus sign to collapse the container again.

Details Pane

The details pane changes to show the contents of the container selected in the scope pane. In other words, the details pane shows the results of the currently selected scope. The details pane can display information in a number of different ways, called views. You can access the standard views—large or small icon, list, and detail—through the View menu.

 Note The View menu also lets you customize the columns that are shown in the scope and details panes. In the details pane itself, you can rearrange columns and click a column heading to reorder rows alphabetically or chronologically.

In addition to the standard views, you can also create a taskpad view to show in the details pane. A taskpad view is a dynamic HTML (DHTML) page that presents shortcuts to commands available for a selected item in the scope pane. Each command is represented as a task that consists of an image, a label, a description, and a mechanism for instructing the snap-in to run that command. Users can run the commands by clicking a task. Figure 8-2 shows an example of a taskpad view.

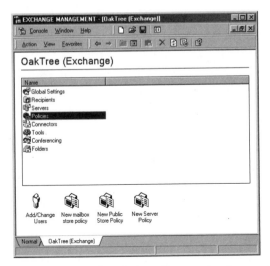

Figure 8-2. *Taskpad views let you develop custom work environments.*

You can use taskpad views to

- Include shortcuts to all of the tasks a specific user may need to perform.
- Group tasks by function or user by creating multiple taskpad views in a console.
- Create simplified lists of tasks. For example, you can add tasks to a taskpad view and then hide the console tree.
- Simplify complex tasks. For example, if a user frequently performs a given task involving several snap-ins and other tools, you can organize in a single location shortcuts to those tasks that run the appropriate property sheets, command lines, dialog boxes, or scripts.

Snap-In Root Node

The snap-in root node is the uppermost node in the snap-in; it is usually named based on the product or task that it is associated with. MMC supports stand-alone and extension snap-ins. A stand-alone snap-in, such as Exchange System, provides management functionality without requiring support from another snap-in. Only one snap-in root node exists for each stand-alone snap-in. An extension snap-in requires a parent snap-in above it in the console tree. Extension snap-ins extend the functionality provided by other snap-ins.

Containers and Objects

Exchange 2000 Server is a great example of an object-based, hierarchical directory environment. All of the little bits and pieces that make up Exchange are objects that interact with one another to some degree. The objects that you see in the scope and details panes can be divided into two types:

- **Containers** Containers can contain both other containers and non-container objects. Container objects can also appear in the details pane. They are used to logically group all of the objects that make up a management environment. An administrator uses the container objects to organize the tree and then to navigate through it.

- **Leaf objects** A leaf object is simply an object that cannot contain other objects. Some common leaf objects with which an administrator works daily include servers and connectors.

You manage all of the objects in an MMC console through the use of property sheets. A *property sheet* is a dialog box that you open by selecting an object and then choosing Properties from the Action menu. It consists of one or more tabs that contain controls for setting a group of related properties. Figure 8-3 shows the property sheet for a server object in the Exchange System snap-in.

Figure 8-3. *Property sheet for a server object.*

How MMC Works

The MMC interface permits snap-ins to integrate within a common management console. This gives all snap-ins a similar look and feel, although they may perform their tasks in different ways. The console itself offers no management functions; it merely acts as a host to the snap-ins. Snap-ins always reside in a console; they do not run by themselves.

Snap-Ins

Each MMC tool is built of a collection of instances of smaller tools called MMC snap-ins. A snap-in is the smallest unit of console extension and represents one unit of management behavior. The snap-in may call on other supporting controls and dynamic link libraries (DLLs) to accomplish its task.

Snap-ins extend MMC by adding and enabling management behavior. They can provide this behavior in a number of ways. For example, a snap-in might add elements to the container tree, or it might extend a particular tool by adding shortcut menu items, toolbars, property sheet tabs, wizards, or Help to an existing snap-in. There are two basic types of snap-ins:

- **Stand-alone snap-ins** provide management functionality even if they are alone in a console with no other supporting snap-ins. They do not rely on any other snap-ins being present. The Exchange System snap-in is an example of a stand-alone snap-in.

- **Extension snap-ins** provide a variety of functionality, but only when used in conjunction with a parent snap-in. Some extend the console namespace, while others simply extend context menus or specific wizards.

Note   Many snap-ins support both modes of operation, offering some stand-alone functionality and also extending the functionality of other snap-ins.

Packages

Snap-ins are usually shipped in groups called packages. For example, the Microsoft Windows 2000 operating system itself includes one or more packages of snap-ins. Additionally, other vendors might ship products composed entirely of packages of snap-ins. Grouping snap-ins into packages provides convenience for downloading and installation. It also permits several snap-ins to share core DLLs so that these DLLs do not have to be placed in every snap-in.

Custom Tools

MMC provides functionality for creating custom management tools. It allows administrators to create, save, and then delegate a customized console of multiple snap-ins tailored for specific tasks. Administrators can assemble these specific snap-ins into a tool (also called a document) that runs in one instance of MMC. For example, you can create a tool that manages many different aspects of the network—Active Directory, replication topology, file sharing, and so on. After assembling a tool, the administrator can save it in an .MSC file and then reload the file later to instantly re-create the tool. The .MSC file can also be e-mailed to another administrator, who can then load the file and use the tool.

Custom Consoles

One of the primary benefits of MMC is its support for customization of tools. You can build custom MMC consoles tailored for specific management tasks and then delegate those consoles to other administrators. These tools can focus on the particular management requirements of various administrator groups. For example, suppose that you have a group of administrators who need to be able to manage the connectors that let your Exchange organization communicate with a legacy Microsoft Mail organization and with a legacy Lotus cc:Mail system. Suppose also that you do not want these administrators to have access to other management functionality in your Exchange organization. You could easily create a customized console that provided only the wanted capabilities. You could also extend any console already used by these administrators to include the additional management capabilities.

More Info   Obviously, there is a lot more to MMC than we can do justice to in a single chapter, especially when the chapter is really about using the Exchange System snap-in. For more information on MMC, start with the Help file available from any console window. If you want more, check out the *Microsoft Windows 2000 Server Resource Kit* (Microsoft Press, 2000).

Using the Exchange System Snap-In

The Exchange System snap-in provides a graphical view of all of the resources and components of an Exchange organization. No matter how many administrative and routing groups or servers you have set up, you can manage them all from a single Exchange System console window. Use this window, and the property sheets of all of the objects in it, to navigate the Exchange organizational hierarchy and perform the various tasks associated with Exchange administration.

You will use both container and leaf objects to administer an Exchange organization. Most objects in the Exchange System console window—both container and leaf—have a property sheet that allows you to configure various parameters for that object and make it act in the way that will best serve the organization's needs. You can open an object's property sheet by selecting the object and choosing Properties from the Action menu. You can also right-click an object and choose Properties from its shortcut menu. You use property sheets to both configure and administer Exchange Server.

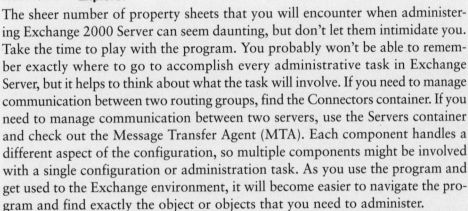

Real World Explore!
The sheer number of property sheets that you will encounter when administering Exchange 2000 Server can seem daunting, but don't let them intimidate you. Take the time to play with the program. You probably won't be able to remember exactly where to go to accomplish every administrative task in Exchange Server, but it helps to think about what the task will involve. If you need to manage communication between two routing groups, find the Connectors container. If you need to manage communication between two servers, use the Servers container and check out the Message Transfer Agent (MTA). Each component handles a different aspect of the configuration, so multiple components might be involved with a single configuration or administration task. As you use the program and get used to the Exchange environment, it will become easier to navigate the program and find exactly the object or objects that you need to administer.

Learning the contents and layout of the various property sheets in the Exchange System snap-in is a key part of learning how Exchange Server works. Once you know how to organize tasks that match the way Exchange Server is structured, you will find that your administrative tasks flow more easily.

To administer an Exchange environment with the Exchange System snap-in, you must be logged on to Windows 2000 under a domain user account that has administrative privileges for Exchange Server. Until you specifically grant other user accounts privileges to administer Exchange Server, the only accounts with permission to do so are the account that you were logged on with when you installed Exchange 2000 Server and the Exchange service account. For more information on how to assign permissions within Exchange Server, see Chapter 21.

Examining the Exchange Hierarchy

The top of the hierarchy in the scope pane of the Exchange System snap-in is the snap-in root node that represents the Exchange organization. It has a small globe icon with an envelope in front of it, as shown in Figure 8-4. In this example, the snap-in root node is named OakTree (Exchange). All of the Exchange containers are held within this node. There are eight primary containers directly within the snap-in root node. The sections that follow describe each of these containers.

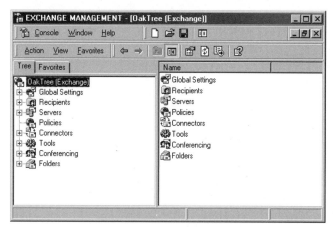

Figure 8-4. *The Exchange hierarchy.*

Note What you see in the main Exchange System scope pane depends upon whether you have configured multiple administrative groups and whether you have configured the Exchange System snap-in to display administrative groups. If you have only one administrative group and have not changed the default settings, you will see the eight containers discussed here. If you have multiple administrative groups and you have configured the Exchange System snap-in to display those groups, you will not see the Servers, Policies, Connectors, Conferencing, and Folders containers in the main display. Instead, you will see a container named Administrative Groups that in turn holds a container for each administrative group defined in your organization. Each of those administrative group containers will hold the five missing containers, since each of those items can be configured at the level of the administrative group. You will learn a lot more about working with administrative groups in Chapter 12.

Global Settings Container

The Global Settings container holds objects governing settings that apply to your entire organization. Inside this container, you will find two objects. The first, Internet Message Formats, defines the formatting for SMTP messages sent over the Internet. Chapter 16 discusses the use of this object in detail.

The second object in the Global Settings container, Message Delivery, is used to configure message defaults for your organization. You can open the property sheet for this object by selecting the object and choosing Properties from the Action menu. The Defaults tab, shown in Figure 8-5, lets you set message limit defaults for your organization. You can set the maximum size, in kilobytes, for both incoming and outgoing messages and the maximum number of recipients that can exist on a server.

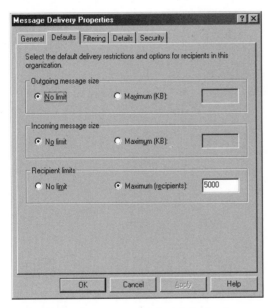

Figure 8-5. *Setting messaging defaults for your organization.*

The Filtering tab, shown in Figure 8-6, lets you create filters for handling messages from particular SMTP addresses. For each SMTP address that you enter here, you can specify whether messages from that address should be deleted or dropped into a custom folder. This is a great way to block unwanted messages (spam) from reaching your recipients or to automatically group all messages from a recipient into a single location.

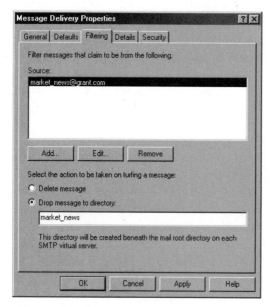

Figure 8-6. *Setting messaging filters.*

Recipients Container

The Recipients container is used to manage server settings that apply to recipients in your organization. You can define recipient policies, manage address lists, and even modify address templates. All of these actions are covered in Chapter 9.

Servers Container

The configuration objects held within the Servers container will depend upon how you have set up your organization. If your organization has only one administrative group, your Servers container holds one container for each of the servers in your organization. If your organization has more than one administrative group, you will find the containers for the individual servers inside those administrative group containers.

Regardless of how your organization is configured, the server containers are where you will perform a good bit of your Exchange administration. Within each server container, you will find configuration objects for managing the protocols, connectors, and storage groups configured on the server. The next several chapters of this book cover the various aspects of server management in detail and from a few different perspectives. In particular, you will learn to manage server components in Chapters 11, 12, and 13.

Policies Container

The Policies container holds objects that define various system policies that may be implemented for your organization. If you have only one administrative group, the Policies container appears as a primary container under the organization. If you have multiple administrative groups, a Policies container will appear for each group inside the group container.

Policies are a new feature in Exchange 2000 Server, designed to enable flexible administration of large numbers of Exchange objects. A policy is a collection of configuration settings applied to one or more Exchange 2000 Server objects of the same type. An administrator can define a policy that controls the configuration settings across many servers, mailboxes, or public folders. Once a policy has been defined and implemented, you can change the configuration of all of the objects the policy covers by editing the policy and applying the changes.

A policy that controls configuration settings can span multiple servers. Once this type of policy is defined and implemented, you can change the configuration of multiple servers by editing the policy and reapplying it. You can use policies in the following ways:

- Create a new object and add it to an existing policy.
- Add an existing object to an existing policy.
- Create a new policy and add it to an existing object.

Note There are actually two types of policies: system and recipient. System policies are created and applied to a server, a mailbox store, or a public store. These are the policies that appear in the Policies container in MMC. Recipient policies are applied to mail-enabled Exchange objects (any object with at least one e-mail address) to generate e-mail addresses. These policies appear in MMC as the Recipient Policies container inside the Recipients container. Chapter 9 discusses recipient policies.

Connectors Container

The Connectors container holds configuration items for each of the connectors available within your organization. If you have only one administrative group, the Connectors container appears as a primary container under the organization. If you have multiple administrative groups, a Connectors container will appear for each group inside the group container.

The objects within the Connectors container represent both connectors between routing groups in your organization and connectors to foreign messaging systems. Chapter 13 covers connectors between routing groups, and Chapter 15 describes connectors to foreign messaging systems.

Tools Container

The Tools container holds objects that help you manage your Exchange organization. You'll find three containers within the Tools container. The Site Replication Service container lets you configure replication with existing Exchange 5.5 sites, using the Active Directory Connector. This topic is covered in Chapter 14.

The Message Tracking Center object is actually a shortcut for opening the Message Tracking Center, which lets you track specific messages in your organization. The Monitors container holds objects that let you monitor the status of servers and connections in your organization. Both of these objects are covered in Chapter 23.

Folders Container

The last container in the hierarchy is Folders. The Folders container holds the public folders hierarchy and the folders' properties, but not their contents. It also contains the system folders, a list of folders that Exchange users do not see. The system folders hold the Offline Address Book and other system configuration objects. If you have only one administrative group, the Folders container appears as a primary container under the organization. If you have multiple administrative groups, a Folders container will appear for each group inside the group container. You will learn more about configuring folders in Chapter 10.

Customizing an Exchange System Console

The Exchange System snap-in is actually a saved console file that connects to a Windows 2000 domain controller to get configuration information regarding your Exchange organization. In certain instances, however, you may want to direct the snap-ins to a particular domain or domain controller. For example, you might want to connect to a specific domain in a Windows 2000 forest or to different domain controllers in different Windows 2000 forests to manage different companies or divisions. You might also want to create custom consoles for novice administrators or administrators to whom you want to give only limited access to Exchange resources. Fortunately, MMC makes all of this pretty easy.

To create a custom console or redirect an Exchange console to another domain controller, the first thing you need to do is to open MMC directly. The easiest way to do this is with the Run command on the Start menu. Enter *MMC* at the prompt. A blank MMC window opens, as shown in Figure 8-7. Next, choose Add/Remove Snap-In from the Console menu. This opens the dialog box shown in Figure 8-8. Here you can add any number of snap-ins to customize your console.

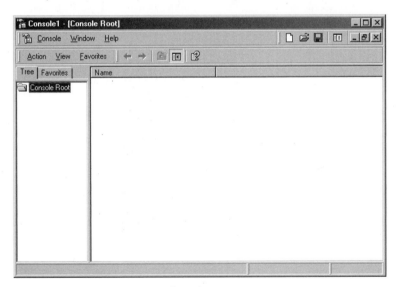

Figure 8-7. *Opening MMC directly.*

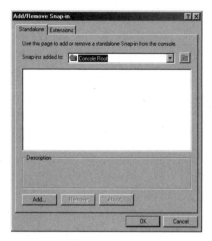

Figure 8-8. *Adding stand-alone snap-ins to a console.*

Real World **Connection Requirements**

The Exchange System snap-in interoperates with Exchange 2000 Server using local procedure calls (LPCs) or remote procedure calls (RPCs). A *procedure call* is an application programming interface (API) that connects to another program and runs using various data interface points. LPCs run on the same machine, so when you run the Exchange System snap-in on the Exchange server to which you are connected, you have invoked LPCs. RPCs run as a session-layer API between two different networked computers. RPCs are an open standard and can run over multiple protocols, such as NetBEUI, SPX, Banyan Vines, and TCP/IP. When you run the Exchange System snap-in on a computer that is different from the Exchange server to which you are connected, you have invoked RPCs. This means that to connect to a server, the Exchange System snap-in must be installed on the Exchange server itself or must be connected to an Exchange server via a network connection that supports RPCs.

Now let's look at creating a console that duplicates the functionality of the System Manager icon found on the Start menu, but allows you to redirect the connection to another domain controller. Click the Add button to open another dialog box that lists the stand-alone snap-ins available on your system. This dialog box is shown in Figure 8-9.

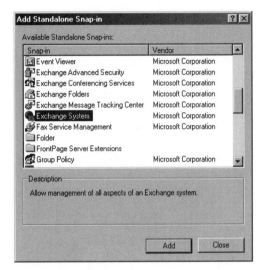

Figure 8-9. *Choosing from the available snap-ins.*

From the list of available snap-ins, choose Exchange System, and then click Add. The Change Domain Controller dialog box, shown in Figure 8-10, opens. In the list of domain controllers, choose the controller to which you want to direct the connection. You can also choose to direct the connection to any writable domain controller, in which case the connection will be made to the first domain controller to respond whenever you open the new console. When you are satisfied with your selection, click OK. Once you exit the remaining dialog boxes, you are taken back to the console window and can start using your new console. Remember to save it if it is a console you will want to use in the future.

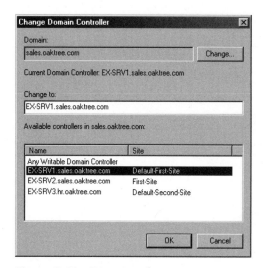

Figure 8-10. *Directing the connection to another domain controller.*

Instead of choosing the full Exchange System snap-in from the list in the Add Standalone Snap-In dialog box (refer back to Figure 8-9), you can choose one or more snap-ins that serve a more limited purpose:

- **Exchange Advanced Security**   creates a console with only the tools for managing the Key Management Service (KMS) . You can find details on using the KMS in Chapter 21.

- **Exchange Conference Management Service**   creates a console displaying only the tools for managing Exchange 2000 Server's online collaboration features, including chat and IM. You can find details on using these features in Chapters 18 and 19.

- **Exchange Folders**   creates a console with only the tools for managing public folders. You can find more on this in Chapter 10.

- **Exchange Message Tracking Center**   creates a console displaying only the message tracking features. You'll learn more about using this tool in Chapter 23.

Summary

This chapter provided a basic introduction to the tools used to administer an Exchange 2000 Server organization. The primary tool that you will use to administer Microsoft Exchange 2000 Server is the Exchange System snap-in for the Microsoft Management Console, which provides a graphical environment for configuring the various services and components of an Exchange organization. Within this snap-in, you work primarily with the property sheets of objects. Chapter 9 begins a series of chapters that look at specific aspects of Exchange administration. In it, you will learn how to create and manage the basic Exchange recipients.

Chapter 9
Creating and Managing Recipients

Sending and receiving information is the foundation of messaging, of groupware, and, of course, of Microsoft Exchange 2000 Server. In this chapter, we start looking at the message transfer process within an Exchange system. Exchange 2000 Server is based on a multitude of messaging components, but with some analysis, it becomes apparent how these components interact to create an enterprise-wide messaging system.

Recipients are objects in the Microsoft Windows 2000 Active Directory directory service that reference resources that can receive messages through interaction with Exchange 2000 Server. Such a resource might be a mailbox in the mailbox store where one of your users gets mail, a public folder where information is shared among many users, or even a newsgroup on the Internet.

No matter where a resource resides, however, a recipient object for that resource is always created within Active Directory on your network. One of your main tasks as an administrator is to create and maintain these recipient objects. Therefore, in addition to discussing mailboxes and message transfer, this chapter explains how to create and manage various types of messaging recipients; it also discusses tools that allow you to search for and organize recipients.

Understanding Recipient Types

It is tempting to think of a recipient as a mailbox or simply as an object that can receive a message, and as you administer your organization, it may be convenient to take that view. But it is important to understand the ways in which the underlying architecture affects how you work with recipients in Exchange Server.

In Exchange Server, a recipient object does not receive messages. Instead, it is a reference to a resource that can receive messages. This is a subtle but important distinction. Recipient objects are contained in and maintained by Active Directory.

The resources that those objects reference could be anywhere. One resource might be a mailbox for a user in your organization. A mailbox resource would be contained in the mailbox store of a particular Exchange server and maintained by its Information Store service. Another resource might be a user on the Internet. In this case, the recipient object would contain a reference to that resource, along with rules governing the transfer of messages. Four types of recipient objects are available in Exchange:

- **User** A user in Windows 2000 is any individual with logon privileges on the network. With regard to Exchange Server, each user in Active Directory can be mailbox enabled, mail enabled, or neither. A *mailbox-enabled* user has an associated mailbox on an Exchange server. Each user mailbox is a private storage area that allows an individual user to send, receive, and store messages. A *mail-enabled* user is one that has an e-mail address and can receive, but not send, messages.

- **Contact** A contact is essentially a pointer to a mailbox in an external messaging system, most likely used by a person outside the organization. This type of recipient points both to an address to be used to deliver messages sent to that person and to the properties that govern how those messages are delivered. Contacts are most often used for connecting your organization to foreign messaging systems, such as Microsoft Mail, Lotus cc:Mail, or the Internet. An administrator creates contacts so that often-used e-mail addresses are available in the Global Address List as real names. This makes it easier to send mail because users do not need to guess at cryptic e-mail addresses.

- **Group** A group in Windows 2000 is an object to which you can assign certain permissions and rights. Users who are placed in a group are automatically given the permissions and rights of the group. Exchange 2000 Server uses the concept of mail-enabled groups to form distribution lists. Messages sent to a group are redirected and sent to each member of that group. Groups can contain any combination of the other types of recipients, including other groups. These groups allow users to send messages to multiple recipients without having to address each recipient individually. A typical group is the one named Everyone. All Exchange recipients are made members of the Everyone group. When a public announcement is made, the sender of the announcement simply selects the Everyone group and is not forced to select every user's mailbox from the Global Address List.

- **Public folder**   A public folder is a public storage area, typically open to all users in an organization. Users can post new messages or reply to existing messages in a public folder, creating an ongoing forum for discussion of topics. Public folders can also be used to store and provide access to just about any type of document. The concept of a public folder as a recipient is difficult to grasp because the repository for information is shared. One way that a public folder is used as a recipient is when it is configured for a Network News Transfer Protocol (NNTP) news feed. Under this arrangement, the information from the newsgroup is sent to the public folder recipient and can then be viewed by Exchange users in the organization.

Although a public folder is a type of recipient, it performs many more functions than just transferring or receiving messages. For that reason, this chapter focuses on the other recipient types: users, contacts, and groups. Chapter 10 is devoted to a full review of the features, functions, and administration requirements of public folders.

Users

Exchange 2000 Server is more tightly integrated with Windows than any previous version. In fact, the tool used in Windows 2000 Server to create user accounts, Active Directory Users and Computers, is also the tool used to create and manage mailboxes for your users. Exchange-related configuration details show up as extra tabs on the user's property sheet. This means that Exchange administrators and Windows 2000 administrators need to work together now more than ever. Although many Exchange administrators hate the idea of giving up control of mailbox administration, it is usually the best course of action. Because all of the user-related functions of mailboxes can now be managed from within Active Directory Users and Computers, it makes sense to let one accounts administrator handle all user-related tasks from a single location. There are two possible mail configurations for users: the mailbox-enabled user and the mail-enabled user. Each of these configurations is detailed in the sections that follow.

Mailbox-Enabled Users

Mailboxes—the mainstay of any messaging system—are private, server-based storage areas in which user e-mail is kept. Every user in your organization must have access to a mailbox to send and receive messages. Most enterprises require that all associates be able to participate in sending and receiving e-mail because it is one of their primary methods of communication. In Exchange 2000 Server, a user with a mailbox is referred to as a mailbox-enabled user. Mailbox-enabled users can send and receive messages, as well as store messages on an Exchange server. One of your principal tasks as an administrator is to create and configure mailboxes for users.

Creating a New Mailbox-Enabled User

When Exchange 2000 Server is installed, several extensions for the Active Directory Users and Computers snap-in are installed as well. As a result, whenever you create a new user, you are automatically given the chance to create a mailbox for that user. To create a new user in Active Directory Users and Computers, make sure the Users container is selected, and then choose New User from the Action menu. This starts the New User Wizard, the first two screens of which are shown in Figure 9-1.

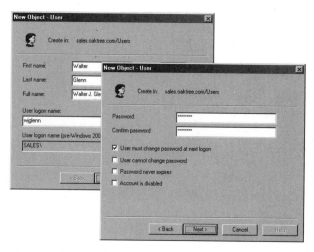

Figure 9-1. *Creating a new user account with Active Directory Users and Computers.*

If you have worked with Windows 2000, you are probably familiar with the process of creating and naming a new user and giving that user a password. This is what you do in the first two screens of the wizard. However, Exchange adds a third screen, titled Create Exchange Mailbox, which appears after you have entered the typical user information (Figure 9-2). Here you can choose whether to create a mailbox, and you can also enter an alias (an alternate means of addressing a user that is covered later in this section) and indicate the Exchange server and the storage group on that server where the new user's mailbox should be created. Once you are done, click Next to display a summary screen for the new user. When you click Finish on this screen, the new user and mailbox are created.

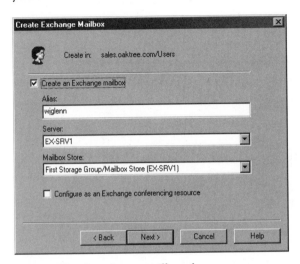

Figure 9-2. *Creating a mailbox for your new user.*

Creating a mailbox for an existing user is just as easy as creating one for a new user. Simply select any existing user in the Users folder in Active Directory Users and Computers, and choose Add Mailbox from the Action menu. This command opens the Create Exchange Mailbox screen of the wizard, allowing you to add and configure the mailbox for the user.

Configuring Mailbox Properties

No matter which method you use to create mailboxes, you configure them in the same way—with the user object's property sheet. To do so, select any user object in Active Directory Users and Computers, and then choose Properties from the Action menu. The property sheet for a Windows 2000 user has quite a few tabs. The next several sections cover the tabs that pertain to Exchange mailbox configuration.

Note Several of the tabs that Exchange Server adds to the user object's property sheet hold advanced properties and are therefore not displayed by default when you open a user's property sheet. To see these tabs, choose Advanced Features from the View menu of Active Directory Users and Computers before you open a property sheet.

General Tab

The General tab, shown in Figure 9-3, is where you configure basic user information. The first name, middle initial, and last name that you enter here are used to generate a display name, which is the name of the recipient as it appears in the Active Directory Users and Computers console. The rest of the information on this tab further identifies the recipient. It is all available to users when they browse the Global Address List.

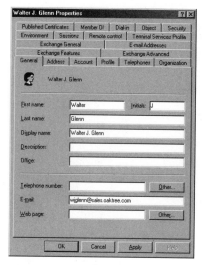

Figure 9-3. *Assigning user information on the General tab.*

Organization Tab

The Organization tab, shown in Figure 9-4, is used to configure additional information about the user's position in the company. You can use this tab to specify a user's manager and a list of people who report directly to the user. Click the Change button to display a list of recipients in the organization. All of the information configured on this tab is available in the Global Address List.

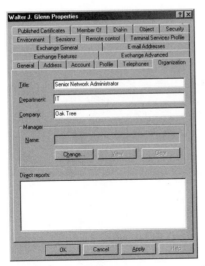

Figure 9-4. *Describing a user's position in the organization by using the Organization tab.*

Exchange General Tab

On the Exchange General tab, shown in Figure 9-5, you can configure general properties governing the Exchange mailbox associated with the user. The mailbox store that the user belongs to is displayed here but cannot be changed. The alias is an alternate means of addressing a user and is used by foreign messaging systems that cannot handle a full display name.

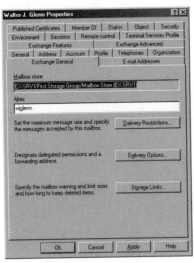

Figure 9-5. *Configuring general mailbox-related properties.*

You will also find three buttons on this tab that lead to more important settings. Click the Delivery Restrictions button to open the dialog box shown in Figure 9-6. You can set limits on the size of messages that can be transferred out of or into a particular mailbox. If an incoming or outgoing message exceeds its respective limit, it is not sent or received, and the sender of the message receives a nondelivery report. The Message Restrictions area allows you to restrict the messages coming into the selected mailbox. The default is to accept messages from everyone. You can specify that messages be accepted only from designated senders or that messages be accepted from everyone except a list of specific users. Choose the option you want, and click Add to select from recipients listed in the Active Directory.

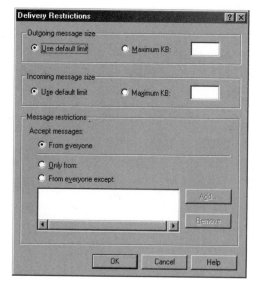

Figure 9-6. *Setting restrictions on a mailbox.*

Note Setting general limits for an entire site or server at the same time is much more efficient than setting them for each individual user. Setting limits for a particular mailbox is one way of dealing with users who need to send large messages or who simply let messages accumulate.

Click the Delivery Options button on the Exchange General tab to open the dialog box shown in Figure 9-7. This dialog box allows you to give Exchange users other than the primary user *delegate access* to the mailbox. This type of delegate access is called Send On Behalf Of permission. By clicking the Add button, you can grant this permission to any recipient in Active Directory. Users included in this list can send messages that will appear as though they came from the selected mailbox. Any messages sent include the names of both the primary mailbox user and the user who actually sent the message. This permission might be used by an assistant who needs to send a message from a manager who is out of the office.

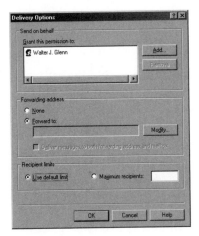

Figure 9-7. *Setting delivery options for a mailbox.*

Note   Send On Behalf Of permission can also be helpful in troubleshooting. If you assign this permission to yourself, as administrator, you can send test messages from any recipient in the organization. This practice can be a great way to test connections from remote servers. We recommend that you use test mailboxes created for this purpose and not actual user mailboxes. Many users would consider this type of extended access to their e-mail an intrusion.

You can also use the Delivery Options dialog box to assign a forwarding address for a mailbox. Any messages sent to the mailbox are routed to the mailbox of the designated alternate recipient. You can also specify that messages be sent both to the primary mailbox and to the alternate recipient. Exchange Server will deliver a separate reference to the message to each mailbox, so deleting the message from one mailbox does not cause it to be deleted from another. Finally, you can specify the maximum number of recipients to which a user can send a single message. By default, there is no limit.

Click the Storage Limits button on the Exchange General tab to open the dialog box shown in Figure 9-8. This dialog box lets you set parameters for storage limits and deleted item retention time. Often, users send and save huge attachments or are simply negligent about cleaning out their mailboxes. Either of these situations can cause a great deal of disk space to be consumed on your server. Fortunately, administrators can set any of three storage limits on a mailbox:

- **Issue Warning At** Specifies the mailbox size, in kilobytes, at which a warning is issued to the user to clean out the mailbox.

- **Prohibit Send At** Specifies the mailbox size, in kilobytes, at which the user is prohibited from sending any new mail. This prohibition ends as soon as the user clears enough space to fall back under the limit.

- **Prohibit Send And Receive At** Specifies the mailbox size, in kilobytes, at which the user is prohibited from sending, receiving, or even editing any mail. All the user can do is delete messages. This prohibition ends as soon as the user clears enough space to fall back under the limit. To do this, a user must delete items from his or her mailbox and then empty the Deleted Items folder. When a user sends a message to a recipient who is prohibited from receiving any new messages, a nondelivery report is generated and returned to the sending user. Prohibiting the sending and receiving of mail is a pretty strong measure for an administrator to take. We recommend that you implement this solution only if you experience continued problems that you cannot otherwise resolve.

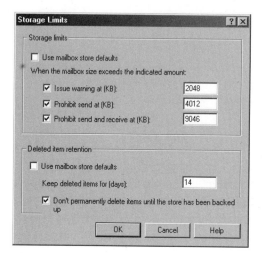

Figure 9-8. *Setting storage options for a mailbox.*

Exchange 2000 Server also includes a feature that gives users a certain amount of time to recover items that have been deleted from their Deleted Items folder. When a user deletes a message using a client application such as Microsoft Outlook, that message is placed in the user's Deleted Items folder. Only when the user deletes the item from the Deleted Items folder is it actually removed from the user's personal folders. However, the deleted item is still not actually deleted from the mailbox store. Instead, it is marked as hidden and is kept for a specified amount of time. During that period, the user can recover the item with the client application. Note that the ability to recover deleted items requires Outlook 8.03 or later.

The Deleted Item Retention area of the Storage Limits dialog box specifies the retention time for deleted items. You can either use the default value that is configured for the entire mailbox store or override it with a different value for the selected mailbox. If you choose to override the value, you can also specify that deleted messages not be permanently removed until the mailbox store has been backed up.

E-Mail Addresses Tab

The E-Mail Addresses tab, shown in Figure 9-9, lets you configure how the mailbox is addressed from different types of messaging systems. When you create a mailbox, four types of addresses are configured by default: cc:Mail, Microsoft Mail, SMTP, and X.400. You can add, remove, or edit addresses as you please. A mailbox can have multiple addresses for a single type. For example, a mailbox for the Web site administrator Jane Doe may have two SMTP addresses: jdoe@company.com and webmaster@company.com. Mail addressed to these two addresses will be placed in the same mailbox.

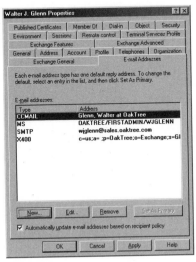

Figure 9-9. *Viewing e-mail addresses for a mailbox.*

Note You can change addresses manually for each mailbox. You can also change the addressing configuration of the address spaces at the site, using the Site Addressing object, and have those changes flow down to individual mailboxes.

Exchange Features Tab

The Exchange Features tab, shown in Figure 9-10, lets you enable and disable certain collaboration features of Exchange 2000 Server for an individual mailbox, including instant messaging (IM).

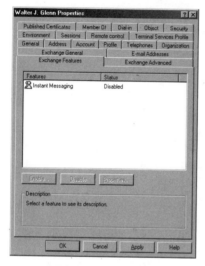

Figure 9-10. *Viewing Exchange features for a mailbox.*

Exchange Advanced Tab

The Exchange Advanced tab, shown in Figure 9-11, lets you configure a number of miscellaneous features that the Exchange designers decided were advanced for one reason or another.

The simple display name is an alternate name for the mailbox. It appears when the full display name cannot be shown for some reason. This situation often occurs when multiple language versions of the Exchange System snap-in are used on the same network.

By default, all recipients except public folders are visible to users via the Global Address List. You can select the Hide From Exchange Address Lists option to hide the mailbox from that list or from other lists created in the Exchange System snap-in. The mailbox will still be able to receive mail; it simply will not be included in address lists.

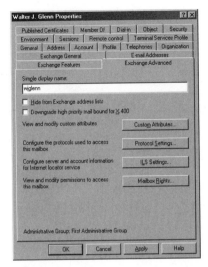

Figure 9-11. *Setting advanced Exchange mailbox features.*

If you select the Downgrade High Priority Mail Bound For X.400 option, the current mailbox cannot send high-priority messages to X.400 systems. If the user sends a high-priority message, Exchange Server will downgrade it to normal priority.

In addition to these settings, you'll also find four buttons on the Exchange Advanced tab that lead to separate dialog boxes with more configuration options. These buttons are covered in the sections that follow.

Custom Attributes Button   Clicking the Custom Attributes button displays the Exchange Custom Attributes dialog box, shown in Figure 9-12. This dialog box lets you enter information about a mailbox in 15 custom fields. These fields can be used for any information you need to include that isn't available on the other tabs. All of these fields are available to users in the Global Address List. By default, these fields are labeled extensionAttribute1 through extensionAttribute15, but you can customize their names to suit your needs. Just select a field and click Edit to enter a new value.

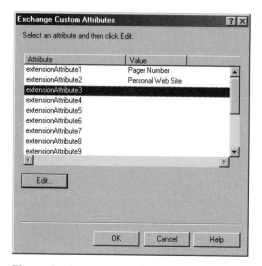

Figure 9-12. *Entering additional recipient information by using custom attribute fields.*

Protocol Settings Button Click the Protocol Settings button to display the Protocols dialog box, shown in Figure 9-13. This dialog box allows you to enable or disable individual Internet protocols for the selected mailbox. The protocols that you can configure (if installed) include HTTP (Web), IMAP4 (mail), NNTP (news), and POP3 (mail). To check the settings for each, select the protocol and click the Settings button. Here you can make simple changes, such as enabling protocol for the mailbox, as well as more complex changes, such as modifying other parameters for that protocol. You will learn more about Internet protocols and how to configure them for sites, servers, and mailboxes in Chapter 17.

ILS Settings Button Click the ILS Settings button to display the ILS Settings dialog box. If you use Microsoft NetMeeting in your organization, this dialog box is for you. NetMeeting allows users to collaborate on documents by using audio, video, and a shared whiteboard. Use the ILS Settings dialog box to set up your Internet Locator Service (ILS) by configuring the ILS Server and Account fields. Once you've done so, users can contact and set up meetings with the user of this mailbox.

More Info For more information on using NetMeeting in your organization, see *Official Microsoft NetMeeting Book* by Bob Summers (Microsoft Press, 1998).

Mailbox Rights Button The Permissions dialog box, shown in Figure 9-14, appears when you click the Mailbox Rights button. It lets you assign various access rights to a mailbox. By default, the Exchange Admins group, the Exchange Servers group, and the mailbox's user are given rights to the mailbox. You can add any user in Active Directory to this list by clicking the Add button.

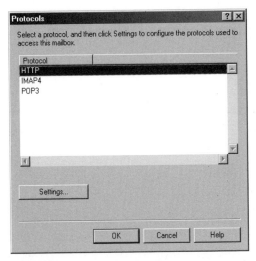

Figure 9-13. *Configuring Internet protocols for a mailbox.*

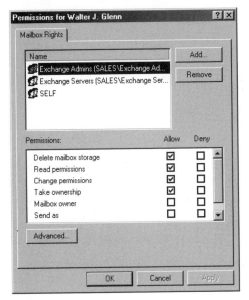

Figure 9-14. *Configuring rights on a mailbox.*

You modify the particular rights of any user in the list by selecting the user and selecting or clearing the Allow and Deny check boxes beside the individual mailbox rights. Here are the rights you can assign:

- **Delete Mailbox Storage** Allows a user to delete the actual mailbox from the information store. This right is given only to administrators by default.

- **Read Permissions** Lets the user read mail in the mailbox. You could use this right alone to allow a user to read another user's mail but not to send, change, or delete messages in the mailbox.

- **Change Permissions** Allows a user to delete or modify items in the primary user's mailbox.

- **Take Ownership** Allows a user to become the owner of a mailbox. By default, only administrators are given this permission.

- **Mailbox Owner** Allows a user to access a mailbox and to read and delete messages. It also allows the user to send messages using the mailbox.

- **Send As** Lets a user send messages as though that user were the owner of the mailbox. This is another type of delegate access that can be assigned only by an administrator. It differs from the Send On Behalf Of type of delegate access in that the sender's real identity is not sent along with the message.

- **Primary Mailbox Owner** Differs from the Mailbox Owner right in that only one user can be the primary mailbox owner.

Member Of Tab

The Member Of tab of a user's property sheet, shown in Figure 9-15, lists the groups to which the user currently belongs. You can add a group by clicking the Add button and then making a choice from the available lists. Not only can you manage a group from a user's property sheet, but you can also manage a group from the group's property sheet. For more information, see "Groups" later in this chapter.

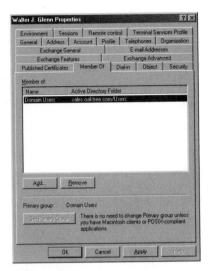

Figure 9-15. *Viewing the groups to which a mailbox belongs.*

Mail-Enabled Users

A mail-enabled user is simply a user that has an e-mail address but does not have a mailbox on an Exchange server. This means that the user can receive e-mail through its custom address but cannot send mail using the Exchange system. You cannot enable mail for a user while creating the user. The only way to create a mail-enabled user is to first create a new user that is not mailbox enabled and then to enable mail for that user. To enable mail for an existing user, select that user in Active Directory Users and Computers and choose Enable Exchange Mail from the Action menu. This opens the dialog box shown in Figure 9-16. Simply enter an e-mail alias and click Modify to choose the type of e-mail address you want to enter for the user. You can create many popular types of addresses, such as SMTP, Microsoft Mail, and Lotus cc:Mail, or you can even create a custom address. Once you enable mail for a user, you can configure the mail settings just as you would for a mailbox-enabled user.

Figure 9-16. *Enabling mail for a user without giving the user a mailbox.*

Contacts

Contacts are objects that serve as pointers to resources outside an Exchange organization. You can think of a contact as an alias that contains an address for that outside resource and rules for handling the transmission of messages. Whenever a user sends a message to a contact, Exchange Server forwards the message to the appropriate foreign messaging system. Contacts have many of the same attributes as mailboxes and can be viewed in the Global Address List.

Creating a Contact

To create a new contact, choose New Contact from the Action menu of Active Directory Users and Computers. This command opens the New Object - Contact dialog box (Figure 9-17). Enter a full name and a display name, much as you would for a typical user.

When you click Next, the dialog box shown in Figure 9-18 opens. Enter a display name in the Alias field, click Modify, and select the type of foreign address you want to create. If this seems like the same process you used to create a mail-enabled user previously, you are right. In fact, a contact is like a mail-enabled user that does not have the right to log on to the network. When you're done, click Next to display a summary page. Click Finish on the summary page to create the new contact.

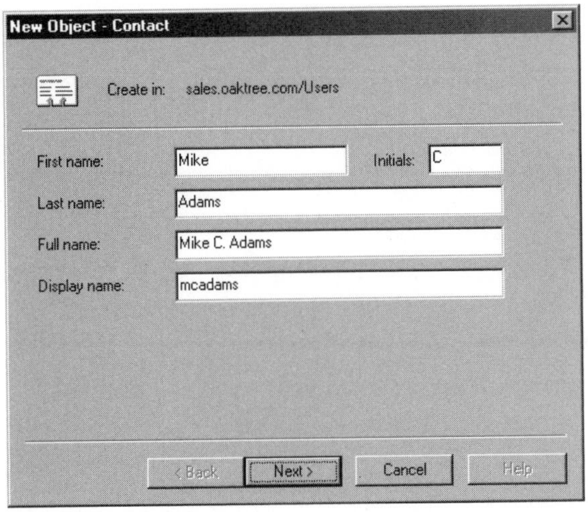

Figure 9-17. *Creating a new contact.*

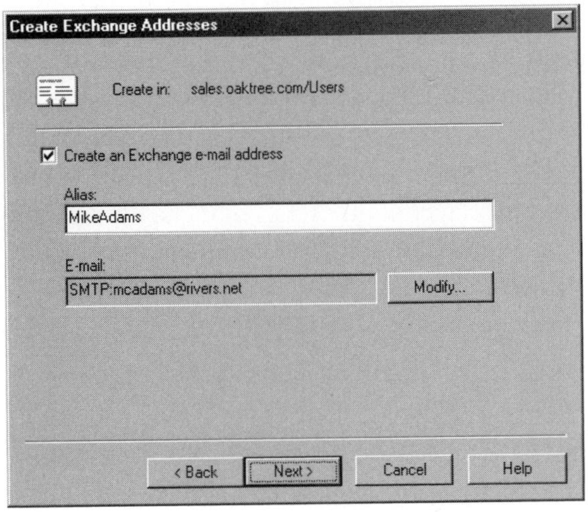

Figure 9-18. *Defining the contact's e-mail address.*

Configuring a Contact

Like all other objects in Active Directory, contacts are configured by means of a property sheet. Most of the tabs for contacts are identical to those for mailbox-enabled users, although contacts have noticeably fewer of them. You will, of course, encounter a number of differences:

- On the Exchange General tab of a contact's property sheet, you can change the alias and address. You can also set delivery restrictions. You cannot, however, set storage limits or delivery options, since contacts do not have storage on the Exchange server.

- On the Exchange Advanced tab, you cannot configure protocol settings or mailbox rights, since no mailbox is associated with the contact.

Groups

In Windows 2000, a *group* is a container of sorts that can hold users and other groups. You can assign permissions to a group that are inherited by all of the objects in that group. This makes the group a valuable Windows 2000 security construct. Exchange 2000 Server also uses groups for another purpose. A group can be mail enabled and then populated with other mail- or mailbox-enabled recipients to make a distribution list, a term you may be familiar with from earlier versions of Exchange Server. A group can contain users, contacts, public folders, and even other groups. When you send a message to a mail-enabled group, the message is sent to each member of the list individually. Groups are visible in the Global Address List.

Creating a Group

Creating a new mail-enabled group is easy. Choose New Group from the Action menu of Active Directory Users and Computers. This command starts the New Group Wizard, as shown in Figure 9-19. Enter a group name that describes the members the group will contain. You must also choose a group scope and a group type. The group scope defines the level at which the group will be available in Active Directory. The group type defines whether the group is for security or distribution purposes. A security group can be mail enabled and used for distribution purposes, but a distribution group cannot be used for security purposes. When you're done, click Next.

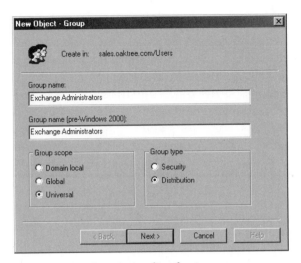

Figure 9-19. *Creating a distribution group.*

On the next screen of the New Group Wizard, you can specify whether a mail address should be created for the new group, and you can enter an alias name. If you are creating a group to be used as a distribution list, you must create an e-mail address. Once you click Finish in this screen, the new group is created and you are ready to add members. This process is described in the next section, along with other ways of configuring groups.

Configuring a Group

You configure a group in the same way that you configure other recipients—with a property sheet. Many of the tabs are identical to those of the same name for user objects; refer to the "Users" section earlier in this chapter for details on those tabs. Some of the tabs found on a user's property sheet simply don't exist for a group. This section covers the three Exchange-related tabs that do differ for a group.

Members Tab

The Members tab lists every member of the group. Use the Add button to access the Active Directory list, from which you can add new members to the group. You can use the Remove button to remove selected members.

Managed By Tab

The Managed By tab, shown in Figure 9-20, lets you assign an owner to the group. The owner manages the group's membership. By default, the administrator who creates the group is the owner, but you can designate as owner any user, group, or contact in the Global Address List. If you give ownership to another user, that user can use an Exchange client or Outlook to modify the group's membership and does not need access to Active Directory Users and Computers. You can relieve yourself of a great deal of work by specifying owners for the groups you create. As groups grow larger, they can consume a considerable amount of management time.

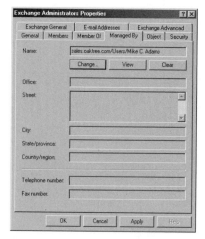

Figure 9-20. *Specifying a group owner.*

Exchange Advanced Tab

The Exchange Advanced tab, shown in Figure 9-21, holds several configuration options that may be familiar to you, such as a simple display name and the Custom Attributes button. You can also, however, configure several options that are specific to distribution lists:

- **Expansion Server**   Whenever a message is sent to a group, the group must be expanded so that the message can be sent to each member of the group. The Message Transfer Agent (MTA) service of a single Exchange server performs this expansion. The default choice is Any Server In Site. This setting means that the home server of the user sending the message always expands the group. You can also designate a specific server to handle expanding the group, which is a good choice if you have a large group. In this case, expansion could consume a large amount of server resources, which can compromise performance for busy servers.

- **Hide Group From Exchange Address Lists**   If you select this option, the group is not visible in the Global Address List.

- **Send Out-Of-Office Messages To Originator**   If you select this option, users can configure Exchange clients to reply automatically to any messages received while they are away from their offices. When this option is selected, users who send messages to the group can receive these automatic messages. For particularly large groups, it's best not to allow out-of-office messages to be delivered because of the excess network traffic they generate.

- **Send Delivery Reports To Group Owner**   If you select this option, the owner of the group is notified whenever an error occurs during the delivery of a message to the group or to one of its members. This option is not available if the group has not been assigned an owner.

- **Send Delivery Reports To Message Originator**   If you select this option, any error notifications are sent to the user who sent a message to the group. If the Send Delivery Reports To Group Owner option is also selected, both the sender and the owner are notified.

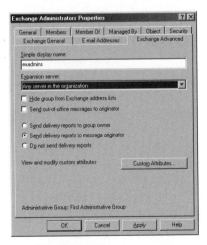

Figure 9-21. *Setting advanced properties for a group.*

Real World Using Message Restrictions on Groups

The Message Restrictions area of the Delivery Restrictions dialog box (displayed by clicking Delivery Restrictions on the Exchange General tab) is often much more useful for groups than for individual users. In large organizations, groups can grow quite large, sometimes holding thousands of users. Because of the possibility of misuse, it is usually not a good idea to provide general access to groups this large. Imagine the increase in traffic if your users sent messages to thousands of users every time their kids had candy bars to sell or they found a good joke. Placing delivery restrictions on large groups allows you to limit access to the groups to a few select, responsible users.

Another potential risk is that someone from the Internet could e-mail everyone in your company, using a group's SMTP address. Imagine what your job would be like on the day that an anonymous person e-mailed malicious information to the entire company. Limiting access to the group will also help prevent this type of unwanted mail from occurring.

Searching for Recipients

As your organization and the number of recipients in it grows, scrolling through lists of recipients to find the ones you need can become quite time-consuming. Fortunately, the Active Directory Users and Computers snap-in can help. This section describes how to use filtering and search tools to make finding a recipient easier.

Filtering Recipients

If you are looking for certain types of recipients, try filtering the recipient objects that are displayed in the Users folder. By default, all types of recipients are shown when you select the Users folder, including public folders. You can filter that view so that only selected types of recipients are shown. For example, you can choose to view only public folders or only contacts. Filtering your recipient view can be useful if you are looking for a specific recipient and the list based on recipient type is not very long, or if you need to select all recipients of a certain type.

To apply a filter, select the Users folder in Active Directory Users and Computers and choose Filter Options from the View menu. You can also click the Filter Options button (the one that looks like a funnel) on the toolbar. The dialog box shown in Figure 9-22 opens. The default setting is to view recipients of all types. Select the Show Only The Following Types Of Objects option, and check the types of recipients you want to view. When you click OK, the Users folder displays only those types of recipients.

The Filter Options dialog box also lets you specify how many recipients should be displayed per folder. Be careful with this one, however. If you set the number too low, many important items may not be shown. Also, keep in mind that the filter options you set apply to the entire Active Directory hierarchy, not just to the Users folder. This means that if you set the filter to show only users and groups, for example, no computers will show up in your Computers folder until you reset the filter.

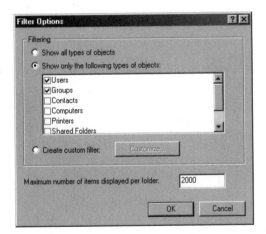

Figure 9-22. *Setting recipient filtering options.*

Another powerful service the Filter Options dialog box offers is the ability to configure custom filters. Select Create Custom Filter and click the Customize button to open the dialog box shown in Figure 9-23. You can create a custom filter based on combinations of just about every field in all the tabs that you use to configure a recipient. Click the Field button to choose a field from the drop-down menu. Use the Condition drop-down menu to choose conditions, such as Begins

With or Is (Exactly), and then enter the value under Value. Click Add to add your criterion to the list. You can enter multiple criteria for searching. Figure 9-23 shows a filter that will find all recipients whose city is Huntsville, whose department is Sales, and whose ILS settings are not present.

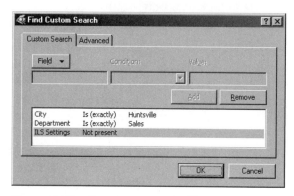

Figure 9-23. *Creating a custom filter.*

Finding Recipients

Active Directory Users and Computers also provides a recipient search tool that allows for some pretty sophisticated searching criteria. You open this tool by choosing Find from the Action menu. The Find Users, Contacts, and Groups dialog box appears (Figure 9-24).

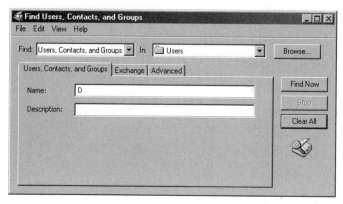

Figure 9-24. *Finding recipients in Active Directory Users and Computers.*

Use the Find field to specify what types of objects you want to find. The default is to find users, groups, and contacts. Use the In field to specify the folder in which you want to perform the search. The default is to search in the Users folder. Enter any part of a name or description and click Find Now to begin the search. The search shown in Figure 9-24 will return all users whose name begins with a "D." The dialog box expands to display the results (Figure 9-25). You can manipulate objects in the search results just as you would in the main Active Directory Users and Computers console, by right-clicking them to access their shortcut menus.

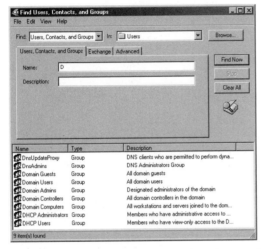

Figure 9-25. *Displaying the results of a search.*

You can also use a few advanced options to narrow down your search. The Exchange tab in the Find Users, Contacts, and Groups dialog box lets you specify that you want to view only Exchange recipients in your search results, and it even lets you set the specific types of recipients you want displayed. The Advanced tab provides custom filtering that works in same way as the custom filtering in the Filter Options dialog box, discussed in the previous section.

Real World   Using the Find Tool

The Find feature is one of the most useful tools in Active Directory Users and Computers. We find ourselves using it regularly to manage recipients. Using Find is much handier than using even the custom filtering choices, and it's certainly quicker than scrolling through long lists of recipients in the main Active Directory Users and Computers window.

Templates

A *template* is a recipient object that is used as a model for creating other recipient objects of that type. Every recipient type except public folders can serve as a template. To create a template, create a recipient object as you normally would. Enter any information that you want to use in the model. If, for example, you are creating a mailbox-enabled user template for new employees, you might enter all of the organizational, phone, and address information for your company.

> **Note** When you create a recipient to use as a template, you will probably want to hide the recipient from the address book, using the Exchange Advanced tab on the template's property sheet. That way, users won't be able to view it in the Global Address List. You will always be able to see it in Active Directory Users and Computers. You should also name your template in such a way that it is both easy to find and easy to distinguish from regular recipients.

To use a template to create an individual recipient, select the template in Active Directory Users and Computers and then choose Copy from the Action menu. The New Object Wizard opens, letting you create the new object. All the information that you entered as part of the template becomes part of the new object, and you can reconfigure the new object using its property sheet, as you would expect.

Recipient Policies

A *policy* is a collection of configuration settings that can be applied across any number of objects. Changing a policy enacts the change on every object to which the policy applies. There are two types of policies in Exchange 2000 Server: system policies and recipient policies. System policies apply to server objects like databases and servers. Recipient policies apply to recipient objects like users and groups and are the focus of this discussion. Because policies can make universal changes across dozens or even hundreds of servers in your organization, they also play a large role in Exchange security.

Exchange 2000 Server includes a single built-in recipient policy used to generate e-mail addresses automatically for mail-enabled Exchange objects, such as users, groups, contacts, public folders, stores, and system attendants. You can create new policies at any time.

Recipient policies employ a "background apply" implementation to make configuration changes. You create a policy by defining the settings for that policy and associating that policy with one or more recipient objects in Active Directory. The policy is then actually applied at a later time, based on the schedule of the Address List service running under the System Attendant.

Creating a Recipient Policy

You create new recipient policies using the Exchange System snap-in. Open the Recipients folder, and then select the Recipient Policies folder inside it. Choose New Recipient Policy from the Action menu to create the new policy. This command opens the property sheet for the new policy, with the General tab showing (Figure 9-26).

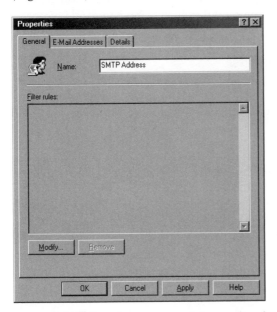

Figure 9-26. *Creating a new recipient policy.*

In the Name field, type a name for your recipient policy. Next click the Modify button to open a Find dialog box similar to the Find Users, Contacts, and Groups dialog box. Select the types of recipients to which you want this new policy to apply on the General tab of this dialog box, and then, on the Advanced tab, enter any custom filter settings you like, using field-level recipient attributes. Once you have defined your search criteria, click Finish to display the results in the Find window. Click OK when you finish defining your policy members. You then return to the General tab of the policy's property sheet, where you will see the filter rules you specified.

Click the E-Mail Addresses tab (Figure 9-27). Use the options on this tab to configure rules for generating e-mail addresses for the members of the new recipient policy. The current rules are listed under Generation Rules. Make sure that the necessary addresses are selected for this set of recipients. Exchange Server uses the rules in this list to generate addresses automatically for any recipient to which this policy applies. You can create a new address generation rule by clicking the New button and choosing an address type, or you can modify an existing address generation rule by selecting the rule and clicking the Edit button. If you create a new address generation rule of the same e-mail type as an existing rule, you can make it the primary address for members of the policy.

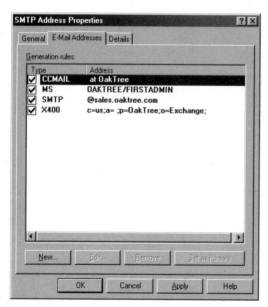

Figure 9-27. *Defining rules for generating e-mail addresses.*

The Recipient Updating area of the E-Mail Address Policy tab allows you to select specific tasks you want Exchange Server to perform when updating recipients. Click Set Existing E-Mail Addresses As Secondary Addresses if you want the updated address to become the primary address shown in the From field of e-mail sent by recipients to which this policy applies. Click Over-ride All Automatically Generated E-Mail Addresses if you want to replace all existing addresses created by the recipient policy. Once you have configured the new address generation policy, you can modify it at any time on this tab.

Creating an Exception to a Policy

Once you have created a policy for a group of recipients, you can override the addressing settings for individual contacts. This is known as creating an *exception* to the policy. You do this using the Active Directory Users and Computers snap-in. Find the recipient or recipients for which you want to create an exception, and open their property sheets. Switch to the E-Mail Address Policy tab, and modify the e-mail address settings, using the same techniques you used when creating the address for the policy. This manual setting overrides any recipient policies in effect.

Address Lists

Address lists are a clever feature of Exchange 2000 Server that allow you to group recipients in the Global Address List according to attributes. Essentially, address lists allow you to add a hierarchical structure to the otherwise flat view provided by the Global Address List.

As you can see from the console shown in Figure 9-28, a number of address lists are preconfigured in the Exchange System snap-in. A separate list is configured for each type of recipient, including conferencing members, containing all of the recipients of that type. There is also a Global Address List that displays all recipients in the organization. It is this list that client software typically uses to display an address book for the organization.

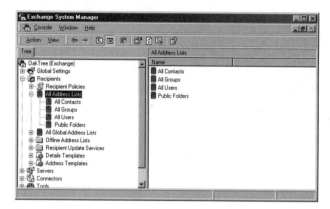

Figure 9-28. *Address lists that are preconfigured in the Exchange System snap-in.*

As you might have guessed, you can also create your own address lists that group recipients in any way you like, to make it easier for users to find the recipient they are looking for in your organization. You can create a new top-level address list right in the All Address Lists folder, or you can create an address list inside an existing address list.

Suppose you wanted to create a new regional address list structure that included only users with mailboxes and that grouped users first by state, then by city, and then by department. Your first step is to create a new top-level address list named Regional. To do this, you select the All Address Lists folder in the Exchange System snap-in and choose New Address List from the Action menu. This opens the dialog box shown in Figure 9-29.

In the Address List Name field, enter *Regional*, and then click the Filter Rules button. This brings up the dialog box shown in Figure 9-30, which, if you've read the rest of this chapter, you should be getting comfortable with by now. On the General tab, select Show Only These Recipients, and then select Users. When you do this, the Show Only Users That Have A Mailbox option activates. Select it too. When you are done, click OK to return to the Create Exchange Address List dialog box.

You have now created the folder that will hold the regional address lists you intend to create. Next you need to create a separate address list for each state. You do this by following the same procedure you used previously. Name each address list for the state, of course. When you get to the Find Exchange Recipients dialog box, where you select user types, this time go to the Advanced tab after you select Show Only Users That Have A Mailbox. This tab is shown in Figure 9-31. Here you can filter recipients based on field-level attributes. In the figure, we have already selected the user attribute State, the condition Is (Exactly), and the value Alabama.

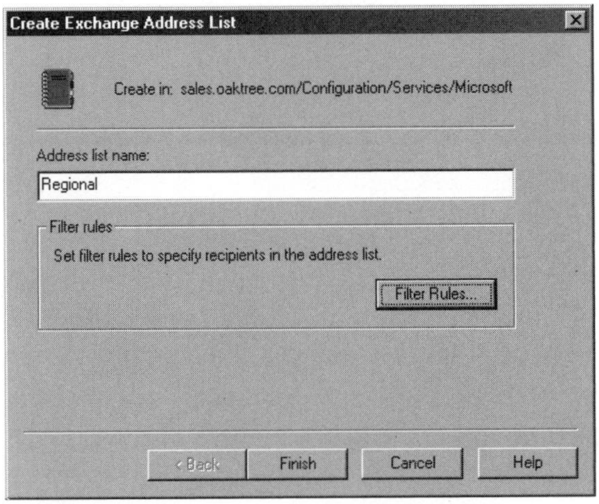

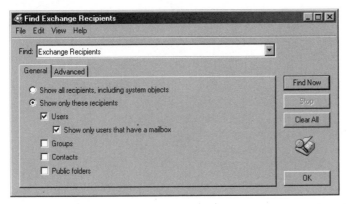

Figure 9-29. *Creating a new address list.*

Figure 9-30. *Selecting the user types contained in an address list.*

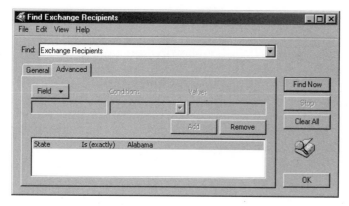

Figure 9-31. *Customizing a filter based on user attributes.*

Once you have configured the address lists for the states in your organization, you can create address lists for cities within those states, using the same procedure. Figure 9-32 shows an example of what the address list structure might look like when you're done.

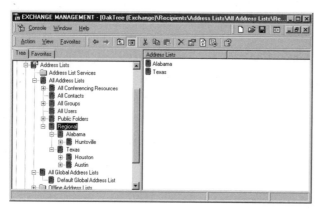

Figure 9-32. *Viewing your new address list structure.*

Address lists can be quite useful in large or complex organizations. Users can open these lists in client applications and find information on recipients quickly. Administrators can use the lists in the Exchange System snap-in to help organize recipients.

Summary

This chapter has discussed how to work with recipients, the destination of all Exchange interactions. You learned about three of the four basic types of recipients in Exchange 2000 Server: users, groups, and contacts, including how to create and configure each of them. You also learned how to search for recipients in various ways, how to create a template that can serve as a model for creating recipients, how to create policies that you apply to recipients, and how to create address lists that group recipients in different ways. Exchange clients use address lists to generate address books. The next chapter looks at the fourth type of recipient available in an Exchange organization: the public folder.

Chapter 10
Using Public Folders

Sharing information is a powerful means of facilitating workgroups and teams. When members of a team are located in geographically distant locations, the ability to share information is even more important. Microsoft Exchange 2000 Server offers that powerful groupware foundation through its implementation of public folders.

In Chapter 9 you learned how to create and manage three of the four basic types of Exchange recipients: users, groups, and contacts. This chapter covers the fourth type of recipient: the public folder. To begin our look at the shared storage architecture of an Exchange Server system, this chapter explores how a user views shared storage and describes how to create, manage, replicate, store, and access public folders in an Exchange organization.

Understanding Public Folder Storage

Public folders are wonderful things, providing centralized storage of virtually any type of document or message and allowing controlled access by any user in the organization. Public folders provide the basis of workflow applications for Exchange 2000 Server.

To manage public folders, you will use the Exchange Folders snap-in as well as the Microsoft Outlook 2000 client. You can create public folders using either of these tools. Much of the creation and management of public folders occurs in the Outlook client because most users work solely in this client, and the administration of public folders was developed to reflect the application with which the users work.

When you create a public folder, that folder is placed in the public folder store of a particular Exchange server. Any Exchange server that has a public folder store can host a public folder. A server might not have a public folder store if, for example, you have made it a mailbox server or dedicated it to some other specific task. A public folder is created in the public folder store of one server but can then be replicated to the public folder stores of multiple additional servers. In a typical organization, the public folders do not all exist on one server; rather, they are distributed across several servers.

An Exchange organization can host multiple *public folder trees*, with each tree consisting of a separate hierarchy of public folders. Within a public folder tree, the folders at the first level are referred to as top-level public folders. When a user creates a top-level public folder, it is placed in the public folder store on that user's home server. When a user creates a lower-level public folder, it is placed in the public folder store containing the parent folder in which the new folder is created. In addition, each public folder can be replicated to other servers in the organization. As you can see, this situation can get complicated. Public folders exist on different servers, and some public folders have instances on multiple servers.

> **Note** In previous versions of Exchange Server, an organization could have only one root-level public folder (and, therefore, one hierarchy), named All Public Folders. In Exchange 2000 Server, you can create multiple root-level public folders, called public folder trees, that appear alongside (or in place of) the All Public Folders tree. Each public folder tree uses a separate database on an Exchange server. Unfortunately, only the initial tree is visible from within MAPI clients such as Microsoft Outlook. Other trees can be viewed only from Outlook Web Access (OWA), Windows Explorer, or another application through the Installable File System (IFS). You will learn how to create new public folder trees later in this chapter.

To ensure that information about public folders is distributed throughout the Exchange system, Active Directory maintains a public folder hierarchy for each public folder tree. This is a single hierarchical structure that contains information about all of the public folders in that tree. The public folder hierarchies are automatically made available to every Exchange user in the organization.

A public folder is considered to have two parts. The first part is the public folder's place in the public folder hierarchy. The second part is the public folder content—the actual messages inside the public folder. The contents of a public folder exist on a single server, unless you specifically configure the content to be replicated to other servers.

Real World   Dedicated Public Folder Servers

Some administrators prefer to use dedicated public folder servers. A *dedicated public folder server* is one from which the mailbox store has been removed. Dedicated public folder servers are useful in large organizations in which large amounts of public data and frequent access to that data consume a great deal of server resources. To use dedicated public folder servers in your organization, follow the steps listed below. When you finish these steps, you're ready to create your public folders.

1. Decide which servers you want to have as your dedicated public folder servers.

2. Remove the mailbox store from the servers you've chosen to be dedicated public folder servers. To do so, simply find the Server container for the appropriate server in the Exchange System snap-in and delete the Mailbox Store configuration object from that server's Information Store container. Be careful when deleting the mailbox store from existing servers; any mailboxes in the store will also be deleted.

3. Remove the Public Folder Store configuration object from all of your organization's servers that will not host public folders. To do so, delete the Public Folder Store configuration object from the server's Information Store container. If the public folder store you want to remove already holds public folders, you must make sure that current replicas of those folders exist on other servers before deleting the object.

Using Public Folders in Microsoft Outlook 2000

Your users—and you—can use the Microsoft Outlook 2000 client both to create public folders and to manage certain public folder properties. This section covers both of these topics. You can also create and manage public folders using previous versions of the Outlook and Exchange clients. Although this section focuses on the use of Outlook 2000, most of the techniques described will work with these other clients as well.

Creating a Public Folder in Outlook

Creating a public folder using Microsoft Outlook is quite easy. Figure 10-1 shows the main Microsoft Outlook window, with the folder list displayed and the Public Folders item expanded.

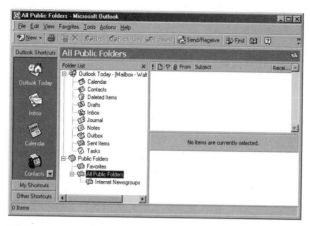

Figure 10-1. *The Outlook 2000 window, showing the public folder hierarchy.*

To create a public folder, ensure that the All Public Folders object (or the folder inside where you want to create the new folder) is selected and choose New Folder from the File menu. The Create New Folder dialog box opens (Figure 10-2). Enter the name of the public folder that you want to create, choose the type of items that folder should contain, select the folder in which it should be created, and click OK. You can set the types of messages that can be posted in a new folder, including appointment items, notes, tasks, and mail items. The default is the type of item that can be posted in the parent folder.

Figure 10-2. *Creating a public folder.*

Real World   Subscribing a Public Folder to a Mailing List

A mailing list service is similar to a newsgroup but is run completely within e-mail. Each subscriber receives a copy of the other subscribers' comments in his or her own Inbox. A public folder has an e-mail address and can subscribe to a mailing list just like any other recipient, as long as your Exchange server has access to a list service server via Simple Mail Transport Protocol (SMTP). To create a public folder and have it subscribe to a mailing list, you need to have permission to add public folders from the Exchange client. You also need to be assigned the Exchange Permissions Admin role.

First create the public folder, following the procedure just described or using the one given in the section "Creating a Public Folder in Exchange System" later in this chapter. Next use the Exchange System snap-in to assign yourself the Send As permission on the folder. Find the SMTP address of the folder (using the E-Mail Addresses tab on the folder's property sheet), and write it down. Then switch to the General tab and select the Show In Address Book option.

Go back to the Exchange client and create a "subscribe" message to the list service to which you want the public folder to subscribe. You will need to view the From field of the message box, so choose From Field from the View menu. In the From field, enter the SMTP e-mail address that you wrote down for the public folder. The list service may have specific instructions regarding what to place in the contents of the message. A typical message is Subscribe *<folder>*, where *<folder>* represents the name under which you want the public folder to subscribe. This name will appear in responses sent from the public folder to the mailing list. The list service should respond with a welcome message or a request for a confirmation message.

Now that the public folder is successfully subscribed to the list service, you can hide the public folder from the address book. It was shown only to ensure that the e-mail address would be resolved the first time that the list service responded.

Managing Public Folders in Outlook

After you create a public folder, you can configure it in several ways. The management of a public folder occurs in two places: the Outlook client and the Exchange System snap-in. Because users can create public folders, it is advantageous to allow them certain managerial responsibilities, which is why part of the management occurs in the client.

When a user creates a public folder, that user automatically becomes the folder's owner. The owner is responsible for the folder's basic design, which includes its access permissions, rules, and association of electronic forms. To perform this management, the user can simply open the property sheet for a particular public folder in Outlook. Public folders can also be managed to a certain degree from within the Exchange System snap-in, but the Outlook option means that the user can do everything from within one application.

General Tab

The General tab of a public folder's property sheet, shown in Figure 10-3, allows you to change the name of a public folder and enter an optional description of that folder. You can also choose the name of an electronic form that should be used to post new items to the folder. By default, the generic Post form is selected. Finally, you can specify that Exchange Client views of the folder be generated automatically. Exchange Client and Outlook process forms in different ways. This option provides compatibility in Exchange Client for folders created in Outlook.

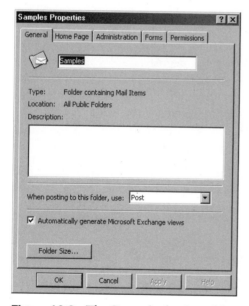

Figure 10-3. *The General tab of a public folder's property sheet in Outlook.*

Administration Tab

You use the Administration tab, shown in Figure 10-4, to set various options governing a public folder's use. The settings on this tab include the following:

- **Initial View On Folder**   Specifies the initial Outlook view that is used whenever the public folder is opened. Available views include the default Normal threaded view as well as views grouped by discussion subject, topic, and poster.

- **Drag/Drop Posting Is A**   Defines what happens when an item is dragged into a public folder. Options include Move/Copy and Forward.

- **This Folder Is Available To**   Specifies whether the folder is accessible by anyone who has appropriate permissions or only by the folder owners.

- **Folder Assistant**   Lets you create rules that apply to new items placed in the folder. Rules include such actions as automatically replying to or rejecting messages based on the posting user or subject. For more information on using rules, see Chapter 21.

- **Moderated Folder**   Allows you to establish one or more moderators for the folder. A *moderated folder* is one in which a moderator must approve all newly posted items before they are made available to the public. Click this button to configure the folder's moderators. Keep in mind that users' posts to the folders will not appear immediately in a moderated folder For this reason, you may want to configure an automatic reply to messages posted to moderated folders, letting users know that the moderator has received their message. You can do so by using the Reply To New Items With area and configuring either a standard or custom response.

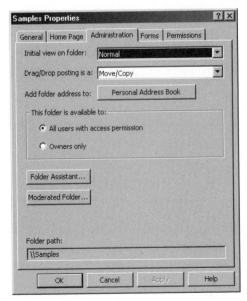

Figure 10-4. *The Administration tab of a public folder's property sheet in Outlook.*

Forms Tab

The Forms tab, shown in Figure 10-5, allows you to specify the forms that can be used in conjunction with the public folder. The forms specified on this tab appear as the choices in the drop-down list for the When Posting To This Folder, Use option on the General tab (refer back to Figure 10-3). You can also manage any associated form from this tab.

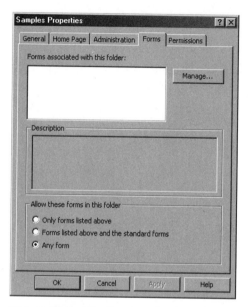

Figure 10-5. *The Forms tab of a public folder's property sheet in Outlook.*

More Info Some of this section's discussion of folder management in Outlook may seem cursory. This is because the subject of associating electronic forms with public folders is a bit outside the scope of this book. For excellent information on using Outlook 2000 and electronic forms, check out *Programming Microsoft Outlook and Microsoft Exchange* by Thomas Rizzo (Microsoft Press, 1999). This book provides information on using Outlook 2000 and Exchange Server to create custom collaborative environments.

Permissions Tab

The Permissions tab, shown in Figure 10-6, allows you to assign permissions to users on the current public folder. Each user can be assigned one of several roles, and each role has a set of permissions associated with it. The available permissions are as follows:

- **Create Items**   Allows the user to post items in the folder.
- **Read Items**   Allows the user to open any item in the folder.
- **Create Subfolders**   Allows the user to create subfolders within the folder.
- **Edit Items**   Specifies which items in the folder the user can edit. The None option indicates that a user cannot edit items. The Own option indicates that the user can edit only items that he or she created. The All option indicates that a user can edit any item in the folder.
- **Folder Owner**   Grants the user all permissions in the folder, including the ability to assign permissions.
- **Folder Contact**   Specifies that the user is to receive copies of any status messages regarding the folder, including nondelivery reports.
- **Folder Visible**   Permits the user to see the folder in the public folder hierarchy.
- **Delete Items**   Specifies which items in the folder the user can delete. The None option indicates that a user cannot delete items. The Own option indicates that the user can delete only items that he or she created. The All option indicates that a user can delete any item in the folder.

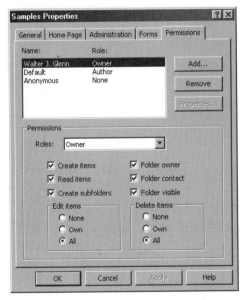

Figure 10-6. *The Permissions tab of a public folder's property sheet in Outlook.*

You can modify the permissions associated with any given role. Table 13-1 shows the available roles and the default permissions granted for each role.

Table 13-1. Default permissions for public folder roles

Role	Create	Read	Edit	Delete	Subfolders	Owner	Contact	Visible
Owner	Yes	Yes	All	All	Yes	Yes	Yes	Yes
Publishing editor	Yes	Yes	All	All	Yes	No	No	Yes
Editor	Yes	Yes	All	All	No	No	No	Yes
Publishing author	Yes	Yes	Own	Own	Yes	No	No	Yes
Author	Yes	Yes	Own	Own	No	No	No	Yes
Nonediting author	Yes	Yes	None	Own	No	No	No	Yes
Reviewer	No	Yes	None	None	No	No	No	Yes
Contributor	Yes	No	None	None	No	No	No	Yes
None	No	No	None	None	No	No	No	Yes

Using Public Folders in the Exchange System Snap-In

The previous section described how to configure public folders using the Outlook client. You can also create and configure public folders in the Exchange System snap-in. Certain tools for managing public folders are available only in this snap-in. In addition, only in Exchange System can you create and modify the top-level public folder hierarchies known as public folder trees.

Creating a Public Folder Tree

Creating a new public folder tree involves three steps. First you must create a new top-level root folder that will house the new tree structure. Second you must create a new public folder store on the server to hold the contents of that new tree structure. Finally you must connect the new top-level folder to the new public folder store. The sections that follow describe these steps in detail.

Creating a New Top-Level Root Folder

The first step in creating a new public folder tree is to create a new top-level root folder. You should name this folder for the structure you wish to create. For example, if you are creating a tree for use only by executives, you might name the new top-level root folder Executives.

Each top-level root folder you create exists on the same level as the Public Folders tree and has its own database on each Exchange server that contains replicas of any of the folders in the tree's hierarchy. To create a new top-level root folder, first select the Folders container for the administrative group in which you want to create the folder, as shown in Figure 10-7. If you have only one administrative group, or if you have Exchange System set not to display administrative groups, the Folders container should appear directly under the root node.

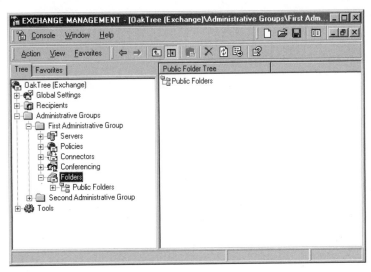

Figure 10-7. *Creating a new top-level root folder.*

Once you have selected the Folders container, choose New Public Folder Tree from the Action menu. This opens the property sheet for the new folder (Figure 10-8). Enter a name for the new tree in the Name field. Click the Select button to open a dialog box that lets you set the mail-enabled public folder container. A mail-enabled container is simply one to which messages can be sent. Unless you have specially configured your Active Directory users containers, you will probably set this container to Users. Once you are finished, click OK to close the property sheet and create the new public folder tree.

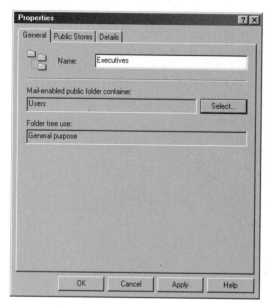

Figure 10-8. *Naming the new public folder tree.*

Creating a New Public Folder Store

Public folders reside in the public folder store. Each public folder tree uses its own database in the store. Once you've created the new top-level root folder for a tree, you must then create a new public folder store to hold that tree. In the Exchange System snap-in, locate the container for the storage group on the server on which you want to create the new tree, as shown in Figure 10-9. You will create the new public folder store in this storage group.

Once you have selected the storage group, choose New Public Store from the Action menu. This opens the property sheet for the new store (Figure 10-10). Enter a name for the new store in the Name field. Click the Browse button to open a dialog box that lets you associate the new store with a public folder tree. Select the tree you created previously. Once you are finished, click OK to close the property sheet. Exchange System will prompt you to mount the new store once it has successfully been created. Click Yes to mount the new store.

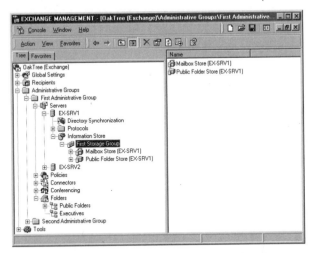

Figure 10-9. *Choosing the storage group for the new public folder store.*

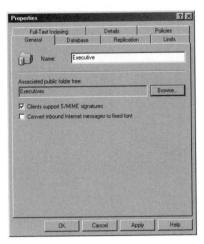

Figure 10-10. *Naming the new store and associating it with the public folder tree.*

Connecting to the Public Folder Store

The final step in creating the new public folder tree is to go back to the top-level root folder that you created earlier and associate it with the new public folder store. In the Exchange System snap-in, find and select the top-level root folder in the main Folders container. Then choose Connect To from the Action menu. This opens the dialog box shown in Figure 10-11, which displays the available public folder stores. You should see the one you just created. Select this store and click OK. The store is connected to the public folder tree and is listed on the Public Stores tab of the property sheet for the top-level root folder.

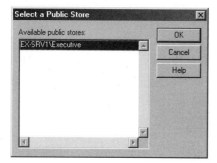

Figure 10-11. *Connecting the public folder tree to the public folder store.*

Note If you just created the new top-level root folder, you may find that the Connect To command is not available on the Action menu. If this happens, exit and restart the Exchange System snap-in to enable the Connect To command.

Once you have created and connected a new public folder tree, you may want to set permissions governing which users can make changes to the root level of that tree. To do so, just open the property sheet for the top-level folder and switch to the Security tab. By default, only the Domain and Exchange Administrators groups have permissions to modify the root folder. Click the Add button to specify permissions for additional users.

Creating a Public Folder in the Exchange System Snap-In

In previous versions of Exchange Server, you could create public folders only using an Exchange client, such as Microsoft Outlook. Exchange 2000 Server lets you create public folders using the Exchange System snap-in. The process is quite easy.

The first step in creating a new public folder is deciding where to create it. In the Exchange System snap-in, select the public folder tree in which you want to create a new folder. If you want to make a new top-level folder in that tree, create the folder right in the top-level root folder. Otherwise, select the folder in the tree in which you want to create a new subfolder, as shown in Figure 10-12.

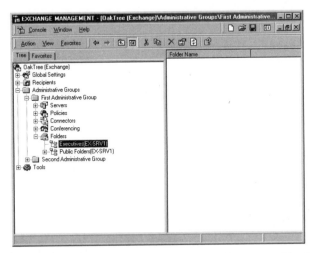

Figure 10-12. *Selecting a location for the new public folder.*

When you have selected the parent folder, choose New Public Folder from the Action menu. This command opens the property sheet for the new public folder (Figure 10-13). All you really have to do to create a new public folder is enter a name in the Name field and click OK. The Exchange System snap-in will create the new folder, and users with the appropriate permissions should find it immediately accessible. If you like, you can also enter a description for the new folder. At the bottom of the General tab for a public folder, you'll also find an option named Maintain Per User Read And Unread Information For This Folder. If you select this option, the folder itself will keep track of and mark as read messages that each individual user of the folder has read. Since most clients (including Outlook) keep track of this information themselves, it is usually not necessary to enable this option.

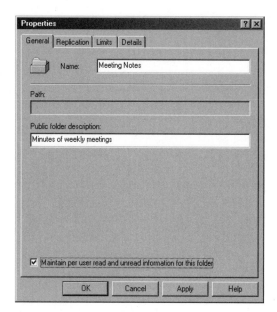

Figure 10-13. *Naming a new public folder.*

Once you have created a new public folder, you still need to mail-enable the folder and configure the public folders' mail-related settings for your organization. To mail-enable a folder, select the folder in Exchange System and choose All Tasks Mail Enable from the Action menu. The command should take effect immediately, although you will get no feedback from Exchange System after executing it. Once you have mail-enabled a folder, that folder's property sheet will include several extra mail-related tabs, including Exchange General, E-Mail Addresses, and Exchange Advanced. These tabs work like the equivalent tabs for other recipients and allow you to perform such functions as setting delivery options and restrictions, changing the display name and alias, and setting custom attributes. Because Chapter 9 covers the use of these tabs with other types of recipients, we won't describe them here.

You should, however, be aware of two important settings that are added to the General tab of a folder's property sheet when you mail-enable that folder. The first setting governs whether or not you want the public folder to be visible in address books so that users can send mail to it. The second setting governs whether you want the name that is visible in address books to be the same as the public folder name or a different name that you specify.

Managing Public Folders in the Exchange System Snap-In

You manage public folders at two levels within Exchange System. At the level of the public folder store, you specify general parameters for how that public folder store should handle public folders. At the level of the public folder itself, you specify properties that govern that folder and often override settings made at the store level.

Managing Public Folders at the Public Folder Store Level

The properties of public folders that you manage at the public folder store level govern the default behavior of all of the public folders in the public folder store. You access these properties using the property sheet of the Public Folder Store object, found in the container for the storage group in which the public folder store is configured. Most of the tabs on this property sheet govern public folder replication, which is discussed in detail later in this chapter. The tab that we are concerned with here is named Limits and is shown in Figure 10-14.

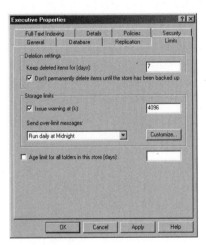

Figure 10-14. *Configuring limits for a public folder store.*

Exchange 2000 Server supports a great feature called deleted-item recovery. When a user deletes a message from a folder, that message is marked as hidden and is actually retained for a certain number of days on the server before being permanently deleted. Within that period, known as the *deleted-item retention time*, the user can recover the item. To do so, however, the user must be using Microsoft

Outlook 8.03 or later. To enable this feature for the public folder store, simply set the number of days that you want to keep deleted items on the server. The default setting is 0. In addition, you can specify that items not be permanently removed from the public folder store until at least one backup has occurred.

You can also use the Limits tab to set a default storage limit for all public folders in the public folder store. This storage limit indicates how large (in kilobytes) a public folder can become before a warning is issued to the folder's contacts. You can override this storage limit at the folder level for individual folders, as you'll see a bit later in this chapter.

The final limit that you can set on the Limits tab is the default number of days for which items are kept in the public folders in the public folder store. The default is no age limit at all.

> **Note** Although age limits make sense for folders that have time-sensitive data, such as an internal classified ads folder or a newsfeed from the Internet, they should be used with caution because most Exchange users expect to be able to retrieve their data indefinitely. Note that public folder age limits work in combination with deleted-item retention time. Suppose that you set a 20-day age limit on your public folders and a 10-day deleted-item retention period. Then suppose that a user deletes an item on day 19—one day before it would automatically expire. The deleted-item retention period, which applies only to user-deleted messages, starts at this point. If the item is recovered within the deleted-item retention period, the age limit for the newly recovered item is reset to add 20 more days.

Managing Public Folders at the Folder Level

You can also manage public folders in Exchange System on a folder-by-folder basis, using the folder's property sheet. Some of the tabs on a folder's property sheet deal only with public folder replication, which is covered later in this chapter. The General tab, which you saw previously in the discussion of creating a public folder, lets you change the description of the folder and the option for maintaining per-user read and unread information. As with the public folder store's property sheet, we are interested primarily in the Limits tab (Figure 10-15) at this point.

The Limits tab defines messaging limits for the public folder. Any setting made at the public folder level overrides the setting made for the public folder store. You can define the following limits on this tab:

- **Storage Limits** Indicates the amount of disk space, in kilobytes, that a folder can take up before a warning is issued to the folder's owner. This setting works like the setting at the public folder store level, discussed previously.

- **Deleted Item Retention** Defines the number of days that deleted messages are retained in the folder before being permanently removed. You can use the default defined for the public folder store or override that setting for this particular folder.

- **Age Limits** Specifies the maximum number of days that a message remains in this public folder before it expires. If not specified, the default set at the public folder store level applies.

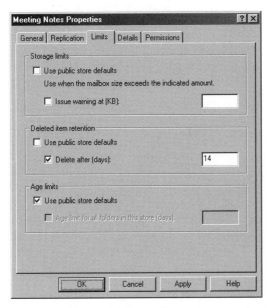

Figure 10-15. *Configuring limits for a single public folder.*

Note Exchange System provides a way to propagate the configuration settings for a parent folder to all of its subfolders. Select the parent folder in Exchange System and choose the Propagate Settings command from the Action menu. A dialog box appears that lets you choose the settings that you want to propagate to all subfolders. Once you've propagated the settings to the subfolders, you can change the settings for any particular child folder.

Replicating a Public Folder

The contents of public folders are not replicated to other public folder stores in your organization automatically. If you want replication to occur, you must set it up manually, on a per-folder basis. You can configure each public folder individually to have replicas on multiple public folder stores. When you set up replication for a parent folder, its child folders are also replicated by default, although you can change this for individual child folders.

Public folder replication follows the multimaster replication model, in which every replica of a public folder is considered a master copy. In fact, there is no easy way to distinguish a replica from the original after replication occurs.

After you've decided which folders you want to replicate, you manually create and configure the replicas. The method for doing this involves pushing replicas from one public folder store to other public folder stores, using the property sheet of the public folder that you want to replicate. To set up replication for a public folder, open its property sheet in Exchange System and then switch to the Replication tab (Figure 10-16).

This tab lists any public stores that already contain a replica of the public folder. Click the Add button to open a dialog box that lists the available public stores in your organization that do not have replicas of the folder. Select the store to which you want to replicate the folder and click OK. The public store is added to the list of stores that contain replicas.

Below the list of public folder stores, you'll find a drop-down menu named Public Folder To Replicate. Use this menu to schedule the replication of the public folder to the other public folder stores. You have several options here:

- **Never Run**   Essentially turns off replication of the public folder, which is handy if you want to stop the replication temporarily to do something like troubleshoot a bad connector.

- **Always Run**   Essentially keeps replication going all of the time. Because this option would cause excessive traffic, it is generally a poor choice. However, it can be useful when you first configure a new replica and you want it to be created as soon as possible. In this situation, turning on the Always Run option ensures that the content will be replicated quickly. Be sure to set the schedule to something more reasonable afterward, however.

- **Run Every 1, 2, or 4 Hours**   Causes replication to occur at the defined interval.

- **Use Custom Schedule**   Allows you to define a custom schedule for replication. Click the Customize button to bring up a dialog box with a calendar of hours you can use to set up the replication schedule.

- **Use Default Schedule**   Causes the folder to replicate according to the default replication schedule set for the public folder store to which the public folder belongs. This option is the default.

Other options on the Replication tab let you see the last replication message Exchange Server generated regarding the current public folder and set the priority that replication messages concerning this folder should have in your Exchange system.

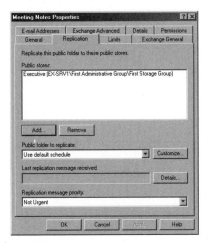

Figure 10-16. *Configuring replication for an individual public folder.*

Once you have created replicas of a public folder and configured how replication should behave at the folder level, you can also configure how replication should behave at the public folder store level. To do this, open the property sheet for the Public Folder Store object and switch to the Replication tab (Figure 10-17).

You can take two actions on this tab. The first is to configure replication defaults that apply to all of the folders in that store. You do this with a drop-down menu like the one used to configure a schedule for an individual folder, as described in the previous section. The value you specify here will apply to all of the folders in the store, unless you specify something other than the Use Default Schedule setting on an individual folder's property sheet. In other words, if you set a schedule for an individual folder, that schedule overrides the setting on this tab.

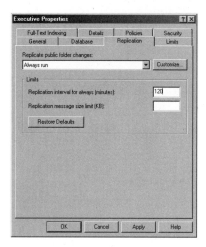

Figure 10-17. *Configuring replication for an entire public folder store.*

The second action you can take on the Replication tab for a public folder store's property sheet is to define limits for replication. By default, no limits are defined. If bandwidth between servers is a consideration, you can specify the maximum time, in minutes, that replication is allowed to go on when it occurs. You can also define the maximum size, in kilobytes, of a single replication message.

Note When folders are replicated, conflicts are possible if users work with different replicas. Exchange has a way to handle replica conflicts intelligently and automatically. The Exchange server allocates revision numbers to all messages posted in a public folder. Using the assigned revision number, the server identifies conflicts as they occur. A conflict may occur when two revisions of the same message are sent from two separate servers to a single server during replication. The server places the conflicting revisions in the replica so that you can resolve the conflict yourself by integrating the revisions or, better yet, by having the authors of the messages work it out themselves. The server then replicates these revisions throughout the organization.

Real World **Client Access**

When a client requests a public folder, the request is processed by the closest Exchange server. If the server doesn't store the public folder or a replica of the public folder locally, the server queries the other servers in the routing group. If no servers in the routing group store the public folder, the server queries other routing groups. The configuration of the connector between routing groups determines whether or not it accepts such public folder referrals. The following connectors have the ability to refuse public folder referrals:

- Routing Group
- SMTP
- X.400
- X.25

You can therefore configure these connectors to control which links in your routing topology handle public folder traffic. Connectors are discussed in further detail in Chapter 13.

Summary

Public folders provide centralized storage of virtually any type of document or message and allow controlled access by any user in the organization. As such, they provide the basis of workflow applications for Exchange 2000 Server. In this chapter, you learned what you need to know to set up a good public folder system in your Exchange organization, including how to create public folders, how to manage them with the Outlook client as well as with the Exchange System snap-in, and how to create multiple public folder trees in your Exchange organization. You also learned how to set up replication so that your public folders can be copied to public folder stores on other servers. Now it's time to turn to another aspect of the Exchange storage architecture. In Chapter 11, you will learn how to configure and manage Exchange 2000 Server storage groups.

Chapter 11
Using Storage Groups

In the previous two chapters, you learned how to create and manage the various types of recipients in Microsoft Exchange 2000 Server. In this chapter, we turn our attention to storage groups. We'll look at the issues involved in planning multiple databases and discuss when you should and should not use circular logging, how to create storage groups, how to create and delete a store, and how to mount and dismount a store.

Review of Exchange 2000 Storage Architecture

Chapter 2 described the storage architecture of Exchange 2000 Server. This section will refresh your memory by summarizing the main points of that architecture. Refer back to Chapter 2 if you need more details.

A storage group in an Exchange system consists of a set of up to six databases. All of the databases in a storage group use the same transaction log files. Each database in Exchange 2000 Server comprises two files: the rich text file (the .EDB file) and the native content file, or streaming file (the .STM file). Both of the these files are managed as one unit by the Store process (Store.exe). The native content file can hold any type of content in its original form. Information is read into and out of the native content file by Exchange Installable File System (ExIFS), a kernel mode component that provides very fast streaming.

Benefits of Using Storage Groups

These days, it is not uncommon to find Exchange 5.5 databases that are well over 20 GB in size. The time necessary to back up these databases can exceed several hours. The problem with this is not the time it takes to back up the database, but the time it takes to *restore* such a large database. During the restoration, of course, your users' productivity goes down the drain. In Exchange database planning, the old cliché is a good one: *Always plan for failure so that you can succeed.* You'll find that prudent use of storage groups will help you succeed during disaster recovery.

In implementing storage groups and allowing multiple databases per Exchange server, Microsoft has made some tremendous changes to the Extensible Storage Engine (ESE) database architecture. These changes significantly enhance recoverability and minimize unproductivity when an Exchange database becomes corrupted. In addition, storage groups offer several key benefits:

- Each server can host more users than before.
- Each database can be backed up and restored individually.
- Each server can host multiple businesses.
- A separate store can be used for special mailboxes.
- Circular logging can apply to individual storage groups.

These points are discussed in the sections that follow.

Increased User Support

Probably the largest benefit of storage groups is that they allow you to spread users across databases and storage groups on the same Exchange 2000 server. This means three things: (1) you can support more users on a single server than was possible in Exchange 5.5, (2) you'll have less downtime when a database becomes corrupted, and (3) you can host more users on an Exchange server because you can keep your databases to a manageable size.

Within a storage group, you can have up to six databases. Each server can house up to four storage groups. Thus, each server can have a maximum of 24 databases.

However, when you run the Information Store Integrity Checker (Isinteg.exe) on a database, you must dismount that database. In addition, Isinteg.exe needs a second database for temporary use. Therefore, if you have six databases operating in a given storage group, you will have to dismount a second database so that Isinteg.exe can run properly. If you limit the number of operating databases to five in a single storage group, then you will always have room to run Isinteg.exe without having to dismount a second store.

Having your users spread out across multiple databases means that only a subset of your users is affected if one of your databases goes off line for some reason. The other users can continue to work because their databases are up and running. A database that is offline is considered to be dismounted. Its icon appears with a red down arrow in the Exchange System snap-in, as shown in Figure 11-1.

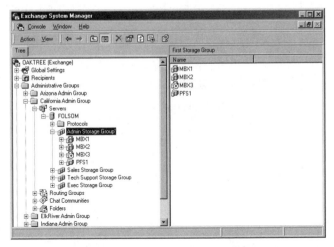

Figure 11-1. *Online databases and an offline database (MBX3) in a storage group.*

Individual Backup and Restore

Because each individual database can be mounted or dismounted, you can back up and restore databases individually while other databases in the same storage group are mounted and running. Consider a scenario in which you have created five mailbox stores in the same storage group, one for each of five departments. If one of those stores becomes corrupted, the other four can remain mounted while you restore the fifth store from backup and then mount it again. You are not required to dismount all of the stores in a storage group in order to restore one of them. And if one store becomes corrupted and cannot be mounted, it does not stop other stores in the same storage group from being mounted and available to users.

Hosting of Multiple Businesses

If you manage e-mail for multiple businesses, you can host them on a single server. You can create an individual store for each business or even devote a storage group to a business, if needed. In either case, Exchange 2000 Server keeps the information for each business completely separate in its respective store, unlike Exchange Server 5.5.

Having the stores separate and distinct allows you to set up different administrative schedules for the businesses. For instance, some administrators may want to have full backups performed every day while others may need only weekly full backups. Some may want to have each department hosted in a separate store, while others may be happy to house all of their users in the same store. This flexibility makes it easier to meet your customer's needs.

Support for Special Mailboxes

While it is not widely recommended, you can take a special mailbox or set of mailboxes and create them in their own store. One instance when this might be useful would be for a journalizing recipient that receives copies of all appropriate e-mails in your organization to comply with local laws or industry-specific regulations. Another instance might be for a project team that is working with highly sensitive and mission-critical company information. Their work might warrant the use of a separate store or public folder tree.

Circular Logging for a Single Storage Group

You may need to control the transaction logs for some storage groups because of limited disk space. It could be the case, for example, that information held in one native content file is expendable while information held in a different native content file is not. Because you are limited to recovery at the last full backup when using circular logging, you could place your expendable information (such as a history of companywide memos) in one public folder in one storage group for which you permit circular logging, and you could place your users' e-mails in a different storage group that has circular logging turned off. That way, you'll be able to focus your disaster recovery efforts on the most important information. For a description of how circular logging works, refer to Chapter 2.

Planning Storage Groups

In most new installations, whether they are migrations or new installations, planning is the part that gets the least attention. We can't emphasize enough that poor planning leads to poor implementation and increased administration over the long term. If you were to record the types of support activities you perform each day for a month and then review them, you might find that 50 percent or more of them could have been avoided with better planning and implementation. I know you're thinking that you don't have the time to do good planning. But if you don't, you'll end up using the time you saved dealing with the unforeseen troubles caused by your migration to Exchange 2000 Server.

Real World **Network Administration at Its Best**

We know of one Exchange administrator who faithfully accomplishes the following activities on a regular basis. He developed this list by taking a thorough look at his daily activities and proactively planning ways to avoid common "fires." Needless to say, his Exchange network runs smoothly and he feels ready for any disaster that might occur. To some of you, these tasks might seem like overkill. But we would encourage you to withhold your judgment as you examine these steps. We think this is nothing less than outstanding administration.

On a daily basis, he checks his logs—all of them. He checks the application, security, system, directory, and other logs. If he sees any warnings or cautions, he checks them out and resolves them that day, if possible. He also checks his backup software logs each day to make sure the backups worked. He performs an incremental backup every day except Friday. In addition, he runs Server Monitor for critical services on his Exchange servers and sends Link Monitor bounce messages every hour to his company's regular vendors and customers. (In all, eight Internet SMTP servers are sent bounce messages.) If the link goes down, he often knows about it before anyone else and can troubleshoot it and (sometimes) fix it before his users even knew something is wrong. (To learn more about Link Monitor and Server Monitor, see Chapter 23.)

On a weekly basis, he performs a full backup of all of his servers and makes sure on Monday that they were successful. If not, he starts another full backup on Monday as he is leaving work. He also checks his antivirus software for updates and uses their network software to update his servers and his users' workstations.

Every month, he runs a series of System Monitor charts, logs the activities, and then prints a report for each server, placing it into an ever-expanding notebook. These charts measure the health of his servers and run for three days at 10-minute intervals. With them, he is able to predict how the addition of a service or a new group of users will affect each of his servers. And when he requests new hardware, he has the numbers and the credibility to back up his request.

In addition, each month he performs a trial restore for each tape backup device that he uses. Since he performs backups on three different servers, he does three trial restores. Here is how he does it. He takes 15 percent of the information that is currently being backed up and copies it to another location on the same server. Often, he'll create a temporary folder named Test. Then he backs up this temporary folder, noting the size and number of files. After the backup and verify operation is complete, he deletes the Test folder and then restores it from the tape backup. When the restore is complete, he compares the size and number of files in the restored folder to those in the original Test folder. If they match, he knows his tape backup system is working. If they don't match, he has some trouble-shooting to do.

Once a month, he also restores his Exchange databases to an offline server that is configured in roughly the same way as his production server. He then makes sure that those databases work on the offline server. This exercise has given him (1) the confidence that he can do a solid restore quickly and efficiently, and (2) the knowledge that his backup system really is working. The time to learn how to restore your Exchange databases is not when the storm is raging and you're on the phone with Microsoft technical support. It's better to do so when everything is calm and you can make mistakes with an offline server.

Also, every four to six weeks, he offers end-user training, usually on topics that have dominated his support calls. This type of "customer service" approach has led to a steady decline in help desk calls because he has developed smarter users who can perform some very basic troubleshooting themselves, such as making sure that everything is plugged in or that the printer is on line.

On a quarterly basis, he drains his uninterruptible power supply (UPS) batteries and makes sure that his UPS software cleanly shuts down his servers. It's better to find out that your UPS software isn't working during a test than during a power outage. A good way to corrupt your Exchange database is to experience an unexpected power outage and have your UPS cut power to your Exchange server instead of shutting it down cleanly.

Moreover, on a quarterly basis, he checks for firmware updates and revisions for all of his servers. If there is a new update, he installs it. For his users, he'll check for updates or service packs for the various applications that his firm uses. If new updates or service packs have been released, he tests them with a few trusted users and, barring anything negative, pushes the updates out to the rest of his network. Finally, he checks the cooling fans on all of his servers quarterly to make sure they aren't getting weak.

Because of his good planning, he has the trust of his superiors. He has taken the time to tell them what he is doing and why. Consequently, he has been able, over time, to implement many standards that have contributed to a smoothly running network. Being proactive in his planning has helped him achieve a situation in which he spends a good portion of his time being proactive about the upcoming changes his network will experience instead of just putting out fires.

Planning for Disk Space

Let's take a look at some planning issues. We'll trust you to not skim this section. Since this chapter focuses on storage groups, we'll confine our discussion to planning for disk space, multiple databases, and multiple storage groups. For a broader look at how to plan for Exchange 2000 Server, refer back to Chapters 5 and 6. When planning disk space capacities for your Exchange 2000 server, you need to consider several key factors:

- The number of users to be housed on a given Exchange server
- The types of users to be housed on a given Exchange server
- The average size of an e-mail and an attachment, and the number of attachments that your users will need to send and receive
- The number and size of public folders

The next two sections describe how to calculate the disk space needs of your Exchange server.

Calculating Disk Space for E-Mails and Attachments

Messaging activity by your users is going to be difficult to forecast. Some users send and receive only a few e-mails each day. Others are at the opposite end of the spectrum, sending and receiving lots of e-mails each day, some with large attachments. Obviously, given the same hardware specifications, you can house more light users in a single mailbox store than you can heavy users. Although it may seem trivial to do so, it's best to develop some type of classification system for your environment and then run the numbers to determine how many users you want per store, per storage group, and finally, per server. If you can get a semi-accurate picture of your current messaging usage, you'll be better able to predict hardware and storage group needs.

A good way to do this is to pick a random sample of your users—at least 15 percent—and then conduct an audit of their current e-mail usage. Be sure they are saving copies of their sent e-mails in the Sent Items folder so that you can get an idea as to how many e-mails they are sending each day and the size of their e-mails as well. You can also see how many e-mails had attachments and, by opening the e-mails, you can see the sizes of the attachments. Security concerns might keep you from getting the information you need from some users, and in those cases you can give them a short survey to fill out.

Once you've collected your data, you need to analyze it. This part simply involves running some numbers. Consider this example: Assume that you conducted your analysis on 45 users (out of 300 users) over a 60-day period, and you find that the average number of e-mails per day for each user is 14, with 2 attachments. Let's further assume that the average size of each e-mail is 1 KB and the average size of each attachment is 200 KB. The numbers would look like this:

- 14 e-mails × 1 KB = 14 KB per day in e-mail
- 2 attachments × 200 KB = 400 KB per day in attachments
- Total average disk space usage: 828 KB per day (414 KB for the store, 414 KB for the transaction logs)
- 828 KB × 300 users = 248,400 KB, or 248.4 MB, of disk space per day for all 300 users. Over a two-month (60-day) period, there will be 44 working days, so 10,929 MB, or 10.9 GB, of disk space will be needed.

This final figure of 10.9 GB is somewhat misleading because the transaction logs will not be retained forever. Eventually, the ESE will delete the old logs, freeing up disk space to be used again by the transaction logs. Therefore, let's assume that the ESE keeps only a week's worth of logs, or 5 × 414 KB = 2070 KB. Thus, after two months of activity, you will need only 5,466,870 KB, or 5.4 GB (44 days × 414 KB average usage × 300 users, plus 2070 KB for the logs) of disk space to run Exchange 2000 Server.

We're not done yet. All we have established is the amount of disk space needed to record e-mails and attachments. We still need to look at public folders and backup throughput.

Calculating Disk Space for Public Folders

To illustrate how to determine the space needed for the public folders, let's assume that each user posts an average of three documents per day to your public folders, each with an average size of 6 KB. (Although this document size might seem large, refer to Chapter 16's discussion of the Web Store, which allows any type of document to be held in an Exchange 2000 database. You will see storage of multiple types of documents in Exchange happening more and more.) We would calculate the public folder disk space like this: 3 posts × 300 users × 6 KB × 2 (because each post is recorded once in the store and once in the transaction log). This scenario comes out to 10,800 KB (10.8 MB) per day of disk space for your users to post to their public folders. Over 44 days, you will need 237,600 KB

(237.6 MB) plus 27,000 KB for the transaction logs (3 posts × 300 users × 6 KB average size × 5 days), giving you a grand total over a two-month period of 264,600 KB (264.6 MB) of disk space needed for your public folders. Thus, you would need 5.46 GB for e-mails and 264.6 MB for public folders, or approximately 5.7 GB of total disk space for a two-month period. We're still not done planning, however. We now need to see how to use these numbers in planning for our storage groups.

Planning for Multiple Storage Groups

Once you've gotten a handle on your disk space needs, you need to consider how many storage groups you need. One factor you need to think about is the varying priorities of the work your users do. Let's assume that 20 of your 300 users perform work that is absolutely mission-critical. Perhaps they are sales staff who take orders over the phone or who process customer orders that are placed in a public folder that is exposed on your Web site. Let's assume that if these users are down for even 15 minutes, your company loses in excess of $50,000. In this type of situation, you should consider splitting these users into two groups and hosting each group in its own mailbox and public folder store. Hosting them in their own storage group, however, is not necessary.

The reasoning behind this recommendation is that if the other databases become corrupted, these users could continue to operate without disruption because you can dismount and restore one or any combination of stores while another store runs in the same storage group. And if one group's database needs to be restored, it would be a fast restore because it would be much smaller than the companywide database in which the other 280 users are hosted. In addition, since these users are spread over two databases, the other half of the group can continue to work and remain productive. Hence, plan your storage groups with disaster recovery in mind more than disk space usage considerations.

Planning for Backup Throughput

Another consideration when planning your storage groups is the type of throughput you need when you do a restore. Let's assume that you have purchased a tape drive with a maximum throughput of 10 GB per hour, or 166.6 MB per minute. At that rate, restoring the databases from tape backup would take about 35 minutes, if all the users were housed in the same database. When you factor in the time needed to diagnose the problem, find the tapes, and do the backup, you can reasonably assume that your users would be without e-mail and public folders for one to two hours, depending on the nature of the problem and how fast you can get to a point at which a restore operation can be performed.

In some companies, being down for one or two hours is no big deal. In others, it could spell disaster. Therefore, you'll need to determine how long your users can be without Exchange services while you are performing a restore. Discussions with your manager can help you formulate the amount of downtime that is acceptable in the event of a disaster.

Suppose that as a result of these discussions, you determine that no one is to be without Exchange services for more than 30 minutes. To plan how to stay within this maximum downtime, you would take the restore time you calculated in the previous section and divide it by the maximum downtime allowed by management policy. This calculation will determine the number of stores you'll need to create on your Exchange 2000 server. To determine the minimum number of storage groups you will need, divide the number of stores by 5 (the number of stores per storage group).

> **Note** Even though we can have six stores per storage group, we've chosen to use five groups to avoid having to dismount a second storage group to run Isinteg.exe. (See the discussion earlier in this chapter.)

In our example, we know that it will take 35 minutes to restore data for 300 users. However, this number reflects keeping data for only two months. Most companies keep data much longer than this. So, if in our running example, we set our data retention policy to a more realistic period of one year, we'll need to multiply our numbers from above by 6 to gain an accurate restore picture for one year's worth of data. Thus, restoring databases holding a year's worth of information would take 210 minutes, or 3.5 hours. Now, how would you handle this? Well, you'll want to be able to restore the databases within 15 minutes to give yourself plenty of time to meet your company's 30-minute downtime policy. Therefore, you would need to create a minimum of 14 separate mailbox stores and 14 separate public folder stores (210/15). This assumes, of course, that the databases will be relatively the same size. If some databases turn out to be much larger than the restore time goal, it would be wise to create additional stores or move some user's mailboxes to create store sizes that will meet your goals.

In this scenario, you would need at least 5 storage groups to accommodate 28 stores. Since we have a maximum of four storage groups per server, you'll need two Exchange 2000 Servers to accommodate these databases. It would be best to load balance the databases as much as possible between the two servers. Also, since the system uses one set of transaction logs per storage group, increasing the number of storage groups would prevent the buildup of a large number of transaction logs per storage group, although it would cause an overall increase in the number of transaction logs for the entire system.

Understanding Storage Group Architecture

This section takes a look at some of the limits to storage groups and examines the purpose and role of each file that makes up the transaction logs. When you create a new storage group, a corresponding folder is created by default in the C:\Exchsrvr directory. Then, when you create a new mailbox or public folder store in that storage group, the files for that store are placed in the storage group's folder. The details pane in Figure 11-2 shows the default files that are created when you create a new mailbox store. The purpose of each of these files is as follows:

- **E01.chk**   Checkpoint file
- **E01.log**   Current transaction log
- **MBX1.edb**   Rich text file
- **MBX1.stm**   Native content file or streaming file
- **res1.log**   First reserved transaction log
- **res2.log**   Second reserved transaction log
- **tmp.edb**   Temporary transaction log

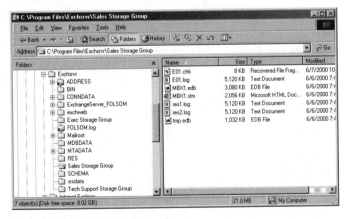

Figure 11-2. *Default files of a storage group.*

You can see from Figure 11-2 that the total amount of disk space for the initial creation of one mailbox store is approximately 19.5 MB. As additional stores are created in the storage group, however, the amount of disk space needed is not as dramatic. For instance, notice in Figure 11-3 that additional stores have been created in the Tech Support Storage Group. There are two mailbox stores (MBX1 and MBX2) and two public folder stores (PFS1 and PFS2). However, there is only one set of transaction logs for all four of these stores. The only additional disk space required to create these stores is the space taken up by the stores themselves. Each storage group has one set of transaction logs, whether the group is housing one, two, or even six stores.

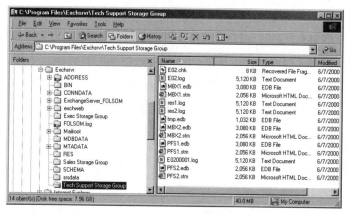

Figure 11-3. *A storage group with four stores and one set of transaction logs.*

For a more complete discussion of storage group architecture and transaction logs, see Chapter 2.

Creating a Storage Group

Creating a storage group is quick and painless. Remember that you cannot create more than four storage groups on any given Exchange 2000 server. Attempts to do so will result in an error message.

To create a storage group, open the Exchange System snap-in and navigate to your server object. Right-click the server object, point to New, and choose Storage Group from the submenu (Figure 11-4). The property sheet for the new storage group appears (Figure 11-5). As you type in the name of the storage group, you'll notice that it is entered in all three fields simultaneously. This step ensures that there aren't any mistakes in the transaction log location or the system path location.

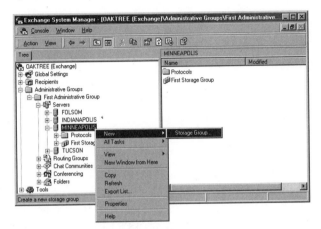

Figure 11-4. *Creating a storage group.*

The property sheet also allows you to select the Zero Out Deleted Database Pages and Enable Circular Logging options. The Zero Out Deleted Database Pages option tells the storage group to write zeros to deleted pages within all of the stores inside the storage group during an online backup. Select this option if you want to be sure that deleted data cannot be recovered. This will add overhead to your backup process and slow down your backup routine, but it will increase the security of your deleted data. The Log File Prefix field can be used to specify a prefix to be placed at the beginning of each log file. This feature allows you to store all of your log files in the same location and still identify which logs go with which storage groups.

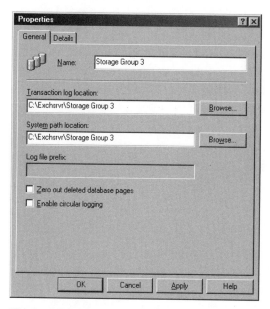

Figure 11-5. *Property sheet for a new storage group.*

The Enable Circular Logging option enables circular logging for the storage group. Consider enabling this feature only for those storage groups that do not hold mission-critical data. Circular logging does reduce the number of transaction logs created by the ESE's Store process, but it eliminates the ability to recover your databases up to the point of a disaster. With circular logging enabled, you can recover only to the last full backup. Consider carefully the full implications of losing the most recent data in your Exchange databases before selecting this option.

The Details tab of the storage group's property sheet allows you to enter notes about the storage group, such as who created it and what its purpose is.

Creating a Store

You can create two kinds of stores in a storage group, a *mailbox* store for messages and a *public folder* store for public folder use. Each store will have its own .EDB and .STM files. You can't create a store until you have created a storage group. When you first install Exchange 2000 Server, it creates a storage group named First Storage Group (which you can rename) as well as a mailbox store and a public folder store inside that storage group.

Creating a Mailbox Store

To create a new mailbox store, right-click the storage group in which you would like to create the store, point to New, and then choose Mailbox Store. Figure 11-6 shows the property sheet that appears. On the General tab, enter the name of the mailbox store, and then click the Browse button next to the Default Public Store field to see a list of public folder stores with which you can associate the mailbox store (Figure 11-7). Choose a public folder store from the list, and click OK.

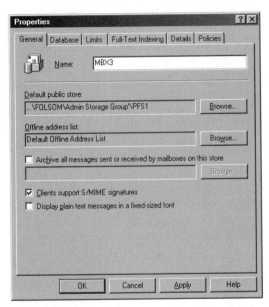

Figure 11-6. *General tab of the property sheet for a new mailbox store.*

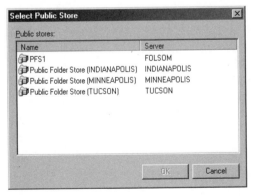

Figure 11-7. *Selecting a default public folder store for the new mailbox store.*

Note Selecting a public folder store to associate with the new mailbox is required because each Exchange user must have a default public folder store for public folder access. Selecting a public folder store here does not limit the user's ability to access other public folder stores or public folder trees. Instead, it provides an entry point into the whole public folder area.

After selecting a public folder store to associate with your mailbox store, click Browse next to the Offline Address List field to choose a default offline address list for users homed in this store (Figure 11-8). Users will still be able to download other offline address lists; this option simply specifies the default. For more information on offline address lists, see Chapter 9.

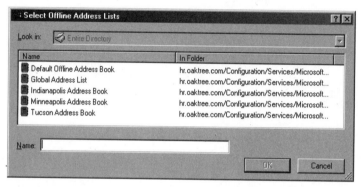

Figure 11-8. *Selecting a default offline address list for the new mailbox store.*

If you want the mailbox store to support Secure/Multipurpose Internet Mail Extensions (S/MIME), select the Clients Support S/MIME Signatures check box. (See Chapter 20 to learn more about S/MIME and when you would want to use it.) And if you want all incoming messages converted to 10-point Courier, select the Display Plain Text Messages In A Fixed-Sized Font check box.

On the Database tab of the property sheet (Figure 11-9), you can specify where you want the two files that make up this store to be physically located. Even though you can navigate to a remote share point on another server, Exchange 2000 Server will not allow you to map either of your files to a network share. However, you can create a volume mount point and specify it as the location for either of your files. This can be helpful if you know that a particular database will house large files or many files, since you can create a special partition for them. You can also specify the time at which you want the store maintenance utilities to run for this particular store.

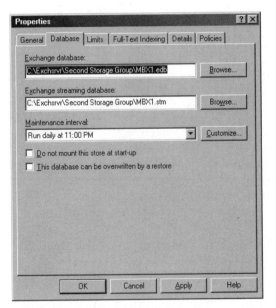

Figure 11-9. *Database tab of the property sheet for a new mailbox store.*

The Do Not Mount This Store At Start-Up check box allows you to specify that the store not be mounted at startup. The default is to have the store mounted when Exchange services start. Finally, you can select the This Database Can Be Overwritten By A Restore check box. This option relates to the database's globally unique identifier (GUID).

Each database has a GUID. This GUID is stored in the ESE database in one of the general purpose tables. (For more information on ESE, consult Chapter 2.) The database GUID, along with its physical path on the hard disk drive, is also stored in Active Directory. When the Store.exe process starts, one of its tasks is to attempt to mount the database. Before mounting the database, however, the Store.exe process compares the database GUID it finds in the database to the database GUID for that database in Active Directory. The directory paths are also compared.

If everything matches, the database is mounted. If there is a mismatch in any of the information, the Store.exe process refuses to start up the database. This failure can occur if the database files are moved from a different server or directory to their present location. The reason the Store.exe process requires the GUID to match is to prevent a database from being accidentally moved to a different location and having it start up under a different storage group with different transaction logs.

If the This Database Can Be Overwritten By A Restore check box is selected, the Store.exe process assumes you really want to move the database to this present location. So at startup, the Store.exe process will "fix" the database by changing the GUID in the database to the GUID that is in Active Directory; then at the next mounting, the GUIDs will match and the database will mount. Finally, the check box is cleared as part of this process.

Note If there is no database found in the path when the Store.exe process is trying to mount the database, it will prompt you with an option to create a new database. The This Database Can Be Overwritten By A Restore check box is really only invoked when the Store.exe process finds a database in the path it is instructed to look in and finds what it believes is the *wrong* database because the GUID is different.

This check box functions similarly during a restore. During the AddDatabase() call, Ntbackup passes in the GUID, database name, and storage group name to the Store.exe process. If these match, then the Store.exe process passes back the locations where the files should be restored. If the GUID doesn't match, the Store.exe process looks at this check box, and if selected, it passes the database back to the backup process where the database files should be written.

Note By moving databases around and selecting the This Database Can Be Overwritten By A Restore check box, it is possible to create multiple, different databases with the same GUID on your Exchange 2000 Server. If you try to mount both databases, only one will mount because of the conflicting GUIDs. Under no circumstances does Microsoft recommend keeping two databases with the same GUID or "swapping" databases for any reason. Unexpected and undesirable results can occur.

The Limits tab (Figure 11-10) allows you to set deleted-item retention times and storage warning limits for the mailbox store. You can also set these options globally by creating a mailbox policy under the Policies container. Values set via a policy cannot be overridden at the server level.

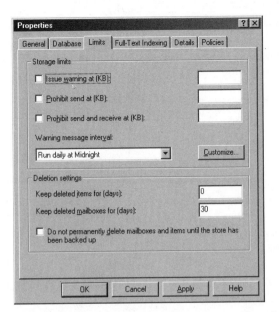

Figure 11-10. *Limits tab of the property sheet for a new mailbox store.*

The Full-Text Indexing features will be dimmed during the creation of your mailbox store. However, after the store has been created, you'll be able to enable full-text indexing by right-clicking the store in the Exchange System snap-in, pointing to All Tasks, and choosing Create Full Text Index. Once this index is created, additional objects will appear under the Full-Text Indexing container (Figure 11-11) and the features on the Full-Text Indexing tab will be available for configuration. For more information on the architecture of full-text indexing, see Chapter 2. To learn more about how to work with full-text indexing, see "Creating a Full-Text Index" later in this chapter.

On the Details tab of the mailbox store's property sheet, you can enter administrative notes about the mailbox store, such as who created it and its purpose. The Security tab, which will show up only on the property sheet of a successfully created mailbox store, lists the permissions for the users and groups that have access to the mailbox store. It's best to leave these at their default values unless you have specific reasons for altering them. Finally, the Policies tab lists any group policies that apply to this database. You cannot configure the group policy from this location, however.

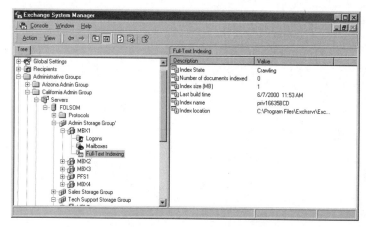

Figure 11-11. *Objects in the Full-Text Indexing container for Mailbox Store.*

Creating a Public Folder Store

Creating a public folder store is similar to creating a mailbox store, with certain significant differences. One item to note is the relationship between the public folder store and a public folder tree. You cannot associate more than one store in each storage group with a given public folder tree. If you attempt to do so, you'll receive the message in Figure 11-12.

Figure 11-12. *Public folder store error message.*

You must associate individual public folders with a public folder tree. Depending on the type of client that will be using the public folder, you are not required to keep all of your public folders in one large, monolithic hierarchy that is replicated to every server in the organization. In Exchange 2000 Server, you can create public folder trees for various reasons: for projects, by department, or by location, to name just three. Bear in mind that additional public folder trees are not accessible by MAPI clients and can be accessed only by applications (such as Microsoft Word, Excel, or PowerPoint), Web-based clients, and ExIFS. In this section, we'll use an example of a tree that will contain public folders for an

Exchange 2000 migration project. Each store will deal with different aspects of the migration: planning, implementation, troubleshooting, and so on. Dividing up the folders for a project allows you to assign permissions to the folder for just those users who need it, thus isolating this information from the rest of the network. Figure 11-13 shows the creation of the Exchange Migration Planning public folder for the Exchange 2000 Migration Project public folder tree.

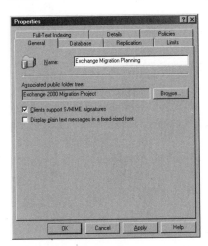

Figure 11-13. *Creating an Exchange Migration Planning public folder.*

Note   Each public folder store must be associated with a public folder tree. The confusing part is that you cannot associate more than one store on a given server with the same tree. Hence, associations are done on a per store/per server/per tree basis. For example, if you want to associate two different public stores created on the same server with the same tree, you won't be allowed to do this. Instead, you'll need to create the two public stores on two different servers and associate them with the same tree.

When you click the Browse button next to the Associated Public Folder Tree field, you see a dialog box listing all of the public folder trees that do not have a public folder store associated with them on your local server (Figure 11-14). Note that this list is based on all of the public folder trees in your organization, not just the ones on the local server. You'll want to develop your own naming convention for your public folder trees before you begin your migration or new installation of Exchange 2000 Server. A lack of planning at this stage will likely result in public folder trees that are misnamed or too similarly named, which will lead to confusion in the long run.

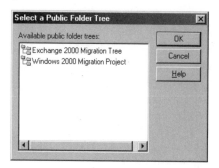

Figure 11-14. *Selecting a public folder tree to associate with the new public folder store.*

On the Database tab of the public folder store's property sheet, shown in Figure 11-15, you can select the locations where the physical databases should be created and the maintenance schedule for the store. You can also force manual mounting of the public folder store by selecting the Do Not Mount This Store At Start-Up check box.

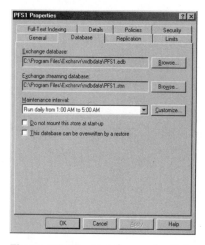

Figure 11-15. *Database tab of the property sheet for a new public folder store.*

The Replication tab, shown in Figure 11-16, has several nice features. Here's where you schedule when replication of the public folder store should occur. Make your choice from the Replicate Public Folder Changes drop-down list; the selections include the following:

- Always Run
- Never Run
- Run Every Hour
- Run Every 2 Hours
- Run Every 4 Hours
- Use Custom Schedule

The default for Always Run is every 15 minutes. However, in the Limits area, you can enter the exact interval at which you want replication to occur when Always Run is selected. For instance, suppose that you have a companywide memos folder that is constantly being updated with new customer information. If you would like replication of this folder to occur every 30 minutes instead of every 15 minutes, you would enter *30* into the Replication Interval For Always (Minutes) field. This is much easier than selecting Use Custom Schedule in the Replicate Public Folder Changes list and then setting replication to occur every 30 minutes, although that is also a valid way to accomplish the same task.

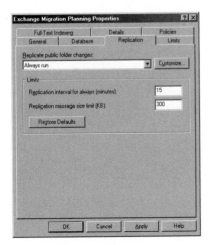

Figure 11-16. *Replication tab of the property sheet for a new public folder store.*

If you are concerned about the size of the replication messages sent between your servers, you can adjust the value in the Replication Message Size Limit (KB) field. The default is 300 KB, but you can lower this limit if your connection is either slow or unreliable.

The Limits tab, shown in Figure 11-17, is where you set storage limits, deletion options, and age limits. The Keep Deleted Items For (Days) option specifies how long you want to retain items that have been deleted from this public folder. The items will remain hidden in the database for the number of days you specify, allowing you to recover them, if necessary.

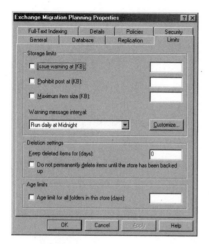

Figure 11-17. *Limits tab of the property sheet for a new public folder store.*

Suppose, for example, that you've set the deleted items option to 90 days. On May 1, you delete a posting titled March Memo. The deleted posting is stripped of its permissions, marked as hidden, and stamped with a future date and time that is exactly 90 days from the second that you deleted it. Now suppose that on July 18 you need some information that was in the March Memo. All you need to do is use your Microsoft Outlook client to recover the deleted item back into the public folder. The posting will be given its permissions back, the future deletion timestamp will be stripped from the object, and the memo will be available for use again. If you retrieve the information you need and then delete the March Memo item again, the same process will occur and another timestamp will be affixed to the object, indicating that it will be deleted in 90 days.

In addition, you can force the store to retain deleted items until the store has been backed up. To do so, select the Do Not Permanently Delete Items Until The Store Has Been Backed Up check box. You can also set age limits by entering a value in the Age Limit For All Folders In This Store (Days) box. Items that exceed this value based on the date and timestamp will expire automatically during the next garbage collection interval.

The Full-Text Indexing tab is dimmed during the creation of the public folder store, but the Details tab is not. On the Details tab, you can enter information about the store, such as its purpose or organizational information that might pertain to the store. Figure 11-18 shows an example of how the Details tab might be used.

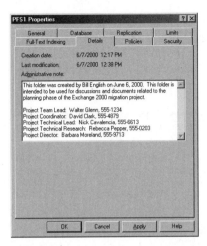

Figure 11-18. *Administrative notes for a public folder store.*

Also, in Figure 11-18, you'll notice a Policies tab. This tab will inform you about the Exchange policies that are currently being applied to this public folder store. Exchange Server has two kinds of policies: system and recipient. System policies are created to apply to servers, mailbox stores, and public stores. To learn more about public folder store policies, refer to Chapter 12.

Moving Transaction Log Files and Database Files

In Exchange Server 5.5, Microsoft provided the Microsoft Exchange Optimizer, a graphical wizard that enabled the movement of databases from one location to another. In Exchange 2000 Server, this has become a manual process that requires careful attention on your part as you move your files. Because all of the stores reference the same set of transaction logs, you can't move a single store in a storage group to another location without moving all of the other stores along with it. However, you can move individual files within a database to a separate location, which we will discuss in just a moment. When you attempt to move either the transaction log file location for a storage group or the stores within a storage group, you'll see the warning message shown in Figure 11-19, which will warn you that your current backups will be useless after the move. The reason moving a database invalidates current backups is that the transaction logs that have been backed up have the database path hard-coded in their headers. If you move a database, the headers in the backed-up copies of the transaction logs will still point to the old location for the database. Thus, a recovery process won't work because it won't be able to find the database that the transaction logs were supporting. See Chapter 2 for more information on this topic.

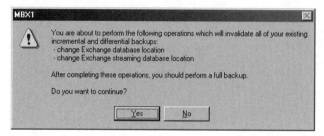

Figure 11-19. *Warning message that you see when you attempt to move a database.*

Since Microsoft recommends that your transaction log and stores be held on different spindles, you can relocate your transaction log files, your store databases, or both by using the General tab of the property sheet for the storage group in question (refer back to Figure 11-5). Simply select the new location where you want the files or databases to reside, and the following happens:

1. All of the stores are dismounted.
2. The selected files or databases are moved.
3. The stores are remounted.

As we mentioned a moment ago, you can select a store's database files to reside in two different places. To relocate a store's database files, use the Database tab on the store's property sheet (refer back to Figure 11-9). First dismount the store, and then enter the new directory location for the database files. You are not required to place them both in the same location. And, as we mentioned earlier, you can host databases on a volume mount point. Once you've chosen the new directory location and selected OK, the databases will be moved and Active Directory will be updated. This action also updates the headers in the transaction files automatically. The store should mount as it normally would.

Deleting a Store or Storage Group

Before you can delete a store or storage group, you must first remove its contents. Therefore, you'll need to delete your mailbox and public folder stores before deleting a storage group.

Deleting a Mailbox Store

Before you delete a mailbox store, you should first back up all of its data to ensure that you can later restore any important information that was inadvertently deleted. After finishing your backup, make sure that you have moved to another store any mailboxes you need to keep. If you're going to delete only one store, you can move its mailboxes to another store in the same storage group. Of course, if you're planning to delete the entire storage group, plan to move the mailboxes to a store in a different storage group. You can delete the mailbox store by right-clicking it in the Exchange System snap-in and choosing Delete.

If there are any messages in the SMTP queue awaiting outbound delivery, you will receive an error message informing you of this circumstance. If you choose to delete anyway, you will be given the option of selecting a new store to be used as the inbound queue for the SMTP messages. Any messages that have been encrypted by the Key Management Service (KMS) will not be deleted, and you will be directed to reconfigure the KMS to use a different mailbox store. Once you've done so, you'll be able to delete the encrypted messages in the queue.

Deleting a Public Folder Store

Deleting a public folder store is a bit more complicated than deleting a mailbox store. First, the store you are deleting must not be the last or only store that contains the public folder tree. If it is, you will not be able to delete the public folder store. Second, this store must not be the default public folder store for any mailbox stores or users. To determine whether this is the case, you'll need to look at the property sheet of each mailbox store to see if any of them are using the store you want to delete as their default public folder store. If any are, you'll want to reconfigure the mailbox store to use a different default public folder store. Third, if the public folder store to be deleted maintains the only replica of one or more folders, you will receive a warning that all data will be lost if you do not first replicate the data to another store.

Deleting a Storage Group

When there are no longer any stores associated with the storage group, you can delete it by right-clicking the group in the Exchange System snap-in and choosing Delete.

Creating a Full-Text Index

The information store creates and manages indexes for common key fields for faster lookups and searches. When you enable full-text indexing, the index is built before the client search, thus permitting faster searches. Full-text indexing makes it easy for Outlook users to search for documents, including text attachments, in the information store. Each information store can be indexed individually for flexibility. For a discussion of how indexing works, refer to Chapter 2.

To enable indexing, right-click the store you want to index, point to All Tasks, and choose Create Full-Text Index. Even though your selection is Create Full-Text Index, all you are doing at this point is enabling the indexing feature for this store. You'll be prompted for a location in which to create the catalog. Once you have specified the location, click OK and the indexing objects are created. You will see these new objects inside the Full-Text Indexing object (Figure 11-20).

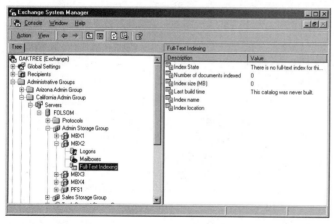

Figure 11-20. *Objects created with Full-Text Indexing.*

Initially, the Index State object will indicate that no full-text index was ever created for this store. In addition, the Last Build Time object will indicate that the catalog was never built. Thus, even though the indexing objects have been created, you still don't have a full-text index.

To create a full-text index, right-click the store object, point to All Tasks, and then choose either Start Full Population or Start Incremental Population. Start Full Population indexes all existing data, and Start Incremental Population indexes only information that is new or modified since the last full population. Depending on the amount of information in your store, this process could take from several minutes to several hours.

Once the index is populated, you will see that the value for the Number Of Documents Indexed container rises, as does the value for the Index Size (MB) container. You will also be able to discern when the last build time was for this store and the current location of your index databases.

Summary

This chapter has given you the information you need to administer storage groups in your Exchange organization. You should now understand the storage group architecture and be able to create and manage storage groups and stores. You should also know how to enable indexing and create a full-text index for a store. In the next chapter, you will learn how to implement and administer routing groups.

Chapter 12
Using Routing and Administrative Groups

In earlier versions of Microsoft Exchange Server, both the routing boundaries and the administrative boundaries were defined by the site. In Exchange 2000 Server, these two functions are broken out into routing groups and administrative groups. A *routing group* is a collection of Exchange 2000 servers that enjoy permanent, high-bandwidth connectivity. Routing groups are most often based on the physical topology of your network. Administrative groups are purely logical and are used to group individual administrative functions together to fit a company's organizational criteria. In this chapter, you will learn how to define and administer routing groups and administrative groups in Exchange 2000 Server.

Administrative Group Concepts

Administrative groups are used to define the administrative topology for large companies with many locations, departments, divisions, Exchange servers, and Exchange administrators. They are logical in nature, which means that you can define a group based on geography, department, division, or function. For instance, if your company has 14 offices in 14 countries, it is likely that you will have one or more Exchange servers in each location, with an Exchange administrator in each location as well. It might be best, in this scenario, to create an administrative group for each of your 14 locations so that the local Exchange administrator can administer the local Exchange servers. Another possible arrangement would be for one group to manage all of the routing group functions, another to manage all of the public folder functions, and still another to manage all of the recipient policy functions. With administrative groups, members of the larger Exchange 2000 administration team can specialize in one area of administration, even if your Exchange 2000 organization is worldwide.

An administrative group makes it easier to assign administrative permissions. After you have set the permissions for the administrative group object, any objects that are created or moved into the object will inherit its permissions. Hence, it is easiest to set permissions for an administrative group first and then to create objects inside the group and have them inherit the group's permissions. As always, it's best to set permissions at the highest object level and then have those permissions flow down the object hierarchy.

Objects that can be created in an administrative group include the following:

- Policies
- Routing groups
- Public folder trees
- Servers
- Conferencing services
- Chat communities

Choosing an Administrative Model

Essentially, there are three administrative models that you can use to organize your administrative groups: centralized, decentralized, and mixed. For the purposes of our discussion, we'll create a fictitious company called Oaktree, Inc. Oaktree has seven offices in three regions, as shown in Figure 12-1.

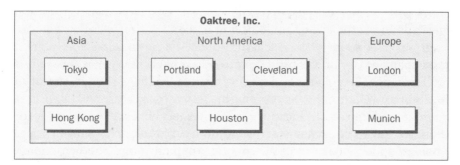

Figure 12-1. *Oaktree, Inc.*

Centralized Administrative Model

In the centralized administrative model, one group maintains complete control over all of the Exchange servers. You might have only one group or a few tightly controlled groups for administrative purposes. Your routing group topology does not need to be the same as the administrative topology, which means that you can have multiple routing groups that reflect your physical topology while maintaining centralized administrative control in one administrative group. Figure 12-2 illustrates how this would work for Oaktree, Inc.

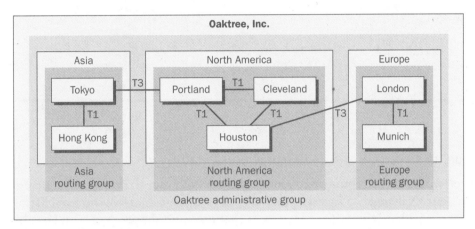

Figure 12-2. *Centralized administrative model.*

> **Note**   The fact that there is a high-speed connection between each of these geographical locations has no impact on the administrative model. All of the servers could be in the same administrative group, even if there was only an 8-Kbps connection between each location.

Decentralized Administrative Model

In the decentralized administrative model, each location has its own team of Exchange administrators and allows them administrative control over any objects placed inside their administrative group. These groups are often based on geographical locations or on the departmental needs of the company. Each of these groups can contain policies, servers, public folder trees, and other objects specific to the group. Figure 12-3 illustrates how this would work for Oaktree, Inc. We would set up an administrative group for each of the three continents and have a group of Exchange administrators, each of whom manages the Exchange servers in his or her own geographical area.

If you are migrating from Exchange Server 5.5 and you had multiple sites in your Exchange 5.5 organization, you will be forced into using a decentralized model of administration during the migration. Each Exchange 5.5 site will be created as a separate administrative group in Exchange 2000 Server.

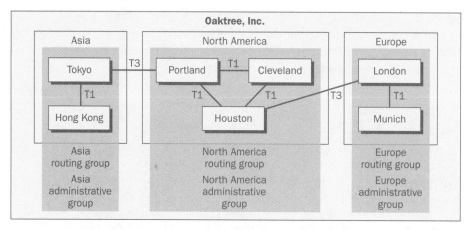

Figure 12-3. *Decentralized administrative model.*

If you would like to centralize administration for both your Exchange 2000 servers and your Exchange 5.5 servers, you'll need to set permissions on the administrative groups that limit administration of that group to those whom you specify. This action won't really incorporate the Exchange 5.5 servers into one administrative group, but it will limit administration to one group of administrators. The only way to really achieve the centralized model described previously is to migrate all of your Exchange 5.5 servers to Exchange 2000 Server.

Note Native mode means that there are no more legacy Exchange servers running on your network. Native mode for Exchange 2000 Server is separate and distinct from native mode for Microsoft Windows 2000. For more information on native mode—what it is and how it works in Exchange 2000 Server—see Chapter 14.

Mixed Administrative Model

The mixed administrative model is best for restricting certain administrative functions to certain people while not creating specializations for every administrative function. In this model, you create administrative groups by function rather than by geographical location or departmental boundaries. For instance, you might create an administrative group whose only child object is policies. In this scenario, you can restrict to a handful of people the ability to create new policies or alter existing policies for your Exchange 2000 organization. However, all other administrative functions remain under the default First Administrative Group and are not placed in their own administrative group.

You can also use this model to combine specialized administrative functions and geographical considerations into one administrative model. For instance, you might create an administrative group to manage the routing groups, a second group to manage policies, a third group for the Atlantic division, a fourth group for the European group, and a fifth group to manage all of the public folder trees. Figure 12-4 illustrates what this would look like for Oaktree, Inc., retaining a decentralized model for day-to-day administration but centralizing the public folder trees into one administrative group and the policies into another administrative group.

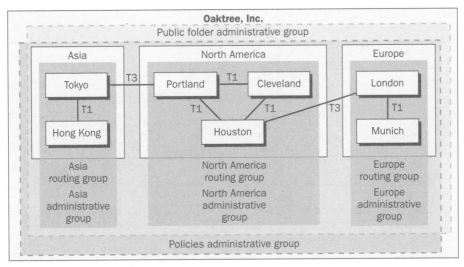

Figure 12-4. *Mixed administrative model.*

Administrative Groups and Permissions

Exchange 2000 Server permissions are based on the Windows 2000 Active Directory directory service and the Windows 2000 permissions model. This means that you can assign permissions to a user or group by object, child object, or object class.

When you create an object in Windows 2000, it inherits its parent's permissions by default. Inheritance allows permissions to flow down the object hierarchy so that child objects do not need to have their permissions manually assigned. In addition, when you need to change permissions for an entire range of objects, all you need to do is change the permissions for the parent object, and the child objects will inherit those permissions automatically.

Real World **Be Aware of How Permissions Flow in the Configuration Naming Partition**

By default, members of the Enterprise Admins group will have full control over your administrative groups. The Domain Admins group will also have significant permissions on these objects. Figure 12-5 shows an Active Directory Services Interface (ADSI) Edit console window that illustrates how these permissions are ultimately inherited from the configuration context. (ADSI Edit is a resource kit tool.)

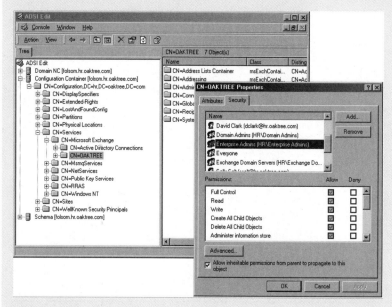

Figure 12-5. *ADSI Edit console, showing permissions inheritance for administrative groups.*

Because Exchange 2000 Server holds much of its information in the configuration partition of Active Directory, you'll notice that your Exchange 2000 organization is created in this partition. To Active Directory, the organization object is just another object to which default permissions flow.

If your climate is such that there is a sharp division between the activities of the Exchange administrators and the domain administrators, you'll need to create an Exchange Admins group and give this group full control over all aspects of your Exchange 2000 organization and limit the depth and scope of permissions for the Domain Admins group. You will have to do this manually on the organization object itself. In addition, you'll need to block inheritance of permissions from the Windows 2000 configuration partition and reassign permissions at the organization level for all of your Exchange 2000 Server objects.

For additional information on how to block permissions inheritance, refer to *Microsoft Windows 2000 Security Technical Reference* (Microsoft Press, 2000).

The permissions model in Exchange 2000 Server has been expanded to give administrators additional control over how permissions flow to containers and objects. This control is accomplished through customized inheritance, which allows you to specify that only certain objects can inherit permissions. Figure 12-6 illustrates these specialized permissions choices. You can specify inheritance for the following:

- This object only
- Inherit only
- This object and subcontainers
- This object and children objects
- Subcontainers only
- Children objects only
- This object, subcontainers, and children objects
- Subcontainers and children objects

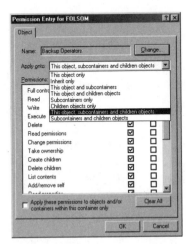

Figure 12-6. *Permissions for Exchange objects.*

Creating an Administrative Group

Because Exchange 2000 Server is installed in many small and medium-sized companies, the Administrative and Routing Group interface is disabled by default. To see these groups, navigate to the General tab of the organization's property sheet, as shown in Figure 12-7, and then, in the Administrative Views area, select Display Routing Groups and Display Administrative Groups, as desired.

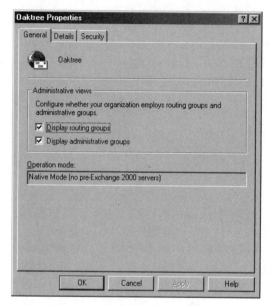

Figure 12-7. *Enabling the Administrative and Routing Group interface.*

Note Although Figure 12-7 shows the interface in native mode, you can also select these configurations in mixed mode. You do not need to be in native mode to see the routing and administrative groups.

Note that if your Exchange 2000 server is installed in an existing Exchange 5.5 site, the Administrative and Routing Group interface is enabled by default. Each Exchange 5.5 site will appear as a separate administrative group in the Exchange System snap-in. For more information on how Exchange 2000 and Exchange 5.5 servers can coexist, refer to Chapter 14.

Once you have enabled the Administrative and Routing Group interface, you can begin to set up your administrative groups. To do so, open the Exchange System snap-in, right-click the Administrative Groups container, point to New, and choose Administrative Group. Figure 12-8 illustrates the property sheet you will be working with. Simply enter your administrative group name and make any notes you desire on the Details tab, and you're done. You've created an administrative group.

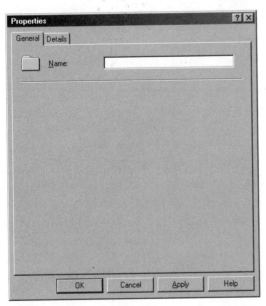

Figure 12-8. *Property sheet for a new administrative group.*

Once you have created an administrative group, you can turn your attention to creating child objects for the group. By default, no objects are created in the group. When you right-click the group, the shortcut menu allows you to create four new containers:

- Routing Groups container
- Public folders container
- Chat communities container
- Policy container

Creating a New Container

To create a new container that this administrative group will administer, choose the type of container you want to create from the shortcut menu (Figure 12-9). Once you make your selection, the container is created for you inside the administrative group. No wizard appears to create any of these containers. You'll also find that there are no properties to set because this is just a container. You can think of it as a box that will hold other boxes—nothing more, nothing less. Once created, the actual properties will be set on the routing groups themselves.

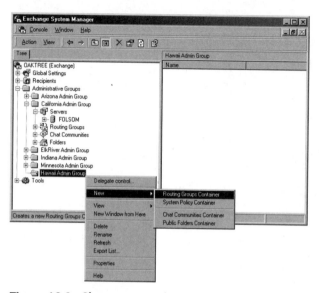

Figure 12-9. *Shortcut menu for a new administrative group, showing the types of containers you can create.*

Note Although Figure 12-9 shows four choices, sometimes you will see only three. The option to create a public folders container will not appear if the administrative group is new and no other containers have yet been created inside it. Once you create a new container, such as a new Routing Groups container, you'll see the option to add a public folders container when you attempt to create a second container. The option to create a public folders container will also not appear if you have already created a container of this type, since each administrative group needs only one public folders container.

Server Objects and Administrative Groups

In Exchange 2000, servers are always installed by default into the First Administrative group under the Server container. (The First Administrative group is given this name by default; you can change the name to fit your overall naming convention for administrative groups.) You'll notice that we don't have the option to create a Server container under a new administrative group and then move servers from the First Administrative group into the new administrative group. This is by design.

When a new administrative group is created, a Server container for the group is automatically created but not displayed in the Exchange System snap-in. This can be seen in our example with the Hawaii Admin group. In Figure 12-10, if we look at this administrative group in the Active Directory Sites and Services snap-in (running Show Services Node), you can see that both a Server container and an Advanced Security container have been created in the Hawaii Admin group, even though these don't appear in the Exchange System snap-in. However, once a server is installed into the administrative group, the server object will appear in the Exchange System snap-in. Therefore, you must create your administrative groups before installing your Exchange 2000 servers if you plan to have those servers spread across multiple administrative groups.

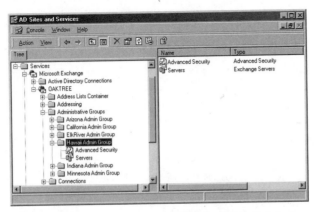

Figure 12-10. *Server object under the Hawaii Admin group in Active Directory Sites and Services.*

Exchange 2000 Policies

Policies are a new feature in Exchange 2000 Server and are designed to increase administrative flexibility while reducing administrative effort. A *policy* is a set of configuration parameters that applies to one or more Exchange objects in the same class. For example, you can create a policy that affects certain settings on some or all of your Exchange servers. If you ever want to change these settings, all you need to do is modify the policy and it will be applied to the appropriate server's organization.

There are two types of policies: system policies and recipient policies. *System policies* apply to a server, a mailbox store, or a public folder store. These policies appear in the Policies container under the administrative group responsible for administering the policy (Figure 12-11).

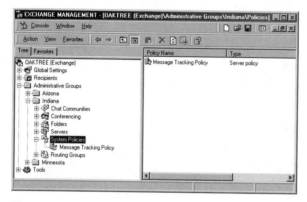

Figure 12-11. *System policy object.*

Recipient policies apply to mail-enabled objects and specify how to generate e-mail addresses. They appear under the Recipients container as recipient policy objects (Figure 12-12).

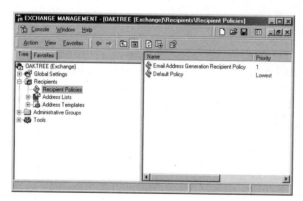

Figure 12-12. *Recipient policy objects.*

Creating a Policy

Generally speaking, creating a policy involves navigating to the appropriate Policies container, right-clicking the container, and then selecting the kind of policy you want to create. Recipient containers provide only one option: recipient policies. Policy containers in administrative groups give you the option of creating any type of system policy: a server policy, a mailbox store policy, or a public folder store policy.

When working with system policies, be sure to create the policy object in the administrative group that will be responsible for administering the policy. Failure to do so could lead to the wrong people having administrative control over your critical policies. Let's take a look at how to create each of the four types of policies, starting with server policies.

Creating a Server Policy

A server policy will enforce message tracking and log file maintenance settings. It is not used to enforce security or other settings on the servers in the administrative group. To create a server policy, right-click the System Policies container, point to New, and then choose Server Policy. You will see the New Policy dialog box (Figure 12-13), where you specify the tabs that will appear in the policy's property sheet. With a server policy, you'll have only one choice: the General tab. Check the box for this tab, and then click OK. You'll see the configuration box where the policy will be created.

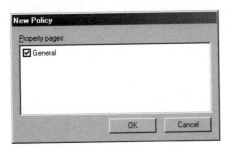

Figure 12-13. *New Policy dialog box.*

Next you need to enter the name of your policy on the General tab of the policy's property sheet. As Figure 12-14 shows, there are actually two General tabs. The first is for naming the policy. Choose a name that describes the task the policy is intended to accomplish, such as Message Tracking Policy or Enable Subject Logging Policy. Good naming at this stage will save you time in the long run because you won't need to look at the policy's properties to determine what the policy does.

The General (Policy) tab (Figure 12-15) is the actual policy that is applied to the Exchange servers in your organization. It is named General (Policy) because you are potentially configuring the General tabs of the property sheets of all of your servers. (We discuss how to apply this policy to servers throughout your organization later in this chapter.) If you compare this tab to the General tab in a server's property sheet, you will find that they are identical, except for the identifying information at the top of the tab.

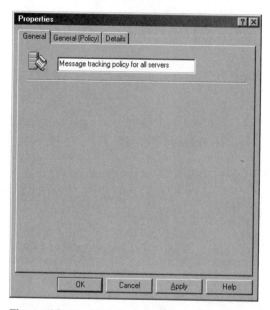

Figure 12-14. *Naming a policy on the General tab.*

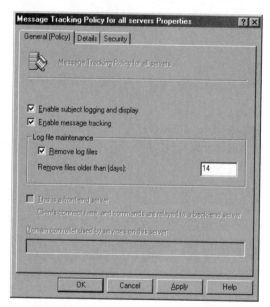

Figure 12-15. *General (Policy) tab.*

On the General (Policy) tab, you can enable subject logging and display for all of your Exchange 2000 servers. This setting works in tandem with the Enable Message Tracking option. Together, these two settings ensure that messages passed in your organization can be tracked. Enabling these two options is useful for troubleshooting if some users are not receiving messages from other users. You can track the message through your organization to determine where it is getting stuck to pinpoint where your transport problems exist. For more information on message tracking and subject logging, refer to Chapter 23.

You'll notice that the lower third of the General (Policy) tab is dimmed. In your server's property sheet, this area allows you to enable front end server services for the server. However, you cannot set a policy to make all of the Exchange servers front end servers. If you need a group of servers to act as front end servers, you'll have to configure each server's property sheet. For more on front end/back end architecture, see Chapter 2.

Once a policy is in force, it cannot be overridden at the local server level. The message tracking policy we've been using as an example was set on the Indianapolis server in the Indiana administrative group. However, we applied it to all three servers in the organization—Indianapolis, Minneapolis, and Tucson. Figure 12-16 illustrates that the message tracking options are dimmed in the property sheet for the Minneapolis server because these values have been set by a policy.

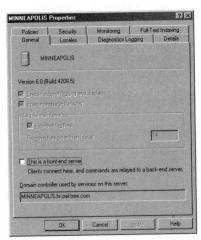

Figure 12-16. *Property sheet for the Minneapolis server, showing dimmed message tracking options.*

At this point, you might be wondering how we applied the policy to the three servers. Here are the steps you need to take to apply your policy once it has been created. After creating a server policy, you can apply that policy to any combination of servers in your organization. Simply right-click the policy object, and then choose Add Item. You see a dialog box listing all of the servers in your Exchange organization in the upper part of the box (Figure 12-17). To apply the policy to a server, highlight the server and then click Add. The server will be moved to the lower part of the dialog box. Repeat this procedure for all of the servers to which you want the policy to apply. Once you click OK, the policy is applied immediately to those servers. To verify this, select the policy object you just created in the Exchange System snap-in. The servers you added should appear in the details pane (Figure 12-18).

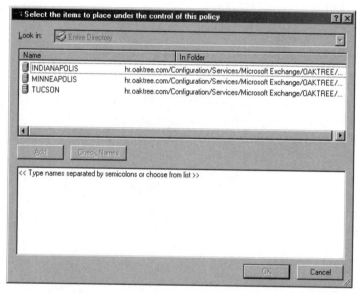

Figure 12-17. *Selecting servers to which the policy will apply.*

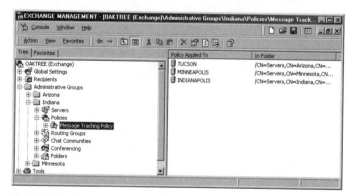

Figure 12-18. *Servers to which the selected policy applies.*

To remove a server from a policy, follow these steps:

1. Navigate to the server policy object in the Exchange System snap-in.
2. Highlight the server you want to remove in the details pane.
3. Right-click the server and choose Remove From Policy.

Should you make changes to an existing policy after you have saved your changes, you will be presented with a message box asking if you want to apply the changes in the policy to all of the objects immediately. You can select either Yes or No. Selecting Yes will force the policy to be applied immediately to the target objects. Selecting No will cause the policy changes to be applied at normal replication intervals.

Creating a Public Folder Store Policy

Public folder store policies encompass a number of configuration options, including maintenance schedules, limits, and full-text indexing. They are applied on a per-store basis across public folder tree boundaries.

The procedure for creating a public folder store policy is similar to the one for creating a server policy, described in the previous section. However, you have the option of specifying five tabs on the property sheet for a public folder store policy:

- General
- Database
- Replication
- Limits
- Full-Text Indexing

On the General (Policy) tab, you can enable support for Secure/Multipurpose Internet Mail Extensions (S/MIME) and specify that text should be converted to a fixed-sized font (10-point Courier). On the Database (Policy) tab, you can specify when you would like daily maintenance to run on your public folders. On the Replication (Policy) tab, you can specify how often you would like replication of public folders to occur as well as the replication size limit and the number of minutes that equates to the Always interval. On the Full-Text Indexing (Policy) tab, you can specify the update interval and the rebuild interval for your public folders. Finally, on the Limits (Policy) tab (Figure 12-19), you can specify storage limits, deletion settings, and age limits for all items in all folders in the public folder store.

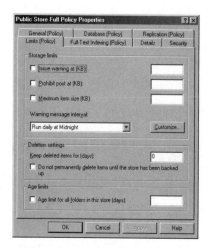

Figure 12-19. *The Limits (Policy) tab of the property sheet for a public folder store policy.*

To apply the policy to your public folders, you'll need to associate it with them just as you did for the server policy in the previous section. By default, no policy is actually applied to its intended recipient; you must associate it with the object by choosing Add Public Store from the policy's shortcut menu.

Unlike server policies, which have only one tab on their property sheet, a public folder store policy can have up to seven tabs. This doesn't mean that you have to use all of the tabs in a given policy. If you would like to add tabs to or delete tabs from an existing public folder store policy, all you need to do is right-click the policy and choose Change Property Pages. Then choose the tabs you want to add or delete, and configure them as needed.

Creating a Mailbox Store Policy

A mailbox store policy allows you to configure a number of settings for mailboxes, including the default public folder store, the maintenance schedule, a message journaling recipient that will receive copies of all e-mails that flow through the organization, and full-text indexing. When creating a mailbox store policy, you can choose to include the General, Database, Limits, and Full-Text Indexing tabs in the policy's property sheet.

Note Message journaling is a concept that was introduced with Exchange 5.5, Service Pack 1. Essentially, it sends copies of most e-mails to a common recipient for use later in either legal or governmental proceedings. This feature is most often enabled when a company is forced to retain all its e-mails to meet government regulations or for legal purposes.

On the General (Policy) tab, you can specify a default public folder store for the mailbox stores that will be associated with this policy. This ability is very handy if you need to create a large number of mailbox stores and want to associate most or all of them with a particular public folder store. The General (Policy) tab also allows you to specify the default offline address list that your selected mailbox stores will use. You can choose to archive messages on this store. In addition, you can enable client support of S/MIME signatures and a fixed-sized font for all incoming messages.

The only item you can set on the Database (Policy) tab is the time at which daily maintenance will run. If you are creating a public folder store policy as well, consider staggering their maintenance times to allow for better system performance during the online maintenance routine. In your planning, be sure to consider other routines that run during off-hours too, including backup programs, online defragmentation of the database, and replication.

> **Note**   The major tasks that the store runs for online maintenance include making sure that the correct free/busy and offline address book folders exist for an administrative group and, if they don't exist, creating them; purging database indexes that were previously created but haven't been used recently; deleting items over the time limit that have exceeded the deleted items retention time (called a hard delete); expiring items in public folders over their age limit; purging deleted mailboxes from the store that are over their retention limit; and detecting mailboxes that are no longer connected to a user object as well as detecting mailboxes that have been reconnected to a user.

On the Limits (Policy) tab (Figure 12-20), you can specify storage limits and deletion settings. Based on mailbox size, you can also choose when you would like the System Attendant service to notify users that they have exceeded their limits. Using the Customize button to create a customized schedule allows you to set more than one time during a 24-hour period when users exceeding their limits will be notified by system e-mail that they need to take action to reduce the size of their mailbox.

When you apply a mailbox store policy, you do so on a store-by-store basis, not on a per-storage-group or per-server basis. Also, the mailbox store does not need to be mounted for you to be able to associate it with the policy.

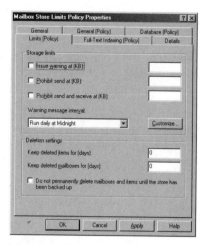

Figure 12-20. *The Limits (Policy) tab of the property sheet for a mailbox store policy.*

Creating a Recipient Policy

A recipient policy is essentially a way to create an LDAP filter rule for address-generation purposes. With this filtering tool, you can specify what kind of e-mail address is generated for each recipient object. For instance, you can indicate that your users based in Minneapolis who have the string of characters "Minneapolis" in their City field should be given an SMTP address of msp.hr.oaktree.com instead of the default hr.oaktree.com, and the policy will change the SMTP addresses for all corresponding Minneapolis users. With the LDAP filter rules, you finally have the flexibility and administrative control you need to create the exact e-mail addresses your organization requires.

Instead of specifying each recipient object that you want to associate with the policy, you use the LDAP filter rules to define the type and class of the recipient objects to associate with the policy. Once you have created the policy, it is applied in the background, based on the time schedule set in the Address List service run by the System Attendant.

One huge advantage of using recipient policies is the ability to set multiple SMTP or X.400 addresses for each user in your organization. If your company has several divisions, each of which is known in the marketplace for its own brand name, you can create a policy that will assign multiple, dissimilar SMTP addresses to each mail-enabled user to ensure that your users get all of their e-mail, regardless of which domain name it is addressed to.

Let's take a look at how to create this type of policy, and then we'll see how to configure it. To create a recipient policy, navigate to the Recipients container, right-click the Recipient Policies subcontainer, and choose New Recipient Policy. Figure 12-21 shows the initial dialog box that appears.

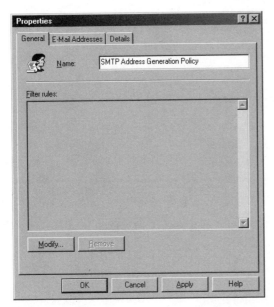

Figure 12-21. *General tab of the property sheet for a recipient policy.*

On the General tab, you can click Modify to change the filter rules. When you do so, you are presented with the Find Exchange Recipients dialog box (Figure 12-22). This is the same dialog box that you see when you use the Find command in Active Directory, except that here your choices create the filter rules that will select the addresses to which the policy will apply.

The Storage tab of the Find Exchange Recipient dialog box (Figure 12-23) lets you apply this policy to all mailboxes, only to mailboxes on a certain server, or only to mailboxes in a certain store. This feature gives you added flexibility in applying the policy.

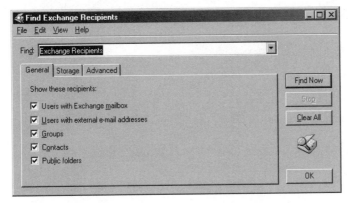

Figure 12-22. *Find Exchange Recipients dialog box.*

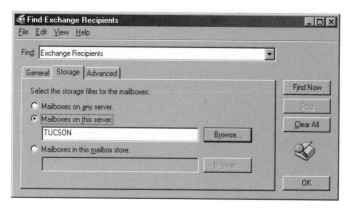

Figure 12-23. *Storage tab of the Find Exchange Recipients dialog box.*

On the E-Mail Address Policy tab, you can choose which e-mail addresses you want to have created for your user objects. By default, an SMTP address and an X.400 address are created for each recipient object. Exchange 2000 Server requires both an X.400 address and an SMTP address for each mail-enabled object. You cannot disable the generation of these two address types.

Managing Policy Conflicts

It is possible that two different policies will conflict when applied to the same object. When this occurs, the default behavior is for the newer policy to replace the older policy. However, if the Do Not Allow The Removal Of This Policy From The Items It Applies To check box is selected, the newer policy will not be able to override the older policy, and you will receive a message indicating that the object has been placed under the control of a conflicting policy (Figure 12-24). You will then be asked if you want to remove the object from the control of the conflicting policies. Choosing Yes will apply the new policy, and choosing No will keep the old policy.

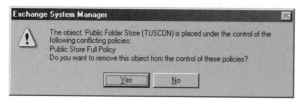

Figure 12-24. *Message indicating a conflicting policy.*

Creating and Administering Routing Groups

As you've seen, an administrative group is a collection of server objects that are grouped together to allow administrative activities to be performed on those objects as a unit. By contrast, a routing group is a collection of servers that enjoy permanent, high-bandwidth connectivity. The links between routing groups are assumed to be either slow or unreliable. Connectors are used to connect routing groups over these slow WAN links. Thus, while administrative groups are logical in nature, routing groups are determined by the physical topology of your network.

Routing groups allow you to specify the routes that messages will take to get from the sender to the recipient within your organization. By implementing costs on the connectors, you can channel the physical path you want messaging to take in your organization. For more information on the architecture of routing groups, refer to Chapter 3.

Creating a Routing Group

You will need to create routing groups if you have two or more servers that are connected over a slow or unreliable WAN link. You can create routing groups in either mixed mode or native mode. Although routing groups do not need to be mapped to administrative group boundaries in native mode, they cannot span administrative groups in mixed mode. This limitation is imposed by the way in which Exchange 5.5 interoperates with Exchange 2000 Server. As long as Exchange 2000 Server is in mixed mode, it will retain its ability to interoperate with Exchange 5.5. And since you cannot move servers between sites in Exchange 5.5, you cannot move them between routing groups or administrative groups in Exchange 2000 Server.

You'll create your routing groups inside the Routing Groups container. If your situation warrants it, you can create new Routing Groups containers in other administrative groups. You can create only one Routing Groups container per administrative group, but you can create multiple routing groups in each Routing Groups container.

To create a routing group, simply right-click the Routing Groups container, point to New, and then select Routing Group. Enter the name of the new routing group on the General tab, and click OK.

Your new routing group will consist of two child objects, Connectors and Members (Figure 12-25). The Connectors container is where you will create your Routing Group Connectors (for details, see Chapter 13), and the Members container is where you will place the server objects that are members of the routing group.

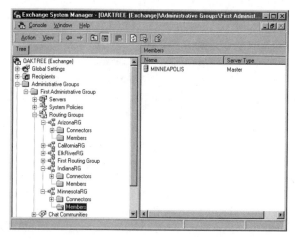

Figure 12-25. *Objects in a new routing group.*

If you need to connect to a foreign e-mail system, you can do so by installing either an X.400 Connector or an SMTP Connector, most likely the former. (See Chapter 22 for information about how to connect to a foreign system.) These connectors can also be used to connect routing groups within your organization, but it is best to use the Routing Group Connector for this purpose. The Routing Group Connector can be used only inside your organization to connect your routing groups. It cannot be used to connect to a foreign e-mail system.

Administering a Routing Group

Two of your primary tasks in administering a routing group will be to create new routing groups and to add one or more servers to a routing group. When you add a server to a routing group, you are, in effect, telling Exchange 2000 Server that the server being added has high-speed, permanent connectivity to the other servers in the group. Although no minimum bandwidth floor is hard-coded into the Exchange operating system, the suggested absolute minimum is a 64-Kbps connection that is available at all times.

> **Note**   Be sure to test your WAN links before implementing Exchange 2000 Server. A leased line of 64 Kbps might offer more *permanent* bandwidth than a T1 that is often saturated with non-Exchange traffic. A prudent approach is to account for all other traffic on your WAN links and then use the amount of bandwidth left over to determine whether you have permanent, high-bandwidth connectivity.

To add a server to a routing group, follow these steps:

1. Navigate to and select the Members container for the routing group to which the server currently belongs (by default, the First Routing Group).

2. Drag the server into the Members container of the destination routing group.

> **Note**   When you remove a server from a routing group, you are actually removing the SMTP virtual server or the X.400 service through which that server communicates and having the service re-created in the new routing group.

By default, all of the servers created in your organization belong to the First Routing Group, which is the default routing group that is created when Exchange 2000 Server is initially installed. However, you might well need additional routing groups based on your physical topology.

To rename a routing group object, simply right-click the routing group, choose Rename, and enter the new name. To delete a routing group, you must first move all of the servers that are members of the doomed routing group to other routing groups. You cannot delete a routing group that has server objects residing in the Members container. After you have moved all of the servers, right-click the routing group and choose Delete. Click Yes to confirm the routing group deletion.

Summary

In this chapter, you have seen how to create and manage both administrative and routing groups. When it comes to routing groups, the containers themselves are not that difficult to manage. However, creating and managing the connectors between routing groups is not always easy and oftentimes presents additional challenges to the administrator. It is the challenges of routing group connectors to which we will turn our attention in the next chapter.

Chapter 13
Connecting Routing Groups

Chapter 3 discussed the message-routing architecture of a Microsoft Exchange 2000 network. It also discussed routing groups and how they can be used to group together servers that enjoy permanent, high-speed connectivity. Further, it described the link state algorithm, a link propagation protocol that replaces and improves upon the Gateway Address Routing Table (GWART) of Exchange Server 5.5. In Chapter 12, you learned how to create and administer routing groups and administrative groups. What you need to know now to make it all work is how to create and administer the individual connectors and the link state information that is generated automatically. That is the focus of this chapter.

There are really only three connectors that you can use to connect your routing groups: the Routing Group Connector, the SMTP Connector, and the X.400 Connector. The Routing Group Connector is the one you will use most often to connect your routing groups. You will use the SMTP Connector for Internet mail messaging. Let's take a look at how to set up and administer each of these connectors. (The X.400 Connector is discussed in Chapter 3.)

Routing Group Connector

The Routing Group Connector is, in most environments, the best choice for connecting routing groups. It is easy to administer and uses the Simple Mail Transport Protocol (SMTP), which means that it can be used even when bandwidth is either slow or unreliable.

The Routing Group Connector is a unidirectional connection from one server in one routing group to another server in a different routing group. Therefore, if bidirectional communication is necessary, you'll need to create two connectors to form the logical, bidirectional link between the two routing groups.

Because Routing Group Connectors are always one-way connections, after you have created one end of the connector, you'll be prompted to have Exchange Server automatically create a Routing Group Connector in the remote routing group. If you choose to do so, the connector that is created in the remote routing group will inherit the settings you have chosen for the local connector, with some exceptions.

First, on the General tab of the Routing Group Connector (Figure 13-1), if the remote routing group has more than one server, Exchange Server will select the These Servers Can Send Mail Over This Connector option and then select each SMTP virtual server for this configuration. If any of the virtual servers that have been created on the target servers are incompatible with message transfer over this connector, you'll need to either manually remove those servers from this list or configure the other connector manually.

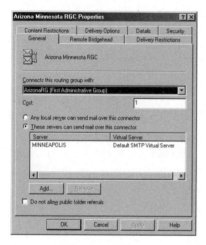

Figure 13-1. *Specifying servers that can send mail over this connector.*

Second, on the Remote Bridgehead tab (Figure 13-2), Exchange Server will list all of the SMTP virtual servers as target servers. Again, if you have an SMTP virtual server that cannot be a target server, you'll need to either remove the server from the list or configure the connector manually.

If your Exchange 2000 organization includes Exchange 5.*x* servers and those servers reside in a separate Windows NT 4 domain, you can have this Routing Group Connector connect as an account in the NT 4 domain. Remember that a Routing Group Connector will look like a site connector in the Exchange 5.*x* organization and that it functions in the same way as the Override tab of the site connector.

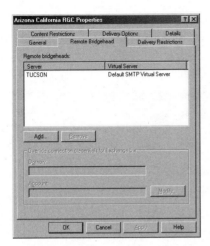

Figure 13-2. *Specifying target servers for this connector.*

The Routing Group Connector uses a bridgehead server, which acts as the gateway through which messages flow into and out of the routing group. As with the Site Connector in Exchange Server 5.5, you can configure the Routing Group Connector to use multiple target bridgehead servers. Unlike the Site Connector, however, in which you assign a cost to each target server, a Routing Group Connector contacts the target servers in a sequential order that you specify. The obvious advantage of identifying multiple servers as bridgehead servers is that if one bridgehead server goes down, Exchange 2000 Server will choose another through which to transmit the message.

The Routing Group Connector uses SMTP as its transport protocol, giving it a higher tolerance than the Site Connector in Exchange Server 5.*x* for lower-bandwidth and higher-latency environments. The Site Connector uses TCP to initiate and maintain a connection to the target bridgehead server and then uses remote procedure calls (RPCs) to invoke the connector's functions. RPCs incur much overhead and require higher bandwidth and greater permanency to maintain their bindings. In contrast, although the Routing Group Connector passes SMTP commands through a TCP session, the commands don't make RPC calls to the target server. Instead, SMTP sends a series of discreet commands that can tolerate lower bandwidth and less permanency than RPCs can. For a more complete discussion of SMTP, please see Chapter 17.

When you upgrade an Exchange 5.5 bridgehead server that is configured with a Site Connector, you'll find that the connector is upgraded to a Routing Group Connector that communicates over RPC to Exchange 5.*x* servers yet uses SMTP to communicate with other Exchange 2000 servers.

The Routing Group Connector contains several features not available in the Site Connector in Exchange Server 5.5. First, you can create a schedule to define when messages will pass over the connector. In addition, you can schedule messages based on size (for instance, any message over 2 MB) so that you can send them when bandwidth usage is lower.

Note Microsoft recommends having at least 64 Kbps of available bandwidth for a connection handled by a Routing Group Connector. Also, no encryption is currently available between the bridgehead servers.

Real World   Resolving Target Server IP Addresses for Bridgehead Servers

When a bridgehead server (BHS) that hosts a Routing Group Connector receives a message destined for a server in the other routing group, the BHS takes several steps to resolve the IP address of the target BHS. The BHS contacts DNS and attempts to resolve the IP address of the mail exchanger (MX) record of the target machine. If multiple MX records exist, it considers the preference values when deciding which BHS to resolve to. If no MX record exists, the BHS queries DNS for an address A record and attempts resolution. When using Microsoft Windows 2000 DNS, all Windows 2000–based servers automatically register A records in DNS. If no A record exists, the BHS attempts to resolve the IP address using the NetBIOS name resolution process.

Note To learn more about the DNS and Windows 2000, refer to *Microsoft Windows 2000 TCP/IP Protocols and Services Technical Reference* (Microsoft Press, 2000) and *Active Directory Services for Microsoft Windows 2000 Technical Reference* (Microsoft Press, 2000).

Creating a Routing Group Connector

To create a new Routing Group Connector, right-click the Connectors container (it appears as a folder) located under the Routing Group container in the Exchange System snap-in, point to New, and then select Routing Group Connector. On the General tab, enter the name of the connector and then select the routing group to which you would like this connector to connect (Figure 13-3).

You can also select either Any Local Server Can Send Mail Over This Connector or These Servers Can Send Mail Over This Connector. The first option is the default and allows any server in the routing group to use the connector for sending messages destined for a server in the other routing group. The second option is a way to reserve the connector for certain virtual servers in the routing group. When you select this option, you'll be able to specify the virtual servers in the routing group that can use this connector.

Tip   Be sure to select a virtual server that will send mail to the destination routing group. For instance, assume that you have a group of external users who send their messages into the organization using Transport Layer Security (TLS) and that you've set up an SMTP virtual server to accept mail on a second IP address over port 25. This SMTP virtual server requires a certificate for authentication. Let's now assume that there are no such configurations for the local users on your LAN. If you were to choose this virtual server as the only server to send mail over the Routing Group Connector you are creating, messages sent by the local users would be rejected because the message would be routed back to the second IP address of the server and the SMTP server would be looking for TLS security and certificates. In this scenario, you want to be sure you *don't* select this virtual server for your Routing Group Connector.

At the bottom of the General tab, you can select Do Not Allow Public Folder Referrals. Selecting this check box means that if a client cannot access or find a public folder replica in the local routing group, the client will not be allowed to look for it in the public folder servers in the other routing group over this Routing Group Connector.

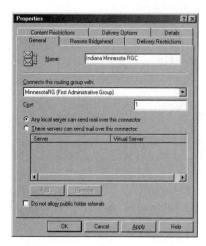

Figure 13-3. *General tab of the Routing Group Connector's property sheet.*

Remote Bridgehead Tab

On the Remote Bridgehead tab (refer back to Figure 13-2), you can specify one or more servers in the remote routing group with which this connector will attempt to establish a connection before sending messages. The servers are contacted in order, starting at the top of the list. Also, if the destination server has more than one SMTP virtual server configured, you'll need to select the one that will allow messages to be sent across the connector you are setting up.

Delivery Restrictions Tab

On the Delivery Restrictions tab (Figure 13-4), you can indicate who can use this connector, either by specifying that all messages are to be rejected except for those from a select list of users or by specifying that all messages are to be accepted except those from a select list of users. You'll find that you cannot enter Active Directory directory service distribution groups here. Instead, you can enter only mail-enabled users and contacts.

> **Tip** To select more than one user from Active Directory, highlight the first user in the Select Recipient list and then use the down or up arrow on your keyboard to select a contiguous list of users. To select a discontiguous list of users, hold down the Ctrl key and then use your mouse to highlight all the users you want to add to this list.

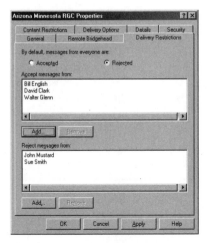

Figure 13-4. *Delivery Restrictions tab of the Routing Group Connector's property sheet.*

Real World   Giving Priority to Messages from Certain Users

When used in conjunction with the cost assigned to the connector itself, the Delivery Restrictions tab can be configured to give messages sent via the Routing Group Connector from a certain group of users a higher priority than messages sent from other users. For instance, suppose that your sales staff and pre-sales support staff are located in two different cities that also represent two different routing groups. Let's further assume that most of your orders come in over the telephone and that when members of your sales staff have a technical question about a product, they need to send that question via e-mail to the pre-sales support staff. In this scenario, you might want to set up two Routing Group Connectors. The first would be a connector with a cost of 100 that would accept messages from any user and forward them on as appropriate but would reject messages from members of the sales staff. The second connector would have a cost of 1, and it would reject all users except for the members of the sales staff, who would be listed on the Delivery Restrictions tab. This arrangement would cause the sales staff's messages to be sent to the other routing group faster than messages from other users.

Delivery Options Tab

The Delivery Options tab, shown in Figure 13-5, allows you to specify when messages can flow through the connector. This ability is especially helpful if you're using the connector over a slow or unreliable WAN link. By selecting the Use Different Delivery Times For Oversize Messages check box, you can hold larger messages until the times you set, presumably when the connector is experiencing little traffic.

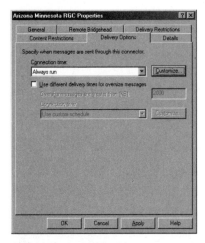

Figure 13-5. *Delivery Options tab for the Routing Group Connector's property sheet.*

Content Restrictions Tab

On the Content Restrictions tab, shown in Figure 13-6, you can set the priorities, types, and sizes of messages that can pass over this Routing Group Connector. Under Allowed Types, selecting the System Messages option allows the transmission of all non-user-generated messages, including directory replication, public folder replication, network monitoring, and delivery and nondelivery report messages. In the Allowed Sizes area, you can restrict messages to those less than a specified size.

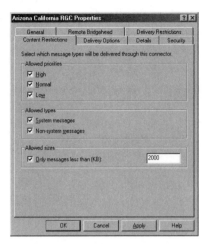

Figure 13-6. *Content Restrictions tab for the Routing Group Connector's property sheet.*

SMTP Connector

As with the Internet Mail Connector (IMC) in Exchange Server 5.5, the primary use of the SMTP Connector in Exchange 2000 Server is for external communication, either to the Internet or to a non–Exchange 2000 environment. Like the Routing Group Connector, it is a unidirectional connector.

When connected to the Internet, the SMTP Connector uses a smart host (another SMTP server to which messages are sent for routing) or MX records in DNS for next-hop routing. When configured internally between two routing groups, the connector relays link state information between routing groups but still depends on the MX records in DNS for next-hop information.

The SMTP Connector is different from the Routing Group Connector in that it can use encryption and authentication. If encryption is necessary for some of your messages, you'll need to use the SMTP Connector. Another feature of the SMTP Connector is its ability to authenticate in a remote domain before sending a message to it. Like the Routing Group Connector, the SMTP Connector lets you schedule messages to be sent at a time when bandwidth usage is low.

The SMTP Connector allows you to create scopes that permit only certain servers in your Exchange organization to use the connector. Instead of limiting the replication of this connector to the servers inside the scope, you can now choose to allow either all servers in the organization to use this connector or only the servers in the local routing group (Figure 13-7).

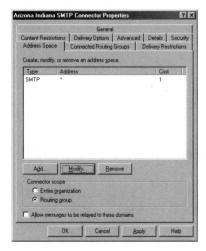

Figure 13-7. *Configuring the scope of the SMTP Connector.*

Finally, you'll want to use the SMTP Connector if your bandwidth is less than 64 Kbps and higher than 16 Kbps. If your sole reason for choosing the SMTP Connector is that you want to use SMTP between your routing groups, choose the Routing Group Connector instead. The Routing Group Connector uses SMTP as its transport protocol.

Creating an SMTP Connector

You create an SMTP Connector in the same manner as you create a Routing Group Connector: right -click the routing group, point to New, and choose SMTP Connector. Once you've done so, you're presented with the connector's property sheet with the General tab displayed (Figure 13-8), where you will name the connector and make some choices regarding DNS. The Use DNS To Route To Each Address Space On This Connector option causes the connector itself to work with DNS to make direct connections to the destination SMTP server, based on the MX records and preference values. If you would rather forward mail upstream because multiple direct connections either take too long or are too costly, select the Forward All Mail Through This Connector To The Following Smart Host option. You can enter either the fully qualified domain name (FQDN) of the smart host or its IP address here. If you choose to enter the IP address, you must place it inside brackets—for example, [192.168.2.200]. Also, the value you specify here will override the value in the Smart Host setting on the Advanced Delivery dialog box, which you display by clicking Advanced on the Delivery tab of the SMTP virtual server's property sheet.

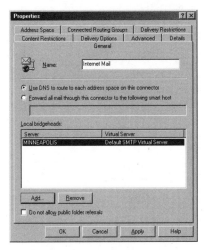

Figure 13-8. *General tab of the SMTP Connector's property sheet.*

Delivery Options Tab

The Delivery Options tab of the SMTP Connector's property sheet has one feature that the property sheet for the Routing Group Connector doesn't have: Queue Mail For Remote Triggered Delivery. This feature allows clients to connect periodically to your Exchange 2000 server and download messages. To make this process secure, your clients must connect using an account in your domain. When you click the Add button to specify the accounts that are authorized to use TURN/ATRN, you'll find that only local domain accounts are available. This restriction occurs because it is your Exchange 2000 server that is holding mail for others to retrieve, and hence they need to be authenticated in your domain. Therefore, you need to specify which Windows 2000 accounts can download mail. The client must issue a TURN command to trigger the download from Exchange 2000 Server.

Advanced Tab

Figure 13-9 shows the Advanced tab of the SMTP Connector's property sheet, which has a number of important configuration options that you'll need to consider as you set up the connector. First, you can set the SMTP Connector to send HELO instead of EHLO. Traditionally, when an SMTP client connects to an SMTP server, the first command that is sent is the HELO command. This command starts the session and identifies the sender of the coming message. By default, Exchange 2000 Server sends the EHLO command, which is a start command that also indicates that the Exchange 2000 server is able to use the Extended SMTP (ESMTP) commands. Not all SMTP servers are capable of communicating using these extended commands. If you need to connect to an SMTP server that doesn't understand ESMTP commands, select this check box to have Exchange Server send the HELO start command instead. To see a list of SMTP commands, refer to Chapter 17.

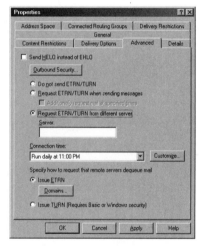

Figure 13-9. *Advanced tab of the SMTP Connector's property sheet.*

Also on the Advanced tab, you can use the Outbound Security button to provide authentication credentials to the remote domain. The Do Not Send ETRN/TURN option prevents this connector from requesting a dequeuing off a remote server. This option is selected by default. When selected, it permits this connector to be used only for basic sending and receiving of messages via SMTP; no remote dequeuing requests can be made. You'll want to leave this option selected most of the time.

If you want to send a dequeuing message along with other messages that are being sent to an SMTP server, select the Request ETRN/TURN When Sending Messages option. If you choose this option, you can also request dequeuing at certain times by selecting the Additionally Request Mail At Specified Times check box and then choosing the dequeuing time under Connection Time. You would use these settings, for example, when your Exchange server connects to another Exchange server via a dial-up connection. Once connected, your Exchange server would send any mail destined for the receiving server. Within the same session, a request would be sent to the other Exchange server to dequeue any messages that are destined for mailboxes located within your Exchange environment.

To request dequeuing from a server other than the one to whom the message was sent, select the Request ETRN/TURN From Different Server option and then enter the server's name. Select this option when you have one server that will handle your outbound messages and another server that holds your inbound messages for your organization.

If you would like to request that dequeuing occur at certain times, select the Connection Time drop-down list and choose one of the default options, or click the Customize button and set the schedule that is needed. You might use this setting if your Exchange server did not have a permanent connection to the Internet and you wanted to retrieve your e-mail from your ISP periodically, using a dial-up connection.

Finally, under Specify How To Request That Remote Servers Dequeue Mail, select either the Issue ETRN option or the Issue TURN option. To use ETRN, you must have a static IP address, whereas with TURN, you do not need a static IP address. In addition, ETRN requires that the domain to be dequeued be specified, so if you click on the Domains button, you can add the local domain name that you want dequeued.

Address Space Tab

When you connect to a foreign system, you must specify an address space that the connector will use. An *address space* is a set of address information associated with a connector or gateway that specifies the domains to which this connector will send messages. Typically, an address space is a subset of a complete address; usually, it is just the domain name.

You specify the address space on the Address Space tab of the connector's property sheet (Figure 13-10). If this SMTP Connector will be used for your organization's Internet mail, you can choose "*" as the address space, which means that any string of characters will be valid and messages can be routed to any domain over this connector.

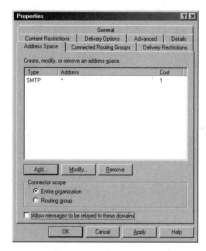

Figure 13-10. *Address Space tab of the SMTP Connector's property sheet.*

You can specify address spaces for SMTP, X.400, Lotus cc:Mail, Microsoft Mail, Lotus Notes, and Novell GroupWise types of addresses. If the address space that you need to use is not one of these types, select Other and enter the address space.

You can prevent messaging relay by not selecting the Allow Messages To Be Relayed To These Domains check box. This will ensure that unsolicited e-mails cannot be routed through your SMTP server back out to the Internet. However, if this SMTP Connector is being used as a relay point between two foreign SMTP systems, select this check box and add the destination name of the domain to which messages should be relayed to the address space area above.

Finally, if you want to limit the use of this SMTP Connector to those servers that are members of the same routing group, select the Routing Group option in the Connector Scope area. The default is to allow all servers in the organization to use this connector. Since servers that are not in the same routing group are assumed to exist across either a slow connection or a nondedicated connection, it is a good idea to enable this setting to keep servers in remote routing groups from routing messages to the Internet or a foreign mail system over this connector.

Real World   **Setting Up the SMTP Server as a Relay Server**

Let's assume that your organization is known by two different names in the marketplace: oaktree.com and sugarmaple.com. Let's further assume that you want all messages to enter the organization through the SMTP Connector on a server that is a member of the oaktree.com domain. Here are the steps you would take to make sure that all messages for both domain names are routed correctly:

1. Enter an A record in DNS for this server's host name and IP address.
2. Enter two MX records in DNS, one for each domain, both pointing to this server's IP address.
3. Create the SMTP Connector for the oaktree.com domain.
4. Add sugarmaple.com as a valid address space.
5. Select the Allow Messages To Be Relayed To These Domains check box.
6. Create an MX record and an A record in your internal DNS tables to point to the internal SMTP server that is serving the sugarmaple.com domain.

Now messages addressed to either sugarmaple.com or oaktree.com will be routed to the same server, and those messages addressed to sugarmaple.com will be relayed to the sugarmaple.com Exchange 2000 server.

Connected Routing Groups Tab

If you do not configure an address space on the Address Space tab, you must use the Connected Routing Groups tab to indicate which routing groups are connected to the local routing group. The purpose here is to inform the connector which routing groups are adjacent to it to enable internal routing of messages. The routing groups are recorded by administrative group membership, so your choice will always involve selecting the administrative group as well. If your organization is small, with one routing group and one administrative group, enter an address space on the Address Space tab and leave this tab blank.

Link State Administration

This section takes a look at how to manage the link state information for your Exchange system. Refer to Chapter 3 for a discussion of how the link state protocol works.

Administration of link state information takes place inside the protocols, not the connectors, and is mainly a function of queue management. We will be most concerned with the SMTP protocol (Figure 13-11), since it is used by both the Routing Group Connector and the SMTP Connector.

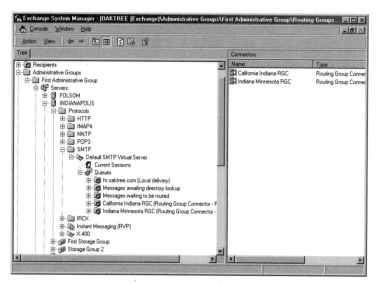

Figure 13-11. *SMTP queues in Exchange System.*

Before launching into our discussion, let's look at the topology for a network that we will use as an example. Figure 13-12 shows that our fictitious company, hr.oaktree.com, has offices in four cities: Folsom, Tucson, Minneapolis, and Indianapolis. It also shows the user located in each city that we will use to illustrate messaging and connectivity. We are assuming that each connector's cost is equal to 1. Furthermore, the Routing Group Connectors are named by state, such as California Arizona RGC for the link between Folsom, California, and Tucson, Arizona. And finally, the servers are named after their location, so that we have four servers: Tucson, Folsom, Minneapolis, and Indianapolis.

It is important to note that each server's display of the overall routing topology will be different because not all of the routes or connectors are displayed in Exchange System for any given server. Take a moment to familiarize yourself with this topology before reading on.

When ssmith sends a message to benglish, it must pass through the Folsom server. Figure 13-13 shows a trace of a message sent from ssmith to benglish, listing the path it took. The reason the message does not pass through Minneapolis is that it is not the lowest-cost route. By default, routing will occur over the route with the lowest cost, which in this case is Indianapolis to Folsom to Tucson, for a total cost of 2.

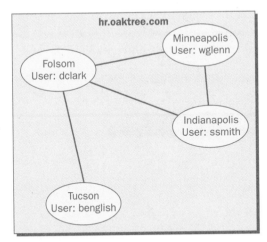

Figure 13-12. *Routing topology for hr.oaktree.com.*

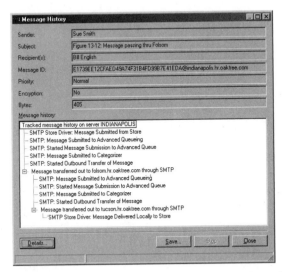

Figure 13-13. *Trace of a message passing through the Folsom server.*

Now that you've familarized yourself with our ficticious company, let's look at how the Link State protocol works when a link goes down. We'll cover four different scenarios and illustrate how the Link State protocol is administered.

Scenario 1: First Link Is Unavailable

A message sent from ssmith to benglish must travel over two separate links (Indianapolis/Folsom and Folsom/Tucson) and through three different servers (Indianapolis, Folsom, and Tucson). Let's assume that Folsom has gone off line for some reason and that ssmith sends a message to benglish. As Figure 13-14 shows, the message is initially placed in the outbound queue for the California Indiana RGC.

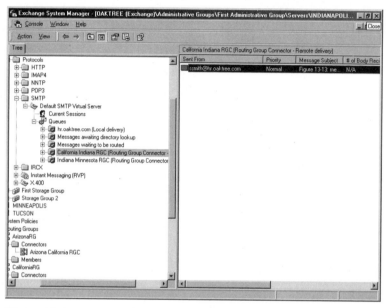

Figure 13-14. *Message held in the outbound queue of the California Indiana Routing Group Connector.*

Managing Messages in Outbound Queues

When a message is held in an outbound queue, it doesn't automatically appear in the contents pane (the right pane). The reason for this is that if messages are accumulating in the queue, enumerating those messages for display could take anywhere from several seconds to several minutes once you've selected the queue. Instead, Microsoft has given us a handy way of knowing that something is wrong with the queue. As you can see in Figure 13-15, the icon in the scope pane (the left pane) for the California Indiana routing group queue has changed to show that it is in the retry state, and the details pane contains a reminder that the queue needs to be enumerated.

Enumerating a queue simply involves right-clicking anywhere in the contents pane to reveal the shortcut menu shown in Figure 13-15. Choosing Enumerate 100

Messages from this menu causes the first 100 messages in that queue to be enumerated. Since our sample queue contains only one message, enumerating the queue displays a single message, as shown back in Figure 13-14.

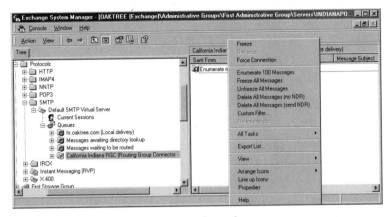

Figure 13-15. *Enumerating an outbound queue.*

Once you can see a message in the queue, there are several things you can do with it. First, you can freeze the message. If you do so, the message will remain in the queue, even if the link starts working again. Freezing a message is handy if you know that a particular message in the queue is either quite large or very unimportant and you want to hold it back until the rest of the messages have been sent. When you unfreeze the message, it is sent immediately. You can freeze and unfreeze a message by right-clicking the message itself and making your selection from the shortcut menu (Figure 13-16).

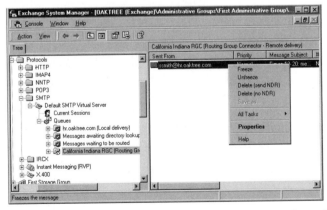

Figure 13-16. *Shortcut menu for messages in an outbound queue.*

The shortcut menu also allows you to delete a message in an outbound queue. When doing so, you can specify either that a nondelivery report (NDR) be sent to the originator or that no NDR be sent. Figure 13-17 shows the NDR the originator will receive if the message is deleted with the Delete (Send NDR) command.

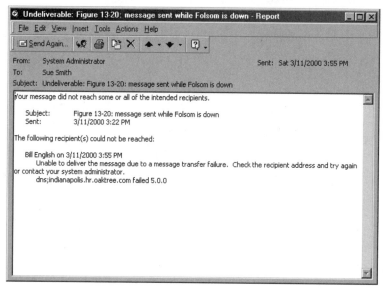

Figure 13-17. *NDR sent to the originator of a deleted message.*

Creating a Custom Filter for Messages   You can perform additional message management by right-clicking the queue itself and choosing Custom Filter. In the Custom Filter dialog box, shown in Figure 13-18, you can filter messages for the Delete (Send NDR), Enumerate, Freeze, and Unfreeze actions.

If you choose Enumerate in the Action list box, you can specify how many messages should be enumerated. The default is to enumerate the first 100 messages. In the Select Messages That Are area, you can filter the queued messages based on a combination of characteristics, such as whether they are frozen, their size, their age, their originator, their recipient, and whether they have experienced delivery failure (Figure 13-19). Once the messages are sorted, you can apply any of the four actions to the filtered messages.

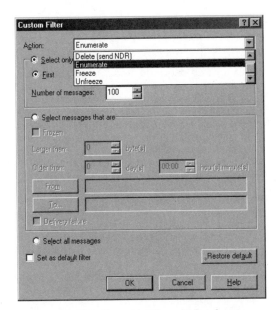

Figure 13-18. *Custom Filter dialog box.*

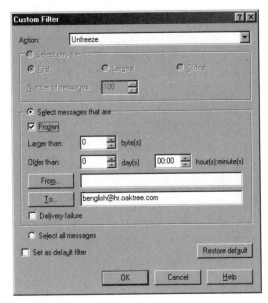

Figure 13-19. *Unfreezing messages to a certain recipient.*

For instance, if all of the messages in a queue have been frozen and the link is operational again, you could filter the messages to unfreeze only those addressed to a certain recipient or distribution group. This gives the administrator maximum flexibility in how messages are managed in a queue once a link becomes operational again. When you click OK, the action you've chosen is applied to the filtered messages. Once you have created a customized filter, you can make it the default filter for a certain action. Check the Set As Default Filter check box to do so.

Resuming Normal Operation

Just because the messages have been sent doesn't mean that the link state information is back to normal. Once Folsom is up and running, the messages might transfer, yet the connector icon will still show the link as being in a retry state (Figure 13-20). This is nothing to be alarmed about. Wait a few minutes and check the queue again; you'll usually find that the icon shows the queue in a normal state.

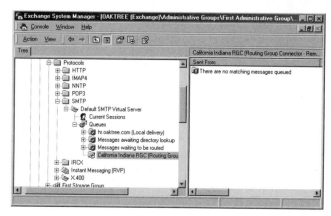

Figure 13-20. *Empty queue in a retry state.*

Scenario 2: Destination Link Is Unavailable

We've seen what happens to a message when the first hop becomes unavailable. Now let's take a look at what happens to a message when the final hop becomes unavailable. In this scenario, ssmith sends another message to benglish, but this time the Tucson server is unavailable.

When ssmith sends the message, it is routed from Indianapolis to Folsom, where it waits until the Tucson server comes back up or the message's expiration time is reached, in which case the user is sent an NDR. Figure 13-21 shows the message sent from ssmith sitting in the outbound queue of the Folsom server's Arizona California RGC.

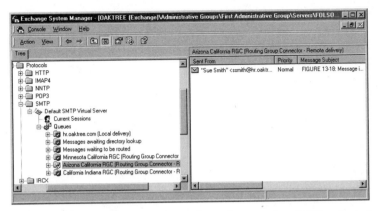

Figure 13-21. *Message in the outbound queue for California Arizona Routing Group Connector.*

Scenario 3: Alternate, Higher-Cost Route Is Available

One of the features of the link state protocol is its ability to detect when part of the overall route is down and reroute a message over a higher-cost link. For this scenario, let's increase the connector cost between Folsom and Indianapolis to 100. Figure 13-22 shows the new topology. Now suppose that benglish in Tucson sends a message to ssmith in Indianapolis.

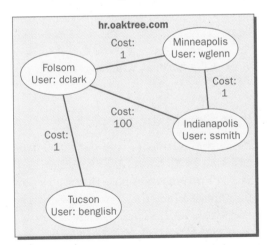

Figure 13-22. *New topology for hr.oaktree.com.*

Given the connector costs, normal routing for this message would flow through Minneapolis. Let's say, however, that the link between the Minneapolis and Folsom routing groups is down. This will force messages to be routed over the higher-cost link between Indianapolis and Folsom. Figure 13-23 shows the results of a trace of the message.

If you are ever in doubt as to which path a message has taken, track the message. For more information on how to do so, consult Chapter 22.

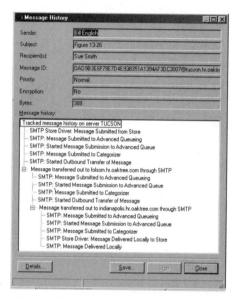

Figure 13-23. *Trace of a message routed over the link between Indianapolis and Folsom.*

Scenario 4: Message Has Multiple Destinations

If a message is sent to both internal and external recipients, a temporary queue is set up for each external domain name as well as each internal Exchange 2000 server that hosts a recipient of the message. For instance, suppose that we've sent a message to a group of fictitious domain names. When the message is sent, the advanced queuing engine creates the necessary queues. The link state protocol does not concern itself with these outbound SMTP queues to external domains. Its only concern is keeping link state information current for the internal servers. Figure 13-24 shows the various queues that have been created for this message. (Since these domain names are fictitious and therefore don't really exist, all of the queues are in a retry state.)

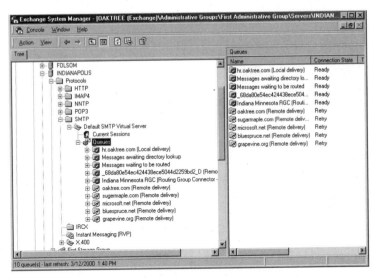

Figure 13-24. *Multiple outbound queues for domain names.*

Summary

In this chapter, you've learned how to administer and manage the Routing Group Connector, the SMTP Connector, and the X.400 Connector. In addition, you've seen how link state information enables message routing for different situations. For instance, you saw that the link state protocol is smart enough to know when a link is down and hold messages until it comes up again.

This protocol is one of the best new features of Exchange 2000 Server. Another feature of Exchange 2000 Server is its ability to coexist with Exchange 5.*x* servers. Since it is likely that you are running Windows NT 4 and Exchange 5.5, the issues of coexistence with Windows 2000 and Exchange 2000 during a migration will be important to you. These issues are the subject of Chapter 14.

Chapter 14
Coexisting with Exchange Server 5.5

Microsoft Exchange 2000 Server is architecturally different from all previous versions of Exchange Server because of its integration with the Active Directory directory service. Many companies will need to migrate from Exchange Server 5.5 to Exchange 2000 Server. During this time, the two versions will need to interoperate. To make the migration go more smoothly, Microsoft has created a couple of services—enhanced connectors that make coexistence with Exchange Server 5.x seamless and reasonable. They provide added flexibility and scalability that was not really possible in earlier versions of Exchange Server. Knowing how these two tools can assist you will go a long way toward making the migration a smooth and relatively painless one for both you and your users.

Coexisting with Earlier Versions of Exchange Server

In this chapter, the word "coexistence" describes a configuration in which different versions of Exchange Server are installed in the same Exchange organization at the same time. This type of configuration is known as a *mixed-mode* configuration. Running Exchange 2000 Server in mixed mode means that Exchange 2000 Server can interoperate with all previous versions of Exchange Server and accommodate the differences between the various versions.

When running in mixed mode, rules that apply to earlier versions of Exchange Server also apply to Exchange 2000 Server. Moreover, after you have installed Exchange 2000 Server, you can install additional Exchange 4.x or 5.x servers into your organization if needed, although you will need a new version of the Setup program to install a server running an earlier version of Exchange Server.

Real World   Mixed Mode vs. Native Mode

While running Exchange 2000 Server in mixed mode allows you to interoperate with Exchange 5.5 systems, running Exchange 2000 in native mode means that you've closed the door on interoperability with previous versions of Exchange. Here are some guidelines to determine whether you are ready to switch to native mode:

- You no longer have Exchange 5.5 servers in your organization.

- You have no plans to add Exchange 5.5 servers to your organization in the future—for example, as a result of a merger or the acquisition of a company with Exchange 5.5 servers.

- Your organization will never require interoperability between your Exchange 2000 servers and previous versions of Exchange Server. (Connectors can provide connectivity between your servers; however administration of servers is limited to Exchange 2000 servers.)

- Your organization does not use any connectors or gateway applications that run only on Exchange Server 5.5.

To switch to native mode in the Exchange System snap-in, navigate to the organization that you want to switch to native mode, right-click on the organization's name and select Properties. On the General tab of the organization property sheet, change the operation mode to Native Mode.

It is important to remember that once you have switched to native mode, your Exchange 2000 organization is no longer interoperable with Exchange 5.5 systems and the change cannot be reversed.

During the Exchange 2000 Server setup, you are given the option of either joining the existing site or creating a new organization. Since you can have only one Exchange 2000 organization per Active Directory forest, you'll need to decide if you should install your first Exchange 2000 server into your Exchange 5.x site. If you do, the existing Exchange 5.x organization name will be replicated to Active Directory as the Exchange 2000 organization name. If you choose not to install Exchange 2000 Server into your Exchange 5.x organization, you'll need to choose a unique organization name and you'll be forced to use a connector to transfer messages between the two organizations. In this case, you will have two separate Exchange organizations, and they will connect to each other as foreign e-mail systems.

In a mixed-mode organization, the Exchange System snap-in shows all Exchange servers installed in the organization, but non–Exchange 2000 servers appear as transparent objects. For example, in Figure 14-1, the Folsom server is an Exchange 5.5 server.

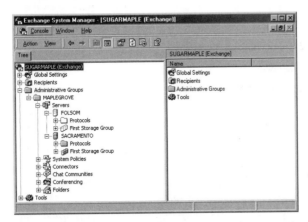

Figure 14-1. *An Exchange 5.5 server (Folsom) in the Exchange System snap-in.*

When the first Exchange 2000 server is installed into an existing Exchange 4.x or 5.x organization, two additional services are installed automatically: Site Replication Service (SRS) and the Active Directory Connector (ADC) service. These two components work together to provide replication between the Exchange 4.x and 5.x servers and Exchange 2000 Server. Intrasite replication occurs using remote procedure calls (RPCs), and intersite replication is handled via directory services (mail-based) transfer. A connection agreement is automatically established in the ADC service between Active Directory and the SRS database to allow directory replication to occur. (Connection agreements are discussed later in this chapter, in the section "Active Directory Connector.") The other Exchange 4.x and 5.x servers will see the Exchange 2000 server as just another 5.x server.

Coexisting with the Exchange 5.x Directory

As we discussed in Chapter 4, Active Directory has three naming partitions: configuration, schema, and domain. In this section, we will primarily be concerned with the configuration and domain naming partitions of Active Directory and how SRS and the ADC service allow the Exchange 5.x directory and the configuration and domain partitions of Active Directory to coexist. (The authors recognize that Exchange 4.x is built on directory services as well. However, for the sake of this discussion, we will use the phrase "Exchange 5.x" to refer to all previous Exchange systems, including both the 4.x and 5.x platforms.) Let's spend some time looking at each of these services.

Site Replication Service

Site Replication Service (SRS) is responsible for replicating Exchange 5.x site and configuration information to the configuration naming partition of Active Directory when an Exchange 2000 server belongs to an existing Exchange 5.5 site. This allows the Exchange 2000 server to be represented in the Exchange site server list so that earlier versions of Exchange Server can send messages to and receive messages from the Exchange 2000 server.

SRS consists of a service that is activated and a database that is initialized when the first Exchange 2000 server is introduced into a legacy Exchange site. Activation can also occur when an Exchange 5.5 directory replication bridgehead server is upgraded to Exchange 2000 Server. If you install additional Exchange 2000 servers into the Exchange 5.5 organization, they will include SRS, but it will be disabled. The components of SRS are as follows:

- Site Replication Service application (Srsmain.exe)
- Site Consistency Checker (runs as part of Srs.exe)
- SRS database (Srs.edb) and transaction logs (ESE98 format)

Even though SRS is similar to the Exchange 5.5 directory service, its Name Service Provider Interface (NSPI) is disabled to prevent Microsoft Outlook clients from connecting to and using the Exchange 2000 directory for name resolution. If the NSPI was activated, Outlook clients could attempt name resolution in the wrong directory, leading to name resolution errors.

SRS must also run LDAP in order to communicate with Active Directory. Because the Microsoft Windows 2000 operating system also uses LDAP and locks the well-known port 389 for its own use, SRS defaults to using port 379 for its LDAP communications. No special configuration is needed for SRS to communicate with Active Directory using LDAP.

Unlike the ADC service, which we will discuss in a moment, SRS automatically installs its own connection agreement (ConfigCA). The agreement is between SRS and Active Directory rather than between Active Directory and the Exchange 5.5 directory. ConfigCA is the pathway through which SRS on the Exchange 2000 server passes configuration naming data to Active Directory. This is a read-only agreement, and it can be seen in the Active Directory Connector Management snap-in, shown in Figure 14-2. (Read-only and other types of agreements are discussed more fully in the section "Active Directory Connector.")

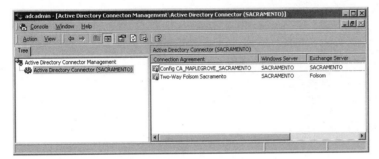

Figure 14-2. *Read-only connection agreement in the Active Directory Connector Management snap-in.*

To communicate with Exchange 5.x servers, SRS uses RPCs. Thus, to the Exchange 5.x servers, Exchange 2000 Server, via SRS, looks like another Exchange 5.x server. If an Exchange 5.x bridgehead server is upgraded to Exchange 2000 Server, SRS will notice this and communicate with that bridgehead server using SMTP.

Since SRS is a read-only service, meaning that it can't be configured, there isn't a great deal to manage. However, a couple of points are worth noting. First, this is a two-way connection agreement that cannot be modified. Second, you'll recall that the agreement is between Active Directory and SRS. This can look confusing when you first encounter the interface because the agreement reports the Exchange server and the Windows 2000 server as the same server. You'll be creating a connection "between" the same server because the server hosting the Exchange 2000 server that is installed into your Exchange 5.5 site is also a domain controller in the Windows 2000 Active Directory. This is most clearly seen on the Connections tab of the property sheet for the connection agreement, as illustrated in Figure 14-3.

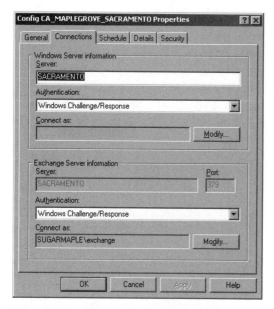

Figure 14-3. *Connection agreement "between" the same server.*

Site Consistency Checker

The Site Consistency Checker (SCC) is an updated version of the Knowledge Consistency Checker from Exchange Server 5.5 and runs inside SRS. It ensures that knowledge consistency is maintained for sites and administrative groups when interoperating between Exchange Server 5.5 and Exchange 2000 Server. In addition, in a large organization with many Exchange 5.5 sites, a triangulation of replication links, which would create duplicate replication paths, could be created as sites are migrated from Exchange Server 5.5 to Exchange 2000 Server. The SCC ensures that as new replication links are created, triangulation is avoided in the link topology.

SRS Database

SRS uses the Extensible Storage Engine (ESE) database technology. You'll find that it installs the same set of databases and transaction logs as a storage group. By default, these files are stored in the Exchsrv\srsdata folder. Unlike the stores in a storage group, the SRS database cannot be mounted or dismounted, but you can start and stop SRS in the Services utility.

Active Directory Connector

The Active Directory Connector is a service that runs on your Windows 2000 domain controller and allows you to synchronize your Exchange Server 5.5 and Windows 2000 directories. Unlike SRS, which replicates information between an Exchange 5.x organization and the configuration naming partition in Active Directory, the ADC service replicates information between the Exchange 5.x directory and the domain partition in Active Directory.

The ADC service comes in two versions: one ships with Windows 2000 Server, and the other ships with Exchange 2000 Server. The Windows 2000 version of the ADC service allows directory information in your Exchange Server 5.5 organization to be replicated to the Windows 2000 Active Directory. The Exchange 2000 version of the ADC service not only lets you synchronize Exchange Server 5.5 directory information with Windows 2000, it also works with SRS. If you've installed Windows 2000 Active Directory Connector, Exchange Server automatically updates it to the Exchange 2000 version when you install Exchange 2000 Server.

After you've synchronized the directories, as described in the sections that follow, Windows 2000 Active Directory generates the Global Address List of mail-enabled users for those users who connect to the Exchange 2000 server. Users connecting to the Exchange Server 5.5 directory will continue to access the Global Address List from the Exchange Directory Store.

Planning Connection Agreements in Active Directory Connector Service

You configure synchronization between your two directories by defining connection agreements that the ADC service manages. A *connection agreement* is just that—an agreement that you manually instantiate to define how directory information is synchronized between the two directories. You will define at least one *primary* connection agreement and one or more *nonprimary* connection agreements. The agreements must contain server names, objects to synchronize, target containers, and a synchronization schedule.

Connection agreements are either *one-way* or *two-way*. As the name implies, a one-way connection agreement allows directory information to flow in only one direction—from the directory you specify to the directory to which the connection agreement connects. For example, if a connection agreement is configured as one-way from directory D1 to directory D2, any changes made to objects in the D1 directory will be replicated to the D2 directory. However, changes made to objects in the D2 directory will *not* be replicated to the D1 directory. A two-way connection agreement allows replication to flow in both directions. Hence, changes made to objects in either directory are replicated.

When setting up your connection agreements, you will strive to match one or more containers in one directory with one or more containers in the other directory. Your environment, future plans, and network administrative model will all affect your choice. For instance, you can synchronize the default Recipients container in your Exchange 5.5 site with one Active Directory container—perhaps the Users organizational unit (OU). In this scenario, any subcontainers in the Recipients container will be created automatically under the Users OU, as shown in Figure 14-4.

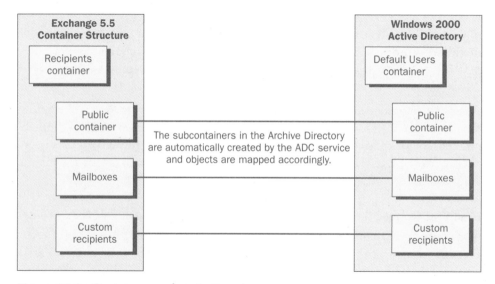

Figure 14-4. *Container synchronization.*

You can also synchronize from one Exchange container to multiple Active Directory containers by choosing to replicate one object class to one Active Directory OU and another object class to another Active Directory OU. For instance, if all of your Exchange 5.5 recipients were created in the default Recipients container, you could choose to replicate your user objects to a Users OU in Active Directory and your custom recipients to a Contacts OU, as shown in Figure 14-5.

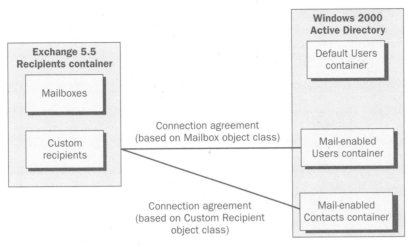

Figure 14-5. *Object class synchronization.*

By the same token, you can synchronize multiple Exchange containers with multiple Active Directory containers or synchronize multiple Active Directory containers with multiple Exchange containers. Moreover, you can configure each connection agreement to synchronize single or multiple object types. This service gives you the opportunity to rearrange your object hierarchy in Active Directory.

Installing the ADC Service

You install the ADC service from the ADC folder on the Exchange 2000 companion CD-ROM. During the installation, the installation wizard prompts you to choose the Microsoft Active Directory Connector Service Component, the Microsoft Active Directory Connector Management Components, or both (Figure 14-6). Selecting Microsoft Active Directory Connector Service Component installs the ADC service (Adc.exe). Selecting Microsoft Active Directory Connector Management Components installs the Active Directory Connector Management snap-in into a separate Microsoft Management Console (MMC).

The user account that you log on with to install the ADC service must have the ability to modify the schema; otherwise, you'll receive the error message in Figure 14-7. However, if Exchange 2000 Server is already installed somewhere in your Windows 2000 forest, schema modifications are not necessary when installing the ADC service, since the schema has already been extended.

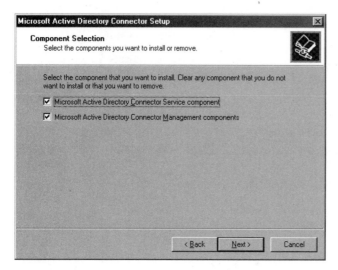

Figure 14-6. *ADC service installation choices.*

Figure 14-7. *Permissions needed to modify the schema.*

Next, the installation wizard asks for a location for the installation files and for the administrator name and password in the Windows 2000 domain. The final installation screen asks you to finish the installation.

Note After you've migrated all of your directory information to Windows 2000 and fully implemented Exchange 2000 Server, you'll no longer need the Active Directory Connector service because you'll no longer have any Exchange 5.5 servers. If you choose to uninstall the ADC service, you must first delete all of the connection agreements you defined on the local server. Best practice would be to do this after you have switched your Exchange 2000 organization to native mode.

Real World   Questions to Consider Before Deploying the ADC Service

Before deploying the ADC service, ask yourself the following questions to determine the best way to configure it for your needs.

Do you want to administer all of your directory objects from Active Directory?

You can manage all of your Exchange Server 5.5 and Active Directory objects with one tool: Active Directory Users and Computers. This approach will require a one-way connection agreement from Windows to each of your existing Exchange sites. If your Exchange team and network team need to administer their areas separately, choose a two-way connection agreement. Final decisions should involve representatives from all of your teams.

Do you want to use Exchange Administrator to manage your Exchange Server 5.5 environment until your migration is finished?

If you want to continue using Exchange Administrator, you need to define most of your connection agreements as one-way from Exchange. This arrangement requires only a single-point connection agreement from one of your sites because the Exchange Directory Service will replicate any new or modified objects into the site hosting the Exchange end of the connection agreement. This scenario is beneficial if you want to reduce management time and replication traffic.

Do you want to be able to create new accounts in both your Windows 2000 and Exchange directories?

You might want the flexibility of creating new accounts in either directory if you're in a decentralized administration model where each department or division manages its user groups or if your migration will take place over a long time (six months or more). This scenario requires a two-way connection agreement (that is, the ADC service must regard each directory as write enabled), and you must carefully coordinate which team creates which user accounts. You also need to consider the security and administrative implications if you're giving users outside your organization LDAP access with write privileges to either of your directories.

Configuring the Active Directory Connector Service

Once you've installed the ADC service, you'll need to create the primary connection agreement. To do so, launch the ADC service snap-in by choosing Active Directory Connector from the Microsoft Exchange menu. Right-click the server name, point to New, and choose either Recipient Connection Agreement or Public Folder Connection Agreement. For our discussion in this chapter, we'll use Recipient Connection Agreement. Creating the Public Folder Connection Agreement is similar to creating the Recipient Connection Agreement.

You'll need to give your connection agreement a name that describes the function it will serve. Figure 14-8 illustrates how to name a two-way agreement.

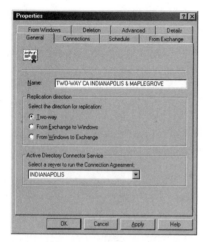

Figure 14-8. *Naming a two-way connection agreement.*

Connections Tab On the Connections tab shown in Figure 14-9, we've configured the Connect As values for each server because these two servers are in different domains and we are writing from each directory to each directory. If you have different domains, which will usually be the case when migrating from 5.x to 2000, you will need to enter Connect As values for each directory to which you would like to write information that is generated in the other directory.

You can also specify the port number that will be used by Exchange Server 5.5. You'll need to change this port number if your Exchange 5.5 server is running on a Windows 2000 domain controller. When Windows 2000 boots up, the Active Directory LDAP services start before any Exchange services, and the LDAP service locks port 389 (the default LDAP port) for its own use. If you leave the port number at 389 for the ADC service to use in this scenario, it will fail to bind to the Exchange directory because of a port number conflict. Most administrators are choosing port 390 in this situation.

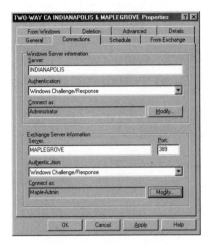

Figure 14-9. *Connections tab of the ADC service property sheet.*

Tip If you're running Exchange Server 5.5 on a Microsoft Windows NT 4 server, be sure to specify the domain name in front of the Windows NT 4 user name that you use to log on to the domain (for example, *domain name\username*). If you don't specify the domain name, you'll receive an 8026 error message in the Event Viewer application log informing you that the bind was unsuccessful.

Schedule Tab You configure the replication interval for the connection agreement on the Schedule tab (Figure 14-10). Setting the replication interval to Always will cause the connection agreement to replicate every 15 miutes. You can force the entire directory to replicate the next time the software runs the agreement, whether it runs on a predetermined schedule or not, by selecting the Replicate The Entire Directory The Next Time The Agreement Is Run check box. Selecting this option sets the *msExchServerXHighestUSN* attribute to 0 and the *msExchDoFullReplication* attribute to True for the connection agreement.

From Exchange and From Windows Tabs The From Exchange tab (Figure 14-11) and the From Windows tab (Figure 14-12) let you set which containers and objects in your Exchange 5.5 site will replicate to Windows 2000 Active Directory and vice versa.

By default, each Exchange site has one Recipients container. If you've created multiple subcontainers under the Recipients container, you have several options for replicating your objects to Windows 2000. If you want to retain the same container structure in Active Directory, create one connection agreement and choose the Exchange site as the source container. Active Directory will automatically create the same container structure in its directory and populate it accordingly. If you want to consolidate several Exchange containers into one container in Active Directory, create one connection agreement and individually choose each of the containers as the source, pointing them to the same container in Active Directory.

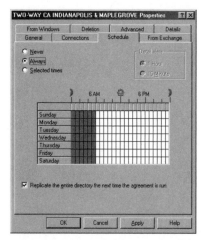

Figure 14-10. *Schedule tab of the ADC service property sheet.*

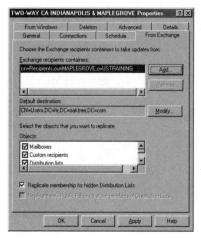

Figure 14-11. *From Exchange tab of the ADC service property sheet.*

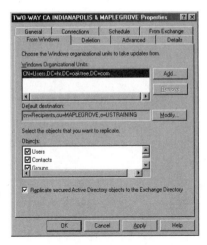

Figure 14-12. *From Windows tab of the ADC service property sheet.*

If you want to have complete control over each container (for example, if you want to have the mailbox container replicate every 30 minutes but have the custom recipient container replicate every 12 hours), create a separate connection agreement for each container, specifying your source and target containers.

Tip   If you want to change your structure entirely, you have two options:

- You can choose one connection agreement, replicate your Exchange containers to one Active Directory container, and then manually move the objects within the Windows 2000 containers after they exist in the Active Directory.

- You can create multiple connection agreements and have each connection agreement process one Recipients container (or object type) and point it to a specific OU in Active Directory. Generally speaking, unless you have a specific reason to choose the previous option, it's best to use this technique, since it is both easier and limits the possibility of human error when moving objects from one container to another.

On the From Windows tab, you can select the Replicate Secured Active Directory Objects To The Exchange Directory check box. Normally, any object with any Deny access control entry (ACE) set would not be replicated to your Exchange 5.5 directory. Selecting this check box disables the filtering of objects based on the specified Deny ACE, so that those objects are replicated from Windows to your Exchange 5.5 directory. Deny ACEs can be set on the Security tab of the object in question.

Deletion Tab The Deletion tab (Figure 14-13) lets you specify how you want the target directory to manage deleted objects in the source directory. You can either have the deleted object replicated to the target directory or have it cataloged in the appropriate import file format. If you choose to delete the objects, the target directory's tombstone setting will determine when the object will be deleted. If you choose to catalog the deletion list, you'll need to manually perform a directory import and choose to have all of the objects being imported deleted during the import process.

> **Note** *Tombstoning* affixes a future date and time to an object after deletion so that all copies of the object in the directory will be deleted at the same time. This practice prevents replication services from backfilling a deleted object into the directory and presenting it as though it had never been deleted.

Remember that Windows 2000 strips an object of its permissions after you delete it. If you think you might want to use a deleted object again, keep it in the deletion list and then import it again when you need the object.

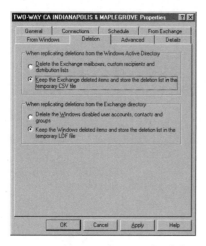

Figure 14-13. *Deletion tab of the ADC service property sheet.*

Advanced Tab On the Advanced tab (Figure 14-14), you need to configure several important values. First, in the Paged Results area, you can change the number of entries per LDAP page. Increase this value if your Exchange 5.5 server is running on a Windows 2000 domain controller. You want to do this because both Active Directory and the ADC service will be using LDAP to send and receive queries.

Paging improves performance by grouping together objects to be replicated before each replication request. Larger page sizes (containing more objects per page) require fewer LDAP requests to complete replication of all objects, but they also require more memory to operate. Setting the page size to 0 results in no replication, so do this only if you want to disable the connection agreement.

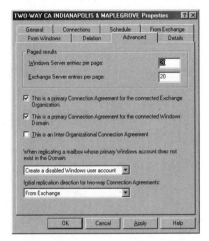

Figure 14-14. *Advanced tab of the ADC service property sheet.*

Be sure to give careful attention to the check boxes for configuring primary agreements. The This Is A Primary Connection Agreement For The Connected Exchange Organization option is the default. A primary connection agreement will attempt to create new objects in the target directory when synchronizing objects from one directory to another. Furthermore, if a mailbox in Exchange Server 5.5 has no primary user account, and no corresponding Windows 2000 user account exists in Active Directory, a primary connection agreement will create a new user account as part of the replication of the mailbox.

A nonprimary connection agreement doesn't create new objects in the Exchange Server 5.5 directory and instead replicates only attributes between the Exchange Server 5.5 mailbox and its corresponding Windows 2000 user object. Furthermore, if the connection agreement is nonprimary, the ADC service establishes replication only if you've designated a primary user account on the mailbox's General tab. If no primary user account is designated for the Exchange 5.5 mailbox and no corresponding Windows 2000 user object exists, a nonprimary connection agreement won't attempt to create the user object in Active Directory.

Having multiple two-way, primary connection agreements to multiple Exchange Server 5.5 sites from one Active Directory container means that each new object you create in the Active Directory container will replicate to each Exchange Server 5.5 site directory. This scenario will create multiple instances of the same object in your Exchange Server 5.5 organization. The Exchange 5.5 Directory Service will then replicate these objects throughout the organization. If you need to synchronize multiple Exchange sites with one container in Active Directory, configure your connection agreements as one-way from Exchange, with only one two-way connection agreement. This configuration will allow newly created objects in Active Directory to be replicated to your Exchange 5.5 directory without incurring multiple instances of that object.

If you want to create multiple connection agreements from the Active Directory to the Exchange Server 5.5 directory, it's best to set only one connection agreement as primary and the rest as nonprimary. Do this by clearing the This Is A Primary Connection Agreement For The Connected Windows Domain check box on all but one of your connection agreements. The overall effect will be that an object created in Active Directory will be created only once in the Exchange 5.5 directory. You'll need to consider which Exchange 5.5 sites should receive the newly created Active Directory objects.

The most complicated scenario is one in which you need to have certain objects that are created in Active Directory replicated to certain Exchange 5.5 sites and other objects created in Active Directory replicated to other Exchange 5.5 sites. If this is your situation, consider creating separate primary connection agreements from different Active Directory containers to each Exchange 5.5 site. Although doing so will increase the complexity of your ADC service administration, it will allow you to specify which Active Directory objects are replicated to which Exchange 5.5 site.

Associated with the This Is A Primary Connection Agreement For The Connected Windows Domain check box is the setting This Is The Primary Connection Agreement For The Connected Exchange Organization check box, used for replicating a mailbox object that has no corresponding primary user account in Active Directory. This check box controls whether an object is created in the Windows 2000 domain if no user account match exists between the two directories. The When Replicating A Mailbox Whose Primary Windows Account Does Not Exist In The Domain drop-down list becomes unavailable if you clear the check box. Use this setting if you need to migrate several mailboxes and you're sure that some of the mailboxes don't have user accounts in Active Directory.

The This Is An Inter-Organizational Connection Agreement check box should be selected if the connection agreement is being made between two Exchange organizations, which would be the case when uploading directory information from an Exchange 5.x organization to a Windows 2000 Active Directory whose schema has already been extended with an Exchange 2000 directory. It is also selected when you are replicating your 5.x information to an Active Directory that has *no* Exchange 2000 organization defined, and thus whose schema has not been extended to include Exchange 2000 objects.

You would not want to select this option if you have installed an Exchange 2000 server into an existing Exchange 5.5 organization. In this case, the Exchange 2000 organization and the Exchange 5.5 organization are the same.

When replication is scheduled to occur within a two-way connection agreement, you can choose the direction in which replication will occur first in the Initial Replication Direction For Two-Way Connection Agreements check box.

Summary of ADC Options

- If you're coming from a single Exchange 5.5 site, create one connection agreement to retain the same container structure in Active Directory.

- To consolidate multiple Exchange Server 5.5 containers into one container in Active Directory, create one connection agreement and choose each of the Exchange containers individually as a source.

- To have complete control over the synchronization of each Exchange 5.5 container as it replicates to Windows 2000 Active Directory, create a connection agreement for each source container.

- To substantially change your container model, either configure one connection agreement, move all of your source objects into one Windows 2000 container, and then manually move the objects within the Active Directory, or set up multiple connection agreements that specify each source and destination container.

Setting the Default Policy for the ADC Service

By right-clicking the Active Directory Connector Management snap-in in the MMC console, you can configure which attributes of each object you want to replicate to the other directory. As was mentioned previously, a nonprimary connection agreement replicates only the attributes of an object to the other directory. This property sheet lets you choose the attributes you want to replicate.

Working with Sites, Administrative Groups, and Routing Groups

In order for Exchange 2000 and Exchange 5.x organizations to coexist, you will need to leave Exchange 2000 Server in mixed mode. Remember that there is no direct relationship between mixed mode and native mode in Windows 2000 and mixed mode and native mode in Exchange 2000 Server. In other words, you can have all of your servers running Windows 2000 in native mode but still have Exchange 2000 Server running in mixed mode to permit interoperability with one or more Exchange 5.x servers.

Mixed mode offers compatibility with previous versions of Exchange Server, but it also has its limitations. Be aware of these, which include the following:

- Exchange 5.x sites appear as administrative groups in the Exchange System snap-in.
- You cannot move mailboxes easily between administrative groups.
- You cannot move servers between administrative groups.
- Members of a routing group must come from the same administrative group.

In other words, when running in mixed mode, Exchange 2000 administration is similar to Exchange 5.x administration, with the site boundaries defining your routing and administrative boundaries.

The last bullet point above is particularly important. In mixed mode, each routing group must be created in the administrative group in which the servers exist. This is because Exchange 5.x sites have a one-to-one relationship with administrative groups. Although you can place your Exchange 2000 servers into routing groups that exist in different administrative groups, you cannot assign a server to a routing group that is held under a different administrative group than the administrative group of which the server is a member. For example, if Server1 was created in the Minneapolis administrative group, it cannot be a member of the Arizona routing group unless the Arizona routing group is created inside the Minneapolis administrative group. (See Chapters 12 and 13 for a discussion of how to implement administrative and routing groups.)

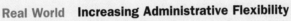

Real World   Increasing Administrative Flexibility

One way to increase your administrative flexibility in mixed mode is to subdivide an Exchange 5.x site. Assume that sufficient bandwidth exists between three locations each hosting three Exchange servers, to place all the servers in the same Exchange 5.5 site. Let's further assume that of these nine servers, five are running Exchange 2000 Server and four are running Exchange Server 5.5.

When a user on an Exchange 5.5 server sends a message to a user on an Exchange 2000 server, the Exchange 5.5 Message Transfer Agent (MTA) routes the message directly to the Exchange 2000 server. From an Exchange 5.5 server's perspective, the routing process works the same as it always has. Now suppose that a user on an Exchange 2000 server sends a message to a user on an Exchange 5.5 server. Because Exchange 2000 Server can operate under different rules, you can subdivide the administrative group into several routing groups and force the message from the Exchange 2000 user to travel along a certain path before it gets to the Exchange 5.5 server. This works because the ADC service and SRS do not replicate routing groups and intra-administrative group connectors to the Exchange 5.5 environment.

After switching your organization into native mode, your servers and routing groups will no longer be tied to the administrative group. Thereafter, you'll have full flexibility in routing messages in your environment and in the kind of administrative model you implement.

Handling Other Coexistence Issues

Let's take a brief look at some other issues surrounding coexistence between Exchange Server 5.5 and Exchange 2000 Server.

Proxy Address

After a server joins an existing Exchange site, the proxy address settings for addresses such as SMTP, X.400, cc:Mail, and Microsoft Mail are copied to a recipient policy for users in that administrative group. This ensures that the same proxy addresses are generated for all users in the administrative group. This policy cannot be removed, and it will be the highest-priority policy in the system, meaning that any other recipient policies that conflict with it will not be enforced.

Foreign E-Mail Connection

Because SRS replicates site and configuration information between the Exchange 5.x and Exchange 2000 systems, it is possible for users in one system to use a connector in the other system to send messages. For instance, Exchange 2000 Server does not ship with a connector for Professional Office System (PROFS). If you need connectivity between Exchange 2000 Server and a PROFS system, you'll have to retain an Exchange 5.x server and use its connector to send and receive messages with your Exchange 2000 organization. Exchange 5.x will act as the transport backbone in this situation.

Messages

Messaging works between Exchange Server 5.x and Exchange 2000 Server because Exchange 2000 Server retains an instance of the MTA in its default installation. Exchange 2000 Server does have its own version of the MTA, with the main difference being that the Exchange 2000 MTA uses LDAP to perform directory lookups, rather than the Directory API (DAPI) used by the Exchange 5.5 MTA.

If two or more Exchange 2000 servers are installed into the same site, they will detect each other automatically and use SMTP as their message transport. This allows them to take advantage of such features as the advanced queuing engine, routing, and link state algorithms. In addition, remember that SMTP is asynchronous and can operate at very low bandwidth.

Tip   If two or more Exchange 5.x sites exist with low bandwidth between them, you can use the SMTP routing in Exchange 2000 Server to your advantage. First, install an Exchange 2000 server into each site, and then increase the connector cost on the current Exchange 5.x site connectors. Subdivide your Exchange 5.x site, and place each Exchange 2000 server in its own routing group. Then create a routing group connector between the two routing groups. This path will now be available to the Exchange 5.5 servers, and they will use this new, low-cost path to route messages from one to the other.

The advantage of this technique is that it allows you to use the link state information and the asynchronous nature of SMTP to route messages between your Exchange 5.5 servers. Since SMTP is more tolerant of low bandwidth and high latency, you might find this to be a good method to reduce the number of non-delivery reports (NDRs) to your users and ensure a better transfer success rate over slow or unreliable connections.

User Data

When working in a mixed-mode environment, you need to consider a few issues related to private and public user data. One deployment issue is that of delegate access to another's private mailbox. In a mixed mode environment, delegate access can be established in Exchange Server 5.5 only when users are in the same private information store on a single server or when the delegate's mailbox and the origination mailbox are on different servers. The Emsmdb32 DLL will not allow delegate access between users' mailboxes if they reside in different mailbox stores on the same physical server.

You can replicate individual public folders between Exchange 5.5 and Exchange 2000, and clients can access either replica because there is very little difference between public folders in the two systems. In addition, the public folder hierarchy is replicated between all versions of Exchange Server.

Recall that Exchange 2000 supports multiple public folder trees, whereas Exchange 5.5 has one monolithic tree. The default public folder tree in Exchange 2000, Public Folders, can be seen by MAPI clients, such as Microsoft Outlook. Other public folder trees cannot be seen by these clients.

The data content of a public folder can also be replicated between public folders, but note that permissions set in Exchange 2000 Server are not represented in Exchange 5.5. If you need to house secure information in your public folder trees in Exchange 2000, migrate the users who will need access to that information to Exchange 2000 as well, and then set up an independent tree and secure it accordingly.

Outlook Web Access

In Exchange 5.5, the rendering process of Outlook Web Access (OWA) occurs inside Internet Information Services (IIS), which retrieves the data from the information store and then renders it back to the client in the form of Active Server Pages (ASP). In Exchange 2000, this rendering takes place in the Exchange 2000 Information Store process. Because of this change, it is no longer possible to customize the ASP files to change the basic user interface. However, you can use the Exchange 2000 OWA component in other applications.

If you have applications that use customized ASP files in Exchange 5.5, consider making the Exchange 5.5 OWA the "front end" of an Exchange 2000 server. Users will make their HTTP calls to the Exchange 5.5 OWA, which will check the Exchange 5.5 directory for the requested data. That request will be forwarded to the Exchange 2000 server, where the data will be retrieved and sent back to the client via the Exchange 5.5 OWA server.

Duplicate Accounts

The Active Directory Cleanup Wizard (Adclean.exe) is designed to merge duplicate accounts into one account when you migrate multiple directories or merge them with Active Directory. If you are migrating user accounts from more than one source, it is possible that you will encounter duplicate user accounts. This duplication can occur, for example, when you are merging multiple domains into Active Directory or when you are importing multiple user lists into Exchange 2000 Server. It can also occur if you need to install Exchange 2000 Server before you are able to upgrade your PDCs to Windows 2000. During the upgrade process, duplicate accounts will be created in Active Directory.

The Active Directory Cleanup Wizard will search Active Directory for duplicate Windows NT accounts that reference the same user. After finding the duplicates, it will offer suggestions for eliminating the duplicate accounts. Once you have made your selections, the wizard will merge the multiple accounts into one account, along with their attributes and properties.

The wizard looks for active accounts and disabled accounts that reference the same object. It also looks for active accounts and contacts that reference the same object. When looking for active and disabled accounts, the wizard searches for identical security identifiers (SIDs) on more than one object in the attributes *msExchMasterAccountSid, objectSid*, and *SIDHistory*. If it finds a match, the objects are merged.

How are two or more objects created with the same SID in Active Directory? Let's assume that you have created an ADC between your Windows NT 4 domain and Active Directory. On the Advanced tab of the ADC service property sheet, under When Replicating A Mailbox Whose Primary Windows Account Does Not Exist In The Domain, you have selected Create A Disabled Windows User Account. This means that when you synchronize a mailbox in Exchange Server 5.5 that doesn't have a primary Windows NT account in its domain, a disabled user account is created for it in Active Directory.

Even though it is a disabled account, Active Directory gives it a new SID. In addition, Active Directory writes this new SID into an attribute called *msExchMailboxSecurityDescriptor*, but it retains the old SID in the SID history attribute of the object. When the Windows NT 4 account is moved to Active Directory, the SID from that account already exists in Active Directory as part of the other object's SID history. Hence, it is necessary to merge these two accounts.

When matching an active user object and a contact object, the wizard compares the attributes *cn* and *displayName*. In addition, it compares the attributes *mailNickname (Alias)* and *SamAccountName (Login ID)* for possible duplications. If there is a duplication in either pairing, you will be given the option to merge the accounts. These types of duplications occur most often when you have an X.400 Connector to a foreign e-mail system.

With the Active Directory Cleanup Wizard, you can do the following:

- Identify duplicate objects to be merged
- Review and modify merge operations
- Export and import lists of accounts
- Use command-line options to run the wizard

Let's look at each of these options more closely.

Identify Duplicate Objects to Be Merged

You can instruct the wizard to search Active Directory for duplicate accounts. You can do this at one of three levels. First, you can have the wizard search the entire forest for duplicate accounts. If you don't want to search at the forest level, you can specify containers and subcontainers that you want the wizard to search. Figure 14-15 shows an example of this type of search.

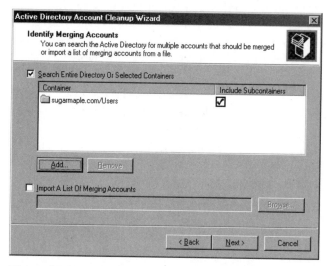

Figure 14-15. *Searching containers and subcontainers for duplicate accounts.*

The container that you select will show up under Container. The check box to search all subcontainers is selected by default. If you do not want the wizard to search the subcontainers, you'll need to clear this box before starting your search.

If you know which accounts you want to merge in Active Directory, you can select them manually instead of having the wizard search Active Directory for them. If you plan to do this, the target object must already exist, because you'll be merging a source object with the target object. After the merge is complete, the source object will no longer exist. Figure 14-16 demonstrates this technique.

If one account is inactive and the target account is active, these accounts must belong to the same forest, and the domains must be in native mode. If the domains are not in native mode, when you attempt to select the second name for the merge process, regardless of whether it is the source or target account, you'll receive the error message shown in Figure 14-17.

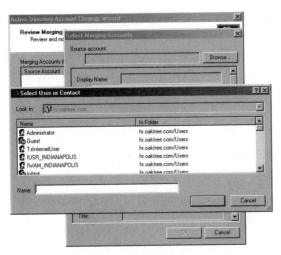

Figure 14-16. *Selecting merge accounts.*

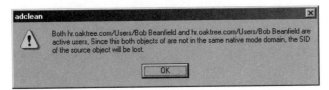

Figure 14-17. *Error message: Source SID will be lost.*

After you have chosen the two accounts to merge into one, you will be given the choice to either merge the accounts immediately or have them exported to a .CSV file from which you can import and merge them at a later date. Once the merge is complete, the log entries of the merge will be shown on the last screen of the wizard and will also be recorded in the Adclean.log file in your Exchsrvr\bin directory. Figure 14-18 shows what the log file looks like.

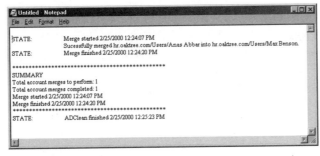

Figure 14-18. *Adclean.log file report.*

Another way to identify duplicate users is to create a list, using the wizard's export/import function. You can modify this list and then import it back into Active Directory.

A couple of restrictions apply to manual account merges. First, the target object must be an active user. If you select an inactive user as your target object, you will be reminded of this restriction and will be forced to choose an active user. An active user is one whose account is enabled.

Second, you cannot merge two users who are both mail enabled. This is because their mailboxes cannot be merged in Exchange 2000 Server. Hence, your source object must not be mail enabled in order for this process to work. And third, if both accounts are active, they must belong to the same domain. You cannot merge two active objects that are not in the same domain.

Review and Modify Merge Operations

Once you've identified the duplicate accounts, you should review and, if necessary, modify merge operations that the wizard is ready to perform. Perform this task before you begin merging accounts in Active Directory. Once the merge process is complete, you cannot undo the operation. Here are some guidelines to keep in mind:

- Make sure the correct accounts are selected. For example, you might want to confirm that the correct target and source accounts are selected.

- If more than two accounts represent a user, make sure that the merge operations are configured to occur in the correct order. This ensures that the correct attributes are merged into the final active user account.

- Export your list of merge operations to a .CSV file. This allows you to view multiple target and source accounts and their attributes at the same time.

Export and Import Lists of Accounts

You can export duplicate accounts to a .CSV file for review and modification before performing the merge process. You might want to do this if you suspect that your Active Directory contains a large number of duplicate accounts. Exporting to a .CSV file is handy in the following circumstances:

- You do not have time to review and then run the merge process but would like to review the list later—perhaps off-site.

- You prefer to view and modify the list in a .CSV file.

- You are ready to perform the merge but desire a premerge list of the accounts to be merged during the process.
- You have been saving deleted accounts in a .CSV file and want to delete them during an import process.

After you have exported the information to a .CSV file, you can make your adjustments and then use the file as a source for the merge process.

Use Command-Line Options to Run the Wizard

If you would rather start the merge from the command line than from the graphical interface, use Table 14-1 to help you.

Table 14-1.   Command-line options for the Adclean command

Option	Description	Example
/?	Displays the available MS-DOS command-line options.	`Adclean /?`
/S	Searches for duplicate accounts and saves them as a list of merge operations in a .CSV file in your working directory.	`Adclean /S` Searches your entire forest for duplicate accounts. The amount of time this takes depends on the size and number of duplicate accounts in Active Directory. To specify the containers that are searched, see the /C option.

/C	Used with the /S option to specify the containers that you want to search for duplicate accounts. The result of this search is a Merge.csv file that contains a list of merge operations found when searching the containers designated in the Container.csv file you have created. This Merge.csv file is saved in your working directory.	`Adclean /S`
		`/C:D:\Exchsrvr/BIN/`
		`    <ContainerFileName.csv>`
		where D:\Exchsrvr/BIN/.
		
		<ContainerFileName.csv> is the location of the .CSV file that contains the locations of the directory containers you want to search. Before you can use the /C option, you must manually create a .CSV file in an application that supports the creation of this type of file (such as Notepad). This file must have the word "containers" on the first line and must then list the paths of the containers you want to search on subsequent lines. In the previous example, the text in the <ContainerFileName.csv> file might be as follows:
		`Containers`
		`server1.east.airlines.`
		`    international.com/Users`

(continued)

Table 14-1. *continued*

Option	Description	Example
/M	Performs the merge operations listed in the .CSV file in the working directory.	`Adclean /M` A merge with only the /M option specified will merge only duplicate accounts from the .CSV file in the directory in which Adclean.exe is installed.

/O	Used with the /M option to merge duplicate accounts based on a .CSV file that you specify.	`Adclean /M`
		`O/:D:/Exchsrv/BIN/`
		`    <MergeFileName.csv>`
		where D:/Exchsrv/BIN/.
		
		<MergeFileName.csv> is the location of a file that contains the list of merge operations you want to perform.

Other Considerations

You should be aware of a couple of other considerations when using the Active Directory Cleanup Wizard. First, if the source object is mail enabled and the target object is not, the mail-enabled attributes will be transferred to the target object. Second, the SID and the SID history of the source user account is transferred to the SID history of the target user account. The SID of the target user account is retained as the object's primary SID. And finally, attributes are transferred in the following manner:

- If the attribute does not accept multiple values, the attribute on the target object remains and the values on the source object are discarded.
- If the attribute does accept multiple values, the values for that attribute are merged, and both remain on the target object.
- If the attribute on the target object is not allowed, it is not transferred and the values are discarded.

Summary

In this chapter, you have learned how to manage a network in which Exchange 5.5 servers coexist with Exchange 2000 servers. Our focus has been on working within a given network. It is often necessary, however, to coexist with other types of systems, through connectors. This is the topic of the next chapter, where you will learn how to connect to foreign X.400 and Microsoft Mail messaging systems.

Part IV
Clients

Chapter 15
Overview
of Exchange Clients

Up to this point, we have focused primarily on the server aspect of the Exchange environment, because this book is primarily about administering Microsoft Exchange 2000 Server. However, a server does not operate in a void; clients must connect to it to complete the picture.

This is the first of three chapters that examine the deployment of clients in an Exchange organization. This chapter introduces you to the main types of clients that you may find in your Exchange environment:

- Microsoft Outlook 2000
- Microsoft Outlook Express
- Microsoft Outlook Web Access
- Exchange Client
- Microsoft Schedule+
- Standard Internet mail clients
- UNIX clients
- Macintosh clients

Each of these can be used as a client in an Exchange organization. Because the focus of this book is Exchange 2000 Server, and because each of these clients has a wide range of functionality and features, we do not describe each client in depth. Instead, this chapter simply introduces the major types of Exchange client software. Chapter 16 covers the Outlook 2000 client in detail.

Microsoft Outlook 2000

Microsoft Outlook 2000 is the latest version of Microsoft's premier messaging client. Originally introduced with Exchange Server 5.0, Outlook combines the functionality that was previously contained in Exchange Client and Schedule+

(both of which are described later in this chapter) to deliver a complete messaging, scheduling, and contact management solution. Outlook clients can also work with public folders to share information.

In addition to providing all the functionality that formerly required both Schedule+ and Exchange Client, Outlook also supports add-ins. *Add-ins* are program modules that, as their name implies, can be seamlessly added to the Outlook environment to extend the functionality of the product. The Schedule+ add-in, for example, provides compatibility between Schedule+ and the Outlook Calendar. The ability to use add-ins makes Outlook a strategic product for Microsoft because third-party developers can use Outlook as an application development platform. One example of a third-party add-in is a product named Pretty Good Privacy (PGP), which allows a user to send encrypted and signed messages using the PGP protocol. PGP is used mainly for Internet mail.

Outlook 2000 is a component of Office 2000 and will become widely used as organizations upgrade to this newest version of the popular office suite. It is included in all five Office 2000 packages: Microsoft Office 2000 Small Business, Microsoft Office 2000 Standard, Microsoft Office 2000 Professional, Microsoft Office 2000 Premium, and Microsoft Office 2000 Developer. Outlook 2000 is also shipped with Exchange 2000 Server. As shown in Figure 15-1, Outlook 2000 looks much like previous versions of Outlook. However, it includes several new features, including the ability to

- Publish a personal or team calendar as a Web page using a single command
- Use the Activities tab on a contact item's property sheet to track and dynamically view all activity related to a contact, such as e-mail, appointments, and tasks
- Use Mail Merge to manage mass mailings for e-mail, fax, and print distribution to all of your contacts or only to those selected based on information contained within a set of contact fields
- Support not only POP3 and SMTP but also IMAP4, LDAP, NNTP, S/MIME, HTML Mail, vCard, and iCalendar
- Use the Outlook Bar to create a shortcut for any file, Web page, or folder
- Use Outlook Today to customize an overview of your e-mail, calendar, and task information in a single location to provide a quick look at the events for the day

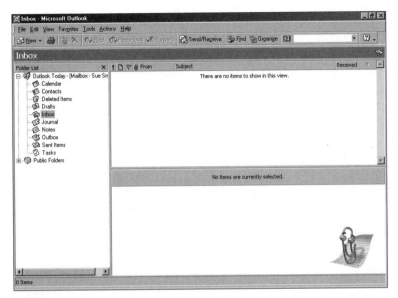

Figure 15-1. *The basic Outlook 2000 client.*

Although this book focuses on using Outlook 2000 with Exchange 2000 Server, let's look at all of the features that Outlook provides on its own:

- **Messaging** E-mail has become a way of life. Outlook provides a single, universal Inbox for all of a user's messaging needs. Users can send and receive messages using a variety of servers. The servers supported include Exchange Server; Microsoft Mail; Internet-based SMTP, POP3, and IMAP4; and a variety of third-party messaging servers. Messages can be created in three formats: plain text, rich text, and HTML.

- **Scheduling** Life today is so fast-paced that most people use some kind of calendar/planner. Outlook's Calendar feature allows you to manage appointments and recurring events for yourself or another user on an Exchange server. You can even schedule users across the Internet through the use of iCalendar group scheduling

- **Contact management** Too many people keep track of their contact information for friends, relatives, and co-workers in some paper-based phone book that has scratched-out entries and entries with arrows pointing to other entries with more updated information. In essence, it is an inefficient and messy method. You can keep track of clients, staff, or any other category of people and their contact information within

Outlook. This information can include phone numbers, addresses, birth-days, anniversaries, and anything else you may need to make note of for a contact.

- **Journaling** There's an old business quip that is often used to settle busi-ness disputes: The person with the most documentation wins. Having a record of every type of contact with a co-worker, a client, or anyone else could come in handy later on. Outlook's Journal Feature can keep track of every phone call, fax, and e-mail sent and associate it with a specific contact.

- **Notes** We have all been in situations in which we've had to jot down an address or phone number but had no paper and pen handy. The Notes feature of Outlook gives you the electronic equivalent of sticky notes. Use Notes to record information you need to keep that doesn't exactly belong in a contact, calendar, or e-mail item.

- **Tasks** Did you forget to call someone back? What about that report you promised your boss—it was due today! Outlook's Tasks feature gives you the ability to create tasks, assign them to yourself or others, and establish due dates. You'll never miss that important deadline again.

E-Mail Service Options

Outlook 2000 can be used with the following service options, each of which provides a different set of features for use in different circumstances:

- **No E-Mail** When you choose to use Outlook 2000 in this mode, you can use only the contact, task, and schedule management features of Out-look, meaning that it functions as a stand-alone personal information manager (PIM). Although this mode supports Internet mail, much like the Internet Only service described next, you are not prompted to set up support for any Internet mail accounts. Even though the client machine, by default, is not used for mail, it must have a personal folder, or .PST file, to store information used by the other features.

- **Internet Only** This service provides the same functions as the No E-Mail service, but it also makes Outlook act as an Internet mail client. If you choose this option, you can use messaging in addition to Outlook's contact, task, and schedule management features. In this mode, an Out-look 2000 user can access mail by connecting to any server that sup-ports POP3, SMTP, or IMAP4 clients. Some of the functionality of

Outlook, such as the use of voting buttons, is unavailable in this mode. A client machine must have a personal folder, or .PST file, in order to store messages.

- **Corporate or Workgroup**   The Corporate or Workgroup service is designed for use over a local area network (LAN) with Exchange Server, Microsoft Mail, or another third-party, LAN-based mail system such as cc:Mail or Lotus Notes. It provides the complete set of Outlook features. With some mail servers, the client machine does not need to have a personal folder, or .PST file, when using this service option because the messages are stored on the server. For example, no personal folder file is needed if the mail server is Exchange 2000 Server. However, if the mail server is Microsoft Mail, a personal folder file is needed to store retrieved messages. Users are free to maintain a personal folder file even if they are not required to do so. They must be aware that this file exists only on their hard drive; it is their responsibility to back it up properly to avoid losing mail if the file becomes unusable. In addition, personal folder files are not, by default, protected from prying eyes. However, users can password-protect these files if they so desire.

The various service options are very similar with respect to the features they offer. Table 15-1 lists the features available in Outlook and indicates how each option implements that feature.

Table 15-1.   Outlook features in each service option

Feature	No E-Mail Option	Internet Only Option	Corporate or Workgroup Option
Calendar, Contacts, Journal, Notes, Tasks	Local use only	Local use only	Local and Exchange-based access
Support for POP3 or IMAP4 mail	Can be set up, but is not set up by default	Yes	Yes
Support for Exchange 2000 Server	Can be set up via POP3 or IMAP4	Via POP3 or IMAP4	Native
Fax support	No	Yes	No

When making a decision as to which service option is right for your users, follow these guidelines:

- Choose the No E-Mail option if they plan on using only the PIM features of Outlook.

- Choose the Internet Only option if they send and receive all of their e-mail through an ISP that uses Internet standards such as POP3, SMTP, and IMAP4.

- Choose the Corporate or Workgroup option if they use Exchange 2000 Server, Microsoft Mail, or a third-party MAPI e-mail service.

Chapter 16 takes a more in-depth look at administering Outlook 2000 in an Exchange Server environment.

More Info   For more details on installing, using, and supporting Outlook 2000, see *Running Microsoft Outlook 2000* by Alan Neibauer, (Microsoft Press, 1999).

Outlook Today

By default, a page named Outlook Today is shown first when you start Outlook 2000, as shown in Figure 15-2. Outlook Today presents a sort of snapshot view of Outlook, including your new messages, active tasks, and some calendar information. You can customize Outlook Today to show the information you want.

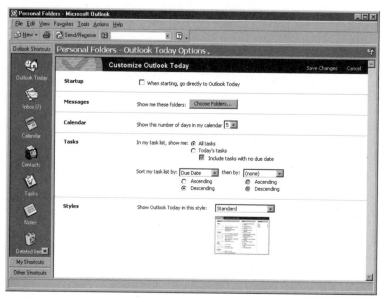

Figure 15-2. *Customizing the view of Outlook Today.*

Real World   Digital Dashboards

The page loaded for Outlook Today is really just a Web page generated by Outlook. Microsoft has introduced a new idea it calls the Digital Dashboard, which is essentially a highly customized Outlook Today page that consolidates personal, team, and corporate information into a single location. It is designed to give users (or what Microsoft calls *knowledge workers*) a single point of access for all the information they might need during the course of a day's work. Figure 15-3 shows a Digital Dashboard customized for use in the health care industry.

A Digital Dashboard starter kit is shipped with Exchange 2000 Server to get you started building your own dashboards. To learn more about Digital Dashboards, you can also check out *http://www.microsoft.com/DigitalNervousSystem/km/ DigitalDashboard.htm.*

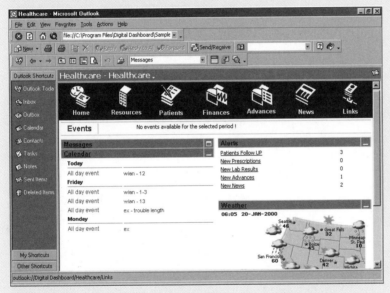

Figure 15-3. *Digital Dashboard designed for a health care worker.*

Microsoft Outlook Express

Outlook Express, shown in Figure 15-4, is a subset of the standard Outlook product. It ships and installs with Microsoft Internet Explorer and is the default mail reader for Microsoft Windows 98. It allows users to retrieve and send mail messages, participate in Internet newsgroups, and access directory information over standard Internet-based protocols. Outlook Express cannot take advantage of most of the collaboration features that Exchange 2000 Server provides, such as native access to public folders and calendaring. Let's look at its three main capabilities—messaging, news reading, and directory service lookup—and see how they differ from their counterparts in Outlook.

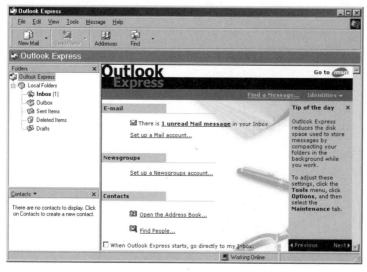

Figure 15-4. *Outlook Express.*

Messaging

E-mail support within Outlook Express is similar to that of the Internet Mail Only option in Outlook: it supports only messaging over the POP3, IMAP4, and SMTP protocols. When Outlook Express interacts with Exchange 2000 Server for retrieving messages, it does so over either the POP3 or IMAP4 protocol. This means that while Outlook Express can use Exchange 2000 Server as its messaging server, it is not a native Exchange 2000 client. In addition, using Outlook Express to access an Exchange 2000 mailbox does not provide the groupware messaging present in Outlook, such as native access to public folders and Outlook forms.

Outlook Express provides support for multiple e-mail accounts, letting users retrieve messages from multiple servers and view them all in a single Inbox. It also allows multiple users to have their own individual identities for messages, contacts, and tasks. Some basic rules functionality is available through the Create Rule From Message command on the Messages menu (Figure 15-5). Outlook

Express can impose some client-side rules for handling incoming mail, but you cannot use it to create server-side rules, as you can with the Rules Wizard in the full Outlook 2000 product.

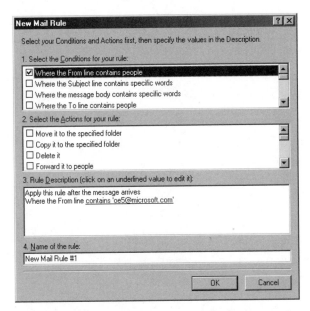

Figure 15-5. *Creating a rule in Outlook Express 5.*

News Reading

Outlook Express can act as a news reader for Internet newsgroups via any NNTP-compliant news server, such as Exchange 2000 Server. It can access Exchange 2000 public folders as newsgroups over NNTP. However, when using Outlook Express to access Exchange 2000 public folders, you need to consider the client application that created the entry in the public folder. If the entry was created by an NNTP-compliant news reader, such as Outlook Express, all contents of the entry are available to Outlook Express. If, however, the entry was created by a native Exchange client, such as Outlook 2000, access to that entry with Outlook Express (and with any other NNTP-compliant news reader) is really effective only with public folders containing note items. When Outlook Express accesses a public folder as a newsgroup containing any other Exchange message type (contact item, calendar item, journal item, or task item), it shows only the name of the entry and the information found in the notes portion at the bottom of all Outlook message types.

Performing Directory Service Lookups

Many companies on the Internet provide information about various Internet users. For instance, if you wanted to find out the e-mail address of John Smith, it would be possible to query various directory service providers to see if they have any record of his e-mail address or other information about him. Outlook Express makes the directory service queries via LDAP.

Outlook Express does not access LDAP-based information by querying an Exchange 2000 server specifically. Because Exchange 2000 Server relies heavily on Active Directory, an LDAP query would be directed to Active Directory via LDAP over TCP port 389 to seek information about a user. The client could be configured to present any LDAP queries to an Exchange 2000 server or to any domain controller in your Windows 2000 Active Directory. For more information on LDAP, POP3, IMAP 4, and NNTP, see Chapter 17.

Outlook Web Access

Outlook Web Access (OWA) is a way of accessing mail and scheduling information from an Exchange server, just as you would from Outlook, through a standard Web browser, such as Microsoft Internet Explorer 3 or later and Netscape Navigator 3 or later. The version 3 or later browsers are necessary to support the functionality required by HTML 3.2, such as frames, advanced scripting, Secure Sockets Layer (SSL), and Java.

OWA is a way to access e-mail over port 80 from a browser. You can install OWA when you install Exchange 2000 Server. Thereafter, a user can access several of the functions available through Outlook, using the browser. Users can have access to functionality for basic e-mail, basic calendar and group scheduling, basic public folders, and collaborative applications. OWA is not intended to replace the full-featured Outlook messaging client for 16-bit Windows operating systems or Macintosh. The following are some of the items that are *not* available when using OWA:

- Personal address books (because they are stored on your workstation)
- Spelling checker
- Replied and forwarded flags in list view
- Message flags and Inbox rules
- Three-pane view

- Dragging and dropping to a folder
- Searching for messages
- WordMail and Microsoft Office integration
- Viewing free/busy details
- Task lists and task management
- Exporting to a DataLink watch or other devices
- Outlook forms
- Synchronizing local offline folders with server folders
- Access to your .PST file

Outlook Web Access simulates the look and feel of Outlook 2000, as shown in Figure 15-6. The universality of the browser client makes OWA an attractive choice in environments that have a diverse mix of clients (such as Windows, Macintosh, and UNIX) and that require a shared messaging client. OWA is extremely beneficial for users, such as information systems staff, who move around to different workstations frequently during the day. They can simply check their mail using OWA instead of creating a mail profile on each of the workstations.

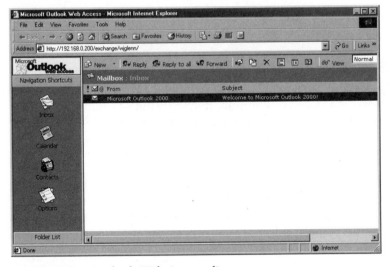

Figure 15-6. *Outlook Web Access client.*

There is no specific integration between Microsoft Office or Internet Explorer and OWA, and OWA does not provide any task management capabilities. OWA does allow users to access Exchange public folders and to query Active Directory for mail-enabled objects.

Exchange Client

Exchange Client was the default client for Exchange Server from the first release of the Exchange product until Exchange Server 5.5 was released. It is available in 32-bit Windows, 16-bit Windows, MS-DOS, and Macintosh versions. Exchange Client delivers many of the functions that are inherent in the Exchange system, such as messaging and the ability to access public folders. It does not have scheduling capabilities built into it, so it depends on Schedule+ (covered in the following section) to provide this capability.

The versions of Exchange Client for Macintosh and for 16-bit Windows are not comparable, feature for feature, to the 32-bit Windows version of Exchange Client. However, both the Macintosh and 16-bit Windows versions do include e-mail, personal calendaring, tasks lists, and group scheduling. If you have been using Exchange Server in your environment for a while, you might have Exchange Client on some, most, or all of your client machines. Exchange 2000 Server fully supports Exchange Client, but the client will not be enhanced in subsequent releases of Exchange Server, and it does not allow access to some of Exchange 2000 Server's more advanced features.

Schedule+

Schedule+ was the default program used for scheduling and contact management for Exchange Server until Exchange Server 5.5, in which it was replaced by the group collaboration capabilities of Outlook. Both Schedule+ 1.0 and Schedule+ 7.0 are available in 32-bit Windows, 16-bit Windows, and Macintosh versions. Users moving to Outlook from Schedule+ can import their existing calendar data so that nothing is lost in the transition.

Schedule+ clients can still be used with Exchange 2000 Server, but Schedule+ will not be enhanced in subsequent releases of Exchange Server. You can use Schedule+ in an Exchange environment that also includes Outlook users. The two client applications can access the same calendaring information, but Outlook provides some additional functionality, such as the following:

- Journal feature
- Notes feature
- Integrated contacts
- Additional views

- Advanced custom view capabilities
- Task delegation
- Advanced printing options
- Public folder with calendars

Standard Internet Mail Clients

One of the goals of Exchange 2000 Server is to continue to comply with the standards being used by the Internet community. Because Exchange 2000 Server is compliant with several popular Internet protocols, it can be used as the messaging server for third-party e-mail clients, provided that the clients are also compliant with those protocols.

If you are running third-party Internet mail client software as either a POP3 client or an IMAP 4 client, you can use Exchange 2000 Server as your messaging server. Although Outlook Express is a Microsoft product, it is a good example of the type of software we're talking about here. Outlook Express really has nothing specifically to do with Exchange Server; you could use it to get your e-mail from your local ISP and to read newsgroup messages from a UNIX-based news server somewhere on the Internet. In the case of Outlook Express, Exchange Server might never even enter the picture.

Non-Windows Platforms

In our discussions of clients using Exchange 2000 Server, we've usually assumed that they've been running on a Windows operating system. How do non-Windows operating systems connect with Exchange 2000 Server? Let's look at two other popular operating systems: UNIX and Macintosh.

UNIX Clients

No Outlook client exists for the UNIX operating system, so UNIX users have one of two choices for connecting to Exchange 2000 Server:

- **Internet mail client**   A UNIX-based, third-party Internet mail client can be used to access messages from Exchange 2000 Server over either the POP3 or IMAP4 protocols.
- **Outlook Web Access**   Because OWA runs in a standard browser, UNIX users can access their e-mail using their own Web browser.

Macintosh Clients

Macintosh clients have three choices for accessing Exchange 2000 Server:

- **Outlook 8.2.2** Microsoft's Outlook client for Macintosh provides functionality similar to that of its 32-bit Windows counterpart. A new release of Outlook is in the works to enable Macintosh users to take advantage of more of the functionality of Exchange 2000 Server.

- **Internet mail client** Like UNIX users, Macintosh users can access Exchange 2000 Server with their own POP3 or IMAP4 e-mail clients.

- **Outlook Web Access** OWA is also accessible from a Macintosh-based Web browser.

As you can see, the client choices for the UNIX and Macintosh operating systems are extensive. Exchange 2000 Server gives the user a variety of ways to access messages, regardless of the operating system.

Choosing a Client for Exchange Server

In a philosophical sense, choosing a client for Exchange Server is easy. Outlook 2000 is the most current version of the Outlook client; it provides the greatest amount of functionality, and it is designated by Microsoft as the official client for Exchange Server. Outlook 2000 is bundled with Microsoft Office 2000 and with Exchange 2000 Server. Although Exchange 2000 Server supports Exchange Client and Schedule+, they are no longer being enhanced with new features and cannot access all of the services that Exchange 2000 Server provides. Standard Internet e-mail clients also miss a great deal of the functionality that Exchange offers, but they are fast enough to be used efficiently over the Internet.

As they say, however, your mileage may vary. You may have a large installed base of Exchange Client users, and upgrading them can be a significant administrative task. Some or all of the people in your organization may already have an e-mail program that they like and, rather than going through the pain of change, may choose to forgo the advanced features available with Outlook. Any of these factors might contribute to a decision to support non-Outlook clients as part of your Exchange environment or to use Outlook Web Access.

You may also have such a widespread mix of client platforms that you need to use the most generic client possible: the Outlook Web Access client. Or you may need to use OWA to service the messaging needs of some of your users and use the complete Outlook product for other users. Client machines can also use standard Internet POP3 and OWA clients to access your Exchange Inbox over the Internet.

The bottom line is that Outlook 2000 will allow you to take advantage of all that Exchange 2000 has to offer, but other preexisting clients, while potentially missing some newer features, are supported and work with Exchange 2000 Server as well.

Summary

Exchange 2000 Server can support a wide variety of clients, including Outlook, Outlook Express, Outlook Web Access, Exchange Client, Schedule+, and standard Internet e-mail clients. Outlook 2000 is currently the most widely used client for Exchange 2000 Server because it provides the most functionality and is the clear upgrade path for forthcoming Exchange clients.

Outlook Express is a capable client for Exchange 2000 Server as long as the server supports the POP3 or IMAP4 protocol. Outlook Web Access is a good client to use when your organization supports non-Windows-based clients such as UNIX and Macintosh or when your users need to access the server over the Internet. Exchange Client and Schedule+ are still functional alternatives in the Exchange environment, although upgrading to Outlook gives you more functionality. The next chapter takes a more in-depth look at deploying and using Outlook 2000.

Chapter 16
Deploying Outlook 2000

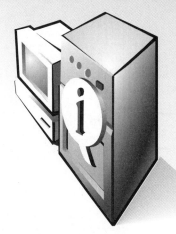

Microsoft Outlook 2000 is the latest version of Outlook. Because it is a component of Microsoft Office 2000, Outlook 2000 will become widely used as organizations upgrade to this newest version of the popular Office suite. It is included in all five Office 2000 packages and is also shipped with Microsoft Exchange 2000 Server. This chapter looks at some of the issues an administrator faces when deploying Outlook 2000, including installation, using Outlook 2000 off line, and enabling multiple users.

Installing Outlook 2000

Installing client software is one of the most repetitive tasks you face as an administrator. However, it's one that you've got to perform because a client/server system such as Exchange 2000 Server will not work unless both sides of the equation are in place.

Because this book focuses on Exchange Server, we will not provide detailed instructions for installing Outlook 2000. We'll simply give an overview of the installation methods available, explaining some of the options you or your users have when performing a standard Outlook installation on an individual machine. We'll then introduce the Office Custom Installation Wizard, which allows you to create customized installations for your users.

More Info   This chapter focuses on Outlook 2000 from an administrator's view, but Outlook is a pretty complex program. If you want to learn more about using Outlook 2000, read *Running Microsoft Outlook 2000* by Alan Neibauer (Microsoft Press, 1999).

Standard Outlook Installation

Like most Microsoft programs, Outlook 2000 installs with a setup wizard—in this case, the new Windows Installer. Windows Installer is a powerful new utility that allows you to customize just about every aspect of an installation and also takes care of adding and removing components after an installation. Figure 16-1 shows the component selection window of Windows Installer. For each component of Outlook 2000, you can elect to

- Install the component to run from the local hard disk. If disk space is abundant, many administrators choose to install every available component to run in this way.

- Install the component to run over the network from a shared access point. If disk space is an issue, this option will conserve space.

- Set the component to install the first time the user attempts to use it. This is a favorite choice for those that are somewhere in between the two choices above. If a user never needs a certain component of Outlook, it is never installed and doesn't waste space. On the other hand, those components that are used constantly are installed locally. This option also saves the administrator time during the initial install.

- Not install the component at all. This simply means that the user will have to run the installer again to install the component. You can also use this option to prevent the user from installing certain components, as long as you don't make the installation files available.

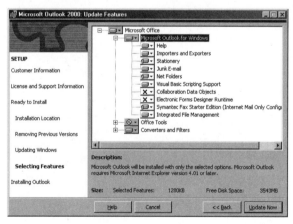

Figure 16-1. *Specifying which Outlook 2000 components to install.*

After you've selected the components to install, Windows Installer takes care of the rest of the installation with little or no intervention on your part. Once the installation is complete, you need to choose a mode for running Outlook 2000. There are three choices, as shown in Figure 16-2:

- **Internet Only**   This service option makes Outlook act as an Internet mail client to any server that supports POP3, SMTP, or IMAP4.

- **Corporate or Workgroup**   This service option is designed for use over a local area network (LAN) with Exchange Server or another third-party, LAN-based mail system such as Lotus Notes. It provides the complete set of Outlook features.

- **No E-Mail**   This service option causes Outlook to act as a stand-alone personal information manager offering only contact, task, and schedule management features.

Chapter 15 discusses each of these options in more detail.

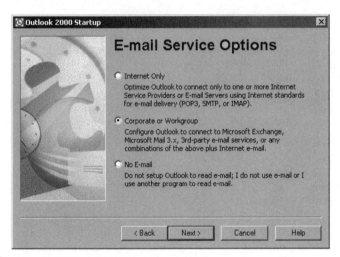

Figure 16-2. *Choosing an operating mode for Outlook 2000.*

Note   To function correctly, Outlook 2000 requires that Microsoft Internet Explorer 4.01 or later be installed on client computers.

When you've selected an e-mail service option, Outlook starts up and prompts you to configure the user's e-mail account. In an Exchange organization, this configuration involves providing the name of the Exchange server and the user name.

Customizing Outlook Installation

As an administrator, you can customize the setup of Outlook 2000 in three ways. You can run the Setup program with command-line switches, use a setup information file to answer various setup questions and then specify the setup information file using command-line switches, and customize an installation of Outlook with the Office Custom Installation Wizard. This section briefly discusses these options.

Using Command-Line Switches

You can customize the setup of Outlook somewhat by using various switches. Most of the switches involve the use of a Microsoft Installer (.MSI) package file. Table 16-1 lists the available command-line switches.

More Info   For more information on using switches to modify your Outlook installations, see Knowledge Base article Q202946.

Table 16-1.   Command-line switches for installing Outlook 2000

Switch	Use
/a <msifile>	Creates an administrative install point using the .MSI file for client installations.
/f [options] <msifile>	Repairs the Outlook installation using various repair modes.
/g <language ID>	Specifies the language to be used. English, which is the default, is ID 1033.
/I <msifile>	Specifies the name of the .MSI file to be used during installation. This switch cannot be used with the /a switch.
/j [options] <msifile>	Creates an icon that can be used later to install a feature not configured during setup.
/l [options] <logfile>	Specifies the log file used during installation and switches to be passed to the Windows Installer.
/x <msifile>	Uninstalls Outlook.
/q [options]	Specifies the amount of information to be presented on screen during the installation.
/wait	Indicates that the installer should wait for the installation to complete before exiting.
/settings	Specifies the path and settings file to be used for the automated installation.

Using a Setup Information File

If a file named Setup.ini exists in the same directory as Setup.exe, or if the */settings* *<inifile>* switch specifies an .INI file with a different name, that file will be used to modify the default behavior of the setup. Because this file can specify all of the parameters you would normally provide at the command line, it is useful for a number of reasons:

- You can avoid typographical errors at the command line.
- You are not subject to limitations on the length of the command.
- You can enforce specific settings, even with an interactive installation.

The file is merely a text document and can be opened with Microsoft Notepad or any other text editor. Like other .INI files, each line represents one aspect of the installation. To include a comment, type a semicolon at the beginning of each comment line.

More Info   The format of the settings file is described in the Setup Reference workbook (SetupRef.xls), which is included with the *Microsoft Office 2000 Resource Kit* (Microsoft Press, 1999).

Using the Office Custom Installation Wizard

The Office Custom Installation Wizard, shown in Figure 16-3, works with Windows Installer to let you tweak almost every detail of the installation process. You can

- Define the path where Outlook 2000 is installed on client computers
- Set the installation options (run from hard disk, install on first use, don't install) for individual components of Outlook 2000
- Define a list of network servers for Windows Installer to use if the primary installation server is unavailable
- Specify other products to install or other programs to run on the user's computer when the Outlook installation is done
- Hide selected options from users during setup
- Add custom files and Windows registry settings to the installation
- Customize desktop shortcuts for Outlook 2000
- Set user default options
- Use Office profile settings created with the Profile Wizard for Office 2000 to preset user options

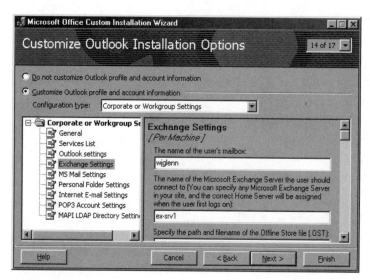

Figure 16-3. *Customizing an Outlook installation with the Office Custom Installation Wizard.*

To accomplish all of this, the Windows Installer uses two types of files: an installer package (an .MSI file) and an installer transform file (an .MST file). The installer package contains a database that describes the configuration information. The installer transform file contains modifications that are to be made as Windows Installer installs Outlook. The package file never changes; it is essentially a database that helps Windows Installer relate various features to actual installation files. The transform file is what the Office Custom Installation Wizard helps you create. It allows you to create unique setup scenarios that all use the same installation files. In other words, you could create different installation routines for different departments but use only one network installation point.

More Info The Office Custom Installation Wizard is included on the CD-ROM that accompanies the *Microsoft Office 2000 Resource Kit*. It is also available on line at *http://www.microsoft.com/office/ork/2000/appndx/toolbox.htm*. The resource kit provides detailed information on using the wizard.

Systems Management Server

Systems Management Server (SMS) is a Microsoft application specifically designed to help administrators address the needs of larger user communities. The *Microsoft Office 2000 Resource Kit* (available in both book form and on line) contains instructions for creating installation packages and configuration files that can be used by SMS. The resource kit also contains a sample package definition file (PDF) that can be used with SMS to distribute the customized version of the executable client setup file to the users on your network. The PDF is a text file that includes the setup parameters necessary to install Outlook 2000 using SMS. The sample PDF is as follows:

```
[PDF]
Version=1.0

[Package Definition]
Product=Microsoft Outlook 2000 9.0
Comment=Microsoft Outlook 2000 for Windows
WorkstationAccess=UserRead, UserWrite, GuestRead, GuestWrite
SetupVariations=Typical, Custom, Manual, Uninstall

[Typical Setup]
CommandName=Typical
CommandLine=OFF9SMS.BAT /TYPICAL
UserInputRequired=FALSE
SynchronousSystemExitRequired=TRUE
SystemTask=FALSE
SupportedPlatforms=Windows NT (x86), Windows95

[Custom Setup]
CommandName=Custom
CommandLine=OFF9SMS.BAT /CUSTOM "New Custom Setup File.MST"
UserInputRequired=FALSE
SynchronousSystemExitRequired=TRUE
SystemTask=FALSE
SupportedPlatforms=Windows NT (x86), Windows95

[Manual Setup]
CommandName=User input required
CommandLine=OFF9SMS.BAT /MANUAL
UserInputRequired=TRUE
SynchronousSystemExitRequired=TRUE
SystemTask=FALSE
SupportedPlatforms=Windows NT (x86), Windows95

[Uninstall Setup]
CommandName=Uninstall
CommandLine=OFF9SMS.BAT /UNINSTALL
UserInputRequired=FALSE
SynchronousSystemExitRequired=TRUE
SystemTask=FALSE
SupportedPlatforms=Windows NT (x86), Windows95
```

(continued)

```
[Setup Package for Inventory]
InventoryThisPackage=TRUE
Detection Rule Part 1=File 1
Detection Rule Part 2=AND
Detection Rule Part 3=File 2

[File 1]
File=MSO9.DLL
Collect=FALSE
CheckSum=
CRC=
Date=
Time=
Byte=
Word=
Long=
Token 1=
Token 2=
Token 3=
Token 4=

[File 2]
File=outl2000.ini
Collect=FALSE
CheckSum=
CRC=0, 204, 20996
Date=
Time=
Byte=
Word=
Long=
Token 1=
Token 2=
Token 3=
Token 4=

[Last Modified]
Date=12-31-98
Time=10:14:09
```

You must accomplish two steps before distributing Outlook 2000 to your client systems. First you must create a package. The package consists of the PDF just discussed and a package source folder containing all of the files necessary for the installation. After you've created the package, the second step is to create an advertisement to distribute the package. An advertisement consists of the package as well as a list of all client systems on which you want the package installed (called a collection). SMS provides flexibility and granularity so that you can install the package only where you want it. For example, you may decide to install the package only on client systems that meet minimum memory and hard disk parameters and ignore all other systems. The job can also be set to run only after a certain time period and, if not voluntarily accepted by the user within that time frame, it can be configured to become a mandatory installation that the user cannot stop or defer to a later time period.

Real World   Creating Your Own Installer Packages

In addition to using SMS and the Office Custom Installation Wizard to create installer packages, you can also create your own installer packages using Veritas' Winstall LE, included with Microsoft Windows 2000 Server. With this software, you can create a package that represents your installation of Outlook or any other program.

The way it works is simple. Winstall takes a "before" snapshot of a system without Outlook on it. This snapshot consists of a file system listing and a registry listing. It then prompts you to install the application in question—Outlook, in this case. Once the installation is complete, Winstall takes an "after" snapshot. From the two snapshots, Winstall generates a difference file consisting of a list of files that are installed (and their proper locations) as well as the registry entries that should be added, deleted, or changed as a result of the Outlook installation. This installation information is written to an .MSI file. Winstall stores this file, a copied set of the installed files, and a .REG file containing the registry changes on a shared folder on a server. When you run this .MSI package, the Outlook files are placed in their appropriate locations and the registry is modified. There are no wizards to walk through and no options to choose. The end result is a reproducible installation that takes far less time than installing Outlook 2000 manually.

Should you choose to modify the installation, you can modify the .MSI file with Winstall LE, or you can start over and re-create a new .MSI package by installing Outlook 2000 with a different set of options.

Supporting Outlook 2000

Many of the features of Outlook 2000 are especially relevant in a book about Exchange 2000 Server because they involve interaction between the Outlook 2000 client and Exchange Server. These features include the ability to work while disconnected from the Exchange server and to let more than one user work with a specific computer. This section discusses these topics.

Using Outlook 2000 Off Line

Exchange Server and Outlook 2000 form the two ends of a powerful communications system. Most of the time, people communicate while the programs are in direct contact with each other so that the give and take of the process can proceed freely.

Recall from Chapter 1, however, that communication with messaging systems such as Exchange Server is *asynchronous,* which means that one party can send a message without the other party's being available to receive the message. Even though messages and replies might fly through your Exchange Server environment as rapidly as they do on the telephone, there is no requirement that the recipient be available when a message is sent or that the sender still be on line when the message is received.

This simple fact means that you can also use the Outlook 2000 client without being connected to the Exchange server. You can read messages in the local folders or create messages that are stored in your Outbox and sent when you reconnect to Exchange Server. This powerful feature makes users more productive in many situations that are typically thought of as downtime. (For example, you've probably seen people sitting on planes answering their e-mail.)

You can work off line with Outlook 2000 without modifying the software in any way. In fact, when you start Outlook 2000 off line, the environment looks almost the same as it does when you are connected to an Exchange server. The folder list displays all of the folders for your mailbox, and you can create messages as though you were connected. Of course, the Outlook 2000 client must previously have been connected to the Exchange Server at some point, and the folders must be marked for synchronization for the folder hierarchy to be the same as the one you see when you work off line.

By default, however, public folders are not displayed in the folder list when you are working off line. To understand why this is so, you must learn about a process called synchronization.

Synchronizing a Mailbox

Synchronizing a mailbox is a simple process from the user's perspective, but to accomplish it the system must perform several complex tasks. When Exchange Server synchronizes the contents of a folder on an Outlook 2000 client machine with the contents of the matching folder on the Exchange server, the system makes a copy of any messages that exist in only one location and places them in the other location. Exchange also synchronizes messages that have been deleted in one location but not in the other location.

The standard, default folders (Inbox, Outbox, Deleted Items, Calendar, Sent Items, Contacts, Tasks, Drafts, Journal, and Notes) in your Outlook mailbox are synchronized automatically, as long as you have set up a location in which to store the contents of these folders. By default, Outlook works with folders on the Exchange server. To work with these folders when you are disconnected from Exchange Server, you must set up an offline folder for them, as described next.

> **Note**   Folders that you add to your mailbox are not synchronized automatically. You must explicitly set up synchronization for them, as described later in this chapter in the section "Synchronizing Public Folders."

Setting Up an Offline Folder   To enable synchronization, you must set up an offline folder for your Outlook client. The offline folder is stored in a file that has the extension .OST. You create an offline folder in one of two ways: implicitly, by enabling offline access, or explicitly, by creating the folder.

> **Note**   When you first configure a new installation of Outlook 2000, you are asked the simple question, "Do you travel with this computer?" If you select Yes, Outlook 2000 sets up an offline folder with the default name in the default location as part of the installation process.

To enable offline access and implicitly set up an offline folder, you simply have to try to open the offline folder settings by pointing to Synchronize on Outlook's Tools menu and choosing Offline Folder Settings. Outlook informs you that offline folders are not enabled and asks if you want to create an offline folder (an

.OST file). If you choose to do so, Outlook opens the Offline Folder File Settings dialog box, shown in Figure 16-4. Click OK to create the .OST file in the default location. (You can also put it anywhere you want.)

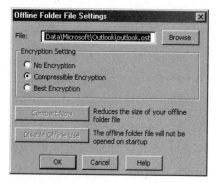

Figure 16-4. *Setting up an offline folder in Outlook 2000.*

Once it has created the file, Outlook opens the Offline Folder Settings dialog box, shown in Figure 16-5, where you specify the folders to be synchronized. By default, all of the normal personal folders are configured for offline use, but you can selectively disable those that you do not want synchronized. You can also set advanced filters to specify exactly what files to synchronize in each of these folders.

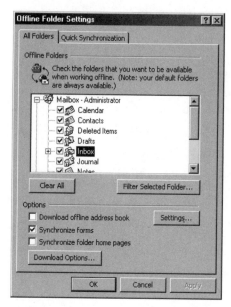

Figure 16-5. *Specifying the folders to synchronize.*

Finally, you can use the Quick Synchronization tab of the Offline Folder Settings dialog box, shown in Figure 16-6, to create smaller groups of folders that take less time to synchronize than the whole group. For example, you might create a group that synchronizes only your Inbox and Outbox. Any groups you create on this tab will show up as commands on the Synchronize submenu of Outlook's Tools menu.

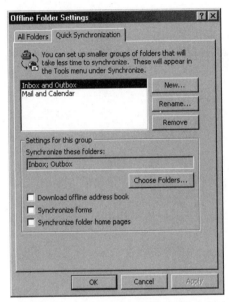

Figure 16-6. *Creating smaller groups of folders to synchronize quickly.*

Synchronizing Offline Folders Automatically   When you start Outlook 2000, it determines whether the client computer is connected to an Exchange server. You can create messages, delete messages, and perform other standard functions while off line. The next time you start Outlook and connect to an Exchange server, Outlook and Exchange Server automatically synchronize the contents of your offline folder. Folders set for synchronization in Outlook 2000 are identified by a blue double-arrow symbol at the lower left of the folder's icon in the folder list, as shown in Figure 16-7. Folders not set for synchronization, such as the Notes folder shown in the figure, do not have the symbol.

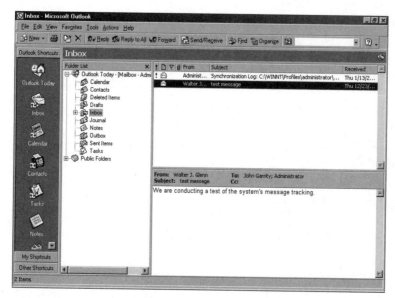

Figure 16-7. *Folder list identifying folders to be synchronized.*

You can also specify other types of automatic synchronization for your offline folder. To do so, choose Options from the Tools menu and display the Mail Services tab (Figure 16-8). You can choose from three options for synchronizing the contents of your offline folder:

- **When Online, Synchronize All Folders Upon Exiting** This option is useful if you regularly work off line because when you choose it, you do not have to remember to explicitly synchronize the contents of your offline folders before you disconnect from the Exchange server. The downside to choosing this option is that logging off from Outlook may involve waiting while synchronization occurs.

Note You can stop the synchronization process by right-clicking the progress indicator for the synchronization in the Outlook status bar at the bottom of the main Outlook window and then clicking the Cancel button in the shortcut menu.

- **When Online, Automatically Synchronize All Offline Folders Every X Minutes** You can keep your offline folders updated by specifying that they should be synchronized on a regular basis. This option includes a field that allows you to specify how frequently this automatic synchronization should occur.

- **When Offline, Automatically Synchronize All Folders Every X Minutes**
  At first, this option may seem a bit confusing. After all, how can you synchronize off line folders when you are off line? Outlook allows you to use a remote dial-up connection to send and receive messages—or to synchronize mailboxes—while you are off line. Because transmission over a dial-up connection is usually much slower than over a direct connection, choose this option with care.

If you choose one or more of these options, the type of synchronization you specify will occur in addition to the default synchronization that takes place every time you reconnect to Exchange Server. The options you specify here will remain in effect until you explicitly turn them off.

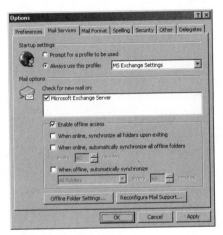

Figure 16-8. *Setting automatic synchronization options.*

Synchronizing Offline Folders Manually   Although your offline folders are synchronized with the matching folders in Exchange Server automatically whenever you connect to the Exchange server and you have several other options for automatic synchronization, you still might want to synchronize your offline folders manually from time to time. When you point to Synchronize on the Tools menu, you have several options, as shown in Figure 16-9.

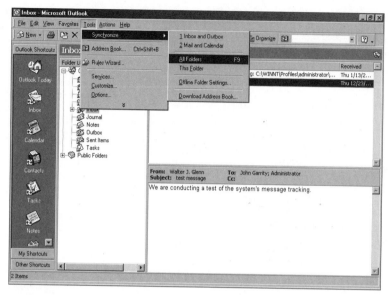

Figure 16-9. *Synchronize submenu of the Tools menu.*

You can choose to synchronize all of the folders that are enabled for offline operation, to synchronize only the selected folder, or to synchronize any of the sets of folders you have configured on the Quick Synchronization tab. (Refer back to Figure 16-6.) You also have the option of downloading the address book for your Exchange server. When you choose Download Address Book, you are given the choice of downloading a detailed version of the address book, containing a complete set of information about the recipients it contains, or a minimal version that contains only a list of the recipients (Figure 16-10).

Figure 16-10. *Downloading address book information.*

Because an offline address book can be very large, you can also choose to download only the changes that have been made since you last downloaded the address book. This option can significantly reduce the time that the download takes. You can improve the speed of the download further by not downloading the full details of the address book. As the dialog box notes, however, this partial download prevents you from sending encrypted messages through remote mail, because the digital IDs for the address book are not downloaded.

Real World   **When Synchronization Doesn't Work**

Despite the fact that you've configured everything correctly on your Outlook 2000 client, at times your folders may not synchronize automatically when you reconnect. If Outlook determines that you have a slow connection, it automatically stops synchronization from occurring. You can still synchronize either all folders or a specific folder by pointing to Synchronize on the Tools menu and choosing the appropriate menu item.

It is possible that other errors may prevent synchronization. A synchronization log file, as shown in Figure 16-11, is always placed in the Deleted Items folder of the offline folder. Check this log for error codes that may help you solve synchronization problems.

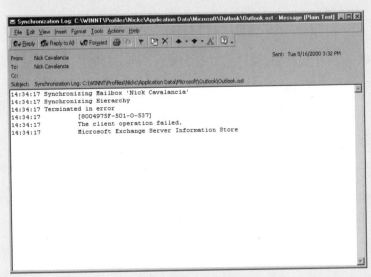

Figure 16-11. *Synchronization log indicating that an error occurred.*

Disabling Offline Use of Your Mailbox Whenever you enable your Outlook 2000 client for offline use, you automatically enable the standard folders in your mailbox for offline use. The only way to disable offline use of your mailbox folders is to disable offline use for your Outlook client. You can disable offline use by choosing either Services or Options from the Tools menu in Outlook 2000.

To disable offline access through the Services dialog box, choose Microsoft Exchange Server, click the Properties button, and display the Advanced tab. Clear the Enable Offline Use check box.

To disable offline access through the Options dialog box, display the Mail Services tab, clear the Enable Offline Access check box, and then click Apply or OK. (Refer back to Figure 16-8.)

These two methods have the same effect. You will no longer be able to use Outlook 2000 with the contents of any of your Exchange-based folders if you are not connected to an Exchange server. If you open Outlook with offline access disabled when you are not connected to an Exchange server, you receive a message that Outlook could not open your default e-mail folders, and Outlook opens with your default file system instead.

Note Disabling offline access after you've created an offline folder does not delete the offline folder. It is not deleted until you explicitly delete it.

Synchronizing Public Folders

As we mentioned earlier in this chapter, the standard mailbox folders are automatically enabled for offline access. You can verify this capability by displaying the property sheet for one of the folders in the mailbox, such as your Inbox. One of the tabs in the property sheet is labeled Synchronization. (This tab is discussed in the next section, "Shaping Synchronization.") However, if you display the property sheet for a public folder, you do not see the Synchronization tab, because public folders, by default, are not enabled for offline access. Public folders typically contain large amounts of information that would clog your client machine. In addition, the contents of public folders are often subject to change, making synchronization difficult. (See the Real World sidebar "Public Folder Synchronization Conflicts" later in this section.)

You can, however, easily enable a public folder for offline access. Simply move the public folder to the Favorites list in the Public Folders container of the folder list. You can make this change by dragging the folder into the Favorites folder or by pointing to Folder on the File menu and choosing Add To Public Folder Favorites. When you drag a public folder to the Favorites folder, it has the same name as the original public folder. When you choose Add To Public Folder Favorites, you see the dialog box shown in Figure 16-12. This expanded list of options allows you to give the folder in the Favorites list a different name and to specify whether the hierarchy of subfolders should be moved with and maintained in the folder as new subfolders are added to the main Favorites folder. When you add a folder to the Favorites list by dragging the folder, only that folder is added to the list.

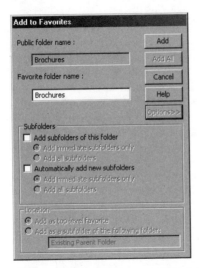

Figure 16-12. *Adding a public folder to the Favorites list.*

When you designate a public folder as a Favorite, you do not move it from its established place in the public folder hierarchy; you simply add the folder to your list of Favorites. When a public folder is in the Favorites list, the property sheet for the folder contains a Synchronization tab. You can remove a folder from the Favorites list by selecting it in the list and then deleting it.

Real World **Public Folder Synchronization Conflicts**

Conflicts can arise if more than one person is using and modifying the items in a public folder off line. If you change an item in a public folder while you are off line, when you synchronize that folder, Exchange Server checks the timestamp on the existing version of the item. If the timestamp for the item is later than the original timestamp on the item you have changed, it means that someone else changed the contents of the folder item since you last downloaded it. If this type of conflict occurs, you receive a message that includes copies of all conflicting versions of the item. It is up to you to resolve the conflict, either by combining all of the versions of an item into a single version and then clicking Keep This Item or by clicking Keep All to keep all versions of the message (Figure 16-13).

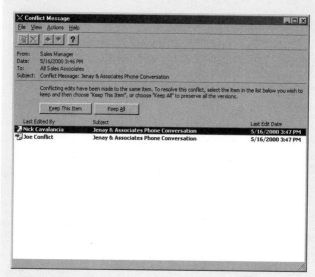

Figure 16-13. *Specifying how to resolve a conflict.*

This procedure is more complicated than it sounds. A user may find it difficult to decide whether to keep an existing item or overwrite it, and the wrong decision could have negative results. For this reason, you should place controls on who is allowed to download and modify public folders, through the standard Exchange security system.

Shaping Synchronization

After you have enabled offline access for your Outlook client, you can shape the way that each folder synchronizes with Exchange. If a folder is enabled for off-line use, the property sheet for the folder contains a Synchronization tab, as shown in Figure 16-14.

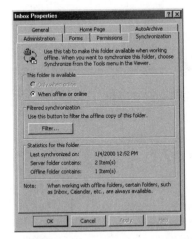

Figure 16-14. *Synchronization tab of a folder's property sheet.*

You can make a folder available off line by selecting When Offline Or Online in the This Folder Is Available area at the top of the tab. By default, a public folder that has been added to the Favorites list is enabled only for online access, so you must explicitly change this setting if you want to enable synchronization for the folder.

When you indicate that a folder is available for offline or online access, you have the option of creating a filter for the synchronization process. Click the Filter button to display a dialog box that allows you to define filtering conditions (Figure 16-15). This dialog box has several tabs that allow you to define a complex condition. After you set up a filter, Outlook uses the conditions described in the filter to control which messages are synchronized between the Outlook client and the corresponding folders in Exchange Server. Keep in mind that these limits are imposed on all future synchronization attempts but have no effect on any messages that currently reside in the offline message store.

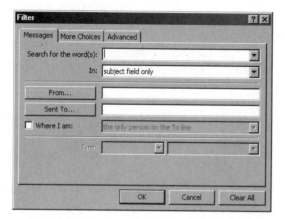

Figure 16-15. *Filtering messages to be synchronized.*

Filtering is an enormously useful tool for getting all of the benefits of offline access without incurring the excessive overhead caused by synchronizing less important messages. You could create a filter that disables synchronization for any messages that have large file attachments, for example, or you could synchronize only messages from your boss. Be careful to remember when you have synchronization filters on. In an offline folder, there is no indication that the messages presented in the folder are not the complete set of messages stored in the matching Exchange folder.

Deciding Whether to Copy or Synchronize

Synchronization is no more than a sophisticated way to copy messages automatically between folders on the Exchange server and the offline folder on an Outlook 2000 client. For your Inbox, Outbox, and other mailbox folders, synchronization works well. But should you use the process for public folders?

Public folders can serve a wide variety of purposes. A public folder can be a simple repository of static information, such as a library, or it can be a dynamically changing discussion group. You can copy the contents of a public folder to your mailbox simply by dragging the folder into the Mailbox container in your Outlook folder list. When should you copy and when should you synchronize the contents of a public folder?

The longer you have the contents of a public folder away from the Exchange server, the more likely it is that you will have a conflict when you reconnect—that is, you will have made changes to your offline copy while others will have changed the version on the Exchange server. Although public folders do have a way to detect conflicts, as we described earlier, you must resolve those conflicts manually, which can be time-consuming.

In deciding whether to copy or synchronize a public folder, you should carefully analyze how the folder is intended to be used off line. If its contents are meant only to be read, you probably will find that a simple copy operation works well. If you will be making changes in the contents of the folder, you should seriously consider preventing later conflicts by applying filters to the synchronization process so that you modify only the messages that are unlikely to be modified by other users.

Enabling Multiple Users in Outlook 2000

The capabilities of Outlook 2000 and the capabilities of Exchange 2000 work in conjunction with each other. Outlook is a client, and Exchange is a server. When an Outlook client is connected to an Exchange server, the client is representing a single user. In some situations, however, the same Outlook client can be used to support multiple users at different times. This section explores the scenarios in which this situation can occur.

Understanding Outlook Profiles, Exchange Mailboxes, and Windows 2000

Before you learn how to implement multiple users with Outlook, you need to understand the differences between an Outlook profile and an Exchange mailbox as well as how both of these entities interact with Microsoft Windows 2000 accounts.

A *profile* is a client-side configuration. An Outlook profile is a set of information services configured for a particular user or purpose. The Exchange Server information service in a profile includes a reference to an associated Exchange server and mailbox. When a user starts Outlook, he or she uses the information in an Outlook profile to establish a connection with a particular Exchange server.

Normally, each client machine has a single, default Outlook 2000 profile. When a user starts Outlook on that machine, the default profile is used to determine which Exchange mailbox will be used on the server side of the environment. If a user is starting Outlook for the first time or is using a machine that does not have a profile, he or she is prompted to create a profile before fully logging on to the associated Exchange server. To see the profile that your Outlook client is currently using, choose Services from the Tools menu of Outlook 2000. You will see the dialog box shown in Figure 16-16.

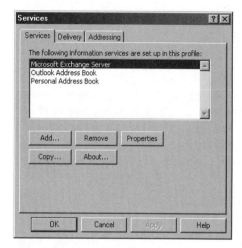

Figure 16-16. *Viewing the current profile from within Outlook 2000.*

Sometimes a single profile on an Outlook client is not enough. The following section discusses situations in which more than one profile is required.

Creating Multiple Profiles with Outlook 2000

You might want to use more than one Outlook profile for any of several reasons. Perhaps you are using Outlook on a machine that you share with other users. Having separate profiles allows each profile to reflect the various mailboxes and configuration information for a given user. You might also be using a machine under different circumstances (such as in the office and on the road), making it desirable to be able to select a profile based on your current situation.

When you first log on to Outlook 2000, you are prompted to create a profile, which is used as the default profile. To create an additional profile, right-click the Outlook icon on your desktop and choose Properties from the shortcut menu. The property sheet shown in Figure 16-17 opens.

This property sheet is almost identical to the one available in Outlook 2000 when you choose Services from the Tools menu. (Refer back to Figure 16-16.) The one big difference is that this property sheet has a Show Profiles button. Clicking this button displays a list of the profiles on the machine, as shown in Figure 16-18.

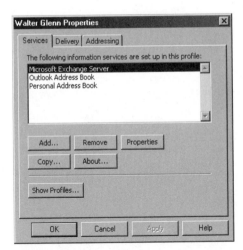

Figure 16-17. *Outlook 2000 property sheet containing the Show Profiles button.*

Figure 16-18. *A list of mail profiles.*

To add a new profile, simply click the Add button, which starts the Inbox Setup Wizard. This wizard prompts you for the values needed for a profile, including the name of the target Exchange server and the mailbox that the profile will use on that server. The Inbox Setup Wizard also asks if you will be using this machine while traveling—and if so, it will set up an offline folder. You can also delete or modify existing profiles in this dialog box.

At the bottom of the Mail dialog box, you can specify a user profile to be used as the default profile for this client machine. Outlook uses this default profile to connect to an Exchange server, unless you specify otherwise. The use of a default profile can be somewhat cumbersome, however, because it requires you to display the Outlook property sheet when you want to use a different profile. Instead, you can have Outlook prompt you for a profile every time you start Outlook. To enable this feature, choose Options from the Tools menu in Outlook 2000. In the Options dialog box, display the Mail Services tab (Figure 16-19).

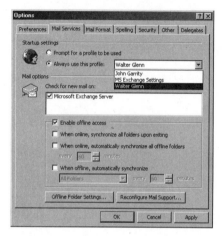

Figure 16-19. *Specifying a startup profile in Outlook 2000.*

In the Startup Settings area are two radio buttons. Always Use This Profile is selected by default, indicating that Outlook should start up with a specific profile. You can indicate any profile as the default profile, and it will override any setting you made in the Mail dialog box. (Refer back to Figure 16-18.)

The Prompt For A Profile To Be Used radio button tells Outlook to prompt you for a profile every time you start the program. If you select this option, a dialog box appears every time you start Outlook (Figure 16-20), allowing you to select the profile to use.

Figure 16-20. *Selecting a profile when starting Outlook 2000.*

Providing Access to Different Exchange Mailboxes

The Outlook profile described in the preceding section includes client-side configuration information. But remember that Outlook is the client portion of a client/server system. You still need the appropriate user privileges to access the server side of the equation in Exchange Server.

Exchange security is based on the Windows 2000 security model. Each Exchange object has an access control list (ACL) consisting of a discretionary access control list (DACL) and a system access control list (SACL). These lists are used in conjunction with the user's access token to either grant or deny access. For instance, before an Outlook client can access an Exchange server, the user must log on to a network and receive a ticket from the Windows 2000 domain controller. This ticket is used to gain entrance to the Exchange server. Figure 16-21 illustrates this process.

More Info   For more information on the security concepts presented here, please consult the *Windows 2000 Server Distributed Systems Guide* in the *Microsoft Windows 2000 Server Resource Kit* (Microsoft Press, 2000).

If you specify a different Windows 2000 user name with each profile, you can use multiple Outlook profiles to access different Exchange mailboxes. In some situations, however, you may want to allow an individual to access different Exchange mailboxes while using the same Windows 2000 user name. For example, you may want a receptionist to be able to open the mailbox of another receptionist who has called in sick for the day.

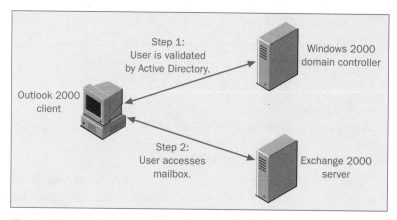

Figure 16-21. *Using the Outlook client to connect to an Exchange 2000 server.*

A mailbox in Exchange is really just a storage place in an Exchange server's private store provided for a mailbox-enabled user. When you create a mailbox, you can give other Windows 2000 users permission to access it. You can grant this permission from the Active Directory Users and Computers snap-in by opening the property sheet for the user and then displaying the Exchange Advanced tab. On this tab, click the Mailbox Rights button to open the Permissions dialog box shown in Figure 16-22. When you click the Add button, you see a list of Windows 2000 users and groups. You can select one or more of these entities and then click OK to grant them access to the mailbox. You can also delete accounts from the list, but you can never delete the primary account for the mailbox.

Note If you do not see the Exchange Advanced tab, you need to enable the Advanced view in Microsoft Management Console by choosing the Advanced command from the View menu.

You can also allow other users to see any of the folders in your mailbox by granting them permission through the standard property sheet for a folder in Outlook. If users have permission for a specific folder or if their Windows 2000 accounts have been granted permissions on the mailbox, they can open the folder by choosing Other User's Folders from the Open submenu of the main File menu. They can also add the mailbox to their profile by using the option on the Advanced tab of the Microsoft Exchange Server property sheet. They simply click the Add button in the top portion of the Advanced tab and select the mailbox they want to add.

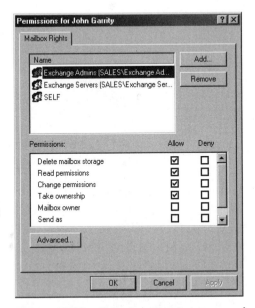

Figure 16-22. *Granting permissions to other Windows 2000 users.*

Using Outlook to Delegate Mailbox Access

The previous section described how the administrator controls access to another user's mailbox using Active Directory Users and Computers. Using Outlook, users can grant privileges to other users without contacting the administrator. They can grant these privileges by right-clicking the folder (such as Calendar), choosing Properties, and then adding the appropriate user on the Permissions tab, as shown in Figure 16-23. These permissions are similar in nature to Windows 2000 ACLs, except that they are Exchange-specific and can be assigned only to certain mail-enabled Active Directory objects. There is no one-to-one correlation between the permissions you see here and the Windows 2000 permissions.

Figure 16-23. *Granting access using Outlook.*

In addition, a user can use the Delegates tab of the Options dialog box (available from the Tools menu) to delegate access to the folders in his or her mailbox. The user can also assign different levels of permissions for each folder. The person being granted delegate access will receive e-mail indicating that permissions have been granted and detailing what level those permissions are.

Once the privileges have been assigned to another user, that user can access the folders by pointing to Open on the File menu and choosing Other User's Folder In Microsoft Outlook. This option is commonly used by administrative assistants checking their bosses' schedules or in situations in which a mailbox represents a conference room, a TV, a company car, or any other resource that can be checked out. In these cases, the Calendar is used to track resource use. By providing a few users the ability to modify the resource's Calendar, and the rest of the company the ability to review it, you can maintain a centralized location for companywide resource tracking.

Setting Up Roving Users

A *roving user* is a user who does not have a fixed physical location and may consequently log on to many different machines. To accommodate such a user, you could set up a user profile on each of the machines he or she might use, but this solution may be impractical. Another way to address this situation is by creating a roving user profile.

> **Note**   In Windows 2000 parlance, these users have *roaming profiles*. Exchange
> Server calls them *roving profiles*.

The configuration information for a roving user is stored on a shared disk on a network server, allowing this information to be accessed from any machine that can connect to the network. When you set up a roving user profile on a machine running Windows 2000, client machines that log on to the network with that profile look on the shared disk for configuration information. The common access to the storage of a roving profile eliminates the need to have this profile stored on many machines. When you enable roving users in Windows 2000, that's all you have to do. Outlook 2000 will automatically support roving Exchange users. For more information about setting up a shared user profile on Windows 2000 and various clients, refer to the documentation for those products.

You can also accommodate roving users through Outlook Web Access and the Web Store. These features are discussed in Chapter 17.

Summary

Outlook 2000 is the preferred client for Exchange 2000 Server. This chapter has covered how to deploy Outlook 2000 in your organization, describing the various installation options, how to support offline use of Outlook 2000, and how to set up profiles and provide access to other users' mailboxes. Outlook is a full-featured client that can be used in conjunction with Exchange Server, even when the client machine is not directly connected to an Exchange Server. A single Outlook client can support many users, and a single user can roam to different machines and use Outlook on each of those machines to check his or her mail.

The next chapter looks at how to access e-mail, public folders, and calendars over the Web using Outlook Web Access. It also discusses the protocols that form the foundation upon which so many Exchange 2000 Server services operate.

Chapter 17
Supporting Outlook Web Access and Internet Protocols

This chapter covers the Simple Mail Transfer Protocol (SMTP), Post Office Protocol version 3 (POP3), Internet Message Access Protocol version 4 (IMAP4), and Outlook Web Access (OWA). At first glance, these might seem the sort of dry topics that only a true geek would appreciate. In reality, however, a good understanding of the basic Internet protocols will greatly assist your efforts in troubleshooting and understanding the Microsoft Exchange 2000 Server architecture.

SMTP is the native transport protocol for Exchange 2000 Server and is used by the Routing Group Connector, by the SMTP Connector (for Internet mail), and for general communications between Exchange 2000 servers. The other protocols—POP3, IMAP4, and OWA—are considered different ways to access the Store process. Understanding the advantages and limitations of each protocol will benefit your planning, implementation, and troubleshooting efforts.

Simple Mail Transfer Protocol

Because it is impossible to provide an in-depth analysis of SMTP in this book, this section concentrates on the parts of SMTP that are most relevant to administering and troubleshooting Exchange 2000 Server.

Simple Mail Transfer Protocol (SMTP) has its roots in the File Transfer Protocol (FTP). Before SMTP was originally defined in RFC 561, it was customary to copy messages to their destination as simple files, using FTP. The problem with this technique was that it was sometimes difficult to discern who had sent the file and who the file was being sent to, due to the lack of identifying information. What was needed was the ability to pass information between two hosts while identifying who the sender and recipient were.

In 1973, the beginnings of such a message structure was defined, containing some header fields and the body of the text. Further refinements came in RFCs 680, 724, and 733 before the current standard in RFC 822 was issued. Now each header line consists of a field name terminated by a colon and followed by a field body. For a message to be valid, the creation time, source, and destination fields must be filled in. Other optional fields, such as received, subject, reply-to, and return-path, can be filled in as well. As the message passes from one Message Transfer Agent (MTA) to the next, these required fields are enumerated and then added to the message header, allowing the recipient to see how the message was transferred through the mail system.

More Info For more information on the standards for transferring messages, refer to "F.400/X.400 Standard: Data Networks and Open System Communication Message Handling Systems," from the International Telecommunication Union at *http://www.itu.org*.

The SMTP design is based on a communication model that follows these basic steps:

1. The user makes a mail request to a sender-SMTP.

2. The sender-SMTP establishes a two-way transmission channel to a receiver-SMTP.

3. The sender-SMTP generates SMTP commands and sends them to the receiver-SMTP.

4. The receiver-SMTP sends response commands to the sender-SMTP.

For example, if User1 would like to send mail to User2 over SMTP, the sequence of events would be as follows (assuming that both users are running the SMTP service on their computers):

1. User1 contacts User2 and establishes a two-way transmission channel over TCP port 25, using the HELO command.

2. User1 sends a MAIL command indicating the sender of the mail. This is how we know who sent the e-mail.

3. User2 sends an OK reply.

4. User1 sends a RCPT command identifying the recipient of the mail. This is how we know who the recipient of the e-mail is.

5. User2 sends an OK reply.

6. User1 sends the mail.

7. User2 sends an OK reply.

8. User1 sends the QUIT command.

9. User2 sends an OK reply and then terminates the connection.

The commands from the sender and receiver are always sent one at a time, and one reply is sent for each command. SMTP does not support multiple commands sent as a batch to another SMTP host. Table 17-1 lists the more common SMTP commands and their purpose.

Table 17-1.   Summary of SMTP commands

Command	Description
HELO	Identifies the sender-SMTP to the receiver-SMTP based on host names.
MAIL	Initiates mail transfer with indication of originator (reverse path argument). If routed through a relay agent, the first host in the list is the most recent relay agent. Nondelivery reports generated by the receiver-SMTP are sent back using this command.
RCPT	Identifies one of the recipients (forward path argument). Multiple recipients are specified by multiple use of this command. The forward path can optionally include a list of relay hosts, but it must include the final destination mailbox.
DATA	Indicates that message data is ready to be sent in 128-ASCII-character codes.
RSET	Resets mail transfer. Received mail data is discarded.
VRFY	Asks the receiver-SMTP to verify that the mail address identifies a user.
EXPN	Asks the receiver-SMTP to confirm the identity of a mailing list and return the membership of that list.
HELP	Requests help on a command.
NOOP	Requests the receiver-SMTP to send an OK.
TURN	Reverses roles of sender and receiver.
QUIT	Requests termination of connection. The receiver-SMTP must send an OK and then close the transmission channel.

7-Bit ASCII Character Set

SMTP commands are sent in the American Standard Code for Information Interchange (ASCII) 7-bit character set. This fact is important because the TCP architecture assumes an 8-bits-per-byte transmission channel.

E-mail started in the United States and at first was used to send text only. Because the entire English alphabet and standard English punctuation marks can fit into the 128 (2^7) possible combinations of 7 bits, the 8th bit was used as a parity bit, giving some extra redundancy in error checking.

The first 128 characters in the ASCII character set define the 26 letters of the English alphabet in both lowercase and uppercase and the more common punctuation marks that might be used in everyday messaging. Messages that use only these characters are said to be 7-bit ASCII.

Extended ASCII Character Set

Because there are many more than 128 characters in the international alphabets, the extended ASCII character set defines 256 characters, accommodating most European alphabets. Defining this many characters means using the 8th bit for character generation instead of for parity. The problem with doing so is that SMTP doesn't permit the use of the 8th bit. Thus, even if you could find an SMTP MTA that would pass all 8 bits, the 8th one would be lost because the protocol itself works only with 7 bits. The solution to this problem has been to fit 8 bits into 7 bits at the sending end and then extract them at the receiving end. Since bits don't compress very well, we add some extra bytes so that the bit combination is cleanly divisible by 7.

We accomplish this task by taking 7 bytes, each with its underlying 8 bits, lining them up sequentially at the bit level, repackaging the bits so that 7 bits equals 1 byte, and then sending the bytes across the line. For instance, if you have 7 bytes, each with 8 bits, you could line up the bits and create 8 bytes of 7 bits each. At the receiving end, the bits are repackaged into 7 bytes of 8 bits each.

Uuencode is a UNIX-based utility that repackages a file with 8-bit data into another file with 7-bit data so that it can be ported across SMTP. The recipient invokes uudecode to convert the data back to an 8-bit standard.

MIME Format

In today's world, we aren't just sending text back and forth. Instead, we are sending files from a wide variety of PC applications and languages. This level of complexity is where Multipurpose Internet Mail Extension (MIME) comes in. MIME provides a way to send more than just text across the Internet. It is a standard that allows multiple files of various content types to be encapsulated into one message. RFCs 2045 through 2049 currently define MIME and are considered to be one single standard.

MIME works by concatenating all of the attachments, placing separators between them. Each body part specifies a content type that indicates the kind of file it represents, and it also indicates how the file is encoded for transfer through the mail system.

Each content type consists of both a top-level media type and a corresponding subtype. It is possible to define additional types other than those specified in the RFCs to accommodate proprietary formats. Table 17-2 lists the more common top-level types and their corresponding subtypes. Each of the five discrete types corresponds to a single file. The composite types can encapsulate discrete or other composite contents.

Table 17-2.   Top-level media types

Media Type		Subtypes
Discrete	Text	Plain, rich text, enriched
	Image	Jpeg, gif
	Audio	Basic
	Video	Mpeg
	Application	Octet-stream, Postscript
Composite	Multipart	Mixed
	Message	RFC 822

Exchange Server 5.5 is based on the X.400 protocol, which is considered to be a *closed* backbone message transfer system. By this we mean that in an X.400 backbone, you need to explicitly define all of the peer MTAs on the network or over the Internet. SMTP, on the other hand, is considered to be an *open* message transfer system because any computer running SMTP will generally accept connections from any other computer running SMTP, and these peer connections do not need to be specified in advance. Because Exchange 2000 Server's default transport protocol is SMTP, it has greater interoperability with foreign e-mail systems than Exchange Server 5.5 does.

Each SMTP server acts as its own MTA, routing messages to the next SMTP server based on the mail exchanger (MX) records it finds in the DNS. SMTP transfers messages over a TCP port 25 connection.

SMTP Service Extensions

In November 1995, RFC 1869 was published, containing several extensions to the SMTP command structure. These extensions are registered with the Internet Assigned Number Authority (IANA), and they allow the receiver-SMTP to inform the sender-SMTP of the service extensions it supports. The purpose of this revision in the SMTP standard was to make SMTP adaptable in the coming years. When SMTP is extended, it is referred to as ESMTP.

When working with extensions, the sender-SMTP sends an EHLO command in place of the HELO command. The receiver-SMTP can respond by indicating which extensions it supports. If it does not support any extensions, it sends an error response.

Exchange 2000 Server takes advantage of these extensions by using the ETRN command, which is the extended version of the TURN command. This command asks the computers not only to reverse roles but also to verify the remote host name so that hosts other than the one for which the messages are intended cannot retrieve the messages. Because of the host name verification, which includes the domain name, ETRN is used to trigger mail delivery for a specific domain rather than a specific host.

Exchange 2000 Server and the SMTP Service

SMTP is really the heart of Exchange 2000 transport services. When you install Microsoft Windows 2000, a base SMTP service is automatically installed as part of Internet Information Services (IIS) 5. The base SMTP service supports many of the ESMTP commands. Although there is only one SMTP service, you can configure multiple virtual SMTP servers on each Exchange 2000 server. Each virtual server can be started, stopped, or paused independently of other virtual servers. However, stopping or pausing the SMTP service itself will affect all of the virtual servers. (See the next section, "SMTP Virtual Servers," for more information.)

When the SMTP service is running, new connections can be accepted from users. When it is stopped, all users' connections are severed. When the SMTP service is paused, each virtual server continues to service currently connected users but will not accept new users.

When you install Exchange 2000 Server, it extends the base SMTP service to add functionality, including the following:

- Commands to support link state information (X-LINK2STATE)
- The advanced queuing engine
- The enhanced message categorization agent
- The Installable File System (IFS) store driver

Figure 17-1 shows a sample log file for the SMTP service as it records the sending of a message from the local server to a remote server. Notice that some of the commands, such as X-LINK2STATE and XEXCH50, are unique to Exchange 2000 Server and are considered ESMTP commands. You can see how the log file allows you to use the SMTP commands to troubleshoot SMTP services. (The log file is discussed further in the section "Configuring and Administering a Virtual Server," later in this chapter.)

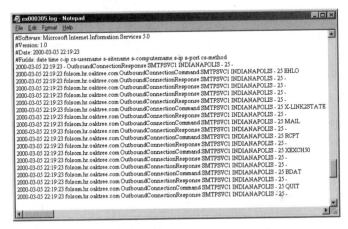

Figure 17-1. *Sample log file.*

SMTP Virtual Servers

As we mentioned earlier, in Exchange 2000 Server, you can create multiple SMTP virtual servers on the same physical server to provide separate configurations for different messaging services. In most cases, additional virtual servers are not needed. However, if you are hosting multiple domains or want to have more than one default domain name, you can create multiple virtual servers to meet your needs. From the end user's perspective, each virtual server appears as a separate SMTP server.

Another reason to create multiple virtual servers is to satisfy different authentication requirements for different groups of users. You can create as many virtual servers as you need to handle the different configurations. Every virtual server on any one single physical server must belong to the same routing group. Multiple virtual servers won't increase your thoughput, but they are very handy if you need to configure different options for different sets of users.

Each virtual server has its own distinct configuration, including IP address, port number, and authentication settings. Each Exchange 2000 server has at least one virtual server that listens on port 25 on all IP addresses.

To create a new virtual sever, launch the Exchange System snap-in and, under the server object, navigate to and expand the Protocols container. Right-click the SMTP container, point to New, and then choose New SMTP Virtual Server. The New SMTP Virtual Server Wizard starts (Figure 17-2) and asks you to enter the name of the virtual server. Choose a descriptive name, since this is the name the object will have within Exchange System.

The next screen of the wizard asks you to select an IP address for this new virtual server (Figure 17-3). Be sure to select an address that is different from the IP address of the default SMTP server. Each virtual server requires its own unique IP/port number combination. Once you've made your selection, click Finish to create the new virtual server.

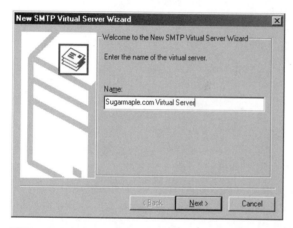

Figure 17-2. *First screen of the New SMTP Virtual Server Wizard.*

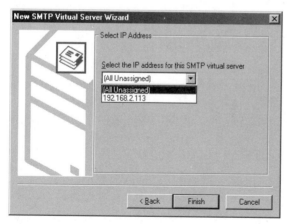

Figure 17-3. *Selecting an IP address for the new virtual sever.*

Tip   The IP address you specify will need to have been bound to the server before you attempt to create the virtual server. Also, be sure to add an address (A) record and an MX record in DNS for this virtual server.

Configuring and Administering a Virtual Server

Once you've created the virtual server, you can configure its property sheet by right-clicking the virtual server and choosing Properties. On the General tab (Figure 17-4), you can enable logging on this virtual server so that you can track user connections. Four formats are available for log files:

- **W3C Extended Log File Format**   The default log file format for IIS and SMTP. Information is written to an ASCII text file. Unlike other formats, you can choose what is written into the log and can limit the size of the log file itself. There are usually multiple entries for a single transmission.

- **Microsoft IIS Log File Format**   Information is written to a comma-delimited ASCII text file. Once the data is written it cannot be changed, and the log format is not customizable. There are usually multiple records for a single transmission.

- **NCSA Common Log File Format**   Information is written to an ASCII text file in the National Center for Computing Applications (NCSA) format. Once the data is written, it cannot be changed, and the log format is not customizable. There are usually multiple records for a single transmission.

- **ODBC Logging**   Information is written to an open database connectivity (ODBC) compliant database.

On the General tab, you can also limit the number of users who connect to this virtual server by selecting the Limit Number Of Connections To check box and then entering the desired limit. You can also limit idle connections to a certain number of minutes to conserve system resources.

Finally, the General tab allows you to change the IP address to which the virtual server is bound without creating a new virtual server. If you need to change the port number, click the Advanced button, and then make your changes in the Advanced dialog box (Figure 17-5). Note that you can also assign multiple combinations of IP address and port number to the same virtual server, which gives you maximum administrative flexibility. Selecting All Unassigned allows the virtual server to respond to any requests that are not handled by other services.

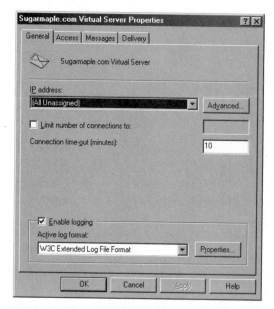

Figure 17-4. *General tab of the property sheet for a virtual server.*

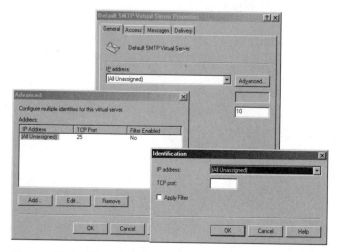

Figure 17-5. *Changing the port number of a virtual server.*

Enabling Message Filtering The Filter Enabled column in the Advanced dialog box indicates whether message filtering is enabled. You can enable filtering by selecting the Apply Filter option in the Identification dialog box (Figure 17-5), which you display by clicking either Add or Edit in the Advanced dialog box. When message filtering is enabled on an SMTP virtual server, the server will not accept e-mail from any domain on the message filtering list. Message filtering is defined globally but is enabled for individual IP addresses. Before you can enable message filtering, you must first create a message filter list.

To create a message filter list, open the Exchange System snap-in, and select the Global Settings container. Right-click Message Delivery, and choose Properties. On the Filtering tab, click Add to display the Add Sender dialog box (Figure 17-6). You must include the @ symbol at the beginning of the domain name. This dialog box will not accept IP addresses or bare domain names.

On the Filtering tab, you can also choose to archive the filtered messages for later review, filter any messages with a blank sender, and specify that senders should not be notified that their messages are being filtered.

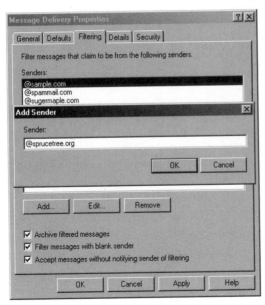

Figure 17-6. *Adding a domain name to the message filter list.*

Note Any changes you make to a virtual server will not take effect for a few minutes because the metabase update service needs time to replicate the changes to the IIS metabase. This service replicates changes made in Active Directory to the IIS metabase, allowing you to make changes to a virtual server without a permanent connection to each system involved in the update.

Configuring Access Properties On the Access tab (Figure 17-7) of the virtual server's property sheet, you'll find a number of important configuration options. Clicking the Authentication button displays a dialog box that allows you to choose Basic Authentication, Anonymous access, and Integrated Windows Authentication or a combination of these options. You can also specify here that Transport Layer Security (TLS) encryption be enforced based on the domain name, which you'll need to enter.

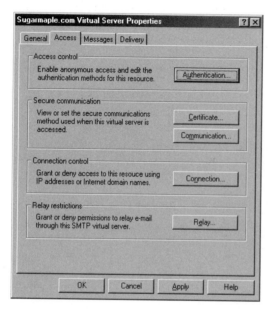

Figure 17-7. *Access tab of a virtual server's property sheet.*

> **Note** Integrated Windows Authentication (IWA) requires a valid Windows 2000 user name and password. It authenticates users by relaying their information directly to the domain controller. Once users are authenticated, they access objects in their security context. IWA was called Windows NT Challenge/Response in IIS 4.

The Secure Communication area of the Access tab has two buttons: Certificate and Communication. If a certificate is not yet installed on this server, you can create a default one, using a wizard that you start by clicking the Certificate button. Once a valid certificate is installed, you can require that communication take place over a secure channel. You do so by clicking the Communication button. In the Security dialog box (Figure 17-8), you can require both secure channel communication and 128-bit encryption. If external users who need high security are sending e-mails to this virtual server, consider using both encryption and certificates.

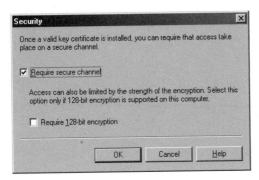

Figure 17-8. *Security dialog box.*

By clicking the Connection button in the Connection Control area of the Access tab, you can specify the domain name or IP address of computers to be given access to or excluded from the virtual server (Figure 17-9).

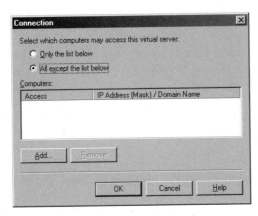

Figure 17-9. *Connection dialog box.*

Finally, clicking the Relay button in the Relay Restrictions area of the Access tab allows you to indicate which SMTP servers can relay messages through this virtual server (Figure 17-10). You can specify the servers by domain name or IP address. You can also establish an exception to these restrictions by selecting the Allow All Computers Which Successfully Authenticate To Relay, Regardless Of The List Above check box. This option could be used to allow vendors outside your company (each with their own SMTP domain name) to use your Exchange server as their messaging relay to the Internet once they authenticate to prove they have permission to do so.

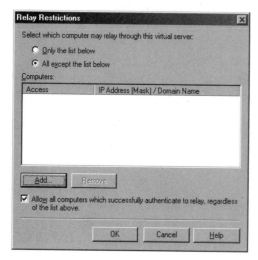

Figure 17-10. *Relay Restrictions dialog box.*

You can restrict relay abilities based on a single IP address, a range of IP addresses, or a domain name (Figure 17-11). You must choose one method per entry in the restrictions list, so if you want to restrict message relay based on both IP address and domain name, you'll need to make two entries.

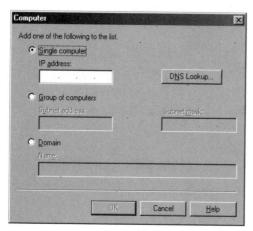

Figure 17-11. *Adding a computer to the relay restrictions list.*

Configuring Messaging Limits and Badmail Behavior   The Messages tab of the property sheet for a virtual server holds configuration choices governing message size limits and badmail behavior (Figure 17-12). *Badmail* is defined as mail that cannot be delivered or returned. The default directory for badmail is \Exchsrvr*mailroot**vsi* #\badmail (where *vsi* # is the specific virtual server; for instance, vsi 1 is the default SMTP virtual server). You can change the location of the badmail directory only by configuring the metabase properties directly. You cannot change the default directory through Exchange System. Usually, when a message is undeliverable, the sender receives a nondelivery report (NDR). You can also designate that a copy of all NDRs be sent to the e-mail address of your choice.

Caution   Be sure that you don't select the M: drive for your badmail directory. Doing so will cause conflicts with Exchange administration and transport services and will cause messages to stop flowing.

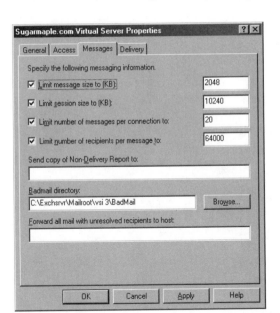

Figure 17-12. *Messages tab of a virtual server's property sheet.*

If you have another mail server, such as a UNIX-based server, in your organization that handles the same domain as your SMTP virtual server, type the host name for that server under Forward All Mail With Unresolved Recipients To Host. When your Exchange server receives e-mail for a user that it can't resolve, it will forward the e-mail to this host. For example, if the SMTP virtual server and a

UNIX e-mail server both serve the oaktree.com domain, Exchange Server may receive e-mail intended for UNIX users. When Exchange Server can't find these users, it will know to forward these messages to the designated host in the other system.

Configuring Delivery Information The Delivery tab of the virtual server's property sheet lets you configure outbound e-mail retry and expiration values as well as outbound connection values and security information. If this virtual server will be connecting to another virtual server, be sure to make the outbound security settings match the inbound security settings on the other virtual server.

The Advanced Delivery dialog box (Figure 17-13), displayed by clicking Advanced on the Delivery tab, has several interesting options. The Masquerade Domain option allows you to indicate a different domain name to be placed in both the Mail From and From fields of all outgoing messages. The Mail From field is found within the SMTP message header and denotes the domain the message came from, while the From field is found in the body of the message and denotes who the message is from. When a message's Mail From field is modified, the modification remains through delivery.

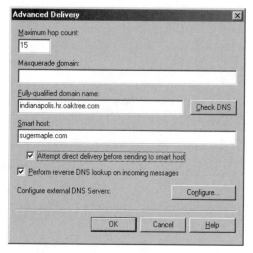

Figure 17-13. *Advanced Delivery dialog box.*

For instance, if your server is hosting the sales.hr.oaktree.com domain inside of the oaktree.com domain, the default entry in the Mail From field would be sales.hr.oaktree.com. If you would like to change this to oaktree.com, type that information in the Masquerade Domain field. All outgoing messages will then appear to come from the oaktree.com domain, and any NDRs will be sent back to the oaktree.com domain.

In contrast, the From field, which the Masquerade Domain field also modifies to denote (in our example) the alternate domain of oaktree.com, applies only to the first hop. This means that if the message has to pass through a number of messaging systems to reach its destination, it will revert to its original domain name after the first hop. The Maximum Hop Count option, which sets the maximum number of Received header lines that an SMTP server will accept on incoming messages before returning an NDR to the message originator, is configured here too.

Selecting the Attempt Direct Delivery Before Sending To Smart Host option directs Exchange 2000 Server to attempt to deliver messages directly to the destination SMTP server. Should this attempt fail, the messages are forwarded to the smart host for delivery. Selecting the Perform Reverse DNS Lookup On Incoming Messages option causes Exchange 2000 Server to attempt to verify that the client's IP address matches the domain name submitted by the client in the HELO/EHLO command. If the reverse DNS lookup is successful, the Received header is not changed. If it is unsuccessful, the Received header indicates "unverified" after the IP address. If reverse DNS lookups are affecting performance, consider clearing this check box. This feature is disabled by default.

Troubleshooting SMTP

There are really only two ways to troubleshoot problems with SMTP. First, make sure that the virtual server settings are correct. For instance, be sure that the IP address and port number assignments do not conflict with those of other virtual servers. Second, enable logging on the SMTP server, and then read the log files to see if an error code or error reply has been recorded. This information can help you pinpoint the cause of your problem.

Post Office Protocol 3

POP3 was developed in response to SMTP and is designed for workstations that don't have the resources to maintain both SMTP services and a message transfer system. In addition, continuous connectivity to the network for each workstation, which is necessary for an SMTP host to operate correctly, is impractical in many instances.

POP3 permits a workstation to dynamically access a server that is holding mail for it. It does not allow extensive manipulation of mail on the server. Instead, it is used to download mail from the server. Once the mail has been downloaded, the server deletes its copy of the messages unless you have set your POP3 client to keep a copy of the message on the server. POP3 is a very small, fast, lean protocol that is really for mail retrieval only. To send mail, a POP3 client uses a normal SMTP connection to the destination mail server or a local SMTP relay server.

POP3 has both a client side and a server side. The server starts the POP3 service by listening on TCP port 110. When a POP3 client wants to use this service, it establishes a TCP connection with the server and then receives a greeting from the server. The client and server then exchange commands and responses until the connection is either closed or aborted. Like SMTP commands, POP3 commands are not case sensitive and can contain one or more arguments. A POP3 session between the server and the client will progress through several stages:

1. Once the TCP connection has been opened and the POP3 server has sent a greeting, the session enters the Authorization state. In this state, the client must identify itself to the POP3 server.

2. Once the client has successfully been authenticated, the session enters the Transaction state. During this phase, the server gathers the client's mail and, in response to requests from the client, sends mail to the client. The client's mailbox is locked to prevent messages from being modified or removed until the session enters the Update state. A series of commands and responses usually passes between the client and server during this phase.

3. When the client issues a QUIT command, the session enters the Update state. In this state, the POP3 server releases any resources it is holding on behalf of the client and sends a good-bye message. Messages are then deleted from the server, and the TCP session is terminated.

Table 17-3 summarizes the POP3 commands.

Table 17-3.   Summary of POP3 commands

Command	Description
USER	Supplies user name for mailbox
PASS	Supplies password for mailbox
STAT	Requests the number of messages and total size of message
LIST	Lists the index and size of all messages
RETR	Retrieves the specified messages
DELE	Deletes the specified message
NOOP	No action required
RSET	Rolls back message deletion
QUIT	Updates (commit) message deletion and terminates connection

Administering POP3 in Exchange 2000 Server simply involves choosing the number of users that can connect to each POP3 virtual server, indicating whether POP3 is assigned to a specific IP address or to All Unassigned, and setting message encoding instructions for the virtual server. All of these settings in the POP3 virtual server work the same as in other protocols and are described throughout this chapter.

Internet Messaging Access Protocol 4

In POP3, once a message has been downloaded from the server, it is, by default, deleted from the server. This deletion is a real disadvantage for users who move from workstation to workstation because mail they have already downloaded remains on the workstation to which they downloaded it. IMAP4 was developed to allow users to leave their mail on the server and to allow remote access to messages. Thus, IMAP4 extends the functionality of POP3 to allow both offline and online storage of messages.

In addition, IMAP4 allows user-initiated storage of messages and nonmail messages, permits users to manage their own configurations, and allows the sharing of mailboxes. This protocol allows a client to manipulate mail messages on a server as though it were a local mailbox, unlike POP3, which can do little more than copy a message from a POP3 server to a local mailbox.

When a client connects to an IMAP4 server, it does so over TCP port 143. The IMAP4 server is always in one of four states. For each state, the client can issue a limited number of commands to the server. Some commands transition the server into the next state. It is a protocol error for the client to issue a command that is not appropriate to the present state of the server. Figure 17-14 shows the IMAP4 states for an IMAP4 server as they are described in RFC 2060. Table 17-4 lists the more common IMAP4 commands.

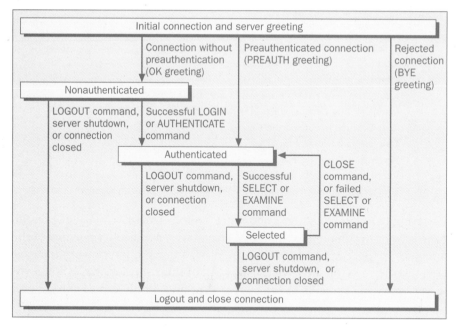

Figure 17-14. *IMAP4 states as described in RFC 2060.*

Table 17-4. IMAP4 commands

Command	Description
CAPABILITY	Requests a listing of the functionality of the server
AUTHENTICATE	Indicates an authentication mechanism
LOGIN	Identifies a client with user name and password
SELECT	Selects the mailbox to use
EXAMINE	Selects a mailbox in read-only mode
CREATE	Creates a mailbox
DELETE	Deletes a mailbox
RENAME	Renames a mailbox
SUBSCRIBE	Adds a mailbox to the server's set of active mailboxes
UNSUBSCRIBE	Removes a mailbox from the server's set of active mailboxes
LIST	Lists a set or subset of mailboxes
LSUB	Lists subscribed mailboxes
STATUS	Requests the status of a mailbox
APPEND	Adds a message to a mailbox
CLOSE	Effects pending deletions and closes a mailbox

(continued)

Table 17-4.   *continued*

Command	Description
EXPUNGE	Effects pending deletions
SEARCH	Searches a mailbox for messages satisfying a given criterion
FETCH	Fetches specified body parts for a given message
STORE	Changes the data of specified messages in a mailbox
COPY	Copies a message to another mailbox
NOOP	No action required
LOGOUT	Closes the connection

Administering IMAP4

IMAP4 is, for the most part, self-administering. You may want to consider a couple of items, however. Figure 17-15 shows the General tab of the property sheet for the IMAP4 default virtual server. Because IMAP4 has the ability to request public folders, Microsoft's implementation of this protocol lets you choose whether to show public folders to the client. In addition, you can enable fast message retrieval here, which will cause Exchange Server to approximate the message sizes, rather than calculate their exact size. This estimation is done only if the clients do not need to know the exact message sizes for retrieval.

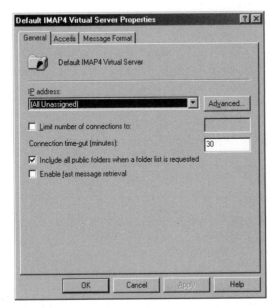

Figure 17-15. *IMAP4 default virtual server properties.*

Network News Transfer Protocol

Because Network News Transfer Protocol (NNTP) is growing in popularity, it would be wise for us to take a brief look at the architecture of this protocol. We'll then discuss the more pragmatic aspects of administering NNTP on your network.

NNTP Architecture

NNTP specifies a way to distribute, query, retrieve, and post news articles on the Internet. A client wanting to retrieve a subset of articles from the database is called a *subscriber*. NNTP allows a subscriber to request a subset of articles rather than requiring the retrieval of all articles from the database. Before NNTP was developed, two methods of distributing news items were popular: Internet mailing lists and the Usenet news system.

An Internet mailing list, commonly known as a *list server*, distributes news by the use of distribution e-mail lists. A subscriber sends a message to the distribution list, and the message is e-mailed to all of the members of the list. But sending a separate copy of an e-mail to each subscriber can consume a large amount of disk space, bandwidth, and CPU resources. In addition, it can take from several minutes to several hours for the message to be fully distributed, depending on the size of the list and the physical resources available to propagate it. Maintaining the subscriber list also involves significant administrative effort, unless a third-party program is used to automate this function.

Storing and retrieving messages from a central location instead of sending an e-mail to each subscriber can significantly reduce the use of these resources. The Usenet news system provides this alternative. In addition, Usenet allows a subscriber to select only those messages he or she wants to read and also provides indexing, cross-referencing, and message expiration.

NNTP is modeled on the Usenet news specifications in RFC 850, but it is designed to make fewer demands on the structure, content, and storage of the news articles. It runs as a background service on one host and can accept connections from other hosts on the LAN or over the Internet.

When a subscriber connects to an NNTP server, the subscriber issues the NEWS-GROUPS command to determine whether any new newsgroups have been created on the server. If so, the server notifies the subscriber and gives the subscriber the opportunity to subscribe to the new newsgroups. After this, the subscriber is connected to the desired newsgroup and can use the NEWNEWS command to ask the server whether any new articles have been posted since the subscriber's last connection. The subscriber receives a list of new articles from the server and can request transmission of some or all of those articles. Finally, the subscriber can either reply to a news article or post a new article to the server by using the POST command.

NNTP uses TCP for its connections and SMTP-like commands and responses. The default TCP port for NNTP is 119. An NNTP command consists of a command word followed in some cases by a parameter, and commands are not case sensitive. Each line can contain only one command and may not exceed 512 characters, including spaces, punctuation, and the trailing CR–LF (carriage return/line feed) command. Commands cannot be continued on the next line.

Responses from the server can take the form of a text response or a status response. Text responses are displayed in the subscriber's client program, whereas status responses are interpreted by the client program before any display occurs.

Each status response line begins with a three-digit numeric code. The first digit of the response indicates the success, failure, or progress of the previous command. Table 17-5 lists the meaning of different values for the first digit. The second digit in the code indicates the function response category. These categories are listed in Table 17-6. The third digit indicates the specific response.

Table 17-5.   Meaning of first digit of status response code

First Digit	Meaning
1xx	Informative message
2xx	Command OK
3xx	Command OK so far; send the rest of it
4xx	Command was correct but couldn't be performed for some reason
5xx	Command not implemented or incorrect or a serious program error occurred

Table 17-6.   Meaning of second digit of status response code

Second Digit	Meaning
x0x	Connection, setup, and miscellaneous messages
x1x	Newsgroup selection
x2x	Article selection
x3x	Distribution functions
x4x	Posting
x8x	Nonstandard (private implementation) extensions
x9x	Debugging output

In general, the 2xx codes are sent upon initial connection to the NNTP server, depending on the posting permissions. Code 400 is sent when the NNTP server discontinues service, and the 5xx codes indicate that the command could not be performed for some unusual reason. Table 17-7 lists some common codes you might encounter when troubleshooting NNTP connections.

Table 17-7. Common NNTP status response codes

Code	Meaning
100	Help text
190–199	Debug output
200	Server ready; posting allowed
201	Server ready; no posting allowed
400	Service discontinued
500	Command not recognized
501	Command syntax error
502	Access restriction or permission denied
503	Program fault; command not performed

NNTP Commands

It isn't possible here to go into detail about each NNTP command. However, several of the commands that you will see in both the event log and the output log file are worth describing in case you ever need to troubleshoot an NNTP connection. Figure 17-16 illustrates some of these commands.

Figure 17-16. *Log file for NNTP service.*

The ARTICLE, BODY, HEAD, and STAT commands refer to the retrieval and transmission of a news article. The HEAD and BODY commands are identical to the ARTICLE command, except that they return either the header lines (HEAD) or the body text (BODY) of the article. No text is returned with the STAT command. Instead, this command returns the message ID to the subscriber.

The ARTICLE command has two forms: one that is followed by the message ID of the article to display and one that is followed by either a parameter or no parameter. In the first form, the ARTICLE command displays the header, a blank line, and then the body text of the specified article. The subscriber obtains the message ID from a list that is provided in response to the NEWNEWS command.

The second form of the command, ARTICLE *<message-id>*, displays the header, a blank line, and then the body text of the message. The subscriber chooses the message number from the range of articles provided when the newsgroup was selected. If the number is omitted, the current article is assumed. Some of the error responses that might occur with this command include the following:

- "420 no current article has been selected"
- "423 no such article number in this group"
- "430 no such article found"

The GROUP command must be followed by the name of a newsgroup. Newsgroup names are not case sensitive. If the group requested no longer exists, the subscriber receives the error message "411 no such news group." If the requested group does exist, the subscriber receives the article numbers of the first and last articles in the group, along with an estimate of the number of articles in the group. This number is not guaranteed to be accurate.

The LIST command returns a list of valid newsgroups and associated information. Each newsgroup is sent as a line of text that looks like this:

> *<group> <last> <first> <p>*

where

> *<group>* is the name of the newsgroup
>
> *<last>* is the number of the last known article currently in that newsgroup
>
> *<first>* is the number of the first article currently in the newsgroup
>
> *<p>* is either "y" or "n," where "y" indicates that posting is allowed and "n" indicates that posting is not allowed

It may be possible to receive a "y" in the *<p>* portion of the response and still not be able to post to that newsgroup because the newsgroup either is moderated, is restricted, or has gone offline for some reason.

The NEWSGROUPS command is followed by the date and then the time and then an optional *<distributions>* parameter. It lists newsgroups that have been created since the date and time specified. The date is specified as six digits in the *yymmdd* format. For the year, the closest century is assumed as the first two digits. Hence, 86 would mean 1986, and 30 would mean 2030. The time parameter is sent as six digits in *hhmmss* format, with the hours calculated on a 24-hour time clock. The time zone is assumed to be the server's time zone unless the token GMT appears, in which case both the date and the time are evaluated at the 0 meridian.

The optional *<distributions>* parameter is a list of distribution groups. For instance, the distribution portion of net.oaktree is "net." This parameter causes the distribution portion of the article to be examined for a match with the distribution groups listed. Only those that match the specified groups will be listed.

Administering NNTP

NNTP in Exchange 2000 Server is used to create asynchronous group discussions. You can configure it to communicate with external NNTP servers to make popular Usenet groups available internally to your users. NNTP in IIS replaces the Internet News Service in Exchange Server 5.5. When you install Exchange 2000 Server, it enhances NNTP in Windows 2000, giving it the ability to communicate with other news servers through newsfeeds.

You can create multiple NNTP servers within your organization in a master-subordinate layout. This enables clients to connect to a collection of servers and still maintain accurate views of newsgroup content. Creating a collection of servers provides scalability for a large user base, such as an ISP, and fault tolerance if a subordinate server should go offline.

Even though the master server controls the article numbers and maintains synchronization with the subordinate servers, clients always connect to the subordinate news server. DNS configuration automatically distributes the client load equally across subordinate servers. Since each subordinate server provides a newsfeed to the master server, a newly posted article will first be sent to the master server and will not appear on the subordinate server until the master server sends the article to all subordinate servers.

Real World   Setting Up a Master-Subordinate Newsfeed
To set up a master-subordinate newsfeed, perform the following steps:

1. Create the newsgroup on the master server.

2. Create the newsgroups on the subordinate servers.

3. Create a newsfeed from the master server to each subordinate server.

4. Create a newsfeed from each subordinate server to the master server.

Configuring an NNTP Virtual Server

To configure the NNTP virtual server, in the Exchange System snap-in navigate to your server object, expand the Protocols container and then the NNTP container; right-click the default virtual server. Figure 17-17 shows the General tab of the NNTP virtual server's property sheet.

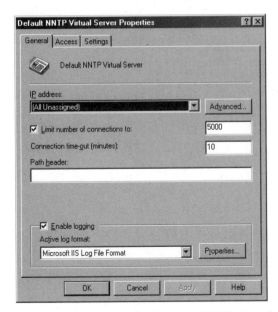

Figure 17-17. *General tab of an NNTP virtual server's property sheet.*

By default, an NNTP server communicates over TCP port 119 or via Secure Sockets Layer (SSL) using TCP port 563. When multiple virtual NNTP servers are present, each must be assigned a unique IP address and/or TCP/SSL port combination.

The default number of connections to an NNTP server from other NNTP hosts is 5000. Adjust this number based on your server's resources and the number of concurrent NNTP connections you expect. The Path Header text box enables you to specify the name of the server to append to the NNTP path header. The default is the fully qualified domain name (FQDN) of the computer. A client can examine the path header to see the route a message has traveled from a source client through various news servers to the destination news server.

The Settings tab allows you to set limits on articles that are posted and to enable control messages and moderated newsgroups (Figure 17-18). This tab also allows you to prevent other servers from pulling articles from this server. The default is to allow them to do so.

Control messages are used by NNTP hosts to communicate with one another, to create and remove newsgroups, and to cancel messages that have already been posted. For example, if you create a new newsgroup, the host providing the newsfeed sends a control message to hosts receiving the newsfeed, indicating that a new newsgroup has been created. NNTP then uses this information to determine whether a new newsgroup should be added under the newsgroup object.

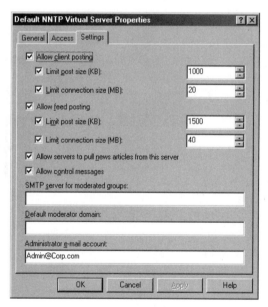

Figure 17-18. *Settings tab of an NNTP virtual server's property sheet.*

The Administrator E-Mail Account text box on the Settings tab lets you specify an e-mail address that will receive NDRs when messages are not successfully delivered to the newsgroup moderator. To enable the sending of NDRs, create a new DWORD value named MailFromHeader with a value of 1 in the registry key HKEY_LOCAL_MACHINE\SYSTEM\CurrentControlSet\Services\NntpSvc \ Parameters\.

NNTP Server Objects

Listed underneath the NNTP virtual server in the Exchange System scope pane are five objects, as shown in Figure 17-19. Let's take a brief look at each one.

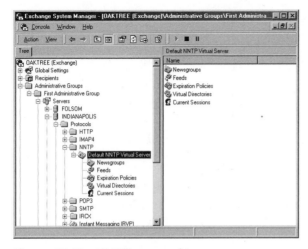

Figure 17-19. *NNTP server objects.*

The Newsgroups object lists the newsgroups that are currently configured on this server, plus the three control newsgroups.

The Feeds object lists inbound and outbound feeds. You set up each feed with a wizard that asks, in part, which role you want the feed to play: Peer, Master, or Slave. By default, each feed uses "*" as a wildcard to denote that all newsgroups on the remote server will be involved with the feed. You can enter individual newsgroups manually if you're interested only in a subset of the newsgroups on the remote server.

By right-clicking the Expiration Policies object, pointing to New, and then choosing Expiration Policy, you can run through a simple wizard to specify how long newsgroup messages should be retained. The time interval is set in hours and can be a maximum of 9999 hours, or just under 14 months.

The Virtual Directories object allows you to set up a virtual root and then map that root to a file system, a remote share, or an Exchange public folder database (Figure 17-20). Start the wizard by right-clicking the Virtual Directories container, pointing to New, and then choosing Virtual Directory. This wizard allows you to select a different server to which this virtual root will write. Using this option, you can have the root written to the file system of a remote server.

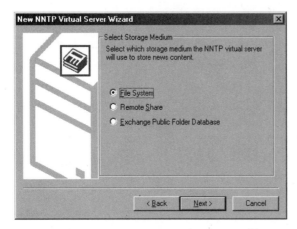

Figure 17-20. *Mapping a virtual root to a file system.*

Finally, you can monitor users' current sessions with the Current Sessions object. Simply highlight the Current Sessions object to see all of the users who are engaged in a current session with this NNTP virtual server listed in the details pane. From here, you can forcibly disconnect individual users by right-clicking the user and choosing Terminate. You can forcibly disconnect all users at once by right-clicking any user in the list and choosing Terminate All.

Lightweight Directory Access Protocol

Lightweight Directory Access Protocol (LDAP), while not unique to Exchange 2000 Server, is still a foundational protocol without which it could not operate. LDAP has its roots in the X.500 Directory services and was first defined in RFC 1487. By now LDAP has been through three revisions, and the current standard is defined in RFC 2251.

The X.500 Directory Access Protocol (DAP) originally required an OSI stack. The current version of LDAP runs over TCP/IP and is thus more adaptable in today's market. In addition, an LDAP server can query a non-LDAP server. Earlier versions of LDAP provided for a client to send queries to a front-end processor at the server that converted the LDAP query to a DAP query and presented that to the server. Version 3 no longer requires this conversion. Moreover, earlier versions of LDAP specified the object classes and attributes as part of the protocol, making the directory static and nonextensible. With LDAP version 3, clients can query a server to discover the object classes and attributes, and the protocol no longer defines what you have come to know as the schema.

LDAP version 3 also allows for X.509 certificates as well as Connectionless LDAP (CLDAP), which is well suited for applications that need to make simple queries and get fast responses. CLDAP uses user datagram protocol (UDP) as the transport protocol at the transport layer.

In LDAP version 3, the client transmits a request to the server describing the query to be performed on the directory. The server performs the query and return the results to the client. There is no requirement in the RFC for synchronous behavior by either the server or the client, which means that multiple requests and responses may be passed between the client and server in any order, provided that the client eventually receives a response for every request.

An LDAP client assumes that there are one or more servers that jointly provide access to a Directory Information Tree (DIT). The tree is composed of entries with names, each of which must have one or more attribute values that form its Relative Distinguished Name (RDN), which must be unique among all its siblings. The concatenation of the object hierarchy names above the RDN form the entry's Distinguished Name (DN), which is, by default, unique in the tree. An example of a DN is: CN=Bill English,DC=HR,DC=Oaktree,DC=com

Each attribute is actually a set of attributes, each of which is a defined type that has one or more associated values. The attribute type is identified by a short, descriptive name and an Object Identifier (OID). The attribute type governs whether there can be more than one value entered in a given attribute field, what rules the syntax must conform to, and other functions. The schema is a collection of attribute type definitions, object class definitions, and other information.

An LDAP server must provide information about itself and other LDAP servers hosting the same directory. This information is represented as a group of attributes located in the root DSA-Specific Entry (DSE), which is named with the zero-length LDAPDN. You can retrieve these attributes by performing a base object search of the root with the filter "objectClass=*". The root DSE *must not* be included if the query performed is focused on a subtree as its starting point.

All message exchanges are encapsulated in a common envelope, the LDAPMessage. The only common fields in the envelope are the message ID and the controls. The following list offers the commands for LDAP version 3 that are sent inside the LDAPMessage:

- BindRequest
- BindResponse
- UnbindRequest
- SearchRequest
- SearchResultEntry
- SearchResultDone
- SearchResultReference
- ModifyRequest
- ModifyResponse
- AddRequest

- AddResponse
- DelRequest
- DelResponse
- ModifyDNRequest
- ModifyDNResponse
- CompareRequest
- CompareResponse
- AbandonRequest
- ExtendedRequest
- ExtendedResponse

If the LDAP search is operating over a connection-oriented transport such as TCP, the server will return a sequence of responses in separate LDAP messages containing zero or more SearchResultEntry responses, one for each entry found during the search. The client will know that all the results have been returned by the server when the server sends the SearchResultDone message. Each entry in a SearchResultEntry will contain all the attributes specified in the field of the search request. Return of any attribute is subject to access control and other administrative policies.

Outlook Web Access

OWA provides an environment for users to access both public folder store and mailbox store data using a browser. With OWA, clients based on UNIX, Macintosh, and Windows can view and work with any public folder, mailbox, Global Address List (GAL), or calendar.

Note For UNIX users, OWA is the primary Outlook solution for e-mail, calendar, and collaboration functionality.

The Web Store

The OWA client in Exchange 2000 Server is dramatically different from the one in Exchange Server 5.5. One of the most important changes is the introduction of the Web Store.

The Web Store integrates knowledge sources by providing a single repository for the management of e-mail messages, documents, Web pages, and other types of data. It supports offline access, remote client access, and a range of APIs. The Web Store brings together file system services, database services, and collaboration services into a single integrated package, making it easier to find, use, and share information.

The Web Store supports HTTP, Web Distributed Authoring and Versioning (WebDAV), and Extensible Markup Language (XML), and each folder in the Web Store has a unique URL associated with it. Figures 17-21 through 17-24 illustrate how the same documents in the Web Store can be accessed through different interfaces. First, Figure 17-21 shows OWA accessing a public folder named Company Documents in the Web Store. Figure 17-22 illustrates how Office 2000 integrates with the Web Store and allows users to access documents in the Company Documents public folder. Figure 17-23 shows that these same documents can be accessed via Outlook 2000. Finally, Figure 17-24 shows how these documents can be accessed via the M: drive in Windows Explorer.

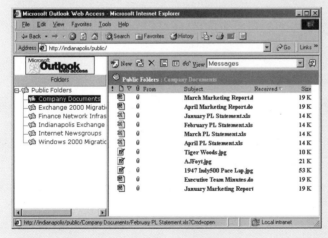

Figure 17-21. *Accessing the Company Documents public folder with OWA.*

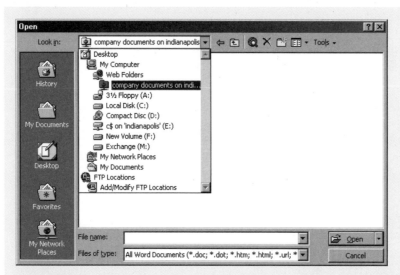

Figure 17-22. *Accessing the Company Documents public folder with Office 2000.*

Tip Web folders are built into Microsoft Office 2000 and are added to Microsoft Windows NT 4 and Windows 98 systems when you perform a full installation of Microsoft Internet Explorer 5 or when you install Office 2000. You can create a Web folder by adding a network place in My Network Places in Windows 2000 or in the My Computer—Web Folders section of Windows NT 4 and Windows 98.

Figure 17-23. *Accessing the Company Documents public folder with Outlook 2000.*

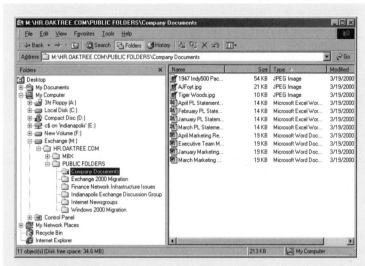

Figure 17-24. *Accessing the Company Documents public folder via drive M: in Windows Explorer.*

Some of the improvements to the performance and functionality of OWA in Exchange 2000 Server include the following:

- Support for embedded items and ActiveX objects.
- Support for public folders that contain contact and calendar items.
- Support for multimedia messages. OWA allows an audio or video clip to be embedded directly into a message and then sent to the recipient.
- Support for named URLs instead of GUIDs.
- Support for Internet Explorer 5.

OWA is not designed to be an advanced e-mail and collaboration utility. Therefore, before you deploy this feature, consider some of its limitations:

- Offline use is not supported. A user must connect to an Exchange server to view information.
- It does not support digital encryption, signatures, or Secure Multipurpose Mail Extensions (S/MIME).
- It does not permit discontinuous days to be shown side by side in the calendar. In fact, many views for meetings and task list management are not available in OWA.

- It does not support Outlook 97 forms.
- It does not support synchronization of local offline folders with server folders.

More Info It is beyond the scope of this book to cover the default Web server settings. For more information, refer to *Microsoft Windows 2000 Server Resource Kit* (Microsoft Press, 2000).

You administer OWA through the Internet Information Services snap-in. Once you have opened up the Internet Information Services snap-in and expanded your server to see its subordinate objects, you'll see the three virtual roots that Exchange creates when it is installed: Exchange (*http://server/exchange*), Public (*http://server/public*), and Exadmin (*http://server/exadmin*). These virtual roots point to the ExIFS roots—either the Mbx folder (Figure 17-25), the public folder, or the root for Exchange administration (Figure 17-26).

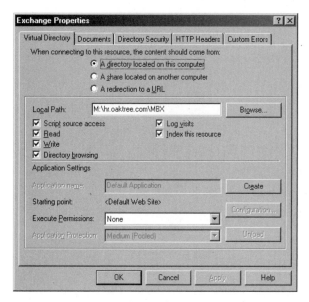

Figure 17-25. *Virtual root that points to the Mbx root.*

OWA has been redesigned to support many more users per server. The most important factor in determining user load is the type of activities your users will perform on the server. We suggest that you start with a trial deployment and use it to develop a baseline for enterprise deployment. Use the Performance Logs and Alerts snap-in to create this baseline. Specific items that you'll want to monitor include logons per day, number of messages read, and session time. Table 17-8 outlines the counters that you should use to obtain a baseline for an OWA server.

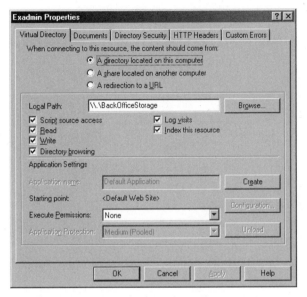

Figure 17-26. *Virtual root that points to the Exadmin root.*

Table 17-8.   Counters for developing a baseline for an OWA server

Object	Counter/Instance	Description
Processor	% Processor Time	Indicates how busy the processor is
System	Context Switches/Sec	Indicates the rate at which the processor is switching between threads
Process	% Process Time/Store % Process Time/Inetinfo % Process Time/Lsass % Process Time/Mad	Indicates how much of the computer's CPU is being used by Exchange Server, IIS, and the security system (including Active Directory)
Physical Disk	Disk Reads/Sec Disk Writes/Sec Current Disk Queue Length	Indicates the level of activity of the physical disk
Memory	Available Bytes Page Reads/Sec Page Writes/Sec Page Faults/Sec	Indicates how much memory is in use and how much is being paged to disk

Because Exchange 2000 Server does not use Active Server Pages (ASP), ASP and MAPI bottlenecks are no longer an issue, as they were in Exchange Server 5.5.

The remaining bottlenecks include the standard hardware constraints of the CPU, memory, disk, and network.

OWA also works with front end/back end (FE/BE) servers, which can give you load-balancing features if you have a large number of users utilizing OWA. In terms of ports and firewalls, you'll need to have only port 80 open on your firewall, which in most installations is a standard port to open. OWA does work with SSL over port 443, and it also supports Kerberos. The unified namespace for users to access mail is *http://<servername>/mail*. The e-mail account namespace on each server would then be *http://<servername>/mail/exchange/<mailbox>*. These URLs work only with FE/BE configurations.

When using FE/BE servers, the front end server functionality is determined by the authentication method that you use. For instance, if you use Basic Authentication, the front end server authenticates the user by verifying the user name and unencrypted password. Exchange 2000 Server then establishes a local security context for the user and connects as that user from the front end server to the back end server. Basic Authentication works only if the security properties for each user exist on the front end server and if each user is granted the Log On Locally right.

If authentication information needs to be encrypted and cannot be determined by the front end server, the server must be able to pass the authentication request to another server. This capability is available only with Kerberos authentication, not NTLM (Windows NT Challenge/Response), and it requires Internet Explorer 5 or later running on Windows 2000 at the client end. Thus, if you require Kerberos authentication for OWA users, they must be running Internet Explorer 5 on Windows 2000. Table 17-9 lists the different authentication methods possible with IIS. You'll want to test these methods in your lab before deploying OWA.

Table 17-9. IIS authentication methods

Authentication Method	Benefits	Disadvantages
Anonymous	Supported by all clients; an easy way to allow access to unsecured public folders.	Does not provide security on an individual basis. All anonymous authenticated users can access any content to which the Anonymous user account (IUSER_*Computername*) has access.
Basic	Supported by most clients; works through proxies and firewalls.	Password is sent as clear text unless the SSL protocol is used to encrypt it.

(continued)

Table 17-9.   *continued*

Authentication Method	Benefits	Disadvantages
Digest	The password is sent as a hashed value, which works through proxies and firewalls. This method works with all HTTP 1.1 compliant browsers.	Password is unencrypted in the Windows 2000 domain controller. Also, this method does not work through front end servers.
Certificate	Very secure; supported by a broad range of clients.	Requires you to create, obtain, and manage certificates and then deploy them to the clients.
Integrated Windows	The password is sent as an encrypted value for highest security.	Supported only by Internet Explorer 2 and later. It does not work through HTTP proxies, and it works through a front end server only when the client is using Internet Explorer 5 on Windows 2000.
Distribute Password, Membership Basic	Not compatible with Exchange 2000 Server.	

Summary

In this chapter, you have learned some of the basics of SMTP, IMAP4, POP3, NNTP, and OWA. You have learned how to read the more common commands of these protocols and how to log the interaction between the server and client for troubleshooting purposes. You have also seen how the Web Store can become the single repository for all types of data and how users can access that data from most types of client utilities, including a browser, Windows Explorer, an Office 2000 application, or Outlook 2000. This chapter has dealt primarily with static types of information. In the next two chapters, you will learn how to enhance the use of static information by using real-time collaboration applications, such as Instant Messaging and Chat Services.

Part V
Functionality

Chapter 18
Administering
Chat Service

As users become more sophisticated in their use of technology, their expectations of what they should be able to do with technology increase. Online collaboration technologies, such as instant messaging, chat services, and data conferencing, are quickly becoming standard methods for business communications rather than being viewed as a novelty.

Traditional e-mail systems cannot deliver dynamic data and information transfer on demand. Most people currently use the telephone for this function. Real-time collaboration services combine the immediacy of the telephone with the functionality of e-mail without the necessity of creating a formal opening and closing to the message.

The winners in the marketplace in the next 10 years will be those that manage information well. Although producing a quality product will still be important, it will take smart information management to remain competitive. For example, at one time Microsoft had close to 1000 paper forms; now it is down to fewer than 60. By managing information electronically instead of on paper, it has saved at least $40 million annually. Using electronic forms for its 401(k) plan alone saves $1 million each year. Companies will find that they can become more competitive by reducing overhead costs through the use of electronic forms.

Real-time collaboration is a part of this overhead reduction. For instance, it allows companies to hold meetings attended by staff in widely dispersed locations, thus reducing travel expenses. In addition, the use of data conferencing allows people in different locations to work closely on a project without the need for extensive travel or relocation. And members of the sales force can use these technologies to be more responsive to their customers. Collaboration technologies offer small and large companies alike the opportunity to make quantum leaps in information management, leading to better customer service and higher profits. In this chapter, we will be focusing on Chat Service and how to administer it. The next chapter covers the highly popular instant messaging technology.

More Info To learn more about how Microsoft has implemented collaboration technologies to become more competitive and profitable, see *Business at the Speed of Thought* by Bill Gates (Warner Books, 1999).

The different collaboration services are designed for specific types of interactions. Instant messaging is meant for users who need real-time, one-to-one conversations. Chat services are available for users who need to communicate as a group in real time, such as a discussion forum. And data conferencing services allow prearranged electronic conferences at which users share multimedia information as they converse during the conference. Table 18-1 outlines the various collaboration technologies and how they are intended to be used. (Note that since conferencing is an add-on product to Microsoft Exchange 2000 Server, we will not cover it in this book.)

Table 18-1. Comparison of collaboration technologies

	Instant Messaging	Chat Service	Data Conferencing
Primary use	Instant messaging	Chat	Data conferencing
Meeting style	Closed	Open forum	Invitation only
Meeting structure	Immediate/ad hoc	Ad hoc/semistructured	Organized
Client type	Vendor-specific	Standards based	Based on T.120 standard
Client facilities	Basic	Basic	Advanced
Primary deployment	Corporate	Service provider	Corporate

Understanding Microsoft Exchange Chat Service

Microsoft Exchange Chat Service provides an environment for online group discussions. One Chat server can handle anywhere from a few users up to 20,000 concurrent users in one chat room. Each administrative group in the Exchange System snap-in can have only one Chat Communities container in which multiple virtual chat communities can be created. Each chat community can host multiple chat rooms, or channels, and can be governed by its own administrative controls.

The Chat Service of Exchange 2000 Server is based on the Internet Relay Chat (IRC) protocol, which supports real-time conversations between two or more users. With IRC, people meet on channels to talk in groups or privately about specific topics. Extended IRC (IRCX) is a set of extensions developed by Microsoft that enhances the functionality of the IRC protocol and adds new commands that you can use to manage users and channels on a Chat server.

Chat Service operates independently of other servers running Chat Service, using separate user and channel lists. Users contact Chat Service over TCP port 6667, which is usually the port number assigned to the first chat community. Port 7000 is also available, although other port numbers can be used if necessary. Any IRC-based client that is RFC 1459 compliant, such as mIRC (*http://www.mirc.com*) or PIRCH (*http://www.pirch.com*), will work.

Channels

A *channel* is a virtual place where people meet to engage in conversations. When a user joins a channel, the user can read anything that is typed to members of the channel. Channels are also called chat rooms.

There are two types of channels: registered and dynamic. *Registered channels* are created by the system administrator and are permanent. They can be divided into two categories: those that start when someone joins the channel and those that start automatically when Chat Service starts. Any started channels that are not secret or hidden are visible and can be displayed in a chat client with the List or Listx command.

Dynamic channels are temporary channels that a user creates from the client by using the IRC Join command or the IRCX Create command. A *channel host* manages a channel from the chat client. Only dynamic channels have channel hosts. The first person to join a channel automatically becomes the channel host. This status can be shared with other chat users. The user who is the channel host is referred to as a *channel operator* or *chanop*.

You should be aware of one other role in a chat community, and that is the *sysop*. A sysop is a user who monitors and controls a chat community's dynamic channels—as well as any registered channels to which the sysop has been given permissions—from a chat client. The sysop can also close a channel by using the IRC Kill command without having owner privileges on that channel. Sysops have no special permissions in a channel unless Chat Sysop Joins As Owner is selected on the channel's Modes tab.

To prevent someone from impersonating a sysop, only a sysop's nickname can begin with the following strings: "sysop," "orwell," "ChanServ," "CodeServ," "HelpServ," "MemoServ," and "NickServ." For example, any user can use the nickname "marysysop," but only a sysop can use the nickname "sysopmary." The terms "system" and "service" cannot begin or be contained in any nickname, including that used by a sysop.

You can configure channels to be either secure or cloneable or both. A secure channel is one to which access is restricted. You can restrict a channel to allow only authenticated users, invited users, or users who enter the correct password. In addition, you can restrict channels with Active Directory security settings by identifying only a group of user accounts or a selected number of group accounts as channel users. Finally, channels can be moderated, meaning that only those who have been granted a "voice" can speak.

A cloneable channel is a registered channel that automatically duplicates itself when its member limit is reached. Any security settings that are configured for the initial channel will be duplicated in the new channel.

Controlling User Connections to a Chat Community

You can control who can connect to a chat community and who cannot in two basic ways. *User classes* let you control connection by a group of users without the need to create a formal group in Active Directory. *User bans* enable you to control access on a per-user basis. Let's discuss each of these briefly.

User Classes

You can group users into classes and then assign Chat Service permissions and restrictions to those classes. In addition, you can control users' ability to create or join dynamic channels, restrict a class of users from logging on to a chat community, or become a channel owner or host. Class membership is based on one or more of the following criteria:

- Whether the user is logged on as an authenticated user or as an anonymous user
- The nickname, user name, domain name, or IP address of the user
- The time of day

When a user logs on to Chat Service, the service searches the existing classes in alphanumeric order by class name. If the user matches any of the selection criteria for a defined class, Chat Service adds the user to the first matching class and applies that class's restrictions to the user. If a user meets the criteria for more than one class, the user is added only to the first class that produces a match.

To create a user class, start the Exchange System snap-in, right-click the Classes folder under the chat community, point to New, and then choose Class. Figure 18-1 shows the General tab of the property sheet for a new user class. Enter the class name, and then configure the member scope by either completing the three fields for the identity mask or by specifying the IP address and subnet mask.

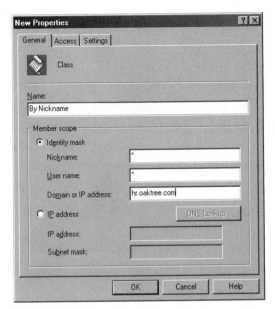

Figure 18-1. *General tab of the property sheet for a new user class.*

In the Identity Mask options, both the asterisk (*) and the question mark (?) are considered wildcard characters. It is important to understand that Chat Service considers all three fields when applying a user class. Table 18-2 give some examples.

Table 18-2.   Examples of identity masks

Nickname	User Name	Domain or IP Address	Result
Crude	*	*	The user class comprises all users with the nickname of Crude from anywhere.
?	*	*.net	The user class comprises all users originating from a .net domain.
*	*	*	The user class applies to all users connecting to Chat Service.
*	US*	*	The user class comprises users whose user name begin with US.
*	*	hr.oaktree.com	The user class comprises users coming from the hr.oaktree.com domain.

Figure 18-2 shows the Access tab for the user class property sheet. Here you can further define the class based on the users' logon state and then, in the Restrictions area, stipulate what users who belong to this class cannot do. You can also enable the user class for certain times of the day—perhaps when the users are most likely to be using Chat Service.

The Hide Class Members' IP Addresses And DNS Names check box is a way to prevent one chat user from launching an attack on another chat user. A user who knows the IP address of another client can send large amounts of data directly to that client's connection, flooding it. You can reduce the likelihood of direct client attacks by masking a portion of each user's IP address or DNS host name.

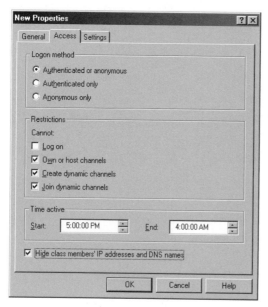

Figure 18-2. *Access tab of the property sheet for a new user class.*

The Settings tab (Figure 18-3) sets protection levels to prevent attacks from bringing down your server. There are four choices for the attack protection level: None, Low, Medium, and High. If Chat Service receives one of these messages, it temporarily suspends the user's session. After the delay expires, the service resumes normal message processing. As shown in Table 18-3, each attack protection level corresponds to a delay time in seconds, based on the type of message or event. The attack protection delay is added to the message processing delay, which you set on this tab, and the channel lag delay, which you set with the Prop command (discussed in the Real World sidebar "Preventing Chat Service Attacks").

In the Limits area, you can enter the following values:

- **Maximum IP Connections**   Regulates the number of connections per IP address for this user class. (This limit does not affect sysops and chat administrators.)

- **Maximum Channels User Can Join**   Regulates the number of concurrent channels that a user can be chatting on. The server tracks this number based on a user's nickname. All channel messages are funneled through the same port number on both server and client.

- **Output Saturation Limit (KB)**   Indicates the maximum amount of data that the server will buffer for a client before dropping the client connection.

Table 18-3.   Attack protection levels

Message Type or Event	None	Low	Medium	High
Data	0	1	2	3
Invitation	0	2	4	5
Join	0	2	3	4
Wrong channel password	0	2	4	5
Standard message, such as a Privmsg, Notice, or Whisper command	0	1	2	3
Message from host to channel	0	1	1	2

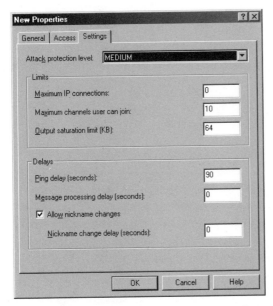

Figure 18-3. *Settings tab of the property sheet for a new user class.*

In the Delays area, you can configure the Ping Delay (Seconds) parameter. The PING message is used to test whether an active client is present at the other end of a connection. In a sense, it is a heartbeat that is sent from the server to the client after the configured number of seconds of inactivity. Any client that receives a PING message must respond as quickly as possible with a PONG message. This indicates to the server that the client is still there and is alive. If the client fails to respond, the server severs the connection to the client. You can set this timeout value to any value between 15 and 3599 seconds. Both the PING and the PONG message packets are only 83 bytes, so unless you manage a large number of users using Chat Service, this activity should have a minimal effect on your bandwidth.

In the Delays area, you can also configure the Message Processing Delay (Seconds) option, which regulates the amount of time the server waits before processing the next message from all clients. The default is 0, but you can set it for up to 10 seconds. Finally, the Nickname Change Delay (Seconds) option regulates how often (in seconds) a user can change his or her nickname.

Real World   Preventing Chat Service Attacks

Microsoft's Chat Service includes security features that can help you reduce and, in many cases, prevent attacks on your Chat servers. You need to defend yourself against three types of attacks: flooding attacks, clone attacks, and direct client attacks.

Flooding Attacks   Flooding attacks occur when an attacker floods a Chat server by sending a large amount of information to be processed, exceeding the capacity of the Chat server. An attacking user can also cause another user's screen to scroll too fast, making it impossible to follow a chat session.

You can specify an output saturation limit on a per-class basis to control flooding on the server. This limit specifies the maximum amount of data that the server can buffer for a client before the server drops the client connection.

The server can also drop sysop connections. The saturation limit for sysops is hard-coded at 1 MB.

Other types of flooding attacks require different measures. For example, an attacker can send users a continuous stream of short messages that are too small to reach the Auto Ignore Flooders limit but are large enough to make the recipients' screens scroll so quickly that the screen is unreadable.

You can control this type of flooding by applying a delay to user connections. A delay is the period of time, measured in seconds, that the server waits before processing the next message from a client. This value is set in the Message Processing Delay box on the Settings tab.

Channel lag adds an additional delay to any message sent to a channel. This lag is added to any other delay that is in effect. To set the channel lag, use the IRCX Prop command. You can set a value of from 0 to 2 seconds. The default setting is 0 (no lag). Actual lag times can vary by plus or minus 1 second. To issue the Prop command, perform these steps:

From a chat client, log on to the server as a chat administrator or chat sysop.

Type */prop <channel> <property> :<lag value>*. For example,

/prop #mychannelname lag :2.

Clone Attacks   A clone attack occurs when an attacker establishes several connections to a server from a single IP address and sends multiple, frequent messages to each connection. Although each individual load is not large enough to cause the connection to be dropped, the combined effect can prevent the server from accepting new connections from other users.

You can prevent clone attacks by limiting the number of connections per IP address within a user class. Sysops and chat administrators are not affected by this limit. The Maximum IP Connections option is the setting to use in this situation.

Direct Client Attacks   Direct client attacks occur when a chat client launches an attack on another client. A user who knows the IP address of another client can send large amounts of data directly through the Internet to flood that client's modem connection. By enabling IP/DNS masking, which masks a portion of each user's IP address or DNS host name, you can reduce the attacker's chances of success. The partial address or host name enables users to know the general location of other chat clients without exposing those clients to possible attack.

If a user has a DNS host name, the server masks the first portion of the host name. For example, benglish@hr.oaktree.com is published as benglish@xxxxx.oaktree.com. If a user has no DNS host name, the server masks the last number of the IP address. For example, the address 192.168.2.200 is published as 192.168.2.xxx.

Sysops, channel owners, and channel hosts (including chat administrators) can see each user's full IP address or DNS host name so they can, if necessary, remove or ban users from Chat Service or a specific channel. Channel owners and hosts can see the full IP address or DNS host name only of users in their channels. Select the Enable The Masking Of IP Addresses And DNS Names check box on the Access tab of the user class's property sheet to enable this feature.

User Bans

User bans restrict individual users from accessing a specific chat community. If a user attempts to access a banned community, the user is refused. The user can be restricted by nickname, user name, or both. The chat community protected by the ban is identified by either the domain name or IP address. User bans are community specific, meaning that a user banned from one community may be able to access another community on your server.

To ban a user, navigate within the Exchange System snap-in to the chat community from which you want to ban the user, right-click the Bans container, point to New, and then choose Ban. As Figure 18-4 shows, you can ban a user based on nickname, user name, domain name, or IP address. You can also configure a time frame during which the ban will be active. These settings work the same as they do for user classes.

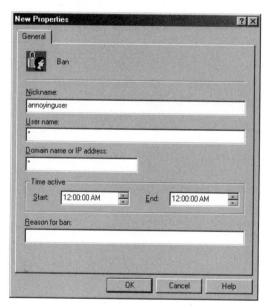

Figure 18-4. *Ban settings for a chat community.*

Tip To ban an entire group of users from a chat community, create a group in Active Directory Users and Computers, add the user accounts to that group, and then ban the group. You can control individual user access to a chat community in a number of ways. Here is a list all of the different ways to control user access to Chat Service; each is described elsewhere in this chapter.

- Limit the number of user connections
- Allow only authenticated users
- Impose restrictions on a group of users
- Ban individual users
- Disable all access to the chat community
- Disconnect users from Chat Service completely

Creating and Managing Chat Communities

When you install Chat Service, a chat community named Default-Chat-Community is automatically created for the First Administrative group. You can rename the community if necessary, and you can also create additional chat communities under other administrative groups.

Creating a Chat Community

To create a chat community, start the Exchange System snap-in, right-click Chat Communities, point to New, and then choose Chat Community. As you can see in Figure 18-5, you can modify several important properties.

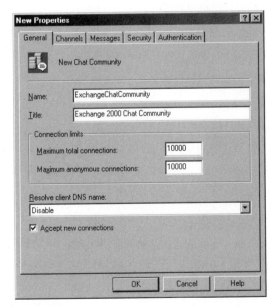

Figure 18-5. *General tab of a chat community's property sheet.*

On the General tab, name the new community. Remember that the name must not contain any spaces or end in a number. The title of the community should be short yet descriptive. The title appears in the tab heading in the client chat window and is a friendly name for the chat community. It is limited to 63 characters. The topic of a specific channel within the community can be longer, indicating more fully what the chat discussion is about. The topic is available to chat clients if they look at the room properties.

You can also set your connection limits on this tab. Be sure that the value set for Maximum Anonymous Connections is less than the one for Maximum Total Connections. The default for both is 10,000, and the range for both is 0 to 99,999,999.

Finally, you can specify whether you want client DNS names resolved. This can be considered a security measure. In the drop-down list, you can choose between Disable, Attempt, and Require. Selecting Disable directs the server not to attempt IP-to-host-name resolution of the chat client. This is the least secure option, especially if the community is available to clients on the Internet.

The Attempt selection directs the server to try host-name-to-IP resolution. If a valid DNS name is returned, the server allows the client to connect to the chat community.

Finally, the Require selection directs the server to look up and resolve the IP address of an incoming chat client. If no valid DNS name is returned, the client connection is refused. This is the most secure option.

Figure 18-6 shows the Channels tab. Use this tab to configure channel defaults and to allow dynamic channels for a chat community. The Language field identifies the default language for the chat community. Use the language codes specified in International Standards Organization (ISO) 639. If needed, you can also include the ISO 3166 country code. The entry is limited to 31 lowercase characters.

When selected, the Allow An Owner Or Host For Channel check box permits any user who creates a persistent or dynamic channel to become the channel owner or host.

The Number Of Users Allowed In Channel field allows you to set the maximum number of users allowed on any dynamic channel in the chat community. The default is 25. The value must be between 0 and 99,999. A value of 0 permits unlimited membership in the channel.

The Chat Sysop Joins As Owner check box grants owner status to chat users with sysop permissions when they join a dynamic channel. Registered channels are not affected by this setting.

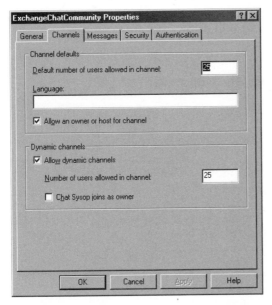

Figure 18-6. *Channels tab of a chat community's property sheet.*

On the Messages tab (Figure 18-7), you can specify a message of the day or a message to be displayed to users who issue the Admin command. The latter message should display information about the server.

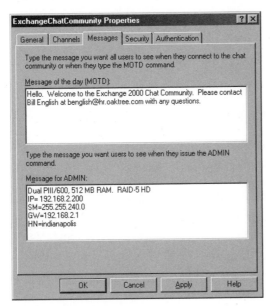

Figure 18-7. *Messages tab of a chat community's property sheet.*

The Authentication tab is used to configure the authentication methods for the chat community. These methods use Active Directory security features for all user accounts.

Connecting a Chat Community to a Server

The next step in creating a chat community is to connect the chat community to a server. In the Exchange System snap-in, navigate to the IRCX container under the server object that will host the chat community, right-click IRCX, and choose Properties. On the property sheet (Figure 18-8), click Add. In the Add Community list, select the name of the chat community you want added to the server. Select the Enable Server To Host This Chat Community option. In the IP Address field, be sure to enter a unique IP address for each community. The default TCP port is 6667.

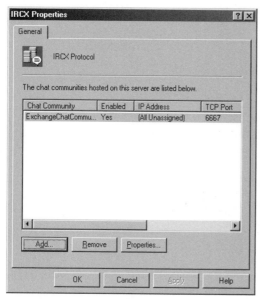

Figure 18-8. *Connecting a chat community to a server.*

Creating a New Channel

Each chat community will need at least one channel through which chat conversations can occur. You can create secure and/or cloneable channels. (For a discussion of these concepts, please see the section "Channels," earlier in this chapter.)

To create a new channel, open the Exchange System snap-in, right-click the Channels container under the chat community, point to New, and then choose Channel. The property sheet for the new channel appears. On the General tab (Figure 18-9), you will need to name the channel and enter the topic, the subject (if needed), and the content rating of the channel.

By selecting the Create This Channel When The Service Starts check box, you will ensure that the channel is always available when Chat Service is running. If this box is not selected, the channel will become visible only when someone joins it.

> **More Info** For more information about content ratings and the Platform for Internet Content Selection (PICS), please go to *http://www.w3.org*.

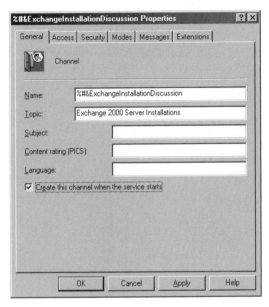

Figure 18-9. *General tab of the property sheet for a new channel.*

Channel Names

A channel name can contain between 1 and 200 characters. If the channel is cloneable, avoid ending the name with a number to prevent name conflicts with cloned channels.

Each channel name must begin with a valid prefix (#, &, %#, or %&). A prefix consists of one or two characters that identify the type of channel:

- A pound sign (#) or ampersand (&) denotes an IRC channel.
- A percent sign (%) followed by a pound sign (#) or an ampersand (&) denotes an extended channel. Extended channels have names that contain characters encoded in Unicode Transformation Format 8 (UTF-8), and these channels are visible only to clients supporting the IRCX protocol, such as Microsoft Chat version 2.5.

Note If the chat client supports the IRCX protocol, the channel name can include double-byte character set (DBCS) characters. Names made up of DBCS characters are limited to 100 characters.

In addition, IRCX supports the use of Unicode characters encoded in UTF-8. Because Unicode provides an extended character set, users running an IRCX-compatible client can participate in chat sessions in any language.

Channel Modes

You can configure four channel modes on the Access tab (Figure 18-10). These modes control a channel's visibility to users. They are as follows:

- **Public** Nonmembers can obtain all information about the channel (except for text messages) from a chat client by using the IRC List command.

- **Private** Nonmembers can obtain only the name, number of members, and PICS property of the channel from a chat client by using the IRC List command.

- **Hidden** A hidden channel is the same as a public channel except that it cannot be found by using a List or Listx command. If you know the exact channel name, however, you can obtain all of the properties of this type of channel from a chat client by using IRC and IRCX commands.

- **Secret** Nonmembers cannot use queries to locate the channel.

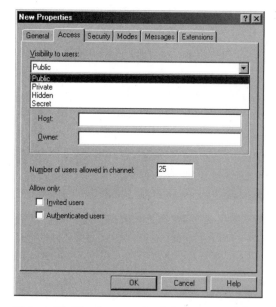

Figure 18-10. *Access tab of the property sheet for a new channel.*

You can configure additional channel modes on the Modes tab (Figure 18-11). Among the settings you can configure are the following:

- **Allow This Channel To Be Cloned**   A cloneable channel is a registered channel that duplicates itself when its member limit is reached. For example, if you create a cloneable channel named Exchange2000 with a member limit of 10, the 11th user who tries to join Exchange2000 is placed on a new channel called Exchange20001. The limit is 99 clones. Each clone retains the properties of the original channel but is a separate channel.

- **Moderated**   Moderated channels are often used for small chat events. A chat user joining a moderated channel cannot post messages to the channel without permission but can see messages posted by the designated speakers. A channel host can use the command /mode <channel_name> +v <nickname> to grant speaking permission to a specific user.

- **Auditorium**   Auditorium channels are often used for large chat events, such as department meetings. Because of the large user list, users cannot send messages to each other and can see only messages posted by the designated speakers. This limitation helps to maintain control of the event. Speakers, however, can see and send messages to any event participant on the channel. Only channel hosts are notified when participants join or leave an auditorium channel.

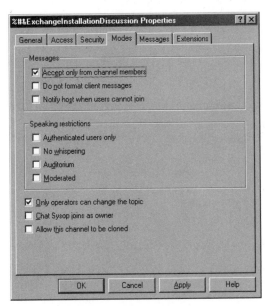

Figure 18-11. *Modes tab of the property sheet for a new channel.*

Access to a channel can also be limited to invited users or to authenticated users. These settings allow for a persistent yet private channel that is available when needed.

Filtering Chat Messages

On the Extensions tab, you can employ a profanity filter on a channel to block objectionable language during the chat. If a profanity filter is not listed on this tab, no words will be banned in conversations on the channel. This filter can ban words in all messages, including whispers and invitations on both dynamic and registered channels. At the server level, you can also apply individual filters to private messages, invitations, quit messages, part messages, channel names, and nicknames.

To use the profanity filter, you must first create a list of restricted words. After creating this list, you can apply the filter to an individual registered channel or you can filter conversations on all of the dynamic channels in the chat community. When a message is sent that contains a filtered word, the entire message is blocked and a private message is sent to the channel member who sent the message, warning that an offensive word was used and requesting that the word not be used again. To create a list of restricted words, perform these steps:

1. Start the Exchange System snap-in.
2. Navigate to the IRCX folder for the server hosting the chat community whose messages you want to filter for offensive language.
3. Right-click IRCX, and then choose Properties.
4. From the list, choose the chat community whose messages you want to filter.
5. Click Properties, and then click Extensions.
6. If the Profanity Filter extension does not appear in the Extensions list, click Add. If the Profanity Filter extension does appear, go to step 9.
7. In the Add Extension dialog box, select the Profanity Filter (PFilter) extension from the Extension list.
8. Stop and then restart the Microsoft Exchange Chat Service.
9. Right-click IRCX, and then choose Properties.
10. On the property sheet for the IRCX protocol, choose the chat community whose messages you want to filter, and then click Properties.
11. Click Extensions.
12. On the Extensions property sheet, click Add.

13. On the community's Extensions tab, verify that the Profanity Filter extension is selected in the window. Click Properties.

14. On the Community PFilter property sheet, click Edit Filters.

15. In the Edit Filters dialog box, click Add Filter.

16. In the Add New Filter dialog box, type a name in the Filter Name box.

As Figure 18-12 shows, you can create additional filters and then apply them to various types of chat communications. This gives you flexibility as to which filters are applied to which kind of chat communication. In the figure, we have set up an obscenities filter for private messages, a crude filter for channel names, and a slang filter for nicknames. The default filter applies to all dynamic channels.

Of course, you can set up multiple filters for different kinds of languages and different groups. For example, you might set up one filter for the entire company listing certain kinds of words, such as obscenities, for all types of chat messages. A second filter could be set up just for nicknames. The point here is that each filter has a different word list, so anytime you need to apply a different word list to messages in your chat network, you'll need a different filter.

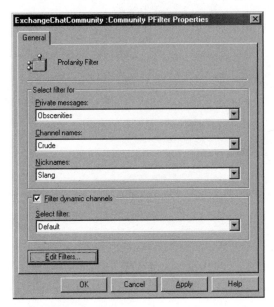

Figure 18-12. *Chat filter properties for different chat groups.*

Transcribing Chat Messages

Chat Service has a transcription extension that will transcribe conversations that occur on one or more registered channels and then save these transcriptions to a directory named after the community. Each transcript file is saved to a folder with the same name as the channel.

Each transcript file contains all messages sent publicly to a channel within a 24-hour period (12:00 A.M. to 11:59 P.M.). Because some characters allowed in channel names are not allowed in directory names, characters are replaced as shown in Table 18-4. Figure 18-13 shows part of a typical transcript.

Table 18-4. Characters replaced during chat transcription

Character	Replaced With
\ (backslash)	~1
. (period)	~2
" (quotation mark)	~3
/ (slash)	~4
[(open bracket)	~5
] (close bracket)	~6
: (colon)	~7
; (semicolon)	~8
= (equal sign)	~9
, (comma)	~10
~ (tilde)	~~

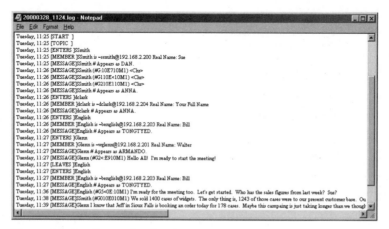

Figure 18-13. *Example of a chat transcript.*

To set up transcription for a chat community, add the Tscript extension to the community, in the same manner as described for the profanity filter in the previous section.

When a user first joins a channel that has transcription enabled, the user is informed of that fact immediately upon entering the chat room (Figure 18-14). By default, the transcripts are placed in the C:\Exchsrvr\Chatdata\Transcript folder. You can change the location of your transcripts in the channel transcript extension properties. Once you've made the change, you must stop and restart the Microsoft Exchange Chat Service before the new configuration will take effect. Also by default, only public messages are transcribed.

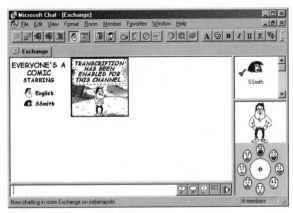

Figure 18-14. *Message indicating that transcription has been enabled.*

Monitoring Chat Service

Although it is beyond the scope of this book to offer an exhaustive review of all of the counters for Chat Service, several are noteworthy. Tables 18-5 and 18-6 indicate which objects and counters you should employ to monitor different aspects of your Chat server. Be sure to set up capacity and performance logging at the same time so that you can analyze both sets of data simultaneously.

In the two tables, you'll notice that we rarely give numeric benchmarks against which to judge your numbers. Instead, you should establish your own baselines by regularly monitoring these counters on your servers. For instance, you might want to schedule monitoring for the second Monday through Wednesday of every month. Doing so will enable you to judge what values are high for each counter.

Table 18-5.   Monitoring physical resource capacity

Counter	Description
% Processor Time (Processor object)	This counter should not exceed 90 percent. It measures the percentage of time that the CPU is engaged in processing nonidle threads. Chat Service is CPU intensive, and excessive usage indicates an attack on the server or a need for additional hardware. Compare this counter with other counters discussed here and in Table 18-6.
Available Bytes (Memory object)	This counter shows the amount of physical memory available to processes running on the server. If less than 10 percent of the memory is available, it can indicate excessive processing, a software error, or a need for additional RAM.

Table 18-6.   Monitoring Chat Service

Counter	Description
Authentication Failures (Microsoft Exchange Chat Community object)	This counter shows the total number of failed authentication attempts by users trying to connect to the Chat server. A high number may indicate an attempt to breach security on your server.
Active DNS Logon Threads (Microsoft Exchange Chat Service object)	This counter shows the total number of worker threads waiting to process DNS lookup requests. A high number may indicate a DNS server failure.
Client Timeout Related Disconnects (Microsoft Exchange Chat Service object)	This counter indicates the total number of clients disconnected because of a PING timeout. A high number may indicate a network lag or a client computer malfunction.

Removing a Chat Community

You can remove a chat community from a server in one of three ways. The method you choose will depend on the outcome you desire. All three methods will disconnect current users from the chat community.

If you want to remove a chat community's association with a server, remove the chat community from the IRCX property sheet by selecting it and clicking Remove, as shown in Figure 18-15. If you want to disable a chat community temporarily, retaining the community's association with the server and also retaining the community and its configuration for future use, clear the Enable Server To Host This Chat Community check box in the property sheet for the chat community. Finally, if you want to remove a chat community entirely from a server, delete it from the chat community's container.

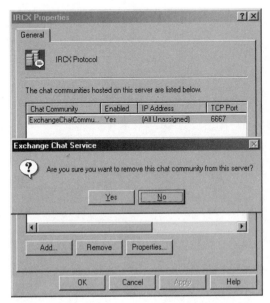

Figure 18-15. *Removing a chat community from the IRCX property sheet.*

Disabling a Chat Community

There may be times when you want to disable a particular community without deleting it. You can do this by clearing the Accept New Connections check box, as illustrated in Figure 18-16. You can put the community back into service again by selecting this box. This process is dynamic and does not require stopping and starting Chat Service.

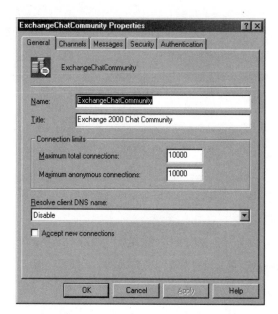

Figure 18-16. *Disabling a chat community by clearing the Accept New Connections check box.*

Migrating from Exchange Chat Server 5.5

If you are using Chat Server 5.5, the chat service in Exchange 5.5, you may have some settings or configurations that you want to migrate when you install Chat Service. The Chat migration tool enables you to create a new chat community on an Exchange 2000 server with the same name as Chat Server 5.5 that preserves most of the settings and configurations.

Tip The Chat migration tool will not migrate Chat Server 5.5 extension data. This means that if you had a profanity filter or a transcript extension with your Chat Server 5.5, you will need to re-create them in Chat Service.

The new chat community that the migration tool creates will be completely different from your Chat Server 5.5. In addition, if your Exchange Server 5.5 installation consists of one Chat Server 5.5 spanning two or more Exchange servers, you need to understand that this type of chat installation is not supported by Microsoft Exchange 2000 Server.

Using the Chat migration tool, you can create chat communities on each of your Exchange 2000 servers. Each of the Exchange 2000 chat communities on each of the Exchange 2000 servers in your domain will operate separately, with separate user lists and channel lists. To migrate to Chat Service from the previous version, perform these steps:

1. Install Windows 2000 Server on your target machine, creating a new domain or configuring it as a member server of an existing domain. Remember that the source of the migration tool is the Exchange 5.5 server running Chat Server 5.5. The target of the migration tool is the server running Chat Service.

2. If you are installing Exchange 2000 into a group of Exchange 5.5 servers that spread Chat Server 5.5 over two or more servers, upgrade all of the machines to Windows 2000 Server first, creating a new domain or configuring each as a member server of an existing domain. All of the machines must be in the same domain.

3. The actual services used by Chat Service and Chat Server 5.5 have the same display name, Microsoft Exchange Chat. Therefore, if you are installing Chat Service on a machine on which Chat Server 5.5 is already installed, you must do the following:

   • Manually modify the name of service for Chat Server 5.5 on your Exchange 5.5 server.

   • Reconfigure the ports so that Chat Server 5.5 is not using the default port 6667 or the alternate default port 7000.

> **Note**   If you do not complete these steps, Exchange 2000 Setup will fail to install Chat Service.

4. Install Chat Service on each target machine.

5. Run the Chat migration tool (Chatmig.exe) and specify the target. The target must be the administrative group to which you want to migrate.

After you run the Chat migration tool, a new chat community is created on the Exchange 2000 server with the same name as the Exchange Server 5.5 Chat server. It will have similar server, channel, ban, and class configurations. Until you are ready to fully switch over to the Exchange 2000 server, both chat services can run simultaneously.

If you are installing Exchange 2000 Chat Service on a new server, copy the migration tool from the \Exchsrvr\Bin directory on the target machine to the source machine. Run the Chat migration tool, identifying the Chat Server 5.5 directory as the source and the Chat Service directory as the target.

> **Tip** You can check the Chatsetup.log file that the migration tool produces to see whether any problems occurred during the migration. This log will be located in the \Exchsrvr directory.

Configuring and Managing the Chat Client

Microsoft Exchange 2000 does not support Microsoft Chat 2.0 and earlier, so if you're running one of these versions you'll need to install the Microsoft Chat 2.1 client. This client can be found on the Exchange 5.5 Service Pack 3 CD-ROM in TechNet. The client installs easily with little up-front configuration. However, once it is installed, there is much that you can configure at the client end.

When the chat client starts, the user is presented with a dialog box consisting of two tabs. The first tab asks which server and community the user wants to connect to, and the second tab allows the user to update or modify his or her personal information (Figure 18-17). Once the user clicks OK in this dialog box, the user sees the message of the day.

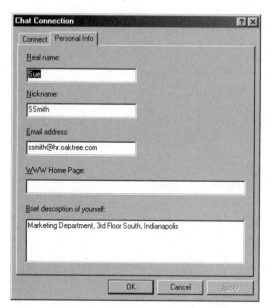

Figure 18-17. *Personal Info tab for a chat connection.*

Logging On with Dynamic Channels Enabled

When a user logs on to Chat Service and dynamic channels have been enabled for the chat community, if the user specifies the same name of a chat room that is currently up and running, the user will be joined to the room. Figures 18-18 and 18-19 demonstrate that users SSmith (Sue Smith) and English (Bill English) have both logged on to the Exchange chat room. This is also seen in the Chat Room List, shown in Figure 18-20. Notice also, that when English joins the room, previous messages are not copied into his Chat client.

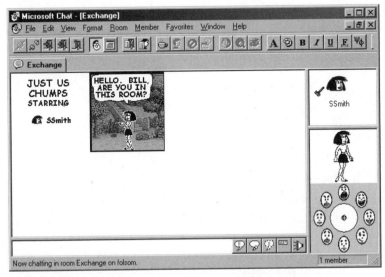

Figure 18-18. *SSmith logs on to Chat Service.*

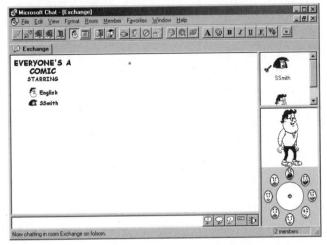

Figure 18-19. *English logs on to Chat Service.*

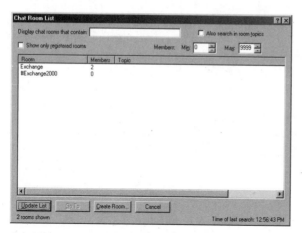

Figure 18-20. *Chat room list showing two members in the Exchange room.*

Logging On with Dynamic Channels Disabled

If dynamic channels have been disabled for the chat community, the user must manually join a room to engage in chat conversations, even if he or she selected a specific room during the logon process. Initially, the user is placed into a generic room, called Room1. From there, the user can join other rooms and engage in chat conversations with other online users.

Discovering Current Rooms and Usage

Chat users can find out which rooms are available and occupied by choosing Room List from the Room menu. The Chat Room List dialog box appears, as shown in Figure 18-21. This dialog box lists all available rooms, shows how many members are currently in each room, and displays the room's topic, if available. From this box, a user can create a new room by clicking the Create Room button and then configuring the Create Chat Room dialog box (Figure 18-22). This button is available only if dynamic channels have been enabled for the chat community.

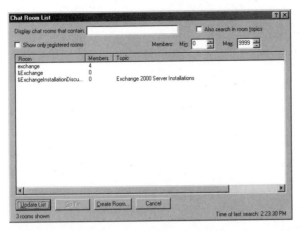

Figure 18-21. *Chat Room List dialog box.*

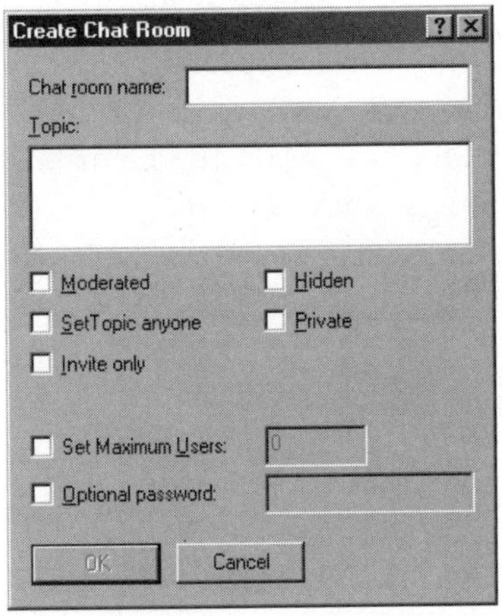

Figure 18-22. *Create Chat Room dialog box.*

Understanding the Chat Interface

Figure 18-23 shows the basic user interface for the Microsoft Chat client. In this window, users can discern which room they are chatting in by looking at the name shown on the tab. The lower part of the window displays a box that is a single line in height, where the user types messages to the other room members.

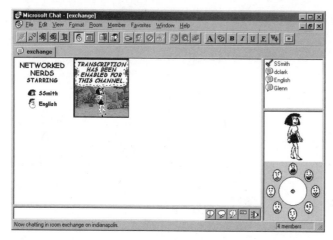

Figure 18-23. *Microsoft Chat client interface.*

The largest part of the window is where messages are displayed. Since this interface has two basic settings—comic strip or text—messages appear in either a comic strip format (Figure 18-24) or as plain text (Figure 18-25). Users can toggle between the two settings by clicking the appropriate button on the Chat bar. Message history is lost when a user toggles from one setting to another.

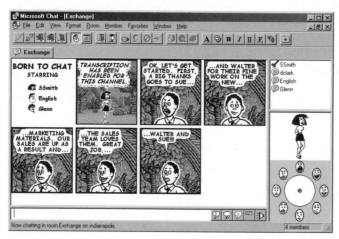

Figure 18-24. *Messages in comic strip form.*

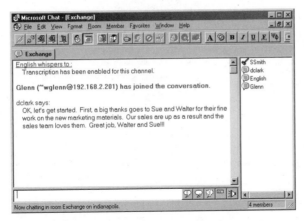

Figure 18-25. *Messages in plain text form*

The right side of the Chat window lists the other room members. Figure 18-26 shows the shortcut menu that appears when you right-click a room member's name. Most of the menu items are self-explanatory, but a few are worth discussing here. First, Get Profile displays the character that the member is using. Get Identity displays the character along with the member's e-mail address.

Figure 18-26. *The shortcut menu for chat room members.*

In the plain text view, the Get Profile command shows whatever the member has entered into the Brief Description Of Yourself box in the member profile. The Get Identity command returns the member's e-mail address in text form.

The host of the chat room can also use the shortcut menu to eject a user and relay this information to the other room members through a system message. Kicking a user out does not prevent that user from reentering the room. A host can eject a user permanently by choosing the Ban/Unban command.

Users can also inform other users that, even though they are still in the chat room, they are temporarily unavailable. They can do this by choosing Away From Keyboard from the Member menu and then specifying the message that is sent to the other members. Figure 18-27 illustrates such a message. In this case, dclark has left his workstation for a few minutes but has forgotten to change the default message, which is "gone fishing."

Figure 18-27. *Message to group members indicating that a member is temporarily unavailable.*

Configuring Individual Settings on the Chat Client

Users can configure the settings of their chat client to enhance their experience of Chat Service. To see the configuration options in Microsoft Chat, choose Options from the View menu (Figure 18-28).

As you can see, users can set individual content ratings that might be more or less restrictive than the settings for the group ratings. They can also restrict the types of communications they see, such as whispers, chat invitations, or net meeting requests.

On the Comics View tab, users can customize their fonts and select their page layout settings. The Character tab (Figure 18-29) allows users to select the character they would like to have represent them in the chat room. They can also choose the default facial expression in the lower right corner of this tab. The black dot can be moved within the circle, making possible many combinations of expressions.

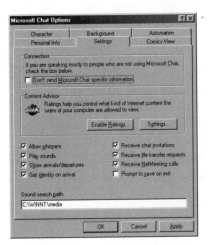

Figure 18-28. *Settings tab of the Microsoft Chat Options dialog box.*

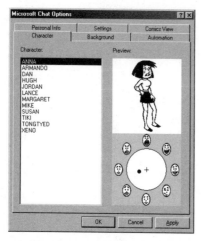

Figure 18-29. *Character tab of the Microsoft Chat Options dialog box.*

The Automation tab (Figure 18-30) allows a user to configure an automatic greeting that is displayed whenever that user is the host of the current chat and another member enters the room. Users can also ignore messages from flooding attackers by using the options in the Auto Ignore Flooders area. By default, if Microsoft Chat receives four messages from the same user within a five-second interval, it will consider these messages to be flooding and ignore them. Finally, users can create hot keys that are tied to message macros, allowing users to send repetitive messages. This is useful for emotional expressions such as "LOL," which means "laughing out loud." Instead of typing those three letters, a user can create a macro that sends the message automatically when invoked.

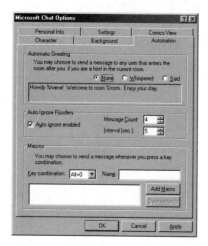

Figure 18-30. *Automation tab of the Microsoft Chat Options dialog box.*

Summary

In this chapter, you have learned how to create chat communities and configure Chat Service in Exchange 2000. You have also learned about the benefits of implementing Chat Service in your environment and seen how it can make your users more productive. The next chapter looks at another real-time collaboration technology: instant messaging. If you liked Chat Service, you're going to love instant messaging because it represents the future of business communications. So let's turn to the Chapter 19 and get going!

Chapter 19
Supporting Instant Messaging

The previous chapter discussed how to configure and administer Microsoft Chat Service, which allows users to engage in online group discussions. Chat Service is one of the two real-time collaboration (RTC) services that ship with Microsoft Exchange 2000 Server. This chapter covers the other RTC service—Microsoft Exchange Instant Messaging (IM). As you'll see, Instant Messaging offers instant, one-to-one communication between users.

> **Note** Data and video conferencing are also RTC technologies that can be run with Exchange 2000 Server. However, since conferencing is an add-on product to Exchange 2000 Server, we will not cover it in this book.

Instant messaging is a bit like using e-mail and a bit like using a telephone. Like e-mail, the communication is in text form rather than being spoken. Like a telephone conversation, an instant message conversation takes place instantly and in real time. Instant messages are also not recorded in the information store; therefore, they are not saved after they leave the screen. Once they are gone, there is no way to recover them.

The benefits of using IM include the following:

- It reduces telephone tag. Rather than leaving voice mail messages for someone who is out of the office briefly, you can check another user's presence information to determine when he or she returns, and then send a message and wait for the reply.

- It allows users to multitask—for example, a person could work on a Word document and answer questions via instant messages at the same time.

- It breaks down the traditional barriers to communication, such as geographic boundaries. For example, if the person you need to communicate with is in a different city, you don't need to pick up the phone to make a call. Instead, you can check the presence information of the user with whom you wish to communicate and, if that person is on line, exchange messages while working.

Instant Messaging uses an emerging technology that can be tricky to understand. We'll begin by looking at the IM architecture, and then we'll see how messages are passed from one IM user to another.

Instant Messaging Architecture

When Microsoft first started to consider incorporating instant messaging capabilities into the Exchange product, it identified several market requirements that such a service would need to incorporate. Table 19-1 lists these requirements and indicates how the IM architecture has met each one.

Table 19-1. Market requirements for Instant Messaging

Market Requirement	How Implemented
Perform at large installations	Scalable architecture
Allow communication between businesses	Federated architecture
Work with firewalls	Firewall compatibility
Provide security and privacy	Authentication and access control list (ACL) mechanisms
Leverage existing infrastructure	Integration with Microsoft Windows 2000 and Exchange 2000 Server
Offer interoperability between products	Use of standard protocols, such as HTTP, LDAP, and WebDAV

Rendezvous Protocol Architecture

All IM communication occurs over the rendezvous protocol (RVP). RVP is an extended subset of the WebDAV protocol, which is an extension to HTTP 1.1. As such, RVP can leverage existing technologies, such as firewall support and proxy servers. In addition, the issue of client authentication need not be addressed in RVP, since it has been settled within HTTP.

RVP is designed to enable subscriptions and notifications within an organization and across multiple organizations and businesses, whether over a LAN connection or over the Internet. Instant messaging clients always communicate with IM servers, but IM servers are not required to communicate directly with each other. Therefore, many different servers can be installed within separate Active Directories.

RVP allows for *watchers* to obtain *presence information*, for *presentities* (we will use the term "user" in place of "presentity" henceforth) to determine which watchers are obtaining their presence information, and for instant messages to be sent to *instant message inboxes* inside the current domain or to a different domain.

The *home server* is the IM server responsible for maintaining current presence information for any user assigned to it and for issuing *notifications* of changes in a user's status to any *subscriber*. Messages sent to a user must first pass through the user's home server. The instant messaging client software represents the user to the home server and acts as the inbox for that user.

In order for a client to find the correct IM server to perform the requested tasks, such as updating a user's presence information or sending an instant message, it must first perform a DNS service (SRV) record lookup for the domain containing the IM server. The domain can be either local or remote, but it must support SRV records. The SRV lookup returns the host name of the IM server responsible for that domain. If no SRV record exists, DNS searches for an address (A) record for the IM server.

The client then connects to this server and sends it a request for some type of action. If the server is the user's home server, it handles the request. If the server is a *routing server*, it either proxies the request or uses HTTP to redirect the client to a specific home server. To improve the speed of lookups, the client caches the destination home server for a period of time.

Because all this activity occurs over HTTP and port 80, RVP allows presence information and instant messages to be transmitted over the Internet between dissimilar networks and domains.

RVP is an asynchronous protocol that requires little bandwidth to operate. Therefore, network bandwidth should not be an issue when considering where to place the IM servers, except in environments with exceptionally heavy message usage. However, it's generally best to place the IM servers near the users who subscribe to them.

All IM communication between clients and servers uses an extended subset of the WebDAV commands. Table 19-2 lists the commands that Instant Messaging uses.

Table 19-2. WebDAV commands used by Instant Messaging

Command	Description
SUBSCRIBE	Asks the home server of the target user to send back presence information and to update that information should it change.
UNSUBSCRIBE	Asks the home server of the target user to stop sending presence information.
PROPPATCH	Updates or patches a property of the target user. Most often used for updating the subscriber's status, such as changing between offline, online, and busy.
PROPFIND	Retrieves a property or set of properties for subscriptions. Most often used to obtain status information when first logging on.
NOTIFY	Used in server-to-server communications to update the remote server regarding subscriber's status changes. Also used to send instant messages between users.

Instant Message Addressing

Once a user account is enabled for Instant Messaging, you can display the Exchange Features tab of the user's property sheet, select Instant Messaging, and click Properties to see the addresses that are used behind the scenes by IM (Figure 19-1). For more information about enabling an account for IM, see the section "Giving Users Access to Instant Messaging" later in this chapter.

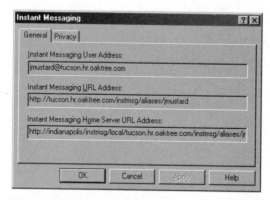

Figure 19-1. *Instant Messaging addresses for a user account*

Instant Messaging uses URLs to route messages to users. It is important to understand what these URLs represent and why they are constructed as they are. Each user has two URLs: a home server URL and a default URL.

At this point, you might be wondering why we are using URLs at the desktop for the instant messaging client. Think of the instant messaging client as a mini-browser that registers itself with the home server when it logs on and is assigned a port number above 1024. It connects to the home server at port 80, so that it can send messages to and receive messages from the IM home server.

The home server URL for the user in Figure 19-1 is *http:// Indianapolis/instmsg/ local/tucson.hr.oaktree.com/instmsg/aliases/jmustard,* and it is parsed in the following manner:

- **Indianapolis**   The home server to which the user will connect.

- **instmsg**   A virtual directory that is created dynamically in the Web site chosen to be associated with the home server.

- **local**   Reserved for future use. There is no immediate use for this tag; it does not mean that the URL is pointing to a local resource.

- **tucson.hr.oaktree.com**   The routing server from which messages will arrive. This section indicates the source of incoming messages only. Outgoing messages can be routed through different routing servers when, for example, a message is destined for a user in another domain.

- **instmsg**   References the router's virtual directory. This path is good for keeping track of how to send messages back along the same path if it is best to do so.

- **aliases**   Specifies the type of account, not the alias attribute for a user account. In the future, IM will be able to include groups, printers, and other addressable entities, such as cell phones.

- **jmustard**   Gives the Windows 2000 logon name of the user.

Tip Configure the IM domain to be the same as the SMTP domain. This will make Instant Messaging easier for your users and will simplify naming conventions used on your network. See the section "Configuring DNS for Instant Messaging" later in this chapter to learn how to configure the IM domain.

Instant Message Authentication and Client Logon

Although users can authenticate to their home server, RVP does not require them to do so. Authentication for IM users is accomplished using either Windows Integrated Authentication (WIA) Challenge/Response or the Digest authentication method. (WIA was formerly known as Windows NT LAN Manager, or NTLM.)

The Digest authentication method verifies that both parties share a secret (that is, a password) without communicating this secret in the open to each other. This scheme can be used by clients on non-WIA platforms, such as UNIX. Kerberos is not used as part of the authentication process.

> **More Info**   The Digest authentication method is outlined in RFC 2617, "HTTP Authentication: Basic and Digest Access Authentication."

When a user logs on to IM, the following processes occur, all of which are transparent to the user:

1. The user's computer queries DNS for an SRV resource record for the RVP protocol, and DNS returns the resolution referring the user to the routing server.
2. The user connects to the IM router.
3. The IM router queries Active Directory for the user's IM home server.
4. The IM router returns the home server's URL address to the user.
5. The IM user uses the home server URL address to connect to his or her IM home server.
6. The IM home server validates the user's Active Directory user name and password.

When a user logs on to Instant Messaging, the user doesn't use the regular logon profile. Instead, the Microsoft Internet Explorer profile is used. This profile's logon uses NTLM authentication, which cannot pass through a proxy server. Thus, if the user's browser is configured with the address of a proxy server, you'll need to configure an exclusion for the IM server's IP address, as described in the section "Users Can't Log On," later in this chapter.

> **Tip**   If the Internet Explorer settings need to be changed, you'll need to exit the instant messaging client and restart it before the new Internet Explorer settings will take effect for the client.

Presence Information

Presence information is information regarding whether an individual is online, out of the office, or busy, as illustrated in Figure 19-2. By checking another user's presence information, an individual can determine whether that user would be likely to read an instant message immediately.

When a user logs on, this fact is sent as a status notification to the IM server, which then passes this knowledge to those who have subscribed to presence information for that user. A user subscribes to presence information for another user by adding that person to his or her contact list, causing the local instant messaging client to send a *subscription message* to the new contact's home server. The home server is then responsible for sending the subscribing user a status notification whenever the presence information for the new contact changes. Figure 19-3 shows the current presence information for a user's contacts.

An instant messaging client has seven presence settings:

- Online
- Invisible
- Busy
- Be Right Back
- Away From Computer
- On The Phone
- Out To Lunch

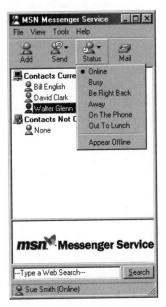

Figure 19-2. *Presence information settings.*

Instant Messaging is not meant to be used to know the current status of everyone in an organization but is rather a way to track the presence of individual team members. It is common for users to list their boss and several other team members as well as a few external contacts in their instant messaging client. If the contact list becomes too large, the client interface becomes less attractive, and the number of status notifications that update presence information can rapidly add up. It is recommended that each user maintain no more than 1000 contacts. Most users will need to list only 15 or 20 users in their contact list.

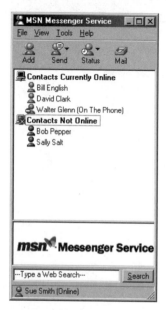

Figure 19-3. *Presence information for a user's contacts.*

Message Flow

This section outlines the basic events that occur when a user sends an instant message to another user. The process depends upon whether the recipient is within the same domain as the sender or in a different domain.

Message Flow Within a Domain

First, let's assume that we have one IM routing server, Tucson, and one IM home server, Indianapolis. Furthermore, let's assume that David is sending an instant message to Sally. Figure 19-4 illustrates the steps involved in sending the message.

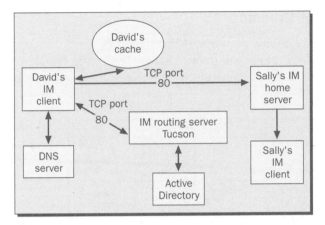

Figure 19-4. *Message flow within a domain.*

When David clicks Send, if the IM DNS information is not cached in David's memory, the instant messaging client contacts the DNS server to obtain the IP address of the server offering the IM service on the network. The DNS server looks up the IM routing server in the DNS tables, where it is specified with an _rvp SRV record for the RVP protocol. (For more information on how to set DNS up for Instant Messaging, see "Configuring DNS for Instant Messaging," later in this chapter.) The DNS server returns the IP address to David's instant messaging client software.

Next, David's instant messaging client software creates a TCP connection to the IM routing server—Tucson, in our example—over TCP port 80. The instant messaging client is assigned a port number above 1024.

After making the TCP connection, the instant messaging client sends a request to the IM routing server, essentially asking it to send an instant message to Sally. The IM routing server does not send the message directly but instead looks up Sally's user account in Active Directory, obtains the corresponding home server URL from her account properties, and returns that URL to David's instant messaging client software.

David's instant messaging client then makes another TCP connection over port 80 to Sally's home server and transmits the message, which uses a combination of HTTP and Extensible Markup Language (XML) to transport the message.

Finally, once the home server receives the message, it transmits the message immediately to Sally's instant messaging client software, which displays the message on the screen for her to read.

Message Flow Between Domains

When it comes to message flow between domains, IM really shines. To understand this process, let's use our previous example with one change—Sally and David are now in different domains at different companies. Figure 19-5 illustrates how a message would flow.

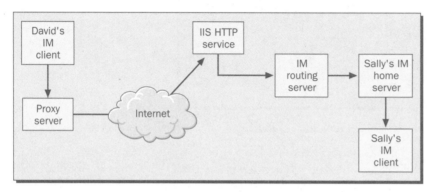

Figure 19-5. *Message flow between domains.*

When David sends a message to Sally, David's client software uses his Internet Explorer settings and sends the request to the proxy server, since the URL is a foreign domain. Finding the destination domain involves the same process on the Internet as finding a home page on a Web site.

At the receiving end, Sally's Internet Information Services (IIS) server receives the request because it is coming in over port 80. IIS looks at the URL and determines that its destination is the IM virtual directory (which exists on the IIS server but points to the routing server) that was set up when the IM routing server was installed. IIS forwards the request to the virtual directory, which in turn routes the message to the routing server because of the virtual directory assigned to the routing server.

Once the routing server receives the request, it would normally want to send the home server URL back to the client, but in this case David is in a different domain on a different network across the Internet. Sending the home server URL back to David is therefore impractical for a host of reasons, not the least of which is that it would consume too much time. Instead, the routing server reverse-proxies the request to the home server, which forwards the message to Sally's instant messaging client software.

Configuring DNS for Instant Messaging

Configuring DNS for Instant Messaging is a straightforward, three-step process. First you must enter an address (A) record for each IM server into the database. You've probably created this type of record for other servers, so it should not be a new activity.

Second, if you're going to have routing servers, consider giving them the host name of "im." Although this is not a standard, nor is it required, Microsoft recommends that the routing servers be given this name so that their fully qualified domain name (FQDN) is im.*domainame*.com (for example, im.microsoft.com). If everyone follows this standard, users can guess at the SMTP address to which they should send instant messages for recipients in other domains. For instance, you could send an instant message to a friend at Microsoft, user1, making an educated guess that the internal routing server's FQDN is im.microsoft.com. Thus, you would send the instant message to user1@im.microsoft.com, and if Microsoft has given its routing servers the name of "im," the message will be routed to that routing server over port 80 and will land in the instant messaging client of user1.

Tip   In a single-server environment, you may want to alias your server's host name with "im," thereby retaining your naming convention internally while still being compatible with other instant messaging installations on the Internet. Be sure that your ISP's DNS records have an FQDN mapping for the IM alias to your incoming IP address for port 80. You will set up the SRV record on your own DNS and will host two virtual servers on the same physical server: a virtual routing server and a virtual home server. If you do not want to configure a routing server, use the "im" FQDN as the host header for your default Web site to have messages routed into your server.

Third you need to create an _rvp SRV resource record for the RVP protocol to enable it to work over port 80. This record should map directly to the routing server. When the instant messaging client attempts to log on, the client first queries DNS for an _rvp SRV resource record. If such a record exists, the client contacts that server, and is then referred to its home server. This SRV record makes it possible for a user's e-mail address and IM address to be the same.

Contrary to what you might have read elsewhere, CNAME records are not necessary when configuring DNS for Instant Messaging. Moreover, aliases are not needed, although in a single-server environment, an alias might be helpful for interoperability on the Internet, as was mentioned in the previous tip.

More Info   See the Windows 2000 Advanced Server DNS documentation for specific information about creating DNS resource records.

> **Note** If you have multiple IM routers identified with the same IM domain, you will need to create multiple A records, one for each router. You can use a DNS round-robin scheme to advertise a single FQDN, with each server binding to a unique IP address.

Real World **Advanced Configuration of DNS to Work with Instant Messaging**

If you meet any of the following criteria, you'll want to be sure to read this section:

- You're an Internet service provider (ISP)
- You're hosting several different companies or domains on the same physical server, all of which want IM services
- You want to implement Instant Messaging without using a routing server

We will look at three different scenarios, describing how best to use three of the basic IM components—the routing server, the home server, and the SRV record—to achieve a specific goal.

Scenario 1: You want to host multiple domains for separate companies on a single physical server, and you're either unwilling or unable to use SRV records and routing servers.

You can implement Instant Messaging in this scenario as follows: Give the physical server the host name "im," and then place an A record in each DNS lookup zone that maps the server's IP address to each FQDN (im.*domainname*.com). Be sure that the name of the server after the @ sign is identical to the FQDN of the home server. This configuration causes the instant messaging client to contact the home server and establish a connection for IM.

This technique is not the best way or even a recommended way to implement IM. Consider this configuration only if it is the only choice available to you.

Scenario #2: You want to host multiple domains for separate companies on a single physical server, and you're using SRV records, one home server, and no routing servers.

To implement IM given this scenario, first give all of the IM servers an A record in DNS. Second create one SRV resource record in each DNS lookup zone that references one home server. Then have the users log on with their domain name minus the "im" designation. Creating a SRV resource record for each domain name causes the users in each DNS domain to be routed to the same home server.

Scenario #3: You want to host multiple domains for separate companies on a single physical server and you're using routing servers with SRV records and one home server.

This scenario is the preferred method of implementing IM. Give the routing server a host name—again, "im" is recommended—and map the SRV resource record in DNS to this server. Give the home server an A record in DNS. As user accounts are enabled for IM, their URLs will be created, indicating to the routing server where to refer the client when they log on.

Installing and Configuring Instant Messaging

To deploy Instant Messaging, you'll first need to have Exchange 2000 Server running on Windows 2000, along with IIS 5. Typically, IM is installed on a member server, but it can also be deployed on a domain controller.

Instant Messaging has two server components: a home server and a routing server. These are really two types of virtual servers. The home server hosts IM user accounts and is the server through which users send and receive instant messages. It is also the server that communicates presence information. The routing server forwards or redirects messages and presence information to home servers on the network. Hence, when an IM routing server receives an instant message addressed to a user, it locates the user in Active Directory and uses the IM settings in the user account to forward the message to the user's home server.

In a single-server environment, an IM routing server is not necessary. In fact, home servers can route messages just as routing servers do. As your organization grows, however, your need for a routing server will increase as well. Best practice suggests that if you create two or more home servers, you should create at least one IM routing server.

To configure and manage Instant Messaging, you need high-level permissions. To manage IM users, you must be a member of the Domain Admins security group for the domain that hosts the users. To manage the global IM settings in the Exchange System snap-in, you must also be a member of the Exchange Admins security group. Global settings include the firewall topology, the proxy server configuration, and the configuration of the IM home and routing servers.

Client Requirements

IM users can run the instant messaging client under Windows 95 or later, Windows NT 4, or Windows 2000. The following software must be installed to use Instant Messaging:

- Internet Explorer 5 or later, which can be downloaded from *http:// www.microsoft.com/one/ie/*

- The Microsoft proxy client if you communicate outside of your Exchange organization

- Exchange Instant Messenging Service, which can be found in the \Instmsg\I386\Client directory on the Exchange 2000 Server CD-ROM

You can deploy IM in a configuration that is similar to a front end/back end (FE/ BE) deployment of Exchange 2000 Server. This configuration involves having a bank of IM routing servers at the front end to act as the primary point of contact for IM services. These servers redirect clients to the appropriate home server for the IM user receiving a message. This type of "bridgehead" server configuration allows one or more front end servers to provide a unified view of the IM topology by having all incoming messages sent to im.*domainname*.com and all internal messages sent to *username@domainname*.com.

Internet users can contact an IM bridgehead server through a public URL. When an instant message comes into the IM bridgehead (routing) server, the server performs a lookup in Active Directory and maps the public URL to the private URL, which contains the name of the home server of the IM user. The bridgehead server then passes back to the Internet client the name of the home server, and the Internet client creates a communications link to the home server.

Note Future versions of Instant Messaging will allow the bridgehead servers to relay messages on behalf of the client to hide the internal IM topology.

The IM service depends on Active Directory to locate the home server for an IM user. The home server need not be the same physical or virtual server as the mailbox server for the user. The IM service creates additional demand on the network subsystem of a server, so it is probably best in most scenarios for the IM server to be a dedicated server. Each IM server is capable of hosting up to 200 transactions per second. It is estimated that an IM server, under normal load conditions, should be able to host 15,000 users simultaneously.

Working with Firewalls

If you are deploying IM on a LAN that sits behind a firewall, you'll need to configure the Firewall Topology tab in the Instant Messaging Settings Property Sheet.

> **Note** When considering the use of Instant Messaging across company boundaries, be aware that the RVP protocol is built on WebDAV and thus, by default, transmits over port 80. Since most firewalls already allow this type of traffic, a reconfiguration of the firewall is rarely needed. Using IM over port 80 does not create additional security considerations in a company's security model.

To identify which IP addresses are protected by your corporate firewall, expand the Global Settings object, right-click Instant Messaging Settings and choose Properties. On the Firewall Topology tab (Figure 19-6), you can enable Instant Messaging to work through a firewall by selecting the This Network Is Protected By A Firewall check box. Selecting this check box will enable the IP Address Ranges Protected By This Firewall settings, and you'll be able to enter the internal IP address range that is behind the firewall.

In addition, to route outgoing IM messages through a proxy server, you need to enter its IP address in the HTTP Proxy Server area of the tab. Select the Use A Proxy Server For Outbound Requests check box, and specify the IP address of the proxy server and an open port number (usually port 80, since this is going over HTTP).

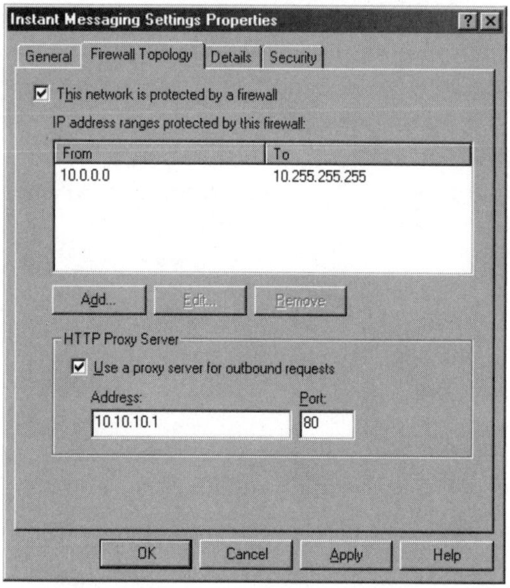

Figure 19-6. *Firewall Topology tab of the Instant Message Settings property sheet.*

Installing the Instant Messaging Service

As an overview, here are the steps for setting up Instant Messaging. The sections that follow cover each of these steps in detail:

1. Create at least one home server.

2. If you are creating more than one home server, you must also create at least one IM routing server.

3. If you're going to use HTTP Digest authentication, set the appropriate password policy on the domain controller.

4. Give users access to the service.

5. Distribute the instant messaging client to your users.

Creating a Home Server

To create a home server, in the Exchange System snap-in, navigate to the server you want to establish as a home server, and right-click the RVP container, found under the Protocols container. Point to New, and then choose Instant Messaging Virtual Server. The New Instant Messaging Virtual Server Wizard starts.

The wizard is short, consisting of only six screens. The first screen is a welcome screen, and the second asks you to enter the display name of the new server (Figure 19-7). The name you assign should identify whether the server is a home server or a routing server. The third screen asks which Web site you want to associate with this IM server. When Instant Messaging is installed, it will create a virtual directory under the Web site that you have chosen and will name it Instmsg. It is through this virtual directory that messages will be routed.

> **Note**   The choice of which Web site to associate with an IM server is an important one. You must have one IIS Web site for each IM home server that you create. If you plan on installing multiple IM virtual servers on one machine, you must first create a new IIS Web site for each IM virtual server.

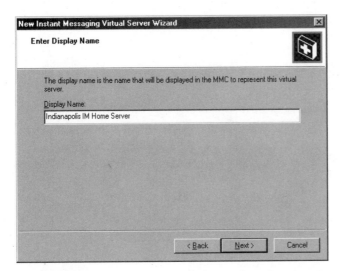

Figure 19-7. *Naming a new home server in the New Instant Messaging Virtual Server Wizard.*

The fourth screen asks you to indicate the domain name to which the server will respond. Even though it asks for the DNS domain name, you must enter only the server's host name, *without* a period—for example, "minneapolis" instead of "minneapolis." If you place a period in the name in this screen, Instant Messaging will try to use a proxy server, even if none exists.

The fifth screen asks whether you want to allow this server to host user accounts. If you do, select the check box; if you do not, clear the check box. When this check box is selected, you are indicating that this server should be an IM home server. When it is not selected, you are creating a routing server. The last screen is the Finish screen.

Creating an Instant Message Routing Server

Remember, before you can create the IM routing server, you'll need an IIS Web site to host it. You can set one up as a virtual directory under the IIS default Web site.

To create the IM routing server, start the New Instant Messaging Virtual Server Wizard, as described in the previous section, and step through its screens. The DNS domain name you specify on the fourth screen will identify the IM router on the network. The form of the name should be *server_name.domain_name*.com. Placing periods in this name will not point the users to a proxy server because the virtual server is not hosting user accounts. Figure 19-8 shows the property sheet for the Tucson IM routing server.

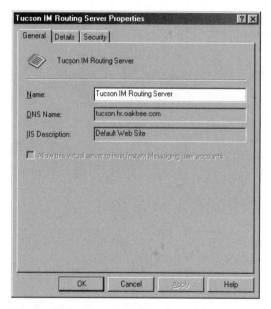

Figure 19-8. *Property sheet for an IM routing server.*

Accept the defaults in the wizard, and then check your DNS to ensure that you have the necessary DNS resource records for the IM router. Each router must have an A record in DNS. For information on how to configure DNS for Instant Messaging, refer to the section "Configuring DNS for Instant Messaging," earlier in this chapter.

Setting a Password Policy

By default, Instant Messaging uses Windows Integrated Authentication (WIA). Incorporating WIA into your IM deployment will allow users to use Instant Messaging without entering an additional user name and password.

However, if you need to authenticate through a proxy server or if you're running an instant messaging client on a different operating system, such as UNIX, you'll want to use the Digest authentication method instead. When using this method, IM must be able to retrieve unencrypted user passwords from Active Directory. Hence, you'll need to change the password policy on the domain controller to store the passwords in a reversible, encrypted format. To change the password policy, follow these steps:

1. Start Active Directory Users and Computers.
2. Right-click the domain organizational unit, and then choose Properties.
3. On the Group Policy tab, select Default Domain Policy, and then click Edit.
4. Open Computer Configuration.
5. Expand Windows Settings, then Security Settings, and then Account Policies.
6. Select Password Policy.
7. Double-click Store Password Using Reversible Encryption For All Users In The Domain.
8. Select the Define This Policy Setting check box and the Enable radio button, and then click OK.

Giving Users Access to Instant Messaging

To give a user access to Instant Messaging, you assign the user to an IM home server. You make this assignment on the property sheet for the user's account in the Active Directory Users and Computers snap-in, as follows.

Open the organizational unit in which the user account resides, right-click the user's account, and choose Exchange Tasks from the shortcut menu. The Exchange Task Wizard starts. On the second screen of the wizard (Figure 19-9), select Enable Instant Messaging and click Next. On the next screen, you're asked to select an IM home server as well as the domain name to be used if the DNS SRV lookup fails. The wizard then associates the user account with the selected home server; you'll see the results on the Completing The Exchange Task Wizard screen (Figure 19-10). You will also see the user's logon and private and public URLs.

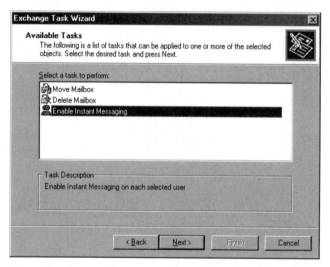

Figure 19-9. *Enabling Instant Messaging for a user account.*

Note   If you need to enable IM on multiple user accounts, you can select them in Active Directory Users and Computers and then perform this operation only once. Hold down the Ctrl key and click on the users you want to configure. Then right-click the group and proceed with the Exchange Tasks Wizard. To enable IM for all of your user accounts at one time, select the entire list by highlighting the first user account, and then holding down the Shift key and clicking the last user in your list. Once the users are selected, you can enable IM for all of them with the Exchange Tasks Wizard.

Figure 19-10. *Completing The Exchange Task Wizard screen.*

Distributing the Instant Messaging Client Software to Your Users

To distribute MSN Messenger (the instant messaging client software that ships with Exchange 2000 Server) to your users, you must copy Mmssetup.exe from the \Instmsg\I386\Client\Usa directory on the Exchange 2000 Server CD-ROM to a distribution point on your network (assuming that you want the U.S. version). It then must be installed on your users' workstations, like any other application. The installation is easy, and the space used is minimal.

More Info For information on how to deploy software to multiple users' workstations without having to touch each workstation, consult the *Microsoft Systems Management Server Resource Guide* (Microsoft Press, 1999) or the *Microsoft Windows 2000 Server Resource Kit* (Microsoft Press, 2000).

Managing IM Users

Once you have installed and configured Instant Messaging, management of individual users is simple. This section discusses how to disable a user's access to IM and change a user's home server. It also discusses finding an IM user on the network and controlling external access to IM users.

Reconfiguring Instant Messaging for an Individual Account

There may be times when you want to disable a user's access to the IM service. You can do so with the Exchange Task Wizard for the user's account, just as you did to enable Instant Messaging for the user. In this case, however, you choose Disable Instant Messaging (Figure 19-11), which disassociates the user's account from the IM home server.

On the same screen, you can also associate the user's account with a different IM home server by selecting Change Instant Messaging Home Server and then stepping through the remaining screens. If you change the home server for a user, the user will need to exit the instant messaging client software and then reconnect to establish a new connection to the new home server. In addition, the user may experience problems receiving instant messages until this new information is replicated to all of the domain controllers in Active Directory.

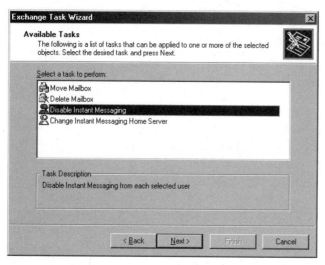

Figure 19-11. *Disabling Instant Messaging for a user's account.*

Another way to disable a user's access to IM is on the Exchange Features tab of the user's property sheet. Simply click the Disable button, and you'll see the status change from Enabled to Disabled.

Finding IM Users on the Network

Sometimes, you'll need to find an IM user on your network. To do this, you'll need to perform an advanced search of Active Directory, since the IM information is held as a set of attributes to the user's account. To use the advanced find feature, start Active Directory Users and Computers and, from the Action menu, choose Find Users, Contacts And Groups (Figure 19-12). Click the Field down arrow and choose User to see a list of all of the attribute fields that can be queried for the user object. Choose the Instant Messaging attribute you want to query, and then wait for the results to be returned. This list could potentially be long, so be patient as it is built by the LDAP services.

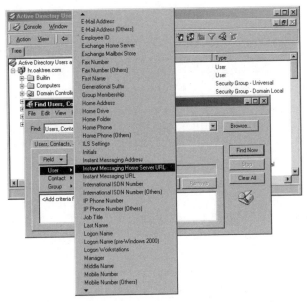

Figure 19-12. *Advanced find feature in Active Directory Users and Computers.*

Controlling External Access to Users

In many environments, privacy for IM users is a concern. You may find that you want to control which groups of users and servers can access an IM user's presence information and send messages to that user. To control access by other users, display the Exchange Features tab of the user's property sheet, select Instant Messaging, and click Properties. Display the Privacy tab of the Instant Messaging property sheet to set privacy options for the user's account (Figure 19-13).

Figure 19-13. *Privacy tab for an IM user.*

This tab allows you to place limitations on IM services for the user account by starting either "wide open" or "totally closed," so to speak. For instance, when the Allow Access Only From These Servers And Users option is selected, you can click Add to add a user or group account to the list. This means that no one, except those who are listed in this box, can obtain presence information and send IM messages to this account. Enter the name of the group or user in the Add User Or Computer box, and then click OK. Repeat this step for each user or group you want to add to the list.

On the other hand, if you want to restrict only a few users from obtaining presence information and instant messaging privileges for this user's account, select the Allow Access By All Servers And Users Except option, and those users who you place in the list will be the only ones restricted for this user account.

Managing IM Servers

There will be times when you want to perform administrative functions on your IM servers, such as moving your IM data files to another location on your server. This section describes how to perform this and other IM server functions, including how to remove an IM server, how to take a server off line, and how to limit user connections to an IM server.

Removing an IM Server

Generally, you'll remove Instant Messaging from a server if you are consolidating IM users on another server or if you want to move IM services to a larger, faster, more robust server. Removing an IM server can be done in one of two ways:

you can remove the IM virtual server or you can remove the IM service entirely. If you might want to install another IM virtual server at some point, you should just remove the IM virtual server. If you know that this server will not be used for Instant Messaging in the future, you should remove the IM service entirely.

To remove the IM virtual server, start the Exchange System snap-in, right-click the IM virtual server and choose Delete. You'll be given a choice as to where the IM users hosted by this server should be moved (Figure 19-14).

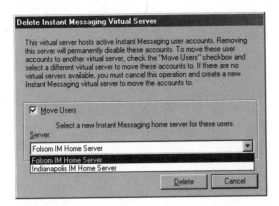

Figure 19-14. *Removing an IM virtual server.*

Notice that the Move Users check box is selected by default. If the server you are deleting is an IM routing server that is not hosting IM user accounts, you can clear this check box and then click Delete.

To remove IM services altogether, you use the Add/Remove Programs tool from within Control Panel. Select Microsoft Exchange 2000 and click the Change/Remove button. The Exchange 2000 Installation Wizard starts. On the Component Selection screen, select Remove Microsoft Exchange Instant Messaging Service. Then step through the rest of the Installation Wizard as usual.

Taking an IM Server Off Line

To take an IM server off line, you must stop the corresponding IIS virtual server. You do this in the Internet Information Services snap-in: simply right-click the virtual IIS site, and then choose Stop. All IM services on the Web site will stop, and users will see messaging halt abruptly.

To place the IM server back online after maintenance is completed, start the IIS virtual server again.

Limiting User Connections and Logging User Activity

If your IM server is becoming saturated with its message load, you can limit the number of users who can connect to the IM server simultaneously for services. In the Internet Information Services snap-in, display the Web Site tab of the Web site's property sheet (Figure 19-15). In the Connections area, click Limited To, enter the maximum number of simultaneous connections, and then click OK.

On the same tab, you can also enable logging to keep track of user activity on an IM server. The default format for the log files is the W3C Extended Log File format. For more information on how logging works and the different formats available, see Chapter 17.

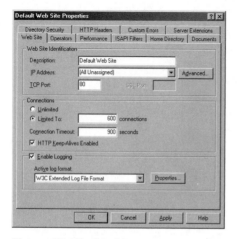

Figure 19-15. *Limiting user connections and enabling logging.*

Moving Data Files

You can designate a new location for the IM data and log files on the property sheet for the RVP Instant Messaging protocol folder (Figure 19-16). Changing the location here does not automatically move the existing databases and log files. Instead, Instant Messaging creates new databases and files in the new location after you stop and restart the service. To continue using the same databases and transaction logs, you'll need to manually copy the files to the new directory and then restart the virtual Web site in IIS.

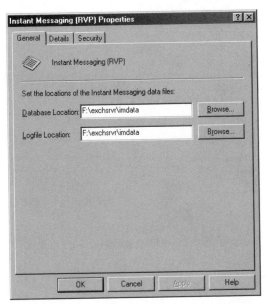

Figure 19-16. *Designating a new location for the IM database and log files.*

Managing the IM Client

For the purpose of this discussion, we will focus on the MSN Messenger client software. Although there are other clients that can work with Instant Messaging, the MSN Messenger client is included free on the Exchange 2000 Server CD-ROM. You don't need client access licenses or installation licenses to use this product.

Installing the client is quick and straightforward. Once you've installed it, you can configure several settings. You can see most of these configuration options by choosing Options from the Tools menu.

General Tab

On the General tab (Figure 19-17), you'll find three basic areas: General, Notifications, and My Display Name. The settings in the General area are self-explanatory. The Notifications area allows users to customize the sounds and visual prompts that notify the user when an instant message arrives or a contact logs on. The My Display Name area allows a user to change his or her display name for privacy on the Internet or when messaging in another domain.

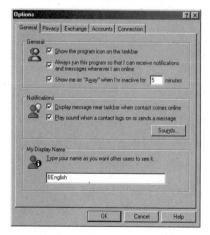

Figure 19-17. *General tab for the Options dialog box of the MSN Messenger client.*

Privacy Tab

The Privacy tab (Figure 19-18) is an important one. You should be aware, however, that the list of users you see here simply shows the results of actions taken in other areas—both in Active Directory and in the MSN Messenger client. Recall that you use the property sheet for a user's account in Active Directory to specify which other users and groups can send messages to that user or can see the user's presence information. Those settings are displayed here.

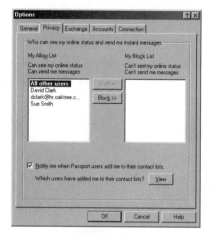

Figure 19-18. *Privacy tab for the Options dialog box of the MSN Messenger client.*

This tab can be a bit confusing, because you might find yourself looking for functionality that isn't there. For instance, you might want to select names and enter them into one of the lists, but it really doesn't work that way. This screen just shows you the *results* of actions you've taken in Active Directory and other parts of the client.

You'll also find that you cannot restrict who can subscribe to the user's presence information on this tab. (This can be done in Active Directory for domain user accounts.) Instead, you can block only users who have already subscribed. To do so, you first need to subscribe to that user. Then right-click the user name in your subscription list and choose Block from the shortcut menu (Figure 19-19).

The reason there is no list of names to select from is that Instant Messaging doesn't work with a common set of user accounts generated by Active Directory. Given its ability to work over the Internet in a federated fashion, the architecture allows anyone to subscribe to anyone. Only after you learn of a user's subscription to your presence information can you block that user from subscribing to your presence information and from sending you messages. Blocking also prevents the local user from sending instant messages to the blocked user or from obtaining subscription information about that user.

Figure 19-19. *Blocking a user in the MSN Messenger client.*

> **Note** Blocking a user applies only to Instant Messaging. It does not apply to e-mail or Chat Service.

The user who is blocked is not notified of this fact. The blocking user will simply disappear from the blocked user's subscription list. If the blocked user attempts to resubscribe to the blocking user, the Add User Wizard allows the blocking user to be added, but the blocking function immediately removes the blocking user again. In other words, the wizard will appear to have been successful, but the subscription will not take effect.

Exchange Tab

On the Exchange tab (Figure 19-20), you can configure the IM user logon name as well as select the service to which the MSN Messenger client will connect. The MSN Messenger Service option requires Internet access. If you want to enable Instant Messaging over the Internet without involving the MSN network, select the Microsoft Exchange Instant Messaging option, and the MSN Messenger client will first attempt to log on with the local home server. Federated IM services will still be available over the Internet.

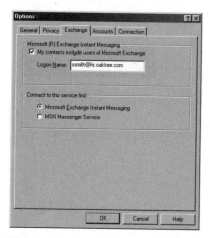

Figure 19-20. *Exchange tab for the Options dialog box of the MSN Messenger client.*

Accounts Tab

MSN Messenger Service account information is configured on the Accounts tab. If your users are connecting to the MSN Messenger Service, you'll need to configure this tab accordingly. If not, you can ignore it.

Connection Tab

The Connection tab allows you to configure proxy services for those who are dialing in. Remember that, by default, the instant messaging client will use Internet Explorer's profile when logging on. For those who dial in, it might be necessary to configure proxy services. The fields on this tab are self-explanatory and should be configured as needed.

Sending and Receiving Instant Messages

Users can send and receive instant messages in the MSN Messenger client. They send a message by right-clicking the name of the user to whom the message should be sent and choosing Send An Instant Message. The dialog box in Figure 19-21 pops up, and the user enters the message in the lower box and clicks Send to send the message.

Figure 19-21. *Sending an instant message.*

At the receiving end, the user simply needs to enter a reply and click Send (Figure 19-22). The MSN Messenger client retains the conversation for as long as the Instant Message dialog box is open. Once it is closed, the messages are gone forever because they are held only in RAM, never on disk or in a database on the Exchange 2000 server.

Figure 19-22. *Replying to an instant message.*

Some users may want to save or print an Instant Messaging conversation for future reference. To do so, they must select and copy the conversation and then paste it into a different program, such as Notepad. The Instant Message dialog box does not have print or save capability. Users can scroll back to earlier messages that they want to copy.

Finally, the Instant Message dialog box contains a one-to-one conversation. If one user is having three simultaneous conversations with three co-workers, that user will have three separate Instant Message dialog boxes open on the desktop and will need to switch back and forth between them to engage in those conversations. There is no way to combine multiple conversations into a single interface at this time.

Troubleshooting Instant Messaging

Although we can't cover every possible problem that may occur with Instant Messaging in this chapter, several common scenarios are worth discussing here. We also cover how to use the logs and Network Monitor to troubleshoot a problem.

User's Can't Log On

Client logon is one of the main areas that might require troubleshooting. It will also be one of your most frustrating problems. Here are some things to check as you troubleshoot client logon problems.

First, since the user's IM profile is derived from the user's Internet Explorer profile, be sure that the FQDN of the routing and home servers as well as the Instant Messaging domain name are excluded in Internet Explorer. To accomplish this, navigate to the Connections tab of the property sheet for Internet Explorer, click the LAN Settings button, and then click the Advanced button (Figure 19-23). Enter the FQDN of the routing and home servers and the Instant Messaging domain name. If these addresses are not excluded and IE is configured to use a proxy server, the instant messaging client will be sending its logon request to the proxy server.

More Info   Exclusions can be set for all users by configuring a group policy. For more information on how to create and configure group policies, see the *Microsoft Windows 2000 Server Administrator's Companion*, by Charlie Russel and Sharon Crawford (Microsoft Press, 2000).

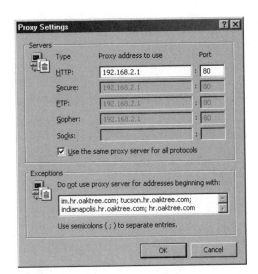

Figure 19-23. *Proxy settings for Internet Explorer, showing excluded addresses.*

Second, be sure that, if you have a routing server, (1) there is a SRV resource record in DNS for this server, (2) the client's logon is to the DNS domain that the routing server resides in, and (3) if you are using MSN Messenger, the version is 2.1 or later. Earlier versions of MSN Messenger will not work with Exchange 2000 Instant Messaging.

Finally, be sure that the client has IP connectivity and name resolution. You should be able to Ping the routing server, the home server, and the DNS server. In addition, you should be able to Ping the host name of each of these servers (Figure 19-24) and receive back its FQDN along with its IP address. If you receive back *only* the host name and IP address, something is wrong with DNS resolution. Troubleshoot as necessary.

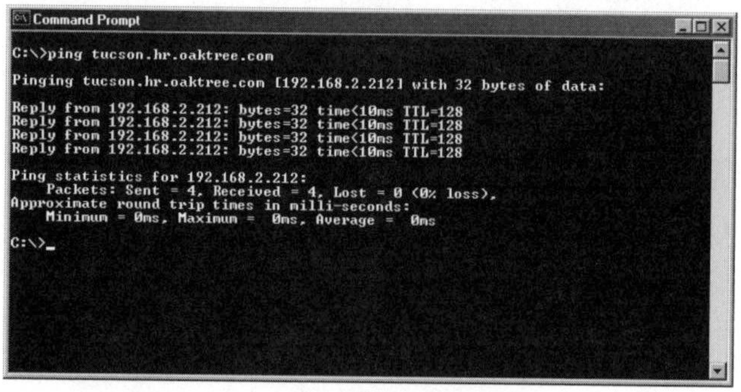

Figure 19-24. *Pinging to check for FQDNs.*

At this point, you might be wanting to reach through the pages of this book and let us know that your IM users still can't log on. If that's the case, consider the following points.

First, if you have recently deleted and then re-created your routing virtual server, you need to make sure that you allow Active Directory to replicate these changes. If you can't wait for that to happen, you can manually force replication by using Active Directory Sites and Services. Navigate to the connection object under the server object that needs to be updated, right-click the object, and choose Replicate Now. Most likely, you will need to repeat this step for each server in your domain. Also—and this must be done *before* you create the new routing server— you must delete the Instmsg virtual directory in the associated Web site that was created when you created the last routing server. When you create the new routing server, it will create a new Instmsg virtual directory that will cooperate with your new virtual server. And remember, since IM does most of its lookups to the Global Catalog (GC) server, you will need to be patient and wait for the GC to update before attempting to log on with the messenger client.

Second, do not use alias names in DNS for your routing server. If your routing server's host name is something other than IM, either use the host name for that server (we used Tucson in our examples) or else add a second A record that resolves the IM host name to the IP address of the server that will host the routing virtual server. But do not attempt to alias the host name of IM to your server's host name and then have the routing virtual server point to the IM host name.

Third, when you delete and then re-create a routing virtual server, the new information is not automatically updated in the user's properties. You will need to disable and then reenable IM in your users' accounts in order for them to receive the new routing server information. Again, since the messaging client does most of its lookups in the GC, you'll need to be patient to allow the GC to update as well.

Fourth, be sure your IM clients are using a password for their logons. The IM service will not accept a client logon request that contains a blanket password.

Best practice is to follow these steps:

- Create the virtual server or servers that you think you need.
- Install the instant messaging client on one machine.
- Test with that user to make sure she or he can log on.
- Deploy IM to a larger group of 10 or 15 and make sure it is working before you roll it out to your entire company.

The overall point here is this: any change you make in one of your virtual servers affects the virtual directory entries in IIS, the users' properties, the GC servers, Active Directory, and DNS. Make sure you have accounted for all of the "domino effects" that a change to a virtual server will cause.

Instant Messaging Client Suddenly Disappears

If the instant messaging client disappears suddenly from users' screens, it means either that the IM home server's Web site has stopped or that the World Wide Web Publishing Service has stopped. Once the service or the Web site is restarted, users may need to log on again to establish a new connection to IM on the IM server.

Users Can Send Messages to the Internet but Cannot Receive Messages From the Internet

You might find that your users are able to send instant messages to one another and to users on the Internet but that they cannot receive messages from the Internet. In addition, if they log off and immediately try to log back on, they receive the error message shown in Figure 19-25. This problem can mean that the Web site associated with the routing server has been stopped or that the World Wide Web Publishing Service on the routings server has been stopped. Restarting the service should restore full communications.

Figure 19-25. *Logon failure message.*

Using the IIS Logs and Network Monitor For Troubleshooting

One of the best ways to troubleshoot an IM issue is to look at the logs that IIS generates. You can use Network Monitor along with the IIS logs to troubleshoot a logon problem. To see the location of the log files, go to the Web Site tab of the property sheet for the IM Web site (Figure 19-26), and click the Properties button within the Enable Logging area to display the logging properties (Figure 19-27).

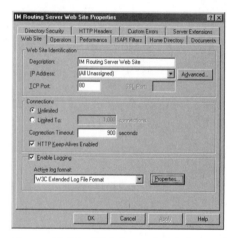

Figure 19-26. *Web Site tab for the IM Web site.*

These log files are very helpful in determining the nature of an error and how to troubleshoot the problem. (Bear in mind that the timestamp in these files is always Greenwich mean time.) For instance, Figure 19-28 shows part of a log file from a test network. It indicates that users are getting some (404) responses to their SUBSCRIBE requests, meaning that the server is not being found. A corresponding packet trace in Network Monitor shows the same error message (Figure 19-29).

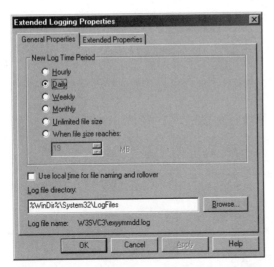

Figure 19-27. *Logging properties, showing log file location.*

Figure 19-28. *IIS log containing 404 errors.*

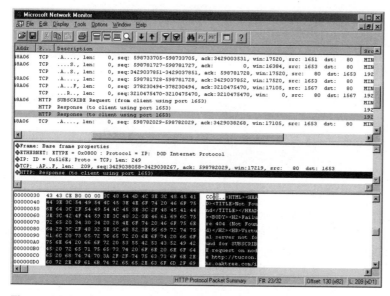

Figure 19-29. *Trace log showing 404 error message.*

This error is due to an incorrect SRV record in DNS and the incorrect placement of a host header name in the default Web site for the routing server, Tucson. Or it is due to incorrect information being returned from one or more Global Catalog servers that have not been fully updated with new IM virtual server information. At the client end, the logon screen was returned almost instantaneously, indicating that the client's first step—to contact DNS and get a resolution on the SRV record—did not work.

In many cases, you can use the IIS logs in conjunction with packet traces in Network Monitor to quickly diagnose a problem. Once you know what the HTTP error is, you can reference the error code and then begin the process of isolating the incorrect configuration and making the necessary changes.

More Info For a good list of the HTTP error codes, along with descriptions, please consult Dilip Naik's book *Internet Standards and Protocols* (Microsoft Press, 1998).

Summary

In this chapter and the previous one, you have learned about Chat Service and Instant Messaging. You have seen how to install and configure these services to meet your organization's needs. This type of communication is the wave of the future, and users will be asking for it more and more.

In the next chapter, we turn our attention away from the real-time collaboration technologies to consider the topic of how to install and manage Exchange 2000 Server on a cluster server

Chapter 20
Managing Exchange 2000 Server in a Cluster Environment

E-mail is a mission-critical application that is used by employees every day. Customers are interacting with your company more and more by e-mail. Employees expect to log on at all hours of the day to send and answer e-mail. And with the increase in flextime and telecommuting, e-mail has become the central way in which many employees communicate. If you need to be reminded about the importance of e-mail, just ask yourself what happened the last time that your e-mail system went down. It wasn't pretty, was it?

If all of this rings true for you, then you should read this chapter. If you pass this chapter by because you don't have a server cluster in your environment, you might very well miss a tremendous technology that could make your e-mail system much more reliable and stable. As you'll see, Microsoft Exchange 2000 Server extends clustering to combine multiple *virtual* servers into a single solution.

We think that clustering will be more strongly considered as an important network function once IT professionals understand the new features and enhancements to traditional clustering technologies. This chapter will help you understand those features. It also describes how to install and work with Exchange 2000 Server in a cluster environment.

Introduction to Windows Clustering

A server cluster is a group of independent servers running Cluster service and working together as a single unit. Clusters provide high availability, scalability, and manageability for resources and applications by grouping multiple Microsoft Windows 2000 Advanced servers or Microsoft Windows 2000 Datacenter servers into a single administrative unit.

Note This chapter provides only an overview of the Cluster service in Windows 2000 Advanced Server, concentrating on how Exchange 2000 Server leverages this service. For a more complete discussion of clustering, please consult the *Microsoft Windows 2000 Server Resource Kit* (Microsoft Press, 2000).

Clustered servers share a common storage medium, such as an external drive bank of SCSI drives using a hardware-based RAID solution. Most often, information is written in cross-longitudinal fashion across the set of disks, with parity information, which is, essentially, an on-disk algorithmic backup of the data itself. This type of installation is called *RAID-5* and is very common in the networking world today.

Clustering provides high availability by allowing applications to run on any single server in the cluster. If the host server goes down, the applications are moved to another server in the cluster, where they can continue to run. This movement is, of course, transparent to the users. The users know only that they have connected to the server for e-mail. They do not know which server in the cluster they have connected to. The Cluster service directs their input and output to the correct server in the cluster.

Problems Solved by Clustering

Clustering avoids the problems that can arise due to a hardware failure, such as a blown CPU, bad memory, or the loss of an entire computer. It also allows services to remain alive for users when there is a planned outage, such as routine maintenance, a software or firmware upgrade, or a configuration change.

Clustering also monitors the health of the installed software applications. If it detects problems with a particular application, it may take actions such as attempting to restart the software or even moving the software focus to a different server in the cluster.

Problems Not Solved by Clustering

Clustering does not solve problems related to poor management, such as data not being backed up or poor-quality hardware used to implement RAID-5. Neither does it help in the event of a major disaster, such as when servers are physically destroyed. Because clustering in Windows 2000 depends on the Active Directory directory service and DNS, clustering also does not help if these technologies have been poorly implemented or are not available.

Clustering Terminology

Before we begin our discussion, it's important to understand some of the basic terminology. We'll define some terms in staccato fashion and then move on to other clustering topics.

- **Shared-nothing architecture** Also known as active/passive architecture, the shared-nothing architecture makes one of the physical nodes responsible for running an application while the other servers, or *nodes,* wait on the sidelines for the first physical server to fail so that they can leap into action and take over the application. Only one server works at any given time for an application. This architecture is why clustering has been viewed as such an expensive solution to implement, and it is the model used in Microsoft Windows NT Server 4.

- **Shared-everything architecture** Also known as active/active, the shared-everything architecture gives any physical server in the cluster access to all of the data and application code at any given time and can offer these services to the client as needed. In this scenario, hardware is better utilized; it is the architecture used by the older VAX/VMS servers.

- **High availability** The aim of high availability is to minimize downtime. Windows Clustering is a highly available solution, but it does not guarantee nonstop operation.

- **Fault tolerance** The aim of fault tolerance is to eliminate downtime. Windows Clustering is not fault tolerant. Instead, fault tolerance is usually provided at the hard disk and controller level.

- **Resource** A resource is an entity that provides a service, such as a disk or an IP address.

- **Group** A group is a combination of resources that are managed as a unit.

- **Dependency** A dependency is an alliance between two or more resources and is very common in Windows NT Server 4 and Windows 2000 Server.

- **Failover/failback** These terms refer to the process of moving a resource from one server to another. Failover happens when a problem occurs on the active server and services must be transferred to the passive server.

- **Quorum resource** The quorum resource stores the cluster management data and is usually held on a shared disk.

- **Heartbeat**   A heartbeat is a group of packets that are sent over a private IP network between nodes to detect the health of the other nodes, as well as the applications and services they manage within the cluster.

Advantages of Using Windows Clustering

Windows Clustering has several attractive benefits, including the following:

- **High availability**   With a server cluster, ownership of resources such as disks or IP addresses is automatically transferred from a failed server to the surviving server. The software is restarted on the surviving server, and users experience only a momentary pause in service.
- **Failback**   Windows Clustering automatically rebalances the workload when a failed server comes back on line.
- **Manageability**   You can use the Cluster Administrator (discussed later in this chapter) to manage a cluster as a single system and to manage applications as if they were running on a single server, even though they are running on separate servers.
- **Scalability**   Server clusters can grow to meet increasing demands. For instance, when the overall capacity of the servers in the cluster can no longer meet the demand placed on them by the users, you can add additional servers to the cluster without needing to re-create the cluster itself.

Exchange 2000 Clustering

The clustering solution in Exchange Server 5.5 is a shared-nothing solution that was not met with great enthusiasm in the marketplace because it is costly to implement and because it calls for the existence of one server that does little but wait for a failure on the active server.

Exchange 2000 Server leverages the active/active implementation of clustering, meaning that all of the hardware capacities of each server are exploited. With this implementation, two or more physical machines can be running Exchange services and offering these services on the network. Exchange 2000 Server supports as many nodes as your version of Windows 2000 supports. Windows 2000 Advanced Server supports two nodes. Windows 2000 Datacenter Server supports four nodes. As these numbers increase with future releases of Windows 2000, Exchange 2000 Server will support more nodes accordingly.

Note   Even in a clustered environment, not all components in Exchange 2000 Server are active/active. The Message Transfer Agent, public folder hierarchy, and Chat Service are active/passive, meaning that only one server in the cluster will offer these services to the network at any given time.

Exchange 2000 Server also supports *rolling upgrades,* which means that during an upgrade, the Exchange services are moved to the second node, which continues to offer the services to the network while the Exchange software is upgraded on the first node. When the upgrade is completed on the first node, services are moved back to it and the Exchange software is upgraded on the second node. This activity is all transparent to the user and is one of the ways in which Exchange 2000 Server's clustering capability achieves high availability.

Figure 20-1 shows an Exchange 2000 server cluster installed on two physical servers that share a common storage device. In the Disk Management folder in the Windows 2000 Computer Management snap-in, the external disks appear as ordinary disks on the server that has access to them. In this illustration, disks 1 and 2 are in the external drive bay. They are not mirrored, although in nearly all production environments, you will want to use some type of fault tolerance at the hardware level. Windows 2000 provides the Cluster service so that even though both machines are connected to the shared data, only one server can access that data at any given time.

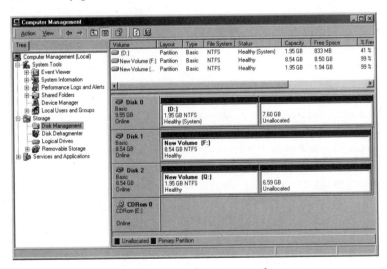

Figure 20-1. *Disk configuration for a server cluster.*

Windows 2000 requires that all data be on the shared drive so that when there is a failover, the surviving node can access that data. The binary files (Exchange system files) are still held on the individual servers in the cluster.

Installing the Windows 2000 Cluster Service

To install Exchange 2000 Server in a cluster environment, you need to be running either Windows 2000 Advanced Server or Windows 2000 Datacenter Server. You must install the Cluster service on each node and then install Exchange 2000 Server. This section gives an overview of the installation process and describes how to prepare for it. Later sections discuss how to perform the actual installation.

Note   We did not run a second network card in the servers for this test environment, but we strongly recommend that you do so. Connect these second cards to a private network that is physically separate from your corporate backbone. In the remainder of this chapter, you will see a number of screen shots from our test environment, which included two servers with Intel Pentium III/500 processors, 256 MB of RAM, 10.1-GB hard drives, and an Adaptec 29160 SCSI card in each server. Our external storage device was a Kingston 2-drive bay with 9.1 GB IBM SCSI-II hard drives. We also had one 3COM 3C905-TX 10/100 network card in each Server. Our software consisted of Windows 2000 Advanced Server and Exchange 2000 Server Release Candidate 2.

More Info   You must install Windows 2000 on two separate physical servers. If you need more information on how to do this, see the *Microsoft Windows 2000 Server Administrator's Companion* by Charlie Russel and Sharon Crawford (Microsoft Press, 2000).

Once you have the appropriate version of Windows 2000 running on both servers, you'll need to set up networking services. The clustered servers require at least two network cards each, one connected to the public network and another connected to a private network consisting only of the clustered servers. This private network is for cluster communications only. Data transfer should be done over the public network.

The Windows 2000 Cluster service recognizes only one network interface per subnet, so be sure to use a separate, private IP addressing scheme for the private network. Also, it is recommended that all nodes in a server cluster use static

IP addresses. If you must use dynamically assigned IP addresses from a Dynamic Host Configuration Protocol (DHCP) server, be sure to lengthen the lease time so the server cluster can continue to operate if the DHCP server becomes unavailable.

> **Note**   Even though it is possible to bind two different IP addresses to the same physical card and use one set as a virtual private network, Microsoft does not recommend this implementation and will not support installations that use only one network card. In addition, it is recommended that the cluster have multiple paths for the private network, to avoid a single point of failure for the cluster heartbeat. You can achieve this by either installing three network cards per server and configuring one card for public traffic and the other two cards for private traffic, such that each private card has a separate cabled backbone to the other node. However, the more common solution is to install two network cards per server and configure one card for private, heartbeat communications and the other card for both public and private communications (mixed).

All nodes in the cluster must be members of the same domain and must be able to access both a Windows 2000 domain controller and a DNS server. The servers' configurations should also be the same—for instance, both servers should either be domain controllers or member servers.

The Cluster service requires a domain user account under which the Cluster service will run. You must create this account before installing the Cluster service because you're prompted to enter the user name and password during the setup process. This account should not be one used by a real person in the domain; for example, it should not be the administrator account.

You'll also need to decide which disk will be your quorum disk before starting the installation. The quorum disk is used to store cluster configuration database checkpoints and log files that help manage the cluster. This database is used to keep track of all of the information regarding the cluster configuration.

> **Tip**   If you are upgrading a server cluster from Windows NT Server 4 Cluster Services, you might find that after the upgrade, no additional entries are being added to the cluster log that was used before the upgrade. This situation occurs because Windows 2000 overwrites the default path for the cluster log in the Cluster.log file, using a default path of %windir%\Cluster\Cluster.log rather than the path that existed in the Windows NT 4 cluster installation. For a resolution of this problem, see Microsoft TechNet article Q246178.

Assigning drive letters to the shared storage device is no small consideration. Each partition must have its own drive letter. Although Windows 2000 allows *mount points,* in which you can mount a file system to an existing directory without assigning it a drive letter, Windows 2000 does not support mount points in clusters. The external storage device must be formatted with the Cluster service and must have a drive letter assigned to it.

Installing the First Node in the Cluster

To install the Windows 2000 Cluster service, you must use the Add/Remove Programs tool in Control Panel. Choose Components, and then select Cluster Service (Figure 20-2). You'll need the Windows 2000 source files handy so that the installation program can copy them to the server's hard disk.

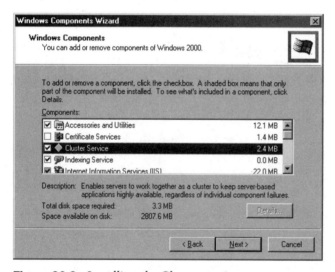

Figure 20-2. *Installing the Cluster service.*

Note If you have never installed the Cluster service before, be sure to read the section on clustering in the *Microsoft Windows 2000 Server Resource Kit* before attempting this installation. Also be sure to have an experienced person either help you with it or be available for questions. A poor Windows 2000 cluster implementation will lead to intermittent problems with the Exchange 2000 installation and management later on.

After the files are copied, the Cluster Service Configuration Wizard starts. The first screen is a welcome screen that has no configuration options. The second screen, shown in Figure 20-3, states that Microsoft won't support hardware configurations that are not on the Hardware Compatibility List and even gives you a link to the list. You must click I Understand before the Next button becomes active.

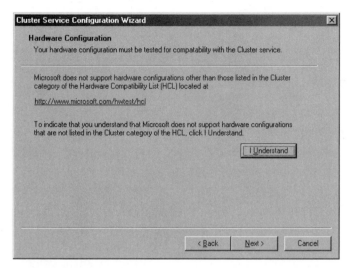

Figure 20-3. *Hardware Configuration screen of the Cluster Service Configuration Wizard.*

The third screen asks whether you are creating a new cluster or joining an existing cluster. Select the appropriate button and click Next. The fourth screen asks you to name the cluster (Figure 20-4). Specify a name of up to 15 characters.

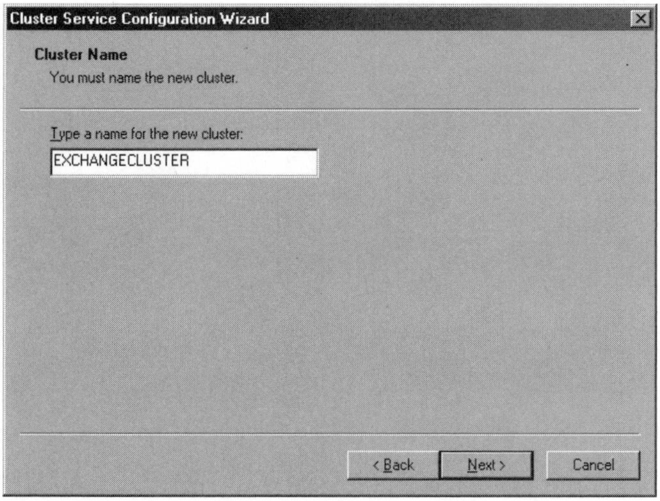

Figure 20-4. *Naming the cluster.*

You're then asked to enter the name and password of the cluster account you created in Active Directory. If the account is not a member of the administrators group, you'll be prompted with a message box (Figure 20-5) informing you of this and asking if you want to give this account administrator privileges. If you click No, you'll be returned to the user name and password screen to enter a different user name and password.

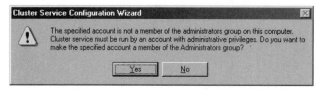

Figure 20-5. *Message regarding administrator privileges.*

If you click Yes, you're presented with the Add Or Remove Managed Disks screen (Figure 20-6), which allows you to select the disks in the external silo that you want to have this server cluster manage. A RAID-5 configuration will appear as a single drive, so you'll need to select the entire disk set. If you are running an external set of drives without fault tolerance, then you can select any combination of drives to be managed by the cluster group. In most cases, you will choose all of the disks.

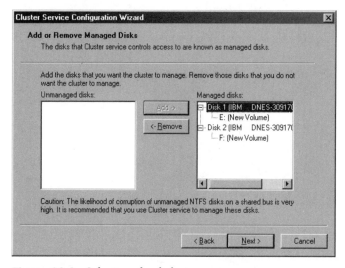

Figure 20-6. *Selecting the disks to manage.*

Next you're asked to designate a partition as the quorum disk (Figure 20-7). Even though the wizard asks you to select either a disk or a partition, you're really selecting just a partition. You'll select it by its drive letter, which means that the partition needs to have been set up in advance and formatted with NTFS. If you are unsure as to which partition you would like to designate at this point, use the Computer Management snap-in to view the disk information. You do not need to stop the wizard to do this.

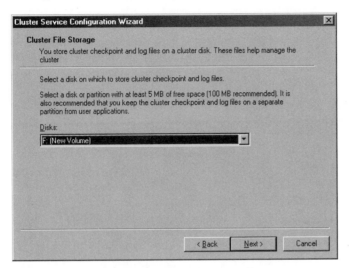

Figure 20-7. *Specifying a quorum disk.*

Note   If you have two logical drives on the same physical disk, the Cluster service will see them as a single resource. In addition, the first partition of the first disk is selected as the quorum resource by default.

The next screen in the wizard contains instructions but no configurable settings. It reminds you that you need a private network for the heartbeat. After reading the text, click Next.

In the Network Connections screen (Figure 20-8), you tell the Cluster service which network card and IP address combination to use for the public network. You'll do the same for the private network on the next screen. Both screens are identical. Notice that you must choose based on the IP address, as there is no way to determine, from this screen, what media access control (MAC) address is burned into either card. If you are using identical cards in the server, you need to have already assigned them each an IP address, and you should select the card based on that.

Notice that you have the choice of using the same card for both public and private communications. If you choose this configuration, you will need only one IP address bound to the card, and this will be the address for both private and public communications. Note, however, that Microsoft does not support this configuration.

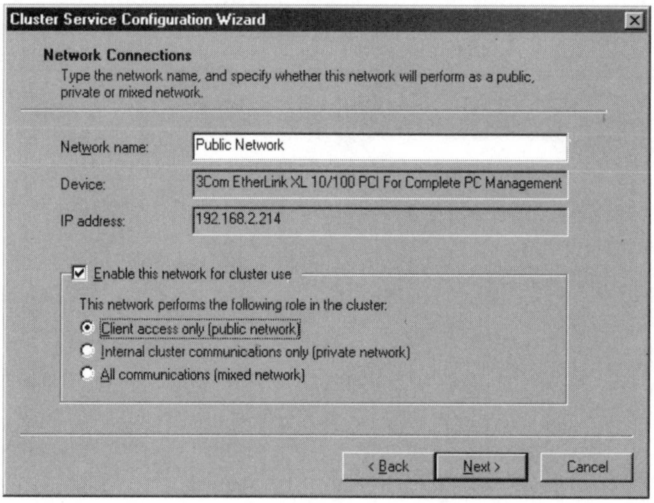

Figure 20-8. *Specifying the connection to the public network.*

After setting up the network card and IP address combinations, you'll need to assign an IP address to the cluster (Figure 20-9). In a two-node cluster, this means that you will likely be using a total of five IP addresses. Plan your IP topology accordingly.

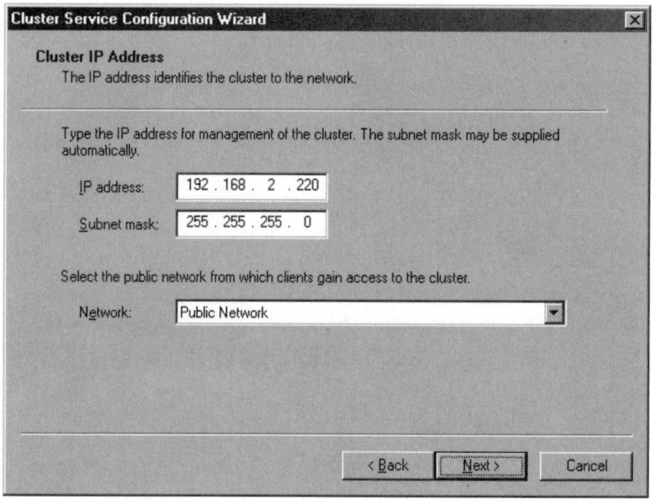

Figure 20-9. *Assigning the cluster an IP address.*

When you click Next in this screen, you are presented with the Finish screen. After you click Finish, the Registry is updated, the log files on the quorum resource are created, and the Cluster service is started on the first node. Then the Configuring Components status screen returns and the Cluster service finishes installing.

Installing the Second Node in the Cluster

Installing the second node is very similar to installing the first node, with a few minor changes. Obviously, you will choose to join a cluster rather than to create a new one in the Create Or Join A Cluster screen.

You'll then enter the name of the cluster and the password of the cluster user account on the Select An Account screen. The name of the cluster account is entered for you. If drive letter conflicts are found during the installation, you'll see a message instructing you to change the drive letters in the second node's configuration before moving ahead with the wizard. Once you've specified this information, the Finish screen appears and the Cluster service is installed on the second node.

Verifying Installation of the Cluster Service

You can verify that the server cluster is installed by opening Cluster Administrator and viewing the active resources, such as the cluster name, IP address, and disk resources (Figure 20-10). In addition, the cluster should have two nodes (ElkRiver0 and ElkRiver2 in the figure). These items show that the cluster exists and is in operation.

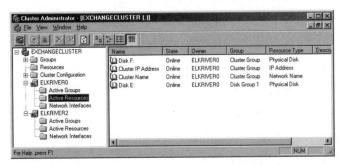

Figure 20-10. *Verifying active cluster resources in Cluster Administrator.*

Once the cluster is operational, you are ready to install cluster resources such as file shares and printer spoolers. You can also install cluster-aware services such as Internet Information Services (IIS), Microsoft Message Queuing, Distributed

Transaction Coordinator, DHCP, and WINS or cluster-aware applications such as Microsoft SQL Server or Exchange 2000 Server.

More Info For information on how to use Cluster Administrator to manage a cluster in Windows 2000, see the *Server Deployment Planning Guide* volume of the *Microsoft Windows 2000 Server Resource Kit* (Microsoft Press, 2000).

Understanding Windows 2000 Clustering Architecture

The Cluster service consists of several components that must cooperate in order for the cluster to function properly. This section briefly describes these components and how they relate to the overall Cluster service.

Node Manager

The Node Manager runs on each node in the cluster and maintains a local list of the nodes that belong to the cluster. It is the Node Manager that sends the heartbeat between the nodes, in the form of a User Datagram Protocol (UDP) packet sent every 1.2 seconds (Figure 20-11).

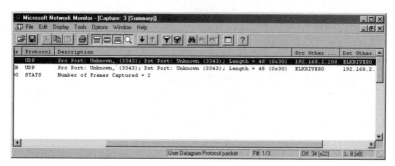

Figure 20-11. *Packet trace showing UDP heartbeat packets.*

Should one of the nodes fail, the other cluster node broadcasts a message to the entire cluster causing all members to verify their current membership list. This is called a *regroup event*. It is essential that all nodes in the cluster have exactly the same view of cluster membership for failover purposes. During the regroup event, the Cluster service prevents write operations to any common disk devices until the membership has stabilized.

Real World   Heartbeat and Failover Architecture

The heartbeat between the servers in the cluster is very important. Understanding how the heartbeat's architecture works will aid in your administration of a cluster environment. We give you here a very basic introduction to how the heartbeat works given two different scenarios. To learn more about the heartbeat and failover architecture, consult the *Microsoft Windows 2000 Server Resource Kit.*

Scenario #1: Public Network Passes the Heartbeat

If a heartbeat is not received within two heartbeat periods and the LAN connection is configured for client-to-cluster communication, the Cluster service initiates a test for each node to determine its ability to communicate with external hosts. By definition, this test includes computers that are on the same subnet as the cluster nodes and that have a connection to a cluster node. The Cluster service uses the PING command to perform this test.

For instance, if the nodes in the cluster are unable to communicate with one another, but one of the nodes is able to communicate with an external host, network connectivity is still good and that node will take ownership of the cluster resources that are depending on LAN activity.

Scenario #2: Private Network Passes the Heartbeat

If the heartbeat is passing over a private LAN, there are no external computers to which a PING command can be sent. In this situation, the Cluster service must use the quorum resource to arbitrate which node should remain up and running.

Configuration Database Manager

The Configuration Database Manager (CDM) maintains the cluster configuration database. This database contains vital information about the cluster itself, such as the cluster node membership and resource types, as well as information regarding the specific resources, such as IP addresses and physical disks. The CDM runs on each node in the cluster, and each CDM communicates with its peers on the other nodes in the cluster to maintain persistent and consistent information across the cluster.

Log Manager

The Log Manager regularly verifies each node's copy of the cluster database to ensure consistency. Working with the Checkpoint Manager, it ensures that the quorum resource's recovery log contains the most recent cluster database information.

Checkpoint Manager

Cluster-aware applications, such as Exchange 2000 Server, use the configuration database to store information. Applications that are not cluster aware can store information in the node registry. The Checkpoint Manager maintains the node registry information, called *checkpoint* information, in the quorum resource recovery log. It also ensures that the quorum resource recovery log contains the most recent cluster database information.

Resource Manager

The Resource Manager is responsible for stopping and starting resources, managing their dependencies, and initiating failover of resource groups. It uses information received from the Resource Monitor to make its decisions.

Failover Manager

The Failover Manager decides which nodes should own which resource group. Once a node is chosen to own a resource group, the individual resources in that group are turned over to the Resource Manager for administration. When resources fail in any given resource group, the Failover Managers on each node work together to make a smooth transition of ownership of resources to another node in the cluster.

The algorithm for triggering a failover is the same whether the failover is planned or unexpected. The only difference is that in a planned failover, the services on the first server are shut down gracefully, whereas they are forcefully shut down in an unexpected failover.

When a node returns to operation, the Failover Manager can decide to move resource groups back to the recovered node. This is called a *failback*. Resource groups must have a preferred owner defined in order to fail back to a recovered server. The Cluster service protects against failback during peak processing times. You can also schedule failback for certain times of the day.

Event Processor

The Event Processor manages communications between applications and the Cluster service. It is the initial entry point for joining a server to a cluster. When a server is coming back on line, it is the Event Processor that calls the Node Manager to begin the process of joining or forming a cluster.

Resource Monitor

The Resource Monitor is a passive communication layer that acts as an intermediary between the Cluster service and the resource DLLs. When the Cluster service makes a call for a resource, the Resource Monitor transfers that request to the appropriate resource DLL. The Resource Monitor runs as a separate process in case the Cluster service fails, so that it can take all of the resources off line and make them available for failover to another node in the cluster.

Installing Exchange 2000 Server in a Cluster Environment

Now that you have taken a brief look at the Windows 2000 Cluster service and have learned how to install and configure this service, you are ready to install Exchange 2000 Server into a cluster environment. We will assume at this point that you understand how to install Exchange 2000 Server on a stand-alone server and that you have read Chapter 7 of this book.

Once you have installed and configured Exchange 2000 Server to run in a cluster environment, you will have created an Exchange virtual server. It is the virtual server to which clients will connect, rather than a specific physical server. The Windows 2000 Cluster service requires that Exchange 2000 Server be completely installed on one node before you install it on the second node. Also, the account that installs the Exchange program must be a member of the Exchange Admins and Domain Admins security groups.

After launching the Setup program, you'll be asked to select the components you want to install. Bear in mind that neither Key Management Service nor the Instant Messaging Service can be installed into a cluster configuration. In addition, you must install Microsoft Exchange Messaging and Collaboration and Microsoft Exchange System Management Tools on a clustered server.

> **Note** Exchange Installable File System (ExIFS) must be assigned the same drive letter on both nodes in the cluster. Recall from Chapter 2 that ExIFS is assigned the M: drive by default. If you're using the letter M for another drive, Setup will select the next available letter for the ExIFS drive. It's best to reserve the letter M for ExIFS. If this isn't possible, make sure that the next drive letter that is available is the same on both nodes.

Once you've completed the component selection screen, Setup will proceed normally. Early in the file-copying phase, Setup will notice that this a clustered server and a message box will appear informing you that it will install a cluster-aware version (Figure 20-12). If you don't see this message, it means that Setup has not noticed that it is installing Exchange 2000 Server onto a clustered server, indicating to you that something is wrong in the cluster itself. There is no particular configuration or problem in Exchange 2000 Server that will cause this message box not to appear, but you'll need to troubleshoot your cluster configuration thoroughly before attempting to install Exchange 2000 Server again.

Figure 20-12. *Message indicating a cluster-aware installation.*

Managing Exchange 2000 Server in a Cluster Environment

Recall that Microsoft Exchange 2000 Server supports active/active clustering. With this configuration, multiple instances of Exchange 2000 Server can run simultaneously in a cluster. To run multiple instances, you need to create multiple resource groups.

A resource group is a container that holds an actual resource. Exchange 2000 Server is an application resource and considers each resource group to be a separate instance, called a virtual server. Thus, after you have installed Exchange 2000 Server into a cluster environment, you need to create a resource group. After that, you create the resources inside the group, such as the IP address and Exchange System Attendant resources.

Creating a Resource Group

When you install Windows Clustering, a default group, called Cluster Group, is created. Microsoft recommends that you not use the Cluster Group to house resources. Instead, you should create new groups for this purpose. To create a new group, within Cluster Administrator right-click the Groups container, point to New, and choose Group. The New Group Wizard starts.

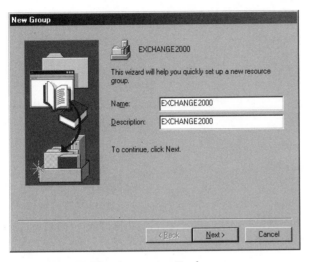

Figure 20-13. *Naming a new Exchange group.*

In the first screen, shown in Figure 20-13, you'll give the group a name and enter a description. In the second screen (Figure 20-14), you'll select the preferred owners of the group and list them in order of priority, top to bottom.

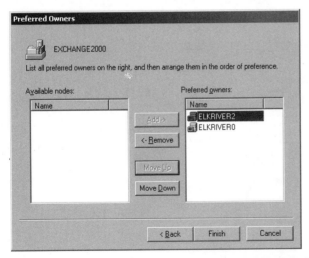

Figure 20-14. *Listing preferred owners for a new Exchange group.*

When you click Finish, the group is created but is off line. The icon for the group will show a yellow triangle with an exclamation point to indicate that it is off line. If you need additional groups to manage additional resources, repeat this process.

> **Note** You must have an independent drive and an IP address for each group that you create. The number of groups that can be created on a cluster is limited to the number of independent drives that are attached to the cluster and the number of storage groups that will exist in each group. Each node can support up to four storage groups, but it is recommended that you use only three and reserve the fourth storage group for recovery of the databases. No resource name in the cluster can be reused. In addition, only one public folder store is permitted in the cluster. Therefore, you must delete the public folder store in any new Exchange group that you create before bringing that group on line.

Assigning Cluster Resources

Each virtual server in an Exchange group must have at least four resources to function correctly: an IP address, a network name, a disk, and the Exchange System Attendant. Let's discuss how to assign these resources to the new cluster group.

Assigning the IP Address Resource To create the IP address resource, right-click the group that you just created, point to New, and choose Resource. The New Resource Wizard starts. First you'll be prompted to enter a name and description for the new resource (Figure 20-15). In the Resource Type drop-down list, select IP Address. If you plan to run the resource in a separate Resource Monitor, select the check box.

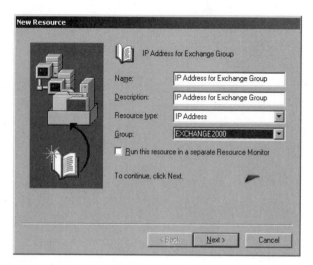

Figure 20-15. *Creating an IP address resource for a new Exchange group.*

> **Note**   The New Resource Wizard is context sensitive and will present the screens necessary to configure and install the type of resource you've chosen.

Next you'll need to specify the possible owners for this resource, as you did when you created the group. Then you'll be given the chance to create dependency resources that must be brought on line first before this resource can start. Generally, you'll want to verify that no resources appear on this screen. On the TCP/IP Address Parameters screen, shown in Figure 20-16, enter the unique static IP address and subnet mask for the virtual server. This will be the IP address for the Exchange virtual server; it does not refer to or bind to the physical card in the server.

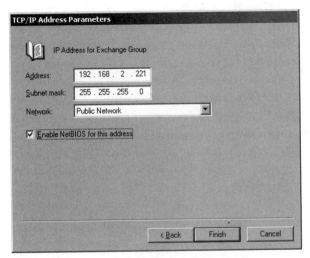

Figure 20-16. *Specifying an IP address for the new IP address resource.*

Assigning the Network Name Resource   To create the network name resource for the resource group, start the process of creating a new resource as you did for the IP address resource. After selecting the possible owners, in the Dependencies screen, under Available Resources, select the IP address resource you just created and then click Add (Figure 20-17). In the next screen, you'll need to enter the network name for the Exchange virtual server. This is the name that will uniquely identify this Exchange virtual server on the network. Click Finish when you're done.

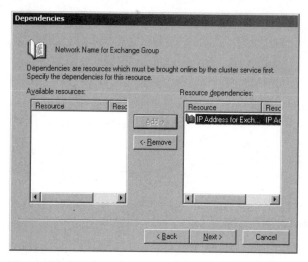

Figure 20-17. *Specifying IP address dependency for a new network name resource.*

Assigning a Disk Resource   To assign a disk resource to a resource group, start Cluster Administrator, click Groups, and select the container that contains the drive you want to move to the cluster group node. Drag the drive into the group container. To verify that the drive is in the container, click the group to see the drive in the details pane, as shown in Figure 20-18. This disk resource will hold the Exchange databases and transaction logs for the virtual server, which you will create as part of this group. You cannot assign a single physical disk or disk set (such as RAID-5) to more than one resource group.

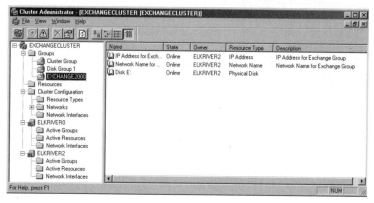

Figure 20-18. *Drive resource in the details pane in Cluster Administrator.*

Real World   **Resource Dependencies When Running Exchange 2000 Server in a Cluster Environment**

It is important to note that you must manually specify the dependencies for the resources installed in a cluster environment. Figure 20-19 shows the dependencies of the various services.

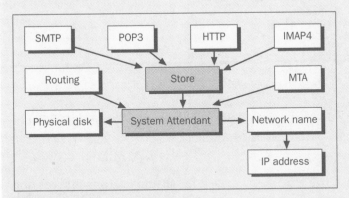

Figure 20-19. *Resource dependencies.*

When installing a resource into a resource group, use this figure to specify which resources depend on another resource. If you start at the bottom with the IP address and work your way up, you will find that all resources depend on the IP address resource being on line to work properly. For instance, the network name resource cannot start unless the IP address resource is running.

Hence, to start the services, you should start at the bottom of the figure and work your way up. Similarly, to stop the services, you'll start at the top of the figure and work your way down.

Creating an Exchange System Attendant Resource   Before you can create the Exchange System Attendant resource, the disk, IP address, and network name must be in the resource group and on line. Once you've installed this resource, the databases and Exchange services are moved to the shared disk. Install the Exchange System Attendant resource as you did the others, choosing Microsoft Exchange System Attendant for the new service and listing both nodes in the cluster as possible owners. On the Dependencies screen, add the network name and disk to the resource dependencies, as shown in Figure 20-20.

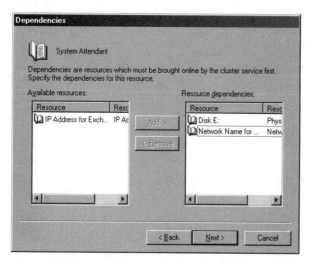

Figure 20-20. *Resource dependencies for the Exchange System Attendant resource.*

The next two screens ask you to choose which administrative group and routing group to place this resource in. Choose the same administrative and routing group that you installed the Exchange servers into. Otherwise, you may have unpredictable results.

Note These two screens may not appear if administrative and routing groups are not enabled in Exchange System.

Once you've selected the appropriate administrative and routing group, the wizard asks for the path to the data directory. This path you enter here should be on the shared resource.

When you click Finish, the data files are moved, the configuration database for the Cluster service is updated, and you will have created the first Exchange virtual server. Figure 20-21 shows how the new cluster group will look in Cluster Manager. Notice that after adding the System Attendant resource, most other Exchange resources are created automatically and installed into the Cluster group.

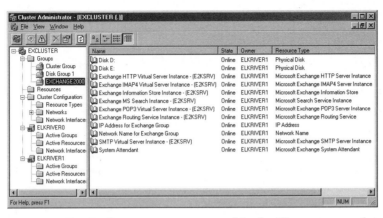

Figure 20-21. *Exchange resources created in the Cluster group when System Attendant resource is created.*

Figure 20-22 shows that the new virtual server that is running inside the Cluster group appears as a separate, physical server in the Exchange System Manager snap-in.

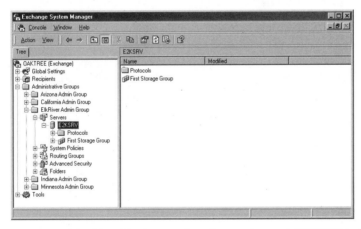

Figure 20-22. *New Exchange virtual server, named E2KSRV in System Manager.*

Information Store Limitations

You'll recall from Chapter 2 that the information store service is limited to six databases per storage group with a maximum of four storage groups. In a cluster environment, you'll need to plan your database and storage group configurations carefully and include the ramifications of a failover. In a nutshell, you don't want to create more databases or storage groups than one node can handle.

For instance, let's assume you have two virtual Exchange 2000 servers running on a two-node cluster. Each one has been configured with three storage groups consisting of four databases per group. Now let's assume that one of your nodes experiences a disaster and goes off line. During the failover process, all the databases will be moved to the other node. However, not all the databases will be mounted because the combined number of storage groups exceeds the hard-coded limit in Exchange 2000 Server. Therefore, design your storage group configuration as if all the nodes in the cluster will run all the databases and storage groups to avoid this type of problem during a failover.

Configuring Full-Text Indexing

When you create the System Attendant resource for the Exchange resource group, the Exchange MS Search Instance is added to the group. To enable full-text indexing, start Exchange System and navigate to the mailbox store. Right-click the mailbox store, and then choose Create Full-Text Index. Verify that the full-text index catalog will be created on the shared storage device, and then click OK. To learn more about full-text indexing, please see Chapter 11.

> **Note** Do not delete the Exchange MS Search Instance from the resource group unless you are sure you will never need it in the future. If you need to reinstall it after deleting it, you'll be forced to delete and re-create the Information Store resource on the virtual server.

Installation Tip

When installing Exchange 2000 Server, you might run across the error message in Figure 20-23 when attempting to add the System Attendant resource. This occurs because the service account is not being granted permissions to the Exchange organization objects. To fix this problem, run the Delegation Of Control wizard by right-clicking on the organization object, then selecting Delegation Of Control. Give the service account full permissions to the organization hierarchy, and the System Attendant resource should install thereafter.

Figure 20-23. *Win32 error caused by permissions not being granted for the service account.*

Summary

This chapter explained how Exchange 2000 Server can run in a Windows 2000 cluster environment and covered the basic administrative and architectural concepts of Windows Clustering. Bear in mind that running a server cluster well requires experience and training. Cluster technologies will be increasingly popular as the active/active architecture is accepted and implemented by more companies.

You've learned how to make your Exchange system's resources highly available by using clustering. Now you need to learn how to configure security for those resources so that only those who need them have access to them. That is the focus of our next chapter.

Chapter 21
Securing Exchange 2000 Server

In today's networks, resources need to be as available as possible. They also need to be as secure as possible. This chapter focuses on the latter. Because Microsoft Exchange 2000 Server is tightly integrated with Microsoft Windows 2000, a major part of this chapter will focus on Windows 2000. Microsoft Windows 2000 supports a comprehensive public-key infrastructure (PKI) to ensure the security of messaging for Microsoft Exchange 2000 Server. Certificate Services and the PKI are the two foundations upon which you will design, deploy, and maintain your public-key security needs.

More Info It is well beyond the scope of this book to cover most of the security concepts associated with Windows 2000. If you would like to learn more about Windows 2000 security, consult the *Microsoft Windows 2000 Security Technical Reference* (Microsoft Press, forthcoming).

Windows 2000 Security Protocols

Windows 2000 provides security via the following security protocols:

- **Kerberos version 5** The default protocol for authentication and logon.
- **NTLM (Windows Challenge/Response)** Provided for backward compatibility with Microsoft Windows NT 4 and earlier, including Windows 3.11.
- **Digital certificates** Used with a PKI deployment; especially useful for authenticating parties outside your organization. The use of digital certificates is becoming more frequent as companies attempt to secure their communications more fully.
- **SSL/TLS (Secure Sockets Layer/Transport Layer Security)** Appropriate for connection-oriented security, such as access to Web-based resources on the Internet.

This chapter focuses on the use of digital certificates and public and private keys to secure messages in Exchange 2000 Server. We'll begin by looking at the public-key infrastructure in Windows 2000.

Understanding the Public-Key Infrastructure in Windows 2000

A PKI deployment involves several basic components. A solid understanding of how these components work is essential to setting up good, basic network security. You can think of the PKI as a collection of resources that work together to provide a secure messaging authentication system. The major components of the Windows 2000 PKI are as follows:

- Certificate Services
- Digital certificates
- Policies to manage the certificates
- Microsoft CryptoAPI and cryptographic service providers (CSPs)
- Certificate stores for storing certificates

This section discusses these components and how they work together to ensure solid Exchange 2000 messaging security. It starts by looking at encryption and public key/private key technology, followed by a description of encryption schemes. Finally, it discusses Certificate Services and the use of certificates.

Encryption and Keys

Basic security starts with encryption. Encryption is the process of scrambling data before sending it over a medium. Encrypting data before sending it to another person makes it much more difficult for a would-be interceptor to read the data than if it was in plain text. Hence, the sender will scramble, or encrypt, the data with a structure called a *key*. Encryption technology uses two types of keys: symmetric keys and asymmetric keys.

Symmetric keys, also known as shared keys, are identical: both the sender and the recipient use the same key to encrypt and decrypt the data. *Asymmetric keys* are not identical: one key is used to encrypt the data and a different key is used to decrypt it. With asymmetric keys, one key is known as the *public* key and the other is known as the *private* key. Exchange 2000 Server uses this type of encryption technology.

The public key is often made public by being published in some central place, such as a public folder or the Active Directory directory service. The private key must be secured so that no one but the owner of that key has access to it. A pair of public and private asymmetric keys is generally referred to in cryptography as a *key pair*.

With key pairs, either key can encrypt or decrypt the data, but the corresponding key is required to perform the opposite function, whether that is encrypting or decrypting. If the key that decrypts the data is not available, the encrypted data will remain encrypted and is, essentially, useless unless the key can be found and employed. Although in theory, either key can perform either function (for example, a private key can be used to encrypt and the public key used to decrypt), Windows 2000 and Exchange 2000 Server implement this technology by having the public key perform the encryption while the private key is used for decryption.

Hence, in Exchange 2000 Server, we are not concerned if someone has our public key, because they can only encrypt data with it. However, the private key must be kept secure, because it is the private key that can decrypt data. The best way to keep a private key secure is to never send it over a medium where a would-be hacker could capture it and use it.

The use of one key to encrypt (the public key) and a different key to decrypt (the private key) forms the foundation of Certificate Services. Table 21-1 summarizes the key types and when they are used.

Table 21-1.   Private and public key usage

	Encryption/Decryption	Electronic Signatures
Sending Messages	Recipient's public key is used to encrypt message contents.	Sender's private signing key is used to apply the signature.
Reading Messages	Recipient's private key is used to decrypt the message contents.	Sender's public signing key is used to interpret the applied signature.

Encryption Schemes

Encryption allows a message to be sent via an insecure channel, such as the Internet, safely. The entire message, including attachments, is encrypted. How is data encrypted? A mathematical function called a key is applied to the data, changing it into an unreadable form. Hence, plain text becomes encrypted, or *cipher,* text. The *strength* of an encryption describes how difficult the encryption is to break, or decrypt. The length of the key determines the encryption strength. Here are some numbers to consider:

8-bit key $= 2^8$ keys $= 256$ keys

56-bit key $= 2^{56}$ keys $= 72,057,594,037,927,936$ keys

128-bit key $= 2^{128}$ keys $= 3.4 \times 10^{38}$ keys

A brute force attack attempting to break a 128-bit encryption and trying one *trillion* keys per second would take 10,819,926,705,615,920,821 years to break the key. Needless to say, 128-bit encryption is very strong. Table 21-2 lists some common encryption schemes.

Table 21-2. Common encryption algorithms

Encryption Type	Description
CAST	A 64-bit symmetric block cipher (which encrypts one block, or set length, of data at a time, rather than a byte) developed by Carlisle Adams and Stafford Tavares. It is similar to DES and supports keys between 40 bits and 128 bits.
DES	Data Encryption Standard. Developed by IBM for the government for use by the National Institute of Standards and Technology (NIST). This standard uses 56-bit keys with a 64-bit symmetric block cipher. It is the most commonly used encryption algorithm.
3DES	Triple DES; encrypts the data structure three separate times.
DH	The Diffie-Hellman method for passing symmetric keys.
KEA	Key Exchange Algorithm, an improved version of Diffie-Hellman.
MD2	Message Digest, an algorithm that creates a 128-bit hash value. It was developed by Ron Rivest of RSA (Rivest, Shamir, and Adleman).
MD4	Another RSA algorithm that creates a 128-bit hash value.
MD5	A better version of MD4.
RC2	Rivest's Cipher, a 64-bit symmetric block cipher.
RC4	An RSA stream cipher (which encrypts one byte or bit at a time) that can use variable-length keys. Microsoft's implementation of RC4 uses either a 40-bit or 128-bit key.
RSA	A commonly used public/private key encryption scheme developed at RSA.
SHA	Secure Hash Algorithm, developed at NIST. It produces a 160-bit hash value and is similar to MD5, but more secure and thus slower.

Certificate Services in Windows 2000

Public and private keys are not enough to guard your sensitive data. For instance, it is possible for someone to obtain your public key—and, by definition, it is available to anyone—and then impersonate a server with which you're communicating. This is easily done if the impersonator is a person internal to your organization. In this scenario, you might believe that you're communicating with Server1 when in fact you're communicating with someone else. Certificate Services is designed to protect against this type of attack.

Windows 2000 certificates form the core of the Windows 2000 public-key infrastructure. You can install Windows 2000 Certificate Services to create a certificate authority (CA) that issues and manages digital certificates. Active Directory maintains information that a CA needs, such as user account names, group memberships, and certificate templates, as well as information about each CA installed in the domain. Active Directory also maintains certificate mappings to user accounts for authenticating clients and controlling access to network resources.

Digital Certificates and the X.509 Standard

Digital certificates verify a user's identity. They are issued by the CA (discussed later in the section "Certificate Authority"). We can trust digital certificates because we trust the source of the certificate, the CA. In addition to issuing the certificate itself, the CA by default creates any public key/private key pair, which is the basis of security in any digital certificate.

Digital certificates generally follow the X.509 standard, which means that they meet the standard criteria for electronic certificates outlined in the X.509 standard. Typically, an X.509 certificate incorporates the following fields:

- Version number
- Serial number of the certificate
- Signature algorithm ID
- Name of the person to whom the certificate was issued
- Expiration date of the certificate
- Subject user name
- Subject public-key information
- Issuer unique ID
- Subject unique ID

- Extensions
- Digital signature of the authority that issued the certificate

SSL/TLS also conforms to the X.509 standard. In Windows 2000, external users' digital certificates can be mapped to one or more Windows 2000 user accounts for permissions to network resources. Windows 2000 then uses the Subject field (the subject user name in the list of fields just given) to identify the user associated with the certificate. In this way, Windows 2000 and Microsoft Certificate Services can map an external user to a user account stored in Active Directory.

The X.509 Standard

The X.509 standard describes two levels of authentication: simple authentication, using a password as the only verification of a claimed identity, and strong authentication, using credentials generated by cryptographic technologies. The standard recommends that only strong authentication be used as a basis for providing secure services.

The strong authentication method specified in the X.509 standard is based upon public-key technologies. The one huge advantage of this standard, and the reason why it is so popular today, is that user certificates can be held within Active Directory as attributes and can be communicated within the directory systems like any other attribute of a user account.

While the X.509 standard does not require the use of a particular algorithm to produce the certificates, it notes that for two users to communicate, they must use the same algorithms during authentication.

Certificate Authority

A *certificate authority* (CA) issues certificates and enables parties to trust each other. The CA's private key is used to sign the certificate, and the certificate is needed to verify the signatures. Because certificates originate from a verified authority, the receiving party can explicitly trust them. For example, a client application can import a certificate to be trusted by a user who is reading data from the application.

Clients and CAs can maintain a list of explicitly trusted certificates. Certificates can also be placed on a certificate revocation list (CRL), which lists certificates

that are explicitly distrusted. In addition, they can be set to expire after a predetermined amount of time.

Certificate Services Architecture in Windows 2000

Figure 21-1 illustrates the components of Windows 2000 Certificate Services.
These components work together, in cooperation with Microsoft CryptoAPI and
the cryptographic service providers, to perform all of the tasks necessary to generate, store, and apply certificates in the enterprise. You can manipulate these
objects and modules in the Certification Authority snap-in. For information on
how to install this snap-in, see the section "Installing and Configuring Certificate
Services" later in this chapter.

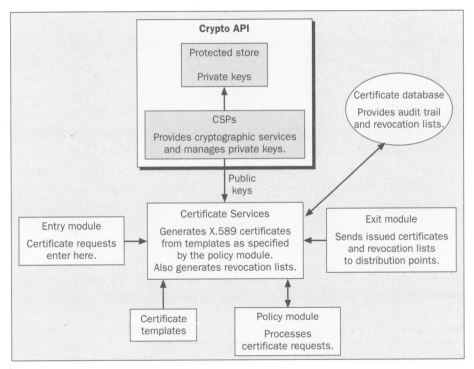

Figure 21-1. *Components of Certificate Services.*

Entry Module

Certificate requests—such as those a user submits via the Web enrollment support page—enter the Entry module of Certificate Services, either through remote
procedure calls (RPCs) or HTTP. The requests are placed in a pending queue until
they are approved or rejected by the Policy module.

Policy Module

The Policy module determines whether a certificate request should be approved, denied, or left pending for an administrator to review. Once the certificate is approved, the Policy module can verify information in the request against various sources, such as Active Directory or an external database. Additional attributes or extensions can be inserted into the Policy module if a customized client application requires them. For example, a signing limit can be inserted into certificates and used by an online purchasing form to determine whether the user can sign for the amount requested.

Certificate Templates

Certificate templates define the attributes for certificate types. You can configure enterprise CAs to issue specific types of certificates to authorized users and computers. When the CA issues a certificate, a certificate template is used to specify its attributes, such as the authorized uses for the certificate, the cryptographic algorithms that are to be used with it, the public-key length, and its lifetime. Certificate templates are stored in Active Directory. Table 21-3 lists the standard certificate types.

Online certificate templates are used to issue certificates to requestors that have Windows 2000 accounts and that support obtaining certificates directly from an enterprise CA. Offline templates are used to issue certificates to requestors that don't have Windows 2000 accounts or that don't support obtaining a certificate from an enterprise CA.

When a CA issues an online certificate, it obtains information about the requestor from the requestor's Windows 2000 account for inclusion in the certificate. When it issues an offline certificate, it includes in the certificate the information that the requestor entered as part of the request, such as a user name, e-mail address, department, and so forth that the requestor entered into a Web form.

Table 21-3. Certificate types

Certificate Type	Description
Administrator	Used for authenticating clients and for Encrypting File System (EFS), secure mail, certificate trust list (CTL) signing, and code signing.
Authenticated Session	Used for authenticating clients.
Basic EFS	Used for EFS operations.

Table 21-3. *continued*

Certificate Type	Description
CEP Encryption	Used to enroll Cisco Systems, Inc. routers for IPSec authentication certificates from a Windows 2000 CA.
Code Signing	Used for code signing operations.
Computer	Used for authenticating clients and servers.
Domain Controller	Used for authenticating domain controllers. When an enterprise CA is installed, this certificate type is installed automatically on domain controllers to support the public-key operations that are required when domain controllers are supporting Certificate Services.
EFS Recovery Agent	Used for EFS encrypted-data recovery operations.
Enrollment Agent	Used for authenticating administrators that request certificates on behalf of smart card users.
Enrollment Agent (Computer)	Used for authenticating services that request certificates on behalf of other computers.
Exchange Enrollment Agent (offline request)	Used for authenticating Microsoft Exchange Server administrators who request certificates on behalf of secure mail users.
Exchange Signature Only (offline request)	Used by Exchange Server for client authentication and secure mail (used for signing only).
Exchange User (offline request)	Used by Exchange Server for client authentication and secure mail (used for both signing and confidentiality of mail).
IPSec	Used for IPSec authentication.
IPSec (offline request)	Used for IPSec authentication.
Root Certification Authority	Used for root CA installation operations. (This certificate template cannot be issued from a CA and is used only when installing root CAs.)
Router (offline request)	Used for authentication of routers.
Smart Card Logon	Used for client authentication and logging on with a smart card.
Smart Card User	Used for client authentication, secure mail, and logging on with a smart card.
Subordinate Certification Authority (offline request)	Used to issue certificates for subordinate CAs.
Trust List Signing	Used to sign CTLs.
User	Used for client authentication, EFS, and secure mail (used for both signing and confidentiality of mail).
User Signature Only	Used for client authentication and secure mail (used for signing only).
Web Server (offline request)	Used for Web server authentication.

Certificate Database

The certificate database records all certificate transactions, such as certificate requests. It records whether requests were granted or denied, and it also holds information about the certificate, such as its serial number and expiration date. Revoked certificates are flagged and tracked in this database as well. You'll use the Certification Authority snap-in to manage the audit trail.

Exit Modules

Exit modules send the certificate to the location specified in the request. Acceptable destinations include LDAP directory services, file systems, and URLs. You can create customized exit modules so that new certificates are sent in e-mail messages or to a public folder on the network. There can be many or few exit modules, depending on your needs. Modules can be written in the Component Object Model (COM) interface to allow any entity or directory to be notified when a certificate is issued. In fact, you could write an exit module to notify a database of a new certificate, for billing purposes.

Brief Summary of Security Objects

At this point, you might be a bit confused as to what we've covered and where a given certificate, key, or file is located. Table 21-4 summarizes this information.

Table 21-4. Location of security objects

Type of Certificate	X.509 Certificate	Key Management Security Database	User's Personal Security Store	Exchange Directory Store
Signing certificate			X	
Encryption certificate			X	
Private encryption key		X	X	
Private signing key			X	
Public encryption key	X			
Public signing key	X	X		
Certificate expiration date	X			
CA signature	X			

Managing the Public-Key Infrastructure

Now that you understand the Windows 2000 public-key infrastructure and are familiar with how Certificate Services works, you need to learn how to install and manage the Certification Authority snap-in. You can use this Microsoft Management Console snap-in to manage one or more CAs. For more information on how to create a customized snap-in, see Chapter 8.

More Info   To learn how to install and manage root and subordinate certificate authorities see *Microsoft Windows 2000 Server Administrator's Companion* by Charlie Russel and Sharon Crawford (Microsoft Press, 2000).

Installing and Configuring Certificate Services

If you do not include Certificate Services as an optional component during the installation of Windows 2000, you can install it at any time by selecting the Certificate Services component in Add/Remove Programs (Figure 21-2). Immediately upon selecting Certificate Services, you're presented with a message box indicating that once Certificate Services is installed, you can't rename this server or move it from the domain.

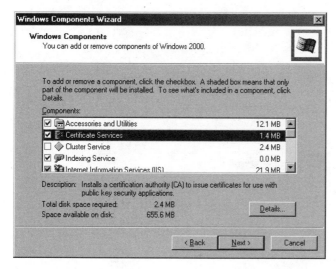

Figure 21-2. *Selecting Certificate Services in Add/Remove Programs.*

On the Certification Authority Type selection screen (Figure 21-3), you're given the chance to choose the type of CA server you want to install. The default is an enterprise root CA. Select the appropriate type for your installation.

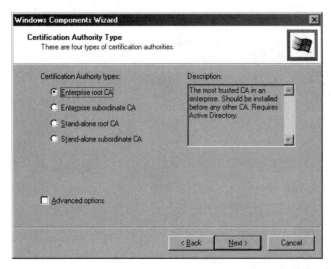

Figure 21-3. *Certification Authority Type selection screen.*

If you want to configure advanced options for the public and private keys, select the Advanced Options check box and then click Next. The screen shown in Figure 21-4 appears. Table 21-5 covers the choices you're given in this screen.

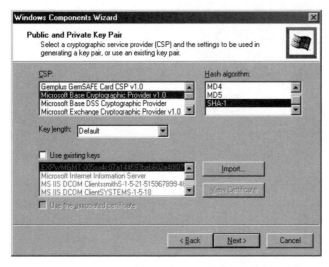

Figure 21-4. *Setting advanced options for public and private key pairs.*

> **Note**   Installing an enterprise CA requires Active Directory services, so the CA computer must already be joined to the Windows 2000 domain.

Table 21-5.   Advanced options for public and private key pairs

Option	Description
CSP	Select the cryptographic service provider to be used to generate the public key and private key set for the CA certificate. The default CSP is the Microsoft Enhanced Cryptographic Provider.
Hash Algorithms	The default is SHA-1, which provides the strongest cryptographic security.
Key Length	The default key length is 512 bits for the Base Cryptographic Provider and 1024 bits for the Enhanced Cryptographic Provider. The minimum key length is 384 bits, and the maximum is 16,384 bits. Generally, the longer the key, the longer the safe lifetime of the private key.
Use Existing Keys	Allows you to choose an existing private key from the list. The existing private key is used for the CA. You might need to use this option to restore a failed CA.
Use The Associated Certificate	Enables the selection of the certificate that is associated with the existing private key that is used for the CA. You might need to use this option to restore a failed CA.
Import	Gives you the ability to import a private key that is not in the Use Existing Keys list. For example, you might import a private key from an archive for a failed CA.
View Certificate	Displays the certificate associated with the private key in the Use Existing Keys list.

Enter the CA identifying information, as illustrated in Figure 21-5, and then click Next. Table 21-6 describes the fields on this screen. The wizard then generates the cryptographic key.

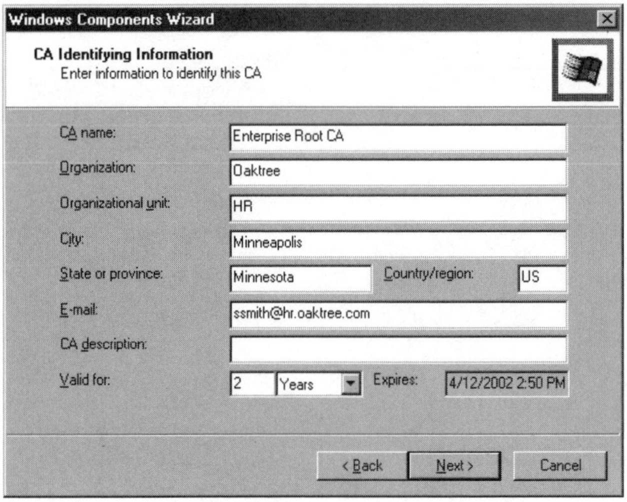

Figure 21-5. *Entering CA identifying information.*

Table 21-6.   Fields on the CA Identifying Information screen

Fields	Value
CA Name, Organization, Organizational Unit, City, State Or Province, Country/Region, and E-Mail	This information is used to uniquely identify the CA. It is included in the Subject field of the CA certificate. Windows 2000 uses the CA name to identify the CA, so each CA name must be unique. All other information can be the same if needed across CAs within your organization. Others can view the Subject field to identify the CA or to find out how to contact the CA.
CA Description	This is an optional field.
Valid For	Enter the duration of the certificate's lifetime for the root CA certificate, and then select either Years, Months, or Weeks. The default is 2 years. This option is not available for subordinate CAs, since their lifetime is determined by the root CA.
Expires	Lists the expiration date for the root CA certificate, which corresponds to the certificate lifetime in Validity Duration.

After the key is generated, Setup needs to know where to put the database. Enter the appropriate path. As Figure 21-6 shows, you can also select the Store Configuration Information In A Shared Folder check box. This option creates a folder that makes information about CAs available to users. It is useful only if you are installing a stand-alone CA and do not have Active Directory.

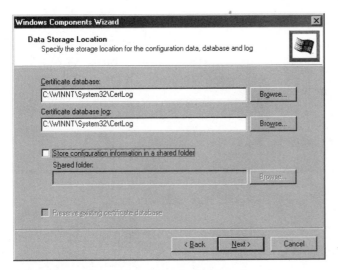

Figure 21-6. *Specifying data storage locations.*

When you click Next, you see a message box indicating that IIS services must be stopped. Just click OK, and the wizard will configure the components. When it is finished, you are done installing Certificate Services. A shortcut to the Certification Authority snap-in appears in the Administrative Tools menu. Figure 21-7 illustrates the basic Certification Authority snap-in.

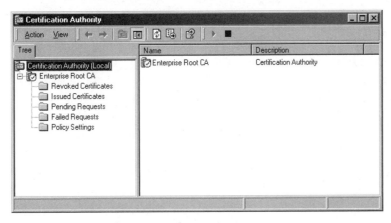

Figure 21-7. *Certification Authority snap-in.*

Installing Web Enrollment Support

By default, when Windows 2000 Certificate Services is installed, the same server will also have installed Web enrollment support (Figure 21-8). You can also choose to install the Web enrollment form on another Windows 2000–based computer. You might do so if the traffic volume for Certificate Services is high and you need to spread the enrollment traffic load over more than one server.

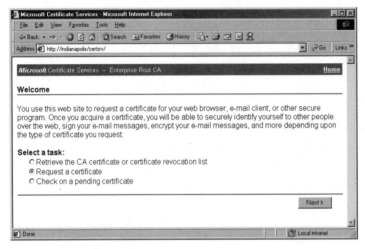

Figure 21-8. *Web enrollment home page.*

The default location for the Web enrollment pages is *<drive*:>\%windir%\ System32\Certsrv, where *<drive*:> is the letter of the disk drive on which the pages are installed. To install the Web enrollment pages on a server other than the one housing Certificate Services, start the Add/Remove Programs tool in Control Panel and select Certificate Services, as though you were installing it. Then, however, click Details and clear the Certificate Services check box (Figure 21-9). Verify that the Certificate Services Web Enrollment Support check box is selected, and then click OK. Follow the wizard to completion.

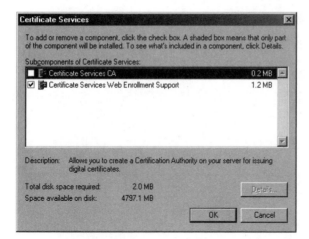

Figure 21-9. *Installing Web enrollment support on a separate server.*

Using the Web Enrollment Pages

Users can access the Web enrollment pages via the URL *http://servername/certsrv*. On the welcome screen, the user has several options. The Retrieve The CA Certificate Or Certificate Revocation List option retrieves the CA's certificate or the most current CRL. When the user selects this option and then clicks Next, a screen appears allowing the user to establish a trust for all the certificates of the CA on the local computer. This task involves installing the certification path for the CA's certificate in the certificate store of the local computer (Figure 21-10). Selecting this option will be most useful when you need to trust a subordinate CA but do not have the certificate of the root CA in your local certificate store.

More often, users will be coming to this Web site to obtain a new user certificate. To begin the process, a user will select the Request A Certificate radio button and click Next. At the next page that appears (Figure 21-11), the user can either request a basic certificate or specify Advanced Request to obtain more than a basic certificate. For information on the advanced options, see the next section, "Making an Advanced Request."

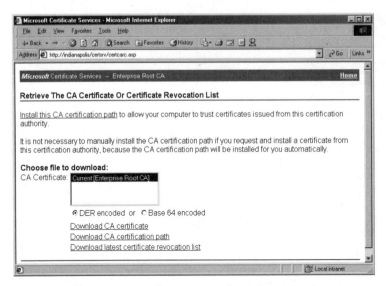

Figure 21-10. *Retrieving the CA's certificate.*

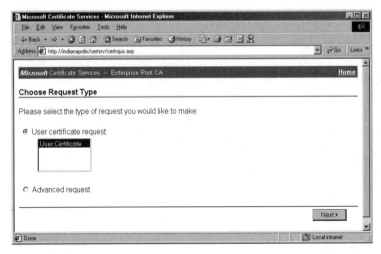

Figure 21-11. *Requesting a new certificate.*

To request a new basic user certificate, the user selects the User Certificate Request radio button and then clicks Next. The User Certificate - Identifying Information page appears. Here the user is asked to enter any additional identifying information that the CA might need to generate the certificate. If no more information is needed, a message indicates this fact (Figure 21-12). In either case, the user can submit the request from this page.

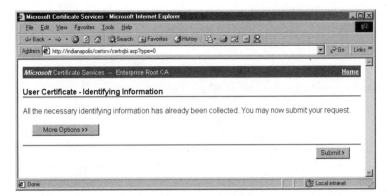

Figure 21-12. *Message indicating system is ready to submit a certificate request.*

Once the user clicks Submit, the certificate is generated. The next support page gives the user the opportunity to install the certificate (Figure 21-13).

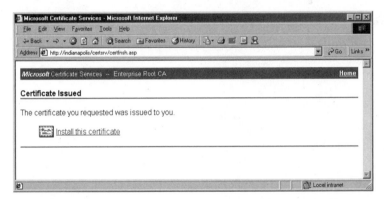

Figure 21-13. *Message indicating system is ready to install the certificate.*

Clicking the Install This Certificate link installs the certificate on the local computer. The certificate is available only to the user for whom the certificate was generated. If other users log on to the computer, they will not be able to use this certificate. The final enrollment page then appears, indicating that the certificate has been installed properly. To verify that the certificate has been created, open the Certification Authority snap-in and select the Issued Certificates folder. The user's certificate will appear in the details pane (Figure 21-14).

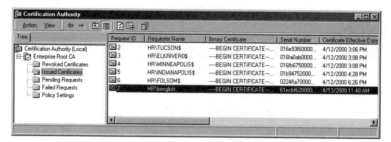

Figure 21-14. *Verifying that a user certificate has been created.*

To verify that the user certificate has been installed, open the Microsoft Outlook 2000 client, choose Options from the Tools menu, and then click on the Security tab (Figure 21-15). In the Certificates And Algorithms area, you will see that the certificate is installed, both for signing and encryption. The hash algorithm and encryption algorithm can be changed, but not the certificate itself.

Figure 21-15. *Verifying that a user certificate has been installed.*

A user can specify a different certificate by clicking the Choose button and making a selection from the choices presented (Figure 21-16). While the list may look like multiple copies of the same certificate, it is not. Each listing is a different, unique certificate, even if it is visually identical to the other certificates listed.

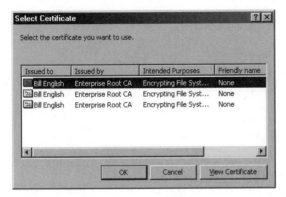

Figure 21-16. *Choosing a certificate for personal use.*

Making an Advanced Request

The Advanced Request option allows the user to specify additional options while making a certificate request. Figure 21-17 shows the three types of requests available. The first choice, Submit A Certificate Request To This CA Using A Form, walks the user through an advanced form. Table 21-7 outlines the options available on this form. You can use this advanced form to request any certificate types supported by the enterprise CA. The second choice, Submit A Certificate Request Using A Base64 Encoded PKCS #10 File Or A Renewal Request Using A Base64 Encoded PKCS #7 File, allows the user to submit a certificate request using a file rather than a form. The file must already exist in base 64, using either the #10 or #7 PKCS encoding format. The last choice, Request A Certificate For A Smart Card On Behalf Of Another User Using The Smart Card Enrollment Station, allows an administrator to create a certificate for a smart card user that can then be installed onto the physical card.

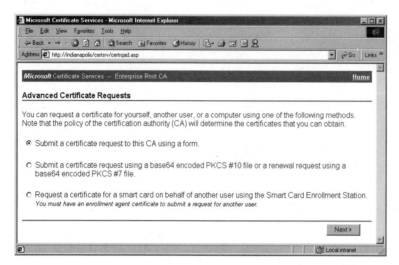

Figure 21-17. *Types of advanced certificate requests.*

Table 21-7. Options on the advanced certificate request form

Option	How to Use
Identifying Information (stand-alone CAs only)	Enter the identifying information that is to appear in the certificate, including name, company, department, city, state, and country/region. Enterprise CAs obtain this information from Active Directory. This information is placed in the Subject field of the certificate when it is issued.
Intended Purpose (stand-alone CAs only)	Choose the intended purpose of the certificate.
Certificate Template (enterprise CAs only)	Select the template to be used when the certificate is generated.
CSP	Choose a CSP. The default is the Microsoft Base Cryptographic Provider or the Microsoft Enhanced Cryptographic Provider, depending on whether the certificate is exportable.
Key Usage	Select the basic purpose of the certificate: Exchange, Signature, or Both. *Exchange* means that the key can be used only for symmetric key exchange. *Signature* means the key is used only for digital signing. The default is Both.
Key Size	Enter a key length from 384 bits to 1024 bits. Minimum recommended key length is 512 bits. When used just for a signature, the maximum length is 16,384 bits. Note that key generation for large signing keys can take a very long time.
Create New Key Set	Leave this option selected (the default) to create a new public and private key for the issued certificate. To enter the container name, click Select The Container Name.

Table 21-7. *continued*

Option	How to Use
Use Existing Key Set	Select this option to generate a certificate that uses an existing key set instead of generating a new one.
Enable Strong Private Key Protection	Select this option to have the system prompt the user for permission before it performs cryptographic operations with the user's private key.
Mark Keys As Exportable	Select this option to enable the private key to be exported. Private keys that are used for digital signing cannot be enabled for export.
Use Local Machine Store	You must be an administrator to use this option because it stores a certificate to be issued in the HKEY_LOCAL_MACHINE subtree of the local machine. The default location for storing certificates is the user's personal certificate store.
Hash Algorithm	Choose the algorithm to use for this certificate. The default is SHA-1.
Save Request To A PKCS #10 File	Select this option to save the request to a file rather than submitting it to the CA. You'll need to enter a filename as well. This option is handy when you want to submit the request file to the CA at a future date.
Attributes	Enter additional attributes for the requested certificate. Consult the Microsoft Platform Software Development Kit for more information about these attributes.

Viewing Information About Certificates

You can view specific information about certificates by navigating to the Issued Certificates folder in the Certificate Authority and then opening an individual certificate. To open a certificate, right-click it and then choose Open. Figure 21-18 shows the General tab of the property sheet for a user certificate. This tab lists the purpose of the certificate, the issuer, the issuee, and the dates the certificate is valid. If you compare the information for a user certificate with the information for a domain controller certificate (Figure 21-19), you'll notice that the purposes are very different. Remember that the purpose of a certificate is derived from its template.

The Issuer Statement button is dimmed in Figures 21-18 and 21-19 because in this case the issuing CA does not provide a statement. If the issuing CA for a given certificate does provide a statement, you can click this button to read additional information about the certificate from the issuing CA's Web site.

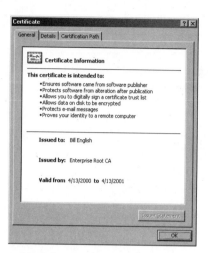

Figure 21-18. *General tab of the property sheet for a user certificate.*

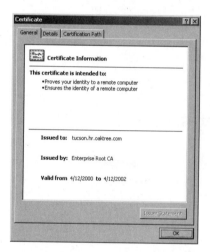

Figure 21-19. *General tab of the property sheet for a domain controller certificate.*

The Details tab shows the information that the certificate contains. When you select an item in the Field column, the contents of that field are revealed in the Value column. Figure 21-20 shows the Public Key field selected, The Value column indicates that it is a 1024-bit key.

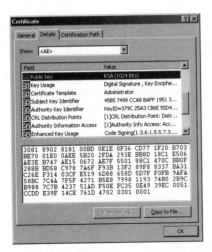

Figure 21-20. *Details tab of a certificate's property sheet.*

The Certification Path tab (Figure 21-21) shows the trust status of the certificate. If there is a problem with either the certificate or the path, a warning will appear in this tab, with information that explains the problem.

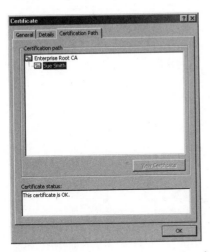

Figure 21-21. *Certification Path tab of a certificate's property sheet.*

On the client side, you can use Outlook 2000 to edit certain certificate properties. With the certificate open, click the Edit Properties button at the bottom of the Certificate's properties to see the sheet shown in Figure 21-22. Here you can change the friendly name and description for the certificate. You can also restrict the purposes for which the certificate can be used. By default, all of the purposes are enabled, but you can manually disable certain purposes or disable all purposes, which would make the certificate invalid.

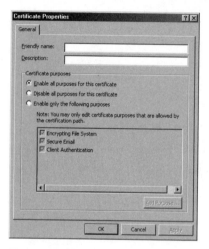

Figure 21-22. *Editing certificate properties in Outlook 2000.*

More Info To learn how to export certificates and private keys, or to learn more about how to back up and restore CAs, consult the *Windows 2000 Server Distributed System Guide*, part of the *Microsoft Windows 2000 Server Resource Kit* (Microsoft Press, 2000).

Securing Messaging in Outlook 2000

Outlook 2000 can be installed in one of two modes: Internet only mode or corporate/workgroup mode. Because the focus of this book is Exchange 2000 Server, we will consider only corporate/workgroup mode, which requires connectivity to an Exchange 2000 server. Refer to the Exchange 2000 Server Resource Kit for information on securing messaging in Outlook 2000 in Internet only mode.

From the client perspective, one question that must be answered is how the Outlook 2000 client knows which certificates to trust. The answer is found in the properties of Microsoft Internet Explorer. When Internet Explorer is installed, a large number of certificates are embedded in the installation. Outlook uses the Internet Explorer cryptographic service provider (CSP) to read these certificates and then determine whether the CA is trusted. To see which CAs are trusted, in Internet Explorer, choose Internet Options from the Tools menu, and then display the Content tab and click the Certificates button. Figure 21-23 shows a partial list of the default trusted root certificate authorities that ship with Outlook 2000 and Internet Explorer 5.

Note   A CSP, or cryptographic service provider, is the actual code that has the algorithms for encrypting data and creating signatures.

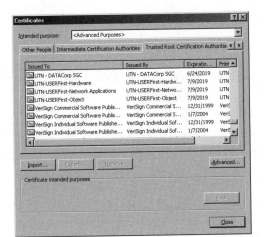

Figure 21-23. *Partial list of trusted root certificate authorities in Internet Explorer.*

Both root CAs and individual users can be added or removed at this location. Let's assume, for example, that we want to remove a root CA's certificate from the list of trusted root CAs. In the Certificates dialog box, shown in Figure 21-23, we would display the Trusted Root Certification Authorities tab, highlight the root CA to be removed, and then click Remove. A message box would then appear confirming this action (Figure 21-24).

Figure 21-24. *Message confirming removal of a root CA in Internet Explorer.*

Initially Trusting a Certificate

If your company implements its own CA or if there are specific CAs that you need to trust that are not embedded by default in IE, you can import their certificates by using the Import button.

You need to think carefully about whether to initially trust a certificate. For instance, if the certificate is included on an installation CD-ROM from Microsoft, you can be sure it's trustworthy. However, if you've downloaded software, such as Internet Explorer, from the Internet, someone may have slipped in a certificate that you don't want to trust. To prevent this, Microsoft uses Authenticode certificates for its software. With these certificates, if any bits have changed, you are notified during installation that the signature is invalid and that you shouldn't install the software.

You can also verify certificates independently by contacting the root CA directly to see if the certificate's serial number is valid. Some CAs include serial numbers on their Web site, or you can contact the system administrator of a corporate CA.

Encryption and Outlook 2000

When both the sender and receiver are using Outlook 2000 along with certificates, their messages are encrypted end to end, meaning that the Outlook 2000 client encrypts them when it sends them and they are not decrypted until opened by the recipient. Encrypted messages in the store remain encrypted. Hence, if someone is able to obtain access to a mailbox on an Exchange 2000 server, the messages are still unreadable because that person does not have the private key to decrypt the message. Only the intended recipient holding the correct private key can decrypt the message.

Here is how Outlook 2000 provides message privacy. First, the sender composes and addresses the message. Outlook then locates the recipient in Active Directory by doing an address book lookup. If the sender has chosen to encrypt outbound messages, Outlook retrieves the recipient's certificate. To see the encryption options, choose Options from the Tools menu in Outlook 2000, and display the Security tab (Figure 21-25).

Figure 21-25. *The Security tab, showing options to encrypt outbound messages.*

Outlook extracts the recipient's public key from his or her certificate and generates a one-time *lockbox*, encrypting all of the data with a one-time, symmetric key and placing it inside this box. The lockbox, along with its contents, is encrypted with the recipient's public key and then sent to the recipient. When the recipient opens the message, the recipient's client decrypts the lockbox, using the recipient's private key, extracts the symmetric key, and decrypts the message with the symmetric key. Then the recipient can read the message.

Digital Signatures and Outlook 2000

Digital signatures are as legally binding as a signature on paper. Digital signatures provide origin authentication, since only the sender holds the private key used to generate the signature. The signature also provides data integrity because the signature is a protected hash of the message, meaning that the document is hashed and then encrypted with the signer's private encryption key and, after verification, it is decrypted with the signer's public key. If even one bit changes during message transmission, the hash will not be the same at the receiving end, and the message will be considered invalid. A given signature is generated for only a single message and will never be used again. Digital signatures work because embedded into each signature is an indicator that explains what hash functions the sender used. The recipient can use the same function and compute the same hash when the message is received. If the hashes match, the signature is considered valid. If the message is encrypted, it must be decrypted before the algorithm can be run to compare the hashes.

S/MIME and Outlook 2000

Secure/Multipurpose Internet Mail Extensions, or S/MIME, was designed by an RSA-led vendor consortium in 1995. Version 3 is in Internet Draft process at the time of this writing. S/MIME allows recipients using non-Microsoft software to see and understand encrypted, secure messages sent from Outlook 2000 users. For more information on S/MIME, please visit the RSA Web site at *http://www.rsa.com/smime/*.

Configuring Outlook 2000 for Secure Messaging

To obtain a certificate, a user can either enter the URL for the Web enrollment forms on the intranet or click the Get A Digital ID button on the Security tab of the Outlook 2000 Options dialog box. This button directs the user to the intranet Web enrollment forms.

Installing Outlook 2000 with the Corporate or Workgroup service option (see Chapter 16) affords several benefits. First, Certificate Services is integrated with Active Directory, meaning that you can specify whether the certificates are placed in Active Directory, in the file system, or both after they are created. To configure this setting, open the property sheet for the CA within the Certification Authority snap-in, display the Exit Module tab, and click the Configure button (Figure 21-26).

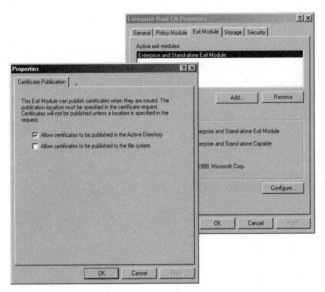

Figure 21-26. *Specifying where certificates are placed.*

The advantage of publishing a certificate in Active Directory is that the certificate becomes an attribute of the user's account, as shown in Figure 21-27. Before a user sends an encrypted message to another user, the client can look up the recipient's account in Active Directory to see whether that recipient has a certificate. If one exists, the message is sent as described previously. In addition, the client periodically (every 24 hours) picks up certificate trust and revocation lists that are published by Certificate Services and applies them as needed. In the absence of a hierarchical CA structure, the client can build a linear trust network of different CAs.

A second advantage of the Corporate or Workgroup service option is that it allows certificate enrollment through Key Management Service (KMS). One attractive feature of this service is its interoperability with legacy clients (Outlook 98 and earlier). Hence, KMS can be set up to issue certificates to clients running several different versions of Outlook, eliminating an immediate need to upgrade a large installed base of Outlook 98 users to Outlook 2000 before beginning to use certificates. Since Outlook 98 supports only version 1 of X.509 certificates, Outlook 2000 and future releases of Outlook will also support version 1 for backward compatibility.

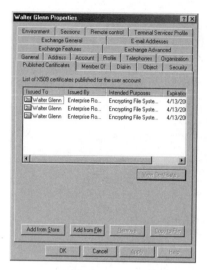

Figure 21-27. *Published Certificates tab of a user's property sheet.*

Enrolling through KMS also provides key recovery, an important feature since approximately 10 percent of all corporate users lose their private encryption keys at some point. The ability to recover a private encryption key is essential because if the key is lost, any existing encrypted e-mail is unusable. For a more detailed discussion of certificate enrollment through KMS, see the section "Enrolling Users with KMS" later in this chapter.

Working with Key Management Service

KMS is an advanced security tool in Exchange 2000 Server that protects data integrity through message encryption and digital signatures. It is an optional component of Exchange 2000 Server that works in close conjunction with Windows 2000 Certificate Services to provide a centralized PKI.

KMS installs its own CSP, which has an embedded Extensible Storage Engine (ESE) database that stores users' private keys so that only KMS has access to those keys. This is necessary, for instance, if a company's messaging is encrypted and an outside legal authority needs to look at certain messages. Having a copy of each user's private key stored inside the KMS ESE database allows users' messages to be decrypted and read.

Certificate Services generates the users' certificates based on requests from KMS and from servers as the trusted third party (TTP) for KMS. The certificate of the

CA is embedded in all of the clients that are enrolled through the KMS and CA. This allows clients to trust each other's certificates because they are all issued under the same CA hierarchy.

Although it is the client that does most of the legwork for security, such as generating the signing key pair, storing the user's keys, reading Active Directory for other users' certificates, and performing both the encryption and decryption of messages, the most valuable tasks that KMS performs is key recovery. The KMS ESE database archives a user's encryption key pair but not the signing key pair. This precaution eliminates any potential for signature forgery by an administrator.

Note   Users' keys and certificates are stored in an encrypted .EPF file in Outlook 97 and earlier. Outlook 98 stores this information in the IE protected store, and Outlook 2000 stores it in the registry.

KMS Architecture

Figure 21-28 illustrates the KMS architecture. As you can see, Active Directory is used to store the trust lists, revocation lists, and user certificates. KMS communicates with Certificate Services through the CA's Policy module. It is the Policy module inside the CA that defines our certificates and the templates that are available for use by the KMS.

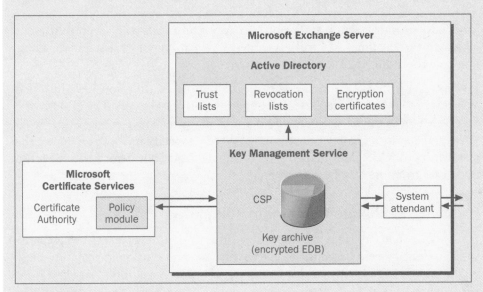

Figure 21-28. *KMS architecture.*

The figure also shows KMS's encrypted ESE database, in which users' encryption key pairs are archived. Part of the encryption scheme for these key pairs is the KMS startup password. There are no applications, at present, that can view the database. The entire object is encrypted.

The Exchange System snap-in controls what KMS can do and is also used to administer KMS. KMS is extended into Active Directory in the form of a Security tab added to the property sheet for each user account, allowing administrators to enroll users or revoke or recover their key pairs individually.

Before you can install KMS, you must be running Windows 2000 Server in your Exchange organization. This section assumes that you have both Windows 2000 and Exchange 2000 Server running in your environment. Neither Windows 2000 Server nor Exchange 2000 Server needs to be in native mode to install KMS.

Note The Exchange 2000 Key Management Service is compatible with Key Management servers running Exchange Server 5.5 Service Pack 1. To upgrade an Exchange 5.5 Key Management server to Exchange 2000 Server, follow the same procedure you would for any non-KMS Exchange server. For more information on how to upgrade an Exchange Server 5.5 Key Management server to Exchange 2000 KMS, see the *Microsoft Exchange 2000 Server Resource Kit* (forthcoming from Microsoft Press).

To conduct a successful installation of KMS, you must take several different actions at specific times. We will cover these installation points first and then outline how to install KMS.

First you must install Exchange Certificate Templates after you have installed Windows 2000 Certificate Services but before you install Exchange 2000 KMS. Second know in advance where you want to place the startup password (we'll cover your options in a bit), since you will need to specify its location during the installation of KMS. And finally, after installing KMS, but before you request a certificate from the CA, be sure to grant Manage permissions to KMS.

Installing Exchange Certificate Templates

Before you can install KMS, you must have at least one enterprise CA that can issue Enrollment Agent (Computer), Exchange User, and Exchange Signature Only certificates. In the absence of this configuration, Exchange 2000 Server will not allow you to install KMS. If you attempt to do so, you'll see the message in Figure 21-29.

Figure 21-29. *Installation error message for KMS.*

To create an enterprise CA, right-click the Policy folder in the Certification Authority snap-in, point to New, and select Certificate To Issue. The dialog box shown in Figure 21-30 appears. In this dialog box, you can choose, by default, from the following templates:

- User Signature Only
- Smart Card User
- Authenticated Session
- Smart Card Logon
- Code Signing
- Trust List Signing
- Enrollment Agent
- Exchange Enrollment Agent (offline request)
- Enrollment Agent (Computer)
- IPSec
- IPSec (offline)
- Router (offline)
- CEP Encryption
- Exchange User
- Exchange Signature Only

Figure 21-30. *Choosing a certificate template.*

Exchange 2000 Server uses three templates for issuing certificates to Exchange 2000 users and computers. The type of template depends on what the certificate will be used for. The Enrollment Agent (Computer) certificate allows KMS to issue certificates on behalf of Exchange Advanced Security users. The Exchange User certificate is used to encrypt mail and digital signatures. The Exchange Signature Only certificate is used for digital signatures only.

Installing KMS

To install KMS, first start the Microsoft Exchange 2000 Server Installation Wizard. In the Component Selection screen, change the install action next to Microsoft Exchange 2000 (the first selection) to Custom. The default is Typical.

Select Install next to Microsoft Exchange Key Management Service. Do the same for any other Exchange components you need, and then proceed with the Exchange installation. Make sure you also select Install next to the Microsoft Exchange System Management Tools. By default, these tools are installed with a Typical installation, but not with a Custom installation. You will be asked to select an administrative group to install KMS into (Figure 21-31). You can have only one instance of KMS per administrative group.

Note If you want to install KMS on a computer that is currently running Exchange 2000 Server, select Change next to Microsoft Exchange 2000 in the Component Selection window. Then select Install next to Microsoft Exchange Key Management Service and click Next.

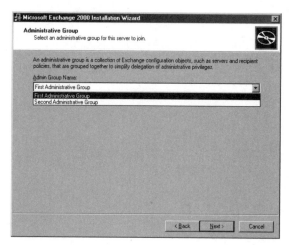

Figure 21-31. *Selecting an administrative group in which to install KMS.*

The next screen in the wizard asks if you would rather type the startup password manually each time you open the KMS management console or have the password written to either a floppy disk or hard disk (Figure 21-32). If you select manual entry, you'll need to write down the startup password that the installation wizard generates. If you elect to have the password written to a disk, you'll be responsible for securing the password and the disk to which it is written. Should any unauthorized person get access to of that disk, he or she would have complete access to KMS, possibly rendering your mission-critical data useless. After securing your password, you can proceed through the file-copying phase and then click Finish.

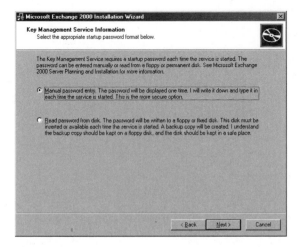

Figure 21-32. *Selecting the startup password option.*

Real World   Changing the Location of Your KMS Password

When you install KMS, you're prompted to specify where you would like the KMS password saved. What you're really specifying is where you would like the Kmserver.pwd file to be saved. You choice is placed in the Windows 2000 registry. You can alter this registry entry if you would like to save the password in a secured folder instead of in its default location.

In the Registry Editor (Regedt32.exe), navigate to the subkey HKEY_LOCAL_MACHINE\Software\Microsoft\Exchange\KMServer, and then double-click MasterPasswordPath. In the String box, type the location where you want to store the password.

If you change this value to a blank, you will need to manually enter the KMS service password in the Startup parameter dialog box every time you start the KMS service.

Granting Manage Permissions to KMS

Once KMS has been installed, the next step is to add the Key Management server computer account to every Certificate Services server that will be issuing certificates to KMS. Then you must assign the Key Management server Manage permissions on the Certificate Services server. Otherwise, you will not be able to revoke certificates.

To grant Manage permissions to the Key Management server, open the Certification Authority snap-in, right-click the name of your CA, and then choose Properties. On the Security tab, shown in Figure 21-33, click Add.

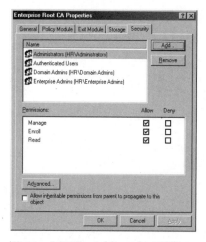

Figure 21-33. *Adding the KMS server account to the CA's security properties.*

In Select Users, Computers, or Groups, select the computer name for every Key Management server in your organization, click Add, and then click OK. On the Security tab, select the computer names you have added, and then select the Allow check box to grant your Key Management servers Manage permissions. Figure 21-34 shows a server with these permissions.

Starting KMS

The next step is to start KMS. You do so in the Exchange System snap-in. When you start the snap-in, you'll notice that there is a new container, Advanced Security, under the administrative group into which you installed KMS (Figure 21-35). To start the KMS server, highlight the Advanced Security container, right-click the Key Manager object in the right pane, and choose Start. You'll then need to enter the KMS password in one of three ways:

- Enter the KMS password in the pop-up dialog box.
- Insert the floppy disk containing the kmserver.pwd file that was created earlier.
- Wait for it to use the kmserver.pwd file that you stored on the hard drive.

This last point is possible only if you modified the registry, as we discussed earlier in the chapter. After you have successfully provided the password, KMS will start.

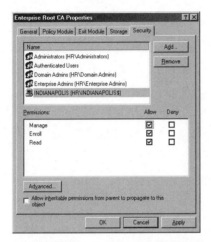

Figure 21-34. *KMS server Indianapolis with Manage permissions.*

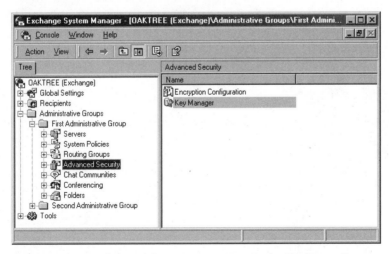

Figure 21-35. *Advanced Security container in the Exchange System snap-in.*

Managing KMS

Now that your KMS server is up and running, you'll need to secure it and learn how to manage the server itself before turning your attention to how KMS issues certificates and works with your users to make their messaging more secure. In this section, we'll look at a number of small but important administrative tasks related to KMS itself.

Adding and Removing KMS Administrators

By default, the only Windows 2000 account allowed to administer KMS belongs to the person who installed KMS. It is highly possible that you'll want to include one or two other administrators in the list of those approved to administer KMS. To add or delete KMS administrators, start Exchange System, click the Advanced Security container, and then, in the details pane, right-click Key Manager and choose Properties. In the Key Management Service Login dialog box, type your administrator password, and then click OK.

> **Note** The default KMS administrator password is *password*. Remember that you have to reenter your password every time you perform a task or click on a tab in the KMS property sheet. This password is *not* the same as the account password. Thus, even though you might be logging on to KMS with your user name, the password you use to do so is different from your logon password in Active Directory.

On the Key Manager property sheet, display the Administrators tab (Figure 21-36), and then click Add. In the Select User box, click one or more users who will have administrative privileges in KMS.

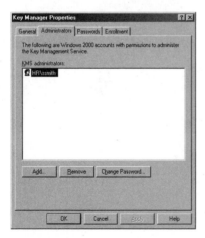

Figure 21-36. *Administrators tab of the Key Manager property sheet.*

In the Set Administrator Password field, type and retype a password for the user you selected, and then click OK. To remove an administrator, highlight the name on the Administrators tab, and then click Remove. Remember that if you add someone to the list of KMS administrators, that person will not be able to access the Advanced Security container in Exchange System until you run the Exchange Administration Delegation Wizard and grant that user Exchange administrator rights. At a minimum, an administrator will need these rights for the administrative group in which the Key Management server is located.

Changing the Administrator Password

As we noted in the previous section, the default administrator password is *password*. You should change the administrator password the first time you start KMS to make the server utility more secure. Whenever you add a KMS administrator, that person will be given his or her own administrator password. KMS administrators can change their passwords at any time.

Note Do not confuse the KMS startup password with the administrator password. The KMS startup password is requested only when you attempt to start KMS.

To change an administrator password, start Exchange System. Click Advanced Security and then, in the details pane, right-click Key Manager and choose Properties. Display the Administrators tab. Select the administrator whose password you would like to change, and then click Change Password. Type the current password, and then type the new password. KMS passwords must be at least six characters long.

Setting Multiple Passwords for KMS Administrative Functions

Use the Passwords tab of the Key Manager property sheet (Figure 21-37) to configure multiple password policies. By default, all KMS operations require only one administrator password, but you can configure certain tasks to require authorization from more than one administrator. Depending on the sensitivity of the task, the number of required passwords can range from one up to the number of administrators listed on the Administrators tab minus one.

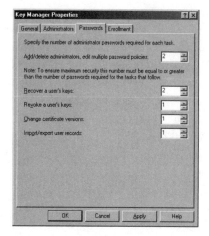

Figure 21-37. *Passwords tab of the Key Manager property sheet.*

In the Add/Delete Administrators, Edit Multiple Password Policies field, click the up arrow or enter the number of administrator passwords required to perform these functions. The default is 1 and the maximum limit is $x - 1$, where x is the total number of administrators. This way you are always able to accomplish KMS tasks, even if someone is out of the office. If needed, type in new values for the number of administrator passwords required to perform each of the tasks listed.

Changing the KMS Startup Password

Every time KMS is started, an administrator must enter the KMS service startup password. You can change both the startup password and its location to keep KMS secure. The location will either be a disk or a place where you write down the password. For example, you might need to change the password and the location if your KMS administrator has recently left the company and you'd like to keep your KMS service startup password as secure as possible.

To change the KMS startup password, start Exchange System. Click the Advanced Security container, right-click Key Manager, point to All Tasks, and choose Change Startup Password. In the Key Management Service Login dialog box, type the KMS password, and then click OK.

In the Change Startup Password dialog box (Figure 21-38), you can choose a location for your new startup password. To record the password manually, click Display This Password Once. This option is the default and is the more secure choice. If you select it, you must write the password down and keep it in a secure place. If you lose this password, you will not be able to start KMS.

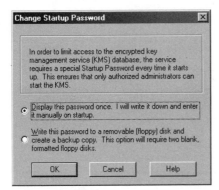

Figure 21-38. *Change Startup Password dialog box.*

To store the new startup password on removable disks, click Write This Password To A Removable (Floppy) Disk And Create A Backup Copy. This option creates two copies of the password. You should store these disks in secure, separate places. Whenever you need to start KMS, one of these disks must be available.

Enrolling Users with KMS

KMS uses Active Directory to enroll users in Advanced Security. This can be done individually, by group, by Exchange administrative group, or by server. The administrator password is required only once per enrollment.

When it enrolls users, KMS requests certificates for them from Certificate Services. The certificates are then used to create two key pairs for every user. One key pair is for digital signatures and is created on the client; the other is for e-mail encryption and is created on the Key Management server. The private digital signature keys are stored on the user's computer.

The first time you enroll users in KMS, it will be necessary to configure token distribution, as described later in the section "Configuring Token Distribution for Enrolled Users Under KMS." In addition, if your users are using Outlook 97 or earlier, you may also need to configure the content version.

To enroll a user via KMS, start Exchange System, right-click Key Manager, and choose Enroll Users. As Figure 21-39 shows, you're given the choice of viewing individual users or entire groups of users.

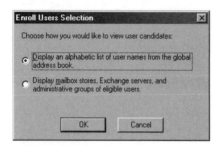

Figure 21-39. *Indicating how to view candidates for enrollment.*

Enrolling Individual Users

To see a list of individual users, select the first radio button, Display An Alphabetic List Of User Names From The Global Address Book. Then click OK. In the Enroll Users dialog box (Figure 21-40), select the users you want to enroll through KMS, clicking Add for each one. When you're done, click Enroll. You'll see a message box indicating that the users were successfully enrolled.

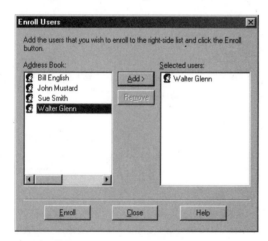

Figure 21-40. *Selecting users to enroll.*

Figure 21-41 illustrates the token the client will receive if you have elected to send it via e-mail. The System Attendant generates the e-mail and sends it directly to the client.

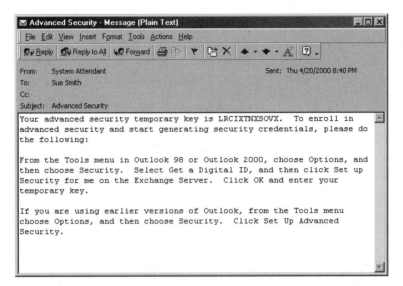

Figure 21-41. *Sending a token to a user via e-mail.*

Enrolling a Group of Users

To see a list of groups of users, select the second radio button, Display Mailbox Stores, Exchange Servers, And Administrative Groups Of Eligible Users. Then click OK. The Enroll Users dialog box appears, listing containers of users. Expand the choices, as shown in Figure 21-42, to enroll users based on their home database. Select the containers whose users you want to enroll, and then click Enroll. All of the users in those databases will be enrolled, and e-mails will be sent to each one if you have elected to send the token by e-mail.

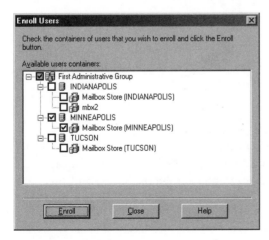

Figure 21-42. *Selecting containers of users to enroll.*

Obtaining User Certificates

Once a user is enrolled and has received his or her token, the user should open Outlook 2000, choose Options from the Tools menu, and display the Security tab. At the bottom of the tab, the user should click Get A Digital ID to begin the process of getting a certificate.

Figure 21-43 shows the welcome screen your users will see when they click this button. Notice that they are asked whether they want to get an S/MIME certificate from a source on the Internet or have security set up for them on the Exchange server. The correct choice here is to set up security on the Exchange server. Once they select that option and click OK, a small dialog box pops up with the user's name in the upper input field. In the Token field, the user should enter the token received from KMS, as shown in Figure 21-44.

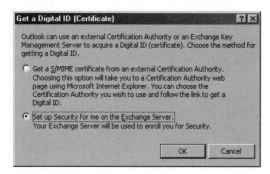

Figure 21-43. *Choices a user has for obtaining a digital ID.*

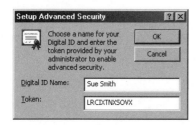

Figure 21-44. *Entering a user's token.*

After the user clicks OK, he or she is prompted to enter a password that will secure the digital ID. This box also contains a reminder that Outlook will not remember the password. The user clicks OK after entering the password and then sees a message indicating that the request has been sent to the Microsoft Exchange Key Management Service and that the user will be notified when the request has been processed. It may take a few minutes for the user to receive a reply from KMS.

KMS notifies the user that the certificate has been issued by sending encrypted e-mail (Figure 21-45). To open the e-mail, the user needs to enter the password created during the request process. The user is then given the option of adding the certificate to the root certificate store, which is part of Internet Explorer and is user specific (Figure 21-46).

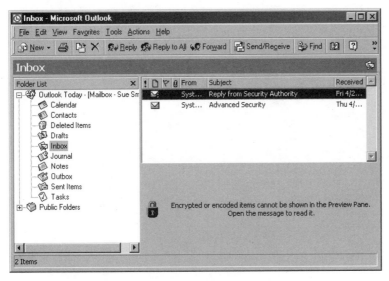

Figure 21-45. *Reply received from KMS.*

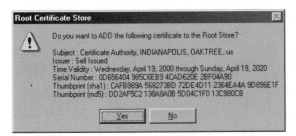

Figure 21-46. *Adding the certificate to the root certificate store.*

Note Once the certificate has been added to the root certificate store, the user is once again asked to enter the password for the certificate. If, at either point, the user clicks Cancel instead of entering the password, the entire operation will be canceled. The user will need to contact you to be reenrolled in KMS. Before doing so, you will need to revoke the user's first set of credentials.

After the user has entered the password, he or she receives an e-mail in Outlook 2000 indicating that the new certificate has been successfully installed (Figure 21-47). The certificate installs itself into the Outlook 2000 client and automatically sets the client to send clear-text, signed messages. Furthermore, as shown in Figure 21-48, the client is set up for S/MIME messaging and a 40-bit RC2 encryption algorithm.

Figure 21-47. *E-mail indicating successful installation of the new certificate.*

Configuring Token Distribution for Enrolled Users Under KMS

An enrollment token is a temporary password that KMS creates for every enrolling user. Users type the token in Outlook to complete the Advanced Security enrollment process. You must decide how the tokens will be distributed to your users.

To choose a token distribution method, start Exchange System and click the Advanced Security object. In the details pane, right-click Key Manager, and then choose Properties. On the Key Manager property sheet, display the Enrollment tab (Figure 21-49).

Figure 21-48. *New security settings in the Outlook 2000 client.*

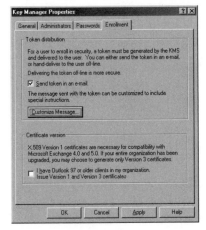

Figure 21-49. *Enrollment tab of the Key Manager property sheet.*

Microsoft prefers that you deliver tokens to users in person. This method is the default and is more secure than delivering them by e-mail. If you choose to use this method, do nothing. When the token appears on your screen, you will then be responsible for recording it and delivering it to the enrolling user. To have tokens sent directly to users by e-mail, select the Send Token In An E-Mail check box. Figure 21-50 shows the default message that KMS sends to users. To change this message, click Customize Message.

Figure 21-50. *Default message used to send tokens to users.*

You have probably noticed that the default message includes %TOKEN%, which is a variable for the actual token that will be sent to the enrolling user. You can remove this placeholder so that the actual token is not sent. If you do so, you will need to deliver the token manually to the user. Note that the tokens always appear on your screen, even when you have configured KMS to deliver them via e-mail.

If you opt to send the e-mail without the token, you can use it to send customized information to your enrolling users. This information can include any special notices or instructions specific to your organization that you may want Advanced Security users to have.

Recovering Keys in KMS

There will be times when you'll need to recover a user's private key. Common scenarios in which this is likely to happen include when users have been imported from another Key Management server or if a user experiences a hardware failure or forgets a password.

Users who have been imported from another Key Management server will need new keys because their certificates will have been revoked. Once they have been imported to a new Key Management server, they can still use their old keys to read old encrypted e-mail. However, those old keys are now bound to a certificate that has been placed on your CRL. Therefore, the users need new certificates and corresponding keys to create new encrypted messages. In the process of exporting and importing users, key recovery is the final step because imported users must have their keys recovered.

Recovery prevents users from losing encrypted e-mail when they lose their existing keys by forgetting their password or by having a media failure. When you recover a key, the user is issued a token. The method of delivering the recovery token is the same as the one you've chosen for delivering enrollment tokens—either by manual delivery or by e-mail. After the user enters this recovery token in Outlook, KMS creates a new key pair for the user. In addition, KMS returns all of the user's old keys. For imported users, a new encryption key pair is generated.

To recover keys for a user, start Exchange System and click Advanced Security. Right-click Key Manager, point to All Tasks, and choose Recover Keys. You are presented with the same choices you saw when enrolling users: you can recover one or more individuals' keys or recover the keys for a group of users. When the process is finished, you see a confirmation window indicating that the keys for all selected users were successfully recovered.

Enrolling Users in Advanced Security Through Active Directory Rather Than KMS

You can enroll individual users to receive a certificate in Advanced Security through Active Directory, rather than through KMS. Enrollment through Active Directory is similar to enrolling users through KMS in the Exchange System snap-in, except that the enrollment applies only to the individual user. In addition, administrators can use Active Directory to recover and revoke keys. This is also done on a per-user basis that is similar to performing the same task in Exchange System.

One advantage of using Advanced Security in Active Directory is the additional detail that is available for each user (Figure 21-51). You can look up an individual's security status (such as Enabled, Disabled, Token Issued, or In Recovery), Key Management server, and the dates his or her certificates were activated and when they will expire.

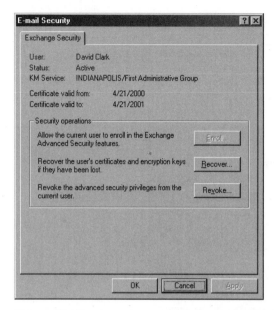

Figure 21-51. *A user's security information in Active Directory.*

To enroll individuals in Advanced Security, recover or revoke their keys, or revoke a certificate through Active Directory, start Active Directory Users and Computers, highlight the Users organizational unit, and then, in the details pane, right-click the user account and choose Properties. On the Exchange Features tab, in the Features column, click E-Mail Security, and then click Properties to display the E-Mail Security property sheet.

Tip You will be required to enter your Key Management Service password.

To enroll the user, click Enroll. If you've chosen to distribute tokens manually, the token will be displayed on your screen so that you can deliver it to the user in person. If you've chosen to distribute tokens through e-mail, click Do Not Send E-Mail to display the token on your screen only, or click Send Enrollment to send it to the user in an e-mail message.

To recover a user's key pairs, click Recover. A temporary token will be generated for the user. You can then choose to either send the token by e-mail or deliver it in person.

To revoke a user's certificates, click Revoke. You will see a confirmation message informing you that the user was disabled from e-mail security.

Understanding How Exchange 2000 Server Integrates with Windows 2000 Security

This section focuses on how Exchange 2000 Server uses the Windows 2000 security features. The Windows 2000 security features can be divided into two broad areas: core operating system features and additional features.

The core operating system features form the basis of a secure implementation of Windows 2000 Server. Those features include the following:

- **Active Directory services**   Unifies Exchange 2000 and Windows 2000 objects into one directory.
- **Kerberos authentication**
- **Access control model**   Gives granular control over Active Directory entries and Exchange objects.
- **Microsoft Certificate Services**   Can be used by other applications to provide security across different layers.

Additional applications that enhance the features of the core operating system include the following:

- **IP Security (IPSec)**   Used for network, remote access, and virtual private networks.
- **Encrypting File System**   Provides additional security for mobile users
- **Security Configuration Analyzer**   Ensures adherence to security policies.

Active Directory

Active Directory in Windows 2000 replaces the Security Accounts Manager (SAM) in Windows NT Server 4 as the security database. However, like an object in the SAM, each Active Directory object is given a 96-digit, pseudorandom security identifier (SID) that is globally unique.

Not all objects in Active Directory are assigned an SID. For instance, a security group has an SID, but a distribution group does not. Likewise, mail-enabled users have SIDs, but mail-enabled contacts do not. Only those objects that have SIDs can be added to the access control list (ACL) of a resource. If an object does not have an SID, it cannot be placed in the ACL. Therefore, non-SID objects cannot access resources guarded by an ACL.

Kerberos Authentication

Kerberos treats Exchange 2000 Server like a service. When a client needs to contact an Exchange server, the client first requests an Exchange service ticket from the key distribution center (KDC). The ticket is then used for authentication to the Exchange server.

The Exchange services also use Kerberos to make a service account log on to a domain controller through the local system account. This account uses computer credentials that change every seven days. The user name of the Exchange 2000 server is added to the Exchange Servers group, which is added to the ACL for the core objects.

Note It is well beyond the scope of this book to cover Kerberos authentication in detail. To learn more about Kerberos authentication, what a ticket is, and how this protocol works, consult the *Microsoft Windows 2000 Server Distributed Systems Guide* in the *Microsoft Windows 2000 Server Resource Kit* (Microsoft Press, 2000).

Access Control Model

The access control model in Exchange 2000 Server follows that of Windows 2000 Server, giving us greater granularity of control for Exchange 2000 Server objects than for Exchange Server 5.5 objects. For instance, you can grant or deny access by container, by item, and at the property level. In addition, Exchange 2000 objects are based on the Windows 2000 NTFS file system and Active Directory objects. By way of illustration, if a user has access to only five out of the ten items in a public folder, the user will see only those five items. Moreover, when a user who does not have access rights to certain attributes performs a search, the user will have only the results that he or she can see.

Note As you migrate public folders from Exchange 5.5 Server, the distribution lists become distribution groups, which do not have SIDs. As a result, you may need to implement new security settings. In addition, public folders created in Exchange 2000 Server will have a Windows 2000 ACL. If the folder is to be replicated to the Exchange Server 5.5 system, be sure to test the folder for access control functions, since the ACLs in Windows NT Server 4 and Windows 2000 Server are different.

IP Security

While KMS provides security on the application layer, IP Security (IPSec) provides security on the IP transport layer; hence, IPSec provides a higher level of security than KMS. In a highly secure environment, IPSec can be used to encrypt information from client to server and from server to server. IPSec works in tandem with Layer 2 Tunneling Protocol (L2TP).

With all of these different security features available, you'll need to consider which type of security you would like to implement. Table 21-8 summarizes some of the encryption and authentication methods commonly used today.

Table 21-8. Common encryption and authentication methods

Services	Method Used	Keys
IPSec	Encryption Authentication Integrity	DES 128-bit MD5 128-bit SHA 160-bit Kerberos
KMS	Encryption Digital signature	DES, 3DES 128-bit RSA 512-bit
EFS	Encryption	DESX 128-bit

Summary

This chapter has covered a lot of ground at the 10,000-foot level. The information could easily be expanded into its own book. As security technologies become increasingly important and common, you will find that many companies are hiring teams of people who focus only on security. In this chapter, you learned how to install and use Certificate Services and Key Management Service, as well as how to perform some of the more common administrative tasks associated with each service. In the next chapter, we turn our attention away from security to learn how to connect Exchange 2000 Server to other messaging systems.

Chapter 22
Connecting to Other Messaging Systems

Microsoft Exchange 2000 Server can connect to a multitude of modern and legacy messaging systems. Until this point, we have focused primarily on working within the Microsoft Exchange 2000 Server environment. You have set up your Exchange system and learned how to deploy and administer all of its components—from routing groups to clients to clustered servers. Exchange 2000 Server is not the only messaging system out there, however. Many types of messaging systems are available today, and you may have to connect your Exchange system to one or more of them. You may, for example, be upgrading from a legacy system or need to establish communications with another company. This chapter covers the basics of connecting Exchange 2000 Server to other messaging systems, referred to as *foreign systems*.

Connecting to Foreign X.400 Systems

X.400 is a messaging standard that is used by many messaging systems. An enterprise that implements X.400-compliant mail systems can support a heterogeneous messaging environment. X.400 uses a strict addressing method that reflects a hierarchical environment. An X.400 address reflects the recipient's position in a messaging hierarchy. For example, the X.400 address for Sue Smith at MicroAge is "c=US;a=;p=MicroAge;o=Phoenix;s=Smith;g=Sue." Each of these parameters represents a particular X.400 value or hierarchical placement: "c=" stands for the country; "a=" represents the Administrative Management Domain; "p=" represents the Private Management Domain and is equivalent to the Exchange organization; "o=" stands for the X.400 organization, the equivalent of an Exchange administrative group; "s=" stands for the surname or last name; and "g=" stands for the given name or first name.

You can use the X.400 connector to connect Exchange 2000 Server to any foreign messaging system that supports the X.400 standard.

More Info To find out more about X.400, look at Request for Comments 1330 (RFC 1330). You can find this online at several Web sites, including *http://www.cis.ohio-state.edu/hypertext/information/rfc.html.*

Real World **Using Other Foreign Gateways**

Many messaging systems use gateways to connect to dissimilar messaging systems. Exchange 2000 Server supports many gateways in the form of connectors. The X.400 Connector, the Connector for MS Mail, the Lotus Notes Connector, and the Lotus cc:Mail Connector are examples of gateways that are built into Exchange 2000 Server. Other vendors provide a variety of gateways for connecting Exchange 2000 Server to external, proprietary electronic mail, fax, voice mail, and other types of systems.

Many connectors are available for Exchange Server, either included with the Exchange Server software from Microsoft or offered separately by other vendors. It is not possible to discuss here every connector that can be used to connect Exchange 2000 Server to foreign systems. For that reason, we'll limit our discussion to the X.400 Connector and the Connector for MS Mail—the X.400 Connector because of the wide acceptance of X.400 as a messaging standard, and the Connector for MS Mail because the process of configuring it is similar to that of other connectors for other proprietary systems. If you need to know the specifics of connecting Exchange 2000 Server to a particular messaging system, consult the Exchange 2000 Server product documentation.

Creating a Service Transport Stack

Creating an X.400 Connector to link Exchange 2000 Server to a foreign X.400 system is not too difficult. The one thing you must remember is that each end of an X.400 Connector must be configured separately. This chapter assumes that the administrator of the foreign system will configure the connector in the foreign system appropriately.

To configure the X.400 Connector in Exchange 2000 Server, you must first create a Message Transfer Agent (MTA) service transport stack. This transport stack is configured for a particular Exchange server and is basically a set of information about the software and hardware that make up the underlying network. The transport stack allows for a layer of abstraction between the X.400 Connector and the network itself.

> **Note**   Transport stacks exist at the server level, and each is associated with a particular Exchange server. In contrast, the connector or connectors that use the transport stack exist at the routing group level. What this means to you is that you can configure multiple MTA transport stacks and X.400 Connectors within a routing group, giving you the ability to balance the load placed on servers by messaging connectors.

There are three different types of MTA transport stacks, each defined by the type of network hardware or software you have configured:

- **TP0/X.25**   Uses an Eicon port adapter to provide both dial-up and direct communication in compliance with the Open Systems Interconnection (OSI) X.25 recommendation.

- **TCP/IP**   Defines specifications for running OSI software, such as X.400 messaging systems, over a TCP/IP-based network. Exchange 2000 Server uses Windows 2000 TCP/IP services.

- **RAS**   Provides an interface for using Remote Access Service (RAS) over standard telephony devices. (This type will appear only if RAS has been installed.)

Because TCP/IP is easily the most commonly installed type of MTA transport stack, we will use it as an example here. However, the configuration process is nearly identical for all three types of MTA transport stacks.

You create an MTA transport stack with the Exchange System snap-in. First navigate to the X.400 object in the Protocols container of the server on which you want to install the stack, as shown in Figure 22-1. Right-click the Microsoft MTA object, point to New on the shortcut menu, and choose TCP/IP X.400 Service Transport Stack. This opens the property sheet for the new MTA transport stack. You will use this property sheet to configure the stack. You're already familiar with the Details tab, which lets you enter an administrative note regarding the object. The other two tabs are discussed in the sections that follow.

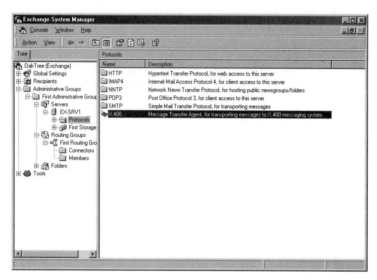

Figure 22-1. *Creating a new MTA transport stack.*

General Tab   Use the General tab, shown in Figure 22-2, to change the display name for the MTA transport stack and to configure OSI addressing information. Unless you plan to allow other applications besides Exchange 2000 Server to use the MTA transport stack, you do not need to worry about the OSI addressing values.

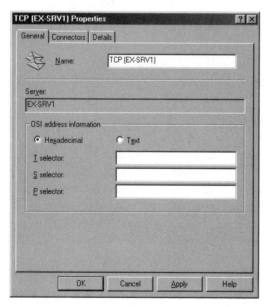

Figure 22-2. *Configuring general properties for an MTA transport stack.*

More Info To learn more about OSI addressing and about configuring other applications to use an MTA transport stack, consult the *Microsoft Exchange Server Resource Kit* (Microsoft Press, forthcoming in 2000).

Connectors Tab The Connectors tab, shown in Figure 22-3, lists all of the messaging connectors in the routing group that are configured to use the current MTA transport stack. When you first create a stack, this list is blank. As you create new connectors that use the MTA transport stack, they are added to the list. After you've created the MTA transport stack, you can find its configuration object in the Microsoft MTA container of the server on which the transport stack was created.

Figure 22-3. *Viewing the connectors that use an MTA transport stack.*

More Info This chapter provides a fairly cursory introduction to connecting to X.400 systems. It should give you the basic understanding you need to configure a foreign connection, assuming that the administrator of the foreign system gives you most of the specific configuration information. If you need more details on the X.400 standard, consult *Introduction to X.400*, an excellent text by Cemil Betanov (Artech House Telecommunications Library, 1993).

Creating an X.400 Connector

After you've created an MTA transport stack, you must create the X.400 Connector itself. To do so, in the Exchange System snap-in, navigate to the Connectors container of the routing group in which you want to create the connector, as shown in Figure 22-4. Choose New TCP X.400 Connector from the Action menu. This opens the property sheet for the new X.400 Connector. The next several sections discuss the tabs on this property sheet.

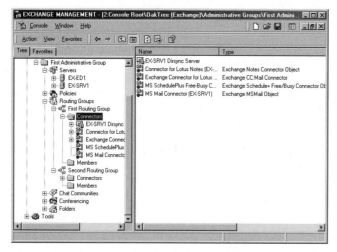

Figure 22-4. *Finding the Connectors container.*

General Tab   The General tab, shown in Figure 22-5, defines basic naming and connection information for the connector. You can configure the following settings on this property sheet:

- **Name**   Gives the name of the connector as it will appear in the Exchange System snap-in. Notice that there is no default value here, as there is for the display names of most other configuration objects. We suggest using a name that includes the type of connector (X.400) and the routing groups, servers, or locations you are connecting. An example might be X.400 Rgroup1 -> Atlanta X.400.

- **Remote X.400 Name**   Indicates the name of the remote server to which the local connector will connect. Click the Modify button to change the remote X.400 name and password. The password can be specified to prevent unauthorized connectors from opening an association to it. If a remote connector has been assigned such a password, you must enter it in this field.

- **X.400 Transport Stack**   Indicates the connector transport stack that the X.400 Connector is currently configured to use. You can change the stack used at any time.

- **Message Text Word-Wrap area**   Contains options that enable or disable word wrap on outgoing messages. Some messaging systems do not allow messages to use word wrap, in which words automatically wrap to the next line rather than trailing off the right edge of a message window when windows are resized. Select Never to disable word wrap on all outgoing messages. This is the default. Select At Column and enter a number to have Exchange Server automatically insert a carriage return at the specified column on all outgoing messages.

- **Remote Clients Support MAPI**   When selected, indicates that the remote messaging system and clients support Messaging Application Programming Interface (MAPI). Exchange Server will then transmit rich text and MAPI characteristics along with messages.

- **Do Not Allow Public Folder Referrals**   When selected, prevents users of the remote system from accessing public folders configured in the local routing group.

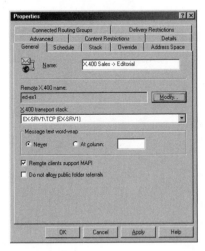

Figure 22-5. *Configuring general connection properties for a new X.400 Connector.*

Schedule Tab The Schedule tab on X.400 Connector's property sheet, shown in Figure 22-6, lets you restrict the times at which the X.400 Connector can be used. By default, the X.400 Connector can be used at any time (Always); for the most part, you will want to leave this value alone. There may be times, however, when you want to limit connectivity, such as on a very busy network or when you need to bring a network down for maintenance.

You can set an X.400 Connector schedule to one of four values:

- **Never** Disables the connector altogether. This setting is useful for bringing the connector down while performing maintenance.

- **Always** Allows connections to be made to and from the server at any time.

- **Selected Times** Allows you to define specific times at which the X.400 Connector is available. This setting can be useful on a busy network. If immediate messaging is not a concern, you can schedule messages to be sent only at specific periods during the day, when network traffic is otherwise low.

- **Remote Initiated** Allows remote servers to connect to the current server, but does not allow the local server to initiate a connection. This setting can be useful if sending outgoing messages immediately is not a big concern but receiving incoming messages is.

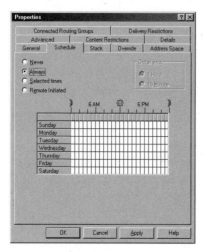

Figure 22-6. *Scheduling the availability of an X.400 Connector.*

Stack Tab Use the Stack tab, shown in Figure 22-7, to specify transport address information about the foreign X.400 system. After you've specified the host name or IP address of the foreign system, you can provide outgoing OSI addressing information, if necessary for the foreign system to which you are connecting.

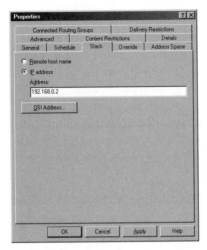

Figure 22-7. *Configuring transport address information for the foreign X.400 system.*

Override Tab   The Override tab, shown in Figure 22-8, lets you configure certain settings that override the local MTA settings when messages are sent over the X.400 Connector. For the most part, you can leave these advanced settings alone, particularly if you are using the X.400 Connector to connect to another Exchange routing group. If you are connecting to a foreign X.400 system, that system's administrator will be able to tell you whether you need to adjust any of these settings.

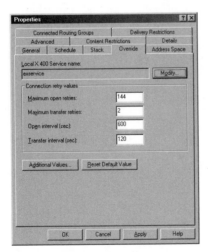

Figure 22-8. *Overriding values for local MTA information.*

You can also override the name and password of your local MTA on this tab. These options are used mainly when the name and password of the local MTA are too long or when they use characters or spaces that MTAs on foreign systems cannot accept. The overriding values are used only for the X.400 connection.

Address Space Tab   Foreign systems typically do not use the same addressing scheme as Exchange 2000 Server. For this reason, the Exchange MTA relies on address spaces to choose foreign gateways over which messages should be sent. An *address space* is the part of an address that designates the system that should receive the message. For example, a typical Internet address takes the form *user@company.com*. Everything after the @ sign is the address space. The format of the address space is enough to tell the MTA that the message should be sent via SMTP.

The Address Space tab, shown in Figure 22-9, allows you to configure an address space for the foreign X.400 system to which you are building a connection. The Exchange MTA compares the destination address of outgoing messages with this address space to determine whether the outgoing messages should be sent over the X.400 Connector.

To add an address space, click Add. The New Address Space dialog box opens (Figure 22-10). This dialog box allows you to specify the type of address space you want to add. Because you are connecting to a foreign X.400 system, you will want to configure an X.400 address space. Click OK.

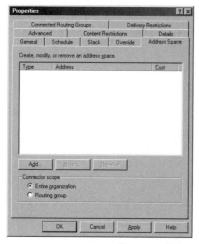

Figure 22-9. *Configuring an address space for the X.400 Connector.*

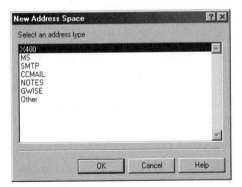

Figure 22-10. *Choosing the type of address space.*

The X.400 Address property sheet appears, as shown in Figure 22-11. The administrator of the foreign system should be able to provide the addressing information that you need to configure here. X.400 addresses are case-sensitive and need to be typed exactly as provided.

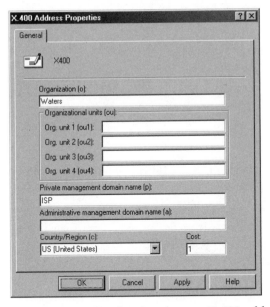

Figure 22-11. *Configuring the new X.400 address space information.*

Connected Routing Groups Tab   The Connected Routing Groups tab of the X.400 Connector's property sheet, shown in Figure 22-12, is used only when you are using an X.400 Connector to connect an Exchange 2000 routing group with an Exchange 5.5 site. (Remember, the Exchange 2000 Routing Group is the equivalent of an Exchange 5.5 site.) Although messaging between the groups can work if you leave the Connected Routing Group information blank and configure an address space for the remote server, Exchange Server will not know that it is communicating with an Exchange 5.5 site. As a result, the two environments will not allow each other access to their public folders. Click New to display a dialog box where you can enter the name of the Exchange 5.5 site to which you are connecting. When you add a routing group, an address space for that group is generated.

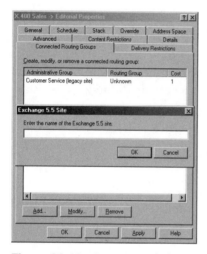

Figure 22-12. *Letting Exchange Server know that you are connecting to an Exchange 5.5 site.*

Delivery Restrictions Tab The Delivery Restrictions tab, shown in Figure 22-13, gives you control over which users can and cannot send messages over the X.400 Connector. You can control this in one of two ways:

- You can choose to prohibit all users from transferring messages over the X.400 Connector except for those whom you specifically allow. This option is represented on the top part of the tab. By default, all users are allowed to use the connector. To allow only certain users, click the Add button and select the users from the address book.

- You can choose to permit all users to transfer messages over the X.400 Connector except for those whom you specifically disallow. This option is represented on the bottom part of the tab. By default, no users are disallowed. To disallow certain users, click the Add button and select the users from the address book.

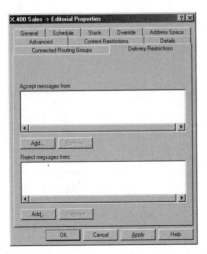

Figure 22-13. *Restricting the use of an X.400 Connector.*

Advanced Tab   The Advanced tab, shown in Figure 22-14, is used to specify options for MTA conformance, links, and message attributes. The settings depend primarily on the specifications of the foreign system to which you are connecting. The following options are available:

- **Allow BP-15 (In Addition To BP-14)**   The Body Part 15 (BP-15) standard is part of the 1988 X.400 recommendation and supports several advanced messaging features, such as the encoding of binary attachments. The Body Part 14 (BP-14) standard is part of the older 1984 X.400 recommendation, which supports fewer features. If you do not select the Allow BP-15 option, only the BP-14 standard will be used.

- **Allow Exchange Contents**   Exchange Server supports the use of Extended MAPI–compliant clients, which in turn support such features as rich text format. Make sure that any foreign X.400 system to which you are connecting supports such features before you allow them to be transferred.

- **Two-Way Alternate**   The two-way alternate specification is an X.400 standard in which two connected X.400 systems take turns transmitting and receiving information. If the foreign system to which you are connecting supports this option, enabling it can greatly improve transmission speed.

- **X.400 Bodypart For Message Text** This option specifies how message text should be formatted. Unless you are communicating with foreign systems that use foreign-language applications, leave this value at its default setting, International Alphabet 5 (IA5).

- **X.400 Conformance area** X.400 standards are published periodically as recommendations. Exchange 2000 Server supports the two primary recommendations: those issued in 1984 and those issued in 1988. Updates have been made to the standard since 1988, but they don't really form a new recommendation. The 1988 recommendation has two versions: normal mode and X.410 mode. The default setting is 1988 normal mode, and you can expect it to work with most foreign X.400 systems.

- **Global Domain Identifier** The global domain identifier (GDI) is a section of the X.400 address space of the target system. It is used to prevent message loops that can occur with outgoing messages. The administrator of the foreign X.400 system will let you know if you need to modify these values.

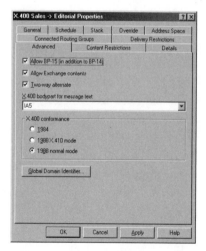

Figure 22-14. *Configuring advanced X.400 properties.*

Once you have finished configuring the property sheet for the connector, Exchange System will remind you that you also need to configure the X.400 Connector on the remote system. If the remote system has already been configured, the new X.400 Connector is ready for use.

Content Restrictions Tab The Content Restrictions tab, shown in Figure 22-15, is used to restrict certain message types. The following options are available:

- **Allowed Priorities area** Only specified message priorities are allowed across this connector.
- **Allowed Types area** You can choose whether this connector supports system messages (like public folder replication messages) or nonsystem messages (like standard interpersonal messages).
- **Allowed Sizes area** Messages sent across this connector can be restricted by message size.

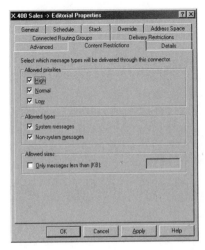

Figure 22-15. *Content Restrictions tab.*

Connecting to Microsoft Mail Systems

The Connector for MS Mail, included with Exchange 2000 Server, enables messaging connectivity and directory synchronization between Exchange 2000 Server and Microsoft Mail for PC Networks. The Connector for MS Mail is similar in configuration and function to other foreign messaging system connectors. It can be used over LAN, asynchronous, or X.25 connections. Microsoft Mail has an extensive history and has optional gateways to many external messaging systems. Exchange Server can connect to an existing Microsoft Mail system and use these gateways. The Connector for MS Mail was created to integrate seamlessly with Microsoft Mail so that if you need to migrate a Microsoft Mail system to Exchange Server, the transition will be transparent to the users. Configuring the Connector for MS Mail is fairly straightforward, but before you learn how to configure it, you should spend a little time learning how it works.

Understanding the Connector for MS Mail

Microsoft Mail is a passive, shared-file messaging system, meaning that it uses a centralized post office composed of shared folders on a network server. Each recipient on the Microsoft Mail system is given access to one of these folders. When one user sends mail to another, the client application formats the message and saves it in the recipient's shared folder. The recipient's client application regularly checks that folder to see whether any new messages have arrived.

When you configure the Connector for MS Mail, a shadow Microsoft Mail post office is created on the Exchange server. This means that the Microsoft Mail system to which you are connecting sees the Exchange server as just another Microsoft Mail system, reducing the amount of effort needed to configure the connection, because no additional software is needed for Microsoft Mail. The server on which the Connector for MS Mail is created will add a service to Windows 2000 that moves messages between post offices, emulating the Microsoft Mail External.exe application. The Windows 2000 service moves the messages between the shadow post office and the Microsoft Mail system for which it is configured.

Unlike Microsoft Mail, Exchange 2000 Server is an active client/server messaging system. The Connector for MS Mail enables the transfer of messages between these two very different types of systems. This connector has three components, each of which duplicates a function performed by a component of a Microsoft Mail system. These three components are as follows:

- **Mail Connector Post Office** A temporary storage area for messages that are being transferred between Exchange 2000 Server and a Microsoft Mail post office. The Mail Connector Post Office does not contain any actual recipient mailboxes; therefore, it is often referred to as a shadow post office. It is the equivalent of a post office in Microsoft Mail.

- **Mail Connector Interchange** A Windows 2000 service that provides routing of messages between Exchange 2000 Server and the Mail Connector Post Office.

- **Mail Connector (PC) MTA**   A Windows 2000 service that provides routing of messages between the Mail Connector Post Office on the Exchange server and one actual Microsoft Mail post office. Only one Connector for MS Mail can be configured on any given Exchange server, but each Connector for MS Mail can connect to multiple actual Microsoft Mail post offices, using a separate Mail Connector (PC) MTA for each post office. The Mail Connector (PC) MTA is the equivalent of a dedicated Microsoft Mail MTA. This component performs the same function as the External.exe application in Microsoft Mail.

When a user sends a message from a Microsoft Mail post office to a recipient on an Exchange server, each of these three components is involved in the transfer. The Mail Connector (PC) MTA receives the message from a Microsoft Mail post office and places it in a queue in the Mail Connector Post Office. The Mail Connector Interchange polls the Mail Connector Post Office at regular intervals. When it finds a message, the Mail Connector Interchange retrieves it, converts it to Exchange format, and places it in the queue for the Exchange Server MTA. The Exchange Server MTA routes the message to the Exchange recipient. When a user sends a message from Exchange 2000 Server to a Microsoft Mail post office, the process occurs in reverse.

Configuring the Connector for MS Mail

The Connector for MS Mail can be configured to work over a LAN connection or over a RAS asynchronous connection. Only one Connector for MS Mail can be configured on any given Exchange server, but each connector can connect to multiple Microsoft Mail post offices.

You use Exchange System to configure the Connector for MS Mail. First, however, you may need to install the connector itself. Check the Connectors container for any given routing group to see what servers the Connector for MS Mail is installed on. If it's installed on the server you want, you need only configure the connector as described in the next several sections. If it's not installed, run Exchange 2000 Server Setup on that server again to add the Connector for MS Mail to the installation.

Once the Connector for MS Mail is installed, its configuration object appears in the Connections container for the appropriate routing group in Exchange System, as shown in Figure 22-16. This container holds the configuration objects for each Connector for MS Mail installed in the group. You configure a Connector for MS Mail by using its property sheet, which you open in the usual manner.

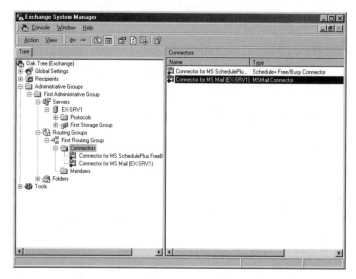

Figure 22-16. *Viewing the connectors for a routing group.*

Interchange Tab   Unlike most of the other property sheets that you configure, the property sheet for the Connector for MS Mail opens to the Interchange tab, shown in Figure 22-17, instead of the General tab. It does this because you must select an administrator's mailbox before configuring any other options on the connector. The Interchange tab also lets you specify how the Connector for MS Mail moves information between Exchange 2000 Server and the Microsoft Mail post office. You can configure the following settings:

- **Administrator's Mailbox**   Designates the recipient who is to receive any delivery status messages associated with the connector, including nondelivery reports (NDRs). You must specify an Exchange mailbox in this field before you can configure other settings for the connector.

- **Primary Language For Clients**   Specifies the primary language that the Microsoft Mail clients will use. The default language is English.

- **Maximize MS Mail 3.x Compatibility**   Microsoft Mail 3.x supports only the earliest versions of object linking and embedding (OLE), the Microsoft standard allowing applications to call the functions of other applications. For example, using OLE, a fully functional Microsoft Excel spreadsheet can be embedded in an e-mail message. When the Maximize MS Mail 3.x Compatibility option is enabled, the Connector for MS Mail creates two versions of each OLE object—one using the older standards and the other using newer standards. Maximizing compatibility allows clients using Microsoft Mail 3.x to view OLE objects, but it can double the size of any message that uses OLE.

- **Enable Message Tracking**   Allows you to use the message-tracking utility in Exchange System to track messages transferred between Exchange 2000 Server and the Microsoft Mail post office. This utility is covered in Chapter 23.

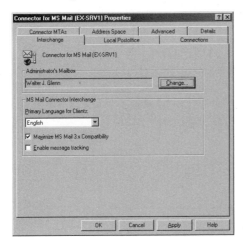

Figure 22-17. *The Interchange tab of the Connector for MS Mail's property sheet.*

Local Postoffice Tab   The Local Postoffice tab, shown in Figure 22-18, is used to configure the Mail Connector Post Office, or the shadow post office. You can set the name of the network (by default the Exchange organization), the name of the post office itself, and a logon password, if you are using RAS to connect.

Figure 22-18. *Configuring the shadow post office on the Exchange server.*

Connections Tab   You use the Connections tab, shown in Figure 22-19, to set up the list of Microsoft Mail post offices that the Connector for MS Mail will serve. At first, the only post office listed is the Mail Connector Post Office, the shadow post office that is maintained on the Exchange server.

Figure 22-19. *Viewing the Microsoft Mail post offices served by the Connector for MS Mail.*

To add a post office to the list, click Create. The Create Connection dialog box opens (Figure 22-20). This dialog box allows you to indicate the name and path of the Microsoft Mail post office to which you want to connect. It also allows you to specify the type of connection: LAN, Async, or Indirect. By default, the Connector for MS Mail attempts to deliver a message to the post office three times before generating an NDR. You can change this value by changing the setting in the Connection Attempts field.

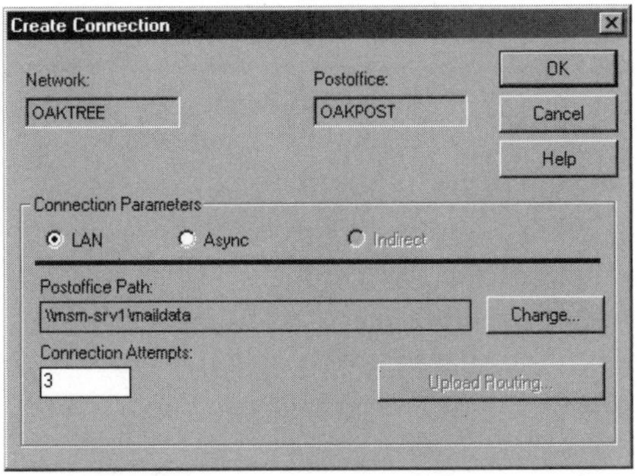

Figure 22-20. *The Create Connection dialog box.*

Connector MTAs Tab   The Connector MTAs tab, shown in Figure 22-21, is used to create a connector MTA to transfer messages between the shadow post office and the Microsoft Mail post office. You must create one connector MTA for each Microsoft Mail post office to which you want to connect.

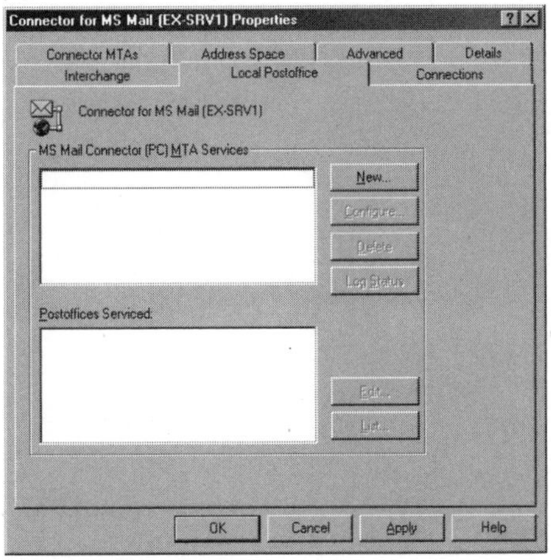

Figure 22-21. *Creating a connector MTA.*

To create a new connector MTA, click New. The New MS Mail Connector (PC) MTA Service dialog box opens (Figure 22-22). You can configure four primary settings in this dialog box:

- **Service Name** Indicates the name of the new connector MTA service you are creating. Give it a name that designates the Microsoft Mail post office that the connector MTA will service.

- **Log Messages area** Contains options for creating a log of messages transferred over the new connector MTA. You can log sent messages, received messages, or both. This option can be valuable when you are setting up an MTA for the first time and want to make sure that the connection is working as it should. It can also be valuable in troubleshooting the connector or in gauging the connector's performance.

- **Polling Frequency area** The Check For Mail Every *XX* Minutes option specifies how often the MTA should check for new messages in the shadow post office. The Update Configuration Every *XX* Minutes option specifies how often the MTA checks for changes to settings that you configure in the MS Mail Connector (PC) MTA Options dialog box.

- **Connection Parameters area** Contains options that indicate whether the MTA should connect over LAN or async. This setting overrides any setting made for the Connector for MS Mail on the Connections tab.

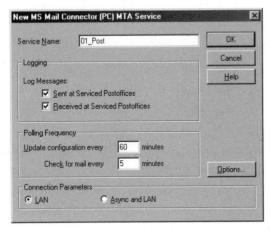

Figure 22-22. *The New MS Mail Connector (PC) MTA Service dialog box.*

Within the Polling Frequency area is an Options button (see Figure 22-22) that, when clicked, displays the MS Mail Connector (PC) MTA Options dialog box (Figure 22-23). In this dialog box the following configuration settings can be changed:

- **Maximum LAN Message Size area**   Contains options that specify whether to limit message size and, if so, the maximum size in kilobytes (KB) that can be transferred over the MTA via a LAN connection.

- **Free Disk Space area**   Contains options that cause the shadow post office to be closed, stopping all transfers to and from it, when the available free disk space in your Microsoft Mail post office drops to the specified level. Once the shadow post office is closed, it won't open again until the free disk space reaches the second level specified.

- **NetBIOS Notification**   When selected, allows Microsoft Mail users to be notified of new messages via a pop-up window.

- **Disable Mailer**   When selected, prevents the MTA from transferring messages between the Microsoft Mail post office and the shadow post office.

- **Disable Mail Dispatch**   When selected, stops the MTA from distributing any directory-synchronization messages. Directory synchronization is discussed in the next section, "Configuring Directory Synchronization."

- **Startup area**   Contains options that specify whether the MTA service starts automatically at system startup or must be started manually by an administrator.

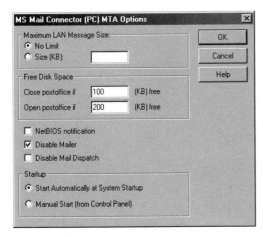

Figure 22-23. *The MS Mail Connector (PC) MTA Options dialog box.*

Real World **Configuring a Microsoft Mail Post Office to Connect to Exchange Server**

On the other side of the system, the Microsoft Mail post office will need to be configured to "see" the new shadow post office on the Exchange server. To configure this post office, follow these basic steps:

1. Open the Admin.exe program and log on as an administrator.
2. Use the arrow keys to select the External Admin menu, and then click Enter.
3. Select the Create menu, and then click Enter.
4. The Enter Network Name prompt appears. Type the Microsoft Mail network name that was configured for the shadow post office on Exchange Server, and then click Enter.
5. The Enter Post Office Name prompt appears. Type the post office name created for the shadow post office on Exchange Server, and then click Enter.
6. The Select Route Type prompt appears. Select Direct because you will not be routing mail through another Microsoft Mail post office to get to the shadow post office. Then click Enter.
7. The Direct Connection Via prompt appears. Select how that connection will occur, and click Enter.
8. At the Create? prompt, select Yes, and click Enter. You can then click Escape until you are prompted to quit and exit the program.

Once you've completed the tabs on the Connector for MS Mail's property sheet, the Exchange side of the configuration is complete. All you have to do is start the new MTA service and your shadow post office will be online and ready to go. The new service will be shown in the Services tool in Control Panel under the name you gave it in the New MS Mail Connector (PC) MTA Service dialog box. Your next step is to go to the Microsoft Mail post offices to which you configured connections and set up external post office entries for the shadow post office. This process is described in the sidebar "Configuring a Microsoft Mail Post Office to Connect to Exchange Server." Then you'll be ready to send a test e-mail from both the Microsoft Mail and Exchange sides of your mail system.

Configuring Directory Synchronization

After you've created the Connector for MS Mail and configured your Microsoft Mail post offices, message transfer between your Exchange organization and your Microsoft Mail system is enabled. Something is still missing, however. Although users can send messages between the two systems, they don't have access to the directory information of the other system. Instead, they are required to know the Microsoft Mail address of the recipient (even for recipients in the Exchange organization, because the Exchange server acts as a shadow Microsoft Mail post office). To allow users to look up directory information in the other system, you must configure directory synchronization between the two messaging systems.

> **Note**   Don't confuse directory synchronization with directory replication. *Directory replication* is the replication of the Active Directory directory service between Windows 2000 domain controllers. *Directory synchronization* is the synchronization of directory information between an Exchange server and a foreign messaging system.

Microsoft Mail native directory synchronization is exceptionally complex because of Microsoft Mail's file-based systems. It uses a program called Dispatch.exe, which is usually run on a separate machine, along with the External.exe program. Dispatch, in turn, launches a program called Nsda. Nsda further launches Reqmain and Srvmain. This cascade of programs is confusing, but it is used for specific reasons. The External program connects to the external post offices configured for that Microsoft Mail post office. Dispatch schedules the connections to those external post offices for directory synchronization. Nsda handles directory synchronization by running Reqmain to request the main directory from the other post office and Srvmain to send the local directory to the other post office.

> **Note**   Remember that Microsoft Mail was initially written in the mid-1980s, when systems had external 33-MHz 80286 chips with MS-DOS and 1 MB of RAM. Although this process may seem overly complex now, it was the only way to get the job done without a minicomputer back then.

Real World   Preparing for Directory Synchronization

Configuring directory synchronization between Exchange 2000 Server and an existing Microsoft Mail network may sound like a fairly easy task—and in theory it is. In the real world, however, things don't always go so smoothly. Often, existing Microsoft Mail networks are unplanned, undocumented beasts that slowly grow over the years in such a way that nobody has a clear idea of how they are set up.

Whether you are implementing an Exchange organization that will coexist with a Microsoft Mail network or planning a migration from Microsoft Mail to Exchange Server, take the time to thoroughly document and clean up your existing Microsoft Mail network. This effort will make it much easier to configure, maintain, and troubleshoot message transport and directory synchronization. The following suggestions will help you get started:

- Document the current Microsoft Mail network. Identify all the existing post offices, including the users of those post offices.

- Document the current directory synchronization topology. Where is the Dirsync server? Which post offices are requestors?

- Have users clean up their existing Microsoft Mail post offices if you plan to migrate messages to Exchange 2000 Server.

- Resolve any outstanding problems on the Microsoft Mail network, ensuring that directory synchronization works correctly before you configure the Connector for MS Mail in Exchange 2000 Server.

In a Microsoft Mail messaging environment, each post office maintains a directory of information about the recipients whose mailboxes exist in that post office. When a network has multiple post offices, a process called Dirsync synchronizes the directory information among the post offices. On the Microsoft Mail network, one post office is set up as a Dirsync server. All other post offices are set up as Dirsync requestors. Three timed events used by the Nsda program, called T1, T2, and T3, govern the synchronization of directory information between the Dirsync requestors and the Dirsync server. Here's how the process works:

1. At the T1 event, every Dirsync requestor on the network sends any changes made to its current directory information to the Dirsync server. The T1 event fires on all post offices.

2. At the T2 event, the Dirsync server starts Dispatch.exe, which in turn starts other processes that combine the directory information from all Dirsync requestors and the Dirsync server into a Global Address List. The Dirsync server then sends that list back to the Dirsync requestors. The T2 event fires only on the Dirsync server post office.

3. At the T3 event, each Dirsync requestor rebuilds its own Global Address List, based on the new directory information from the Dirsync server. The T3 event fires on all post offices. After these three events occur, all post offices on the network use a common address list.

The Mail Connector Post Office on the Exchange server can be configured to act as either a Dirsync server or a Dirsync requestor. Unless you are building a new Dirsync system and want to use Exchange server as the Dirsync server, you should set up the Exchange server as a Dirsync requestor on your current system. The next section describes how to do this.

Configuring Exchange 2000 Server as a Dirsync Requestor

Setting up the Exchange server as a Dirsync requestor is quite simple. In the Exchange System snap-in, navigate to the Connectors container for the routing group in which you want to configure the requestor. Then, on the Action menu, point to New and choose Dirsync Requestor. The property sheet for the new Dirsync requestor opens.

General Tab   The General tab of the Dirsync requestor's property sheet (Figure 22-24) allows you to define the basic properties of the new Dirsync requestor. On this tab you can configure the following settings:

- **Name**   Specifies the name of the new Dirsync requestor. Give it a name that indicates the server on which the requestor is installed and the name of the Microsoft Mail network—for example, *server_name* (Dirsync) *network_name*.

- **Append To Imported Users' Display Name**   When selected, causes the requestor name to be added after each custom recipient that is created by the Dirsync process. This can be very useful in identifying recipients created by a specific requestor.

- **Dirsync Address** Indicates the custom recipient that receives directory synchronization messages. By default, the Dirsync address is set to a hidden administrator's mailbox, $SYSTEM, on the Dirsync server.

- **Address Types area** Contains options that specify the address types the new Dirsync requestor will submit to the Dirsync server during synchronization.

- **Requestor Language** Indicates the language used by the Dirsync requestor. The Dirsync server uses this information in formatting the address lists that it sends back to the requestor.

- **Server** Specifies the Exchange server in the routing group that will act as the Dirsync requestor. The default is the server to which the Exchange System snap-in was connected when you created the requestor.

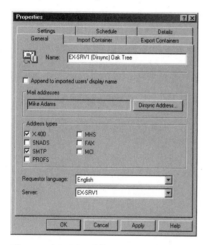

Figure 22-24. *The General tab of the property sheet for a new Dirsync requestor.*

Import Container Tab The Import Container tab, shown in Figure 22-25, is used to define the Recipient container on the Dirsync requestor where addresses that are imported from the Dirsync server should be stored. This option is available only while you are creating the requestor; after the requestor is created, you cannot change the Recipient container. You can also specify what should happen when Exchange Server tries to synchronize a Microsoft Mail mailbox for which a Windows 2000 user account does not exist. Your options are to create a new contact, create a new user account, or create a new but disabled user account. For more on these types of recipients, see Chapter 9.

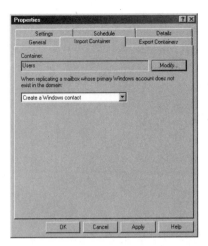

Figure 22-25. *Specifying an Import container for the Dirsync requestor.*

Export Containers Tab The Export Containers tab, shown in Figure 22-26, specifies the Recipient containers whose recipients should be exported to the Dirsync server during the T1 event. Click the Add button to select from a list of Recipient containers to use. You can add as many as you like. By default, users, groups, and contacts are all exported. The Export Contacts and Export Groups options at the bottom of the tab allow you to disable synchronization of contacts and groups.

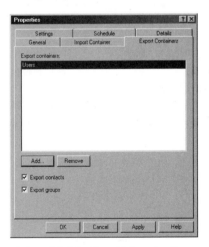

Figure 22-26. *Specifying the Export containers for the Dirsync requestor.*

Settings Tab The Settings tab, shown in Figure 22-27, is used to specify various settings that govern the new Dirsync requestor. The options on this tab are as follows:

- **Dirsync Password** Gives the password for the Dirsync server. You can specify a password on the Dirsync server to prevent unauthorized access to the system. If such a password is in effect, you must enter it here.

- **Participation area** Contains options that indicate whether the Dirsync requestor sends updated directory information to the Dirsync server, receives updated information, or both. This feature can be useful if you have a great deal of directory information being transferred. You can set up separate Exchange servers to receive and send directory information.

- **Template Information area** Contains options that let you import Microsoft Mail templates and export Exchange 2000 Server templates, if your Microsoft Mail post offices use address templates. Templates allow users of one system to manually enter the addresses of the users on the other system on an ad hoc basis each time they create new messages instead of using an address book.

- **Dirsync Information area** Contains options that force the Dirsync requestor to perform an import, an export, or both of every address available on the Dirsync server during the next T1 and T3 events. Select these options for the first time your new requestor enters the Dirsync cycle.

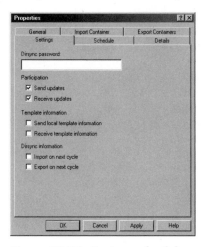

Figure 22-27. *Settings tab of the property sheet for a new Dirsync requestor.*

Schedule Tab   The final tab you need to configure is the Schedule tab. Two Dirsync events, T1 and T3, are important for every Dirsync requestor. The Schedule tab allows you to configure the time at which the T1 event fires—that is, when the requestor sends updates to the Dirsync server. By default, this happens once each night. You do not need to configure a schedule for the T3 event for an Exchange 2000 Server Dirsync requestor, because updates are dynamically committed to the directory as soon as they reach the requestor.

When you finish configuring the Dirsync requestor's property sheet, your Exchange 2000 server will be set up as a Dirsync requestor. You then need to configure the Dirsync server on the Microsoft Mail network with information about the new requestor. For more information on this procedure, refer to your Microsoft Mail product documentation.

Setting Up Exchange 2000 Server as a Dirsync Server

Configuring Exchange 2000 Server as a Dirsync server is even easier than configuring it as a Dirsync requestor. The process requires only three steps:

1. Use Exchange System to configure a Dirsync Server object for the Exchange routing group.
2. Configure a Remote Dirsync Requestor object in Exchange System for each remote Dirsync requestor on the Microsoft Mail network.
3. Configure the remote Dirsync requestors to use the new Dirsync server.

The following sections cover the first two steps of this process. For the third step, refer to your Microsoft Mail product documentation.

Configure a Dirsync Server Object in Exchange System   To configure a Dirsync Server object, first navigate to the Connectors container for the chosen routing group in Exchange System. Then, on the Action menu, point to New and choose Dirsync Server. The Dirsync Server property sheet opens (Figure 22-28).

Note   You will need to configure an MS Mail recipient policy before you can create and configure a Dirsync Server object. To do this, navigate to the Recipients Policy container under the Recipients container. You can either modify the default policy or create a new one. In either case, on the E-Mail Addresses tab, ensure the MS Mail address is correct for Exchange users and select the check box next to the MS Mail e-mail address.

As you can see, there is much less to configure for the Dirsync server than for the Dirsync requestor. The Schedule tab is identical to the other Schedule tabs that you have grown accustomed to by now. You use it to define the times at which the Dirsync server sends master address list updates to remote Dirsync requestors—otherwise known as the T2 event.

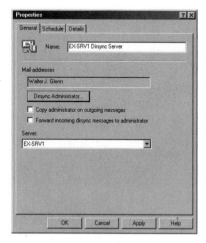

Figure 22-28. *The Dirsync Server property sheet.*

The General tab contains several settings:

- **Name**   Gives both the display name and the directory name of the Dirsync server. Specify a name that includes the name of the Exchange server on which the Dirsync server is being installed.

- **Dirsync Administrator**   Clicking this button displays a dialog box where you can designate a mailbox to which synchronization status messages should be sent.

- **Copy Administrator On Outgoing Messages**   When selected, causes all outgoing synchronization messages from the Dirsync server to be copied to the Dirsync administrator's mailbox during the T2 event. Enabling this option often results in a large number of messages being sent to the administrator's mailbox, but the messages are useful in troubleshooting problems with synchronization.

- **Forward Incoming Dirsync Messages To Administrator**   When selected, causes all incoming messages from Dirsync requestors to be forwarded to the Dirsync administrator's mailbox during the T1 event. Again, this option can be a valuable aid in troubleshooting synchronization problems.

- **Server**   Specifies the Exchange server that will act as a Dirsync server. The default is the server to which Exchange System was connected when you created the Dirsync server.

Configure a Remote Dirsync Requestor Object in Exchange System   For each remote Dirsync requestor on the Microsoft Mail network that the new Dirsync server will serve, you must configure a Remote Dirsync Requestor object in Exchange Administrator. To create the Remote Dirsync Requestor object, navigate to the Connections container and select a Dirsync Server object. Then, on the Action menu, point to New and choose Remote Dirsync Requestor.

The process you use to configure the remote Dirsync requestor is virtually identical to the process you use to configure Exchange 2000 Server as a Dirsync requestor. Refer to "Configuring Exchange 2000 Server as a Dirsync Requestor," earlier in this chapter, for details. After you create a Remote Dirsync Requestor object for each Dirsync requestor on the Microsoft Mail network, remember to configure the actual Dirsync requestors themselves.

> **More Info**   Arriving at a peaceful coexistence between an Exchange organization and a Microsoft Mail network involves more detail than a single chapter can provide. You can find additional valuable information on coexistence and migration issues in *Deploying Exchange 2000 Server* (Microsoft Press, 1998) in the Notes From the Field series.

Summary

In this chapter, you learned how to configure Exchange 2000 Server to transfer messages and synchronize directory information with foreign messaging systems. In particular, you learned how to set up an X.400 Connector to transfer messages with any X.400-compliant messaging system and how to set up message transfer and directory synchronization between Exchange 2000 Server and Microsoft Mail for PC Networks. The next chapter begins the section on maintaining Exchange 2000 Server.

Part VI
Maintenance

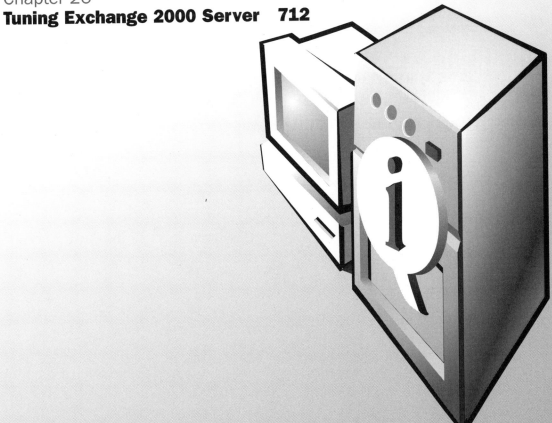

Chapter 23
Monitoring Exchange 2000 Server

One key to running a successful network is keeping a close eye on its operation, especially if you are running a complex system such as a Microsoft Exchange 2000 Server. By keeping close watch over your organization and its components, you can spot potential problems before they occur and can quickly respond to the problems that do occur. Monitoring also allows you to identify trends in network use that signal opportunities for optimization and future planning.

This chapter covers many of the tools that you can use to monitor Exchange 2000 Server. Some of these tools, such as Event Viewer and System Monitor, are provided by Microsoft Windows 2000. Other tools, such as server and link monitors, are part of Exchange 2000 Server itself.

Using Event Viewer

As you may know, Windows 2000 records many events in its own event logs. You can view the logs of both local and remote servers by using the Event Viewer utility, which you can find in the Administrative Tools folder on the Programs menu. Windows 2000 maintains three distinct logs:

- **Application** The application log is a record of events generated by applications. All Exchange 2000 Server services write their status information to this log. If you enable diagnostics logging for any Exchange 2000 components, that information is also recorded in the application log. This log is the most valuable one for monitoring the general health of an Exchange server. Figure 23-1 shows an entry made in the application log following a directory access error.

- **Security** The security log is a record of events based on the auditing settings specified in Active Directory Users and Computers.

- **System** The system log is a record of events that concern components of the system itself, including such events as device driver and network failures.

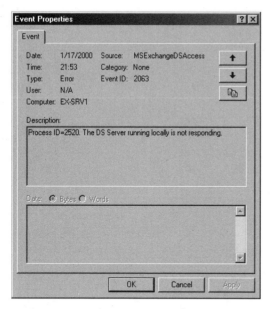

Figure 23-1. *Reviewing an application event created by Exchange 2000 Server.*

Note You may also see additional event logs in Event Viewer based upon the services installed on your server. For example, a server running DNS will show a DNS Service log. Domain controllers may also show a File Replication Service log.

If you have a particular log file that you want to save, you have at your disposal three formats in which to save it. You can save it as a binary event log file with the .EVT extension, as a text file with the .TXT extension, or as a comma-delimited text file with the .CSV extension. Binary files with the .EVT extension can be read only with Event Viewer; the two text files can be read with your favorite ASCII editor/viewer.

You will encounter five types of events in the three logs, and a unique icon identifies each event type so that you can easily distinguish between the information entries and the error entries. Table 23-1 shows these icons and describes each of them. Normally, you will encounter only the first three icons in the table in relation to Exchange Server. The classification of events is controlled by the applications and system and cannot be configured by the administrators.

Table 23-1.   Event types displayed in Event Viewer

Icon	Event	Description
⊗	Error	A significant problem has occurred, such as an Exchange Server service that may not have started properly.
⚠	Warning	An event has occurred that is not currently detrimental to the system but may indicate a possible future problem.
ⓘ	Information	A successful operation has occurred. For example, an Exchange Server service starting successfully may trigger this type of event.
🗝	Audit success	An audited security access attempt—for example, a successful logon to the system—was successful.
🔒	Audit failure	An audited security access attempt—for example, a failed access to an audited file or directory—was not successful.

Using Diagnostics Logging

All Exchange 2000 Server services log certain critical events to the Windows 2000 application log. For some services, however, you can configure additional levels of diagnostics logging. Diagnostics logging is one of the most useful tools for troubleshooting problems in Exchange 2000 Server.

You can modify the levels of diagnostics logging for all services on a particular Exchange server by using the Diagnostics Logging tab of the server's property sheet in the Exchange System snap-in, as shown in Figure 23-2. On the left side of this tab, you'll find a hierarchical view of all of the services on the server for which you can enable advanced diagnostics logging. On the right side, you'll find a list of categories that can be logged for the selected service.

Real World   Size of the Event Viewer Application Log

Diagnostics logging of Exchange 2000 Server components generates many entries in the Event Viewer application log, especially if you have the diagnostics logging level set to Maximum. You should use diagnostics logging only when you are troubleshooting potential problems in specific components, and you should disable it when you are finished. By default, the application log file is set to a maximum size of 512 KB. We generally recommend setting this size to at least 1 MB for general use and even larger when using diagnostics logging. By default, each log file overwrites events older than seven days.

You can configure the default settings for size and overwriting by changing the Maximum Log Size and Event Log Wrapping options on the property sheet for the log. To see this property sheet, in Event Viewer, right-click the log in question and click Properties. The options are in the Log Size area of the General tab. The Maximum Log Size option can be adjusted in 64-KB increments.

You can choose from among three Event Log Wrapping options. They are Overwrite Events As Needed, Overwrite Events Older Than X Days, and Do Not Overwrite Events. (If you select the last option you must clear the log manually.) Make sure that you have set the wrapping option correctly for what you are trying to accomplish. For example, if you have it set to Overwrite Events As Needed, you could lose critical information that might have helped you solve the problem you had when you turned diagnostics on in the first place.

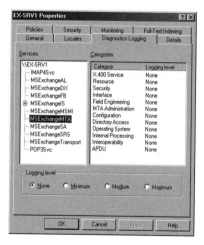

Figure 23-2. *Viewing diagnostics logging categories.*

All of the major services are represented on this property sheet, including the following:

- **MSExchangeCCMC (Microsoft Exchange cc:Mail Connector)**   Use diagnostics logging on this service to troubleshoot problems with message delivery between Exchange 2000 Server and a cc:Mail post office.

- **MSExchangeDX (Microsoft Exchange Directory Synchronization Agent)**   Use diagnostics logging on this service to troubleshoot problems with directory synchronization of foreign mail systems.

- **MSExchangeIS (Microsoft Exchange Information Store service)** You do not actually enable logging for the Information Store service as a whole. The MSExchangeIS item expands, allowing you to enable diagnostics logging individually for the public folder store and the mailbox store and for the various Internet protocols, as shown in Figure 23-3. Use diagnostics logging on this service to monitor background tasks that occur in Exchange, such as information store maintenance.

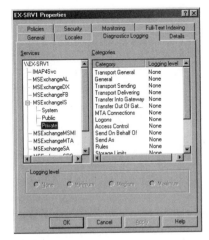

Figure 23-3. *Enabling diagnostics logging for components of the information store.*

- **MSExchangeMSMI (Microsoft Exchange Microsoft Mail Connector)** The acronym MSMI stands for Microsoft Mail Interchange. Use diagnostics logging on this service to troubleshoot problems with message delivery between Exchange 2000 Server and Microsoft Mail post offices.

- **MSExchangeMTA (Microsoft Exchange Message Transfer Agent)** Use diagnostics logging on this service to troubleshoot problems with message delivery and gateway connectivity.

You can enable four distinct levels of logging. All events that occur in Exchange 2000 Server are given an event level of 0, 1, 3, or 5. The logging level you set will determine which levels of events are logged.

Those levels are:

- **None**   Only events with a logging level of 0 are logged. These events include application and system failures.
- **Minimum**   All events with a logging level of 1 or lower are logged.
- **Medium**   All events with a logging level of 3 or lower are logged.
- **Maximum**   All events with a logging level of 5 or lower are logged. All events concerning a particular service are logged.

Real World   **Using High Levels of Diagnostics Logging**

Although diagnostics logging can be a very useful tool in some circumstances, at other times it can be more of a hindrance than a help. Enabling high levels of diagnostics logging, such as Medium or Maximum, can fill up your event log quickly, often hiding important level 0 events in a flood of trivial events. In addition, many events are logged that may seem like errors but actually are not. These events include the routine errors and timeouts that occur in normal Exchange 2000 Server operation.

Finally, many events will be logged that are really not documented anywhere in the product literature. Exchange developers often use these undocumented events to perform diagnostics.

Our recommendation is to leave diagnostics logging set to None for general purposes. If you need to troubleshoot malfunctions of particular services, try setting the diagnostics logging level to Low or Medium for brief periods.

Using Exchange Monitors

Exchange 2000 Server provides server and link monitors that help you watch over your organization by checking the status of servers and connectors. *Server monitors* check the status of designated services, as well as the usage of various resources on a particular Exchange server. *Link monitors* check the status of a connector between two servers. You configure monitoring of both types of objects using the Exchange System.

To view the available monitors, navigate to the Tools container, expand the Monitoring and Status folder, and select the Status container. The available monitors are displayed in the contents pane, as shown in Figure 23-4. The objects shown are those monitored by the server to which you are currently connected. To view the monitored objects on a different server, right-click the Status container and choose Connect To from the shortcut menu. This displays a list of servers from which you can choose.

In addition to specifying what you want to monitor, you also need to configure how you will be notified of any problems with your servers or connectors. This is covered later in the chapter, in the section "Using Notifications."

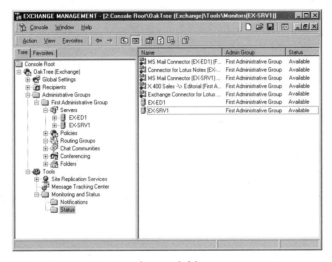

Figure 23-4. *Viewing the available monitors on a server.*

Using Server Monitors

A server monitor checks designated resources and Windows 2000 services on a server to detect critical situations. This type of monitor is created automatically when you install Exchange 2000 Server. Server monitors allow you to monitor the status of six important resources:

- Windows 2000 services
- SMTP queues
- X.400 queues
- CPU utilization
- Free disk space
- Available virtual memory

To configure the resources to be monitored, right-click the server monitor you want to modify in the Status container and choose Properties.

> **Note** In Exchange Server 5.5, you must create a monitor manually for each server, and the Exchange Administrator utility must be running for the monitor to work. In Exchange 2000 Server, server monitors are created automatically, and they run all the time, regardless of whether you keep Exchange System running or not.

Windows 2000 Services

By default, a server monitor checks various Windows 2000 services that affect the performance of Exchange 2000 Server. There is a preconfigured set of such services, which will appear as a default set in the server object's properties in the Status folder (Figure 23-5). You can view or edit the services being monitored by selecting the default set of resources and clicking the Detail button. The services shown in Figure 23-6 all have some impact on Exchange 2000 Server.

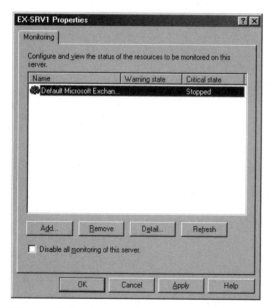

Figure 23-5. *Viewing the resources being monitored.*

Figure 23-6. *Viewing the Exchange-related services that are monitored by default.*

You may want to add additional services, such as an antivirus service or a backup agent so that you are monitoring not only Exchange 2000 Server but also those services related to the overall functionality of Exchange 2000. You can either add these services to the existing list or create a separate set of Windows 2000 services to monitor. To create a separate set, click the Add button on the server's property sheet. The Add Resource dialog box appears, listing the six resources you can monitor (Figure 23-7). Select Windows 2000 Service and click OK. The Services dialog box opens (Figure 23-8). Give the group of services a descriptive name, and add the services you want to monitor by clicking the Add button and selecting them from the resulting list.

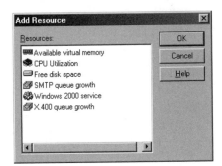

Figure 23-7. *Viewing the resources you can monitor.*

Figure 23-8. *Adding services to be monitored.*

For each group of resources you want to monitor, you need to specify the state the monitor will be in should those resources fail. You have two choices: Warning or Critical. The state you choose determines what notifications are made should the resource cross a certain threshold. (See the section "Using Notifications" later in the chapter.)

> **Tip** At first, you may want to add other Windows 2000 services to be monitored along with the default group of services. However, best practice is to separate additional Windows 2000 services that are to be monitored by creating a new group for them. The state that a monitor triggers will determine which group a particular service belongs in. Should any of the services being monitored in a group fail, one group of monitored services can trigger a Warning state, while the other can trigger a Critical state.

SMTP and X.400 Queue Growth

The server monitor can monitor both the SMTP and X.400 queues for continuous queue growth. With this type of monitoring, the server monitor is looking not for a certain number of entries in each queue but rather for continual growth of the length of the queue over time. When you add monitoring for either type of queue from the server's property sheet, you see the appropriate Queue Thresholds dialog box (Figure 23-9), where you specify the number of minutes of continual queue growth that will cause the server to enter a Warning or Critical state.

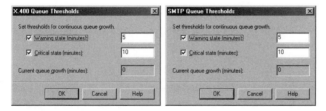

Figure 23-9. *Setting X.400 and SMTP queue thresholds.*

CPU Utilization

A CPU running at a high utilization percentage can indicate either that too many services are running on one server or that the server does not have enough processing power. For this reason, it is a good idea to monitor the server's CPU utilization. You can specify how long the CPU should run above a certain utilization percentage before the server's state changes to Warning or Critical, as well as the threshold utilization percentages, as shown in Figure 23-10.

Figure 23-10. *Setting CPU utilization thresholds.*

Note   The CPU utilization monitoring capability in Exchange 2000 Server is a great enhancement over the CPU monitoring in Microsoft Windows NT 4 and Exchange Server 5.5, in which you have to use Performance Monitor if you want to monitor server CPU utilization. Even then, you can check only for each instance in which the server exceeds the specified CPU utilization and react either the first time or *every* time. It is when CPU utilization remains high over a period of time that you truly have a problem. The CPU monitoring in Exchange 2000 Server gives a more realistic picture of your server's performance.

Free Disk Space

Exchange 2000 Server can suffer adverse effects if it runs out of disk space. That is why it is important to monitor your server's free disk space and be notified when you need to take action by freeing up disk space or replacing drives with larger ones. Disk space is monitored on a per drive basis. You can specify which drive to monitor and the levels of free disk space below which the server will enter a Warning or Critical state (Figure 23-11).

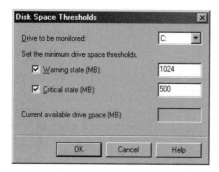

Figure 23-11. *Setting disk space thresholds.*

Available Virtual Memory

Because Windows 2000 uses a virtual memory model (one in which the server's memory consists of the physical memory and a pagefile on disk working together to provide memory services to other system processes), it is important to get an idea of how much memory is available, whether in RAM or on disk. As with CPU utilization, you need to know not only whether the server dips below a certain usage threshold for memory, but whether it remains below that threshold over a period of time. You can specify how long the server's available virtual memory should remain below the specified thresholds before the server's state changes to Warning or Critical (Figure 23-12).

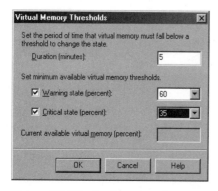

Figure 23-12. *Setting virtual memory thresholds.*

Using Link Monitors

A link monitor is automatically created for each connector present on a server. Like server monitors, link monitors are displayed in the Status container in the Exchange System snap-in (refer back to Figure 23-4). The status of each link monitor is listed as either available or unavailable. Unlike server monitors, there is really nothing you need to configure for a link monitor.

When a link monitor indicates that a connector is unavailable, you can troubleshoot the connector using the Queue Viewer, which is an embedded utility found in the Protocol container in the Exchange System snap-in. For instance, to troubleshoot an SMTP queue problem, you would look at the queues that were created under the SMTP virtual server for the server in question. You may also want to use Exchange Server's message tracking feature, which is described later in the section "Tracking Messages," to see where messages are getting stuck.

Using Notifications

If a server crashes in the middle of the forest and there is nobody to hear, does it make a sound? Monitoring a server is useless if no one is notified when problems occur. Thus, to complete the loop, you need to configure how you want to be notified of specific problems. Exchange 2000 Server gives you the ability to send notifications using e-mail, a script of commands when the monitor enters a given state, or both of these methods. To add a notification, navigate to the Notifications container under Monitoring and Status. Right-click Notifications, point to New, and choose either E-Mail Notification or Script Notification.

Setting Up an E-Mail Notification

If you choose to be notified by e-mail, Exchange 2000 Server provides you with a default detailed e-mail message that lists the current status of all six types of resources that can be monitored. All you have to do to set up e-mail notification is provide information about the resources in question and indicate which state will trigger the e-mail notification (Warning or Critical).

In the property sheet that appears when you choose E-Mail Notification (Figure 23-13), use the Monitoring Server option to specify which server will perform the monitoring function. Choosing a value for the Servers And Connectors

To Monitor option is the most critical step: be careful not to have a server configured to monitor a specific resource with no notifications set up to act upon that monitor. Table 23-2 lists the values for this option and the monitoring scope of each value.

> **Note** We do not recommend that you use an Exchange server to monitor itself. If a Warning or Critical state occurs on a self-monitoring Exchange server, it may be unable to send e-mail to an administrator. Therefore, you should plan on setting up cross-monitoring of your Exchange servers.

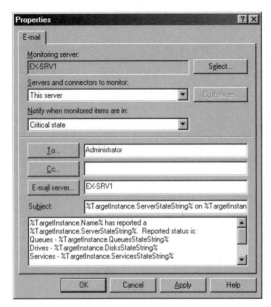

Figure 23-13. *Property sheet for a new e-mail notification.*

Table 23-2. Choices on the Servers And Connectors To Monitor list

Value	Monitoring Scope
This Server	Monitors a specific server for Critical or Warning states.
All Servers	Monitors all Exchange 2000 servers for Critical or Warning states.
Any Server In The Routing Group	Monitors any server in the routing group for Critical or Warning states.

Table 23-2.   *continued*

Value	Monitoring Scope
All Connectors	Monitors all connectors in the Exchange organization for Critical or Warning states.
Any Connector In The Routing Group	Monitors all connectors in a specific Exchange routing group for Critical or Warning states.
Custom List Of Servers	Allows you to create a customized list of servers to be monitored for Critical or Warning states. After you select this option, click Customize to add servers to the list.
Custom List Of Connectors	Allows you to create a customized list of connectors to be monitored for Critical or Warning states. After you select this option, click Customize to add connectors to the list.

The next step is to establish the recipients of the notification message, using the To and Cc fields (Figure 23-13). To provide the name of the e-mail server that will deliver the message, either enter the fully qualified domain name (FQDN) of the SMTP server or click the E-Mail Server button to retrieve a list of available Exchange servers.

If you choose to enter the FQDN of an SMTP server, the SMTP server you specify must allow the Exchange server to send e-mail using anonymous relay. Otherwise, e-mail notifications will not be delivered. A well administered e-mail system will most likely not allow relaying anonymously, so you will need to carefully select the SMTP server that will deliver the notification.

Notice that the subject and message fields in Figure 23-13 are already filled in to provide a default message that informs the recipient of the nature of the notification. You can, of course, modify these fields to meet your own needs, using plain text and Windows Management Instrumentation placeholders.

More Info   For more information about Windows Management Instrumentation placeholders see *Microsoft Windows 2000 Server Resource Kit* (Microsoft Press, 2000).

Note   You can use e-mail to provide both immediate notification as well as a historical record of a problem. You can provide immediate notification by sending a message to an alphanumeric pager or cellular phone via a mail-enabled contact while maintaining a historical record by sending a notification to a public folder.

Setting Up a Script Notification

A script notification differs from an e-mail notification in that it runs an executable file rather than sending an e-mail. This type of notification gives you the flexibility to start a variety of processes, limited only by your need, your imagination, and the existence of the needed executable. For example, if a monitor found that the SMTP queue was growing significantly, perhaps indicating that a VB Script–based e-mail virus was running rampant through your system, you could use a script notification to issue a NET STOP command to shut down all of the Exchange services on your server (Figure 23-14).

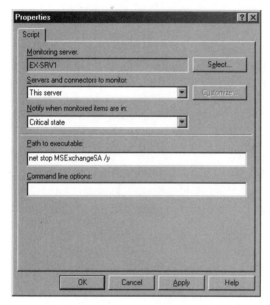

Figure 23-14. *Property sheet for a new script notification.*

Don't forget that you can use a combination of e-mail and script notifications for the same monitored resources. For instance, in the example just given, in addition to having a script notification that shuts down Exchange 2000 Server, you could have an e-mail notification that sends an e-mail to your alphanumeric pager using an SMTP server not running Exchange 2000 Server.

You will most likely have to experiment a bit with the resources you want to monitor and the notifications in order to establish the correct thresholds, the servers and connectors to be monitored, and the recipients who should be notified.

Tracking Messages

Message tracking is enabled at the server level, using the property sheet for the server container. Once message tracking is enabled, Exchange Server keeps a log of all messages transferred to and from the server. Log files are maintained by the System Attendant service on each server. When message tracking is enabled, you can track individual messages by using the Message Tracking Center (MTC), a component of the Exchange System snap-in.

Using the Message Tracking Center

You launch the MTC by first navigating to and selecting the Message Tracking Center container in the Exchange System snap-in, as shown in Figure 23-15. Next choose the Track Message command from the Action menu, which opens the Message Tracking Center dialog box (Figure 23-16). Click the Browse buttons next to the From or Send To boxes to open a standard address book from which you can choose the originator or recipient of the message that you want to track in the MTC. You can also browse for the servers on which you would like to search for the messages. After you enter your criteria, click Find Now to perform the search. Figure 23-16 shows all messages that were sent to John Garrity.

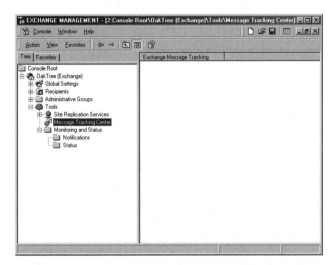

Figure 23-15. *Navigating to the Message Tracking Center container.*

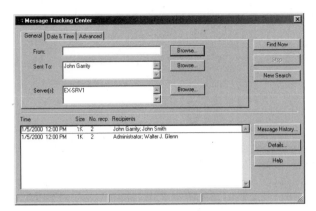

Figure 23-16. *Message Tracking Center dialog box, showing all messages to John Garrity.*

Once the messages that meet your criteria are displayed, you can open the property sheet of any message by selecting it and then clicking Details. Use this method to find the actual message that you want to track. When you find that message, select it and then click Message History to put the MTC to work tracking the history of the message. The results are displayed in the Message History dialog box (Figure 23-17). As you can see, this dialog box displays basic information and a history of the message.

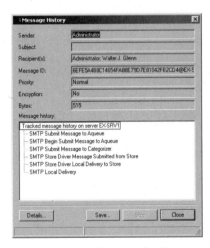

Figure 23-17. *Viewing the history of a message.*

Real World   Performing Advanced Searches

You can perform a more sophisticated search for messages by clicking either the Date & Time tab or the Advanced tab of the main Message Tracking Center dialog box. The Date & Time tab lets you specify a particular date or range of dates for which to search. You can also combine this criterion with criteria entered on the General or Advanced tabs.

The Advanced tab lets you search for a particular message using its message ID. Every message transferred in an Exchange organization has a unique ID that includes the name of the originating Exchange server, the date, and a long series of digits. Choosing this option is best when you want to track one specific message, such as a test message that you create. You can find the ID for any message by viewing the properties of a copy of the message in a mail client.

Using System Monitor

System Monitor is a tool that is included with Windows 2000 and is available in the Administrative Tools folder. System Monitor graphically charts the performance of hundreds of individual system parameters on a computer running Microsoft Windows 2000 Server. When Exchange 2000 Server is installed on a Windows 2000 server, you can chart several Exchange-specific counters as well. Chapter 26 describes in detail how to use System Monitor.

Using SNMP and the MADMAN MIB

Simple Network Management Protocol (SNMP) is a standard, nonsecure communication protocol used to collect information from devices on a TCP/IP network. SNMP was developed within the Internet community to monitor activity on network devices such as routers and bridges. Since then, acceptance of and support for SNMP have grown. Many devices, including computers running Windows 2000, can now be monitored with SNMP.

How SNMP Works

SNMP has a small command set and maintains a centralized database of management information. An SNMP system has three parts:

- **SNMP Agent**   The SNMP Agent is the device on a network that is being monitored. This device is typically a computer that has the SNMP Agent software installed. Windows 2000 includes SNMP Agent software in the form of the Microsoft SNMP Service. (You install SNMP Service by using Add/Remove Windows 2000 Components in the Add/Remove Programs Control Panel tool.)

- **SNMP Management System**   The SNMP Management System is the component that does the actual monitoring in an SNMP environment. Windows 2000 does not provide an SNMP Management System. Third-party SNMP Management Systems include Hewlett-Packard's OpenView and IBM's NetView.

- **Management Information Base**   The Management Information Base (MIB) is a centralized database of all the values that can be monitored for all of the devices in an SNMP system. Different MIBs are provided for monitoring different types of devices and systems. Windows 2000 comes with four MIBs: Internet MIB II, LAN Manager MIB II, DHCP MIB, and WINS MIB. These four MIBs allow the remote monitoring and management of most components of Windows 2000.

Exchange 2000 Server and the MADMAN MIB

Exchange 2000 Server includes a special MIB that you can use to enable an SNMP Management System that manages many Exchange 2000 Server functions. This MIB is based on a standardized MIB named the Mail and Directory Management (MADMAN) MIB, which is detailed in RFC 1566. Microsoft's implementation of the MADMAN MIB meets all the specifications of the standard and adds a few touches of its own. The Exchange MADMAN MIB works by converting the System Monitor counters for the MTA and IMS objects to MIBs, using utilities provided with the *Microsoft Windows 2000 Server Resource Kit* (Microsoft Press, 2000).

More Info   Despite its name, Simple Network Management Protocol is not so simple to use. This chapter offers only a glimpse of it so that you will know that it is available. If you are interested in deploying SNMP in your Exchange organization, consult the *Microsoft Windows 2000 Server Resource Kit* (Microsoft Press, 2000).

Summary

This chapter described how to monitor your network, which is crucial in spotting problems before they grow too large. It also covered many of the tools used to monitor Exchange 2000 Server, including Event Viewer, diagnostics logging, and the various types of monitors that are available. The next chapter turns to another aspect of maintenance: methods for backing up and restoring Exchange servers.

Chapter 24
Backup and Recovery

One key to keeping a reliable network going is planning for what must be done when a piece of that network fails. Nothing is more important than a good backup to ensure that you can recover from failure. This chapter describes how to use the Windows 2000 Backup utility to back up and restore a Microsoft Exchange 2000 server.

Deciding What to Back Up

A great deal of information is stored in an Exchange server. Much of this information resides in the Exchange databases of user messages, public messages, and Active Directory directory services. Some configuration information is stored in the Microsoft Windows 2000 registry; some is stored in various places in the Exchange Server installation path. This section covers the information that you need to include when you back up an Exchange server.

Exchange Stores

The heart of Exchange Server is the public folder and mailbox stores, and these stores are the most critical items to back up. You can back up and restore individual stores or manage the entire storage group at one time. When selecting a store to back up, you are really requesting that a number of files be backed up. Depending on the type of backup chosen (see "Types of Backups" later in this chapter) and the features of the backup software you are using, you will back up one or more of the following items:

- Mailbox store
- Public folder store
- Transaction logs

Like backup software for previous versions of Exchange Server, third-party solutions for Exchange 2000 Server will most likely also be capable of backing up individual mailboxes and individual public folders.

System State

In previous versions of Exchange Server, you backed up not only the information store but also the Exchange directory that maintains information about each mailbox, as well as configuration information about Exchange Server. That information is now stored in Active Directory, so it is necessary to back up your Active Directory. You can back it up using the System State folder within the Windows 2000 Backup utility. The System State folder allows you to specify whether to back up the following resources:

- Active Directory
- Boot files
- COM+ class registration
- Registry
- Sys volume

Exchange 2000 Server Files

It is also important to back up the Exchsrvr folder in your server's file system. Many pieces of information, such as message tracking data, exist within the file system. If these cannot be restored, you may have to recreate parts of your Exchange organization to ensure that the file system contents match the Exchange configuration in Active Directory.

Understanding How Backups Work

Now that you know what to include in a backup, you need some basic information about the backups themselves. This section covers the five basic types of backups that you can perform with Windows 2000 Backup and also discusses a few backup strategies.

Types of Backups

You can perform five basic types of backups with the Windows 2000 Backup utility (and with most other backup utilities). The key difference among these backup types is how each one handles the archive bit that is found in every Windows 2000 file. When a file is created or modified, the archive bit is set to *on*, as shown by the *A* in the Attributes column in Figure 24-1. After some types of backups run, the archive bit is set to *off*, which indicates that the file has been backed up. If, prior to the backup, a files's attribute has been set to archive manually by an administrator, that file will be backed up with the others.

Figure 24-1. *Contents of the Mdbdata folder, showing the archive bit set to* on.

The five types of backups are as follows:

- **Normal**   During a normal backup, all selected files are backed up, regardless of how their archive bit is set. After the backup, the archive bit is set to *off* for all files, indicating that those files have been backed up.

- **Copy**   During a copy backup, all selected files are backed up, regardless of how their archive bit is set. After the backup, the archive bit is not changed in any file.

- **Incremental**   During an incremental backup, all files for which the archive bit is on are backed up. After the backup, the archive bit is set to *off* for all files that were backed up.

- **Differential** During a differential backup, all files for which the archive bit is on are backed up. After the backup, the archive bit is not changed in any file.

- **Daily** During a daily backup, all files that changed on the day of the backup, which are identified by the modified date of the file and not the archive bit, are backed up, and the archive bit is not changed in any file.

Note In this chapter, we will refer to a *full* backup. This is simply a normal backup with all Exchange-related items selected.

When you initially create a backup job, you manually select the files to be backed up. In most backup software programs, including the Windows 2000 Backup utility, these jobs can be saved and reused. In some cases, not all of the files selected are actually backed up. Normal and copy backups back up all of the files selected, but in the case of an incremental, differential, or daily backup, the selected files must also meet the selection criteria of the backup type, as just listed.

All five types of backups apply to Exchange 2000 data, although only three are commonly used: normal, differential, and incremental. Daily and copy backups normally apply only to file-level (Word documents or Excel spreadsheets) backups. The following list describes what happens with regard to Exchange 2000 Server during each type of backup:

- **Normal** The selected Exchange stores are backed up, and the transaction logs for those stores are flushed.

- **Copy** The selected Exchange stores are backed up, but the transaction logs are not flushed.

- **Daily** With respect to Exchange, a Daily backup performs the same backup as a Copy backup.

- **Differential** Only the transaction logs for the selected stores are backed up. Because differential backups are supposed to back up all changes to the stores since the last normal backup, the transaction logs are not flushed so that they can be backed up again during the next differential or normal backup.

- **Incremental** Only the transaction logs for the selected stores are backed up. Because incremental backups are supposed to back up only the changes to the stores since the last normal or incremental backup, the transaction logs are flushed.

Circular Logging

Circular logging enables Exchange Server to conserve disk space by maintaining a fixed number of transaction logs and overwriting those logs as needed. Circular logging should be enabled only if you are performing regular full backups of your Exchange data. Otherwise, you should leave it disabled, allowing Exchange Server to create as many transaction logs as necessary and letting the backups clean up the old logs as they are performed. If circular logging is enabled, you will not be able to successfully perform either a differential or an incremental backup. To check the status of circular logging on your server, navigate within Exchange System to a storage group, right-click it, and choose Properties from the shortcut menu. You will see the Enable Circular Logging check box at the bottom of the General tab of the storage group's property sheet (Figure 24-2). For more information on transaction logs and circular logging, see Chapter 2. Chapter 11 also discusses circular logging with respect to planning storage groups.

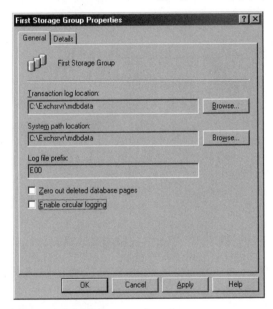

Figure 24-2. *Property sheet for a storage group, showing the Enable Circular Logging check box.*

Backup Strategies

Given the five types of backups covered in the preceding section, most administrators use one of three strategies for backing up a server. These strategies all start with a full backup of the Exchange server, performed on a regular basis—for example, every Sunday. One strategy then continues with full backups daily, another involves performing an incremental backup on all of the other days of the week, and the last calls for performing a differential backup on all of the other days of the week.

- **Full daily backup** Every day of the week, complete a full backup of your Exchange server. If you follow any other backup strategy, you run the risk of having to revert to a backup that is several days or weeks old. An example of a failure would be if your weekly full backup failed in a normal plus daily incremental backup strategy. You would then have to restore all of the previous week's backups. Money spent on large-capacity backup systems (such as DLTs) is money well spent.

- **Normal plus daily incremental backup** On Sunday of each week, perform a full backup of all the files on the Exchange server that you have decided need to be backed up. On Monday, perform an incremental backup that backs up all files that have changed since the full backup. On Tuesday, perform another incremental backup that backs up all files that have changed since the last incremental backup on Monday. At the end of the week, you have performed a full backup and six incremental backups. To restore these backups, you would first restore the full backup and then restore each incremental backup, in order.

- **Normal plus daily differential backup** On Sunday of each week, perform a full backup of all files. On Monday, perform a differential backup that backs up all files that have changed since the full backup. On Tuesday, perform another differential backup that backs up all files that have changed since the last full backup, which occurred on Sunday. Each consecutive differential backup backs up all files that have changed since the last full backup. To restore these backups, you would first restore the full backup and then restore only the most recent differential backup.

In all strategies, plan to use your transaction logs to your advantage. Every backup strategy must incorporate the role transaction logs play in recovering data up to the point of the disaster. Remember, your transaction logs represent what *will* happen to your database in the future. Often they hold committed transactions that have yet to be written to the database. (Consult Chapter 2 for a good discussion of the transaction log architecture.) When a disaster strikes your Exchange server, the information that has been generated in your Exchange organization since the last backup can be recovered from the transaction logs.

For instance, if your server finished a full backup last night at 11:30 P.M., and then at 4:30 P.M. today the disk containing one of your Exchange stores experienced a failure, you would recover today's information from your transaction logs. This ability to recover assumes you have your transaction logs on a different physical disk from the store that experienced the failure. If the logs were on the same disk as the store, you would only be able to recover up to 11:30 last night, when the backup took place. Let's continue this scenario under the premise that the logs are on a separate disk and the disk with the store experiences a failure. To recover, you do a full restore of last night's backup from tape. Then when you start the store.exe process, it will attempt to replay all the transactions in the transaction logs back into the databases. When it is finished playing these transactions back into the database, the service will start and your databases will have been restored to the point in time when your disaster occurred.

When the store.exe process is started under normal (nonrecovery) conditions, such as during a proper shutdown and restart of the Exchange server, all of the transaction logs will be replayed unless the checkpoint file is available. Essentially, that file tells the store process which portions of the transaction logs have already been written to the databases and which have not. If the checkpoint file is available, only those portions of the transaction logs which were not previously written to the database will be written to the database. However, in a recovery situation (like the one mentioned above) a special key is created in the registry by the restore process; it is called the Restore in Progress key. This key controls the startup sequence of the store process and uses the LowLog Number registry entry, rather than the checkpoint file, to act as the checkpoint to determine which logs should be played into the database.

Let's illustrate this important point. Suppose your backups concluded last night at 11:30 P.M., and your disk failure occurred at 4:30 P.M. today. During this period of time, 40 new transaction logs were created, 30 of which had been written to the database and 10 of which had not. Thus, at the point of the system malfunction, the checkpoint file would be pointing to the 31st transaction log.

Now, if you restore last night's backup from tape and then start the store.exe process without the Restore in Progress key present, the store process will start committing transactions from the 31st transaction log to the database. This action will result in a corrupted database because your transactions will be committed to the database out of order and the information in the first 30 transaction logs will be completely lost. Because the key is automatically created by the restore, the LowLog Number points to the first transaction log as the starting point for log replay during the store.exe process startup. The key to the success of the recovery is to use an Exchange-aware backup solution, like the version of Windows 2000 Backup that is included with the installation of Exchange 2000 Server.

Hopefully, you'll see why it is important to make sure that your transaction logs are sitting on a different spindle from your databases, preferably one that has some type of disk fault tolerance, such as mirroring or disk striping with parity. If you lose your databases, you can recover by using the combination of tape backup and transaction logs. If you lose your transaction logs but not your databases, perform a clean shutdown of the store.exe process and your database will be up to date because all of the committed transactions in memory will be written to disk. Hopefully, you can better understand now why it is very important to guard your transaction logs.

Real World **Mission-Critical Backups**

Most companies consider Exchange Server to be a mission-critical application, meaning that unscheduled downtime needs to be kept to a minimum. In these cases, a single daily backup (normal or otherwise) is simply not enough. In the event of a server failure, you'll need your transaction logs as well as your last set of backups, including the full, incremental and/or differentials. An alternative method to ensure you'll have your transaction logs is to perform a normal backup of your Exchange data daily and several differential backups throughout the day. For example, you might perform the normal backup at night, when server usage is lowest. Then throughout the day (at 7:00 A.M., 11:00 A.M., 3:00 P.M., and 7:00 P.M., for example) you could make a differential backup of the transaction logs. Don't worry about the effect on the system of performing differential backups during the day; you'll be backing up only several megabytes of data, which will take just a few minutes, depending on your backup hardware.

The point of using this method is to keep restore time to a minimum. Nobody cares that the backups took four hours last night, but they definitely will care when restoring them takes you four hours. A restore using this method would require only two sessions: the previous evening's normal backup and the latest differential backup. Using this method would, in this example, restore your server's data to within four hours of the crash. You can, of course, schedule the differential backups more or less frequently, depending on your need for relevant, recent data.

Using Windows 2000 Backup

Many Windows 2000 backup products are Exchange-aware, allowing you to perform online backups. The standard Windows 2000 Backup utility included with Windows 2000 lets you perform only offline backups of Exchange Server. When you install Exchange 2000 Server, an enhanced version of Windows 2000 Backup is installed; this version supports online server backups. This section briefly explains how to use Windows 2000 Backup to perform an online backup of an Exchange server.

Real World   Online and Offline Backups

An *online backup* is performed while the Exchange services that are being backed up are still running. In contrast, an *offline backup* is performed while the related Exchange services are not running. The online method has the obvious advantage of allowing users to send and receive messages while the backup is being performed. Current databases and transactions are included in a full online backup. During an incremental or differential online backup, only transaction logs are backed up. The databases don't need to be backed up because all changes are recorded in the transaction logs. You may be wondering how an online backup can safely back up all transactions, especially since the core Exchange services are still online and users are still sending and receiving messages. Consider how transactions occurring during an online backup are handled. If a transaction occurs for an .EDB file that has not been backed up yet, it is processed just as it always is. However, if a transaction occurs for an .EDB file that has already been backed up, it is stored in a *patch file* (.PAT). The patch file is used only during an online backup/restore situation, and there is one patch file for each store that is actively being backed up. The names of the patch files follow the naming convention of their respective .EDB files. For example, if you created a mailbox store and named it PrivateStore1.EDB, the patch file would have the same name with a .PAT extension. When the online backup starts, the patch file is created in the same directory as the database. As the backup is taking place, entries are placed in the patch file as necessary. When the backup is complete, the .patch files are written to tape and then deleted from the Mdbdata directory. Since all stores within the same storage group maintain the same set of transaction logs, Exchange 2000 Server creates a temporary transaction log called E00tmp.log for the other active stores. Once the backup process is complete, the temporary log is renamed to match the log numbering scheme used by Exchange 2000 Server.

More Info   For more information on performing offline backups, see Knowledge Base article Q237767. Although it is based on Exchange Server 5.5, the information is also relevant to Exchange 2000 Server.

Selecting Components to Back Up

You can find Windows 2000 Backup in the System Tools program group, assuming that it was included in the Windows 2000 installation. When the program starts, you can choose to run the Backup Wizard or to go right to the Backup tab and set up the backup yourself. This section describes how to use the Backup tab.

If you choose to use the Backup Wizard, you will make all of the same selections described in this section—you'll just do so in a different fashion. The Backup tab is shown in Figure 24-3.

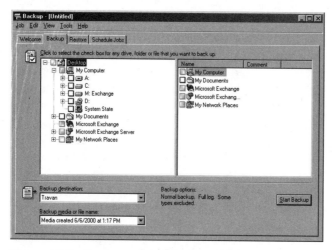

Figure 24-3. *Backup tab in Windows Backup.*

As you can see, the Backup tab shows a hierarchical directory of your entire system. You can back up anything on your server that you like, including Microsoft Exchange Server. To see the Exchange Server items, expand the Microsoft Exchange Server container, as shown in Figure 24-4. You can choose to back up as much or as little of your Exchange organization as you like. As the figure shows in the right-hand pane, you can back up a single database within a storage group, you can back up an entire storage group by selecting the check box next to the storage group in the left pane, or you can back up all of the stores residing on a given server by selecting the Microsoft Information Store check box under the server name in the left pane. You can even back up one database on one server and one on another, should you choose. This provides for a very flexible backup strategy.

Once you have selected all of the components you want to back up, you must specify the destination for the backup. Use the Backup Destination drop-down list to specify whether you want to back up to tape or file. Then, in the Backup Media Or Filename box, specify the tape drive or the drive and filename to which you want to back up. When you're satisfied with your choices, click Start Backup.

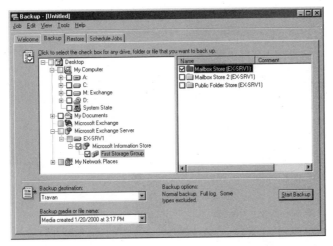

Figure 24-4. *Selecting the Exchange components to back up.*

Setting Backup Information

Once you've selected the components to back up and clicked the Start Backup button, the Backup Job Information dialog box opens (Figure 24-5). Here you need to supply the name of the backup set and indicate whether the backup you are creating should overwrite or append any backup files already existing on the medium.

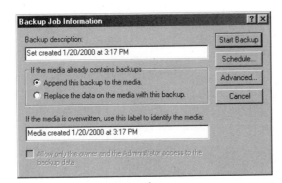

Figure 24-5. *Specifying backup information.*

If you want to perform something other than a normal backup, click the Advanced button to open the Advanced Backup Options dialog box (Figure 24-6). From the

Backup Type drop-down list, you can choose to perform a normal, copy, incremental, differential, or daily backup. You can also use this dialog box to set additional options, such as verifying and compressing data. Click OK to return to the Backup Job Information dialog box. When you are ready to go, click Start Backup and the backup will begin. You are shown the backup progress and, when the backup is finished, a summary.

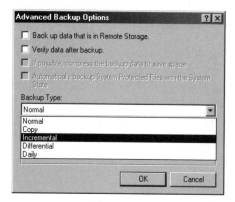

Figure 24-6. *Setting advanced backup options.*

More Info   Obviously, you can do a lot more with the Windows 2000 Backup utility than is presented in this chapter. For more information on using the Windows 2000 Backup utility, refer to your system documentation.

Real World   Automating Backups

Running a backup routine manually can be tedious, especially when you have a large number of servers to back up on a regular basis. Fortunately, Windows 2000 Backup provides a way to schedule backup jobs. Click the Schedule Jobs tab of the Backup dialog box to select a date and create a new backup job. A Backup Wizard walks you through setting up the files you want to back up and any backup options and then lets you schedule a job to run once or at specified intervals.

There is also a command-line alternative to Windows NT Backup: Ntbackup.exe. This command supports several command-line switches that allow you to specify the components you want to back up and the backup settings you want to use. To use the Ntbackup command, you must have previously selected, from within the Backup utility, the items to be backed up and saved those selections into a .BKS file, better known as a selection script. You will need to reference this file on the Ntbackup.exe command line.

After you create a command that performs the desired backup, save it as a batch (.BAT) file, and run it when you need to perform the backup. You can also use the Windows 2000 command-line utility At, shown in Figure 24-7, to schedule the .BAT file to run at specific times. The At utility works in conjunction with the Scheduler service, so this service must be running in order for At to function. You can find more information on using Ntbackup.exe in your Windows 2000 product documentation.

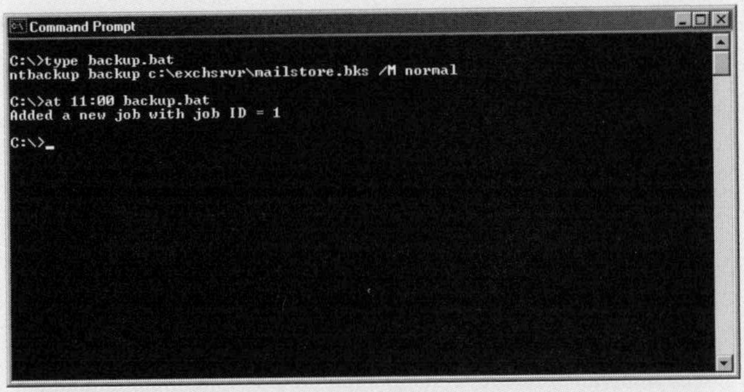

Figure 24-7. *Using a .BAT file and the At command-line utility to schedule a backup job.*

Restoring Backups

Restoring from an Exchange server backup is not a difficult procedure. First, you have to specify which backup set you want to restore. In Windows 2000 Backup, click on the Restore tab. All available backup jobs are displayed, and you simply have to navigate to and select the backup job and the components of that job that you want to restore, as shown in Figure 24-8. You also need to specify whether to restore files to their original location, to an alternate location, or to an individual folder. If you are restoring an Exchange server, you will use the first option. If you are using a backup to move items to another server or to a newly installed server, you will usually use the second option. Restoring to an individual folder is useful if you want to try to find some particular piece of data within the backup job.

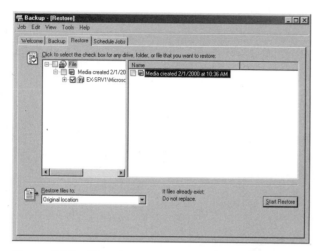

Figure 24-8. *Choosing components to restore.*

When you have made your choices, click the Start Restore button. This opens the Restoring Database Store dialog box (Figure 24-9). Because you can back up any number of Exchange servers from one backup server, you need to use the Browse button to select the Exchange server to which you will be restoring. Click OK when you are done, and the restore will start. When it is done, you will be shown a summary of the job.

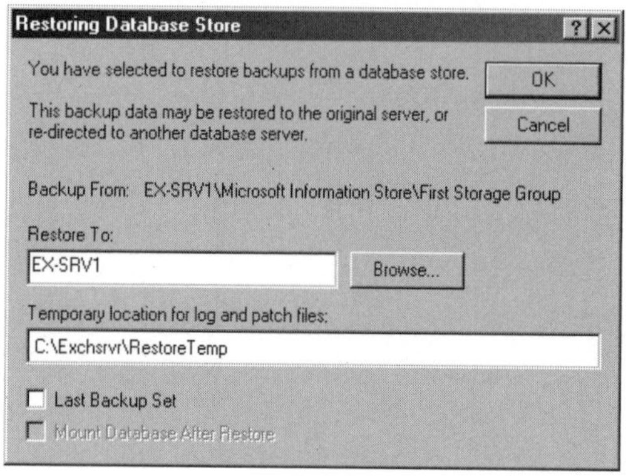

Figure 24-9. *Setting the restore options.*

Note   There are several reasons to restore the data from an Exchange server backup. For example, a user may have deleted something important, or someone may need access to a mailbox that was deleted when its owner left the company. However, when an Exchange server has failed and the Windows 2000 operating system and Exchange files cannot load, more steps are involved. These steps typically involve reinstalling Windows 2000 Server and all of the service packs, joining a domain, restoring the system state data, reinstalling Exchange Server and any Exchange service packs, and finally restoring the Exchange data.

Real World   Using a Recovery Server

The faster and more reliably you can restore your backups, the better. You should therefore test your backups regularly to ensure that they are working as you believe they should. Practicing restoration also puts you in good shape for the real event. You should keep an offline Exchange server, known as a *recovery server*, running for just this purpose. Most administrators never run a restore job until they need to restore an actual server. It's better to routinely restore backup jobs to the recovery server both to test your backup routine and media and to give yourself practice for when the real thing happens. Recovery servers also offer an ideal place to restore databases when what you're really after is a single piece of the database, such as an individual mailbox or a message, and you don't want to restore an entire server.

Summary

Performing routine backups of your servers is your primary defense against losing valuable information in the event that something goes wrong with an Exchange server. This chapter described the process of backing up and restoring an Exchange server, from deciding what files to back up to choosing a strategy and performing the backup, to performing a restore operation. A good backup strategy is important, but you still need to know how to diagnose and fix the problems that occur. The next chapter provides a look at some of the tools you can use to troubleshoot Exchange 2000 Server.

Chapter 25
Troubleshooting Exchange 2000 Server

Nothing is perfect—not your car, your house, or even Exchange 2000 Server. It's no wonder, then, that stores selling car parts and building supplies are successful. Even a stable system like Microsoft Exchange 2000 Server may break down once in a while. Troubleshooting Exchange 2000 Server is a skill that you will develop as you solve real problems on your network. One chapter cannot prepare you for all the possibilities you could face as an Exchange administrator. However, this chapter introduces some of the troubleshooting tools that are available in Exchange 2000 Server and discusses some places to find more information and help with specific types of Exchange problems.

Using Troubleshooting Tools

When you troubleshoot a system as complex as Exchange 2000 Server, your most valuable tool is your understanding of the system itself. This understanding includes knowledge of how Exchange 2000 Server works in general and how your organization is set up in particular. Ideally, this book has given you a good understanding of Exchange 2000 Server and, if you took the advice in Chapter 5, you have completely documented your network. With this knowledge in hand, you are ready to find and repair whatever may go wrong in your organization. This section introduces some of the tools that you will use in the process.

Inbox Repair Tool

Not all problems in an Exchange organization occur on an Exchange server. Many users keep personal folders and offline folders on their client computers. A set of personal folders is stored as a single file with the extension .PST, as shown in Figure 25-1. Multiple sets of personal folders can be stored on a single client. A set of offline folders is stored as a single file with the extension .OST. Like any other type of file, personal and offline folder files can become corrupt. Fortunately, Microsoft Outlook provides the Inbox Repair Tool, which helps you repair corrupt personal and offline folder files.

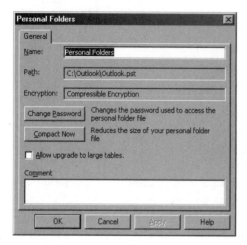

Figure 25-1. *Personal folders stored in a .PST file.*

The Inbox Repair Tool (Scanpst.exe) is installed during a typical installation of Microsoft Outlook, but no shortcut is created on the Start menu. You can find the file Scanpst.exe in the \Program Files\Common Files directory for Outlook 98 and in the \Program Files\Common Files\System\Mapi\1033\NT directory for Outlook 2000. Note that these are default paths that may be changed during client installation.

When you launch the Inbox Repair Tool, a dialog box appears in which you can enter the path and filename of the corrupt file and then click Start (Figure 25-2). However, before you run the Inbox Repair Tool, you should back up the existing file that you are attempting to repair. The Inbox Repair Tool often discards messages that it cannot repair. Without a backup, these messages are permanently lost.

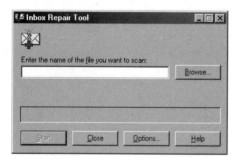

Figure 25-2. *The Inbox Repair Tool.*

The Inbox Repair Tool examines the entire contents of the specified file, as shown in Figure 25-3, discarding messages that cannot be repaired and moving the rest to a specially created Lost And Found folder. When the Inbox Repair Tool finishes running, launch Outlook to access this Lost And Found folder. You should create a new set of personal folders and move any recovered items to these new folders.

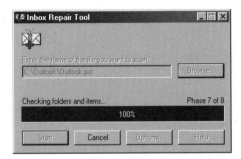

Figure 25-3. *The Inbox Repair Tool scanning a .PST file.*

RPC Ping Utility

Many of the connections among computers in an Exchange organization rely on remote procedure calls (RPCs). Simply put, an RPC calls a protocol that allows a program on one computer to execute a program on another computer. Exchange servers in a routing group rely on RPCs to communicate with one another. Exchange clients connect to Exchange servers by using RPCs. Likewise, the Exchange System snap-in connects to remote Exchange servers via RPCs. Often, connectivity problems in an Exchange organization are the result of bad RPC connectivity.

You can use the RPC Ping utility to confirm the RPC connectivity between two systems as well as to make sure that Exchange services are responding to requests from clients and other servers. RPC Ping has two components: a server component and a client component. You can find both of these components on the Exchange 2000 Server installation CD-ROM in the \Support\Rpcping directory.

RPC Ping Server

The server component of RPC Ping is a file named Rpings.exe, which you must start on the server before using the client component. To run the server component, type *Rpings.exe* at the command prompt. This command runs the server component using all available protocol sequences, as shown in Figure 25-4.

A *protocol sequence* is a routine that allows the return of a ping for a given networking protocol, such as TCP/IP or IPX/SPX. You can also restrict the server component to any single protocol sequence by using the following switches:

- -p ipx/spx
- -p namedpipes
- -p netbios
- -p tcpip
- -p vines

To exit the RPC server, type the string @*q* at the RPC server command prompt.

Figure 25-4. *RPC Ping running on an Exchange server.*

Note You can control which protocols RPC uses on each client to communicate with the Exchange server and in what order by making a modification in the registry. Navigate using Regedit.exe or Regedt32.exe to HKEY_LOCAL_MACHINE\ SOFTWARE\Microsoft\Exchange\Exchange Provider, and modify Rpc_Binding_Order. The protocols used—in their default order—and the corresponding entries in the registry are as follows:

ncalrpc	Local RPC	**ncacn_np**	Named pipes
ncacn_ip_tcp	TCP/IP	**netbios**	NetBIOS
ncacn_spx	IPX/SPX	**ncacn_vns_spp**	VINES IP

For more information on changing your RPC binding order, see Microsoft Knowledge Base article Q163576.

RPC Ping Client

After you launch the RPC Ping server on the Exchange server, you use the RPC Ping client, shown in Figure 25-5, on another computer to test RPC connectivity to that server. There are four versions of the RPC Ping client; the version you use depends on the operating system or the processor on the client. Each of the versions has the same name, Rpingc.exe, and they are found in different subdirectories within the \Support\Rpcping directory.

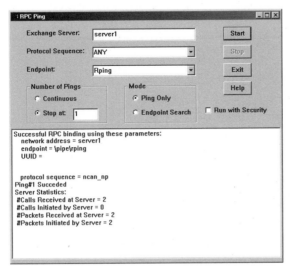

Figure 25-5. *Checking RCP connectivity with Rpingc.exe.*

The options you provide are rather simple:

- **Exchange Server** Specifies the NetBIOS name or IP address (if TCP/IP is used on the network) of the server running the RPC Ping server.

- **Protocol Sequence** Specifies the RPC mechanism that will be used in the test. Options include Any (all protocol sequences are tested), Named Pipes, IPX/SPX, TCP/IP, NetBIOS, and VINES. Set the protocol sequence to correspond to the protocol sequence setting on the RPC server.

- **Endpoint**   Specifies protocol-specific ports that the RPC client uses to communicate with the server. Choose Rping to collect information about RPC Ping client-to-server communication itself. You can choose Store to simulate communications with the Information Store service on the Exchange server, and choose Admin to simulate communications with the Exchange server.

- **Number Of Pings**   Specifies whether to ping the server continuously or a certain number of times. This option is available only if you choose Ping Only mode.

- **Mode**   Specifies the mode. Ping Only means that the ping is returned directly by the RPC Ping server. Endpoint Search returns Pings from detected endpoints.

- **Run With Security**   Verifies authenticated RPCs.

If the RPC Ping from the client is successful with a particular protocol, you'll want to move that protocol to first in the binding order so that the client system will not have any problems connecting to the Exchange server. If the RPC Ping is not successful over any protocols, check for a corrupted RPC.DLL file on the client. There are nine RPC.DLL files used to support RPC for Windows 2000 and Windows NT clients. All of these files are included in the Windows 2000 operating system, just as they are for Windows 95 and 98. For MS-DOS and 16-bit Windows clients, the RPC.DLL files used for RPC are included with Exchange Client. If replacing these .DLL files does not fix the problem, trace the packets between the client system and the Exchange server. A packet analyzer such as Network Monitor, a Windows 2000 utility, can be handy in this situation. For information on using Network Monitor to analyze remote procedure calls on a TCP/IP network, see Microsoft Knowledge Base article Q159298, "Analyzing Exchange RPC Traffic Over TCP/IP."

MTA Check Utility

The Message Transfer Agent (MTA) was responsible for the transfer of all messages outside Exchange Server 5.5. Now, the MTA's use is limited to handling message transfer for the X.400 Connector. The MTA maintains a separate message queue for each X.400 Connector to which it routes messages.

All of the MTA's message queues are stored in files that have a .DAT extension. These files are located in the \Exchsrvr\Mtadata directory on the Exchange server. These files can become corrupted, just like any other files. Corruption of .DAT files typically happens during an improper shutdown of the MTA, such as during a power failure. It can result in message delivery problems and MTA startup problems.

The MTA Check utility (Mtacheck.exe) is a command-line tool that attempts to fix all MTA message queues and the messages that those queues contain. It automatically discards all corrupt messages from the queues, backing up those messages in the \Exchsrvr\Mtadata\Mtacheck.out directory.

When the MTA service starts, it automatically runs the MTA Check utility if it determines that the MTA was not shut down properly. During an automatic check, events are logged to the Windows 2000 application log, and an Mtacheck.log file is created in the \Exchsrvr\Mtadata\Mtacheck.out directory. You can also run the MTA Check utility manually by using the command mtacheck.exe. The utility is found in the \Exchsrvr\Bin directory. The MTA service must be stopped when you run this utility manually. Mtacheck.exe supports the following command-line options:

- **/f** *<filename>*   Logs status information to a file with the specified name
- **/v**   Enables verbose logging and must be used with the /f switch
- **/rd**   Removes all queued directory replication messages
- **/rp**   Removes all queued public folder replication messages
- **/rl**   Removes all queued link monitor test messages

If the MTA Check utility encounters a problem with a queue, you will see an error in the log like the following:

```
Queue '241062' required reconstruction - corrupted queue file
    69 messages recovered to the queue
Other items in the log may consist of the following entry,
which reflects a missing file:
Object 300596 invalid - missing object file
    Object removed from queue '060193'
    MTS-ID: c=US;a= ;p=Lar;l=Seattle019601202001080000CDE
```

After the MTA Check utility completes processing, it will return one of the following messages to show the outcome:

```
Database clean, no errors detected.
Database repaired, some data may have been lost.
<number> queue(s) required repair out of <percent> detected.
<number> object(s) damaged out of <percent> detected.
Database has serious errors and cannot be reconstructed.
Some objects missing from the Boot Environment. Please reload the
files from the BOOTENV directory on the install CD.
```

Figure 25-6 shows the results of running the MTA Check utility on an Exchange server.

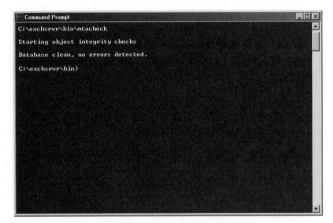

Figure 25-6. *Results of running the MTA Check utility on an Exchange server.*

Eseutil.exe Offline Tool

The public folder store and the mailbox store on an Exchange server begin as empty database files. As messages accumulate, these databases grow. Unfortunately, they do not shrink when messages are deleted. Instead, the emptied space is simply marked as available for use during routine garbage collection performed by the Information Store service. When new messages are stored in the databases, they are written in any available free space before the database enlarges to hold them. This method of using free space can result in single items actually being broken up and stored in several physical places within the database—a process known as *fragmentation*.

During their scheduled maintenance cycles, the Information Store service defragments the databases. It also checks for database inconsistencies every time the server is shut down or started. Because of this routine maintenance, fragmentation itself is not much of a problem on an Exchange server. However, online defragmentation routines do nothing about the size of the databases themselves. To compact the databases, you must turn to an offline utility. Exchange 2000 Server provides an offline defragmentation tool named Eseutil.exe, which you can use to perform database defragmentation while the Information Store service is stopped.

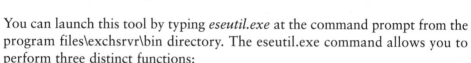

Caution   Eseutil.exe is not meant to be used as a regular tool for maintenance of your Exchange servers. You should use it only when you are in contact with Microsoft Technical Support.

You can launch this tool by typing *eseutil.exe* at the command prompt from the program files\exchsrvr\bin directory. The eseutil.exe command allows you to perform three distinct functions:

- **Defragmentation (/d)**   Defragments the database by moving the used pages in the database into contiguous blocks in a new database. Unused pages are discarded, which is the only way to recover empty space inside the database for other uses. By default, eseutil.exe writes the contents of the database file to a temporary file, tempdfrg.edb. When this process is complete, the temporary database becomes the new database and replaces the original database. While it is possible to place this temporary file on another server across the network, this activity is not recommended since doing so will saturate your bandwidth and could take hours to complete. Once this new database is created, a new signature will be written to the database. As a result, previous transaction logs can no longer be played into the database nor can transactions created after the defragmentation be played into the old database. Therefore, after completing the defragmentation, you should perform a full online backup.

- **Repair (/r)** Examines the structure of the database and attempts to restore broken links. This process is slow and uncertain and should only be used as a last resort. If the repair finds a physical corruption, which will be seen as a -1018, -1019 or -1022 error, the injured page will be removed, resulting in a loss of data for that page. After the repair has completed, you will be instructed to delete all your current transaction logs. This step is necessary because the page numbers in the database will not correspond to the page numbers referenced in the transaction log files. Running a repair also rewrites the database signature.

- **Integrity (/g)** Checks the integrity of a database. The main purpose of this switch is to provide feedback to the development team for debugging purposes. This is a read-only command and does not make any changes to the database. It will check the database index, build a second index in a temporary database (integ.edb), and compare the two.

Other Useful Utilities

There are many other tools you can use to troubleshoot Exchange 2000 Server—too many to cover in detail in this book. Table 25-1 lists some of these tools and briefly describes their use, as well as where to find them.

Table 25-1. Other utilities for troubleshooting Exchange 2000 Server

Filename	Use	Location
Error.exe	Converts store, MAPI, and database error codes to error message strings	\Support\Utils\I386 on the Exchange 2000 Server CD-ROM
Filever.exe	Displays versions of .EXE and .DLL files	\Support\Utils\I386 on the Exchange 2000 Server CD-ROM
Isinteg.exe	Checks the integrity of the information stores	\Exchsrvr\Bin in your Exchange installation
Mdbvue32.exe	Displays information about information stores and .PST and .OST files	\Support\Utils\I386 on the Exchange 2000 Server CD-ROM

Finding Help

As an administrator, you sometimes have problems that you cannot solve by yourself. In these circumstances, knowing where to go for help can save your day. Many sources of information on Exchange 2000 Server are available.

Product Documentation

The product documentation for Exchange 2000 Server is quite good. (Many administrators have never even looked at the product documentation, primarily because they have grown accustomed to shoddy documentation in other products.) This documentation is in .RTF format and is available on the Exchange 2000 Server CD-ROM in the \Docs directory. Open the file Contents.html for a hyperlinked table of contents that allows you to open the various .RTF files.

Microsoft Exchange 2000 Resource Kit

Another invaluable resource for any Exchange administrator is the *Microsoft Exchange 2000 Resource Kit* (Microsoft Press, forthcoming in 2000). It provides comprehensive technical data detailing the planning, deployment, administration, and troubleshooting of Exchange 2000 Server. The resource kit also contains valuable tools designed to make your life as an Exchange administrator easier. Earlier chapters of this book described several of these tools.

Microsoft TechNet

Each month, Microsoft publishes a collection of information and tools called TechNet. TechNet is a CD-ROM subscription that delivers current information on the evaluation, deployment, and support of all Microsoft products. It consists of nearly 300,000 pages of information, including the full text of all Microsoft resource kits and the entire Microsoft Knowledge Base. Each month, subscribers also receive other CD-ROMs that include useful items, such as all of the published service packs for all Microsoft products; server and client utilities, and Microsoft Seminar Online.

TechNet is now also published in an extended version, TechNet Plus, that includes Microsoft software currently in beta testing. Much of the content of TechNet, as well as ordering information for the CD-ROM subscription, is available online at *http://technet.microsoft.com*. Further support mechanisms include contacting the local Microsoft office or using Microsoft Support through *http://support.microsoft.com*.

Internet Newsgroups

Newsgroups offer the chance to interact with other administrators and to get opinions and ideas about your specific problems. Many newsgroups are available on the Internet. Microsoft maintains a public Usenet server that hosts hundreds of newsgroups on many Microsoft products. The address of this server is *http://msnews.microsoft.com*. The following are a few of the Exchange-specific newsgroups available on this server:

- *microsoft.public.exchange2000.administration*
- *microsoft.public.exchange2000.clients*
- *microsoft.public.exchange2000.clustering*
- *microsoft.public.exchange2000.development*
- *microsoft.public.exchange2000.general*
- *microsoft.public.exchange2000.setup.installation*
- *microsoft.public.exchange2000.transport*

Hundreds of people, including Microsoft personnel, read and post to these newsgroups daily. These newsgroups are also replicated by many other Usenet servers and may be available through your own Internet service provider's news server.

Summary

This chapter discussed some of the tools you can use to troubleshoot problems with Exchange 2000 Server, including the Inbox Repair tool, the RPC Ping utility, and the MTA Check utility. It also described other sources of troubleshooting information, such as TechNet and the Microsoft Knowledge Base. The next chapter completes our discussion of maintaining Exchange 2000 Server, with a look at ways to tune your servers for enhanced performance.

Chapter 26

Tuning Exchange 2000 Server

System Monitor is a valuable tool included with Microsoft Windows 2000 and is available in the Administrative Tools folder on the Programs menu. It graphically charts the performance of hundreds of individual system parameters on a computer running Microsoft Windows 2000. When you install Microsoft Exchange 2000 Server on a Windows 2000 server, several Exchange-specific counters are installed into System Monitor that you can track as well.

This chapter describes how to use System Monitor to better understand your Exchange system. This is an overview chapter only. For a more thourough discussion of how the Exchange 2000 counters work together to provide various types of information on performance, consult the *Exchange 2000 Server Resource Kit* (Microsoft Press, forthcoming).

Understanding How System Monitor Works

Although a full discussion of how System Monitor works is beyond the scope of this chapter, this section covers some of its basic concepts and briefly describes how System Monitor works. Because the bulk of your performance-tuning activities will involve the Windows 2000 operating system, our discussion will focus on monitoring Windows 2000.

Performance Monitoring Concepts

Before beginning our discussion, we first need to briefly cover some basic concepts and terms. One thing you'll notice right off the bat is that we are using the terms "performance monitoring" and "System Monitor." *Performance monitoring* is the activity of gathering measurements and data from individual counters that show how a server is performing its activities. *System Monitor* is the snap-in utility in MMC that is used to gather this data.

More specifically, performance monitoring looks at how the Windows 2000 operating system and installed applications use the resources of the system. The four main subsystems that are monitored are the disks, memory, processors, and network components. Later in this chapter, we will look at each of these components and highlight some important counters and measurements for them. In connection with performance monitoring, we need to discuss four concepts: throughput, queue, bottleneck, and response time.

More Info   If you need a more detailed discussion of System Monitor, consult Chapters 5 through 10 of the *Windows 2000 Server Operating Guide,* one of the volumes in the *Microsoft Windows 2000 Server Resource Kit* (Microsoft Press, 2000).

Throughput

Throughput is a measurement of the amount of work done in a given unit of time. Most often, we think of throughput as the amount of data that can be transmitted from one point to another in a given time period. However, the concept of throughput is also applied to data movement within a computer. Throughput can either decrease or increase. When it increases, the load, which represents the amount of data that the system is attempting to transmit, can increase to the point that no more additional data can be transmitted. This is called the *peak* level. If the load begins to decrease, which means that less and less data needs to be transmitted, the throughput will also fall.

When data is being sent from one point to another, or in any end-to-end system, the throughput depends on how each component along the path performs. The slowest point in the overall data path sets the throughput for the entire path. If the slowest point is too slow (which is defined differently in each situation), and a queue begins to develop, that point is referred to as a *bottleneck*, a concept we'll discuss in more detail in just a moment. Oftentimes, the resource that shows the highest use is the bottleneck, and a bottleneck is often the result of an overconsumption of that resource.

Generally, we do not define a heavily used resource in data transmission as a bottleneck unless a queue is also developing for the resource. For instance, if a router is being heavily used but shows little or no queue length, it is not thought of as a bottleneck. On the other hand, if that router develops a long queue (which is defined differently in each situation for each router), it could be said to be a bottleneck.

Queue

A *queue* is a place where a request for a service sits until it can be processed. For instance, when a file needs to be written to a disk, the request to write that file is first placed in the queue for the disk. The driver for the disk then reads the information out of the queue and writes that information to the disk. Long queues are rarely considered a good thing.

Queues develop under various circumstances. When requests for a service arrive at a rate faster than the resource's throughput, or if certain requests take a long time to fulfill, queues can develop. When a queue becomes long, the work is not being handled efficiently. Windows 2000 reports queue development on disks, processors, server work queues, and server message block (SMB) calls of the server service.

Response Time

Response time is the amount of time required to perform a unit of work from start to finish. Generally speaking, response time increases as stress on the resource increases. It can be measured by dividing the queue length for a given resource by the resource throughput. By using the new trace log feature in Windows 2000, you can track a unit of work from start to finish to determine its response time.

Bottleneck

As we mentioned earlier, a *bottleneck* represents overconsumption of a resource. You will experience this as a slow response time, but you should think of it as overconsumption. Finding bottlenecks is a key goal in performance tuning because eliminating bottlenecks makes your system run more efficiently. Moreover, if you can predict when a bottleneck will occur, you can do much to proactively solve a problem before it affects your users. Factors that contribute to bottlenecks are the number of requests for the services of a resource, the frequency with which those requests occur, and the duration of each request.

Collecting Data with System Monitor

Before you can properly tune your Exchange 2000 server, you must first collect data that shows how the server is presently running. Data collection involves three distinct elements: objects, counters, and instances. An *object* is any resource, application, or service that can be monitored and measured. You will select various objects for which you want to collect data.

Each object has multiple *counters* that measure various aspects of the object. Examples include the number of packets that a network card has sent or received in a given time period or the amount of time the processor has spent processing kernel-mode threads. The counters are where the data is actually measured and collected.

Finally, a counter might have multiple *instances*. The most common use of multiple instances is to monitor multiple processors on a server or multiple network cards. For example, if a server has two processors, you can either measure the amount of time each processor is spending processing nonidle threads or you can measure the two processors as one unit, and look at the average. Instances allow greater granularity in measuring performance. It is important to note that not all object types support multiple instances.

Each counter is assigned a *counter type*, which determines how the counter data is calculated, averaged, and displayed. In general, counters can be categorized according to their *generic type*, as outlined in Table 26-1. System Monitor supports more than 30 counter types. However, many of these types are not implemented in Windows 2000 and so are not listed in the table.

Table 26-1. Generic counter types

Counter Type	Description
Average	Measures a value over time and displays the average of the last two measurements.
Difference	Subtracts the last measurement from the previous measurement and displays the difference, if the result is a positive number. If the result is negative, the display is zero.
Instantaneous	Displays the most recent measurement.
Percentage	Displays the result as a percentage.
Rate	Samples an increasing count of events over time and divides the cache in count values by the change in time to display a rate of activity.

More Info For more information on each counter type—its name, its description, and how the formulas are calculated—consult the *Windows 2000 Performance Counters Reference,* one of the reference files installed with the *Microsoft Windows 2000 Server Resource Kit* (Microsoft Press, 2000).

Viewing Collected Data

When you first open System Monitor, you see a blank screen called a *chart view*, which displays selected counters in real time as a graph (Figure 26-1). To see data displayed in the chart, you have to add some counters. Choose Add from the toolbar to open the Add Counters dialog box (Figure 26-2).

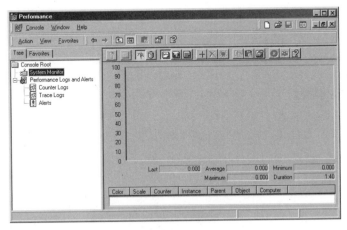

Figure 26-1. *System Monitor chart view.*

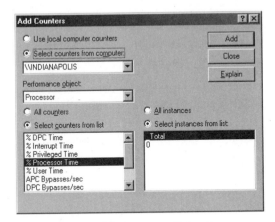

Figure 26-2. *Add Counters dialog box.*

By default, the computer that you monitor is the computer on which you launched System Monitor, but you can monitor remote computers as well. In fact, you can select different counters from multiple computers at the same time. You might do so, for instance, to monitor how a distributed application is running. You can also choose to monitor the same counter on multiple computers for comparative purposes. For instance, in Figure 26-3, we've chosen to monitor the same counter on four servers—Indianapolis, Minneapolis, Tucson, and Folsom—while installing Microsoft Office 2000 on Folsom from the source files on Indianapolis. The two graph lines showing higher levels of processor activity represent the Indianapolis and Folsom servers.

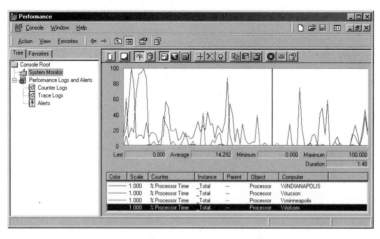

Figure 26-3. *Monitoring the same counter on four servers.*

As you can see in the figure, you can also view digital values for the selected counter by selecting a counter from the list at the bottom and reading the values just under the graph. You can attain the last, average, minimum, and maximum values for each counter selected. In this case, the Folsom server's processor activity was averaging a bit over 14 percent for a period of 1 minute and 40 seconds.

Evaluating the Four Main Subsystems in Windows 2000

Earlier we mentioned the four subsystems that you should always monitor: memory, processor, disk, and network. In this section, we'll briefly discuss each element and offer some advice on tuning these parts of Windows 2000 to optimize their work with Exchange 2000 Server.

One point that applies to all four of these areas is this: Current data is not that helpful unless you have a baseline against which to compare it. This argues in favor of setting up regular monitoring schedules for *all* of your servers and then regularly compiling that data to form a baseline of how your servers operate at off-peak, normal, and peak periods of usage. As an example, if you find that one server is averaging 53 pages per minute, that number won't mean much unless you know the period of time that the average represents and whether it depicts abnormal behavior or is an expected result. The only way to know this comparative information is to have conducted regular monitoring of the server.

Evaluating Memory Usage

Use the counters in Table 26-2 to set up a baseline for your system's memory. When you're monitoring these counters, you will see occasional spikes that you can exclude from your baseline because these short-term values will not be representative of your servers. However, do not ignore these spikes if they are occurring with increasing frequency. This increase could indicate that a resource is becoming too heavily utilized.

Table 26-2.   Essential memory counters

Counter Name	Description
Memory\Pages/Sec	Shows the rate at which pages are read from or written to the disk to resolve hard page faults. This counter is a primary indicator of the type of page faults that can significantly slow down your system. It is the sum of Memory\Pages Input/Sec and Memory\Page Faults/Sec. Microsoft recommends keeping this value below 20.
Memory\Available Bytes	Shows the amount of physical memory, in bytes, available to processes running on the computers. Microsoft recommends keeping this value above 4000 KB.
Paging File(_Total)\% Usage	Shows the amount of the paging file in use during the sample interval, as a percentage. A high value indicates that you may need to increase the size of your Pagefile.sys file or add more RAM. Microsoft recommends keeping this value below 75 percent.

Recall from Chapter 2 that the Extensible Storage Engine (ESE) automatically checks the system's performance and allocates to itself all of the available memory that it anticipates it will need. This allocation means that when you monitor the

Memory\Available Bytes counter, it may hover around 4000 KB, even if there isn't much activity on the server. In addition, you'll find that the Store.exe process allocates a large amount of memory to itself. This action is by design and does not represent a memory leak or a memory bottleneck.

You'll also recall that the DSAccess cache automatically allocates 4 MB to itself (set in the registry) for holding LDAP lookup results from the Global Catalog server. Its size can be monitored with the MSExchangeDSAccess Caches\Total Memory Size counter.

To see memory allocations on a per-process basis, use the Memsnap or Process Monitor tool found under Windows 2000 Support Tools on your Windows 2000 CD-ROM. The Memsnap tool records system memory usage to a log file for later review. It gives just a snapshot of your memory usage, not an ongoing logging of how each process is using memory. Figure 26-4 illustrates what the log file looks like.

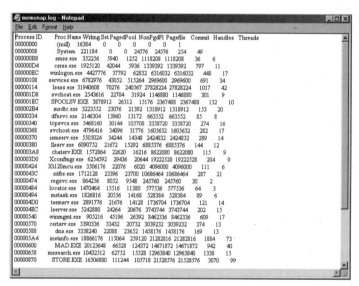

Figure 26-4. *Memsnap log file.*

The Process Monitor (Figure 26-5) provides total and per-process values for nonpaged and paged pool memory. It also monitors the committed memory values shown in the Pmon display for increases, where a process with a memory leak should report an increasing value under Commit Charge.

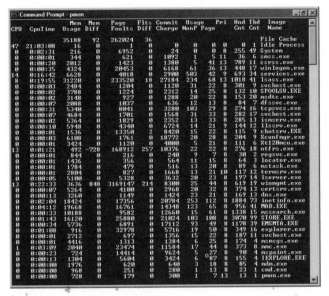

Figure 26-5. *Process Monitor output in a command-prompt window.*

Evaluating Processor Usage

Use the counters listed in Table 26-3 to set up a baseline for your processor usage. The processor always has a thread to process. Most often, the system supplies an idle thread for the processor to process while it is waiting to process an active thread. The Processor\% Processor Time counter does not factor in the idle thread when calculating its value.

Table 26-3.   Essential processor counters

Counter Name	Description
Processor\% Processor Time	Shows the percentage of elapsed time that all of the threads of this process used to execute instructions. An instruction is the basic unit of execution in a computer, a thread is the object that executes instructions, and a process is the object created when a program is run. Microsoft recommends keeping this value to 80 or below (sustained).
System\Processor Queue Length	Shows the number of threads in the processor queue. There is a single queue for processor time, even on computers with multiple processors. This counter shows ready threads only, not threads that are currently running. Microsoft recommends keeping this value to 2 or less.

The most common causes of processor bottlenecks are insufficient memory and excessive numbers of interrupts from disk or network I/O components. During periods of low activity, the only source of processor interrupts might be the processor's timer ticks. Timer ticks increment the processor's timer. These interrupts occur every 10 to 15 milliseconds, or about 70 to 100 times per second. Use the Processor(_Total)\Interrupts/Sec counter to measure this value. The normal range is in the thousands of interrupts per second for a Windows 2000 server and can vary from processor to processor. Installing a new application may cause a dramatic rise in this value.

If you want to improve processor response time or throughput, you can schedule processor-intensive applications to run at a time when system stress is usually low. Use the Scheduled Tasks tool in Control Panel to do this. You can also upgrade to a faster processor with a larger L2 cache. This upgrade will always increase your system's performance, and you can use multiple processors instead of a single processor to balance the processing load.

Two resource kit tools that will help you understand and experiment with processor performance are CPU Stress (Cpustres.exe), which simulates processor workload, and QuickSlice (Qslice.exe), which provides a graphical display of processor usage by a process.

The CPU Stress utility (Figure 26-6) allows you to run up to four threads that endlessly loop. These threads can be run at different priorities and levels of activity. You can use this tool to test how well your processor will sustain a utilization of over 80 percent. Select a number of threads to run, a Thread Priority and Activity level for each, and then use System Monitor to check the processor utilization. You can then test normal server usage to see if it is acceptable while these test threads are running.

The QuickSlice tool (Figure 26-7) gives a graphical representation of how much of the CPU each of the processes is using for any given instance. This tool has no logging feature; it provides only real-time information. Use this tool to see quickly which thread is monopolizing the CPU.

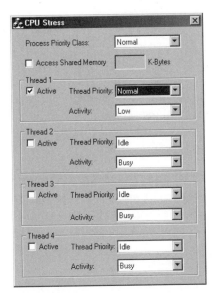

Figure 26-6. *CPU Stress resource kit tool.*

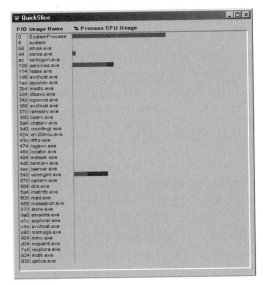

Figure 26-7. *QuickSlice resource kit tool.*

Evaluating Disk Usage

Windows 2000 includes counters that monitor the activity of the physical disk and logical volumes. The PhysicalDisk object provides counters that report physical-disk activity, while the LogicalDisk object provides counters that report statistics for logical disks and storage volumes. By default, the Windows 2000 operating system activates only the PhysicalDisk performance counters. To activate the LogicalDisk counters, go to the command prompt and type *diskperf –yv*. The counters will be activated when you reboot your server.

More Info For more information on the various switches used with the Diskperf command, see Chapter 8 of the *Windows 2000 Server Operations Guide*, one of the volumes in the *Microsoft Windows 2000 Server Resource Kit* (Microsoft Press, 2000).

Table 26-4 lists the counters for evaluating disk performance. They are the same for both the LogicalDisk and PhysicalDisk objects. We've chosen to use the PhysicalDisk object in the table.

Table 26-4.   Essential disk counters

Counter Name	Description
PhysicalDisk\Avg. Disk Sec/Transfer	Indicates how fast data is being moved, in seconds. A high value might mean that the system is retrying requests due to lengthy queuing or, less commonly, a disk failure. There are no benchmark recommendations from Microsoft. Watch for significant variances from baseline data.
PhysicalDisk\Avg. Disk Queue Length	Shows the number of requests that are queued and waiting for the disk to process. Microsoft recommends that this value be 2 or less.
PhysicalDisk\Disk Bytes/Sec	Indicates the rate at which bytes are transferred. It is the primary measurement of disk throughput.
PhysicalDisk\Disk Transfers/Sec	Shows the number of completed read and write operations per second. This counter measures disk utilization and is expressed as a percentage. Values over 50 percent might indicate that the disk is becoming a bottleneck.

Diagnosing a disk as a bottleneck is a tricky process that requires both time and experience. We give some helpful tips here, but for a more full discussion of this topic, please see the works cited earlier in this chapter.

What you want to see in order to diagnose a disk as a bottleneck in your system is either a sustained rate of disk activity that is well above your baseline or an increasing rate of disk activity that represents a dramatic departure from your baseline statistics. In addition, you'll want to see persistent disk queues that are either steadily increasing or that are significantly above your baseline statistics, coupled with *the absence of a significant amount of paging* (less than 20 pages per second). If these factors combine in any other way than those described here, it is unlikely that your disk is a bottleneck. For example, if your system doesn't have enough RAM to accommodate its load, you will find that paging occurs more frequently, creating unnecessary disk activity. If you monitor only the PhysicalDisk object, you might see this activity as evidence that your disk is a bottleneck. Therefore, you must also monitor memory counters to determine the real source of this type of problem.

If you do determine that your disk is too slow, consider taking one or more of the following steps.

1. Rule out a memory shortage, for the reasons just discussed.

2. Defragment the disk, using Disk Defragmenter. For information about using Disk Defragmenter, see the online help for Windows 2000.

3. Use Diskpar.exe from the *Microsoft Windows 2000 Server Resource Kit* to reduce performance loss due to misaligned disk tracks and sectors.

4. Consider implementing a stripe set to process I/O requests concurrently over multiple disks. If you need data integrity, implement a stripe set with parity.

5. Place multiple drives on different I/O buses.

6. Limit the use of file compression or encryption.

7. Be sure you're using the best and fastest controller, disk, and I/O bus that you can realistically afford.

Evaluating Network Usage

Windows 2000 provides two utilities for monitoring network performance: System Monitor and Network Monitor. We will not discuss Network Monitor here. For more information on Network Monitor, see the resource kit books cited earlier in this chapter.

You should monitor other resources, such as disk, memory, and processor objects, along with network objects to obtain an overall perspective on the network objects' results. In addition, you can select which layer of the Open Systems Interconnection (OSI) model you want to monitor. Table 26-5 summarizes the counters and their corresponding OSI layer.

More Info   For more information on the OSI model, see Appendix A in the *TCP/IP Core Networking Guide,* part of the *Microsoft Windows 2000 Server Resource Kit* (Microsoft Press, 2000).

Table 26-5.   Essential network counters and their OSI layer

Counter Name	Description	OSI Layer
Network Interface\ Output Queue Length	Indicates the length of the output packet queue. A queue length of 1 or 2 is often satisfactory. Longer queues indicate that the adapter is waiting for the network and thus cannot keep pace with the server.	Physical
Network Interface\ Packets Outbound Discarded	A high value indicates that the network segment is saturated. An increasing value means that the network buffers cannot keep pace with the outbound flow of packets.	Physical
Network Interface\Bytes Total/Sec	A high value indicates a large number of successful transmissions.	Physical
Network Segment\ Broadcast Frames Received/Sec	You'll need to develop a baseline for this counter and then compare subsequent measurements against it. Since every computer processes every broadcast, frequent broadcasts mean lower overall performance.	Physical
Network Segment\ % Network Utilization	Reflects the percentage of network bandwidth used for the local network segment. A lower value is preferred. For an unswitched Ethernet network, a value under 30 percent is best. Collisions will become a problem at 40 percent.	Physical
IP\Datagrams/Sec	Shows the rate at which datagrams are received from or sent to each interface.	Network

Table 26-5. *continued*

Counter Name	Description	OSI Layer
TCP\Segments Received/Sec	Shows the rate at which segments are received, including those received in error. This count includes segments received on currently established connections. A low value means that you have too much broadcast traffic.	Transport
TCP\Segments Retransmitted/Sec	Gives the rate at which segments containing one or more previously transmitted bytes are retransmitted. A high value might indicate either a saturated network or a hardware problem.	Transport
Redirector\ Network Errors/Sec	Measures serious network errors that indicate the Redirector and one or more servers are having serious communication problems.	Application
Server\ Pool Paged Failures	Indicates the number of times that allocations from the paged pool have failed. If this number is high, either the amount of RAM is too little or the pagefile is too small or both. If this number is consistently increasing, increase the physical RAM and the size of the pagefile.	Application

The Network Interface object is installed when you install TCP/IP. The Network Segment object is installed when you install Network Monitor. To monitor the TCP/IP protocol, use the TCP/IP, UDP, and ICMP objects. (You no longer need to install SNMP to get the IP counters as you did with Windows NT.) Use the NBT Connection object to track session-layer packets between computers. You can also use this object to monitor routed servers that use NETBIOS name resolution.

Application-layer objects include the Browser, Redirector, Server, and Server Work Queue objects on computers running Windows 2000. These objects will help you understand how your file and print services are performing, using the Server Message Block (SMB) protocol.

Using System Monitor to Tune Exchange 2000 Server

It would take an entire book to discuss in depth all of the counters in Exchange 2000 Server and how they can be combined to give you a particular type of report. Instead, we will focus here on the more important counters and offer a few suggestions as to how to use them. We will cover the POP3, IMAP4, Content Indexing, SMTP, and Outlook Web Access counters. If some of the discussion of the POP3, IMAP4, and SMTP protocols is unfamiliar to you, refer to Chapter 17, where these protocols are discussed in depth.

POP3 System Monitor Counters

As you'll recall from Chapter 17, the POP3 protocol allows users to retrieve mail for reading and to delete that mail on the server. The POP3 counters can be classified as to when they are used in a user session: the user's initial connection to the POP3 service, the user's authentication, the transfer of messages between the server and the client, and the user's disconnection from the server. Table 26-6 outlines which counters are used at the various stages. Our focus in this table is on the MSExchangePOP3 object.

Table 26-6. POP3 counters for the MSExchangePOP3 object

Stage	Counter	Meaning
User connects to POP3 server	Connection Total	Total number of connections since the service started. An unusually high rate could indicate that user connections are being dropped unexpectedly, causing your users to reconnect multiple times to retrieve their mail.
	Connections Current	Current number of connected users. Be sure you have enough licenses for these connections.
Server authenticates user	AUTH Total	Total number of successful user authentications. This should be somewhat consistent with the value of the Connection Total counter.
	AUTH Failures	Total number of authentication failures. A high rate indicates user difficulty in authenticating to the domain.
Message transfer	STAT Total	Total number of STAT requests.
	LIST Total	Total number of LIST commands.
	RETR Total	Total number of messages retrieved.
	DELE Total	Total number of messages deleted.
User ends session with POP3 server	QUIT Total	Total number of QUIT commands issued. This should be somewhat consistent with the AUTH Total counter.

IMAP4 System Monitor Counters

The IMAP4 server allows users to retrieve messages from the server and manipulate the messages and folders once they have been retrieved. Like the POP3 counters, the IMAP4 counters are classified by the stages of a user session, including a user's first connection to an IMAP4 server, folder activities, manipulation of files and folders, and disconnection from the server. Table 26-7 outlines these counters and their functions, focusing on the MSExchangeIMAP4 object.

Table 26-7. IMAP4 counters for the MSExchangeIMAP4 object

Stage	Counter	Meaning
Client connects to IMAP4 server	Connections Total	Total number of connections since the server started. As with the POP3 protocol, an unusually large number could indicate that your users are having to reconnect multiple times to retrieve their e-mail.
	Connections Current	Current number of users connected.
Folder activities[1]	LIST Total	Total number of LIST commands.
	RLIST Total	Total number of RLIST commands.
	FETCH Total	Total number of messages fetched to be read by the client.
	COPY Total	Total number of messages copied to another folder by the client. High activity for this counter might indicate that the server is generally overused for e-mail purposes.
	STORE Total	Total number of messages whose data has been changed by a STORE command— for example, when the store flags a message for deletion.
	EXPUNGE Total	Total number of calls to expunge messages that have been marked for deletion.
	CREATE Total	Total number of folders created. This counter, along with the next counter, helps reveal overall user activities on your e-mail server.
	DELETE Total	Total number of folders deleted.
	SELECT Total	Total number of calls to select a particular folder.
User disconnects from server	LOGOUT Total	Total number of logouts from the server. This should be somewhat consistent with the total number of connections.

[1] Note: If the mailbox is local to the server, the client must run a LIST command. If the mailbox is on a remote server, the client will need to run an RLIST command.

SMTP System Monitor Counters

The SMTP server receives messages, categorizes them, places them in queues created for the intended destination, and then delivers them to that destination. Messages can be received from port 25, from the Message Transfer Agent (MTA), or from a local store submission. Table 26-8 lists the counters that are most important with the SMTP service. The main object we are looking at here is the SMTP Server object. Some counters originate in different objects; these are noted in the Counter column.

Table 26-8. SMTP counters for the SMTP Server object

Stage	Counter	Meaning
Messages received from port 25	Messages Received	Total number of message received.
	Inbound Connections Current	Number of simultaneous inbound connections over port 25.
	Pickup Directory Messages Retrieved/Sec	Rate at which messages are being retrieved from the mail pickup directory. An unusually high number could indicate the use of a large distribution list with many mail-enabled contacts.
Messages received from the Exchange Store	MSExchange Transport Store Driver: Store/MSExchange-MTA Submits	Total number of messages received from the Store/MTA and submitted to the Transport Core.
Messages submitted for processing	Total messages submitted	Total number of messages submitted to queuing for delivery.
Messages categorized	Categorizer Queue Length	Number of messages that are currently being categorized or waiting to be categorized. An increasing number could indicate a problem with an event sink. A value of 0 could indicate that the SMTP service is stopped.
	Categorizations Completed Successfully	Total number of messages successfully categorized.
Categorized messages placed in destination queue	Remote Queue Length	Number of messages going to other servers that are waiting to be sent. An increasing number in this queue could indicate a problem with the physical connection to the Internet or between two Exchange 2000 servers. If one queue in particular has a steadily increasing number, you may want to see if the remote SMTP server is available.

Table 26-8. *continued*

Stage	Counter	Meaning
Categorized messages placed in destination queue	Remote Retry Queue Length	Number of messages going to other servers that could not be sent in a former attempt and that will be retried later. A high number here indicates either a physical connection problem or that the remote SMTP server is unavailable.
	Local Queue Length	Number of messages going to local recipients, to the MTA, or to other gateways.
	MSExchangeIS Transport Driver: Current Messages to MSExchangeMTA	Number of messages going to the MTA or other gateways only. This value is included in the Local Queue Length counter.
	Local Retry Queue Length	Number of messages going to local recipients, to the MTA, or to other gateways that could not be delivered in a former attempt and that will be retried later.
	Badmailed Messages	Number of messages that are malformed, such as having a nonexistent destination domain. These messages are delivered to the badmail directory. A high number here could indicate that some addresses for mail-enabled contacts were entered incorrectly.

Content Indexing System Monitor Counters

Content Indexing (CI) in Exchange 2000 Server consists of two basic phases. First is the initial crawl, which can take from hours to days and needs to be done only once. Until this initial crawl is completed, the index cannot be used for searching. Second is the incremental crawl, which is done numerous times after the initial crawl and is used to keep the index up-to-date. An incremental crawl usually completes in less than an hour. Table 26-9 lists the most important counters and the circumstances under which those counters are significant. The object we are most concerned with is the Microsoft Gatherer Projects object. Table 26-10 shows counters for the Microsoft Search Indexer Catalogs object, which can provide important information about indexes.

Finally Table 26-11 lists two of the most used counters for obtaining information about the number and extent of queries against your indexes. The counters in this table are for the Microsoft Search Catalogs object.

Table 26-9. Content Indexing counters for the Microsoft Gatherer Projects object

Stage	Counter	Meaning
Crawl in progress	Crawl in Progress flag	1 if a crawl is in progress, 0 if not.
	Current Crawl Is Incremental	1 if the current crawl is an incremental crawl, 0 if not.
	Document Additions	Number of documents being added to the index since the last crawl.
	URLs in History	Total number of URLs (documents) that CI has detected. This value will climb during the crawl and, once it levels off, will represent the total number of documents to be indexed.
	Waiting Documents	Total number of URLs (documents) that CI has detected that have not yet been indexed. The difference in rate between this counter and the URLs in History counter is essential in determining how long a crawl might take.

Table 26-10. Content Indexing counters for the Microsoft Search Indexer Catalogs object

Stage	Counter	Meaning
Index complete	Index Size	Size of the index.
	Number of Documents	Number of documents in the catalog. This value corresponds to the number shown in the Exchange System snap-in.
Merge in progress	Merge Process	Percentage of completeness for merges. While shadow merges can happen quickly, master merges can take up to an hour.

Table 26-11. Content Index counters for the Microsoft Search Catalogs object

Stage	Counter	Meaning
Ongoing	Queries	Total number of queries that have been run against a catalog.
	Results	Total number of results from queries. Note that one query can return thousands of results, so expect this number to be significantly higher than the Queries value.

Outlook Web Access

Outlook Web Access (OWA) allows users to access their mailboxes over the Internet through a browser, such as Microsoft Internet Explorer or Netscape Navigator. Due to differences in code paths between IE4-level (Internet Explorer 4 and Netscape Navigator) and IE 5.x-level browsers, performance counters in the MSExchange Web Mail object exist in three forms: non-IE5, IE5 and above, and Total, which sums the former two counters. Table 26-12 shows the counters for the MSExchange Web Mail object.

Table 26-12.   Counters for the MSExchange Web Mail object

Stage	Counter	Meaning
User connects over port 80	Web Service: Maximum Connections	Total number of OWA connections initiated since the Web Service (W3Svc) was last started.
	Web Service: Current Connections	Number of OWA users currently connected.
Messages sent over OWA	Message Sends (Total)	Total number of message sends. After OWA submits a message, it is handled by SMTP, and the applicable SMTP counters are affected.
OWA requests flow to and from the store	Epoxy: Client Out Que Len: DAV	Number of requests in the queue from the client to the server.
	Epoxy: Store Out Que Len: DAV	Number of responses in the queue from the server to the client.
	Epoxy: Blocks Allocated: DAV	A secondary indication of outstanding OWA requests. High numbers in these three Epoxy counters may indicate the need for an additional OWA server.
Client disconnects	Web Service: Current Connections	Current number of connections to the Web service. OWA has no logout process. Whether or not the user closes out the browser session when finished, the OWA user context will time out after 60 minutes of inactivity and that user's cached authentication will expire, causing this counter to decrement.

Summary

Monitoring your network is crucial in spotting problems before they grow too large. This chapter described the counters that are important in measuring the four primary subsystems of your Windows 2000 system: the disks, memory, network, and processor. It also examined the more important counters for the SMTP, POP3, and IMAP4 protocols, as well as the OWA and Content Indexing activities. We want to emphasize that regular monitoring of your Exchange 2000 servers will help you detect when something is about to go wrong and can give you some warning so that you can fix a problem before it occurs. Use the information in this chapter to devise a regular monitoring strategy for your system.

Appendix

The following table lists the names of the major Exchange directories and subdirectories created during installation, along with their contents. The path for each directory is shown relative to the root Exchange folder, \Exchsrvr.

Table A-1. Default directory structure for Exchange 2000 Server

Directory	Contents
\Address	Subdirectories used for e-mail address proxy generators
\Address\Ccmail\I386	Lotus cc:Mail address proxy generator
\Address\Notes\I386	Lotus Notes address proxy generator
\Address\Ms\I386	MS Mail address proxy generator
\Address\Notes\I386	Lotus Notes address proxy generator
\Address\Smtp\I386	SMTP address proxy generator
\Address\X400\I386	X.400 address proxy generator
\Bin	Exchange executables and core services
\Ccmdata	Temporary storage used by the connector for cc:Mail
\Conferencing	Video conferencing files
\Connect	Subdirectories used by connectors
\Connect\Ccmail\bin	Binaries for the connector for cc:Mail
\Connect\Msexcimc\bin	Binaries for the Internet Mail Service
\Connect\Msfbconn\bin	Binaries for the MS Schedule+ Free\Busy Connector
\Connect\Msmcon\bin	Binaries for the MS Mail Connector and shadow post office directories
\Docs	Exchange documentation in HTML format
\Dxadata	Directory synchronization database for the MS Mail Connector
\ExchangeServer	Miscellaneous files for global Exchange support
\Exchweb	Components for Outlook Web Access
\Mailroot	Working directories for message transfer
\Insdata	Working directory for the Internet News Service

(continued)

Table A-1. *continued*

Directory	Contents
\Kmsdata	Files supporting Key Management Service
\Mdbdata	Information store database files (Priv.edb, Priv.stm, Pub.edb, Pub.stm)
\Mtadata	Message Transfer Agent database files
\Mtadata\Mtacheck.out	Results of running the Mtacheck utility
\Res	DLLs for Event Viewer and System Monitor
\Schema	XML files supporting the Exchange extension of the Windows 2000 Active Directory Schema
server_name.log	Log files for message tracking

Glossary

A

access control entry (ACE) An object such as a user or group that is present on an access control list.

access control list (ACL) A list of security permissions applied to an object. An ACL for an item normally includes membership (ACEs) and the actions that each member can perform on the item.

ACE See *access control entry.*

ACL See *access control list.*

Active Directory The Microsoft Windows 2000 directory service, which replaces the Security Accounts Manager in Microsoft Windows NT 4. Active Directory consists of a forest, one or more domains, organizational units, containers, and objects. Various classes of objects can be represented within Active Directory, including users, groups, computers, printers, and applications.

Active Directory Connector (ADC) A service that runs on a Windows 2000 domain controller and allows you to synchronize Microsoft Exchange Server 5.5 and Windows 2000 directories. Unlike Site Replication Service, which replicates information between an Exchange 5.x organization and the configuration naming partition in Active Directory, the ADC replicates information between the Exchange 5.x directory and the domain partition in Active Directory.

ADC See *Active Directory Connector.*

address space The part of an e-mail address that designates the system that will receive the message. Typically, the address space is all of the address except the recipient and any delimiter. For example, in the address joe@microsoft.com, @microsoft.com is the address space.

administrative group A collection of Exchange 2000 servers that can be administered as a single unit. An administrative group can include policies, routing groups, public folder trees, monitors, servers, conferencing services, and chat networks. When security settings (permissions) are applied to an administrative group, all child objects in the tree inherit the same permissions as the administration group node.

American Standard Code for Information Interchange (ASCII) A code for representing English characters as numbers, with each letter assigned a number from 0 to 127.

ASCII See *American Standard Code for Information Interchange.*

automatic document property promotion A feature that allows for advanced searches on any document property, such as author, size, or department. When Exchange stores a document in a supported file type, the document's properties are automatically parsed and promoted to the information store. Hence, the properties become a part of the document's record in the database. Searches can then be performed on these properties.

B

BHS See *bridgehead server.*

bridgehead server (BHS) A server that acts as a message transfer point between Exchange 2000 routing groups. This term also refers to a computer hosting a directory replication connector.

C

CA See *certificate authority.*

certificate Public keys that have been digitally signed by a trusted authority (the certificate authority) and that are used to ensure that public keys have not been tampered with. Key Management Service uses a certificate format that complies with the X.509 standard.

certificate authority (CA) An entity that verifies the validity of public keys that have been created for users in the organization through the issuance of certificates. The CA also issues, revokes, and renews certificates.

certificate revocation list (CRL) and **certificate trust list (CTL)** Lists published by Certificate Services that name certificates whose authenticity can be trusted (trust list) or not trusted (revocation list).

channel See *chat room.*

chat community A chat entity within Exchange Server. Each administrative group in the Exchange System snap-in can have only one Chat Communities container in which multiple virtual chat communities can be created. Each chat community can host multiple chat rooms, or channels, and can be governed by its own administrative controls.

chat room A channel within a chat community. A user within a community can log on to any available chat room or even create a new one if dynamic channels are enabled for that community.

checkpoint file A file used to keep track of transactions that are committed to an Exchange database from a transaction log. Using checkpoint files ensures that transactions cannot be committed more than once.

circular logging A logging technique that involves maintaining only previous log files with uncommitted changes on the server. Fully committed transaction logs are removed to save space.

CMS See *Conferencing Management Service.*

Conferencing Management Service (CMS) The network service that coordinates resources for online meetings in the Microsoft Exchange Conferencing Server. Each site normally has an active CMS to allow fast connection for data conferencing users.

Conferencing Server See *Exchange Conferencing Server.*

ConfigCA A special connection agreement implemented as part of the Active Directory Connector that replicates configuration naming partition data from Exchange 5.x sites to administrative groups in Active Directory and vice versa. ConfigCAs work in conjunction with Site Replication Service.

configuration naming partition A partition of Active Directory that stores information regarding how an Exchange 2000 system is organized. Because this information is replicated to all domain controllers in the forest, the Exchange 2000 configuration is also replicated throughout the forest. The configuration information includes the Exchange 2000 topology (such as routing group information), connectors, protocols, and service settings. See also *domain naming partition* and *schema naming partition.*

connection agreement The configuration of information to replicate using the Active Directory Connector. Configuration information includes the servers that participate in the replica-

tion, the object classes (mailbox, custom recipient, distribution list and user, contact, and group) to replicate, the containers and organizational units to use for object placement, and the activity time schedule.

contact A nonsecurity principal that represents a user outside of the organization. A contact generally has an e-mail address, facilitating messaging between the local organization and the remote object. A contact is similar to a custom recipient in Exchange Server 5.5.

CRL See *certificate revocation list.*

CTL See *certificate trust list.*

D

DAV See *Distributed Authoring and Versioning.*

Digest authentication A form of authentication in Internet Information Services in which the password is sent as a hashed value that works through proxies and firewalls. This method works with all HTTP 1.1–compliant browsers, but the password is unencrypted in the Windows 2000 domain controller.

dismount See *mount.*

distinguished name A name assigned to every object in Active Directory that identifies where the object resides in the overall object hierarchy.

Distributed Authoring and Versioning (DAV) An extension to HTTP 1.1 that allows for the manipulation (reading and writing) of objects and attributes on a Web server. Also known as WebDAV. Exchange 2000 natively supports WebDAV. Although not specifically designed for the purpose, DAV allows for the control of data using a filing system–like protocol. DAV commands include PROPFIND and PROPPATCH.

DNS See *Domain Name System.*

domain The core unit in Active Directory. A domain is made up of a collection of computers that share a common directory database.

domain controller A Windows 2000 server that has Active Directory installed. Each domain controller is able to authenticate users for its own domain. It holds a complete replica of the domain naming partition for the domain to which it belongs and a complete replica of the configuration and schema naming partitions for the forest.

domain mode The mode in which an Active Directory domain is operating. A domain can be in either mixed mode or native mode. In mixed mode, the domain has limitations (such as 40,000 objects) imposed by the Windows NT 4 domain model. However, Windows 2000 domain controllers and Windows NT 4 backup domain controllers can coexist within the domain without problems. Switching to native mode, which is irreversible, allows the directory to scale up to millions of objects but requires that all domain controllers be upgraded to Windows 2000.

Domain Name System (DNS) A widely used standards-based protocol that allows clients and servers to resolve names into IP addresses and vice versa. Windows 2000 extends this concept even further by supplying a dynamic DNS (DDNS) service that enables clients and servers to automatically register themselves in the database without needing administrators to manually define records.

domain naming partition A partition of Active Directory that stores all of the domain objects for Exchange 2000 Server and replicates the objects to every domain controller in the domain. Recipient objects, including users, contacts, and groups, are stored in this partition. See also *configuration naming partition* and *schema naming partition.*

domain tree A collection of domains that have a contiguous namespace, such as microsoft.com, dog.microsoft.com, and cat.microsoft.com. Domains within the forest that do not have the same hierarchical domain name are located in a different domain tree. When different domain trees exist in a forest, it is referred to as a disjoint namespace.

DSAccess The Exchange 2000 component that provides directory lookup services for components such as SMTP and MTA. Client requests use the DSProxy service for directory access.

DSProxy The Exchange 2000 component that can proxy (and refer) MAPI directory service requests from Microsoft Outlook clients to Active Directory for address book lookup and name resolution.

E

ECS See *Exchange Conferencing Server.*

epoxy layer See *Exchange Interprocess Communication layer (EXIPC).*

ESE See *Extensible Storage Engine.*

event sink A piece of code that is activated by a defined trigger, such as the reception of a new message. The code is normally written in any COM-compatible programming language, such as Microsoft Visual Basic, Microsoft VBScript, JavaScript, C, or C++. Exchange 2000 Server supports transport, protocol, and store event sinks. Event sinks on the store can be synchronous (meaning that the code executes as the event is triggered) or asynchronous (meaning that the code executes sometime after the event).

EVS See *Exchange virtual server.*

Exchange Conferencing Server A service that allows users to meet in virtual rooms on an Exchange server. Exchange Conferencing Server defines the use of a Conferencing Management Service to coordinate the room bookings and a T.120 multipoint control unit for the actual connection of clients to a conferencing session.

Exchange Interprocess Communication layer (EXIPC) A queuing layer, formerly known as the epoxy layer, that allows the IIS and Store processes (Inetinfo.exe and Store.exe) to shuttle data back and forth very quickly. This layer is required to achieve the best possible performance between the protocols and database services on an Exchange 2000 server. Conventional applications require the processor to switch contexts when transferring data between two processes. Exchange Server 5.5 incorporates protocols such as NNTP, POP3, and IMAP directly into the Store.exe process, so data transfer is very efficient. The Exchange 2000 architecture separates the protocols from the database for ease of management and to support future architectures.

Exchange virtual server (EVS) When using clustered servers, you allocate different resources (such as storage groups) to an EVS. If a node fails, you can move an EVS from the failed node to one of the remaining nodes.

Extensible Storage Engine (ESE) A transaction logging system that ensures data integrity and consistency in the event of a system crash or media failure. Other databases, such as the Active Directory database, also use ESE.

F

failover or **failback** The process of moving a resource from one server in a cluster to another. Failover happens when a problem occurs on the active server and services must be transferred to the passive server. Failback is the process of restoring resources to the active server after they have been temporarily relocated on a passive server.

filter rules LDAP rules created using recipient policies. Filter rules allow you to specify what kind of e-mail address is generated for each recipient object.

firewall A system designed to prevent unauthorized access to or from a private network. A firewall can be made up of hardware, software, or a combination of both. Firewalls can work by blocking certain types of packets or certain applications.

forest A collection of domains and domain trees. The implicit name of the forest is the name of the first domain installed. All domain controllers within a forest share the same configuration and schema naming partitions. To join an existing forest, you will use the Dcpromo utility. The first domain within the forest cannot be removed.

front end/back end An Exchange 2000 configuration in which clients access a bank of protocol servers (the front end) for collaboration information, and these in turn communicate with the data stores on separate servers (the back end) to retrieve the physical data. A front end/back end configuration allows for a scalable single point of contact for all Exchange-related data.

G

Global Address List The list of all Exchange Server recipients in the entire Exchange organization. Exchange uses address lists to hold and organize the names of the recipients associated with the system.

Global Catalog server A server that holds a complete replica of the configuration and schema naming contexts for an Active Directory forest, a complete replica of the domain naming context in which the server is installed, and a partial replica of all other domains in the forest. The Global Catalog knows about every object in the forest and has representations for them in its directory, however, it may not know about all attributes (such as job title and physical address) for objects in other domains.

globally unique identifier (GUID) An attribute consisting of a 128-bit number that is guaranteed to be unique, used by applications that need to refer to an object by an identifier that remains constant. A GUID is assigned to an object when it is created, and it will never change, even if the object is moved between containers in the same domain.

group An object defined in Active Directory that contains other objects such as users, contacts, and possibly other groups. A group can be either a distribution group or a security group, and its scope can be local, domain, or universal. Groups are similar to distribution lists in Exchange Server 5.5.

GUID See *globally unique identifier.*

H

Heartbeat A group of packets that are sent over a private IP network between nodes to detect the health of the other nodes, as well as the health of the applications and services they manage within the cluster.

high availability A quality of a server cluster, in which ownership of resources such as disks or IP addresses is automatically transferred from a failed server to the surviving server. The software is restarted on the surviving server, and users experience only a momentary pause in service. The aim of high availability is to minimize downtime. Windows clustering is a highly available solution, but it does not guarantee nonstop operation.

hosted organization A collection of Exchange services including but not limited to virtual servers (that is, instances of IMAP4, SMTP, POP3, NNTP, HTTP, or RVP), storage space, and real-time collaboration facilities that exist to serve the needs of a single company. A hosted organization is normally used by Internet service providers to host multiple companies on the same physical computer. However, a hosted organization is not limited to a single Exchange 2000 server.

I

IFS See *Installable File System.*

IIS See *Internet Information Service.*

IM See *Instant Messaging.*

IMAP4 See *Internet Message Access Protocol 4.*

Installable File System (IFS) A file system that allows users to place any kind of document in the native content file (the streaming file) and then access it from almost any client, regardless of whether that client is a browser, a MAPI client, or simply Microsoft Windows Explorer.

Instant Messaging (IM) The Exchange 2000 service that allows for real-time messaging and collaboration between users. Clients generally use the MSN Messenger client to log on to Instant Messaging and subscribe to other users.

Instant Messaging home server The IM server responsible for maintaining current presence information for any user assigned to it and for notifying subscribers of changes in a user's status. Messages sent to a user must first pass through the user's home server. The instant messaging client software represents the user to the home server and acts as the inbox for that user.

Instant Messaging routing server A server that either proxies Instant Messaging requests or uses HTTP to redirect the IM client to an appropriate Instant Messaging home server.

Integrated Windows Authentication A form of IIS authentication in which the password is sent as an encrypted value to the highest security level. This form of authentication does not work through firewalls and proxies.

Internet Information Services (IIS)
Microsoft's Web server software for the Windows 2000 operating system. IIS 5 ships with Windows 2000 and is installed by default during a typical Windows 2000 installation.

Internet Message Access Protocol 4 (IMAP4) A standards based protocol for accessing mailbox information. IMAP4 is considered to be more advanced than POP3 because it supports basic online capabilities and access to folders other than the Inbox. Exchange Server 5.x and Exchange 2000 both support IMAP4.

Internet Relay Chat (IRC) A popular chat system developed in the late 1980s that allows multiple users to participate in a chat environment simultaneously. IRC is made up of an IRC server and an IRC client.

IRC See *Internet Relay Chat.*

K

Key Management Service (KMS) An advanced security tool in Exchange 2000 Server that protects data integrity through message encryption and digital signatures. It is an optional component of Exchange 2000 Server that works in close conjunction with Windows 2000 Certificate Services to provide a centralized public-key infrastructure.

key pair, asymmetric A pair of encryption keys that are not identical: one key is used to encrypt the data and a different key is used to decrypt it. With asymmetric keys, one key is known as the public key and the other is known as the private key. Exchange 2000 Server uses this type of encryption technology.

key pair, symmetric Identical encryption keys: both the sender and the recipient use the same key to encrypt and decrypt the data. Also known as shared keys.

KMS See *Key Management Service.*

L

LDAP See *Lightweight Directory Access Protocol.*

Lightweight Directory Access Protocol (LDAP) A standards-based protocol that can be used to interact with conformant directory services. LDAP version 2 allows users and applications to read the contents of a directory database, whereas LDAP version 3 (defined under RFC 2251) allows them to both read from and write to a directory database.

link state algorithm (LSA) The algorithm used to exchange routing status information between Exchange 2000 servers.

LSA See *link state algorithm.*

M

mail-based replication A mechanism to replicate directory information through a messaging transport. This term applies to Exchange 5.x intersite directory replication as well as to Active Directory replication through SMTP.

mail exchanger (MX) record A record in a DNS database that indicates a host responsible for receiving e-mail messages.

MAPI See *Messaging Application Programming Interface.*

Masquerade Domain option An option that allows you to indicate a different domain name to be placed in both the Mail From and From fields of all outgoing SMTP messages.

MCU See *multipoint control unit.*

message tracking A feature of an Exchange server that, along with the subject logging feature, provides a sophisticated way to track messages throughout the Exchange organization, primarily for troubleshooting purposes.

Message Transfer Agent (MTA) The component in all versions of Exchange Server that transfers messages between servers, using the X.400 protocol.

Messaging Application Programming Interface (MAPI) The API used by Microsoft messaging applications such as Outlook to access collaboration data. MAPI, or more specifically, MAPI RPC, is also used as the transport protocol between Outlook clients and Exchange servers.

metabase A store that contains metadata such as that used by IIS to obtain its configuration data. The metabase can be viewed through utilities such as Metaedit.

metabase update service A component in Exchange 2000 that reads data from Active Directory and transposes it into the local IIS metabase. The metabase update service allows the administrator to make remote configuration changes to virtual servers without having a permanent connection to each system.

metadata Data about data. In relation to Exchange, this term can be used in the context of Active Directory and can also be used to describe the structure within the store or the MTA.

MIME See *Multipurpose Internet Mail Extensions.*

mixed mode See *domain mode.*

mount To place an individual store in a storage group online. Stores can also be taken off line, or dismounted. You might dismount a store for maintenance, for example.

MTA See *Message Transfer Agent.*

multipoint control unit (MCU) A reference to the T.120 protocol, which allows clients to connect to data conferencing sessions. MCUs can communicate with each other to transfer conferencing information.

Multipurpose Internet Mail Extensions (MIME) A standard that allows multiple files of various content types to be encapsulated into one message. RFCs 2045 through 2049 currently define MIME and are considered to be one single standard.

MX record See *mail exchanger (MX) record.*

N

Name Service Provider Interface (NSPI) Part of the DSProxy process that can accept Outlook client directory requests and pass them to an address book provider.

namespace A logical collection of resources that can be managed as a single unit. Within Active Directory, a domain defines a namespace.

naming partition A self-contained section of a directory hierarchy that has its own properties, such as replication configuration and permissions structure. Active Directory includes the domain, configuration, and schema naming partitions.

native content file See *rich text file.*

native mode See *domain mode.*

NDR See *nondelivery report.*

Network News Transfer Protocol (NNTP) A standards-based protocol that includes simple command verbs to transfer Usenet messages between clients and servers as well as between servers. NNTP uses TCP/IP port 119.

NNTP See *Network News Transfer Protocol.*

nondelivery report (NDR) A report generated when a message is not deliverable for some reason in Exchange Server. The NDR is returned to the message sender and sometimes to an administrator or automated monitor as well.

NSPI See *Name Service Provider Interface.*

O

object An entity that is described by a distinct, named set of attributes. In the Windows 2000 Active Directory, all network resources are represented as objects that can be centrally administered.

OLE DB An API that allows low-level programming languages such as C and C++ to access dissimilar data stores through a common query language. OLE DB is seen as the replacement for open database connectivity (ODBC). Data stores such as those in Exchange 2000 and SQL Server allow for OLE DB access, which makes application development easier and faster.

organizational unit (OU) An Active Directory container object that is used to organize other objects within a domain. An OU can contain user accounts, printers, groups, computers, and other OUs.

OU See *organizational unit.*

Outlook Web Access (OWA) The Web browser interface to Exchange Server mailbox and public folder data. The

OWA client in Exchange Server 5.x uses Active Server Pages to render collaboration data into HTML, whereas the OWA client in Exchange 2000 uses native access to the store.

OWA See *Outlook Web Access.*

P

PGP See *Pretty Good Privacy.*

PKI See *public-key infrastructure.*

policy A set of configuration parameters that applies to one or more Exchange objects in the same class. For example, you can create a policy that affects certain settings on some or all of your Exchange servers. If you ever want to change these settings, all you need to do is modify the policy and it will be applied to the appropriate server's organization.

POP3 See *Post Office Protocol 3.*

Post Office Protocol 3 (POP3) A standards-based protocol for simple access to Inbox data. All versions of Exchange server except version 4 support POP3. POP3 uses TCP/IP port 110 for client-to-server access.

Pretty Good Privacy (PGP) A public-key technique for encrypting data, developed by Philip Zimmerman. It has become a popular encryption method on the Internet because it is widely available and free.

property promotion See *automatic document property promotion.*

public folder A folder on an Exchange server that is part of a public store made available to multiple users. A public folder can hold messages, documents, and just about any other type of file.

public folder tree A collection of public folders created under the same hierarchical namespace. Previous versions of Exchange Server used only a single tree called All Public Folders. You can define multiple trees in Exchange 2000 Server. Each tree is a unit of hierarchy replication and can be replicated to one or more public stores. A public store can host only one tree. MAPI clients such as Outlook can access only a single tree, called All Public Folders, whereas other clients such as a Web browser, a networking client using the Microsoft Web Storage System, or any NNTP client can access any tree that is defined.

public-key infrastructure (PKI) A collection of resources that work together to provide a secure network authentication system, the major components of a public key infrastructure are certificates and certificate authorities, policies, and cryptographic service providers.

Q

Queue Viewer A tool built into the Exchange System snap-in that allows you to view any message queue. When messages are sent from an Exchange server, they are placed in a message queue, where they wait until it is their turn to go out over the appropriate connector.

quorum resource A resource that stores the cluster management data for a server cluster. It is usually held on a shared disk.

R

Recipient Update service Part of the Exchange System Attendant, this service is responsible for keeping address lists up-to-date and creating proxy addresses for users.

remote procedure calls (RPCs) A reliable synchronous protocol that allows a program on one computer to execute a program on another computer. Outlook clients use MAPI RPCs for accessing mailboxes and public folders.

resource In real-time collaboration, a user object in Active Directory that represents a facility. Resources are stored in the System\Exchange organizational unit in Active Directory.

request for comments (RFC) RFCs are a series of notes about the Internet. Anyone can submit an RFC and, if an RFC gains enough support, it may become an Internet standard. Each RFC is designated by an RFC number. Once published, an RFC never changes. Modifications to an original RFC are assigned a new RFC number.

rich text file One of the two files that make up an Exchange 2000 database. The rich text file (ending in .RTF) holds mail messages and Message Application Programming Interface (MAPI) content, and the native content file or streaming file (ending in .STM) holds all non-MAPI information. The term is also used to describe a file formatted according to a formatting standard defined by Microsoft. RTF files are actually ASCII files with special commands embedded in them to indicate formatting.

routing group A collection of Exchange 2000 servers that can transfer messaging data to one another in a single hop without going through a bridgehead server. In general, Exchange servers within a single routing group are connected by high-bandwidth links. Connectivity among servers in a routing group is based entirely on SMTP.

Routing Group Connector A connector in Exchange 2000 Server that connects routing groups to one another. A Routing Group Connector is unidirectional and can have separate configuration properties (such as allowable message types over the connection). Routing Group Connectors use the concept of local and remote bridgeheads to dictate which servers in the routing groups can communicate over the link. The underlying message transport for a Routing Group Connector is either SMTP or RPC, and it uses link state information to route messages efficiently.

routing service A component in Exchange 2000 that builds link state information.

RPC See *remote procedure calls.*

S

SCC See *Site Consistency Checker.*

schema The metadata (data about data) that describes how objects are used within a given structure. In relation to Exchange Server, this term can be used in the context of Active Directory, but it can also be used to describe the structure within the store or the MTA.

schema naming partition A partition of Active Directory that contains all object types and their attributes that can be created in Active Directory. This information is replicated to all domain controllers in the forest. During the first installation of Exchange 2000 Server in the forest, the Active Directory schema is extended to include new object classes and attributes that are specific to Exchange 2000 Server. See also *configuration naming partition* and *domain naming partition.*

security principal A user who can log on to a domain and gain access to network resources. In Active Directory, a user object is a security principal. A non-security principal is an object represented in Active Directory that cannot access resources within the enterprise.

shared-everything architecture An architecture that gives any physical server in the cluster access to all of the data and application code at any given time and can offer these services to the client as needed. It is also known as active/active archictecture.

shared-nothing architecture An architecture that makes one of the physical

nodes responsible for running an application while the other servers, or nodes, wait on the sidelines for the first physical server to fail so that they can leap into action and take over the application. Only one server works at any given time for an application. It is also known as active/passive architecture.

Simple Message Transfer Protocol (SMTP) A widely used standards-based protocol that allows for the transfer of messages between different messaging servers. SMTP is defined under RFC 821 and uses simple command verbs to facilitate message transport over TCP/IP port 25.

single-instance storage (SIS) A storage technique in which messages sent to multiple recipients are stored only once as long as all the recipients are located in the same database. SIS is not maintained if a mailbox is moved to a different database, even if it still resides in the same storage group. Moreover, it does not span multiple databases in a single storage group.

sink See *event sink.*

SIS See *single-instance storage.*

site In Active Directory, a collection of IP subnets. All computers in the same site have high-speed connectivity—LAN speeds—with one another. Unlike an Exchange site, an Active Directory site does not include a unit of namespace; for example, multiple sites can exist within a single domain, and conversely, a single site can span multiple domains.

Site Consistency Checker (SCC) An updated version of the Knowledge Consistency Checker from Exchange Server 5.5. SCC runs inside the Site Replication Service. It ensures that knowledge consistency is maintained for sites and administrative groups when interoperating between Exchange Server 5.5 and Exchange 2000 Server.

Site Replication Service (SRS) The service responsible for replicating Exchange 5.x site and configuration information to the configuration naming partition of Active Directory when an Exchange 2000 server belongs to an existing Exchange 5.5 site.

SMTP See *Simple Message Transfer Protocol.*

SRS See *Site Replication Service.*

storage group A collection of Exchange databases on an Exchange 2000 server that share the same ESE instance and transaction log. Individual databases within a storage group can be mounted and dismounted. Exchange 2000 architecture allows each server to host up to 16 storage groups, although only 4 can be defined through the Exchange System snap-in.

store The generic name given to the storage subsystem on an Exchange server. This term is used interchangeably to describe the Store.exe process and Exchange databases.

sysop Short for system operator. An individual who manages an online service, such as a bulletin board or chat room.

System Attendant One of the core Exchange 2000 services. System Attendant performs miscellaneous functions (usually related to directory information), such as generating address lists, offline address books, and directory lookup facilities.

system policies General sets of rules created to apply to servers, mailbox stores, and public stores. Once a policy is created, changing the policy changes the rules for all members of that policy.

T

T.120 A standards-based protocol used with Exchange Conferencing Server. Clients such as Microsoft NetMeeting are T.120 compatible.

TCP port In the TCP/IP protocol, a TCP port identifies a logical connection that an application can use to transport data. For example, TCP port 80 is normally used to send HTTP messages.

transaction logs The primary storage area for new transactions made to ESE databases. Data is written to these logs sequentially as transactions occur. Regular database maintenance routines then commit changes in the logs to the actual databases.

U

UPN See *user principal name*.

user In Active Directory, a security principal (a user who can log on to the domain). A user may have an e-mail address and/or an Exchange mailbox, making the object mail enabled and/or mailbox enabled, respectively.

user ban An action that prevents an individual user from accessing a specific chat community. If a banned user attempts to access a community, he or she is refused. The user can be restricted by nickname, user name, or both.

user principal name (UPN) A name that is generated for each object, in the form *username@domainname*. A UPN allows the underlying domain structure and complexity to be hidden from users. For example, although many domains may exist within a forest, users would seamlessly log on as if they were in the same domain.

V

virtual root A shortcut pointer to a physical storage location. Virtual roots are normally defined to allow users and applications to connect with a short "friendly" path instead of navigating a complex hierarchy. IIS uses the concept of virtual roots to expose resources provided by a Web server.

virtual server An instance of any service type normally implemented in IIS. For example, a virtual server can be an instance of FTP, IMAP, Instant Messaging, HTTP, NNTP, POP3, or SMTP. An Exchange 2000 server can host multiple virtual servers of the same type on each computer. Each virtual server can have its own configuration properties, such as bound IP addresses, port number, and authentication type.

W

WebDAV See *Distributed Authoring and Versioning*.

Web Store The database architecture in Exchange 2000. Previous releases of Exchange exposed data such as public folders only through MAPI, whereas Exchange 2000 exposes all of its data through MAPI, HTTP, and Win32 layers. This means that an object stored in a public folder can be retrieved and manipulated through a Web browser or a standard client with a network redirector. The Exchange 2000 store exposes itself to the operating system as an Installable File System, which means that the underlying data can be accessed through a drive letter and, in turn, that this drive and its folders can be shared via a universal naming convention (UNC) path to allow other clients to connect to the data.

X

X.400 A messaging standard that can be used by many messaging systems. X.400 uses a strict addressing method that reflects a hierarchical environment. An X.400 address reflects the recipient's position in a messaging hierarchy.

X.400 Connector A connector that can be used to connect an Exchange system to a foreign X.400 system or to connect two Exchange routing groups over unstable or low-bandwidth (typically less than 16 Kbps) connections.

X.500 A standard that defines how directories should be structured. X.500 directories are hierarchical, with different levels for each category of information. Both Active Directory and LDAP are loosely based on the X.500 standard.

X.509 A standard that defines digital certificates.

Index

Note: Page number in italics refer to figures or tables.

Walter J. Glenn   is a veteran of more than 15 years in the computer industry. He is a Microsoft Certified Systems Engineer (MCSE) and Microsoft Certified Trainer (MCT), who currently splits his time between consulting for small to medium-sized companies and writing on computer-related topics. Walter's publications include *Microsoft Exchange Server 5.5 Administrator's Companion*, *Exchange Server 5.5 MCSE Study Guide*, *Teach Yourself MCSE Windows NT Server in 14 Days*, and *Teach Yourself MCSE TCP/IP in 14 Days*.

Bill English   is a trainer, author, and consultant who specializes in Microsoft Exchange Server. He is a Microsoft Certified Systems Engineer (MCSE), a Microsoft Certified Trainer (MCT), and a Certified Technical Trainer. Bill's hands-on experience ranges from working with LANs as small as 13 nodes to those with over 10,000 users. He served as a Windows NT system administrator in a large multinational company and acted as the lead consultant to Minnesota's major airline in their migration from Novell to Windows NT. Bill currently divides his time between work as a part-time system administrator, an Exchange trainer, and a freelance writer. Bill holds a Bachelor's degree and two Master's degrees; he resides in the Twin Cities with his wife and two children.

The manuscript for this book was prepared and galleyed using Microsoft Word 2000. Pages were composed by Microsoft Press using Adobe PageMaker 6.52 for Windows, with text in Sabon and display type in ITC Franklin Gothic. Composed pages were delivered to the printer as electronic prepress files.

Cover Designer:	Greg Hickman
Interior Graphic Designer:	James D. Kramer
Principal Compositor:	Dan Latimer
Principal Copy Editor:	Cheryl Penner
Indexer:	Liz Cunningham

System Requirements

To follow the procedures described in this book, you must have Microsoft Windows 2000 Server and Microsoft Exchange 2000 Server running on your system. Chapter 7 details the hardware and software requirements for installing Exchange 2000 Server.

The compact disc that accompanies this *Administrator's Companion* contains the complete text of the printed book in a fully searchable electronic form. To install the electronic book you must have Microsoft Internet Explorer 4.01 or later and the proper HTML Help components. If your computer does not have these tools, the e-book setup program will offer to install Internet Explorer 5. For more information on running the electronic book, read the Readme.txt file on the CD.

The compact disc also contains a series of white papers written by experts on Exchange 2000. To read these articles you must have Microsoft Word or Microsoft Word viewer. Microsoft Word Viewer is included on the CD.

Microsoft Press Support

Every effort has been made to ensure the accuracy of the book and the contents of this companion CD. Microsoft Press provides corrections for books through the World Wide Web at

> *http://mspress.microsoft.com/support/*

If you have comments, questions, or ideas regarding the book or this companion CD, please send them to Microsoft Press via e-mail to

> *MSPInput@Microsoft.com*

or via postal mail to

Microsoft Press
Attn: Editor, Exchange 2000 Server Administrator's Companion
One Microsoft Way
Redmond, WA 98052-6399

Please note that product support is not offered through the above addresses.

Microsoft Exchange 2000 Server Support

For support information regarding Exchange 2000 Server, you can connect to Microsoft Technical Support on the Web at

http://support.microsoft.com/support/

In the United States, you can also call Technical Support at (425) 635-7011 weekdays between 6 A.M. and 6 P.M. Pacific time. Outside the United States, please contact your local Microsoft subsidiary for support information. Microsoft also provides information about Exchange at

http://www.microsoft.com/Exchange/

MICROSOFT LICENSE AGREEMENT

Book Companion CD

IMPORTANT—READ CAREFULLY: This Microsoft End-User License Agreement ("EULA") is a legal agreement between you (either an individual or an entity) and Microsoft Corporation for the Microsoft product identified above, which includes computer software and may include associated media, printed materials, and "online" or electronic documentation ("SOFTWARE PRODUCT"). Any component included within the SOFTWARE PRODUCT that is accompanied by a separate End-User License Agreement shall be governed by such agreement and not the terms set forth below. By installing, copying, or otherwise using the SOFTWARE PRODUCT, you agree to be bound by the terms of this EULA. If you do not agree to the terms of this EULA, you are not authorized to install, copy, or otherwise use the SOFTWARE PRODUCT; you may, however, return the SOFTWARE PRODUCT, along with all printed materials and other items that form a part of the Microsoft product that includes the SOFTWARE PRODUCT, to the place you obtained them for a full refund.

SOFTWARE PRODUCT LICENSE

The SOFTWARE PRODUCT is protected by United States copyright laws and international copyright treaties, as well as other intellectual property laws and treaties. The SOFTWARE PRODUCT is licensed, not sold.

1. **GRANT OF LICENSE.** This EULA grants you the following rights:

   a. **Software Product.** You may install and use one copy of the SOFTWARE PRODUCT on a single computer. The primary user of the computer on which the SOFTWARE PRODUCT is installed may make a second copy for his or her exclusive use on a portable computer.

   b. **Storage/Network Use.** You may also store or install a copy of the SOFTWARE PRODUCT on a storage device, such as a network server, used only to install or run the SOFTWARE PRODUCT on your other computers over an internal network; however, you must acquire and dedicate a license for each separate computer on which the SOFTWARE PRODUCT is installed or run from the storage device. A license for the SOFTWARE PRODUCT may not be shared or used concurrently on different computers.

   c. **License Pak.** If you have acquired this EULA in a Microsoft License Pak, you may make the number of additional copies of the computer software portion of the SOFTWARE PRODUCT authorized on the printed copy of this EULA, and you may use each copy in the manner specified above. You are also entitled to make a corresponding number of secondary copies for portable computer use as specified above.

   d. **Sample Code.** Solely with respect to portions, if any, of the SOFTWARE PRODUCT that are identified within the SOFTWARE PRODUCT as sample code (the "SAMPLE CODE"):

      i. **Use and Modification.** Microsoft grants you the right to use and modify the source code version of the SAMPLE CODE, *provided* you comply with subsection (d)(iii) below. You may not distribute the SAMPLE CODE, or any modified version of the SAMPLE CODE, in source code form.

      ii. **Redistributable Files.** Provided you comply with subsection (d)(iii) below, Microsoft grants you a nonexclusive, royalty-free right to reproduce and distribute the object code version of the SAMPLE CODE and of any modified SAMPLE CODE, other than SAMPLE CODE, or any modified version thereof, designated as not redistributable in the Readme file that forms a part of the SOFTWARE PRODUCT (the "Non-Redistributable Sample Code"). All SAMPLE CODE other than the Non-Redistributable Sample Code is collectively referred to as the "REDISTRIBUTABLES."

      iii. **Redistribution Requirements.** If you redistribute the REDISTRIBUTABLES, you agree to: (i) distribute the REDISTRIBUTABLES in object code form only in conjunction with and as a part of your software application product; (ii) not use Microsoft's name, logo, or trademarks to market your software application product; (iii) include a valid copyright notice on your software application product; (iv) indemnify, hold harmless, and defend Microsoft from and against any claims or lawsuits, including attorney's fees, that arise or result from the use or distribution of your software application product; and (v) not permit further distribution of the REDISTRIBUTABLES by your end user. Contact Microsoft for the applicable royalties due and other licensing terms for all other uses and/or distribution of the REDISTRIBUTABLES.

2. **DESCRIPTION OF OTHER RIGHTS AND LIMITATIONS.**

   - **Limitations on Reverse Engineering, Decompilation, and Disassembly.** You may not reverse engineer, decompile, or disassemble the SOFTWARE PRODUCT, except and only to the extent that such activity is expressly permitted by applicable law notwithstanding this limitation.

   - **Separation of Components.** The SOFTWARE PRODUCT is licensed as a single product. Its component parts may not be separated for use on more than one computer.

   - **Rental.** You may not rent, lease, or lend the SOFTWARE PRODUCT.

   - **Support Services.** Microsoft may, but is not obligated to, provide you with support services related to the SOFTWARE PRODUCT ("Support Services"). Use of Support Services is governed by the Microsoft policies and programs described in the user manual, in "online" documentation, and/or in other Microsoft-provided materials. Any supplemental software code provided to you as part of the Support Services shall be considered part of the SOFTWARE PRODUCT and subject to the terms and conditions of this EULA. With respect to technical information you provide to Microsoft as part of the Support Services, Microsoft may use such information for its business purposes, including for product support and development. Microsoft will not utilize such technical information in a form that personally identifies you.

- **Software Transfer.** You may permanently transfer all of your rights under this EULA, provided you retain no copies, you transfer all of the SOFTWARE PRODUCT (including all component parts, the media and printed materials, any upgrades, this EULA, and, if applicable, the Certificate of Authenticity), **and** the recipient agrees to the terms of this EULA.

- **Termination.** Without prejudice to any other rights, Microsoft may terminate this EULA if you fail to comply with the terms and conditions of this EULA. In such event, you must destroy all copies of the SOFTWARE PRODUCT and all of its component parts.

3. **COPYRIGHT.** All title and copyrights in and to the SOFTWARE PRODUCT (including but not limited to any images, photographs, animations, video, audio, music, text, SAMPLE CODE, REDISTRIBUTABLES, and "applets" incorporated into the SOFTWARE PRODUCT) and any copies of the SOFTWARE PRODUCT are owned by Microsoft or its suppliers. The SOFTWARE PRODUCT is protected by copyright laws and international treaty provisions. Therefore, you must treat the SOFTWARE PRODUCT like any other copyrighted material **except** that you may install the SOFTWARE PRODUCT on a single computer provided you keep the original solely for backup or archival purposes. You may not copy the printed materials accompanying the SOFTWARE PRODUCT.

4. **U.S. GOVERNMENT RESTRICTED RIGHTS.** The SOFTWARE PRODUCT and documentation are provided with RESTRICTED RIGHTS. Use, duplication, or disclosure by the Government is subject to restrictions as set forth in subparagraph (c)(1)(ii) of the Rights in Technical Data and Computer Software clause at DFARS 252.227-7013 or subparagraphs (c)(1) and (2) of the Commercial Computer Software—Restricted Rights at 48 CFR 52.227-19, as applicable. Manufacturer is Microsoft Corporation/One Microsoft Way/Redmond, WA 98052-6399.

5. **EXPORT RESTRICTIONS.** You agree that you will not export or re-export the SOFTWARE PRODUCT, any part thereof, or any process or service that is the direct product of the SOFTWARE PRODUCT (the foregoing collectively referred to as the "Restricted Components"), to any country, person, entity, or end user subject to U.S. export restrictions. You specifically agree not to export or re-export any of the Restricted Components (i) to any country to which the U.S. has embargoed or restricted the export of goods or services, which currently include, but are not necessarily limited to, Cuba, Iran, Iraq, Libya, North Korea, Sudan, and Syria, or to any national of any such country, wherever located, who intends to transmit or transport the Restricted Components back to such country; (ii) to any end user who you know or have reason to know will utilize the Restricted Components in the design, development, or production of nuclear, chemical, or biological weapons; or (iii) to any end user who has been prohibited from participating in U.S. export transactions by any federal agency of the U.S. government. You warrant and represent that neither the BXA nor any other U.S. federal agency has suspended, revoked, or denied your export privileges.

DISCLAIMER OF WARRANTY

NO WARRANTIES OR CONDITIONS. MICROSOFT EXPRESSLY DISCLAIMS ANY WARRANTY OR CONDITION FOR THE SOFTWARE PRODUCT. THE SOFTWARE PRODUCT AND ANY RELATED DOCUMENTATION ARE PROVIDED "AS IS" WITHOUT WARRANTY OR CONDITION OF ANY KIND, EITHER EXPRESS OR IMPLIED, INCLUDING, WITHOUT LIMITATION, THE IMPLIED WARRANTIES OF MERCHANTABILITY, FITNESS FOR A PARTICULAR PURPOSE, OR NONINFRINGEMENT. THE ENTIRE RISK ARISING OUT OF USE OR PERFORMANCE OF THE SOFTWARE PRODUCT REMAINS WITH YOU.

LIMITATION OF LIABILITY. TO THE MAXIMUM EXTENT PERMITTED BY APPLICABLE LAW, IN NO EVENT SHALL MICROSOFT OR ITS SUPPLIERS BE LIABLE FOR ANY SPECIAL, INCIDENTAL, INDIRECT, OR CONSEQUENTIAL DAMAGES WHATSOEVER (INCLUDING, WITHOUT LIMITATION, DAMAGES FOR LOSS OF BUSINESS PROFITS, BUSINESS INTERRUPTION, LOSS OF BUSINESS INFORMATION, OR ANY OTHER PECUNIARY LOSS) ARISING OUT OF THE USE OF OR INABILITY TO USE THE SOFTWARE PRODUCT OR THE PROVISION OF OR FAILURE TO PROVIDE SUPPORT SERVICES, EVEN IF MICROSOFT HAS BEEN ADVISED OF THE POSSIBILITY OF SUCH DAMAGES. IN ANY CASE, MICROSOFT'S ENTIRE LIABILITY UNDER ANY PROVISION OF THIS EULA SHALL BE LIMITED TO THE GREATER OF THE AMOUNT ACTUALLY PAID BY YOU FOR THE SOFTWARE PRODUCT OR US$5.00; PROVIDED, HOWEVER, IF YOU HAVE ENTERED INTO A MICROSOFT SUPPORT SERVICES AGREEMENT, MICROSOFT'S ENTIRE LIABILITY REGARDING SUPPORT SERVICES SHALL BE GOVERNED BY THE TERMS OF THAT AGREEMENT. BECAUSE SOME STATES AND JURISDICTIONS DO NOT ALLOW THE EXCLUSION OR LIMITATION OF LIABILITY, THE ABOVE LIMITATION MAY NOT APPLY TO YOU.

MISCELLANEOUS

This EULA is governed by the laws of the State of Washington USA, except and only to the extent that applicable law mandates governing law of a different jurisdiction.

Should you have any questions concerning this EULA, or if you desire to contact Microsoft for any reason, please contact the Microsoft subsidiary serving your country, or write: Microsoft Sales Information Center/One Microsoft Way/Redmond, WA 98052-6399.

Proof of Purchase

0-7356-0938-1

Do not send this card with your registration.
Use this card as proof of purchase if participating in a promotion or
rebate offer on *Microsoft® Exchange 2000 Server Administrator's Companion*.
Card must be used in conjunction with other proof(s) of payment
such as your dated sales receipt—see offer details.

Microsoft® Exchange 2000
Server Administrator's Companion

WHERE DID YOU PURCHASE THIS PRODUCT?

CUSTOMER NAME

Microsoft®
mspress.microsoft.com

Microsoft Press, PO Box 97017, Redmond, WA 98073-9830

OWNER REGISTRATION CARD

Register Today!

0-7356-0938-1

Return the bottom portion of this card to register today.

Microsoft® Exchange 2000
Server Administrator's Companion

FIRST NAME   MIDDLE INITIAL   LAST NAME

INSTITUTION OR COMPANY NAME

ADDRESS

CITY   STATE   ZIP

(   )

E-MAIL ADDRESS   PHONE NUMBER

U.S. and Canada addresses only. Fill in information above and mail postage-free.
Please mail only the bottom half of this page.

For information about Microsoft Press®

products, visit our Web site at

mspress.microsoft.com

BUSINESS REPLY MAIL
FIRST-CLASS MAIL   PERMIT NO. 108   REDMOND WA

POSTAGE WILL BE PAID BY ADDRESSEE

NO POSTAGE
NECESSARY
IF MAILED
IN THE
UNITED STATES

MICROSOFT PRESS
PO BOX 97017
REDMOND, WA 98073-9830